Also by David Cesarani

Justice Delayed: How Britain Became a Refuge for Nazi War Criminals

*f*P

ARTHUR KOESTLER
The Homeless Mind

David Cesarani

The Free Press

THE FREE PRESS
A Division of Simon & Schuster Inc.
1230 Avenue of the Americas
New York, NY 10020

First Free Press Edition 1999
First published in the United Kingdom by William Heinemann
Published by arrangement with William Heinemann

THE FREE PRESS and colophon are trademarks
of Simon & Schuster Inc.

Manufactured in the United States of America

10 9 8 7 6 5 4 3 2 1

Library of Congress Cataloging-in-Publication Data

Cesarani, David.
    Arthur Koestler : the homeless mind / David Cesarani.—1st U.S.
  ed.
        p.   cm.
    Originally published: London : William Heinemann, 1998.
    "Works by Arthur Koestler": p.
    Includes bibliographical references (p.   ) and index.
    1. Koestler, Arthur, 1905–83.—Criticism and interpretation.
  I. Title.
PR6021.04Z613   1999   99-13114   CIP
828'.91209—DC21

ISBN 0-684-86720-6

Contents

Preface

In July 1998 a distinguished panel of writers and intellectuals, including Maya Angelou, A. S. Byatt, Arthur Schlesinger Jr, William Styron and Gore Vidal ranked *Darkness at Noon* by Arthur Koestler as the eighth best novel of the century. To millions of readers around the world Koestler is still known mainly for this literary and political milestone. But there was far more to his life and work than that, much of it deliberately hidden by Koestler, his acolytes and biographers. This book is the first comprehensive evaluation of Koestler's life and work since his death in 1983 and the only one written without his influence over its contents or interventions by those with a stake in his reputation.

The Homeless Mind grew out of an idea for a study of Arthur Koestler as a Jew who exemplified the Jewish experience in Europe during the twentieth century. However, Koestler's life and interests could not be restricted to Jewishness, no matter how central that may have been to his existence, consciously or otherwise. Conversely his Jewishness could not be seen in isolation from the rest of his career. So an investigation into Koestler as Jew broadened into an account of Koestler the man and his achievements as a whole.

Koestler himself wrote four volumes of autobiography covering his life from 1905 to 1940. He was co-writing a fifth volume with his third wife, Cynthia, at the time of his death. Covering the period up to 1956, it was edited by Harold Harris and published posthumously. In addition, Celia Goodman edited the letters and diaries of Koestler's second wife, Mamaine, her twin sister, which encompassed the years 1945 to 1955. A full length biography by Iain Hamilton appeared in 1982. However, Koestler's version of his own life, which furnished the raw material for most biographical and literary studies, needs to be treated with great caution. Although Hamilton had access to the personal papers of Koestler and Mamaine, he was restrained from telling all that they revealed. Hamilton also ran out of time and sympathy when it came to recounting the last decades of Koestler's career: he compressed the years 1965 to 1980 into just a few pages. Since Koestler's death there have been numerous reminiscences mentioning or entirely devoted to him, but these have frequently been partial and were often *parti pris*.

This is the first biographical study to make full use of all the papers held in the excellent Koestler Archive in Edinburgh University Library. The end of the Cold War and the collapse of the Soviet Union also made possible the discovery of certain material which Koestler believed had been lost. In 1939–40, the French Secret Service, the Deuxième Bureau, raided his Paris apartment and removed stacks of documents. These were seized by the Gestapo after the fall of France and transferred to Berlin. When the Red Army conquered the Nazi capital in 1945, the papers were transported to Moscow by the forerunner of the KGB. Koestler thought they had disappeared. In fact, they were stored in the KGB 'Special Archive'. The collection contains 'lost' manuscripts, including the text of his unpublished first novel, and correspondence revealing how the Communist Party network, orchestrated by his first wife Dorothea Ascher and Otto Katz, the grey eminence of the Cominform, extracted him from a Fascist jail in Spain in 1938.

In the course of my research I conducted interviews with many of those who knew Koestler. I treated the results with caution since, over time, Koestler either beguiled or alienated those who came into contact with him. I have tried to keep speculation and psychologising to a minimum, although, given the nature of biography and Koestler's own dalliance with psychoanalysis, it seeps into chapters about his childhood, his sense of self, his relations with women and his death. Wherever possible in the course of building my picture of the man, I have relied on his own diaries, letters, notebooks and published writings, along with those of his contemporaries.

I have run up many debts, professional and otherwise, in the course of researching and writing this book. No one who helped me is responsible for what it contains, but I want to thank them for the many acts of kindness that helped me finish it. I would like to thank, pre-eminently, John Howard, head of Special Collections, Edinburgh University Library when I started my work, his successor, Jean Archibald, and all the hard-working, long-suffering staff operating under their direction. I would also like to thank the archivists of the Beinecke Rare Book and Manuscript Library, Yale University Library; Elizabeth Berman and the library of the United States Holocaust Memorial Museum; the Public Records Office, London; the Jabotinsky Institute, Tel Aviv; and the Central Zionist

Archive, Jerusalem. I owe special thanks to Yoram Mayorek, the head of the CZA, who alerted me to the Koestler Papers in the KGB 'Special Archive' and arranged for them to be microfilmed and despatched to me for my use. The London Library served me as marvellously as it had Koestler. The staff of the Wiener Library and Institute of Contemporary History, with which Koestler was also acquainted, were a constant source of support and I could not have managed without the unfailing and good-tempered assistance of Anne Beale. My colleagues at Southampton University were equally supportive, but I am especially indebted to Tony Kushner, Director of the Parkes Centre for the study of Jewish/Non-Jewish Relations, whose friendship has been a precious asset. At a moment when an expanding family made yet another trip to Edinburgh impossible Sarah Kavanaugh proved a first-rate research assistant.

In Hungary I benefited from the help and hospitality of Andras Kovacs and Maria Kovacs. I would also like to record my thanks to Erzsébet Vezér for her genealogical expertise. Yehuda Don cast his eye over the chapter on Koestler's Budapest and saved me from some howlers. George Lavy kindly translated part of an unpublished manuscript. David Astor, Julian Barnes, Sir Martyn and Lady Priscilla Beckett, John Belloff, Mary Benson, Marion Bieber, Jill Craigie, Quentin Crewe, Anita von Etzdorf, Michael Foot, Martin Goldenberg, Celia Goodman, the late Harold Harris, Josef Herman, Daphne Hardy Henrion, Elizabeth Jane Howard, David Pryce-Jones, Jan Karski, Walter Laqueur, Melvin Lasky, Janetta Parladé, Miriam Rothschild, Hugh Trevor Roper, Louis Waller, George Weidenfeld and Paul Willert either granted me the favour of interviews, informally shared their recollections of Koestler, or just provided one telling anecdote. Peter Robinson helped to inspire this book, jollied me along and made it worthwhile. Victoria Hipps was a wonderful editor whose comments vastly improved the finished product. My friends Bryan Cheyette, Daniel Eilon and David Herman listened to my ideas and helped to keep my spirits up. It will take many years to repay my family for the time which this project has taken away from them and for the love they gave me, despite my absences and frequent despondency. Without my wife, Dawn, whose patience has been heroic, I could not have done it.

This book is dedicated to my father, Henry Cesarani. I first heard Koestler's name bandied about at home when I was growing up. Both my parents had been involved with the Communist Party in the Pink Decade. My mother broke with Communism soonest and it was from her that I heard the phrase 'The God That Failed' and the

word 'commissar' used as a term of abuse. My father's faith was more
durable and gently decayed into stoical support for socialism and its
parliamentary vessels in the United Kingdom. His life story made me
wary of those who dismiss the youthful adherents of the CP in the
1930s and 1940s as gullible, naïve or ludicrously idealistic. To him the
likes of Koestler would always remain 'renegades', but he sedulously
tracked down Koestleriana on my behalf and read it intently before
passing it on. By the end he was debating Koestler's life and thought
with an earnestness that put me to shame. He made me realise how
Koestler's writing had electrified those to whose experiences it
spoke. Koestler hoped that by writing books he would influence
future generations. If it was necessary to avoid having children and
the trivia of family life, that great end justified the means. Perhaps.
By taking the responsibility of parenthood my father had a profound
influence on at least one person: unobtrusively he taught me what
justice means and what it is to live decently. He has not written any
books, but this one is his all the same.

Introduction
In Search of Arthur Koestler

Arthur Koestler was a journalist of genius and an outstanding chronicler of his times. He wrote half a dozen novels, one a classic and several more of enduring value, two superb volumes of autobiography and dozens of elegantly phrased, stimulating and frequently memorable essays on a host of subjects. One cannot fail to stand in awe of his corpus of work, or the intellectual energy and sheer effort that went into it. Yet today he is not as well known as he should be and the time has surely come for a re-evaluation of this remarkable man and his extraordinary career.

The reasons for Koestler's eclipse are not hard to find. Since the fall of the Berlin Wall, the dissolution of the 'Eastern Bloc' and the disintegration of the Soviet Union, those who distinguished themselves on the field of combat during the Cold War have suffered a loss of standing. Ever shortening historical memory means that to those without personal experience of the East–West conflict these personalities lack substance or significance.

To appreciate the scale of Koestler's achievement and his colossal status in the 1950s, it is first necessary to recapture the sense of peril that ran through the Western democracies during the Cold War. Between 1945 and 1950 it was common to believe that the Red Army might roll through Western Europe right up to the English Channel, with or without the aid of internal subversion and insurrection by indigenous Communist parties owing their first loyalty to Moscow. Thanks to its influence among millions of organised workers and the prestige it amassed for its role in the defeat of Nazi Germany, the Soviet Union and Communist doctrine had immense popularity and a vice-like grip over sections of the intelligentsia. It took courage for those whose natural place was on the left, or among intellectuals, to point out the iniquities of Communism and the appalling character of the Stalinist regime. It was even more difficult for those of the Pink Generation, the youth of the 1930s who had enrolled under the Red Banner in huge numbers and with great zeal, but who subsequently saw the flaws in Communist ideology and the threat posed by Soviet totalitarianism. This is precisely what Arthur Koestler did.[1]

Koestler's novel of ideas, *Darkness at Noon*, published in Britain in 1940, was the first intellectual counter-attack to make any significant headway against Communism. During the Second World War, when the Soviet Union was an official, prized and much admired ally in the fight against Nazism, he published a series of essays mercilessly exposing the deformation of Communism and the repressive character of the Soviet system. These writings had a liberating effect on wavering Communists and doubting fellow travellers who had been perturbed by the actions of the USSR in the late 1930s, especially the mass purges in 1936–8 and the Nazi–Soviet pact in 1939. By the force of his arguments and his personal example, Koestler emancipated thousands of people from thraldom to Marx, Lenin and Stalin. He continued this ferocious counter-crusade into the post-war decade, culminating in his inspirational role in the great anti-Communist rally in embattled Berlin in 1950. All of his writing in this era, his five novels, two works of reportage and, above all, his two autobiographical volumes, are informed by a determined anti-Communism. They reached millions of people and, along with George Orwell's *1984*, were probably more responsible for stemming the drift towards Communism than any other form of political education or anti-Soviet propaganda in the sphere of the democracies. The final rout of the Soviet imperium in 1989–90 began with the publication of *Darkness at Noon*.

This alone would be reason enough to re-evaluate Koestler's accomplishments. Yet to concentrate on this aspect of his thinking would eliminate half of his life. From 1955, Koestler devoted his manifold talents and huge energy to the study and popularisation of science. This had a paradoxical effect on his reputation. His formal renunciation of political activism and the publication of a stream of major works focused on scientific subjects during the later 1950s, the 1960s and 1970s lost much of the audience which had eagerly consumed his writing for its political message. Koestler never ceased to be concerned with the 'human predicament' and saw science as the most likely source of a new ethical system and the solution to the endemic problems of conflict in human society, but this was not always clear. So he lost old readers who were disappointed at the retirement of their anti-Communist champion and gained a new readership that was interested primarily in scientific issues.

In a succession of books Koestler probed the sources of creativity, the dynamics of scientific advance, the validity of neo-Darwinian approaches to evolution and theories of the mind. He waged a campaign against what he saw as desiccated, mechanistic and outdated scientific orthodoxies: materialism, behaviourism and reductionism. In the course of this counter-offensive he explored mind-altering drugs, para-science and parapsychology. His growing interest in the paranormal during the 1970s alienated many of those who admired his scientific writing and cast a pall of quirkiness over his entire body of work. His 'vocational change' from politics to science, followed by his defection from conventional science to para-science, lost him his second generation of readers.

His reputation was dealt a final blow by the circumstances of his death. From the mid-1970s he suffered ill-health. To pre-empt a lingering end he opted to take his own life. However, his perfectly healthy wife committed suicide with him, causing shock amongst their friends and giving rise to speculation that he had dragged her down. Within a few years the scandal of their double suicide and a series of posthumous autobiographical and biographical books further reduced his standing. They raked over his stormy personal relationships, exposing his violent treatment of his wives and girlfriends. It was revealed that his antipathy to fatherhood extended to procuring illegal abortions for his lovers. On the eve of the defeat of Communism one of its boldest enemies had been reduced to the level of a half-forgotten crank who was reviled as a philanderer and wife-beater when he was recalled at all.

Yet the trend of scientific and cultural thinking over the last decade provides a further reason for re-evaluating Koestler. At least some of the ideas that earned him a reputation for crankiness have now become more mainstream. Neo-Darwinism is facing severe criticism. There are serious philosophical attempts to ground ethics in biology. Mainstream scientists are even showing a greater interest in para-science. The public certainly is: a recent survey in Britain indicated that sixty per cent of people credit the existence of psychic powers; and television fiction based on the paranormal, such as *The X-Files*, has never been more popular.[2]

Koestler anticipated many strands running through the culture of the 1960s and stumbled across some of the key features of globalisation. As an inveterate traveller and observer in the 1950s and 1960s, he investigated Eastern spirituality and toured the Pacific region. Thanks to these journeys he perceived the interpenetration of East and West, and the growing simultaneity of events in distinct hemispheres well before most other commentators. His grasp of the global predated the phenomenon of 'post-modernity', another intellectual shift which he may be said to have foreshadowed albeit in an inchoate and partial manner.

The 'post-modern experience' is typified by globalisation, deracination, migration, hybridity and distrust of 'grand theory' or the 'exhaustion of modernity'. Koestler's nomadic life-style, transition from one culture to another and his reinvention of himself through his autobiographical writings make his life a classic example of the post-modern odyssey. His intimate encounters with grand theories, notably in the form of Marxism and Fascism, left him with an abiding distrust of the great nineteenth-century narratives of progress, even if he could never fully emancipate himself from them.[3]

The prominence of Jewish intellectuals in the formation of modern thought suggests a clue to the dynamic of Koestler's life and career. Jews, and those taking their inspiration from an interpretation of Judaism, rank high among the progenitors and popularisers of modern as well as post-modern cultural and social theory. They include Georg Simmel, Walter Benjamin, Emmanuel Levinas, Theodor Adorno, George Steiner, Jacques Derrida and Zygmunt Bauman. By virtue of their ethnicity these thinkers experienced marginality and migration: they were obliged to grapple with questions of identity, contingency, inter-textuality and translation. Along with the intellectuals of post-colonialism they were the first to probe the extraterritorial sensibility, deterritorialised identities and the dynamics of Diaspora. Thanks to their vulnerability as members of a historically persecuted minority they were extra-sensitive to currents of modern politics. It should therefore be no surprise that Koestler explored much the same ground, albeit less systematically and to different ends.[4]

In his autobiographical writing Koestler projected himself as a 'typical case history'. Typical, that is, of the generation of young, educated, middle-class Central Europeans born in the decade before the First World War who saw the security of their parents' lives swept away by war, revolution and economic chaos, who were then forced to wander Europe as migrants or refugees, enticed by or caught between Communism and Fascism. Most of those who have been drawn to study his life and work have taken this, his own carefully constructed narrative, at face value. Yet Koestler was anything but typical.[5]

Koestler was a Jew who exemplified the *Jewish* experience in Europe during the twentieth century. This is reflected in his involvement in the Zionist movement, his activity during the

Holocaust, and his writings on Jews and the 'Jewish Question'. It might be seen as reductive to insist that Koestler cannot be understood except as a Jew and there are certainly perils in such an approach. In 1949-50, Koestler himself 'renounced' his Jewishness and consistently played it down thereafter. However, he thought holistically, believed that everything was interconnected and that the whole could be illuminated by throwing a beam of light on any one part. So by his own devices his Jewishness cannot be sundered from the rest of him and vice versa. Jewishness was in fact a key to his personality and his life story. Yet this fundamental part of his make-up has been badly neglected in previous biographical accounts which have taken their cue from his own, doctored version of his life story.[6]

Ethnicity cannot easily be divorced from personality either. Koestler confessed to an inferiority complex (indeed, he jokingly bragged that his was bigger than most), which he blamed on the way he was raised by his parents and their domestic employees. Its expression and squalid effects are beyond dispute: his lack of self-worth dogged his relations with men and women. In a self-defeating pattern he sought out sexual encounters and relationships in order to prove his virility and his attractiveness. Low self-esteem left him vulnerable to the perils of success, too. Financial independence, thanks to the sales of *Darkness at Noon*, and the experience of becoming a celebrity turned him from a rather appealing if nervy young man, who was irritating only because he was eager to please, into an opinionated and quarrelsome bully.

This crippling deficit of self-regard may not be attributable solely to family background, which is where Koestler preferred to locate its origins. Koestler was equally much a victim of the way European society treated its Jewish citizens in the twentieth century. He was a Jew who was never given a chance to belong anywhere, a deracinated intellectual whose roots were treated with a kind of cultural weed-killer. His Jewish identity was that of a member of a stereotyped minority, alternately viewed with exaggerated respect or cosmic contempt. In the years during which he grew to maturity Jewishness was either a badge of contumely or a death warrant. Due as much to his ethnic as to his family background, his life was propelled and ruined by a never-ending quest for a satisfying identity and a home.

This book attempts to disentangle the real Koestler from the mythic version he created. It will reinstate at the centre of his life story the Jewishness of the milieu in which he grew up, the Jewish identity which he embraced in the form of Zionism, his effort to transcend religion and ethnicity via Communism, the reasons for the denial of his Jewishness in his autobiographical writings, and the curious 'return of the repressed' in all his later activities and even his intimate relationships. This search for Koestler parallels his search for belonging, a universal trope of our times − a twentieth-century quest for the Holy Grail.

Chapter 1

'A good Jewish child', 1905–22

Arthur Koestler had a famously unhappy childhood. In his mature years he was quick to ascribe defects of personality to his upbringing and persecuted his elderly mother for her supposed misdemeanours as a parent. Even if Koestler had not directed attention in this direction, the development of psychology and psychoanalysis would require scrutiny of his infancy to get a picture of the man in the process of formation. In fact, Koestler himself was so enamoured of these disciplines that he built them into his self-portrait. As a result the sources we have for understanding his childhood and its effects are largely provided and filtered by him.

Koestler's origins, and his genealogy, are blurred by force of circumstance as well as by his own design. The Second World War and the Holocaust were responsible for the destruction of much of the physical and human record of his family history. Biographers and critics have relied on the partial and highly coloured account which he disseminated himself. However, enough evidence has survived to subject that version to critical examination.

Such an examination reveals that Koestler's upbringing was not so awful or so unusual. His relations with his parents were standard for the era. Nor was he quite the sad, lonely, tortured boy he depicted. The surviving letters he wrote to his mother in childhood and adolescence display the normal range of emotions including love and ambivalence, rather than the unmitigated resentment he described in his published work. These letters and other sources also demonstrate that Jewishness played a far larger part in Koestler's early life than he later admitted.

His memoirs are superb works of artifice, closely adhering to the conventions of autobiography as a genre.[1] They are shot through with the ideas that fascinated him in mid-life, including psychology and the paranormal, and are arranged to illustrate them accordingly. Above all, they consistently play down his Jewish origins. He did not want his life story and its message to seem relevant to just one ethnic group so he toned down the Jewish element and universalised his experiences as much as he could. The overall result is a pre-structured life. Koestler knew what he wanted to record before he sat down to write out his life: autobiography was a political as much as a personal act. From the very moment of his birth, as reconstituted in the narrative of his life, Arthur Koestler was seeking to endow his existence with meaning, to place it, to make it belong somewhere.

I

There is no doubt about one fact of Koestler's life: Arthur Koestler was born in Budapest at 8.30 a.m. on 5 September 1905. He was a large baby, weighing 4.8 kilograms at birth. The labour had been long and hard, a fact which his mother, Adele, would frequently impress upon him as he grew up.

Adele Koestler was thirty-five years old when she gave birth, not a safe age at which to have children in those days. Nor did she have a resilient constitution. She was a dark-haired, pretty, but highly strung woman, who came from an eminent Jewish family in Prague. Adele was born on 25 June 1871 to Jacob and Wilhemina Zeiteles. Her father was a businessman of Viennese origin; her mother, née Reiner, came from Prague.[2] She grew up in Vienna and was destined for bourgeois respectability and a good marriage when her father lost his fortune. It is not clear exactly what occurred, but he appears to have become liable for a large debt incurred by his son-in-law. The Zeiteles family met his obligation, but Jacob left for America, where he worked as an importing agent. Adele was forced to move to the home of her married sister, Rosa Aldor, who lived in Budapest. Her mother, who was of independent means, went with her.

The Hungarian capital was regarded by most Viennese as the back of beyond; its natives, their language, cuisine and culture were seen as one step removed from barbarism. During all the years she lived in Hungary Adele never learned Hungarian properly and read only the German-language *Pester Lloyd* newspaper. She spoke German at home and wrote all her letters in that language. Arthur Koestler blamed her isolation and *declassé* status for the 'chronic headaches, irritability, and nervous tic' that subsequently afflicted her. When Adele was about nineteen years old, her family considered her emotional and psychological state sufficiently serious to warrant a visit to Dr Sigmund Freud. The consultation was not a success.[3]

Adele's misery was well founded. It was bad enough that she was cast among the 'backward' Magyars. Worse, her family could not offer a dowry to potential suitors. She was saved from the ignominy of spinsterhood by Henrik Koestler, a tall, thin, moon-faced textile salesman, who met and married her in 1898. Henrik Kestler (the spelling of the name varied from region to region and from one era to another) was born on 18 August 1869 in Miskolcz, an industrial city with a large and prosperous Jewish population located ninety miles north-east of Budapest. His father, Leopold Kestler, was a Russian Jew who had settled in north-east Hungary in the 1860s. He had married a local Jewish woman, Karolina Schoen, whose father owned a saw mill. Leopold Kestler ran his father-in-law's business until it went bankrupt, then moved his family to Budapest, where they lived in straitened circumstances.[4]

At birth, Henrik was named Heiman or Hyman, a traditional Yiddish appellation, and it can be assumed that he had a routine Jewish upbringing. By the 1860s the Miskolcz Jews were on the way to adopting a modified, modernised form of Judaism, but the orthodox Jews remained a powerful presence in the city. The reform of Judaism went forward slowly and cautiously. Henrik's two names, like the multiple spellings of his patronym, bear witness to the transitional stage reached by the Jews of Central Europe in their collective journey from an essentially pre-modern Jewish social structure and culture to forms that were adjusted to the conditions of modernity. Geographical, linguistic and cultural migration were all part of this transformative process.[5]

As a result of the family's economic difficulties Henrik was forced to break off his education early and take work as an errand boy for a firm of drapers. However, he was energetic and ambitious. He got up each morning at 4 a.m., using the three-and-a-half hours before he left for work to teach himself languages. By means of these exertions he learned English and French, and obtained a position as a salesman. He excelled in that role and was repeatedly promoted until he became a partner in the firm. Henrik Koestler rode the crest of the boom years of Budapest's economic expansion. Around 1889–90 he set up his own firm, travelling widely in Europe, especially England, importing and marketing textile products.[6]

Until the age of nine, Arthur Koestler enjoyed the benefits of a classic bourgeois upbringing. His family took regular holidays to Venice, resorts on the Dalmatian coast, spas in Austria and Lake Balaton in Hungary. There are many family photographs which show the trio posing against aquatic backgrounds or waterfront boulevards lined with imposing hotels. The young Koestler is always in the centre.

The apartment in which they lived in Budapest was large, with room for a maid and a nursery. It was richly furnished in characteristic late-Victorian style with heavy curtains, antimacassars, a great many lace coverings, cuspidors, Meissen china, a polar bearskin rug, a piano and a large variety of potted plants. It was also equipped with the latest recreational technology: a telephone connected to a bureau that dispensed news and music on request. As a child, Koestler would sprawl on a well-padded black leather sofa set against the wall of the living room and listen to extracts from Lehár operettas or the football results.[7]

In photographic portraits from this period Arthur looks a reasonably contented little boy. One, taken when he was around two years old, shows him dressed and combed carefully. He has a mass of curly hair. This luxurious growth disappears when he is about six and he is seen with severe crew-cuts, hair shorn almost to the skull. This was a typical precaution taken with children once they entered school and started mixing with others who might be carrying nits. But it reveals his physiognomy even more clearly: his broad forehead and almost orientally sculpted eyes. Usually one of his parents is lovingly clutching a hand or arm; normally he is smiling.

According to his published recollections, however, the childhood Koestler spent in these plush surroundings and holiday retreats was not a happy one. This was largely because of his mother, who had now burgeoned into a *grande dame* in every sense of the words. Her figure and health never fully recovered from the traumatic circumstances of Arthur's arrival. She became prone to moods and migraines, spending large stretches of time in bed. Her conduct towards her son was erratic. Koestler recalled that 'my mother's love was excessive, possessive and capricious . . . I was constantly tossed about from the emotional climate of the tropics to the arctic and back again.' As he grew older their relationship became increasingly stormy, which coloured all his reminiscences of earlier years. He records infantile rages against Adele, but few of the usual, counter-balancing emotions of love and dependence.[8]

While he remembered little that was positive about his mother, he could recapture his father in loving detail. In his seventies, Koestler wrote a moving account of watching his father shaving in the morning. It is full of the awe and affection of a son for an idealised father who, in fact, was rarely present in his life.[9]

Henrik was a vague and rather distant figure. In one account of his childhood Arthur Koestler comments that 'my father hardly enters the picture'. Henrik's deficient education made him nervous about questioning Arthur on the subject of his schooling, let alone offering encouragement or assistance. Once Arthur had started school his father insisted with quaint naïveté that he should not read when he was at home since too much reading would damage his eyes. The young Koestler threw tantrums and argued until Henrik agreed that before bedtime he could read ten pages of a book of his choice, but no more. Although it must have been frustrating to Arthur the boy, this incident does show that in a confused way his father cherished his health and best interests. Henrik loved his son 'tenderly and shyly from a distance', but could hardly express his affection. Koestler recalled that 'from my earliest schooldays to the end of his life we never established any intellectual contact, and never had a single conversation of an intimate nature. Nor did we ever quarrel; we liked and respected each other with the guarded reserve of strangers thrown together on a train journey.'[10]

From the age of three, Arthur's life was dominated by a series of hired helpers: maids, nannies and governesses who did little to create greater emotional stability. The family's long-serving, and long-suffering, maid Bertha was an unhappy woman of lower-class background whose own illegitimate son had been sent to the country to be raised by relatives. She spun a web of petty rules over the apartment. As the only child, Arthur's natural exuberance and naughtiness often got him into trouble, but there was no one else to share the blame for violations of the domestic order and he was constantly being scolded. Bertha, with Adele Koestler's consent, treated the boy as a recidivist criminal: 'The list of major offences included: to be noisy; to answer back; to offend Bertha; to speak in the presence of strangers without being spoken to; to omit saying "please" and "thank you very much"; to ask for a second helping without waiting for it to be offered. But these were all explicit, identifiable offences; the dark menace of life consisted in acquiring guilt without noticing it.' He seems to have inhabited a Kafkaesque world of unremitting judgement for unknown transgressions: 'the first major fact that took root in my mind was the consciousness of guilt . . . everything was forbidden that was not expressly permitted.'[11]

In his autobiography Koestler paints a nightmarish picture of his infancy and childhood. He records that he was locked in a dark bathroom by his mother at the age of two, was relentlessly punished by the half-educated maid and tormented by sadistic governesses. His mother and father seem to be semi-detached figures who desert him at crucial moments, leaving him with a deep mistrust of human relationships and protestations of fidelity. When he was four or five years old he was subjected to a brutal tonsillectomy. It was performed without advance warning and without anaesthetic. While his parents watched in horror he was strapped into a chair. Then, once they were bundled out of the room, the bloody assault commenced. Koestler never forgot the experience. Many years later he wrote with undiminished anguish: 'These moments of utter loneliness, abandoned by my parents, in the clutches of a hostile and malign power, filled me with a kind of cosmic terror.'[12]

Koestler later claimed that, although he was just a child, this horrible incident convinced him that a world of chaos and pain lay just beneath the veneer of peace, personal security and respectability. 'It was as if I had fallen through a manhole, into a dark underground world of archaic brutality. Thenceforth I never lost my awareness of the existence of that second universe into which one might be transported, without warning, from one moment to the other. The world had become ambiguous, invested with a double meaning.'[13]

In a similar vein he describes the terror he felt when he suspected that he might have to undergo an appendectomy. Until he turned six and started school, in September 1911, he lived in a double state, plagued by suspicion and anxiety that he would be swept from the safe to the unsafe spheres. 'For a long time thereafter, my days divided into dangerous and secure halves. The dangerous half was the morning, when the doctor made the rounds of his patients. The safe half was the afternoon when he received them in his consulting room.' These surgical sagas generated hostile feelings towards his parents. 'It never occurred to me to confess my fears to my parents nor to ask for their protection . . . Since they had sided with Dr Neubauer [who performed the tonsillectomy] and trapped and betrayed me, they could no longer be trusted.'[14]

The antagonism he felt towards his mother, especially, was aggravated by his status as an only child and her peculiar views on child rearing. Adele Koestler was so snobbish and prejudiced against Hungarians that until young Arthur went to school she would not allow him to mix with the local children. 'I grew up without playmates. I was an only child and a lonely child; precious, neurotic, admired for my brains and detested for my character by teachers and schoolfellows alike.' When he started school the other boys asked which of the two Budapest football teams he supported. He had to opt blindly for one over the other since word of neither had penetrated his closeted, over-protected environment.[15]

There were occasions when business acquaintances of his father would come to the apartment to socialise, bringing their families with them. Arthur planned these encounters in minute detail. When he was introduced to the visiting children he turned into 'a frenzied little maniac' and a 'fierce bully', hustling them through the programme of activities he had devised. But he was always conscious that play with the other child had to end. This made him tense and depressed. 'Thus I taught myself early the art of poisoning my pleasures by reminding myself of their ephemeral nature.'[16]

When told that a child would be coming to his home or taken on a social visit, he would fantasise about acquiring a new friend. Adulation was followed by disillusion. His relations with girls were no less strained. For months he harboured an infatuation for a girl called Sarah Berger whom he had met only once. At the age of five, his mother sent him to a 'progressive' kindergarten where at last he could mix with girls. The children actually spent a good deal of time at the school running about half naked, and he developed a puppy love for a little girl called Vera, although his main interest in her seems to have been a fascination for the vaccination marks on her arm. Before long his mother withdrew him from this idyllic, if unconventional, milieu.[17]

II

How far can Koestler's autobiographical recollections be trusted? Were his infancy and childhood really so fraught as to explain his tempestuous personality when he was an adult? In fact, his memoirs certainly should not be taken at face value. His portrayal of his childhood was driven by the great autobiographical models of his day, notably Rousseau, Goethe and Nietzsche. These in effect stipulated that the writer aspire towards complete transparency. Confession was an end in itself, but also served to validate the narrative. The recollection of a shameful incident was the surest sign that the author was not hiding anything or painting a dishonestly flattering self-portrait.[18]

Romanticism, with its interest in the development of individual character, focused attention on childhood, a trend that was reinforced by the development of psychology and psychoanalysis. For Koestler this stress on infancy and juvenile adventures had extra importance. Marxism ordained that the character and destiny of a person was formed by socio-economic forces. By excavating his childhood and stressing the eccentricity of his family, Koestler asserted the role of unique, individual factors in the formation of personality and the unfolding of a life story. Writing autobiography of this type accorded with his interest in psychoanalysis, but was also a sign of his emancipation from Communism and an explicit critique of one of its main doctrines.

Koestler accentuated the psychological factors that both matched his views about human development and the way he wanted to be perceived. He had immersed himself in the theories of Freud, Adler, Jung and other psychoanalytical thinkers. With their guidance he took childhood experiences to explain, and by implication to excuse, adult behaviour. If his autobiography proclaimed his genius as self-made, it sought to pin the blame for his flaws on his upbringing and, in particular, his parents. However, Koestler was his own analyst and provides only the experiences and dreams that sustain his diagnosis.

Finally, he wrote his life story when his ideas about predestination were crystallising. He selected incidents which apparently bore witness to the force of coincidence or the 'language of destiny'. In retrospect, certain happenings may have seemed like signs of unknown cosmic influences manifesting the existence of a 'parallel universe'. But these were not necessarily the most significant developments in his life when they occurred, and those which were fêted in this way may have been assigned exaggerated importance.

While he declaimed against reductionism of any kind, and mechanistic, psychological determinism in particular, Koestler was constantly drawn to deterministic theories. He began *Arrow in the Blue*, the first volume of his autobiography, with a 'secular horoscope' based on the events recorded in *The Times* for the day of his birth. News items and mentioned personalities replaced the stars; they described the 'field of force' into which he was born 'and the influences which were to shape my character and fate'.[19]

This is a useful device for getting the work off to a start but it has a deeper purpose. Koestler was establishing his life as representative, shaped by the forces that would make the twentieth century. 'The clock that struck the hour of my birth also announced the end of the era of liberalism and individualism, of that harshly competitive and yet easy-going civilization which had succeeded in reconciling, thanks to a unique, kindly-callous compromise, the slogan of "survival of the fittest" with that of "laissez faire, laisez aller" . . . I was born at the moment the sun was setting on the Age of Reason.'[20]

He was also exploring the extent to which psychological formation determined all else. This is a theme he develops in several of his novels, notably *Arrival and Departure* (1943) in which a Freudian psychoanalyst demonstrates to a resistance fighter who has escaped from Europe to a neutral country that courage derives from a sense of guilt and the need to make reparations for earlier transgressions.

Bravery is the product of a childhood trauma.

Likewise, in an unperformed play he wrote during the early 1950s he hinted at the way he saw his childhood. Entitled *The Fall of Dr Icarus* the play attempts to stage a psychoanalytic consultation. The analyst, Dr Icarus, tells a client that 'your case would be ordinary to the point of boredom except for one or two ironic twists. A bossy, overbearing, priggish father – mother over-affectionate, frustrated, emotionally unstable. In short, the perfect late Victorian idyll.'[21] Equipped with such a template, Koestler set out to explain the formation of his character and his self-confessed neuroses in terms of infant experiences. How much was selected or moulded to fit the man he became? There are few external sources of validation since most of those who knew him then are dead, but a few papers in his archive and elsewhere shed light on these years.

His mother was certainly upset by the references to family life in the autobiographical essay in *The God That Failed* (1950), a precursor to his first volume of memoirs, *Arrow in the Blue*. She wrote to him in March 1950 complaining, 'have you no nice memories of your childhood and youth?' Why didn't he record some of the nice times, she asked. Koestler replied: 'It never occurred to me that you would mind about the autobiographical family details.' His response clearly implies that he saw nothing to change and nothing to apologise for.[22]

Some confirmation comes from the diary of his companion, later his second wife, Mamaine Paget in December 1949. Arthur and Mamaine were then living at Verte Rive, a villa at Fontaine le Port, on the Seine near Fontainebleau. They invited Adele to stay for Christmas and Koestler used the opportunity to quiz his mother about his past, probably to obtain material for his forthcoming autobiographical essay.

> Last night K. drew his Ma out on the subject of his childhood. He said he didn't seem to remember ever playing with any other children till he was about 14; she said, no, the other children he knew weren't well-brought-up enough, so she didn't want him to go about with them; and, besides, she was afraid he might catch some infection from them. As he continued to pursue this subject she went on the defensive and (according to K) greatly falsified the facts – which he remembers only too well – in an attempt to make out that after all he *did* have some playmates. K's face during this conversation was worth seeing, but fortunately she didn't seem to notice – the sparks of hatred flashed from his eyes, he grinned fiendishly. Afterwards in bed he talked about his childhood till late.

I loathe K's Ma as much as he does and feel singularly little pity for her.[23]

Mamaine is a reliable, if not pristine source. Although she developed a sort of affection for Adele and was a better daughter-in-law than Koestler was a dutiful son, her initial dislike may have clouded her judgement. The exchange between mother and son was also conducted in rapid-fire German, which had to be translated by Arthur. But the upshot is that Adele had not been a terribly proficient mother and young Arthur had endured a pretty miserable time until he started school.

Even so, the stark dichotomies which Koestler constantly draws are open to question. He may have come to hate his mother in adult life, but there are many indications that, like most children, he once loved her as much as he raged against her. The bleak portrait of their relationship was exaggerated to explain and justify his less endearing personal characteristics.

In June 1916, around the time of Adele's birthday, he gave her an affectionate poem addressed to 'Dear Mother'. The eleven-year-old Arthur wrote: 'You should have a long and happy life / all your wishes should come true / You should never be ill.' Rather touchingly, the reason given in the poem for wishing her good health was that medicines were rare and costly due to the war. But thrift and filial adoration are not mutually exclusive virtues. It was also a family tradition that on Adele's birthday he would get up early, dress smartly, go into her bedroom carrying a bouquet of flowers and sing 'Happy Birthday'. As he recalled in a letter to his mother, in June 1921, then 'we all three smothered each other with kisses and, in a festive mood, sat down to breakfast'.[24]

From 1918 Koestler attended a school in Baden bei Wien, a spa town near Vienna, and lived in a boarding house while his parents shuttled between Austria and Hungary. He missed his mother. In one letter he reproved her for not writing to him more frequently, although she was hardly negligent and wrote every few days. He doted on these maternal communiqués. A boy who loathed his mother would hardly complain if he did not hear from her, yet this was the substance of a letter to her in 1918: 'I was at that time, when I received your letter, very desperate, just imagine Mama, for a *full week* I had not received one line from you.' Three years on, and deep into adolescence, his sentiments were no less intense. He complained that he saw his parents infrequently and told his mother that he longed to live with them again: 'Mama, if only we had a flat now and did not need to live separated, the one here, the other there!'[25]

The letters young Arthur wrote to Adele from Baden bei Wien brim with filial devotion. He reported his achievements in the school, such as mastering grammatical German sufficiently well to get into a school play or getting a good report. For his mother's birthday in 1919 he sent his 'sweet Mum' a special birthday letter and a humorous poem:

> I wish you all the very best imaginable;
> A new Rock-manto with a pretty hat,
> Shoes, stockings, blouses, a magnificent new dress,
> And that Fortuna may remain faithful to you for all time.

As a present he sent her fresh fruit, which he had picked himself.[26]

At just the point when a genuinely resentful adolescent boy would have taken the chance to break his ties with his mother Arthur Koestler seems to have done the opposite. He clung to her and sent her highly charged, affectionate letters. This hardly coheres with the portrait of the tormented and tyrannised little boy. The picture he drew of a domineering, selfish mother can only be partly accurate. Nor were his feelings towards his parents as simple as he pretends in his autobiography. If anything, it was precisely the ambivalence that mediated family relations that had most effect in shaping his character.

Guilt was inscribed on his personality. Like most children who cannot understand adult behaviour he blamed himself if domestic harmony foundered. When his mother turned cold he felt responsible. He feared that he was to blame for marital discord or family misfortune. To add to the burden of guilt, he felt he had to strive to win the attention of his perpetually distant father and frequently distracted mother. The result of this was constant self-scrutiny: was he doing the right thing? How could he please mother, father, nanny, governess? Later he projected these emotions on to employers, friends and lovers. Childhood made him into a classic 'schizoid personality' or a 'divided self': tortuously self-conscious, seeing himself through the eyes of others, living in terror of opprobrium, relying on approbation for feelings of self-worth, otherwise convinced he was worthless and empty and, consequently, unable to be alone or inactive for any length of time. Due to their intermittent displays of affection for Arthur, the incessant castigation and the apparent conditionality of their love, he grew up with a mistrust of emotion, an exaggerated rationality, a keen (to the point of painful) self-awareness and acute restlessness due to the unceasing need to prove himself.

Yet his interpretation of other childhood incidents also seems tailored to prefigure his future life story. For example, it seems more likely that he retrospectively attributed to his horrendous tonsillectomy the capacity to empathise with the victims of violence and terror. It helped to justify what some critics considered to be a perverse fascination with torture. In like manner, the rather precocious realisation that secure existence was always shadowed by another, threatening world is more probably an *ex post facto* reading. The notion of worlds existing in parallel is a concept that accorded with his later speculations on the paranormal.

Koestler recalled that his parents' apparent failure to protect him from physical suffering left him with a sense of abandonment. Despite relating certain patterns of behaviour in later life to this incident, such as the empathy with victims, it is striking that he made nothing more of his parent's 'betrayal'. Another lesson of the surgical traumas might have been that if his parents let him down how could he trust anyone else? Distrust of human relationships, duplicity and betrayal emerged as characteristics of his own personality; but this was not a connection he made, or was willing to make, in his autobiographical writings.

He also claimed that because he was deprived of playmates he ran to excess when he had the chance to socialise. However, he could not have been quite as isolated as he suggested. Indeed, he must have been quite a popular child at school, from the age of six onwards, since he made friends who could recall him fondly many years later. Often, during the long summer holidays, Henrik and Adele took a place in the Hungarian countryside, joining forces with Rosa and Siegfried Aldor and their children, Ferenc, Willy and Margit. Willy, the oldest, was quiet and bookish. But Ferenc was a tearaway who stole the neighbour's chickens and even robbed Arthur's father. Ferenc also had a powerful sexual appetite and round about 1918 managed to seduce Arthur's governess, making her pregnant. He was 'the embodiment of forbidden badness, and as a small child I worshipped him'. However naughty they may have been, the Aldor children were another source of relief for the only child Arthur.[27]

Given Koestler's knowledge of psychoanalysis and his predilection for editing his life story, on the basis of the available material it is hard to make meaningful judgements about the influence of infancy and childhood on his later life. The version he provided is suspiciously akin to the clinical etiology of an inferiority complex as understood by Alfred Adler. Adler maintained that every infant is inculcated with feelings of inferiority by virtue of being helpless and dependent, but overcomes these in childhood and turns them to constructive ends by striving for autonomy. Each child develops a 'life style' for coping with the family situation, which defines it for the rest of its life. If the child's efforts to overcome inferiority feelings are successful they translate into 'a good adjustment to the three challenges of life – society, work and sex'. If not, the child/adult suffers from 'over-compensation' in which 'the striving becomes too apparent and leads to varying degrees of maladjustment' that may include competitive-ness, endless perfectionism and striving for sexual conquests.[28]

Whether or not the childhood incidents were true and formed the roots of his personality in a Freudian or Adlerian sense, there is ample external evidence that as a young man Koestler was deeply ambivalent towards his parents, highly self-conscious, guilt-ridden and driven by the need to earn regard in the eyes of others. To this extent his recollections of infancy and childhood may be accurate. But at the same time they served as a smoke screen and an apologia, and cannot be wholly trusted. While he was working on his memoirs he was involved in a string of alcoholic brawls and car accidents, and was detained several times by the police for drunken behaviour. In his autobiography he intended to confess and explain his 'rare' misdemeanours, like his model Rousseau, but without confirming the suspicion held by many people that they were habitual.

III

Koestler stated in his autobiography that 'I was brought up in an assimilated environment without roots in the Judaic tradition. My mind had been fed on Hungarian, Russian, French and English literature; the only Jewish literature as far as I knew, was the Old Testament, and that wasn't literature in the accepted sense.' He claimed that he only encountered orthodox Jews when he started university in Vienna in 1922, and only learned about the Jewish religion from Polish and Russian Jewish students. This is hardly credible since his grandfather, Leopold Kestler, was one of these very Russian Jews. Arthur Koestler himself grew up in the districts of Budapest crowded with Jewish immigrants from Galicia, the hilly, rural marshes of north-eastern Hungary (now divided between Poland and Ukraine) where Yiddish was still spoken extensively.[29]

In 1910, Jews formed five per cent of the Hungarian population. But no less than twenty per cent of Hungary's Jews lived in Budapest where, in 1910, they comprised twenty-three per cent of the capital's 880,000 inhabitants. Most were poor or lower middle class and of recent provenance. But there was an older-established, assimilated and wealthy élite. Over half of all the employers of industrial labour in the city were Jews, as were nearly sixty per cent of all medical practitioners and just over sixty per cent of lawyers. No less than sixty-four per cent of all those engaged in trade, commerce and finance were Jewish. It was not without reason that Viennese anti-Semites contemptuously labelled the Hungarian capital 'Judapest'.[30]

The wealthy Jewish inhabitants clustered in the city's fifth district, the Leopold (Leopoldstadt), in the shadow of the great neo-gothic Parliament building. The large agglomeration of middle-class, lower middle-class and poorer Jews who dominated the free professions, trade and artisanal occupations packed the sixth district, Theresa, and the seventh district, Elizabeth. The bulk of Budapest's less well-heeled Jews lived in the area bounded by Károly körút, Erzsébet körút and Király útca (Street; abbreviation – u.). In this residential area many of the apartment buildings were predominantly Jewish. John Lukacs, the historian of *fin-de-siècle* Budapest, estimates that seventy per cent of those living on Király u., the boundary between the sixth and seventh districts, were Jews. From the 1910s onwards, Dob u., which bisected the seventh district, was virtually synonomous with orthodox, recent immigrants from the country, who persisted in traditional modes of garb, speech and religiosity.[31]

Although they moved around a lot, the Koestlers usually resided within the fifth, sixth and seventh districts. Arthur attended a school on Szív u. which connected the sixth and seventh districts and drew its pupils from both. His grandfather took him on walks up Városligeti fasor, an extension of the heavily Jewish Király u., leading to the City Park, and he played on Erzsébet körút, the great ring boulevard which crossed Király u. at midpoint, just inside the fifth district or inner city. In other words, the 'assimilated' Arthur Koestler grew up in an intensely Jewish social milieu in which orthodox Jews jostled with Neolog (Reform) Jews, and immigrants of varying degrees of Magyarization rubbed shoulders. His childhood pals and school friends were predominantly Jews, such as Eva Zeisel, Sarah Berger, Charley Gluek, Lajos Hershman and Lewis Herman.[32]

How Jewish was his immediate family background? Koestler was circumcised at birth. In 1905 this would necessarily have been a religious ceremony conducted in the family home, hardly a sign that the boy's parents were divorced from 'Judaic traditions'. He recollected: 'My father went to synagogue twice or three times a year in the Festivals and dragged me along.' This was no more and no less synagogue-going than that of the average non-orthodox, Neolog Hungarian Jew and demonstrated a normative degree of Jewish commitment for that period and locale. The youthful Arthur escaped the rigours of a talmudic education, but he admitted that 'I learnt the rudiments [of Judaism] in secondary school. In the Austro-Hungarian empire religious instruction was still obligatory so I learnt the rudiments of the Hebrew alphabet.'[33] This entailed reading the Hebrew Bible, a work with which Koestler subsequently displayed great familiarity.

Until his grandfather died in 1911, Arthur spent much time with the old man. As in the case of Freud, Mahler, Kafka and many other of the 'assimilated' Jews born in Central European cities in the age of Jewish emancipation, his grandfather was an intimate bond with a traditional, almost archaic Jewish past. Leopold Kestler was brought up 'in strict observance of the Mosaic law'. Although his grandfather described the values of his upbringing as 'prejudice', the old Jew remained loyal to the fundamental tenets of Judaism. He allowed young Arthur to eat ham sandwiches, but he declined to do so himself and continued to observe at least some of the Jewish dietary laws. Nor did he shave his beard. Most remarkably, Koestler describes his grandfather as 'always dressed in a morning coat'. He deduced this from the fact that the old man parted the tails before he sat down. Yet a more distinctive feature of a morning coat is the cutaway front and it seems more likely that his grandfather was wearing a frock-coat or a *kapote*, the black, three-quarter-length gaberdeen jacket traditionally worn by orthodox East European Jews. Dressed in this way or not, Koestler's grandfather was a living exposition of traditional East European Judaism.[34]

The adult Arthur Koestler maintained that he only ran into Yiddish speakers when he entered university, whereupon his response was immediately hostile. 'This jargon, with its insinuating, lilting, sing-song that turned every factual statement into an emotional one, repelled me . . . I disliked the language, and the mentality which it reflected, from the first time I heard it, and I have never lost my aversion for it.' This passionate denunciation of Yiddish and all it represents is redolent of the great culture-clash between Western, 'assimilated' Jews and the *Ostjuden*, but it is also probably untrue. It is unthinkable that his grandfather did not know Yiddish and it is probable that he spoke it in his grandson's presence during their

strolls through 'Judapest'. Arthur Koestler's father was given a typical
Yiddish name and it is almost certain that Yiddish was spoken in the
household in which his father grew up.[35]

There is no record that Koestler had a bar mitzvah or confirmation
ceremony. But since he turned thirteen in 1918, just when the
Austro-Hungarian empire was collapsing and chaos reigned in
Budapest, it may well be that the family had more pressing concerns.
All the same, Koestler was familiar with Jewish life-cycle events. He
kept in his personal files a calendar bearing the date of his father's
Jahrzeit, the annual day of rememberance of his death. When his
mother died in London in August 1960, he contacted a rabbi and
ensured that she was cremated according to Reform Jewish practice,
including a short service.[36]

Koestler described himself and his family as assimilated but
'assimilation' in this specific context should not be measured in terms
of proximity to or distance from Jewish religious orthodoxy. Jewish
religious life in Budapest was dominated by the Neolog tendency.
Being Jewish in Budapest meant *not* being orthodox. However,
Mary Gluck, the biographer of Georg Lukács and his circle, notes
that most Jewish intellectuals in *fin-de-siècle* Budapest could recall or
knew their orthodox, immigrant grandparents. This gave them an
acute sense of differential origins and social transformation.[37]

The fact that the children and grandchildren of Galician, Polish or
Russian Jewish settlers all assimilated at the same time in similar
conditions gave them a group identity. As Marsha Rozenblit has
observed with respect to the Jews of Vienna, this sort of assimilation
en masse only succeeded in producing a distinctive sub-culture of the
'assimilated' Jews. This was no less true of Budapest. Jews were
concentrated in a few residential districts, sent their children to a few
excellent gymnasia, mixed in the same overwhelmingly Jewish social
circles and approached the world from basically the same parvenu
perspective.[38]

Jewish identity was also formed by encounters with anti-Semitism.
Koestler claimed that until he reached university 'I had never been
personally victimised or bothered by anti-Semitism, and always
regarded the so-called "Jewish Question" as the same kind of boring
and remote subject as Municipal Autonomy . . .'[39] This is hard to
believe. As long as the Hungarian economy was booming the Jews
were perceived as a major asset. However, from 1899 to 1900
inflation built up as a side effect of rapid growth. Commercial rivalry,
professional jealousy and popular envy combined with Magyar
nationalism in a nasty local variety of anti-Semitism. By 1900, anti-

Jewish feeling in the Hungarian capital was a well-remarked fact of life. In 1883 the metropolitan press reported a sensational trial in the provincial village of Tiszaeszlár in which Jews were falsely accused of the ritual murder of a Christian girl. The following year the first anti-Semitic deputies were elected to Parliament. In 1899 the respected Catholic Party leader Bishop Ottokar Prohászka proclaimed a 'Christian awakening' in Hungary. Although the anti-Semitic parties faded away, the effect of their propaganda did not. Social and athletic clubs, including the famous casinos, began to refuse Jewish applicants. Jewish and non-Jewish students brawled in the university. The city became increasingly segregated at an informal level, with Jewish and non-Jewish residential zones and streets for shopping or promenading that were patronised either by Jews or Gentiles, but not both.[40] If Koestler did not encounter raw anti-Semitism as a child, it may have been because he was enclosed within an overwhelmingly ethnically Jewish milieu.

IV

Koestler started school at the age of six, attending an elementary school at the junction of Andrássy út. and Szív út. in the sixth district. He was a zealous pupil, doing well at arithmetic and languages, including German (which his parents spoke at home), French and English. By the time he was ten years old he had shown such talent for maths and mechanics that it was decided he should specialise in engineering and physics at the Real Iskola (Realschule) in Budapest. Koestler made rapid progress there and was in the top class of his year. He excelled at chess and was well liked. But it may be no coincidence that the subjects which he liked the most, geometry, algebra and physics, offered certainty and stability in contrast to the upheavals and irrationality of his home life.[41]

Having finally escaped the ten-page-a-day regimen imposed by his father, Koestler's reading exploded. He progressed from the tales of Grimm, Andersen, *Struwwelpeter* and *Alice in Wonderland* to *Robinson Crusoe*, *Gulliver's Travels*, *Don Quixote*, *Till Eulenspiegel*, the cowboy stories of Karl May, Jules Verne and Fennimore Cooper. As a precocious adolescent, in addition to the German classics – Rilke, Goethe, Heine and Hölderlin – he devoured Strindberg, Ibsen and Hamsun, who had a deep effect on his aesthetic and social outlook. But his 'principal heroes' were scientists. He read their lives and works *in extenso*: Darwin, Spencer, Kepler, Newton, Mach, Edison, Hertz, Marconi and especially Haeckel, the best-selling popular science writer who embodied nineteenth-century optimism about progress and reason.[42]

Science and scientists promised answers to the mystery of existence and, perhaps, refuge from Koestler's bewildering domestic circumstances. But not everything in the universe could be satisfactorily explained by Haeckel and his like. As a young adolescent Koestler was intrigued by the idea of infinity and eternity. He was familiar with mathematical paradoxes, such as Xeno's paradox which prescribes that if an arrow covers half the distance to its target and then half of that and so on, it will theoretically never arrive. Such unresolved puzzles haunted him, none more so than the concept of infinity. For, until the universe was circumscribed, everything within it was doomed to potential insignificance. Koestler asserted: 'The thirst for the absolute is the stigma which marks those unable to find satisfaction in the relative world of the now and here.' He later traced his search for utopias back to this dissatisfaction, but even if it were true it does not explain why he opted at particular times for particular Utopias.[43]

The outbreak of the First World War, six weeks before his ninth birthday, cruelly disrupted Koestler's life. Henrik realised immediately what the war meant for the family. He was seized by stomach cramps and retired to the sofa in the living room while Arthur brought him a glass of water and bicarbonate of soda. Within a few months his business collapsed and the family were staring at destitution. They moved out of their spacious apartment and took up residence in Vienna, shifting frequently from one boarding house to another.[44]

In 1916 Henrik Koestler's creativity and business acumen spectacularly, if temporarily, restored their fortunes. Arthur Koestler remembered his father as a man of 'shrewdness and childishness, of ingenuity and ingenuousness'. Although he had little formal education and showed scant interest in literature or the arts, Henrik Koestler studied the newspapers intently and read widely in popular science. He was gripped by enthusiasms for new inventions in which Adele showed no interest, or business schemes she could not appreciate. Consequently, he turned to his son for companionship and reinforcement. The 'sole disciple of a lonely prophet' was a hard role for the boy to play and Arthur resented it.[45]

However, Henrik's ingenuity gave the family an Indian summer of prosperity. In one of the Vienna boarding houses where they were lodging he met a chemist who had an idea for manufacturing soap out of clay. The clay deposits in question were mildly radioactive, but curious beliefs about the properties of radium only added to the marketing value of the product. At a time when soap was in short supply any ersatz version would probably have done well, but the grandly named Frybourg Chemical Works more than flourished on the strength of its chief product: 'radioactive soap'. The factory was in the industrial suburb of Buda, so Henrik returned to Hungary, while Adele and Arthur seem to have oscillated between the two capitals before returning to Budapest.[46]

The run of good fortune finally ended in August 1919, amid defeat, revolution and counter-revolution. By the autumn of 1918 the Austro-Hungarian armies had suffered a series of reverses, and morale on the home front was crumbling. Strikes and mutinies broke out in the Hungarian capital. At the beginning of October 1918 the Hungarian government approached the United States, seeking peace terms with the Allied powers. It was understood that the price of peace would be the dissolution of the Habsburg empire and the abolition of the monarchy. At the end of October the Czechs, Slovaks, Croats and Ruthenians threw off rule from Vienna and Budapest. A revolution in the Hungarian capital led to the appointment of a liberal democratic government under Count Michael Károlyi. An armistice was proclaimed on 3 November 1918 and Hungary became a republic. But the momentum for radical change could not be halted: in March 1919 Béla Kun took power at the head of a Soviet-style regime.[47]

Over thirty years later Arthur Koestler had no difficulty recapturing the mood at the start of the war and the revolutionary years of 1918–19. Even though he was Jewish, he was enthralled by Magyar nationalism. Hungarian schools were extremely chauvinistic and drummed a mystical, ethno-cultural nationalism into their students. In 1914, Arthur Koestler was swept away by the nationalistic fervour that accompanied the declaration of war. Four years later he was equally enraptured by the proclamation of Hungarian independence which was made by Count Károlyi from the balcony of a building not far from his father's office.[48]

The thirteen-year-old Koestler (in *Arrow in the Blue* he gives his age as fourteen years) embraced Kun's revolution with naïve, adolescent excitement. He read the Communist press and was amazed by the insights it gave into the lives of workers and peasants of whom he had formerly not been aware. He listened raptly to the agit-prop lectures given by Communists sent into the schools to indoctrinate the children. One of these teachers was his cousin Margit Aldor.[49]

Revolutions always attract youth: they are irreverent towards authority and property, boisterous, noisy and colourful. The Hungarian revolution exemplified these qualities in concentrated form. Koestler adored the bold revolutionary posters, the marching crowds and choruses of revolutionary songs. He rather portentously suggests in his autobiography that his attraction to the brouhaha of the Hungarian commune signified the germ of his gravitation towards Communism in later life. A more modest explanation is that he was simply carried away by the excitement and youthful energy of the revolutionaries. He showed no interest in Marxist ideology until his mid-twenties.

His mother saw the turmoil in a rather different light. One morning she had to use all her courage and wits to repel two Red Army soldiers who attempted to enforce the new housing regulations and make the Koestlers share their two-room boarding-house accommodation. In an intriguing vignette, Koestler depicts the burly, rough-mannered soldiers with phallic rifles and bayonets menacing his mother, who was clad only in a dressing gown. His father was absent and he was the sole male in the house. In describing this incident Koestler portrays his mother in a somewhat more heroic light than was his custom. The epsiode is sexually charged and hints at the erotic tie between son and mother that Koestler acknowledged in private writings.[50]

In April 1919 the Romanian army invaded Hungary in order to topple the Communist regime. It reached Budapest at the start of August and occupied the capital. On 6 August the Romanians supported a right-wing coup that installed a reactionary regime under Admiral Horthy. The new rulers initiated a reign of counter-revolutionary terror. Since many of the revolutionaries had been Jews, anti-Semitic propaganda and violence accompanied the wave of repression. Although Henrik Koestler's business had been nationalised by the Soviet government, he had been retained as its manager. Possibly fearing that this placed him too close to the defeated Communists, he organised the family's rapid departure from Budapest. In any case, the Koestlers were Jews in the midst of a vicious anti-Jewish campaign. They left in such haste that they did not even have the proper travel documents. But in those chaotic, perilous days this counted for little.[51]

By the age of thirteen, Arthur Koestler had lived through a war and a revolution. He had been uprooted from his home and condemned to 'nomadic wanderings'. His father had twice lost his wealth and the family had twice become *déclassé*. During 1914–15, his parents came close to separation and quarrelled frequently in front of their impressionable son. Around the same time he accidentally set fire to the room in the boarding house where they were staying, with traumatic results. Not long afterwards he was twice operated on for appendicitis.[52]

To cope with these emotional crises and upheavals Koestler claimed to have developed a series of psychological defence mechanisms. He convinced himself that he could escape the mire of anxiety, fear and loneliness by sheer will power. *En route* to the appendectomy he experienced a sense of transcendence: he 'felt reconciled and at peace'. In the operating room he asked to be able to hold the ether mask over his face, for him the most terrifying part of the surgical process. In this way he could assert some control over his fate, even if only symbolically. Similarly, he could recall the moment when he supposedly learned to live with loneliness. He was thirteen years old and staying with Rosa Aldor's family. Everyone in the apartment went out to the cinema, leaving him alone. He was initially crestfallen, but then realised that the solitude was quite enjoyable. He took from this experience the lesson that he could cope with being alone, but not for too long. The secret was to reach a balance between the divergent needs of his personality.[53]

In his memoirs Koestler constructed these incidents as turning points in his personal growth. Since the appendectomy, he wrote, 'I have learned to outwit my obsessions and anxieties – or at least to come to a kind of *modus vivendi* with them . . . one accepts one's complexes and treats them with respectful courtesy, as it were, instead of fighting them and denying their existence.' This would have been precocious indeed, if it were accurate. But Koestler's later life demonstrates that he remained under the lash of his obsessions and anxieties. He may have dissected them on paper, but he never defused them. In like manner, his later activities belie his confident assertion: 'As the years wore on, my life gradually fell into a pattern, oscillating like a pendulum, between periods of complete isolation and short bouts of hectic gregariousness.'[54] The notion that Koestler achieved a harmonious existence thanks to self-awareness gained in childhood does not stand up to scrutiny. If he was bold in sharing his analysis of his own youth and correct in his deductions, he was cowardly in declaring the truth about his adulthood and utterly wrong in the proposition that self-analysis had promoted maturity. In certain respects, Koestler never stopped being a child.

V

During 1919 Koestler started at a private school in Baden bei Wien. He lodged in a *Pensionat* or boarding house run by the Ehrmanns, a Jewish family. There were fourteen other pupils, most of them Jewish: Koestler affectionately dubbed them 'the circus'. In his memoirs the years which he spent in Baden are compressed into less than one page. The chapter in which he deals with this period begins with a quotation from Cyril Connolly and in his description of the *Pensionat* Koestler seems to aspire to a Central European version of *Enemies of Promise*.

The impression he gives of these years is unremittingly bleak. He describes himself as being intensely self-conscious, agonising over his appearance and his height. He felt insecure and unworthy, full of self-loathing. His lack of exposure to children left him awkward in company. He felt compelled to construct a 'complete false personality' in order to interact smoothly with the other schoolboys. The 'false' personality was as much a liability as the one it encased. He took on the air of a cocky know-all and was thrashed by the bigger boys when he got too much for them. He concludes that 'everybody who, in his youth, has gone through the purgatory of boarding-school can appreciate the nature of this experience'.[55]

Photographs of Koestler as an adolescent certainly do show a remarkable change of countenance from that of the happy child. The pensive and rather tight-lipped expression of his adulthood is now well-defined. Yet so is the handsome face, marked out by high cheek-bones, which led others to dub him Slavic, and thick, dark, swept-back hair. Even making allowances for the serious pose which portraiture required, this was the look of an introspective youngster. However, several letters which he wrote to his parents from Baden have survived and there is no suggestion in them that he was miserable. On the contrary, he seems to have had a wonderful time.

The family had vacationed in Baden bei Wien before the war, so Koestler was familiar with the town. The boarding house was clean and well run; the school was conveniently located nearby. In the first year Koestler struggled to make up for the disruption to his schooling during the war. He told his mother: 'I see only now what a tremendous advantage it is to be able to do one's studies regularly.' However, by the end of the academic year 1920–1 he was doing so well he could afford to relax. He bragged to his mother that he could cope with the work in under two hours per day. In the summer term, due to the heat, the boys studied from 7.00 a.m. to 11.30 a.m. which left the whole afternoon free to cavort in the Kurpark, the gardens in the centre of the town, play football or listen to the spa orchestra. According to his letters he got on well with the boys of his own age. They played sports together and went on mountain walking expeditions. In the summer of 1922, prior to his university entrance, Koestler took a long walking holiday 'with three very nice colleagues: Kamsarakan, the Armenian, Leschowsky, the star pupil, and Lototzky, who is a Parisian and wears a monocle'. Always careful of his mother's anxieties, he reassured her that *'No mountains are to be climbed at all'*.[56]

Although Koestler was preoccupied by money matters, he does not seem to have been constrained by lack of resources. He went to the theatre regularly and in June 1921 was even taken to the races by family friends.[57] That summer he also went on holiday in Hungary with his father. They travelled from Gastein to Boglar and thence to Földvár, near Lake Balaton. Due to the season there were no rooms available in Földvár, but his father bribed a hotel proprietor to give them accommodation, a trick which mightily impressed the young Koestler.[58]

Around this time he saw more of his father than his mother. Henrik visited Baden several times, his mother rarely. His parents lived rather separate lives, too. Henrik was trying to re-establish himself in business and was travelling a great deal; Adele was used to the routine of living in boarding houses and moved when economic circumstances permitted or necessitated a transfer. It was an unsettling way of life. According to Arthur, he and Henrik each felt 'like an old bachelor who is longing for his own abode'.[59]

The boarding house in Baden did, however, offer the opportunity for full sexual initiation. Since his obsession with Vera's arm Koestler's sexual activity had been muted. Rather predictably, his mother's Victorian prudishness had made him embarrassed by nudity. She convinced him that contact with genitalia, including his own, was dirty if not potentially fatal. Finally, when he was fourteen he learned the facts of life from class-mates; a biology textbook proved handy in confirming the details. Soon after, he discovered the pleasures of masturbation. When he was sixteen he charmed the maid at the boarding house into having sex with him: 'After the initial mishaps, this proved even more delightful.'[60] He continued to practise (and advocate) masturbation whenever other methods of erotic gratification were unavailable, but after this Koestler himself rarely lacked for female admirers or sexual partners.

VI

In youth and adolescence Arthur Koestler's Jewish identity continued to develop in the curious, unique form it commonly took for 'assimilated' Central European Jews. Although he denied suffering from anti-Semitism, it is clear that his family fled Budapest partly to escape the anti-Jewish violence unleashed by Admiral Horthy and his right-wing regime. Thirty years later Koestler remembered the counter-revolution, 'with its organised pogroms . . . its bombs thrown into synagogues' as 'a nasty foretaste of things to come'. In his memoirs he reduced his encounter with anti-Semitism to a dull subject he had heard adults speak about, like 'Municipal Autonomy', but one did not usually scuttle from one's home for fear of the council.[61]

When he embarked on his higher education in Austria Koestler was keenly aware of the disadvantages of being a Jew in post-bellum Central Europe. In August 1922 he told his parents that he had been to the 'Technik', the Technische Hochschule, in Vienna to enquire about the admissions procedure. 'I was told in confidence that it is very difficult as a Hungarian and even more as a Jew to be accepted.' He pleaded with his father to boost his chances by obtaining a recommendation on his behalf from someone in the engineering business.[62]

Other letters he wrote during his stay in Baden show that his Jewish identity was not merely negative. At the start of July 1921, he reported that the Jiddische Volksbühne, the Yiddish Theatre, were to perform in the local theatre. 'Of course, the whole Ehrmann circus goes there.' Initially he was sceptical: he did not have a high opinion of Yiddish, possibly because of the circumstances in which he had heard it spoken previously, the Yiddish argot of Dob út. Afterwards, however, all doubts vanished: 'did they play!! I have never ever seen that before, not at the Burg[theater] and not in the Deutsches Volkstheater. Next year you really must go and look at it.'

He described the play – *Shema Yisroel*, a typical Yiddish melodrama – the set and the acting in great detail: 'one has time to be amazed that it is possible to talk Yiddish without making it sound repulsive. No, the language in which the play is performed is not *Gejuedel* [Jewish jargon], it is a beautiful – yes, however paradoxical that may sound – a really beautiful, pleasant sounding, harmonious dialect.' The play included a wedding and a funeral, which was *de rigueur* for Yiddish melodramas. What is interesting in Koestler's reaction is the

air of familiarity with which he discussed the Jewish rituals. He used
the word 'schüve', a German rendering of the Yiddish 'shivve', the
term for the mourning ritual. 'In the end, of course, *as was to be
expected* [author's emphasis], the rebuilding of Jerusalem was proclaimed from the stage.' His exposure to the Yiddish Theatre recalls
the electrifying effect which it had on another 'assimilated' Jew,
Franz Kafka.[63]

One incident in particular reveals the nature of Koestler's Jewish
identity and the ease with which he bore it. In May 1921 he went
with 'the circus' on a mountain-walking expedition up the Hohe
Wand in Piestingthal. At lunch-time they stopped at a hostel, ate
their packed lunches and drank beer. After three more hours'
hiking they paused at the summit and refreshed themselves at
another inn where Koestler drank two glasses of Most, a kind of
cider. The group set off again and had walked for an hour when
their leader, the school chemistry teacher, got lost. The main party
halted while two lads went ahead to find a landmark. While they
were gone, Koestler developed 'tummy-ache' from the cider and
ran off to relieve himself behind some rocks. When he returned,
the main party had moved on. 'What a mess!' he told his mother.
'There I stand, a good Jewish child, at 1092 metres above sea level,
all on my own and do not know which way to turn.' After a mild
panic, he collected himself, found the landmark by asking a passing
hiker and caught up with the party. 'The lost lamb was greeted with
cheers.'[64]

In this letter Koestler plays with Jewish stereotypes in a way that
would only have been possible if he and his readers had been familiar
with them. Then, as now, Jews were considered to be pre-eminently
urban people who did not excel in sports and who were not
associated with outdoor activities. In fact, Central European Jews
such as Freud did go on country holidays and enjoyed hill or
mountain walking. But the stereotype of the urban ghetto Jew
persisted. It is not accidental that Max Nordau, the Hungarian-born
writer of *Degeneration* (1892), who became a devotee of Theodor
Herzl and a fanatical Zionist, invented the concept of 'muscular
Judaism' in the 1900s in order to challenge the stereotype of the
weedy Jew.

Koestler shows himself to be sufficiently at home with
contemporary Jewish identity both to acknowledge the stereotype of
the weak Jew and undermine it at the same time. A mountain was no
place for a 'nice Jewish boy', although, of course, he could function
perfectly well in that situation. Someone who was not conscious of

being a Jew, who was truly assimilated, or who was uneasy with
Jewish identity (or, equally, unsure that his audience's reaction
would be informed and sympathetic) would hardly have made such
a witty remark in such a natural way.

Chapter 2

Zionism and Palestine, 1922–9

In September 1922, aged seventeen, Koestler matriculated and entered the Vienna Technische Hochschule to study engineering and physics. The three years which he spent at university were blissfully happy. He looked back on them as the *only* genuinely happy, anxiety- and neurosis-free period he ever knew.[1] They were also marked by the first of his great ideological conversions. In Vienna he became a Zionist and entered on the trajectory that would carry him to Palestine in spring 1926, in search of Utopia.

His conversion to Jewish nationalism was partly the result of meeting a series of extraordinary personalities, notably the Zionist firebrand Vladimir Jabotinsky. It did not, however, come out of the blue: Koestler was not as 'assimilated' a Jew as he later claimed. But for the purposes of genre, to fit his life story into a conventional narrative of conversion, he exaggerated the extent of his Damascene revelation. He also played on the psychological theme by attributing his supposed change of heart to charismatic individuals who served as father figures. By contrast, he minimised the effect of his exposure to traditional Jews in Budapest, the rampant anti-Semitism during the White Terror in Hungary or indeed the persuasive quality of the Zionist argument.

When he came to write of these years in his memoirs, composed between 1949 and 1953, his feelings about Zionism and Israel were complicated by the mixed experiences of the three intervening decades. Furthermore, for political reasons he wanted to belittle the origins of his Zionist enthusiasm and the salience of his Jewish identity. It is no accident that his very funny account of his first year in Palestine in 1926–7 seems to be informed by a new auto-biographical trope: that of the *shlemiel*. A well-worn Jewish stereotype in Yiddish culture, the *shlemiel* was popularised among German readers by Heine. The *shlemiel* represented the hapless Jew whose aspirations were constantly thwarted by forces over which he had no control. The *shlemiel* was frequently the victim of attempts to

cross geographical, class, linguistic and cultural boundaries: his comic
fate illustrated the perils of such transgressions.[2]

In fact, Koestler's misfortunes in Palestine were of comparatively
short duration. He spent a painfully lean year after the rejection of his
attempt to join a collective farm and was at times in desperate straits.
But not for too long. This period actually saw him hit upon his
vocation, journalism. By autumn 1927 he was launched on the path
to fame and prosperity as one of the outstanding reporters of the
twentieth century.

I

Like most Viennese students Koestler joined a *Burschenschaft*, a
student society which combined the characteristics of a college
fraternity with the German duelling tradition. But he did not join
any ordinary student association. Following advice given to his
mother by a family friend he enrolled in the 'Unitas' *Burschenschaft*.
According to his recollections he thus inadvertently became a
member of one of the oldest, most prestigious and militant Jewish
student organisations, famous for its Zionist fervour.[3]

The original aim of the Zionist student societies had been to
promote Jewish nationalism and contest the stereotype of the weak
and cowardly Jew. By the time Koestler arrived in Vienna the Jewish
Burschenschaften were not simply fighting a negative image. The
student body was highly politicised, divided between right-wing
nationalists, mainly pan-German and anti-Semitic, on the one side
and socialists, democrats and Jews on the other. Almost every
Saturday morning the *Bummel*, the weekly *Burschenschaften* parade
through the Aula, the cloisters of the university, degenerated into
pitched battles between rival groups of students. An isolated Jewish
student was vulnerable to attack at any moment and it was wise to
align with a protective student association.[4]

The violence was neither aimless nor solely intended to harass
political opponents: it was designed to force certain concessions from
the university administration. The main goal of the Deutsche
Studentschaft, the German nationalist student association, was to
secure the imposition of limits on the number of Jewish students who
could enter the university. The Vienna Technische Hochschule was
the very first institution within the university to cave in to this
agitation. A numerus clausus on Jewish students was introduced in
November 1923: Koestler got in just under the wire.[5]

As a member of Unitas Koestler took part in many of the *Krawalle*, or brawls, wearing his father's bowler hat stuffed with newspaper as protection against blows from the walking sticks that both sides wielded. But Unitas did not just offer physical protection: it provided a psychologically and socially supportive community for Jewish students. The nurture of Jewish pride blended with traditional fraternity pastimes: drinking, singing bawdy songs and chasing girls. As a student, Koestler spent most of his recreational time in the basement headquarters of Unitas in Josephstadt (a district of Vienna in which the Jewish population comprised between ten and twenty per cent of the total inhabitants). There were regular *Knieper*, or drinking sessions, at which the hierarchically divided members of the fraternity sang hoary student drinking songs and newer ones with specially composed Jewish nationalist lyrics. They were also compelled to perform challenges, which invariably ended up with a fault that was 'punished' by the obligatory consumption of further draughts of beer.[6]

Membership supplied him automatically with friends and a sympathetic environment: 'For the first time I experienced that strongest of all social emotions: the feeling of comradeship, the feeling of belonging.' For an allegedly socially deprived child and awkward adolescent he adapted to his new environment with surprising alacrity. He revelled in his nickname of Perqueo, derived from the character in a drinking song whose 'stature was short, his thirst gigantic', and enjoyed a regular supply of girlfriends from the female workers in the local bars, restaurants and shops. His feats as a drinker and womaniser became legendary. When George Weidenfeld entered the diplomatic college of Vienna University and joined Unitas in 1935, he found that Koestler 'had left a trail of apocryphal stories of amorous adventure, intellectual feuds and hard living'.[7]

It may have been the best time of his life so far, but there were still tensions. A contemporary recalls that Koestler 'was already a morose student of life, his face wrinkled with worry – a brooding, suffering youth'. After two years of study Koestler found conventional engineering and physics boring. He preferred to spend his time in the university library reading about the Theory of Relativity, and the new quantum physics. He familiarised himself with such titans as Einstein, Böhr, Heisenberg, Schrödinger and Wolfgang Pauli. He also became absorbed in the work of the anthropologist Lucien Lévy-Bruhl, Freud and the post-Freudians, especially Adler and Jung. The *Burschenschaft* took up more and more of his time. In June 1923 he produced, directed and played in a 'Travesty' called *Madame Pompadour*. A clue to the atmosphere in which the performances were held can be gleaned from the programme notes (which he also wrote): 'It is forbidden to throw oranges and eggs at the artistes . . . Stinkbombs must be left at the cloakroom.'[8]

Koestler was immensely popular and well respected by the other students. In two years he advanced from being a 'Fox' or novice, to being 'Praeses', the chairman of his *Burschenschaft*. At the same time he became chairman of the entire association of Jewish nationalist student societies in Austria. In 1924 he presided over the thirtieth anniversary banquet of Unitas, a splendid occasion, which took place in the hall of a former Habsburg imperial palace.[9]

Sadly, the family fortunes did not mirror Arthur's personal success. In 1919 Henrik Koestler had found new employment with a Viennese import company. He was appointed company president and for a time enjoyed a high salary plus various perks. While Arthur attended the private school in Baden, his father and mother lived in luxurious rented apartments and hotel rooms in the midst of inflation- and poverty-stricken Vienna. Some time in 1921 Henrik decided to set up his own enterprise. For a while it was moderately successful. But the prosperity of an import-export firm at a time of roaring inflation depended heavily on juggling exchange rates, transactions that were vulnerable to illegal manipulation. In 1922 Henrik joined forces with another Vienna-based importer. The man turned out to be a swindler and the partnership collapsed. Fortunately, the venerable company accountant was an honest soul and revealed to Henrik Koestler how the fraud had been staged. Henrik went to the police, who arrested his ex-partner, and stood a good chance of recovering some of his fortune until the aged accountant, his star witness, died. Having earlier turned down a generous out-of-court settlement Henrik was condemned to pursuing the issue through the courts in an increasingly hopeless and financially ruinous quest. The case foundered and by 1924 he was a broken man. Roaring inflation during 1919–24 had eaten up whatever capital had escaped the lawyers' clutches.[10]

Arthur was a helpless spectator to the destruction of his father's health and fortune. In addition to 'aching pity', he felt a growing sense of responsibility for his parents. He now represented their last hope in the world, their guarantee of a peaceful and secure old age. However, his behaviour was diametrically opposed to what one would expect of a dutiful son. Instead of applying himself to his studies with the object of acquiring qualifications and setting up in practice as an engineer, he threw himself into Zionist activism and neglected his university work. He became a part-time volunteer worker in the Vienna office of the Jewish National Fund, the main instrument of Zionist fund-raising. He accompanied Vladimir Jabotinsky on a speaking tour of Austria and Czechoslovakia in 1924 and attended the fourteenth World Zionist Congress with his mentor in September the following year. Soon afterwards he abandoned his studies in favour of a new life in the emergent Jewish homeland in Palestine.[11]

II

Why did Koestler become a Zionist? In *Arrow in the Blue* he depicts his enrolment in Unitas as pure serendipity and his attachment to it as another consequence of his miserable childhood. He describes his devotion to Zionism and his decision to abandon university as emotional and impulsive. Yet, as we have seen, his childhood was not so abysmal and his attraction to Unitas may not have been simply emotive. There is certainly a pattern in his behaviour that was to recur again and again throughout his life, but there is also a logic to his actions. Given his Jewish identity and his awareness of anti-Semitism, it would have been natural to join a Jewish student association and a Zionist one at that. But this was not the impression he wanted to convey thirty years afterwards.

In a 1974 interview he gave an unusually incoherent explanation for his decision to join Unitas. 'When I got to Technical University in Vienna that was a period of rabid anti-Semitism . . . But I think I could have identified just as well with the Hungarian minority. Somewhere it was a romantic attachment which did not have its roots in any Jewish tradition in which I could have been bound up – I was not. But, of course, this vehement anti-Semitism automatically created a Jewish nationalist reaction and through friends of my parents I got recruited into that Zionist fraternity.'[12]

If refuge from and militancy against anti-Semitism was the motive for joining a student society, Koestler could have opted for the socialists. In his autobiography he jokingly dismisses the left-wingers because 'they had no *Burschenschaft*, merely clubs, and were altogether beneath contempt'. But there were other more pertinent reasons why a Jew might not want to enter their ranks. According to Helmut Gruber, a historian of inter-war Vienna, 'For educated and assimilated Jews the Socialist Party, formally on record as a staunch opponent of antisemitism, promised the possibility of being accepted as comrades, of finding an outlet for their commitment to *Bildung* [education] and Enlightenment, and of building a new world of true equality and justice.' However, the Socialist Party 'made quite clear that to enter its ranks meant to abandon all aspects of a Jewish identity. The demand for assimilation was total.'[13]

By 1922 Koestler had experienced the dissonance between being a Jew and a Hungarian. He had witnessed the two worlds of his grandfather's Jewish traditionalism and his father's Magyar acculturation. His Jewish identity was secular and to a large extent negative, but it was part of his sense of self. There were few possible spiritual homes for Jewish youths like him, but the pressure of anti–Semitism made a choice essential. As Gruber writes, 'Identity was an inescapable problem for all Jews save, perhaps, the religious and Zionists.' If Koestler had been true to his psychological reductionism he could have joined any of half a dozen other fraternities that offered comradeship. In fact, he made a specific choice, far less randomly than he implied. It was entirely reasonable and in keeping with his ethnic background for Koestler to have joined a Jewish nationalist student society and become a Zionist.

Perversely, he maintained in his memoirs that he was an ingenu when it came to Jewish nationalism and Zionist student societies: 'neither my parents nor I had ever heard of Zionism.' He claimed that he was converted by two more-senior Jewish students, Otto Hahn and Jacob Teller. They presented him with the standard Zionist argument: the Jews had always been persecuted due to anti–Semitism. There was no point arguing with anti–Semites because their antipathy towards Jews was irrational. For their part, the Jews were a 'sick race'. Thanks to a history of discrimination they had a distorted socio-economic profile. Few Jews were peasants or workers. Rather, they were crowded into certain high-profile economic positions that invariably aroused jealousy and hostility. The only way to cure Jews of this malaise, and all the neuroses associated with being a vulnerable, hated minority, was to return to the land. In Palestine the Jews would reconstitute themselves as a nation like other nations.[14]

Koestler suggests that when he first heard the arguments put by Hahn and others they 'seemed so simple and obvious' that he wondered why he hadn't thought of them himself. But would they have had *any* purchase on him if, as he protested thirty years later, he had barely no Jewish identity and had never been troubled by anti–Semitism? Is it possible that neither Koestler nor his parents had heard of the movement even though Theodor Herzl, the founder of modern Zionism, and his ally Max Nordau, the famous writer, were from Hungary and were celebrated local figures? Hungarian Jews in general, including those who were Magyarised, were hardly ignorant of Zionism. During the relatively tranquil years before the First World War, considerable numbers of 'assimilated' Hungarian Jewish students studying in Vienna signed up for Zionist student associations.[15]

It is much more likely that familiarity with the core elements of Zionism, or at least an empathy with its diagnosis of the modern Jewish condition, explain Koestler's rapid ascent through the ranks of the *Burschenschaft* and his passionate involvement with the right-wing Zionism of Vladimir Jabotinsky. For Koestler did not just elect to join a Jewish nationalist fraternity, he gravitated towards one of the most chillingly logical and aggressive forms of Zionism, one that eschewed the romantic, socialistic, pioneering ethos that in the 1920s was far more popular among Central European Jewish youth.[16]

For several years the World Zionist Organisation had been pre-occupied with the humdrum business of getting immigrants to Palestine and providing the infrastructure to absorb them into the new Jewish society. While it still faced political challenges, Zionism was bedevilled by the lack of funds for settlement projects. Zionist leaders exhorted their followers to devote their efforts to fund-raising. They played down any talk of statehood for the Jews in Palestine since they knew that, given the demographic balance between Jews and Arabs there, such proposals were premature and would incite violent Arab opposition. Calls for statehood would also discomfit the British, who commanded the destiny of Palestine by virtue of a mandate from the League of Nations. As a result, Zionism had become rather a tame affair.[17]

Vladimir Jabotinsky, the Russian-born Zionist maverick, believed the Zionist movement was missing a great opportunity to evacuate Jews from the Diaspora. He was also convinced it should press for a Jewish state on both banks of the River Jordan as, he believed, had been the original intention of the British when they had announced their patronage of a Jewish National Home in 1917. At odds with the movement's leadership, Jabotinsky resigned from the executive of the World Zionist Organisation in 1923 and spread his activist message via articles and speaking tours across Europe. He gave birth to an ideology and a movement known as Revisionist Zionism. To the maximalist territorial vision and militancy, from 1925 Jabotinsky added anti-socialism. He had always been anti-Marxist, but he now took up the cause of middle-class immigrants to Palestine who were excluded from economic influence by the all-powerful Jewish trades unions which controlled the labour market and the large collectivised sector of the economy. This was an explosive mixture.[18]

Jabotinsky acquired disciples in many countries. In Vienna his chief advocate was Wolfgang von Weisl, an alumnus of Unitas and a journalist for the highly respected Vienna *Neue Freie Presse*. Von Weisl was an amazing character who would materialise in spectacular circumstances at crucial moments in Koestler's youth. He was a native Viennese, about ten years older than Koestler. During the First World War he served in an artillery unit of the Austro-Hungarian army and reached the rank of lieutenant. Like Koestler, he oscillated between frenetic activity, often with a military accent, and more contemplative pursuits. During the revolutionary chaos in Vienna in 1918–19 von Weisl helped organise Jewish defence groups. He then settled down to study at the Vienna University medical faculty and qualified as a doctor. During his student days he was a member of Unitas and was busy with Zionist student politics. In 1921 he emigrated to Palestine. At first he worked as a manual labourer, setting a precedent which may have influenced Koestler. He eventually started a medical practice in Tel Aviv, but was also secretly engaged in giving officer training courses to men of the Haganah, the nascent underground Jewish defence force in Palestine.

In 1923 von Weisl returned to Vienna, but did not abjure Zionist work. While resuming medicine he wrote articles for the *Neue Freie Presse* and the Zionist daily, the *Wiener Morgenzeitung*. A year later he was appointed a political correspondent of the Berlin *Vossische Zeitung*, the most respected of the papers in the stable of the Ullstein press house. At around this time he threw in his lot with Jabotinsky. He went back to Palestine in the mid-1920s as the Palestine and Near East correspondent for the *Chicago Tribune* and Middle East correspondent for the Ullstein newspapers.[19]

During his spell in Vienna, von Weisl devoted his charm, charisma and energy to promoting Revisionist Zionism. He courted his old *Burschenschaft* and persuaded its members to endorse Jabotinsky and appoint him an honorary member. Koestler was delegated to present the badge of membership to Jabotinsky who was due to arrive in Austria for a speaking tour in May 1924. The two men got on with each other as soon as they met. Both were highly literate, cosmopolitan, assimilated and, a matter of some importance for the self-conscious young Koestler, short.[20]

Jabotinsky was born in Odessa in 1880 and brought up in a Russified family with little connection to Jewish life. He studied law in Switzerland and Italy, but found work as a journalist back in Odessa. The anti-Jewish riots in Russia in 1904–5 turned him into a professional Zionist and he was at the centre of world Zionist affairs from 1904 onwards. During the First World War he raised a Jewish fighting unit for the Allies in Egypt, later serving as an officer in one of the Jewish battalions formed by the British army in 1917. He ended the war in Palestine and for a time worked with the British administration before accusing it of reneging on its promises to the Jews. He was imprisoned by the British authorities in 1920 for organising illegal Jewish self-defence units to counter Arab rioters. By the time he was amnestied he had become a Jewish national hero. Jabotinsky joined the executive of the World Zionist Organisation, but his impatience and maximalism led to friction with its president, Chaim Weizmann. He soon resigned to form his own party and, ultimately, his own Zionist organisation.[21]

In many respects Jabotinsky's personality was similar to Koestler's. Weizmann, who despite being politically opposed to Jabotinsky liked him personally, wrote that 'he was rather ugly, immensely attractive, well-spoken, warm-hearted, generous, always ready to help a comrade in distress; all of these qualities were, however, overlaid by a certain touch of the rather theatrically chivalresque, a certain queer and irrelevant knightliness which was not at all Jewish'. Jabotinsky was also impatient and had an explosive temper. While he was a gifted writer capable of nuanced literary translations, his political thinking tended towards extremities. Often rhetoric and formal logic substituted for reality. His Zionist programmes, however lucidly expressed and internally coherent, frequently bore no relation to actualities.[22]

Jabotinsky and Koestler were two quixotic characters with much in common. Yet this alone could not explain Jabotinsky's astonishing invitation, so soon after their initial rendezvous, to the young and, to him, all but unknown student leader to act as his secretary and co-speaker during a lecture tour of Czechoslovakia. While Jabotinsky was impulsive he was not politically inept and was unlikely to invite someone to take up such a crucial role unless he was competent and trustworthy. Indeed, Koestler was no Zionist naïf. Nor was he hesitant in his Zionist work. In 1955 Oskar Rabbinowitz, the Revisionist Zionist activist and historian who was feared for his demanding intellectual standards, recalled hearing Koestler speak in support of Jabotinsky at a public debate in Brünn (Brno) during the tour. Rabbinowitz gave no indication that Koestler did anything other than acquit himself well in this demanding part.[23]

If Jabotinsky identified Koestler as an articulate, powerful and tested advocate of Zionism, what did Koestler see in him? Koestler later reflected that Jabotinsky was 'the first political shaman in my life'. He traced his attachment to charismatic ideological leaders back to the strong desire for certainty which had gripped him as a child. He believed then, and for many years continued to believe, that some men 'were guardians of the holy grail, of the one and indivisible secret'. In his pursuit of this ultimate truth and the security it offered, he followed these men until disillusionment or disaster overtook their association.[24]

It is also surely no coincidence that Jabotinsky appeared on the scene just when Koestler's father lost his fortune and began the years of decline. Koestler was forever in search of his father, who had been so physically and emotionally absent in his youth. Jabotinsky was as much a father figure as a 'shaman'. Yet there are father figures and father figures. Why choose one who is a maverick proponent of an extremist ideology? The obvious answer, albeit one which Koestler could not bear to admit, is that Jabotinsky's brand of Zionism made sense to him. It was precisely the logic of Revisionism that made it appealing. His immersion in Zionism was only visceral insofar as a coherent argument, that accorded with reality as he experienced it, excited him.

Despite the rationality of the Zionist idea, in his memoirs Koestler insisted that for him its attraction operated on a gut level: 'emotional commitment came first, and the arguments came later.' Koestler used the account of his initiation into political activity to illustrate his theory about the psychological origin of political allegiances: 'all evidence tends to show that the political libido is basically as irrational as the sexual drive, and patterned, like the latter, by early, partly unconscious experiences.'[25]

Koestler wants us to believe that, although he excelled in representing the Zionist case and became one of its foremost propagandists, his initial attraction to Zionism was muddle-headed. 'To take the plunge was easy; the struggle for clarity that followed was not. It took the best part of twenty-five years.'[26] Yet his pro-Zionist logic was as clear in 1922 as it was in 1947. Only the circumstances changed following the creation of Israel. Koestler did not abandon Zionism because he saw its flaws: it became redundant precisely because it was vindicated. He wrote his autobiography after the goals of Zionism, as he saw them, had been fulfilled and after he had 'renounced' his Jewish affiliations, which had been theoretically premised on a Zionist analysis and which in practice largely rested on Zionist activism. To throw a smoke screen around this logical progression he dismissed his youthful Zionism as a libidinally driven aberration which forced him into a sympathetic relationship with Jews whose beliefs and behaviour he despised.

III

After Jabotinsky returned from Czechoslovakia to his Paris head-quarters, Koestler went back to Vienna. There, he and a group of acolytes set up a branch of Jabotinsky's new Zionist Revisionist movement. Koestler's studies increasingly took second place to his Zionist work: he travelled frequently, addressing Jewish student groups throughout Austria, Czechoslovakia and further afield. But by now his parents' financial situation was adversely affecting him. In a letter to his father he mentioned pointedly that the cost of his travel to a conference of Jewish youth organisations in Czechoslovakia would be refunded. 'Come back soon,' he wrote, 'you know that as long as you are not here I am condemned to being thrifty.'[27]

Koestler was being torn in different directions. When he read about Arab attacks on Jewish settlers in Palestine he was choked with anger; his body muscles tensed and he desperately needed the relief of action. But in the university library, reading books on theoretical physics, he felt a 'sensation of absolute tranquility and peace' or, in Freudian parlance, 'the relaxed quietude and self-dissolving stillness' of 'the "oceanic feeling"'. In October 1925 he dropped out of university and six months later left Europe for Palestine.[28]

This was an extraordinary act in view of the hopes his parents were pinning on him. In subsequent years he explained it in quasi-mystical terms, in the style of a Dostoevsky novel. He had spent an intense evening with a Russian student, who insisted that all lives were predetermined. To prove that there was such a thing as volition, when he got back to his own digs Koestler located his matriculation book, in which his academic progress was logged, and burned it. The book was essential to graduation and was almost irreplaceable. For a moment he was intoxicated by a sense of freedom, but it was soon followed by remorse and depression as the enormity of what he had done sank in. He had only two more semesters to go before graduating; now his career prospects were nil. To make matters worse, he had to solicit money from his parents in order to survive and was forced to lie in the letters he sent them, saying that he was still working hard at his studies. In fact, he was spending whole days in bed and could not bring himself to go to the university.[29]

Several weeks later, he claimed, he resolved to go to Palestine to 'till the earth'. In his autobiography Koestler insisted that the two acts were unconnected. To explain his motives he recalled a dream that he had had at the time and which echoed a childhood fantasy. When he was about five he longed to get hold of a spade and go out into the streets to dig alongside gangs of labourers. It was, in his interpretation, a dream that expressed a desire to escape, 'an urge to run away and burn my bridges'. Perhaps. But in view of his subsequent resolution it might be more convincing to read the dream as anticipating the decision to go to Palestine and, spade in hand, 'till the earth'.[30]

Arguably, Koestler interpreted his own dream not so as to reveal some buried truth, but in order to disguise it. The 'bridge-burning' pattern may be accurate, but it does not explain the particular direction in which he headed once he had reached the other side. This only makes sense if it is seen as a logical extension of his Zionist activism, which was, itself, an outgrowth of his Jewish childhood in Budapest, Baden and Vienna. Significantly, Koestler did not mention that in September 1925, just a few weeks before he torpedoed his career, he had accompanied Jabotinsky to the fourteenth World Zionist Congress in Vienna. This was a turning point in Jabotinsky's life, too, marking his final rupture with mainstream Zionism and the formation of the Revisionist Zionist Organisation. He made a magnificent speech cutting to shreds the timid programme of the Zionist leadership and calling for immediate mass immigration to Palestine, using para-military methods if necessary. Even his enemies were overwhelmed by his lucidity and rhetorical power. Although Jabotinsky was the *sole* representative of his new movement at the Congress (he was later joined by three delegates elected on other tickets), he received a standing ovation from an audience that was overwhelmingly hostile when he rose to speak. The effect of this spectacle on the youthful Arthur Koestler can easily be imagined.[31]

To throw up one's studies to go to Palestine was the sort of stunt Jabotinsky would have favoured. Hundreds of young Jewish people were making similar romantic gestures all over Central Europe.[32] Koestler was, again, typical rather than atypical in his behaviour. The only difference, indicative of a truly quixotic character, was that he followed a Zionist leader who rejected the collective farms that were the chief lure for, and employer of, youthful immigrants who wanted to work in the Land of Israel.

IV

During the years of the British mandate, Jewish immigration to Palestine was managed by the Zionist Organisation according to quotas set by the British-run Palestine Adminstration in consultation with the Jewish Agency for Palestine. From 1922 the quotas were calibrated to Palestine's 'economic absorbative capacity', that is the demand for workers. Since there was still relatively little industry there, immigration depended heavily on the estimated demand for labour in the agricultural sector. To qualify for an immigration certificate it was almost essential for a prospective immigrant to be suited to agricultural employment. The Zionist Organisation ran and funded a network of training farms designed to equip young pioneers with these skills. As 'conquest of the land' through settlement and farming was central to Zionist ideology, pioneering was doubly important. But Koestler had no desire to train as an agricultural worker and, as a disciple of Jabotinsky, was out of sympathy with the socialistic, back-to-the-land ethos of the pioneering movements.

As if his efforts to immigrate were not sufficiently complicated, in 1925 the British authorities revised the rules governing the issue of immigration certificates. Instead of being supplied by British consulates, they now had to be sent from the central immigration office in Palestine, once the quotas for manual workers were agreed with the Jewish Agency. As a result, there were long delays and hundreds of mainly East European pioneers exiting Europe for Palestine via Vienna found themselves stranded in the city.

Several weeks passed before Koestler obtained his immigration permit in March 1926. It was awarded on the pretext that he was a rural labourer although, in fact, officials in the Palestine Office of the Zionist Organisation in Vienna, particularly its director Dr Nahum Blauer, had smoothed the way for him. Koestler was, after all, a leading light in the student Zionist world and had proved himself on the campaign trail with Jabotinsky. He merely had to teach himself rudimentary modern Hebrew in order to pass an examination and he was on his way. If he did seriously intend to work on the land, it may have been merely a desire to emulate his hero von Weisl.

Koestler's parents were in England, where his father was attempting to rebuild his import business, at the time he left the Technische Hochschule. They were still abroad when he deceitfully told them that he was going to Palestine to get work experience as an engineer in order to have a better chance of getting a job back in Vienna. He eventually left on 1 April 1926, amid cheers from the members of Unitas who escorted him to the station and gave him a stirring send-off.[33]

What followed was a grimly comic anticlimax. He arrived in Haifa a few days later where he found the sights of the 'Orient' unexpected, dazzling and confusing. After his first night in the Promised Land he sought out Dr Abraham Weinshall, another of Jabotinsky's followers and at that time the chief organiser of the Revisionist Zionists in Palestine. Weinshall was a Russian Jew, who came from a small town near Baku in the Caucasus. Like many talented Jewish youths he had gone to universities abroad and studied law in Germany and Switzerland. He was a founder of the Zionist student organisation HaHever and during the First World War edited a short-lived Zionist journal in Zurich. After the war he returned to the briefly independent Caucasus region, but left in 1920 after Communist rule was imposed by the Red Army. He settled in Haifa and became an expert in land law. In 1925 he was chairman of the Palestine branch of the Zionist Revisionists and also a member of Haifa's Jewish community council.[34]

Weinshall and Koestler, who was twelve years younger, quickly became firm friends, an alliance which led Koestler to enduring relationships with other members of the Weinshall clan, notably Abraham's brother Jacob, known familiarly as Jascha. But these were not friendships that would be of practical use to him for the moment. He had been assigned to a *kvutzah* – collective settlement – in the Jezreel Valley, about forty miles inland. In ideological terms the settlement was light years away from the Revisionists of Haifa.

Several days after landing in Palestine, Koestler reached his goal: Kvutzah Heftzi-Bah. At that time Heftzi-Bah numbered a few dozen pioneers. Even in the 1970s its total population did not exceed 500 and it often goes unmarked on maps of Israel. The settlement had been founded in 1923 on the lower slopes of Mount Gilboa by Central and East European Jews who had arrived in the 'Third Aliyah', the third major wave of Jewish immigration to Palestine, which lasted roughly from 1919 to 1923.[35]

The members of the Third Aliyah were mainly hard-bitten Marxist socialists. They provided the ideological leaven for some of the most radical social experiments and political movements of the Yishuv, the Jewish community of Palestine. The *kvutzah* was one of these innovations. Sticking to the prototype of the first successful collective settlement at Degania, on the shore of Lake Galilee, the *kvutzah* eschewed the larger communal enterprises known as kibbutzim. Numbers were kept low in order to preserve an intimate family-like atmosphere. Small numbers were also easier to support economically, and the *kvutzot* (plural form) were intended to settle arid, hilly areas that were ignored by the protagonists of large-scale farming.[36]

The pioneers of the Third Aliyah were fanatically dedicated to work on the land. Physical labour was regarded as a medium for personal spiritual cleansing and rebirth, eliminating the 'corruption' of Jewish life in the Diaspora. It was also the key to national revival through regenerating the people and reclaiming their land. The *halutzim*, pioneers, were imbued with a concoction of Marxist dogma about the evils of property and materialism, and a mystical attachment to work on the soil as exemplified in some of Tolstoy's writings. The *kvutzot* expected members to shed all personal interests and identify totally with the collective. They had no private belongings or income. All meals were taken together in a communal hall. Children were raised in collective children's homes.[37] Koestler had stumbled into a community which he could not have been less well equipped to join.

On arrival at Heftzi-Bah, Koestler looked for a certain member of the collective's secretariat, an alumnus of Unitas, who had been warned to expect him. This man was ill, but Koestler was given a meal in the dining hall while another of the commune's leadership took him in hand. Before he had left Haifa, Abraham Weinshall had asked him what he wanted to be and Koestler had replied: 'A wanderer and an author.' The representative of the *kvutzah* now asked him a similar question. Koestler told him that he wanted to join the collective and stay for one or two years, before going to Tel Aviv or taking up politics. In one sentence he doomed his prospects as a pioneer.[38]

The formal procedure for admission was for a prospective candidate to serve a short probationary period of up to two months before being taken on as a candidate. Full acceptance into the *kvutzah* was decided by the entire membership and could take years to achieve. Koestler never made it past the short trial phase. He struggled manfully in the fields, clearing rocks from land that was to be tilled, but his hands soon blistered and his ineptitude was glaringly obvious. 'I did my best to hide my aversion for the spade – that rusty, clotted spade, so different from the gleaming symbol of my dream of freedom.'[39] It was no use. Furthermore, he was ill-served by his prior political activity. Jabotinsky was not yet regarded by the Palestine Jewish labour movement in such extreme terms as in the 1930s, when his followers increasingly adopted the trappings of Central European Fascism, but he was already resented as a critic of collective settlement as a way to 'conquer the land'. In any case, the *kvutzot* expected complete ideological homogeneity. There was no way that Koestler could have fitted in and it is hard to understand how he ever got himself into this ludicrous fix.

When he was told that the *kvutzah* secretariat had decided he was not suitable to become a candidate he experienced 'mixed feelings of dejection and half-conscious relief'. Although he saw that he was not cut out for rural labour he was intensely competitive and hated to fail at anything. As he had demonstrated in his student days, he also possessed rigid ideas of what constituted manliness. In Vienna he constructed a hard-living and hard-drinking persona. Yet in Palestine, confronted by one of the ultimate tests of manhood, he could not make the grade. Years later his rejection still hurt.

There were other reasons, too, which he never quite acknowledged. Koestler confessed that he had 'come under the strange lure of kvutsa life'. He realised that the collective offered him the chance to settle and build firm, permanent relationships. He sensed the 'undefinable feeling of growing roots in an untamed spot, and of growing human ties of a quality unknown elsewhere'. The commune promised even more: a resolution of the tension between the active and contemplative lives that had bedevilled him as a student. In effect, the *kvutzah* offered the ideal praxis: a combination of the life of the mind and physical exertion. Work was intended to be spiritually fulfilling and to push forward the national enterprise. The individual and the nation would both be regenerated through manual labour. The collective demanded self-abnegation, but it was not intellectually sterile. Mind and body, self and others were in perfect harmony. What, then, stopped Koestler from making a bid to stay by working to overcome his physical weaknesses and renouncing his affiliation to Jabotinsky?

Vanity was probably the single most important element. Close behind this were arrogance and impatience. As he indicated to Weinshall and the member of the secretariat, he was already convinced that he was destined for greater things. Nor was he prepared to work his way up slowly and painfully, shovel in hand. His chosen tool was the pen and he wanted to be a writer. He wanted to strut a larger stage than that offered by Kvutzah Heftzi-Bah, something the members of the settlement probably sensed even before Koestler did. He also had mixed feelings about his Jewish comrades. His sense of rejection and his later break with Zionism may have so coloured his attitude towards the pioneers that his subsequent writings about them must be read with caution, but it is still possible to detect equivocation from an early stage in his encounter with the Jews of the new Jewish society.

In 1945 Koestler returned to Palestine for several months to research a novel on the struggle for a Jewish state: this was the second peak of his involvement with Zionism and the Jewish people. The novel, *Thieves in the Night* (1946), is set largely on a kibbutz and Koestler drew extensively on his earlier experiences as an apprentice pioneer. The main character and narrator, Joseph, is a half-Jewish English immigrant who settled on the kibbutz in the early 1930s, after being repelled by the anti-Semitism of English society. The character is heavily autobiographical: some of the most memorable observations and turns of phrase in the novel first appear in Koestler's journalism and he would, in turn, draw on it in memoirs and elsewhere to express his own thoughts about Jewish nationalism and Israel.[40]

The Palestine Joseph inhabits had changed greatly in the ten years since Koestler first arrived and the type of settler was different. All the same, the ambivalence he feels towards his fellow Jews may be taken as indicative of Koestler's attitude in the 1920s. Surveying his comrades in the kibbutz dining hall, Joseph is struck by the 'ugliness of the faces around him'.[41]

By contrast, Koestler's view of the communal settlements was almost wholly positive. In *Thieves in the Night* he wrote approvingly that they embodied the best of the Bible, Marx and Herzl. In his first novel, *The Gladiators* (1938), which was all about man's search for Utopia, the kibbutz was the model for 'Sun City', the experimental, ideal society which Koestler imagined being created by slaves who had freed themselves from the Romans. Only in the late 1940s, after his break with Zionism and the Jewish people, did he add a critical edge to his commentaries on the kibbutzim. At the time he left Heftzi-Bah he actually considered celebrating it in a work of fiction.

V

Koestler was now homeless and broke. All his possessions could be packed into the small suitcase that he lugged down the road out of Heftzi-Bah in the general direction of Haifa. His only plan was to reach the city, make contact with his Revisionist friends and find work. It was the worst possible time to go job hunting in Palestine. The economy had been artificially stimulated by the mass immigration of 60,000 Polish Jews driven out of Poland by economic and legal discrimination during 1924–6. The new arrivals, who were mainly middle class and brought some capital with them, helped promote a building boom in the coastal cities, especially Tel Aviv. But when the Polish government changed and the anti-Semitic policies were toned down, immigration tailed off. Towards the end of 1926 the building trades crashed and the economy went into a deep recession. By 1927 there were 8000 unemployed Jewish workers and twice as many Jews left Palestine as arrived. According to Walter Laqueur, the historian of Zionism, 'By 1927–8 the prospects of Zionism were dimmer and its adherents more despondent than ever before.'[42]

To make matters worse for Arthur Koestler, he belonged to a political faction that was rapidly acquiring pariah status. Its adherents fell outside the comprehensive, if rudimentary, welfare system established to service members of the Jewish labour movement. Revisionist Zionists had none of the connections that enabled East European immigrants arriving via the left-wing parties and pioneering movements to get a toe-hold in the labour market or the predominant, socialised sector of the economy.

It took Koestler three long, hot, dusty days to reach Haifa. Once there, he stayed with Abraham Weinshall and his family for several weeks while he tried to find work. Weinshall was full of ideas which combined entrepreneurship with Revisionist politics, an uneconomic mixture at the best of times. He and Koestler first attempted to set up a Hebrew newspaper for northern Palestine. Called *HaTzafon* (*The North*) it was intended to break the hold of Jerusalem and Tel Aviv over publishing and end the monopoly of the left-wing press. Weinshall, whose Hebrew was far superior to Koestler's, supplied the copy; Koestler trudged the business district of Haifa drumming up the advertising. It was hardly a propitious moment to start a paper, least of all a right-wing one in a town famous as a bastion of Jewish trades unions. In addition, the problems of distribution were fearsome.

The duo also established a Revisionist press agency to rival the left-wing dominated and semi-official news services. It had a modest success and Koestler managed to get several articles published in Zionist newspapers in Europe. He successfully submitted one to the Vienna *Neue Freie Presse*, although he did not get confirmation of this for some time. Despite initial promise neither venture generated sufficient income to support Koestler. To add to his woes, the Weinshalls moved and he had to find rented accommodation.

For three weeks he made use of the course on architecture which he had taken at the Technische Hochschule and worked as an assistant to an Arab architect. However, he was forced to extend himself well beyond his meagre training and was sacked for incompetence. He spent an even shorter spell as a lemonade seller in downtown Haifa. During this humiliating period he was too ashamed even to visit the Weinshalls and hovered on the edge of malnutrition, sharing a fetid room with a married couple in a spartan house in Haifa's German colony.[43]

Now without any income to speak of, Koestler was forced to vacate the room. Over the next few weeks he slept on the floor of a paint shop, in a dentist's surgery and on the tables at the Haifa Revisionist Club. He was beginning to look pretty awful. For days he consumed little more than a handful of olives or dates, some pitta bread and copious amounts of tea. He perfected the art of making cigarettes from stubs discarded on the floor of the Club and bumming smokes off comrades or anyone who looked ripe for a conversation.

Suddenly, at this nadir in Koestler's fortunes, von Weisl materialised, like a *deus ex machina*. He had stopped at the Club *en route* to Jerusalem from the Golan Heights, where he had been covering a story for his new employer, the Ullstein press. Von Weisl treated Koestler to tea and, probably realising his comrade's dire condition, left him in possession of the considerable amount of change from the note he dropped to cover the bill before rushing off. On the strength of this Koestler was able to clean himself up, buy some fresh clothes and visit the Weinshalls again. After discussing his plight with them he decided to head for Tel Aviv, in the hope of finding more job openings in the fledgling Jewish metropolis.[44]

Once again, Koestler made the journey mainly on foot. He arrived just when the recession in Tel Aviv was worsening, although the city still felt like a boom town. It had more than doubled in size over the preceding three years and was bursting with the vitality of the new settlers. The bulk of these were middle class, mainly Russian or Polish Jews, and Koestler seems to have taken an instant dislike to them and the urban society they moulded around themselves. His hunt for work was no more successful than it had been in Haifa. In quick succession he held jobs as a multi-lingual secretary for a tourist agency, a land surveyor's assistant (employed by one of Abraham Weinshall's brothers) and a salesman of advertising space for the magazine of the Palestine Manufacturers' Association. His efforts to maintain the press agency were unavailing and it was closed down.[45]

Koestler's social and business contacts were mainly confined to the small Revisionist faction in Palestine, but he made some new friends, particularly among the habitués of the Hungarian Café, a popular meeting place for intellectuals, artists and writers. One of them was Avigdor Hameiri, born Avigdor Feuerstein in provincial Hungary in

1890. Hameiri combined a secular with a Jewish education and in his teens started writing poetry in Hungarian and Hebrew. He was a Zionist and a writer from an early age. During the First World War he was captured by the Russians and lived in Odessa after his release from a POW camp in 1917. When Zionist activity in Russia was suppressed by the Bolsheviks in 1921, he emigrated to Palestine. Hameiri was an influential figure within the tiny world of Hebrew *belles-lettres* and edited his own literary monthly. He shared a Hungarian background and a love of world literature with the neophyte Koestler, who came to his attention when Koestler translated some of his poems for a German Zionist publication.[46]

Hameiri, too, was a quixotic type and both men got on well despite the disparity in age and experience. Koestler often slept on the floor of Hameiri's flat in north Tel Aviv where the older man lived in poor and cramped circumstances with his wife and child. Both desperately needed a profitable venture, so with two other Hungarians they planned to open a satirical theatre modelled on Central European cabaret. It was a typically fantastic notion and Koestler moved on before the project came anywhere near to fruition. (Against all the odds, Hameiri did eventually enjoy a minor success with 'Kumkum', or the Kettle Theatre.)

More bizarrely, Koestler tried writing Hebrew fairy stories for children. The stories were commissioned by the Jewish National Fund to introduce children to themes in Jewish history and tell them about the Land of Israel. A few were completed and printed in Zionist journals in Central Europe. But this was hardly a career and Koestler's options were running out fast. One of his new friends in Tel Aviv was a Russian-born, Viennese-trained psychoanalyst, Moshe Har Even. They shared a past familiarity with Vienna and the luminaries of psychoanalysis, and a common present that was comprised chiefly of hunger and poverty. Har Even was an Eeyorish character who seemed to absorb Koestler's moods effortlessly. He was also capable of talking blunt good sense and urged him to return to Vienna to complete his studies.[47]

Despite the fact that recent immigrants were deserting Palestine by the hundreds each month, Koestler ignored Har Even's sound advice and persisted. He stayed partly out of pride. For weeks he wrote letters home that bore no relation to his true situation; to give up would have meant confessing failure and deceit. He may also have hung on because he had just enough success to give him a glimpse of a breakthrough. Finally he was sustained by political dedication. Aside from his sojourn in the Jezreel Valley, Koestler lived within the close-knit, fervent Revisionist community. Almost all his friends were followers of Jabotinsky. They were fired with a mission that buoyed them, despite regular set-backs. In later life Koestler denigrated his ideological commitment to Zionism, but without this it is hard to fathom the grim resolution he showed in the face of repeated failure.

In the autumn of 1926 von Weisl made another dramatic intervention in Koestler's life. He was now responsible for a monthly German-language and Arabic publication sponsored by the German legation in Cairo for the purposes of promoting German goods and services. Since he was already stretched covering the Middle East for the Ullstein newspapers, von Weisl summoned Koestler to Cairo to edit the magazine for him. The *Nile and Palestine Gazette* only lasted for three months, but the job enabled Koestler to winter in Cairo in a modicum of comfort and see Egypt. He visited the museums, the archaeological sites and travelled around the countryside in the company of Robert Hoffmann, a German orientalist painter. When the journal was discontinued, von Weisl helpfully retained Koestler as his 'secretary'.[48]

Although the Revisionist network had never managed to fit Koestler with a substantial job, it always managed to tide him over. It worked for him once more in the first weeks of 1927, when Jabotinsky put Koestler's name forward as a candidate for the job of executive secretary to the World Union of Zionist Revisionists (UZR) at its international office in Berlin. In the spring he travelled back to Europe via Alexandria, Constanza and Budapest, where he stopped off to see his parents. While he was there he sold three travel pieces about the Middle East to the *Pester Lloyd*, Budapest's German-language liberal newspaper. The fees covered his onward travel expenses and enabled him to give some money to his parents, who were now living in much reduced circumstances in a single room in a boarding house. He did not stay more than a few days with them or show much interest in their rather pitiful state. Instead, he was more concerned to catch up with a woman he had met *en route* to Europe. This relentless pursuit was typical of his romantic affairs. He had been involved in a number of liaisons in Palestine, one of which almost led to a shot-gun wedding. They were all marked by infatuation, and obsessive involvement, followed by growing lack of interest and rejection. While he was in the thrall of an affair he seems to have been almost unbelievably self-centred.[49]

From May until the end of August 1927 Koestler lived in Berlin. At first he stayed with his uncle, Otto Devrient (Zeiteles), and his

non-Jewish wife, Henne, at their home in the Berlin suburb of
Köpenick. Later he took digs in the slum area of Alexander Platz hard
by the centre of the city, a district densely populated by *Ostjuden*,
Polish Jewish immigrants.

Officially he worked for the World Executive of the UZR, as a
subordinate to Richard Lichtheim, a wealthy and highly cultured
German Jewish Zionist. Lichtheim, who was one of the most
impressive converts to Jabotinsky's creed, was formally a vice-
president of the movement and chief of its Berlin HQ. Koestler's job
was to inform constituents of the UZR of decisions made by its
central policy-makers and to encourage their implementation. But
the UZR had no money to speak of and Lichtheim was so disgusted
with the sloppy funding arrangements that he rarely appeared at
'Head Office'. He resigned after only eight months. Koestler
meanwhile found that the movement could only afford to employ
him part-time and eked out a miserable living, going into the bare
office to fire missives into a vacuum. Berlin, by contrast, was
buzzing. These were the golden years of the Weimar Republic, but
Koestler was too broke to savour the cultural excitement forever
associated with this era of the city's history. For him it was a ghastly,
demoralising phase.[50]

VI

Yet again Wolfgang von Weisl came to the rescue. In September he
was assigned to tour the Far East as a special correspondent for the
Ullstein papers. Since he would be away for over a year a replacement had to be found to cover his beat in the Middle East. He put
forward Koestler who had, by this time, accumulated a fair bit of
journalistic experience notwithstanding his tender age – he was
barely twenty-two years old, and even more boyish in appearance.
Koestler was called for an interview at the imposing Ullstein offices
on Kochstrasse in the heart of Berlin. He was in awe of the place and
not without reason.

The Ullsteins were an old German-Jewish family hailing from
Fürth in Bavaria. Although the family members became less Jewish
over the generations, they were increasingly committed to the
liberalism in Germany that had enabled their social and economic
progress. Leopold Ullstein, the founder of the newspaper dynasty,
had taken over his father's wholesale paper business in the 1860s, but
itched to get into politics or newspaper publishing. In 1877 he
bought the ailing *Berliner Zeitung* and made it a platform for liberal

views. He next founded the *Berliner Abendpost*, an evening paper which kept the presses of the *Berliner Zeitung* employed during the day and recycled its contents. His greatest success came with the *Berliner Illustrierte Zeitung*, which he purchased in 1892. It soon had a circulation of two million, or over three per cent of the entire German population, and was immensely profitable.

In the 1890s control of the house passed to Leopold's five sons. In 1898 they founded the *Berliner Morgenpost*, which soon won a circulation of half a million in Berlin, and added the *Berliner Zeitung am Mittag*, designed to come out at noon and service the districts around Berlin. It too was a commercial hit. The Ullsteins expanded into humorous magazines, journals for intellectuals, women and children. Each new publication brought in train new marketing gimmicks and sales lines. In 1913 they bought the *Vossische Zeitung*, founded in 1705, one of the most revered newspapers in Germany. It was costly to modernise and to run, but it gave them far-reaching influence.

Under the editorship of the left-inclined Georg Bernhard, between 1918 and 1928, the *Vossische Zeitung* preached reconciliation with France, commitment to the League of Nations and support for Weimar democracy. Although the publishing house suffered during the years of hyper-inflation after the First World War, it enjoyed a second phase of expansion in the salad days of Weimar Germany. It could afford to pay very high salaries to editors and journalists, and pampered its 10,000 employees. At the highest levels its reporters and editors had access to ministers and politicians, with whom its papers had a cosy relationship. In 1927 it looked as if everything was going well for the Ullsteins and for Germany. To work for the house was a passport to social status and financial security.[51]

Koestler was interviewed by the head of personnel and the director of the news service. He was certainly young, but he had published articles in the prestigious Viennese *Neue Freie Presse*, the equally weighty Budapest *Pester Lloyd* and numerous Zionist papers. They decided to hire him on a trial basis at a salary of DM200 per month basic, plus what he could earn free-lancing on the side. This was a small fortune to the impoverished Koestler and he was suitably euphoric. But until his first salary cheque came through he remained virtually destitute and he still had to find the means to get back to Palestine.

Penniless, and too insecure to ask for a loan or an advance, he was condemned to a 'grotesque Odyssey' wholly out of character with his new position and status. He scraped together enough cash to get as far as Vienna, where he persuaded the *Neue Freie Presse* to commission a series of articles from him. But this, too, was money in the future rather than in the bank. Fortunately, his comrades from Unitas organised a whip-round and after a night of revelry gave him enough to pay for a river-boat ticket to Budapest. There he sold his books and children's toys, while his parents pawned some of their last valuables to buy him a passage by train and river steamer to Constanza, on the Black Sea, where he would set sail for Palestine.

Although Koestler had left the employment of the UZR, he was still an activist. In Romania he stopped off in Bucharest to meet the local Zionist Revisionist committee with which he had been corresponding from Berlin. It was a doubly useful meeting. When he arrived in Constanza he found that his boat was held up for two days. He was down to his last few coins and would have to go hungry and sleep in the open unless he could get some money. In desperation he cabled his Zionist Revisionist comrades back in Bucharest and they immediately wired him funds. It took Koestler nearly a month to get back to Palestine to embark on his new career as Ullstein's man in the Middle East.[52]

VII

Thanks to von Weisl, Arthur Koestler had found his *métier*. In later life he would write novels, plays, memoirs, essays, literary criticism and popular science, but nothing as consistently excellent as his journalism. If he had a genius it was for reportage. This is evident not just in what he wrote for newspapers, but in his longer works that used a journalistic style. He was an acute observer, combining a clear perception of things and places with an ability to describe them precisely and concisely. He was no less perceptive in evaluating and portraying people, a gift that was nourished by his interest in psychology and psychoanalysis.

The reasons for the consistency of his journalism are easy to fathom. When writing for newspapers he was constrained by fixed rules of procedure. His efforts were subjected to tough editorial scrutiny, against which he had little recourse. The ethic of journalism also forced him to minimise his own opinions and curb overt expressions of personality. Koestler needed and benefited from these disciplines, but sadly he enjoyed journalism far more than he valued it as a mode of expression or a social function. Once his talents were freed from the word-count and the deadline, he tended to become sententious and his writing grew flaccid.

There was no time or room for sentiment once he was established in a house on Rehov Neviim, Street of the Prophets, in the new Jewish quarter of Jerusalem, not far from the Old City. From this base he was expected to cover events in Palestine, Egypt, Transjordan, Iraq, Syria, Lebanon and the Saudi peninsula. Each week he had to file three full-length articles, a mixture of news reports and feuilletons, miniature essays often of a whimsical nature. This was not all. He contributed articles to the *Neue Freie Presse* and Zionist periodicals in Palestine, Europe and the United States.

He did not waste any time. On 2 October 1927 his byline appeared over a full-page illustrated piece about 'Jerusalem Today' in *Die Grüne Post*. From then on a steady stream of articles poured forth on every conceivable subject. They varied from a report on a visit to a workers' colony serving the Jordan hydro-electric works (*Vossische Zeitung*, 17 July 1929), to coverage of a première by the 'Habimah' Hebrew theatre company (*Vossische Zeitung*, 9 June 1929). He reported elections in Tel Aviv (*Vossische Zeitung*, 26 January 1929), a visit to the Holy Land by Rockefeller (*Vossische Zeitung*, 18 March 1929) and wrote an article for one of the *Vossische Zeitung* supplements on the archaeological features of the settlement at Bet Alfa (14 April 1929).

Among his more significant assignments, Koestler interviewed King Feisal of Iraq, Emir Abdullah of Jordan, the Egyptian Prime Minister and the President of Lebanon. He reported on the internecine struggle between the Husseini and Nashashibi clans as they manoeuvred for leadership of the Palestinian Arab national movement, the outcome of which would be critical for the future of the Jewish National Home. He sent back dispatches on the simmering row between Jews and Muslims in Jerusalem over ownership of and access to the Wailing Wall, the surviving portion of the western wall of Herod's temple. In 1928 the dispute led to serious brawls that foreshadowed the country-wide riots against the Jews a year later.[53]

His Zionist ardour was undiminished, but its expression neatly dovetailed with his newfound profession. In 1928 Jabotinsky returned to Palestine after a long, enforced sojourn in Europe. Soon after his arrival he was invited to take up the editorship of a sickly daily paper *Doar HaYom*. Jabotinsky intended making it into a vehicle for Revisionism and brought on to the reconstituted editorial board a host of old comrades including von Weisl and Koestler. Their first task was to modernise the paper, which had previously been directed towards the conservatively minded Jewish settlers of the pre-war era. By introducing the modern techniques and styles of European journalism they hoped to gain readers and sell the Revisionist message.

Within Zionist circles Koestler was now a young man of some importance and stature. Jabotinsky certainly valued his participation and engaged him to write the first editorial for *Doar HaYom*, in December 1928, on the subject of Europe's development since the end of the 1914–18 war. In addition to writing leaders Koestler contributed an occasional column called 'Jerusalem Letters', which he also sold in translation to the New York *New Palestine*.[54] In a lighter vein, Koestler took a leaf out of the Ullstein book and developed a weekend leisure section. This was an astonishing innovation in the po-faced world of Hebrew journalism. He caused mild consternation by introducing a Hebrew crossword puzzle, something previously regarded as too flippant for a serious newspaper. Circulation rose from a meagre 1000 to 2000 in just a few months and within a year the paper was one of the best-selling titles in Palestine. Its very success was the cause of its undoing. In July 1930 the British authorities became alarmed that the hawkish Revisionist message was reaching so wide an audience at a time of great political and communal sensitivity. The publisher was told that, unless Jabotinsky relinquished control, the paper would lose its licence. Jabotinsky was obliged to comply.[55]

By that time Koestler had been long gone from Palestine. In June 1929 he took his annual leave in Europe, as usual. He made sure he saw his parents at least once a year for an extended period, but this time the pull towards home comprised more than filial duty. Despite his increasing income, his prestige, his Revisionist friends and his growing rootedness he had resolved to leave Palestine for good. Why?

In the late 1940s von Weisl recounted to Joseph Nedava, a disciple of Jabotinsky and one of Koestler's early biographers, that 'At first Koestler was enraptured with Zionism. He realised that he had found his spiritual refuge. He roamed the plain of Sharon and the hills of Galilee like a dreamer.' But he was impatient and the economic crisis ground him down.[56]

Yet Koestler's income had quintupled since he was first hired at the Kochstrasse offices and he lived a good life. Although he remitted a substantial proportion of his salary to his parents, there was more than enough to lavish on Palestine's few leisure activities. Jerusalem was an isolated, provincial city with few social or cultural facilities. On most weekends he travelled down to Tel Aviv, where there was more to do there over the sabbath, including cafés, restaurants, theatres, concerts and cinemas, and stayed with Moshe Har Even. For longer breaks, he went riding in the desert areas around Jerusalem or hiking in the Galilee, an area familiar from his time at Heftzi-Bah. He often took his Alsatian dog Jassy with him, the first of many canine companions, which he had acquired on a leave-trip to Hungary.

But he was getting fed up with the small, incestuous Revisionist community in Palestine and he found it difficult to break out. As a foreign Jew he was unacceptable to British colonial society, while the Jewish community was dominated by mainstream Zionists who looked askance at his politics. More seriously, he realised that without a lot of work he was never going to become as fluent in Hebrew as Hameiri or von Weisl. Nor was he inclined to make the effort. He preferred that the new Jewish community of Palestine should Latinise the Hebrew alphabet to make it easier to read and more permeable to European vocabulary. Although this was one of Jabotinsky's pet ideas too, such a notion flew in the face of the cultural and linguistic nationalism which was a cornerstone of the Jewish national revival. Whereas Jabotinsky, by necessity, bent with the wind Koestler rather typically let his impatience and egoism blind him to unpalatable facts. He rationalised his reluctance to embrace Hebrew by denigrating the language and deriding the attachment of Jews to it.[57]

In his memoirs he claimed that his decision to leave Palestine was due to a fundamental disenchantment with Jews, Judaism, Zionism, the Hebrew revival and the entire Palestine project. The Holy Land, he reflected in 1951, 'exerts a strong attraction on eccentrics, prophets, monomaniacs, and reformers; there are probably more cranks to the square mile in Jerusalem than in any other town'. The city combined a 'tragic beauty and inhuman atmosphere'. Its inhabitants were 'poisoned by holiness. . . . The population of the city is a mosaic; but every portion of it is disagreeable.' The various ethnic and faith groups were clannish. 'It was an austere, pharasaic town, full of hatred, distrust, and phoney relics.' Jerusalem testified to 'the destructive power of faith, the failure of man's attempt to come to terms with God, and the resulting unpleasantness of the union of the mortal and the divine'.

Regardless of his social and professional progress, 'I grew increasingly tired of Palestine. Zionism in 1929 had come to a standstill. Immigration had been reduced to a mere trickle.' He had gone to Palestine as an idealistic Zionist youth, but: 'Instead of Utopia, I had found reality; an extremely complex reality which attracted and repelled me, but where the repellent effect, for a simple reason gradually gained the upper hand . . . the Hebrew language.'[58]

Koestler genuinely feared that if the Hebrew alphabet was not Latinised the Jews of Palestine would be cut off from the treasures of European culture. 'Its archaic structure and vocabulary made it totally unfit to serve as a vehicle for modern thought, to render the shades of feeling and meanings of the twentieth century.' However, Nedava recalled that his grasp of written Hebrew was 'rather poor' and it is hard to see how without a better grasp of Hebrew Koestler was in any position to judge whether this was true. The opposite was more likely the case: he was cut off from the treasures of Jewish culture. Prejudice came to the rescue of impatience.[59]

In any case, this was more the view from 1949 than 1929. It was not how he felt when he returned to Palestine on a journalistic assignment for the London *News Chronicle* in 1938. Describing this 'sentimental journey' he recalled: 'I had lived in Palestine before, and I felt rather attached to that romantic, bizarre little country.' He admired the new Jewish districts, with their modern architecture and Central European café life. Until he enquired into Jewish–Arab relations, 'Life in Jerusalem seemed a perfect idyll.' He was even cheerful about Tel Aviv. In places it resembled 'a rather backward quarter in some Eastern European city' but in fact it was 'the antithesis of the ghetto'. True, he was disappointed by the city's cultural life (even though he noted that it already had two theatres and a vibrant Hebrew press) and ascribed this to the insularity imposed on the country by the use of Hebrew; but when in the course of this article he coined the apophthegm that 'self-hatred has been the Jewish form of patriotism', he intended it to be heeded by overly self-critical Palestinian Jews.[60]

Koestler lived in Jerusalem again from January to August 1945. At this time he even contemplated remaining in Palestine. He wrote to his then girlfriend Mamaine Paget that he 'toyed with the idea of perhaps settling here; after a month I find that I love this country more than I ever thought'. Even though the settlement process worked best for sedate families, 'I love it and feel rooted in it – but then my case is different.'[61]

So it appears that Koestler was rather more slowly disillusioned with Zionism and Palestine than he later said. Ironically, he left the country just as it was about to explode and produce some of the most dramatic news stories of the decade. In August 1929 another disturbance at the Wailing Wall signalled the eruption of countrywide assaults by Arabs upon Jews. The Arab uprising was eventually covered by von Weisl, who was stabbed and seriously wounded during the riots.[62] By then, however, Koestler was happily munching croissants in Paris and covering share-price movements on the Bourse. This did not mean he had lost interest in the Jewish Question or that his Jewish identity had suddenly evaporated. Instead, he continued to probe both in a new milieu which raised new issues and demanded different answers.

Chapter 3

Towards the 'New Promised Land', 1929–33

Between June 1929 and December 1932, as a journalist working in Paris and Berlin, Koestler watched European society unravel. Politics became increasingly polarised between the far-Left and the far-Right. Both wings had well-defined attitudes and policies towards the Jews. The Right to a greater or lesser degree blamed them for a range of social, economic and political ills and wished to enact anti-Jewish measures. The Left rejected anti-Semitism, although it was not immune to it, and offered a vision of a society in which the Jews would be equal citizens, secure and fully able to integrate. As Nazism and the other anti-Jewish variants of Fascism gained strength, the anti-Fascist parties of the Left acquired more and more Jewish followers. For them the Left was not merely a temporary shield against Fascism: it offered to solve the Jewish Question in the context of a social revolution. Communists could point to the USSR where anti-Semitism was outlawed, Jews had full equality while still being recognised as a national group, occupied exalted positions throughout society, and even had their own rural settlements and an autonomous Jewish region.[1]

No politically informed Jew could have been unaware of the Communist position on Jewish issues. So the attraction which Communism held for Koestler should not be seen in isolation from his prior commitment to Zionism. Rather, he was turning from one device to resolve the Jewish Question to another. Later he edited his conversion to Communism to make it appear as if there were barely a Jewish aspect, just as he retrospectively modified his conversion to Zionism. To accept this at face value is as dubious as swallowing his de-Judaised account of his childhood, along with his self-professedly naïve embrace of Jewish nationalism.

In 1951 Koestler depicted his departure from Palestine and his drift towards Communism as a fundamental reorientation: 'In subsequent years my interest in Zionism faded, and became absorbed in the larger context of social problems.' Only the Holocaust brought him back to the Jewish Question.[2] This assertion and the absence of discussion about Jewish issues in his recollections of the period 1929 to 1942 may not reflect accurately their role in his life. A passionate involvement of seven years' duration in Jewish affairs could not be dropped instantly, even less when events thrust the fate of the Jews into prominence. On the contrary, Koestler's ideological, political and geographical peregrinations make more sense if they are seen in the light of his complex Jewish identity.

For Koestler, Zionism represented a solution to the dilemma of Jewish existence, but it was not the only option. When he moved from Zionism to Communism the latter was a continuation of the former, a difference of means not ends. Koestler made this explicit in the unfinished memoir which he was working on at the time of his death: 'Nor was there incompatibility, at that time, between devotion to the Promised Land – Palestine – and the Land of Promise – the Soviet Union. The Communist revolution was to solve all social problems on a global scale, but also reserve a niche for the "Jewish National Home" in the world order.'[3]

Koestler's life story was typical in that he was drawn to Communism in the 1930s for the same reason as thousands of other young Jews. It was the most active anti-Nazi political force and proposed to deal with the Jewish Question in a way that many Jews endorsed. Finally, for non-believing, non-Zionist Jews in search of belonging it offered community, comradeship and a cause. Thanks to anti-Fascism the Left attracted a disproportionate number of Jews: it became a very Jewish milieu. By the 1930s the Communist Party, especially, was one element of a Jewish sub-culture. Just as it was wholly logical that Koestler should have become a Zionist because he was a Jew, so was this true of his gravitation towards Communism. In this he *was* a 'typical case history'.

I

Koestler decided to leave Palestine in characteristically impulsive fashion. Instead of forewarning his superiors in Berlin and formally requesting a transfer, he planned to turn up at the Kochstrasse headquarters of the Ullstein press and demand a reassignment. He subjected himself to this nerve-racking procedure because he immodestly fancied that now he was a Middle Eastern 'specialist' his employers would prefer him to stay put. In fact, von Weisl was just slotted back into his old niche and Koestler was offered a reporting job with the Ullstein Paris bureau.[4]

In Paris he was stepping into large shoes. He replaced Alfred Kantorowicz, a theatre critic and writer, who had in his turn succeeded the Ullsteins' distinguished cultural correspondent Kurt Tucholsky. Kantorowicz's and Koestler's paths would cross again in Berlin a few years later. On their first encounter Kantorowicz recalled him as being a 'brilliantly gifted' young man.[5]

Koestler arrived in July 1929. His new job was gruelling and offered none of the opportunities for free-wheeling that he had enjoyed in Jerusalem. Dr Leo Stahl, the bureau chief, was a classic Ullstein press bureaucrat. The office, over which he presided like a schoolmaster, was located in a flat at 23 rue Pasquier, off boulevard Haussmann in the eighth *arrondissement*. The flat also provided accommodation for the junior staff. Apart from trips to the subterranean press room in the Paris stock exchange building, the Bourse, Stahl insisted that all reporting should be done from the office on the basis of information culled from the French newspapers and the wire services.

Koestler began work as soon as he arrived and for months barely saw more than a desk. He put in ten hour days divided into three shifts between 9 a.m. and 11 p.m., with just enough time in the intervals to get a meal at a local restaurant. He usually collapsed into bed in the flat at midnight. After a few weeks he was switched from the mid-morning shift to the 4 a.m to 8 a.m. slot and commenced working in the basement of the Bourse. This was even more physically demanding. Since he felt unable to sleep for just three hours and start work again in the middle of the night, he filled the hours between the late-evening stretch and the early-morning stint by going from café to café sampling Parisian 'night life'. This seems to have involved mainly hanging around brothels or the rendezvous of pimps and prostitutes.

At the office he worked in the company of one other journalist and a secretary – an attractive and talented woman nicknamed Bébé, with whom he inevitably had an affair. During the red-eye sessions in the poky press room underneath the Bourse he was among gnarled veteran reporters, from whom he learned all the tricks of the trade necessary to survive and function effectively. His work load was enormous. He had to scan sixteen French dailies and write a 1000-word overview of the day's main story which was dictated by telephone to Berlin at 5.45 a.m. This was followed an hour later by a second 1000-word piece covering various subjects. He also contributed two articles per month on social, cultural and scientific subjects to the *Vossische Zeitung*.[6]

In addition to the telephone calls to the Kochstrasse, Koestler made a third call to the German Social Democratic Party (SPD) news service. The House of Ullstein could not ignore the trends in German politics and was alert to the dangers posed by the Nazi party, especially after the onset of the economic crisis in the autumn of 1929 and the Nazi electoral breakthrough in September 1930. Although the five brothers who guided its conduct were divided over how best to respond, they agreed that at least some of their resources should be devoted to helping the socialists who were the largest anti-Nazi party.[7]

Years later, Koestler recalled that while he 'had no clear intellectual conception of the relative merits of socialism and Communism' he was unimpressed by the SPD press service. Its cavalier operation suggested that the party had little respect for the intelligence of its supporters, or much appreciation of the potential of the popular press as a political weapon.[8] Koestler's recollection of political indifference at this time is suspicious, given his recent adherence to a Zionist faction that was militantly anti-socialist and abhorred Marxism. He may have meant that he disliked all parties of the Left equally, or that he was already developing an attraction to the noisy, aggressive and colourful Communists as against the rather passive, grey socialists. Whatever the motive, he was beginning to share in the process of ideological polarisation.

For the moment, however, he lived the life of a *petit bourgeois*. He had a set pattern of work and leisure, ate at certain restaurants and with his girlfriends patronised favourite cafés (the Café Weber on the rue Royale was the one he liked best). He bought a car, learned to drive (more or less) and journeyed into the countryside on Sundays. Even though he lived in Paris and worked to the same tempo as the average French white-collar worker, he was not really a part of French society. The Ullstein bureau was an outpost of Mitteleuropa. He and Stahl were Middle European Jews who eloquently represented the ethos of the liberal, Jewish House of Ullstein. 'We were Central Europeans, steeped in German culture, supporters of the Weimar democracy, yet immune against German chauvinism through a hereditary judaeo-cosmopolitan touch.' He met hardly any French people and regarded them with the eye of an anthropologist, simultaneously admiring and despising what he perceived as the individuality, bloody-mindedness and stoicism of the average Frenchman.[9]

He was more enthusiastic about French sexual mores, particularly the institution of the brothel. Koestler was perpetually on the look-

out for sexual opportunities. No sooner had he left Palestine than he
started an affair with Lisa Luria, a teenage girl he met on the boat
from Haifa. Although she was a member of an austere left-wing
Zionist party and had opted to return to Russia, they spent a couple
of frivolous days in Venice before continuing on their separate
ways.[10] He began and ended such relationships with insouciance. So
it was no surprise that he was at ease with the commodification of sex
in the Parisian 'houses' and the separation of sexual activity from
emotional commitment. In his memoirs he chillingly described how
he watched in fascination as French men introduced their wives to
their mistresses, or to their favourite prostitute, as if the meaning of
infidelity were negligible and the pain it caused irrelevant. He never
commented on the balance of power in the male—female relationship
that enabled these sadistic performances, and even lamented the
decline of the brothel in which sexual betrayal and all it connoted
was institutionalised. One reason for his approval of brothels was his
peculiar belief that they helped men to enjoy 'normal' sexual
relations and thereby kept homosexuality at bay. Homophobia
justified the degradation of women.[11]

On one of his rare missions away from rue Pasquier, Koestler
obtained an interview with the Duc de Broglie, the recently named
Nobel Laureate. His article on de Broglie's scientific discoveries was
read appreciatively by Dr Franz Ullstein, one of the partners who ran
the firm. He subsequently engineered Koestler's promotion to
science editor for the Ullstein papers. In September 1930 Koestler
moved to Berlin to take up his new exalted position to which was
added science adviser to the entire Ullstein operation, including
merchandising and book publishing.[12]

He arrived in Berlin on 14 September 1930, the day of the
Reichstag elections in which the National Socialists made their
electoral breakthrough. A year after the Wall Street crash had
provoked an economic crisis in Germany, unemployment there had
more than doubled to reach three million. People were disillusioned
by the failure of the SPD government to improve the economy and
voters flocked to Hitler's youthful new party, which was untainted
by power and promised instant panaceas. The Nazis' share of the vote
jumped from 2.6 per cent in 1928 to 18.2 per cent in 1930; the
number of Nazi deputies in the Reichstag rose from 12 to 107,
making it the second largest party after the SPD.[13]

The atmosphere in the Ullstein headquarters was grim. Over half
the employees were Jews, who knew perfectly well that the Nazi
party's success boded ill for them. The Ullstein papers, impeccably

liberal and anti-chauvinist, had long been a target for Nazi attacks. But it was hard to devise a coherent, effective response. Hermann Ullstein wanted the family's newspapers to take a more aggressive anti-Nazi stand. His brothers were less sure and pointed to the indicators which showed a large part of their readership was leaning towards Hitler. Unbeknownst to Koestler, efforts were made to unite the centrist newspaper proprietors and editors in an anti-Nazi alliance, but they failed. In exile in Britain, Hermann Ullstein later recalled that 'the fear of Hitler lay already too deep in the bones of many of these people. The greatest fear, however, was that of losing their readers.' One proprietor estimated that half the readers of his papers were pro-Nazi.[14]

Instead, editors were ordered to pander to the new political tastes of their readership. Georg Bernhard, the socialist-minded and anti-Nazi editor of the *Vossische Zeitung*, was dismissed. Efforts were made to reduce the number of Jews in prominent editorial positions in order to deflect Goebbels's unceasing taunts about the 'Jewish press'. Koestler, who was himself briefly enmeshed in the power struggle between the brothers and feared that he would lose his job, remembered: 'The building on the Kochstrasse became a place of fear and insecurity which again reflected the fear and insecurity of the country in general.'[15]

Nevertheless, he quickly established himself in his impressive office. He revelled in his high salary and access to all the perks of a senior Ullstein employee, such as the gym where he would work out in the evenings. He dressed well, bought a new car and moved into a plush flat in the smart Neu-Westend district. One who knew him then described him as 'a young dandy'. Above all, he loved his work. In Palestine he had discovered that journalism was his *métier*. In Berlin, it became his vocation. He was not just reporting developments in science, but engaging in public enlightenment. By disseminating scientific discoveries and explanations of the physical universe he believed he was helping to make the world a better place.[16]

Yet there was a tension between his aspirations for science and what scientists were in fact producing, a tension that commingled with his concurrent politicisation. As a youth he had believed that science would bring in its train a complete understanding of the universe and, with that, a sense of calm and security. Instead, the work of physicists like de Broglie, Schrödinger and Heisenberg undermined prior certainties about the nature of the physical world. 'By 1932 the tidy Newtonian view of the universe had been replaced by a kind of expressionistic portrait full of such horrors as "negative energies", "holes in space", and electrons "moving in the opposite sense of time".'[17]

It was the science of the mind, however, that most famously produced disturbing results. On the basis of privileged access Koestler wrote several articles on the pioneering sex clinic established by Dr Magnus Hirschfeld in Berlin. He reproduced Hirschfeld's estimates that there were 1.5 million homosexuals in Germany and that the number of abortions exceeded that of live births. Koestler then explored the paradox that greater sexual freedom did not seem to engender greater happiness, suggesting that much of the sense of dissatisfaction was due to the commercialisation of sex and the exploitation of the erotic in advertising. But Hirschfeld's research and his toleration of sexual preferences that were outlawed in Weimar Germany, coupled doubtless with the fact that Hirschfeld was a Jew, were too much for the Ullstein brothers and the articles were spiked.[18] They were not wasted though. Part of Koestler's indubitable sexual attraction to women was his familiarity with 'sexology', and his ability to talk knowingly and easily about the intimate aspects of sexual anatomy and practice. His 'research' would also later prove a small-scale money-spinner.

However, in 1930s Berlin the public was not ready for either sexology or quantum physics. The popular reaction to the new discoveries was a retreat into conservatism or obscurantism. The Nazis played on the fear of uncertainty by denouncing 'Jewish' science and identifying unwelcome innovation with Freud and Einstein, who were both Jews. Nor was Koestler immune to the popular response. He found himself being drawn deeper and deeper into Marxism, the ultimate statement of nineteenth-century rationalism. Marx's theory of historical materialism purported to lay bare the mechanisms of human history. Friedrich Engels even claimed that dialectical materialism could explain physical processes. Followers of Marxism had creation neatly analysed and packaged for them: it was very reassuring. Koestler later argued that science rescued him from Communism by pitting uncertainty and empiricism against Marxist dogma. Initially, however, his drift to the left may have been due partly to an innate recoil from the science described in his own articles. The onward march of knowledge, as surely as economic crisis and political polarisation, was destroying what remained of the secure bourgeois world in which he had grown up.

On a day-to-day basis Koestler covered developments in applied science and inventions that would improve life. His passion for practical innovations expressed a continuing optimism about science, but it often brought him into contact with cranks whose desperate ventures disturbingly echoed those of his father. By meeting these obsessives and failures one may speculate that he was semi-consciously re-enacting his exchanges with his father when he was a child. While he was science editor he also became interested in research into the paranormal. He never explained where this interest came from, but perhaps it was a variation of his search for the 'key to the universe', now that the scientists seemed to have mislaid not just the key but even the door.[19]

All of Koestler's dreams about science and journalism came together in the greatest assignment of his journalistic career, as the sole correspondent on an expedition to explore and map part of the Arctic from the air using the *Graf Zeppelin* airship to carry a team of geographers and scientists. The Ullsteins had purchased exclusive rights to cover the story and Koestler was the natural choice to represent them. The voyage, which lasted from 24 to 30 July 1931, momentarily caught the imagination of the entire German public for whom the *Graf Zeppelin* was a symbol of progress and national enterprise.[20]

On 21 July Koestler travelled to Friedrichshafen in south-west Germany to join the airborne mission. The Zeppelin was due to carry forty-six people in all: Dr Eckner, the captain, and seven Germans, a four-man Soviet scientific team led by Professor Samoilowich, two Americans, one Swede and thirty crew. When Koestler arrived the mooring site was already mobbed by journalists and photographers: but he was the only one on board when it took off three days later.

The *Graf Zeppelin* flew to Berlin for a rowdy overnight stop and took off again for the Soviet Union, where it paused in Leningrad for the mission to be fêted by local dignitaries. From 26 to 30 July it remained constantly aloft, passing over Karelia, the Barents Sea, the Arctic Circle and Novaya Zemlya. It finally reached Cape Chelyuskin at the tip of the Taimyr peninsula, the northernmost point of Asia, before beginning its return flight. It halted only to rendezvous briefly with a Soviet cargo ship off the coast of Siberia and to drop a mail bag to a remote research station. *En route* the scientists carried out various experiments while the geographers mapped the terrain. Meanwhile, Koestler broadcast to Berlin every two hours while there was radio contact. Since not a great deal happened for long stretches of time, his reports were often lyrical descriptions of the icy waste below. The journey was an escape from the ugly reality of Berlin and German politics, an 'Arctic Nirvana'.[21]

On his return to Berlin Koestler was granted several weeks' leave to write up the expedition and go on an illustrated lecture tour around Germany, Denmark, Sweden and Holland. His coverage of the mission had been outstanding and won him wide public attention. He was rewarded within the House of Ullstein by further promotion. Although only twenty-six years old, he was made foreign editor and assistant editor-in-chief of the mass circulation *Berliner Zeitung am Mittag*. It was the peak of his career: Koestler was now earning RM2000 per month, had two secretaries and a large office. His parents were hugely proud of him and were able to live decently thanks to the money he sent them.[22]

But it was not to last. Beneath the patina of material success Koestler was in emotional turmoil, plagued by a feeling of 'inauthenticity'. He was no less unsettled politically. Both these syndromes found a resolution in Communism.

II

Manès Sperber, a writer on psychoanalysis and a Communist activist, recalled meeting Koestler at the home of a Hungarian family in Berlin in 1930. He had 'a boyish way of boasting about his success' and by his demeanour 'seemed bent on provoking antipathy'. Sperber diagnosed 'a clumsy, overcompensating self-dramatization of an extremely sensitive man who hoped that his mockery would guard him against any hurt'. This insight confirms the unflattering self-portrait Koestler painted in *Arrow in the Blue*: he 'looked and felt like an adolescent' and made up for 'shyness and insecurity' by a braggadocio that only irritated colleagues. He felt compelled to play at being the tough, cynical journalist, but the 'phoney personality overgrew the real one without ever fitting it'. Koestler felt like a sham and, worse, he was convinced others saw through him.[23]

His macho personality was expressed through non-stop womanising. He was constantly trying to prove himself: in the office, in the gym and in bed. Looking back in middle age, he explained his immature conduct as that of a lonely, vulnerable adolescent seeking the comfort of women. But there comes a point when his rationalisations for sleeping around ring hollow. On the one hand he wanted to be the little-boy-lost. On the other he devised an elaborate philosophy to justify his promiscuity (although he was at pains to refute such a description of his sexual athletics). He believed he was engaged in a sophisticated quest for the 'perfect physical and spiritual union' and that he was genuinely in love with each woman he bedded. Once he realised a woman was not 'perfect' he considered it was entirely acceptable to break off the intimate relationship and to expect no bitterness. Indeed, he felt 'powerless' to control his sexual appetite. In a telling phrase he considered that 'falling in love restores one's virginity'. The women he slept with, in the context of respectable Berlin society in the 1930s, may not have seen it in quite the same way.[24]

Koestler characterised his lust and perpetual infidelity as the hapless side effect of a search for the perfect woman, whom he dubbed Helena. He drew a parallel with his political genesis: 'All my life I have had emotional measles: the quest for the secret of the arrow was followed by the search for the knowing shaman, then by the pursuit of Utopia. The longing to embrace the perfect cause turned me into a Casanova of Causes; the phantom chase after Helena followed the same pattern.' The reference to the arrow harked back to Xeno's paradox and the questing arrow fired to the outer limit of the universe. It was also unmistakably a phallic image. His libido and political inclinations were one: 'in Helena's womb, as in Utopia, as in the Perfect Cause, the torment ceased, the arrow came to rest.'[25]

At the same time as he was seeking an emotional home he was in search of political anchorage. Unlike in Vienna or Palestine the Jewish Question was now only one aspect of his politics, but a key element all the same. In Paris he had learned contempt for the corruption and ineffectuality of bourgeois liberal politicians. In his dealings with the German socialists there and, later, in Berlin, he detected an equal degree of 'unprincipled opportunism and spineless compromise'. By contrast, from 1929 he grew to respect the Communists for 'their uncompromising radicalism'. While the old parties were tainted by practical failure and deal-making, the Communist Party had a clean record. The Soviet Union appeared to present a tangible, positive alternative to capitalism and bourgeois democracy. It seemed clear that both were breaking down in the West: it was time to give the East a chance.[26]

Koestler never dwelled on the apparent ease with which he transferred his allegiances to Communism from an anti-socialist Zionist party led by a vehement anti-Marxist ideologue. A clue may lie in his scorn for compromise and his adulation of militancy. From the time he was beguiled by the clatter and colour of the short-lived revolutionary regime in Budapest in 1919 he had preferred activism, slogans and bold designs to the grey business of mundane politics. Jabotinsky was famously tough-talking: he was radical by principle and rigid in practice. His sweeping vision was inspirational, if sparse on the essential minutiae. Koestler was drawn to Communism for many of the reasons that he was drawn to Revisionist Zionism: by the dynamism of the movement rather than the detail of its proposals and by the force of its personalities rather than their policy.

Around 1930 Koestler started reading some of the classic Marxist texts, although it is notable that he never seems to have embarked on *Das Kapital*. Instead, he acquired his knowledge of Marxism through an eclectic variety of sources. He refers most frequently to *The Communist Manifesto*, Marx's *Eighteenth Brumaire of Louis Napoleon* and *The Philosophy of Poverty and the Poverty of Philosophy*, Engels's study of Ludwig Feuerbach, and Lenin's *State and Revolution*. In the late 1940s Simone de Beauvoir commented acidly that he had 'a mediocre Marxist education'. Her verdict was delivered in the wake of the famous row she and Sartre had with Koestler, but it still carries weight. It is confirmed by an earlier incident, in 1934, when Egon Erwin Kisch, the Communist journalist who was a friend and patron of Koestler, defended him against a violation of the party line on the grounds of his 'lack of ideological training'.[27]

Koestler never engaged with Marxism-Leninism at a very high theoretical level. He studied Communist doctrine at a particularly arid phase of its development and seems to have contented himself with appropriating the most mechanistic, deterministic version peddled in the Stalinist era. As an anti-Communist polemicist in later years his speciality lay in disputing with the popularisers and vulgarisers of Marxism rather than the founding figures or their intellectual heirs such as his fellow Hungarian Georg Lukács. Having been a Communist propagandist, he was especially familiar with the dogmatic application of 'dialectical materialism' to politics, history and culture, and became adept at mocking critiques of the party line on one subject or another. It was roustabout stuff, but shallow.

III

Koestler analysed his 'conversion' to Communism several times, chiefly in his contribution to *The God That Failed*, the landmark book edited by Richard Crossman in 1950, and again, with significant variations, in *Arrow in the Blue* in 1951–2. No less than ten per cent of the latter is devoted to it. The purpose of the analysis was admonitory, pedagogic and combative, most explicitly so in *The God That Failed*. In his introduction Crossman disingenuously renounced any intention of 'swelling the flood of anti-Communist propaganda'.

But according to Koestler, writing thirty years later, 'That of course was precisely what we were interested in.' Both publications were conceived and executed during the intense, early phase of the Cold War and Koestler, who was in an apocalyptic mood, constantly refers readers to the Communist menace and the danger of a third world war.[28]

In these works Koestler was reaching out to the widest possible audience to warn them against emulating his erroneous ways. Consequently, he wanted to embody the most general reasons why members of the educated middle classes in the 1930s and 1940s were prone to the appeal of Communism: 'my progress towards the Communist Party followed a typical, almost conventional pattern of that time.'[29] In *The God That Failed* all specific personal and ethnic factors are played down. Koestler waited until he composed *Arrow in the Blue* to integrate his odyssey into his broader and quite eccentric philosophy. He may have done this because his mystical *Weltanschauung* emerged only gradually, but it is equally likely that he had wanted to avoid alienating any of the audience of Crossman's volume. By the time he wrote his memoirs he was less inhibited by his pedagogic obligations: he not only reworked, but mystified, the process by which he became enamoured of Marxism and threw in his lot with the German Communist Party.

The more prosaic, practical and *political* account in *The God That Failed* opens with a general theory of 'conversion'. A 'sick' society produces restless, discontented individuals: his own case was typical of a generation. His father's bankruptcy and the sudden impoverishment of the Koestler family made him sensitive towards the unfairness that allowed some to have enormous riches, while others experienced the misery of destitution. He also felt guilt towards those less well off than himself, a generalised projection of the guilt inculcated in him by his mother and nanny. The post-war inflation completed his disillusionment with bourgeois society. While Freud subverted the values of the bourgeoisie, Marx undermined the principles of capitalism and parliamentary democracy. By the start of the 1930s the economic, political and moral structures of Western society were disintegrating. In contrast, Russia appeared to be the model of a well-regulated economy and society. The values of Marxism seemed vindicated in practice. The spur to his conversion came with the Nazi success in September 1930, when it seemed that only the Communists could stop Hitler. For intellectuals like himself, the Party offered an esteemed role and a place in history.[30]

Two years later Koestler claimed to be dissatisfied with this explanation. At the point in *Arrow in the Blue* where he returned to his metamorphosis, he made substantial changes and additions to the version presented in *The God That Failed*. Some of these were minor. He explained in greater detail that his thoughts and feelings on the social question were crystallised by reading about American agricultural policy and the destruction of food surpluses in order to maintain prices, while in Berlin the unemployed were starving on the streets. This seemed to prove Marx's predictions that periodic crises of over-production were endemic to capitalist economies and that human compassion would always give way to the profit motive. Indignation found an intellectual vehicle in Marxism. He stressed the visceral nature of the process. In a similar vein to the description of his conversion to Zionism he wrote: 'all these ingredients fused into one emotional explosion.' When he finally decided to join the Communist Party, it was an act of rebellion for which the party and the ideology in question were almost irrelevant.[31]

Koestler explained that by July 1931, when he set off on the Arctic expedition, he was already a member of the Society of Friends of the Soviet Union, a Communist front organisation. He was thrilled to arrive in the USSR and during the stop-over in Leningrad experienced the same sensations he had when he entered the sanctum of Unitas. As an official 'friend' of the USSR, he was garlanded by his hosts; every Russian he encountered seemed delighted to see him and received him with a warm embrace. 'Once again I was being accepted into a friendly, fraternal community – but this time the experience of comradeship, the feeling of belonging, was not the cause but the effect of political evolution.' Koestler drew a further parallel between his enthusiasm for Communism and his gravitation towards Zionism: in Russia he had 'the consciousness of having set foot at last in the new land of promise'.[32]

Koestler added a psychological dimension to his conversion. He depicted it as a consequence of his inferiority complex and a symptom of his 'bridge-burning' compulsion. Put in other words, his sense of self-worth was so low that he believed any club that might have him as a member must be worthless too. Any outward success was instantly disparaged as a sham. With the Arctic adventure he had proved himself as a journalist: his work was greeted with acclaim and he was rewarded materially. But to him this merely signified the emptiness of his achievement. Paradoxically, he 'felt suddenly liberated' from the need to prove himself in the realm of journalism and in terms of bourgeois success. Marxism validated this temptation to rebel, the same urge that led him to burn his matriculation book in 1925.[33]

He went still further and gave this behaviour pattern a mystical resonance. In the opening pages of his memoir he hinted at a cosmic interpretation of his life story and now, at the climax of the work, he set out to show how the hidden forces became visible. All the rational explanations for leaving bourgeois respectability and joining the Communists were merely an 'alibi' for a deeper truth.[34]

Koestler revealed that the trigger for his decision actually to join the Communist Party in December 1931 was a poker game that turned sour and a mishap with his car. (From the moment he learned to drive in Paris, cars, and more especially breakdowns and crashes, punctuated Koestler's life.) He had joined a regular card game with colleagues and lost a very large sum of money. On emerging into the winter night he found that the engine of his car, which had been repaired recently, had been wrecked by a sudden freeze. To add to his woes he had an unhappy one-night stand with a woman he didn't really like. All of this led to a moral and physical hangover of major proportions, inducing a sort of 'out of body' experience. He felt he had surrendered his life to trivia and lost touch with his true self. 'I was impatient to reunite my life with my faith, as on that occasion when I had subscribed for the New Jerusalem.'[35]

Joining the Communist Party was very likely to jeopardise his career, yet it was not as irrational as it seemed. It 'proved in the end eminently rational in a world of mass insanity. Had I behaved reasonably, I would in all likelihood have ended up in the crematoria of Belsen.' Looking back, Koestler suggested that he had been privileged to enjoy a special, almost magic insight into the hidden currents of history:

> Now I have always held a perhaps superstitious belief in the significance of events which come in series. When major and minor calamities crowd together in a short space of time, they seem to express a symbolic warning, as if some mute power were tugging at your sleeve. It is then up to you to decipher the inchoate message. If you ignore it, nothing at all will probably happen; but you may have missed a chance to remake your life, have passed a potential turning point without noticing it. It is not an altogether naive superstition if one concedes that such series are often produced by unconscious arrangement . . .[36]

What is one to make of this? In *Arrow in the Blue* weird transcendental hypotheses jostle eerily with incisive empirical explanations of what led thousands of young people into the ranks of the Communists.

One of his formulations has become an oft-quoted explanation of the phenomenon of the so-called Pink Decade: 'In the 1930s conversion to the Communist faith was not a fashion or a craze — it was a sincere and spontaneous expression of an optimism born of despair: an abortive revolution of the spirit, a misfired Renaissance, a false dawn of history. To be attracted to the new faith was, I still believe, an honourable error. We were wrong for the right reasons . . .' Just as convincing is his stripped-down explanation that he became a Communist and left Germany in July 1932 because, foreseeing either civil war or a Nazi victory, 'I did not wait for the end'.[37]

By the time he wrote his memoirs Koestler was no longer happy with mundane elucidations of his experiences. He had discharged his homiletic duty in his contribution to the best-selling *The God That Failed* and was now free to construct a more exotic version of his own life, one that echoed the careers of some of his heroes. Constructing himself as an extraordinary person he wrote that 'apparently crazy adventurers, artists and other emotionally unbalanced people accustomed to living on the precarious edge where the tragic and the trivial planes intersect, jump with alacrity from one to the other'. He remarks, almost casually, that André Malraux had a similar interpretation of events and called such signal happenings the 'language of destiny'.[38] Koestler wanted to be Mr Everyman and Mr Extraordinary at the same time. He wanted his life story to appear commonplace so that it would warn against the perils of Communism, but he also wished to explain his seduction in terms of his unique personality and his even more singular direct line to the supernatural plane of existence.

Whether he was distinguished by a cosmic intervention or not is impossible to say, but there can be no doubt that his Jewishness was a differential factor in his decision-making, even if he only hints at the role it played. In *The God That Failed* Koestler effaced his Jewishness and skated over his Zionism. In *Arrow in the Blue* he drew on his experience with Zionism to help explain his attraction to Communism. But was the parallel limited to the form taken by the encounter with a new faith, new comrades, a new 'promised land' and the emotions it generated?

Koestler was searching for a home, a community and a sense of belonging, but the terminus of his renewed quest could be no more arbitrary than his decision to join Unitas. In Russia he experienced a rare moment when 'intellectual conviction is in complete harmony with feeling, when reason approves of your euphoria, and your emotion is a lover to your thought'.[39] This unity was not just based on anti-capitalism and the warmth generated by a few vodkas. It was solidly founded on his Jewish sensibilities. In a negative sense there was nothing to jar with them. More positively, the Jews in Russia had full equality and the Communists were opposed to both anti-Semitism and Nazism. Truly, this was a 'new promised land'.

Koestler had not stopped thinking about the Jewish Question after leaving Palestine. In December 1929 he had addressed a meeting of Revisionist Zionist students in Paris. Prior to the Zeppelin expedition he approached Franz Ullstein with an extraordinary proposal that he stake a claim over any as yet undiscovered territory in the Arctic on behalf of the future Jewish state. He treats the story jokily, and suggests that he saw it partly as a gimmick. But as his boss pointed out, it was a gimmick that could incur the wrath of the vigilant Nazi press and had to be examined carefully. In fact, Koestler had thought it through. He argued that if a German scientific mission tried to help the Jews, Germany would curry favour with American Jewish opinion which might be translated into financial support for the ailing German economy. This was not as bizarre as it seems at first sight. He was reproducing one of the arguments which Chaim Weizmann made for the Balfour Declaration in 1917, that of winning over American Jewry, and repeating a time-honoured Zionist practice of exploring settlement possibilities for the Jews in places other than Palestine. In the end the plan was vetoed, but Koestler turned it over and over in his mind as he glided above the ice-floes. He had not given up trying to save the Jews.[40]

The remote possibility of a Jewish state in either Palestine or, more wildly, the Arctic pointed to the limitations of a Zionist territorial solution. By contrast, the 'new promised land' offered a real, practical alternative. Russia was not only a home for the Jews, but a power-house for the fight against Nazism. Insofar as Koestler was still thinking about the Jewish Question, here, too, 'intellectual conviction' was 'in harmony with feeling'. Although he explained his dive into the Communist Party in a variety of more or less convincing ways, it appears most logical when it is seen as having a significant Jewish dimension.

IV

On 31 December 1931 Koestler wrote to the Central Committee of the German Communist Party asking to join. He didn't just turn up at a Communist Party meeting to seek membership in the normal way, probably because friends who were already in the Party realised that he was too valuable a recruit to risk to early public exposure and advised him to take a different route.

One of these friends was Alex Weissberg. Weissberg (aka Cybulski) was born in Cracow in 1901. His father was a well-to-do Jewish merchant who gave his children a good education. The family moved to Vienna after the First World War and acquired Austrian citizenship. Weissberg studied maths and engineering at Vienna University, graduating in 1926. From the age of seventeen he was involved with socialist youth movements and the Austrian Social Democrats, but in 1927 he joined the Communist Party. For a time he taught science in Berlin and dabbled in business, for which he had a marked talent. Koestler met Weissberg through his wife, Eva Zeisel, whom Koestler had known as a child in Budapest. His rotund, jovial and rather absent-minded appearance concealed intellectual and physical toughness. When Koestler told him that he was thinking of joining the Party, Weissberg was 'astounded'. 'Koestler', he recalled, 'was a journalist working for Ullstein and he had never shown any revolutionary tendencies.' Weissberg could only assess him on his record as 'a brilliant journalist with all the typical characteristics of his profession'. He was sceptical when the younger man declared that he wanted to work in a factory. While his 'lively temperament and his courage were engaging', they were not the most suitable credentials for a Communist militant. Weissberg knew that Koestler could do a lot for the cause and told him that he would be more use to it on the Kochstrasse than the assembly line.[41]

Manès Sperber, who had joined the Party in 1927, three years before they met in Berlin, was likewise surprised by Koestler's démarche. Koestler 'seemed neither suited nor inclined to join a movement for an extended period of time and thus to give up the role of a spectator'.[42] But Koestler had come under the influence of new shamans and, as on previous occasions, his earlier persona was being radically overhauled.

A crucial role in his conversion was taken by Otto Bihaly, a Yugoslav Communist who had settled in Berlin in the 1920s and achieved respect among left-wing intellectuals for his articles on aesthetics and art criticism. Bihaly went under the assumed name of Pierre Merin, appearing in Koestler's memoirs disguised as 'Peter Maros'. It is not clear how they met, but Koestler was captivated by Bihaly's blend of charm, passion and insight. He fell under his spell much as he had been mesmerised by Otto Hahn, Wolfgang von Weisl, and Vladimir Jabotinsky.[43]

Weissberg and Bihaly counselled Koestler and guided him into the

Party's embrace. His application was handled in cloak-and-dagger style. A few days later he received a reply asking him to attend an interview at a paper mill in a Berlin suburb. There he met Ernst Schneller, a Communist deputy in the Reichstag who also held various covert positions in the Party *'apparat'*. At a second meeting Koestler asked if he could go to live and work in the USSR, but Schneller told him that he could help the cause more if he stayed in his job, influencing editorial policy and passing on information gleaned within the Ullstein operation. Koestler claims with a touch of hyperbole that he thereby 'became, without being fully aware of the fact, a member of the Comintern's intelligence service'.[44]

Schneller issued Koestler with a Party card in a false name and introduced him to the contact who would 'run him'. He would report to Fritz Braude, cover name 'Edgar', assisted by a woman called 'Paula'. Much later, Koestler learned that Braude had actually worked for the Red Army intelligence service, which was quite separate from the Comintern. For about three months, this trio met in Koestler's flat, while he passed on any titbits he had garnered through his work. It was simultaneously a period of instruction for Koestler since he kept making observations that diverged from the party line, causing Braude to 'correct' him. Before long Koestler learned to see things through the lens of official doctrine. Through 'Paula' he also learned that female comrades were not going to accept his amorous advances as readily as women of the bourgeoisie, a fact he rather resented.[45]

Somewhat incongrously in view of his 'undercover' work, Koestler also organised a circle of Communist Party sympathisers employed at the Kochstrasse. One of its members was Alfred Kantorowicz, the journalist whom Koestler had succeeded in Paris in 1929. Kantorowicz, now a free-lance writer, had joined the Communist Party in the autumn of 1931, impelled by the same forces that pressed on Koestler, and was already rising within the party hierarchy.[46] They gathered in Koestler's apartment to discuss events within the Ullstein empire and how best to resist the Nazis who had already formed a cell there. According to Hermann Ullstein, no less than thirty per cent of the staff were Nazi party members or pro-Nazi by 1933. Koestler's band tried to counter their influence and led a protest against the sacking of another left-leaning editor; but by then dread and paralysis ruled the Ullstein headquarters.[47]

In time-honoured Communist fashion Koestler also attempted to suborn other members of staff. He fastened on to a well-connected young aristocrat and before he had really checked him out had confided to him that he was a member of the Party. He asked the youthful nobleman to supply him with information harvested from the lofty social gatherings he attended. However, the younger man proved to be unstable and unreliable. He could not maintain the deception and soon barged into Koestler's office to announce that he had to confess his duplicity to his superiors. To appease his guilt for thereby dropping Koestler in the mire he wanted 'permission' to confess; if he didn't get it he threatened to kill himself. Koestler meekly consented to be exposed. A short time afterwards he was relieved of his position, although the true reasons were suppressed for fear of a scandal. He was paid a substantial sum for the breach of contract and was even allowed to free-lance for Ullstein publications.[48]

In the second volume of his memoirs, *The Invisible Writing*, Koestler invested this episode with a mystical significance. During the first flush of his Communism nothing would have pleased him more than to become totally subservient to the Party. He had begged Braude to be allowed to do more for the cause and, at one point, had even been prepared to go to Japan on Party orders. However, after the clumsy way he handled his mission inside the Ullstein headquarters he thought he would never again be trusted with covert operations. In retrospect he believed that this saved him from becoming a true member of the 'apparat', like Kantorowicz. He could possibly have persuaded his nervous disciple to calm down but he couldn't be bothered: some unknown power inhibited his customary fluency.[49]

In fact, in years to come he would be entrusted with far more secret and dangerous work on behalf of the Party, but this contradiction did not prevent Koestler launching into a mystical explanation for his stupidity. The gesture and its consequences, he argued, conformed to a pattern: 'all the crucial decisions which have altered the course of my life had in the appearance been contrary to reason and yet in the long run had turned into spiritual blessings. It seems as if on these crucial occasions a type of logic were entering into action entirely different from the reasonings of the "trivial plane"; as if one's decisions in these rare moments, however paradoxical or apparently suicidal, followed the commandments of the invisible text, revealed for a split second to the inner self.'[50]

Only Koestler knew what was going through his mind in the moment of 'dreamy certitude' when he let his fate be decided by a sweating, panicky young man with whom he had idiotically entangled his fate. It is probably true that, from the perspective of

1951, his action, or lack of action, was to his benefit. On these grounds he divined the hand of fate at work, the language of destiny. But, in hindsight, and after a sufficient length of time has elapsed, practically anything can be made to seem significant. In the short term, Koestler's behaviour was disastrous and exposed him to years of peril. Seen in this light his memoirs appear less a trustworthy record of the past and more a case study of, and justification for, the odd beliefs about predestination and the split levels of existence which increasingly obsessed him from middle age onwards.

V

Once he was sacked Koestler began to work openly on behalf of the 'new promised land'. This entailed a drastic change of circumstances and a return to the impecunious, unstable life-style he had known in Palestine. There was one difference: having sent his severance pay to his parents he had the comfort of knowing that they would be able to live decently for at least a couple of years. He gave up his apartment in the Neu-Westend and moved into a block of flats in a public housing complex on Bonner-Strasse in the Berlin-Wilmersdorf district. The flats were reserved for artists, writers and workers in the performing arts, and were known as the 'Artists Block' or more popularly as the 'Red Block' because they were dominated by left-wingers. Alfred Kantorowicz, who lived there, recalled that they were a 'Nazi-free island' amid a sea of Fascist supporters. During elections the blocks were draped in the black, red, gold colours of the Weimar Republic, while other tenements were bedecked with flags bearing the swastika.[51]

Installed in the Red Block, Koestler joined the local Communist Party cell. Its leader was none other than Alfred Kantorowicz. The convener was another writer, Max Schroeder. Wilhelm Reich, who was to become a leading psychoanalytic thinker, was also a member. The novelist Gustav Regler, whose career as a Communist would subsequently intersect with Koestler's, became a member of the cell soon after Koestler had moved on.[52]

Koestler was placed in charge of producing propaganda material and for the next three months the cell members were his constant companions in the electoral campaigns, street politics and low-level civil war that racked Berlin during the final phase of the Weimar Republic. Inside the cell he listened to lectures based on the Party line and took part in political education. Outside he canvassed for the Party, joined demonstrations on behalf of rent strikers and drove his car on Party errands. It was also requisitioned for operations by the Party militia, the Roter Frontkämpfer Bund. These secretly armed veterans of the trenches protected Party rallies and meetings. They also acted as bodyguards for Party bosses since political assassinations were rife. On occasions they launched armed attacks on Nazi meeting-places. Mobility was vital for these nocturnal operations and Koestler's car was one of the few at their disposal. Usually one of the militiamen collected and drove it, but one night an unhappy and tremulous Koestler took the wheel on an armed patrol.[53]

Notwithstanding the atmosphere of violence and political crisis, Koestler was happy and relatively relaxed. 'I was no longer alone; I had found the warm comradeship that I had been thirsting for; my desire to belong was satisfied.' He felt that he was closer to 'the absolute cause, the magic formula which would produce the Golden Age'. At the same time, however, he had to conform to Party doctrine and conduct himself in the manner that was expected of the comrades. Despite its rather puritanical approach to sexuality he was soon sleeping with female members of the cell, but noticed a reticence in the discussion of personal and political matters. He learned to express himself with caution, using the circumlocutions supplied by senior Party members, political instructors and Party publications. Within a short time he had entered the 'closed system' of Marxist dialectics and its application through the Party line. Years afterwards he confessed that it was a struggle to confront and write about the way he was in those days: 'Irony, anger and shame keep intruding; the passions of that time seem transformed into perversions; its inner certitude into the closed universe of the drug addict.'[54]

One perverse reason for his contentment was the institutionalisation of guilt. Although intellectuals were welcomed into the Party, they were constantly reminded that they were not members of the proletariat, which was the main agent of history and the bearer of revolutionary hopes. According to the Party, intellectuals were obliged to restrain their penchant for free-thinking, unrestrained enquiry and critique because this would confuse and demoralise the workers who, in any case, intuitively understood the truth and found it articulated by the Party in its doctrinaire statements. Koestler thus laboured happily under a double burden of guilt: he was not of the proletariat and he was constantly tempted to betray them by letting his intellect follow its natural inclinations. He masochistically enjoyed the self-discipline imposed on him: his inferiority complex had found a perfect expression in official ideology. The cell leader replaced the nanny in a pleasingly familiar psychological ménage.[55]

It would be wrong to assume that Koestler had been completely transformed. Institutionalised guilt did not for a moment curb his promiscuity: not even Communism could overcome the elaborate defence mechanism created to justify his relentless pursuit of women. He was sleeping his way through Berlin at the rate of one girlfriend every four to six weeks. He continued to earn good money free-lancing for the *Vossische Zeitung* and now had time to extend his talents in fresh, money-spinning directions. His energy was irrepressible. On top of political activity and free-lancing, while he was esconced in the Red Block he wrote film treatments and a crime story, which was bought by the *Münchner Illustrierte Zeitung* 'for a fairly large sum'. In the meantime, he mixed with the Communist beau monde of Weimar Berlin, meeting some of its best-known writers and artists.[56]

One of these was Johannes Becher, a moderately successful poet and littérateur who was well on his way to becoming the cultural arbiter of the German Communist Party. Becher and Koestler became friendly, and Koestler told him that he was still hoping to emigrate to the USSR.[57] He was frustrated that he could not get an entry visa even though the Party had agreed that he could travel to Russia under the guise of a neutral journalist writing articles about the progress of the Five Year Plan. He had even obtained a contract with the impeccable Karl Dunker Verlag press agency to syndicate the articles. Becher had pull in Moscow via the International Organisation of Revolutionary Writers (IORW), the German branch of which he headed, and quickly sorted out the travel arrangements for Koestler. He clinched a lucrative contract with a Soviet publishing house for Koestler to write a book in which a 'bourgeois' author looked (approvingly) at the Soviet Union. The IORW issued a formal invitation and a visa soon followed. In July 1932 Koestler travelled by train to Russia, filled with the same emotions he had felt when he had left Vienna for Palestine nearly seven years earlier.[58]

VI

He headed for Kharkov, where Alex Weissberg was living with his wife after having been summoned by the Party in 1931 to take up a position at the Ukrainian Physical Technical Institute. Two decades later, Weissberg remembered vividly how Koestler turned up at his flat in Kharkov, brimming with naïveté and enthusiasm for his new mission and the Soviet Union. Weissberg listened patiently while

Koestler confidently explained that he was going to travel to previously unvisited parts of Russia, such as Central Asia. When Weissberg enquired how he planned to finance this adventure, Koestler airly assured him that Becher had arranged for money to be waiting for him in Moscow. Koestler went there, only to return a few days later empty-handed. Weissberg's circumspection was vindicated, but Koestler's zeal was undimmed. He borrowed 500 roubles and disappeared again. When he next showed up he was bubbling with excitement because he had discovered that not only the Russian State Publishing Trust, but also the equivalent publishers in the Ukraine, Georgia, Armenia and the Volga German region, were willing to pay him an advance for his book. He already had enough in hand to set off on the first leg of the voyage and believed he could finance himself in stages by effectively selling the same book several times over.[59]

With 1000 roubles and 1000 words of Russian, but no grammar, he set off. More importantly, however, he was equipped with a letter of introduction from the Executive Committee of the Comintern. This had been arranged for him by Becher, in concert with the head of the propaganda department. The letter was a potent weapon. It warranted the co-operation of the security apparatus, which was virtually the only efficiently functioning agency in the more far-flung areas of the Soviet empire. However, when he booked seats on trains or went to hotels he posed as a 'bourgeois journalist' and displayed accreditation from the Foreign Ministry Press Department. If he had revealed to the staff of the special shops for foreigners that he was in fact also working for the Comintern he would have lost his privileges. This seemed to him a characteristic dualism of Soviet life and politics. In his didactic account of the trip in *The God That Failed* he treated these privileges as simple corruption.[60]

It is not clear exactly how long Koestler's journey lasted. In *The God That Failed* he says that he spent one year in the USSR, of which he was travelling for six months and sedentary for six months in Kharkov and Moscow. In the second volume of his autobiography, the time on the road is reduced to five months. Weissberg, who is admittedly not entirely reliable on such matters, recalled that Koestler returned to Kharkov three weeks after his departure.[61] From the duration of individual legs of the journey, sketchily suggested in *The Invisible Writing*, it seems that Koestler was actually away for between twelve and sixteen weeks. This is a considerably truncated version of his odyssey as described in the first version, but the discrepancies are not accidental.[62]

The story of Koestler's Russian journey occupies no less than twenty per cent of *The Invisible Writing*. He accords it huge importance and gives it an epic quality, so much so that it threatens to unbalance the whole memoir. It was certainly a turning point in his life, although if it began his disillusionment with Soviet Russia and Communism it took a long time to have much effect. More pertinently, the experience he amassed on his trip was one of his assets as an ex-Communist, a source of credibility. Koestler had seen the Soviet imperium up close, places unvisited by other Westerners. His journey gave him authority as a commentator on Soviet affairs and a premium value to those seeking information about Russia. This alone justified the space devoted to it.

Koestler was also writing in a genre. Dozens of Western intellectuals and politicians had made journeys to the USSR, which they had subsequently written up. The pilgrims, investigators and explorers included Sidney and Beatrice Webb, Julian Huxley and G. B. Shaw from England and André Gide from France. Gide caused uproar with his account, *Retour de l'URSS* (1936), because unlike all the others he was critical of what he saw.[63] Koestler was indignant at Gide's 'treason' when *Retour de l'URSS* was published, but by the 1940s he viewed it rather differently. Gide's account became a model for the travel literature of disenchantment to which Koestler's memoir made a striking contribution.[64]

Finally, the thrifty writer hates to waste anything into which he has poured energy and intelligence. Koestler was thrifty in the extreme. He disliked writing letters if he could not keep a carbon copy since this risked the waste of a well-turned phrase. He was adept at cannibalising his own writing and remorseless about publishing the same work several times over. The book on Russia which he eventually completed in 1933, called *Von Weissen Nächten und Roten Tagen*, was only published by the press for the German minority in the USSR and even then in a shortened, heavily censored version. It irked him that, aside from the crass propaganda, all the valuable, exotic reportage was effectively buried. The notes for the trip were long since lost or destroyed, but around 1947 an American visitor to Russia found a copy and sent it to him, so Koestler was able to refer to it when writing his memoirs.[65]

The Invisible Writing recycled *Von Weissen Nächten und Roten Tagen*, partially restoring it in substance, if not in spirit. By this time his attitude to Russia, the trip and himself was completely transformed. The long account in *The Invisible Writing* is *Von Weissen Nächten und Roten Tagen* in the negative: it recovers but inverts the book he wrote in 1932–3. Fortunately a copy was obtained by the British Library in London in 1984 so it is possible to compare the two versions. There is also some outstanding corroborative material from an unlikely travelling companion, which throws light on both the 1933 and 1953 accounts.

His grand tour began with a series of local and more far-flung excursions from Moscow designed to furnish chapters on the Five Year Plan. He visited a synthetic rubber factory in Yaroslavl, then went down the Volga to Gorki. His next trip took him through the Ukraine to the Dniepr Dam, but he was prevented from seeing coal mines in the Donetz basin or collective farms. This was the peak of the famine in the Ukraine and not even a loyal foreign Communist could be trusted to be shown that much. The six articles he wrote on the basis of what he saw were intended to form the central section of the book. However, the Russian masters of the IORW were unhappy with the quality of his work. Paul Dietrich, a member of the German section of the Comintern, advised him how to adjust the pieces to satisfy the Russians and they subsequently passed the first hurdle. They were then accepted by the Foreign Ministry Press Department without demur and parts of them appear in the book where they can be relished today.[66]

Koestler was now ready to research the section detailing Soviet achievements in the Caucasus and Central Asia. In the late summer of 1933 he travelled by train to Ordzhonikidze in the Caucasus. From there he crossed the Caucasus mountains to Tiflis, capital of Georgia. After a fortnight in this lively city, which reminded him of Hungary, he journeyed on to Erevan, the capital of Armenia. Erevan was a pleasant surprise, somewhat reminiscent of Tel Aviv. He then moved on to Baku, capital of Azerbaijan, where he lingered for about three weeks, getting into a complicated affair with a local girl, about which more will be heard. Once he had disentangled himself he crossed the Caspian Sea by ferry and spent a fortnight travelling through Turkestan in Central Asia.

In Ashkhabad, capital of Turkmenistan, he ran into the Black American poet Langston Hughes, whose autobiography, *I Wonder as I Wander*, published in New York in 1956, provides a sardonic log of Koestler's travels. Hughes had gone to Russia in June 1932 at the invitation of International Workers Aid, a Communist front organisation designed to turn celebrities into fellow travellers by involving them in philanthropic projects for the USSR. Once there he was supposed to make a film about the plight of Blacks in the USA, but it ran into production difficulties. Instead, he took up an offer from a leading figure in the Comintern, Karl Radek, to tour Central Asia and write several articles on the condition of the national, ethnic and religious minorities. *En route* he decided, against the advice of his handlers, to visit Ashkhabad. He arrived on 22 September 1932 and checked into the dreary Dom Sovietov, an official Party guest house. Soon he felt isolated and depressed. For days he barely ventured outside his room, whiling away the time playing the small collection of jazz records that he carried around with him. Half-way through a Louis Armstrong recording, 'The door opened and an intense-looking young man, in European clothing, with a sharp face and rather oily dark hair stepped in.' When Koestler introduced himself in English, Hughes, who had been starved of fellow English-speakers for weeks, was delighted.[67]

Koestler put life back into Hughes's languishing newspaper project. He insisted on not only following his brief, but getting Hughes out on the news-beat too. Giving an interesting sign of how he now saw himself, Koestler admonished Hughes: 'A writer must write.' Hughes noted that his new companion was a driven man, pathologically unable to relax, a characteristic which would impress all those who met him. He recalled: 'It was Koestler, really, who started me to work in Ashkhabad. He wasn't happy unless he was doing something useful – if happy then. Even listening to music, Koestler would be thinking about work.' The laid-back Hughes found this zeal a little tiresome, but as an English-speaker was not to be spurned he went along with Koestler until the relentless pace left him fed up and exhausted.[68]

They spent about two weeks prowling around Ashkhabad in search of stories. Hughes languidly observed with a sharp, critical eye, while Koestler tracked down people in the know and fired questions at them in Russian, making copious notes. 'Koestler was a great one for making contacts and, being a Communist party member, very conscientious about uncovering all the facts in hand regarding what the Communists had done in Turkmenistan.' For all his enthusiasm as a convert, the fastidious Koestler could not hide his dismay at the backwardness, poverty and squalor of what he saw. 'He had a German sense of sanitation, and neither Russians nor Turkomens were very hygienic. In fact, Koestler complained that Russian and Asiatic dirt together made a pretty thick layer. And every time he came back to our hotel he would wash. I had not known him long before I heard him say what I was often to hear him repeat. "If the Revolution had only occurred in Germany, at least it would have been a clean one".'[69]

Hughes, who had grown up in poverty in the southern states of America, cautioned that it was not all that bad. But Koestler was not easily able to shake off his bourgeois upbringing. Nor had he totally abjured his pre-Communist values. In Ashkhabad Koestler and Hughes attended the trial of a local Party boss, Atta Kurdov, who was accused of corruption along with almost the entire former leadership of the Turkomen Soviet Republic. He observed the proceedings for several hours and interrogated officials in the regional Party head-quarters to get to the bottom of the affair. It seemed artificial and Koestler suspected that it was a show-trial. According to Hughes, 'The trial disturbed him.'[70]

In addition to Hughes and Koestler there were two other writers in the Dom Sovietov, Shaarieh Kikilov, a Turkoman, and Kolya Shagurin, a Ukrainian who was writing about the Five Year Plan. With tongue in cheek, Koestler declared that all four comprised the 'International Proletarian Writers Brigade' and proposed that they join forces. By now it was getting chilly – it was late October – and Koestler was bored with the place. Hughes recalled that 'Koestler was a restless young man. After ten days or so of continual activity in Ashkhabad, he was ready to move on.' So they resolved to visit Bokhara, Samarkand and Tashkent. They travelled by train via Merv (now called Mary), pausing for ten days to investigate this cold, bleak town and its agricultural hinterland. To keep warm, Shagurin, Hughes and Koestler crammed into one bed in the town's only, and very decrepit, hotel. Koestler was enraged by the shabbiness of it all. 'This filthy hole', he exclaimed to Hughes, 'It will take more than a revolution to clean up this dive. I can't wash in this stinking water. It's been here for a week.' Hughes, who compared it with Negro-only hostels in the Deep South, was more sanguine, but was grateful when Koestler turned his discontent to good use and succeeded in foraging for a car and some food.[71]

The 'Writers Brigade' passed several days in Merv, using it as a base to visit a *kolkhoz*, a collective farm, and Permytab on the Afghan border. Kolkhoz Aitakov was one of the bold new collective farms dedicated to cotton growing. The visitors were welcomed in style and given a tour of the farm, enriched by plentiful information (for Koestler's benefit) on the workings of the labour brigades. Then they were treated to a banquet. Hughes loved every moment of it, but Koestler winced when the guests were invited to pull lumps of meat and other delicacies out of common bowls passed between the revellers. However, even Hughes had difficulty finding any redeem-ing feature in Permytab, which he dubbed 'a distant outpost of hell'.

To reach the place they had to drive for hours across super-heated desert tracks in a car filled with dust. The inhabitants were Baluchis who, despite their formal incorporation into a collective settlement, lived in huts and tents as their ancestors had done for centuries. When the travellers finally arrived they were treated to a tea-drinking ceremony. They sipped the muddy brew nervously from four filthy cups, which were shared between the twenty villagers gathered to meet them. Koestler was relieved to find a white woman, a Jewish doctor from Minsk who was assigned to the medical centre that was virtually the only sign of Soviet modernity. She casually recited all the diseases she had to cope with, mentioning *en passant* that many of the men had syphilis. Koestler almost fainted when he heard this. Hughes later confessed, 'I was a bit upset myself.' When they got back to Merv (which now looked like the acme of civilisation), 'Koestler began to wash his face and hands, his mouth and teeth – not once, but three or four times – emptying the water after each washing, until he had used up the whole pitcher. Then he went to the outside faucet, got more water and washed his body, then rinsed it in a second bowl. Finally, he washed his hands again. Syphilis, dirt, Permytab, the frontiers of the revolution, ugh!'[72]

In his recollections Hughes did not merely poke fun at his fellow traveller. His portrait of Koestler is a fair one because Hughes balances his mockery of the young man's fussiness with admiration for his energy and conscientiousness. After the drive from Merv to Permytab, Hughes was afflicted by cramps and a debilitating headache. Koestler was not much better off, but immediately he arrived he whipped out his notebook and started asking questions. He even went on jotting down facts while learning that he might well have been infected with some ghastly disease from the communal bowls and cups they had been using. To his credit, when he came to write *Von Weissen Nächten und Roten Tagen* he did not disguise what he had seen.

With relief, Koestler and Hughes journeyed on to the ancient exotic city of Bokhara. Hughes now took it easy and bummed notes off his hyperactive partner. But he made an exception when it came to researching about the Jews. He asked Koestler to take him to the Jewish quarter so that he could meet Soviet Jewish citizens for himself: 'With Koestler's help, in the old Jewish quarter of town I gathered a book full of notes.' It is striking that Hughes devoted two pages to the venerable Jewish community of Bokhara, whereas Koestler passed over it in silence. It is as if he was at pains to distance himself from Jews, yet Hughes recounted an incident that illustrates how far Koestler identified himself with his co-religionists. While in Bokhara, a local Jewish journalist conned Hughes into swapping his good American pencil for a useless Russian-made one, claiming dishonestly that he just wanted an American souvenir. '"That Jew!" Koestler said, "I'm ashamed! Ashamed!"' Hughes tried to calm him down, but Koestler stormed off and returned a while later with the lost pencil. Hughes analysed the incident incisively:

I was embarrassed. I had not intended to make an issue of it — a mere pencil. In high school with hundreds of Jewish youngsters I had learned how sensitive some Jewish people can be when another does something considered shameful — just as many Negroes feel keenly any sort of behaviour which they think 'disgraces the race'. But I had not thought of Jewishness at all when I mentioned wishing I had back my pencil. Yet, as soon as I saw Koestler's face, and heard him explode, 'That Jew!' I felt that he thought one of his own had misbehaved, so he set out to do something about it.

The following day Koestler left for Samarkand and Tashkent, leaving Hughes to catch up with him later.[73]

In other ways, too, the Jewish Question stayed with Koestler. In Merv he was taken to see a school and watched a class being taught German. On listening more carefully, Koestler realised that the teacher, a Jew from Minsk, was actually instructing the children in Yiddish. While he was looking over Bokhara and Samarkand, Koestler was aware of following in the footsteps of Arminius Vámbéry whose epic narrative of a journey through Central Asia was published in 1868. He had 'devoured' Vámbéry as a schoolboy and now used him as a point of reference in his memoir. Vámbéry was, in fact, born Hermann Vamberger, a Hungarian Jew with an orthodox background. He had a genius for languages and was employed by the Ottoman Sultan before setting off on his exploration of Central Asia disguised as a Muslim. He eventually converted to Protestantism and held a chair in oriental languages at Budapest University. Vámbéry was a pro-Zionist, who helped Herzl make approaches to the Sultan to secure permission for Jews to settle in Palestine. Did the parallels between himself and Vámbéry escape Koestler?[74]

On the final leg of his journey he visited other remote villages on the Afghan border and spent a week on a state farm recently created in a formerly wild region of Kazakhstan. Hughes and Koestler were briefly reunited four weeks later in Tashkent, capital of the Uzbek Soviet Republic, where Hughes this time stayed in Koestler's hotel room. Koestler dismissed the city in short order: it was 'dirty and ugly and dusty'. More worrying, he observed signs of famine and had discovered that the jails were full of people who seemed to have committed no obvious crime. When he spoke he stared at Hughes intently. Looking back on that confrontation, Hughes mused that it was the point at which Koestler had reached his 'crossroads', his 'turning point from left to right'. Shortly after this meeting Koestler travelled by train back to Moscow. As he was unable to get a room in a hotel there he went on to Kharkov, turning up at Weissberg's flat looking 'as thin as a lath'.[75]

After staying with his friends for two weeks he found accommodation in the Intourist hotel and started work on *Von Weissen Nächten und Roten Tagen*. He had to write in atrocious conditions. According to Weissberg, 'That winter was one of the worst since the end of the civil war. There were frequent power cuts. At one time it was so bad that there was current for only two hours a day, and even then the consumer never knew which two hours.' Swathed in blankets and wearing all his clothes, Koestler sat huddled over a typewriter and struggled to reconcile with Communist doctrine what he had seen with his own eyes. The trip churned up enormous confusion, which even dialectical thinking could not contain. Writing became a form of therapy; it helped him to 'remodel his observations into the desired facts'.[76]

Von Weissen Nächten und Roten Tagen is in two parts. The first seventy pages describe the Zeppelin trip, but with a pronounced Marxist slant. Koestler mocks the financial arrangements for the expedition and the limits insurers put on the distance the airship could travel. This showed how decisive scientific advances would not occur until 'the masses took the conduct of society into their own hands'. He concluded his Soviet-oriented description of the flight by arguing that the Zeppelin craze was fostered by those in power to make people gaze towards the skies rather than at the hunger and iniquity under their noses.[77]

The first two chapters of the second part deal with his sallies from Moscow. There are flashes of Koestler's humour, but it is otherwise dull stuff. The account of the Ukrainian leg of his journey was deleted by the censor.[78] Koestler then moves on to Armenia, devoting several pages to the Armenian genocide of 1915–16, with the message that Armenians found sanctuary only inside the USSR. The chapters on Armenia are stuffed with local colour and facts to show the progress made under Soviet rule. The chapter on Baku tells the story of the oil industry, combining an anti-capitalist homily with vivid passages full of information.[79]

The narrative is liveliest when describing the journey to the Afghan border and scenes in Turkmenistan. Koestler is scathing about the conditions he found in the Baluchi settlement: nothing he had seen in the Middle East was so bad. The only clean buildings, the symbols of modernisation and Soviet power, were the school and the clinic.[80] He gives a detailed picture of Kolkhoz Aitakov to illustrate the transformation achieved by the Soviets. In the chapters about Bokhara he focuses on Hadji Mir Baba, a leading local politician, hero of the civil war, and a virile embodiment of the revolution. He also dwelt at length on the emancipation of women, writing graphically about the harem system in the former Emir's palaces.[81]

What he saw of Russia and the 'achievements' of socialism shocked him. Twenty years later he claimed that it was only thanks to his training in 'dialectical thinking', the 'closed system' of Communist reasoning, that he was able to rationalise the negative aspects: 'it was all so easy to accept while rolling along the single track of faith.' However, even when he no longer had to obey the rules of propaganda his narrative hummed with admiration for the revolution. In *The Invisible Writing*, no less than in *Von Weissen Nächten und Roten Tagen*, he persistently contrasted the primitive conditions of the native peoples dwelling in the benighted corners of the Russian empire with the benefits of modernity which the Bolsheviks brought with them. He depicted several local Communist leaders, like Hadji Mir Baba, in an unblushingly heroic light at the same time as berating himself for his own short-sightedness. He wrote with admiration and affection of the Minister of Education for Georgia, an erudite and cosmopolitan young man who had studied in Berlin, with whom he got drunk and walked arm in arm through Tiflis in a state of 'Dionysian bliss'. He could not make up his mind about the benefits of the revolution. He berated the Soviets for ignoring ancient traditions, trampling venerable cultures and wrecking beautiful medieval cities; but he could not disguise his pride at being part of the great wave of modernisation breaking against the backward shores of Asia.[82]

In his memoirs he was able to develop a number of themes and tell a number of stories which he had himself suppressed during his Communist years. A curious sexual leitmotif emerged in the course of his odyssey. On the train from Moscow to the Caucasus he described how he fought off a large Russian woman who turned out to be an anti-Bolshevik ex-nun. On the train from Tiflis to Erevan he assisted a peasant girl who thought she owed him sexual favours in return, the result of an imbalance of power that so troubled him he was temporarily rendered impotent. In Baku he fell in love with a girl called Nadeshda, but ended up betraying her. She gave him a bout of gonorrhoea, which he saw as symbolic of the relationship. All these female relationships were fraught, threatening and unhappy. To the reader sexuality appears under siege, threatened by castration, impotence and disease. By contrast, his encounters with men are dramatic but overwhelmingly positive. There is even a homoerotic quality to his meetings with Hadji Mir Baba, Oragvilidze, the Georgian Minister of Education, and Langston Hughes.[83]

Writing about Baku, he goes into detail about his affair with the woman called 'Nadeshda Smirnova' and its gruesome *démarche*. At the same time he had bumped into a German comrade called Paul Werner (who was later to appear as Little Loewy in *Darkness at Noon*). Werner ostensibly worked for a trade union, but was really a GPU agent. He told Koestler that Nadeshda and her aunt were suspected of espionage. When Koestler mislaid a cablegram from Berlin he suspected Nadeshda and, even though he was still smitten with her and hoped she would accompany him on the rest of his trip, reported his misgivings to Werner. Having informed on her it could only be a matter of time before the GPU investigated the case. Werner recommended that Koestler take her with him, possibly in order to save her, but she refused. Koestler left on his own and, predictably, lost touch with Nadeshda. He never knew if Werner had acted on the information he had received from him. But in an echo of Koestler's rejection from the *kvutzah*, Werner told him that 'he had been weighed and found wanting'. Koestler's act of betrayal and uncertainty about Nadeshda's fate haunted him for years.[84]

Koestler had hoped to find Utopia in Russia, but he discovered that 'the restless traveller has only one goal: to escape from himself'. It was a hopeless quest. Sundered from all props and distractions, he was brought face to face with himself. He discovered a capacity for political betrayal, which disgusted him. 'What happened to me in Baku made me into a bad Communist, and a bad anti-Communist, and thereby a little more human. I had my first glimpse of the invisible writing.' In fact, when he wrote this Koestler had recorded a number of other 'glimpses', but the Baku débâcle seared him. He learned that he was by nature a rebel, not a revolutionary. He was uncomfortable with power; his potency was not of the sort which animates nation-builders and modernisers.[85]

The tension between what he was going through and what he felt compelled to say, both pragmatically to keep his sponsors happy and out of a sense of conviction because he was still in thrall to Communism, was becoming unbearable. It was worsened by the evident dissonance between reality and its Communist version on his very doorstep in Kharkov. The power cuts and freezing cold were serious enough, but Koestler was irritated by the utter denial of the facts in the local and national Russian press. Nor were there any reports of the famine he saw in rural areas. The chambermaid in his hotel fainted with hunger, but the press said nothing about rationing and food shortages.[86]

When they met in the evenings to play cards, he railed to Weissberg,'The newspapers make me sick. Why don't they tell the truth?' He protested that there was starvation in the countryside, but the journalists only reported 'certain difficulties in the food supply'. 'Really, Alex, it's too much.' This was dangerous talk. Weissberg knew that central planning had created these disastrous problems and to correct them would require a political upheaval, a counter-revolution: 'Although we all thought that way there was no possibility of any sort of opposition or even of modest criticism. All we could do was wait and hope.' For all his bellyaching then, and observations with hindsight, Koestler, too, knew that rapid change was impossible and buckled down to his task. Weissberg observed: 'Koestler realized this perfectly well, and despite the fact that he had become very critical he wrote a pro-Soviet book.'[87]

In February 1933, while he was at the Weissbergs', he heard that the Reichstag, the German parliament building in Berlin, had been burned down. His immediate response was to rush back to Germany since he foresaw that the incident heralded a *coup d'état* by the Nazis (who had come to power constitutionally the previous month after becoming the largest party in the parliament). Weissberg restrained him, pointing out that if the Nazis were really about to abolish democracy and the rule of law he wouldn't evade prison for more than a few days. So Koestler stayed in Kharkov, finishing his book by April 1933. He sent copies to his publisher in Moscow and all the separate publishing houses around the USSR who had 'bought' it. The manuscript was not well received. Despite being 480 pages long it barely mentioned Stalin and the tone was deemed 'too frivolous'. As a result, only a truncated version appeared in German.[88]

While he was waiting for a decision about the book, Koestler moved to Moscow. He arranged meetings with a number of leading Communists including Karl Radek and Nikolai Bukharin. Radek was the head of propaganda for the Comintern and the man who ultimately ran Koestler's superiors; Bukharin was the Communist theoretician who had for a time jointly led the regime with Stalin, only to be ejected by him from the Politburo in 1929 and demoted to a minor research position on the Supreme Economic Council. Koestler detected a weariness in both men, exhausted by conspiracy, war, state building, factional fighting and ideological orthodoxy. Both were to appear in the person of Rubashov in *Darkness at Noon*.[89]

Koestler was not on very good form himself. He was lonely, miserable and at a loose end. Throughout his life as a writer he went into a depression as soon as he had completed a book: this was his first real one. As a distraction he wrote a satirical, science-fiction play called *Bar du Soleil*. He began it while sitting on the terrace of the Café Metropole, inspired by the lyric of a sentimental German song that was being played by the café orchestra: 'tell me fairy-tales of a happy land'. In the play, the first version of which was lost in 1940, the human race appoints a dictator to force humanity to be happy in order to stave off an alien assault predicated on the notion that unhappy planets have no right to survive. The Utopia inaugurated by the 'dilettantes' who comprise the new regime was rather like the Hungarian commune. Its anarchic quality made the play a risky project in Stalin's Russia: Koestler felt like 'a schoolboy drawing obscene pictures on the blackboard'. Symbolically, the play was finished on a train carrying Koestler from Russia to the West.[90]

Despite the official line of the Communist Party, which predicted imminent revolution in Germany, Koestler and Weissberg concluded after the outcome of the last Reichstag elections in March 1933 that National Socialism had established itself there for the foreseeable future. Koestler's boss, Paul Dietrich, told him that the Party thought he would be best used in Paris where the exiled German Communists were assembling to carry on their fight against Nazism.[91] When he heard of his reassignment he 'received the news with immense relief'. He still considered himself a loyal Communist but 'found life in Russia terribly depressing'. After a long and uncomfortable wait for an exit visa, and a two-week sojourn with the Weissbergs, he left Russia. Weissberg's parting words to him at the railway station in Kharkov were: 'Arthur, keep the Soviet flag flying abroad.' In later years Koestler would reproach Weissberg for this adieu, but Weissberg defended himself in terms that Koestler understood only too well: 'We knew what was going on in the land of the revolution even then, but we still defended it.'[92] Not only did Koestler go on

defending Communism, he threw himself into the fray with even
greater zeal.

VII

As soon as Koestler crossed the border he felt a sense of euphoria.
The sight of well-stocked kiosks on the railway station platforms
selling beverages, food and dozens of newspapers filled him with joy.
He stopped off in Vienna for a few days, stayed with Otto Hahn and
met other friends from his Zionist student days. The atmosphere was
very different from the happy-go-lucky early 1920s. The country was
now ruled by Engelbert Dollfuss, a right-wing Catholic conservative
who had suspended parliamentary democracy a few months earlier.
The Austrian Nazis, who were agitating for union with Nazi
Germany, had grown in numbers and influence. Facing them was an
embattled socialist movement which was convinced that armed
resistance would soon be inevitable if either clerical Fascism or Nazi
rule were to be averted. Koestler toured his old haunts with
increasing gloom. But he was still a 'convinced Marxist' and his faith
was only strengthened by what he saw. 'I felt that Vienna was
doomed. But at the time I still believed that the Communist
revolution would eventually resurrect it.'[93] The belief that
Communism was the only adequate riposte to Nazism would
deepen, smothering his doubts about Russia and keeping him in the
Party until early 1938.

While he was in Vienna Koestler sold a diamond ring he had
bought with his rouble earnings in Moscow. This funded a side-trip
to Budapest to see his parents, which led to a further detour since his
mother was spending part of the summer in the Slovakian countryside, in a small town called Kalna where her niece was married to the
local doctor. Twenty years afterwards his memory of this reunion
was dominated by the melancholy knowledge that the 'Final
Solution' swept away most of his mother's family. Rather more
peculiarly, it stuck with him because of the intense irritation he felt
when his mother refused to discuss his recent activities and, instead,
fussed over him as if he were still a boy.[94]

The visit to Budapest turned into a three-month sojourn; all the
anti-Fascist urgency with which he had left Moscow seems to have
evaporated. Instead he was diverted into more amusing and profit-
making projects. His father was, as ever, broke and feverishly
planning impossible new ventures. Arthur proved only slightly less
adept at earning money. He offered the local papers a variety of

articles describing Central Asia, but sold only one. The director of the Budapest City Theatre bought the rights to *Bar du Soleil*, but after closer inspection decided not to produce it. Nevertheless, the advance enabled him to stay on in Budapest. He wrote two detective stories with a friend, Andor Németh, which were sold to 'pulp magazines'. Németh was a minor writer whom Koestler first met in Vienna in 1921. He never produced anything more than literary journalism and a popular historical novel, but Koestler romanticised the older man. The friendship was typical of his male relationships, based on idealisation to the point of infatuation. Their attempts at more ambitious publishing schemes, including another play, all failed.[95]

He also spent time with Attilá József, a self-taught poetic genius of humble origin. József shared Koestler's passion for Marxism and psychoanalysis which he managed to blend in his verse. However, poverty and lack of recognition finally drove him insane and he committed suicide in 1937. In the portraits of Németh and József which Koestler drew many years later, he was both paying homage to lost friends and holding a mirror up to himself.[96]

As he prepared to leave Budapest for Paris it was clear that political trends in Hungary were making his future still more uncertain. Hungary was drifting further rightward as the Third Reich set the political and diplomatic pace in Central Europe. During his stay Koestler was interrogated twice by the Hungarian police, once at the border and once when he went to collect his passport. His cover story had been effective, but it might soon wear thin: Hungary was no longer a safe place for a Communist. Vienna and Budapest were rapidly joining Berlin as inhospitable territory. When he had left Vienna in 1926, then Palestine in 1929, he had had a home base to which to return. By 1933 he was being steadily rendered homeless.

For the deracinated Jew, temporarily cut off from his past and his people by his own volition, for whom the USSR now seemed something less than a 'new promised land', the Communist Party and the spirit of international brotherhood substituted as a home. His ever-deepening involvement in the Party was an expression of his search for identity and belonging, a quest that was typical of so many estranged Jews in the 1930s.

Chapter 4

Retreat from Communism, 1933–8

Koestler was deeply affected by what he saw in Russia. When Manès Sperber met him in Paris in 1933 he remarked that Koestler seemed a changed man. Before Russia, Koestler had looked boyish and untroubled. Afterwards he had a worried expression, his lips were pinched and his lower lip trembled when he spoke: 'while the details of the picture that I had of him since the Berlin days had not changed significantly, the total impression was quite different.'[1] Koestler was struggling to contain the discord between Marxist theory and practice, Communist Party policy and its effects. However, at that time he had no political home except the Party and could see no other way of opposing Fascism except in its ranks. More practically, the Party offered a physical home and employment.

On reaching Paris he joined up with the exile propaganda apparatus directed by Willi Münzenberg, but his political commitment was too shallow to motivate him when the work became dull. Instead, as in Palestine in 1926–7, he took a succession of odd jobs and survived on the verge of poverty. He wrote constantly: journalism, an unpublished novel and hack work on sex books. From 1935 he tried to concentrate on a novel about a slave revolt in ancient Rome. Through this book, *The Gladiators*, he tried to answer his own questions about the fate of the Russian Revolution. He drifted between jobs, countries and into a marriage with a fellow German Communist exile, Dorothea Ascher.

In 1936, following the outbreak of the Spanish Civil War, Münzenberg suggested that he use his journalistic experience and credentials on a mission in Francoist Spain. It was the first of two journeys there, which led to the violently anti-Fascist propaganda book *Menschenopfer Unerhört* (published in French as *L'Espagne ensanglantée*). In February 1937, while reporting on the war for an English newspaper, he was caught by the Fascists and imprisoned pending execution. Only good luck and fast thinking by his friends saved him. After several months he was freed and travelled to

England, where he wrote up his experiences in *Spanish Testament* (1937), the book that finally launched him as a writer.

It is important to see these years clearly since Koestler portrayed them as decisive for shaping his politics and personality: '1936–37 was the turning point, not only in my political orientation but in my whole attitude to existence. In the condemned cell of a Franco prison my former life was to be dissolved and recast in a new shape.'[2] However, he produced several inconsistent narratives of the period, each driven by a different political or personal agenda. In *Spanish Testament* he gave an early account of his incarceration. In *Dialogue with Death* (1942) he revised and expanded the story, dwelling at greater length on his subjective experience. His autobiographical essay for *The God That Failed* (1950) fed in the details that related to his disenchantment with Communism. His full-scale memoir, *The Invisible Writing* (1954), added a mystical dimension, which identified his Spanish experiences as the founding moment of his later philosophy.[3]

When, during the Cold War, he recalled these years he was dogged by a question: why had he remained in the Communist Party after all that he had seen in the USSR? His attempt to find an answer was both personal and pedagogic: Koestler wanted to warn his readers against the continuing lure of Communism. But to have any credibility he had to explain his doubts about Communism and his final break with the movement without making himself look like a naïve idiot.[4] To suggest that a blinding revelation about the fallacies of Marxism prompted his departure from the Party in early 1938 would make him appear foolish; to discuss doubts which lingered for years would make him seem at best irresolute, at worst a hypocrite. Anti-Fascism provided the escape from this dilemma. His narrative constructed a succession of advances towards and retreats from the 'new promised land', in which distressing revelations about the nature of Communism were played against the Party's inspirational anti-Fascist campaign.

On close examination this narrative is not entirely plausible. While each new call to the barricades soon ended in disillusionment, giving fair cause to make the break, there is evidence that his politics adjusted at a glacial rate. The true reason for his vacillation may be found in the condition of homelessness and the quirks of his personality, in pathology rather than politics.

I

Sitting in a café on the boulevard St Germain Koestler recounted to

Sperber the details of his trip although he appeared more interested in talking about 'his personal experiences in exile, about disappointments and difficulties'. Sperber was struck by the immense change he had undergone. It appeared to him that the neurotic, but formerly unreflective Koestler had embarked on an agonising self-appraisal: 'after he had given up dramatizing himself for at least an hour, his real nature, no longer blocked, became visible, and with it his striving for inner integrity.' To Sperber he had acquired 'an uncommon sensitivity and a fear of deception and disppointment; the fear that a pain one cannot prepare for could destroy one's strength to bear it'.[5]

When he arrived in Paris Koestler was to all intents and purposes an exile. Although he revelled in cosmopolitanism and liberation from material possessions, he quickly discovered the corrosive effects of deracination. He realised that he had 'paid the penalty which the loss of one's cultural roots entails through a long time'. And he became an acute observer of the degradation of statelessness: 'poverty and exile make one oversensitive; what a refugee craves most is relief from his permanent feeling of uprootedness.' Koestler, like the other exiles, bitterly resented the reserve of the Parisians and the coolness of the left-leaning French intellectuals, who were expected to display something more than formal expressions of fraternity. 'It depressed me that neither I nor any of my fellow refugees was ever invited to a French home.'[6]

Sperber, too, has movingly reconstructed the plight of the shunned émigré community, but with important additional observations. 'The radical indifference of Parisians and their decided disinclination to be drawn into the life of foreigners or let such persons into their lives guarantees every individual a personal freedom that is hardly known elsewhere. This freedom benefited the exiles, but it also allowed the poorest and the loneliest among them to perish.' Although the Germans were not the only involuntary expatriates in Paris they were 'the most unpopular because they were Germans, Germans and Jews, because they were eminently intrusive and obtrusive, importuning the local population with a warning that it did not care to hear'.[7]

Koestler was a member of this awkward brigade of exiles, overwhelmingly German-Jewish and mostly left-wing. They were his family; this was his home. Unfortunately, he was not a homely type. His childhood exposure to domestic discord and constant moving around was hardly conducive to sedentary life or fixed relationships. He desperately wanted to fit in, become accepted, serve a cause and belong; but he soon felt uncomfortable as an insider. His attraction to the Party and his disillusionment are difficult to disentangle from psychological impulses forged in childhood: the warps in his personality get confused with, and are disguised as, ideological fluctuations. For example, he candidly admitted that he enjoyed his stay in decadent Budapest following his time in ascetic Moscow because 'I have always been hungry for contrast, for a manner of existence directly opposed to the one I was supposed to be leading'.[8]

This was not someone who was cut out for sustained political work, least of all the form of Communist activism which called for idealistic, impersonal, anonymous, stoical, self-sacrificial behaviour. Koestler claimed that through serving the Party and anti-Fascism he discovered the joys of selfless labour as an antidote to mood swings and depression. 'I began to learn that complete dedication to a cause was for me a physical necessity, my only haven from the nagging sense of guilt which early childhood had implanted and my only salvation from becoming that typical and boring phenomenon of our age, the neurotic intellectual stewing in his private limbo.'[9] Sadly, this was as untrue of the 1930s as it was of the 1950s: Koestler was incapable of sticking to one task or one set of beliefs (except his own private philosophy) for any length of time. This foible was exemplified by his relationship with Willi Münzenberg, the most influential man among the German Communist exiles in Paris. He was Koestler's next shaman. Imperceptibly, in a manner that was perhaps not even apparent to Koestler, Münzenberg would determine the course of his life.

Willi Münzenberg was born in Erfurt in 1889, the son of a drunken and brutal innkeeper. His mother died when he was six years old, and his father accidentally shot himself when Willi was thirteen. Münzenberg subsequently made his way in the world alone, taking a string of menial jobs to survive. His early experiences of exploitation and violence steered him in the direction of politics. With the build of a boxer, eyes that twinkled with intelligence and the gift of oratory, Münzenberg was a born leader. He soon took a prominent part in left-wing youth groups and trades union work. After being sacked for his radical activities, in 1910 he made his way to Switzerland. There, he held a variety of unskilled jobs while throwing himself into local left-wing politics. In 1914 he was appointed to run the Swiss Socialist Youth Movement.

During the First World War Münzenberg was a militant pacifist. His work in the international socialist and anti-war movement brought him into contact with the exiled Bolshevik leaders, notably Karl Radek and Lenin. Under their inspiration he became a Communist. In 1918–19 Münzenberg transformed the Socialist

Youth International into the Young Communist International (YCI) and took part in the street battles between the radical Left and the new Weimar government. During spells in prison he wrote pamphlets extolling Bolshevism.

Lenin called Münzenberg to Moscow and in 1921 he became a member of the Executive Committee of the Comintern. He relinquished direction of the YCI, but was charged by Lenin with a new responsibility. Münzenberg had scored great success in organising aid for the victims of the counter-revolutionary terror in Hungary in 1919. Lenin asked him to set up a similar relief campaign for the victims of the famine then raging in Russia. Back in Germany, Münzenberg attended to his new task with zeal and imagination. He created *Internationale Arbeiterhilfe* (IAH – International Workers Aid), bringing together leading writers, artists, scientists and sympathetic politicians of every hue on a 'non-political', humanitarian platform of aid to Russia. Local, national and international committees were set up to co-ordinate a massive relief operation under the patronage of such eminences as Einstein, George Bernard Shaw and Henri Barbusse. Huge sums were raised for Russia, while at the same time people who were not Communists were brought into the Soviet orbit.

Münzenberg was a Communist deputy in the Reichstag from 1924 to 1933, but he was principally an entrepreneurial wizard and a propagandist of genius. He understood how print media and film could be used to mobilise public opinion. The IAH issued a bulletin and later a journal, *Sowjetrussland im Bild*, that acquired a wide readership. He branched out into daily newspapers and monthly magazines. His *Berlin am Morgen* and *Welt am Abend* rivalled the Ullstein press. The monthly *Arbeiter Illustrierte Zeitung* had a circulation of over 420,000 by 1931. The 'Münzenberg Trust', as his ramified operation became known, published books and produced and distributed Russian films. Parallel to the IAH, Münzenberg also ran the League against Imperialism and the World Anti-Fascist Congress. They too generated hundreds of local committees that embraced people from all walks of life and many political persuasions. The subliminal message was always that Communism had the answers to world problems and the USSR was the model to emulate.[10]

Even though Münzenberg's propaganda strategy was highly successful he walked a tightrope within the Comintern. From 1929 to 1934, Communist policy was to fight the bourgeois parties and the socialists as hard as the Fascists. The official line was that socialists merely propped up capitalism and split the workers, delaying the moment of revolution. Therefore they were in effect assisting the Fascists. In Comintern propaganda socialists were abused as 'Social Fascists' and all co-operation with them was forbidden. Münzenberg saw the folly of this approach, but criticised it only implicitly and by deed through the strategy he pursued.

After the infamous arson attack on the Reichstag on 27 February 1933 provided the Nazis with the pretext to assume dictatorial powers and hunt down their left-wing opponents, Münzenberg escaped across the French border and successfully applied for political asylum in France. At 83 boulevard Montparnasse, in a 'tiny blind alley that most pedestrians on the boulevard Montparnasse did not even notice, and in a little house that a builder with a taste for parody seemed to have improvised just for the fun', he re-established his operation.[11]

Münzenberg was now surrounded by only his closest lieutenants: Hans Schultz, his private secretary; Otto Katz, his second in command; Babette Gross, his wife and the former editor of his publishing house; and Jupp Füllenbach, his chauffeur and bodyguard. Through them he directed the new vehicle for his political campaigning: the World Committee for the Relief of the Victims of German Fascism. The Committee raised money to help exiles, but it was also a Communist front organisation and a centre for anti-Nazi propaganda. Münzenberg had raised a standard around which the *émigrés* could gather. One of those who found refuge and work with him was the writer Gustav Regler. He recalled: 'Our offices were like an island where the shipwrecked struggled ashore, somebodies and nobodies and Quixotes, the broken and embittered victims of the new over-lords.'[12]

Münzenberg's first campaign was to prove that the Nazis, not the Communists as they alleged, had started the fire in the Reichstag. His staff gathered information from the Communist underground, the press and other sources to substantiate the charge. Vital circumstantial evidence was provided by Regler, who located ground plans of the Reichstag, which showed that a subterranean passageway led to the office of the President of the Reichstag, which at that time was occupied by none other than Hermann Goering. Other information showed that the man arrested near the scene of the crime, a Dutchman called Marinus van der Lubbe, was incapable of perpetrating the act alone.[13]

While he could be gentle, charming and affable, Münzenberg was a demonic taskmaster as long as there was work to be done bloodying the Nazis. He intended to pre-empt the Nazis' enquiry into the fire and the trial of the alleged culprits by issuing a report of his own. To give it authority he lined up the English Labour Party peer Lord Marley to write an introduction, but he needed facts. During the summer of 1933 he harangued Katz to dig up more information, browbeat new arrivals from Germany for fresh insights and demanded the most explosive prose from those writing the book. Regler recounted that 'Until the very last moment Münzenberg was dissatisfied with our work. I remember him flinging a whole sheaf of corrected proofs at the feet of Katz, who was admittedly a bungler, and stomping out of the office.'[14]

Soon after he reached Paris in mid-September 1933 Koestler went to Münzenberg's office. Following a meeting lasting barely five minutes he was told to begin work the same afternoon. Koestler was immediately bewitched by Münzenberg and 'became deeply attached to him'.[15] Less consciously, he fell under his intellectual influence. Koestler absorbed from Münzenberg an appreciation of propaganda in all its forms. He learned how to evaluate popular feeling and gear political appeals to emotion as well as reason. Münzenberg taught him the formal organisational business of setting up campaigns and roping in the great and the good. More important, he helped him to understand the limits of conventional Communist propaganda and the reasons why Fascism had such a hold over the popular imagination. When Koestler became an anti-Communist he would deploy against his former employers all the tricks he had learned from Willi. He was perhaps Münzenberg's greatest disciple and exponent among the few survivors of the band that gathered at 83 boulevard Montparnasse.

By the time he arrived, the *Brown Book of Hitler Terror and the Reichstag Fire* had already been published, its authorship attributed to the Committee for the Relief of the Victims of German Fascism. The *Brown Book* charted the Nazis' rise to power and analysed the arson attack on the Reichstag in the context of the assault on democracy. It detailed the persecution of writers and artists, Communists, socialists, trades unionists and Jews with such precision and authority that it became a standard source for anti-Nazi propaganda. It was so effective that Goering was forced to refer to it during the trial of van der Lubbe and several other, mainly foreign, Communists, on whom the Nazis wanted to pin the blame for the fire. In the end, Lubbe was convicted, but the most prominent Communists were acquitted. It was an astounding victory. The *Brown Book* attained almost biblical status in the fight against the Nazis.[16]

Münzenberg, who never failed to capitalise on a good thing, immediately put his team to work on a second edition, *The Reichstag Fire Trial. The Second Brown Book of Hitler Terror*. Koestler was delegated to prepare material for this volume (in his memoirs he confuses the two), scouring the British press and reports of parliamentary debates for useful material.[17] The *Second Brown Book* contained added sections on the persecution of Jews as well as Communists, socialists and trades unionists. It too became a work of reference for anti-Nazi propagandists.

In addition, Koestler edited daily bulletins for the British and French press, finely tuned to their respective readerships. For a while he was happy. In his memoirs he maintains that his activism was satisfying because it was sustained: 'these were years of single-minded dedication, filled with purpose, relatively free from doubt, and thus, paradoxically, happy years as well as tormented years'. To be a nameless worker for a great cause 'gave me a feeling of spiritual cleanliness, of innocence regained'. The danger Nazi Germany posed to freedom and peace left no time for reflection on the perils which Soviet Communism equally posed to freedom and peace. Hitler was responsible for his 'second honeymoon with the Party'.[18]

Yet Koestler was barely inside Münzenberg's anti-Fascist headquarters before he resigned from it. He blamed his departure on intrigues by Otto Katz, the suave Sudeten-Czech-born Jew who was Münzenberg's right-hand man. Katz, whose real name was André Simon, supplied the linguistic skills and international outreach that the ill-educated Münzenberg lacked. After a few weeks Katz suggested that Koestler take an obscure job compiling the Committee's 'archive', well away from Münzenberg's magic circle. Koestler thought this was because Katz regarded him as a rival for Münzenberg's favour. It is possible, but unlikely. Katz was a consummate operator who had been at Münzenberg's side since 1926. He had run branches of the Münzenberg empire and knew where the skeletons lay. Furthermore, in 1937 it was Katz who organised the international campaign to rescue Koestler from a Fascist jail in Spain. If he truly feared Koestler it is hardly likely that he would have gone to this trouble. A tortured, shot and martyred Koestler would have been just as useful to the cause and Katz was easily cynical enough to abandon him to such a fate.[19]

It is more likely, as Koestler hints, that Münzenberg and Katz were not entirely comfortable having him around. Koestler was disconcertingly self-conscious, forever striving to please those he admired and flagellating himself psychologically, while at the same time overcompensating by putting on a show of boundless confidence. Regler commented that during the short phases that Koestler did attend the office he 'always had somehow the aspect of a stranger who feels that he has been allowed in on sufferance.' Katz famously remarked to him at this time: 'We all have inferiority complexes of various sizes, but yours isn't a complex – it's a cathedral.' Münzenberg liked him but sensed that he was there for the wrong reasons: he had no use for Koestler's 'puritanism and naïveté'. The Party called for total devotion, but Münzenberg could tell that in Koestler's case 'This urge for subordination and anonymous usefulness was obviously the reverse of a character consumed by ambition and vanity in other fields'.[20]

In Koestler's own words he was a 'psychological freak' and Katz may have been doing him a favour in shifting him away from the high-pressure atmosphere of Willi's office. Whatever the reason, the move tested his resolve to serve the cause in any capacity and revealed that it did not run very deep. Since his brief experience of Zionist politics in Berlin in 1927, he 'never wanted to be a party bureaucrat' and 'had a deep aversion to all kinds of political officialdom'. Even though he was supposedly a loyal and selfless Communist he had no desire to be stuck in a boring, low-profile job and resigned. Later he justified the move as a vital step in preserving his independence, yet this is hardly convincing since he continued to work for the Party in a variety of functions and regularly took money from Party organisations. There is more truth in his admission that he wanted to be 'an amateur Communist'.[21]

So far, Koestler had spent just four months as an anti-Fascist crusader. Regler, who took a truly major role in researching and writing the *Brown Book*, commented that 'Koestler seldom appeared' at 83 boulevard Montparnasse.[22] For all his rhetoric about the Party being his 'home' and his commitment to the anti-Nazi struggle, Koestler still suffered from an inability to be an insider, put down roots and develop a sense of belonging.

II

At this point Arthur's cousins, Ferenc Aldor and his younger brother Willy, came to the rescue. From being a very naughty youth, Ferenc had grown up to become an international businessman. He set up a publishing company which marketed popular reference works on a subscription basis in several countries. Early in 1934 Willy Aldor invited Koestler to collaborate on an encyclopaedia of sexual knowledge. Koestler was now urgently in need of money. He was unable to interest any French publisher in a version of his book on Russia or a novella based on *Bar du Soleil*.[23] Because of his *émigré* status and imperfect French he could not get regular work with a French newspaper. When the Aldors offered him a flat fee of 3000 francs for two months' work he seized the opportunity. 'Sexology' was not an alien subject and it was not uninteresting to him. He had read widely in psychology and psychoanalysis; in Berlin he had investigated Hirschfeld's clinic.

Few critics have bothered to look at Koestler's sexological writings, which is odd, given his reputation as a Casanova. Instead, they have followed the lead he set in his memoirs where he belittled the work as hack writing. Of course it was that, and worse: the Aldor 1933 *Encyclopaedia of Sexual Knowledge*, by 'Drs A. Costler, A. Willy and Others under the general editorship of Norman Haire', contains many passages that were surely included for the sake of titillation. The ponderous title was scarcely more than a device to enable inhibited men and women to buy mild pornography. Yet for those with more serious intentions the book was by no means worthless. It contained many reflections on sexuality which were repeated in works that Koestler acknowledged and gives a sense of why he was so attractive to women. At a time when many men, especially in Anglo-Saxon countries, and a lot of women everywhere were paralysingly inhibited about sex, as well as ignorant of basic anatomical details, Koestler was able to speak about the most intimate bodily features and functions knowingly, reasonably and with a reassuring air of detachment. Moreover, if he practised half of what he preached he would have been an excellent lover.

The *Encyclopaedia of Sexual Knowledge* begins with a chapter on the idea of love from ancient to modern times which argues that an open and honest approach to sex has been submerged by hypocrisy. To remedy this, subsequent chapters describe the male and female genitalia and the development of sexuality in children and youths, taking a very relaxed line towards masturbation. Book II, which deals with intercourse and 'love-play', stresses the importance of patience and practice on the part of men. The third book covers procreation, pregnancy, childbirth and child rearing. There is even a solid chapter on premature birth and miscarriages. Book IV covers contraception, impotence, 'frigidity in women' and menopause. The final books deal with 'sexual aberrations' and sexually transmitted diseases. There is also an appendix on prostitution with a description of French brothels that is remarkably similar to the passages on the same subject in *Arrow in the Blue*. There is plenty of salacious detail, but a high moral tone runs through each chapter: the authors insist that the denigration of sex and the suppression of sexuality tends to exaggerate the importance of sex as a physical act to the disadvantage of sexual relations as part of a broader, loving association of individuals. To modern readers it is sensible: at the time it was written it bordered on the scandalous.[24]

Not without reasons, good and bad, the *Encyclopaedia of Sexual Knowledge* was a best-seller. It sold 16,500 copies in France alone between June 1934 and the end of 1935, and was translated many times over. Such was its success that Ferenc, who was normally unscrupulous about exploiting writers, even topped up the fee paid to his assiduous contributors.[25]

Koestler's next employment was equally improvised, although far less profitable. The Committee for the Relief of the Victims of German Fascism ran a children's home in the grounds of a former royal summer palace, Maison Laffitte, outside Paris. The thirty children it housed were the orphans of Communist activists or had been placed in the care of the Party while their parents were on underground missions inside Germany. Münzenberg asked Koestler to visit the home and write a pamphlet about it for use in an urgent fund-raising campaign. He arrived in the middle of a diphtheria outbreak and ended up staying for two months, acting as an unpaid nurse and teacher, while also observing the home at work. The children, many of them Jewish, were 'a new and amazing discovery' for Koestler, who was fascinated by their 'alien universe'. As well as a pamphlet, the stay produced Koestler's first attempt at a novel.[26]

In his autobiographical summaries of the novel, called 'Die Erlebnisse des Genossen Piepvogel und seiner Freunde in der Emigration' ('The Experiences in Exile of Comrade Piepvogel and His Friends'), Koestler claimed that it was mainly about the dilemmas of conformity and dissidence within the Communist Party. In other words, it marked another stage of his disillusionment with Communism. He characterised it as a *roman-à-clef* on the exile politics of the KPD and identified the central figure as a youth called Ullrich who could not reconcile himself to collective discipline – not unlike Koestler. Ullrich realised, however, that the alternative to the subordination of his 'bourgeois individualism' was to remain outside the collective, homeless and friendless. Unable to reconcile these contradictions, he attempted suicide.[27]

The manuscript, which survived the war in the hands of successively the French, German and Russian secret police, tells a different story. Ullrich is not the central character and from the outset the Jewish tragedy in all its specificity is placed at the heart of the novel. The main character in the opening chapters is Peter Potschewski, a Jewish boy aged nine-and-a-half, whose East European Jewish parents have been driven out of Nazi Germany. The father resembles Henrik Koestler and the father–son relationship echoes Koestler's sad exchanges with his broken parent. The dialogue of these characters is punctuated by Yiddish words or phrases and draws on images from the Hebrew Bible. For example, Potschewski's father refers to life on a farm as 'ein gojisches Paradies' (a non-Jew's paradise) and calls Nazi stormtroopers 'Gewittergojimes' (storm-goyim). When he is about to hand his son into the care of a farmer, the father (named Abraham) feels 'wie Isaak zur Opferung zu führen' (like leading Isaac to the sacrifice). Eventually Potschewski's parents emigrate to Palestine, but he opts to stay in the Party's children's home, tellingly called 'L'Avenir' – The Future.[28]

When he presented the novel before the Schutzverband Deutscher Schriftsteller im Exil, the Association of German Writers in Exile, essentially a Party affair, it was rudely handled. The Association contained some of the most significant writers of inter-war German literature, including Kisch, Regler, Sperber, Anna Seghers and Klaus Mann, as well as exponents of Party orthodoxy such as Rudolf Leonard, the group's chairman, Kantorowicz and Becher. Koestler remembered them as a 'humourless, fanatical and unpleasant lot'. He ascribed their hostility to the theme of dissidence explored in the novel, but it was just as likely that they squirmed at its overt Jewishness. Whatever the reason, the silence of those writers whom he admired hurt as much as the ritual critique of the hacks he despised.[29]

Like Peter, Koestler did not see Palestine as an option but, like Ullrich, he felt the 'new ideas' had become oppressive. He was trapped. However much he felt disconnected from Communism, he needed validation from the movement. It was similar to his experience on the *kvutzah*. Even though he was being judged by people whose values he did not share, his self-esteem was so fragile that any rebuff was devastating. Although the adventures of Comrade Piepvogel won a prize in a Swiss socialist book-club competition, Koestler could not find a publisher for it.

The novel's fate reinforced his sense of failure and sharpened his sensation of being an outsider. He thought of the Party as his family: 'I no longer had any friends outside the Party. It had become my family, my nest, my spiritual home.' Yet for all the security and unhappiness that he accepted as part of family life, he still felt ill at ease in this CP ménage. He asked himself miserably, 'was I always going to remain an outsider, and treated, at best, with tolerant condescension?'[30]

Of course, the real Koestler family had been a particularly dysfunctional one. In it he had felt a prey to his mother's whims, a victim of the authoritarian maid and governess, and abandoned by a distant father figure. He had been *lonely* as a child. If the Party was really to be like his family it, too, had to be dysfunctional. This he neatly achieved by acting provocatively. Despite his readings of Freud, Adler and Jung, he could not see that this was precisely what he *wanted* to feel. He was compelled to recreate the atmosphere of his real family, even if it was unhappy, because it was the milieu in which he was most comfortable.

Koestler was plunged into depression. Self-pity was a condition to which he was prone, but this time he had good cause to wallow in it. He had no more cash and was reduced to working as a menial for a couple in the hotel at 34 boulevard de Belville, where he had lived since April on his earnings from the *Encyclopaedia*. Like his creation Ullrich, Koestler made a feeble attempt at suicide. After making his room airtight with masking tape he turned on the gas and lay down to die. But a copy of the *Brown Book* fell off a shelf on to his head, bringing him to his senses.[31]

Shortly afterwards, Otto Bihaly came to him with the offer of a new job. Bihaly had the idea for a research institute dedicated to understanding the well-springs of Fascism and contributing intellectually to the anti-Fascist campaign. The project appealed to Münzenberg, who agreed to supply the resources it needed. The Institute pour l'étude du fascisme (INFA) was established in a flat at 25 rue Buffon, close to the Seine on the east side of Paris. Around June 1934 Koestler was taken on to manage the Institute's publications and write its bulletin. Later he added the function of 'business manager', soliciting advertising and donations. He received no salary, but at lunch-time along with the five other staff members was fed a thick soup made in the Institute's kitchen. For part of the time that he worked at INFA he was so hard-up that he slept in a barn in a deer park at Meudon-Val Fleuri, near Versailles, a sort of artists' colony cum nudist camp. Apart from the midday soup, he lived on little more than cigarettes, bread and dripping; but he was happy again. 'I was in excellent health and profoundly contented. Work, and a glowing feeling of comradeship and belonging had burnt every trace of self-pity out of my system. At last, I felt, I was leading the life a

Communist should lead, a life of poverty, dedication and obedience.'[32]

The team at INFA was labouring flat out to produce an anti-Fascist exhibition to be presented in Paris with the support of trades unions and the League for the Rights of Man. In June 1934 the Comintern unveiled its new policy of co-operation between Communists and all anti-Fascist groups. At last official policy seemed to have caught up with Münzenberg's tried and tested practice. But the idyll was short-lived. INFA took a critical view of the Party's reductive analysis of Fascism as the last-gasp defence of capitalism by a decaying bourgeoisie. Its researchers wanted to explore the appeal of Fascism to various social groups and the reasons it won consent from workers as well as the middle classes. To guard against 'deviationism', the Party installed a watchdog. This dull, bureaucratic guardian of orthodoxy harassed Koestler and Bihaly. Meetings were called to discuss the line which the exhibition ought to promote. Finally, Party hacks insisted on scrapping the subtle approach and replacing it with crude sloganeering. Koestler, fed up with seeing his ideas trampled on, resigned. Bihaly, who was a more loyal and disciplined Communist, followed him out of the Institute some time later.[33]

Sperber, who also joined the staff, recalled: 'As a consequence of personal arguments – which Koestler had reason to believe were due to ruthless intrigues by the Comintern delegate who was supervising INFA – Koestler, Peter [Otto Bihaly], and a few other fine comrades left the Institute.' It was a double blow for Koestler who 'wanted to devote himself primarily to the cause of the Party, the struggle against the Fascists'.[34]

The demise of INFA was a rude lesson. The Party seemed more interested in narrow orthodoxy than genuine research and preferred to waste talent, energy and idealism rather than engage in open debate. In retrospect, Sperber wrote, 'I do not have happy memories of the INFA period, for it ultimately was a depressing disappointment for so many people who were ready to apply their best energies to a difficult task even under the worst conditions.' Koestler dated his withdrawal from the Party from this moment. As in Russia, he found it difficult to harmonise unfettered enquiry, which he valued on principle and to which he was inclined by temperament, with the Party line. Since he did not have the personality to subordinate his intellect to any organisation or rigid ideology, he realised that his future as a comrade was limited.[35]

If the saga of INFA was depressing, in other respects the summer of 1934 saw a modest improvement in Koestler's fortunes. While he was at the Institute he wrote a series of six articles on the German underground for the left-wing paper *L'Intransigeant*. They were well received and led to invitations to do more writing, mainly for German exile publications such as *Das Neue Tagebuch*. Thanks to his work at INFA and his articles he was received by French intellectuals, including André Malraux. Although most were rather cold, Malraux was passionate and connected with him at once. It was the beginning of an occasional friendship founded on a shared apocalypticism and a mutual penchant for mystification.[36]

In August 1934 Koestler moved into a room in the Hôtel de la Paix, 29 quai d'Anjou on the Île St-Louis in the Seine. If the plumbing in the hotel was noisy, the locale was dreamily peaceful. He was now accompanied by a pretty, dark-haired and serious young woman called Dorothea Ascher, who was also a Communist Party worker. Ascher was the youngest of three children of a Berlin Jewish banker who had converted to Protestantism. She grew up in a comfortable bourgeois home under the watchful eye of a governess who imported the prevailing class system by declaring the kitchen, the domain of the maids and the cook, out of bounds. Along with her sister and brother Ascher rebelled against all that her parents represented and joined the Communist Party at a young age. All three chose work that was socially useful: Dorothea took a job in a kindergarten, her sister trained as a social worker and her brother became a doctor dispensing medicine to Berlin's poor. In 1933 they all left Germany on political grounds, although their Jewish origins would later add to their difficulties with the Nazis. Koestler probably met Ascher at Münzenberg's office, possibly via her sister, who was married to Otto Bihaly. Freed of regular work and with some money coming in from his journalism and from Dorothea, who had a part-time job, Koestler settled down to produce a new novel.[37]

As his subject he chose the slave revolt against Rome led by the gladiator Spartacus in Italy in 73–71 BCE. Although he came across it by accident the story turned out to be ideal as a framework in which to organise his confused thoughts about the Russian Revolution and the Communist Party. Much of his initial work consisted of research for the period detail that would make the novel convincing, but he discovered that the slave revolt allowed him immense scope to explore questions of revolutionary strategy, utopian ideology and the human dimension of history that was so neglected in dialectical materialism.[38]

However, he had barely started when Party business called him away. The first diversion was the campaign over the Saar plebiscite

in November–December 1934. Since 1919 the Saarland, on
Germany's western border, had been administered by the League of
Nations. The area was rich in coal, but the French siphoned off the
earnings from the mines as compensation for war damage sustained
in 1914–18. In January 1935 the League was committed to holding a
plebiscite to allow the Saarlanders to decide their ultimate fate: union
with Germany or France, or maintenance of the *status quo*. For the
exiled German anti-Nazis the vote was a test of Hitler's popularity.
Thanks to the French exploitation of the region there was no chance
that the Saar would choose union with France, but the anti-Nazi
forces hoped to persuade Saarlanders to vote for maintaining the
status quo. Initially the Communist Party was as hostile to this option
as it was to union with Germany since the former would perpetuate
French economic exploitation. The Party leaders got around the
impasse with slogans calling for union with a 'Soviet Germany',
which was fine except that a Soviet Germany did not exist and a
revolution to achieve it was unlikely to come about by the date of
the plebiscite.[39]

Münzenberg drafted Koestler into the battle, sending him to
Saarbrücken to edit a humorous weekly paper that would carry
propaganda. But, like all the activists, he was driven to distraction by
the Party line. Münzenberg also sent Regler, who was a native of the
Saarland, commissioning him to write a quick book to influence the
vote. Regler was bewildered and disgusted by the Communist
campaign, but held his peace like most loyal Party members. It was
an uphill battle from the start. The Saarland was densely populated
with clusters of tightly-knit mining communities and industrial
towns. It was a conservative, Catholic area, which responded well to
the Nazi appeal. The Nazis were well organised and numerically
dominant. Brownshirts trailed the anti-Nazi campaigners around,
threatened them with violence and smashed up their cars. Regler
recalled that 'There were not many of us. We thought of ourselves
as the David who would overthrow the National Socialist Goliath.
There are wishful dreams that defy reason.'[40]

Koestler's efforts were ill-rewarded. After only one issue of *Die
Saar-Ente* the paper was shut down and he was recalled. When the
poll result was announced on 13 January 1935 he was shattered. In an
article for *Das Neue Tagebuch* he had predicted a Nazi victory, but
estimated that thirty per cent of the vote would go for the *status quo*.
In fact, on a massive turnout the Nazis won over ninety per cent of
the vote. Sperber, observing from Paris, saw the true implications. It
showed 'the process by which intimidation is transformed into

seduction and forced subjugation into enthusiastic consent'.[41]

This was a theme which Koestler was to explore in his Spartacus novel. He saw in ancient Rome many parallels to contemporary Europe: the collapse of traditional values, corruption, economic disruption and unemployment, disillusionment with the established parties and the decadence of the ruling class. Yet when Spartacus raised the banner of revolt the mass of slaves and the poor freemen refused to join him. Spartacus seized on Utopian ideas to supply his followers with an ideology, but in the end it failed to inspire them sufficiently. His propaganda was ineffective: he did not read and work the crowd as well as his Roman adversaries. Nor was he prepared to be as ruthless as they were. Rome was able to rally the forces necessary to destroy the slave army.

In the course of his writing Koestler was extricating himself from the thrall of historical materialism. 'Up to now I had been critical of the Soviet leadership and the Comintern bureaucracy, but not of the basic teaching of Communism, which I regarded as historically correct, and as self-evident as the axioms of Euclid. Now, the more engrossed I became in my subject, the more questionable became the very foundations of the doctrine.' It eventually took four years to complete the novel. Apart from a six-month stretch in Zurich, Koestler wrote it in trying conditions, constantly moving about and diverted by the need to undertake paid work. The book became a palimpsest of his political divagations. At the same time it was almost the only fixed point in his life. Writing was always a form of therapy for Koestler; *The Gladiators* represented a long and interrupted series of visits to his conscience. When it was eventually finished, he had made a psychological and political breakthrough.[42]

III

From January to June 1935 Koestler lived with Ascher in a smart flat in Zurich that had been vacated by her brother when he went with his family to live in Russia. Dorothea was receiving five pounds a month from her mother, who lived in Shepherds Bush, London, and Koestler was, for a few months, paid an equal amount by Ferenc Aldor in return for the rights to *The Gladiators*. Out of fear of deportation by the authorities they avoided politics and the months in Switzerland were relatively calm. They were sociable too. Koestler was taken into a circle of writers and intellectuals who gathered around the Swiss-German author Jacob Humm. Here he met the rising Italian novelist Ignazio Silone, Bernard von Brentano and

Julius Hay.[43]

Hay was also a Hungarian Jew but, unlike Koestler, came from a small town where his grandfather had been a wealthy landowner and wool-merchant. Five years older than Koestler, he had thrown himself into the commune in 1919 and afterwards had been forced into exile, living mainly in Germany. He aspired to live by writing, but scraped a living without much literary success until 1932 when his revolutionary play *God, Emperor and Peasant* became a *cause de scandal* in Berlin. It was around this time that he met Koestler. When Berlin became too hot for comfort he moved to Vienna, but was arrested soon after the socialist insurrection in 1934. On his release he made for Zurich to convalesce. Like Arthur and Dorothea, Hay and his girlfriend Micky were almost penniless in a city that was not hospitable to Bohemians. The two men went on desperate shopping expeditions, hunting out affordable food and clothing. On one sally they went into Woolworths where Koestler, whose trousers were almost worn through, purchased the cheapest replacements: a pair of bricklayer's cottons, 'white with thick black seams and a wide variety of pockets, including some that were manifestly designed to hold hammers, footrules and the like'.

To dampen their hunger they went on long walks by the Zürichsee and River Limmat, distracting one another with their respective literary projects. Hay has given a vivid picture of their promenades: 'two young Hungarians – one rather taller than the other, one rather stockier – engaged in the process of killing the lunchbreak and with it the unwelcome pangs of hunger by means of a walk along the Limmatquai. They have problems – the one of a dramaturgical nature, the other of an epic nature.' Koestler was absorbed in *The Gladiators*, a saving grace. 'Had they worried their heads about their own banal little problems they would have succumbed to despair long ago.' Like Koestler, Hay was as disturbed about contemporary politics as historical dramas. 'It is this feeling of responsibility for centuries past and to come that is keeping them on their feet. Each believes in himself and both believe in each other.'[44]

In March 1935 Ascher's German passport expired. Since she was an anti-Nazi *émigré* there seemed little chance of getting it renewed at the German consulate. Without a passport, however, she was stateless and vulnerable to deportation. So Koestler offered to marry her, thereby making her a Hungarian national. Neither believed in the institution of marriage, but they were sufficiently self-conscious and conventional to go through with the announced ceremony on 22 June even after the consulate surprisingly agreed to renew

Ascher's passport.[45] It was quite an occasion since Hay decided to make it a double wedding by marrying Micky, who was now pregnant. The Humms acted as witnesses and loaned the rings for the ceremony. Hay recalled: 'under the solemn stained-glass windows of the registry office we must have presented a curious sight – like a band of Gypsies come to catch up at one go on all the formalities of bourgeois existence that they had neglected for years.' The two couples, with the Humms, witnessed each other's marriages.[46]

This happy band split up before the summer was over. Arthur was unable to remain even moderately faithful to Dorothea and bridled at the constraints of cohabitation. Dorothea, who had a great need to be loved, and could be very demanding, would not accept his infidelity. As she was strong-willed and refused to live according to his rules, they separated and Koestler went to Budapest and Lugano, before returning to Paris in the autumn. Julius Hay travelled to the USSR, where he lived for the next ten years. At times during their walks by the lake both men were silent, but Hay suspected what was going through their minds. In December 1934 Kirov, the Communist Party boss of Leningrad, was assassinated. The murder was the pretext for Stalin to launch a purge of the political élite, initially to destroy his opponents and consolidate his power. Communists watched in amazement as the veteran Bolsheviks Zinoviev and Kamenev were arrested and tried in Moscow the following year. Yet neither confided in the other his doubts about events in Russia: 'in those wordless minutes we fought our fight. Not together – each with himself.'[47]

In Budapest Koestler earned some cash by grinding out a second sex book for the Aldors. Enticingly called *Sexual Anomalies and Perversions. Physical and Psychological Development, Diagnosis and Treatment*, it was actually a distillation of the research by Magnus Hirschfeld. For recreation he saw Németh and József, who was now seriously deranged. His efforts to collaborate with Németh produced nothing of value and his morale slumped badly. Literature offered no escape from his political agonies. Paul Ignotus, the writer and socialist politician, who met him often in those days recalled: 'He was at that time a slightly shaken Communist, disturbed by what he had seen in Russia, but unable to imagine that the Soviet doctrines would not go down in history as the leading ideas of our time, vindicated by general progress and happiness.'[48]

In order to resume work on his novel he accepted an invitation from a wealthy German hostess, Maria Kloepfer, to spend a month in a villa by Lake Lugano. It was a curious interlude that bulks large in his memoirs. Kloepfer was a 'stranded, ageing mermaid' who supported Communist causes. For many years she had offered rooms in her house to left-wing German writers such as Becher, Ludwig Renn and Otto Bihaly. She also happened to be mentally unstable and was haunted by childhood experiences of sexual abuse. Koestler was intensely attracted to her, but was equally powerfully repelled by certain aspects of her physiognomy (she wore braces on her teeth which, for some reason, irritated him). He bridled at the way he felt he was being treated: she patronised him in every way, paying for his meals and pointing out his adolescent vanities. The atmosphere in the villa became so uncomfortable that Koestler suggested she invite Németh who started flirting with Kloepfer, which only aggravated Koestler's ambivalence.

In *The Invisible Writing* this episode is rendered by Koestler like an erotic ghost story. He uses it to illustrate the gradualness of his third conversion, to a belief in the paranormal and the 'language of destiny'. Kloepfer sensed that he was becoming unhinged from Marxist certainties: 'Maria instantly saw through the smirk and the brilliantine; she saw whatever substance there was behind it – and behind the honest substance, the ultimate gaping emptiness: the void of the nineteenth century's scientific materialism.' Koestler characterised her frontal assault both on Marxism and his personal morality, her attacks on determinism and her assertion of free will, as the classic confrontation between nineteenth-century rationalism and mysticism. In other words, she anticipated the dichotomy between the thinking of the Commissar and the Yogi which he would later draw and make famous. But, at this stage, 'I was fighting a rearguard battle of my own, defending my reassuring formulae and equations and raciocinations against the invisible writing that had appeared on my horizon and was closing in on me.' To accept her claims for 'the existence of another plane of reality, inaccessible to the rational mind' would overturn his Communist beliefs and the system of rationality that lay behind them.[49]

This bizarre episode is illuminating for another reason. It shows how Koestler began to exchange one form of determinism for another. He asserts that he clung on to Marxism because he 'was not ready to accept the burden of freedom'. Yet even as he was on the road to rejecting historical materialism, he was warming to the idea that life was determined by unseen forces, the 'invisible writing' or the 'language of destiny'.

Back in Paris, Koestler spent the rest of the year on hack work, writing a chapter for a guidebook published by the Aldors and producing a translation for Editions du Carrefour, the exile publishing house run by Münzenberg. In addition to contributing to *émigré* journals, he tried his hand at another play and some film treatments, none of which succeeded.[50]

Early in the new year, 1936, Koestler got part-time work with a press agency set up by Alexander Rado, also known as Sandor, a stoutly built, sober but kindly Hungarian-born Jew whom he had met in Berlin. Rado was a cartographer by training and combined this with journalism by producing maps for the press. He was also a dedicated Communist and a spy, whose press agency provided a cover for espionage in France and, later, Switzerland where he did crucial work for the USSR during the Second World War.[51] Koestler suspected that Rado was an important figure in the Soviet intelligence community, but put this knowledge to one side. He was glad of the work, which consisted mainly of summarising the news from the foreign press and sending out digests in French and German to 'subscribers' in France, Austria and Switzerland. More important, perhaps, he enjoyed the warmth of Rado's home in suburban Bellevue to which he was regularly invited for much needed meals and company.[52]

The job came to an end in the spring of 1936, but Koestler was commissioned by Münzenberg to write an anti-war novel in the form of a sequel to Jaroslav Hašek's *The Good Soldier Schweik*. With the advance he was able to take rooms in Breedene, a small seaside town in Belgium, near Ostend, which was home to a number of German *émigré* writers including Kisch and Joseph Roth. The novel was never finished: after he had written 100 pages it was submitted to a Party caucus and panned. Then other business distracted him. The Spanish Civil War broke out and, like a warhorse scenting gunpowder, he travelled to Paris to ask Münzenberg to get him into Spain so that he could fight for the progressive Republican government against the reactionary Nationalists.[53]

IV

Within weeks of the insurrection by Nationalist troops under General Franco, Willi Münzenberg was organising aid and volunteers for the Spanish Republican government. He listened patiently while Koestler asked to be sent to Spain, then countered with a proposal that would make better use of his skills. Münzenberg saw that, with his Hungarian passport and the press card he carried from the conservative Budapest paper *Pester Lloyd*, Koestler could get through the barriers which the Nationalists had erected against probing liberal or left-wing journalists. Potentially, he could make a far more valuable contribution on the propaganda front than in the trenches.

Münzenberg's plan was for Koestler to enter the Nationalist-held areas of Spain and locate proof of German and Italian backing for Franco's nationalist forces in defiance of the 'non-intervention' policy adopted by the League of Nations. Since the small *Pester Lloyd* was not likely to send a journalist all the way to Spain, Otto Katz arranged through his extensive contacts in England that Koestler should also act as a special correspondent for the liberal, anti-Franco *News Chronicle*. Equipped with letters of accreditation, a new suit and £200, Koestler left Paris for England. On the night before his departure, Katz took him out to an 'opulent' Czech restaurant in Paris, but Koestler hardly enjoyed the food: 'it seemed like the condemned man's last meal.' On 22 August 1936 he boarded a ship bound for Lisbon, the gateway to the rebel zones of Spain.[54]

When he arrived in Lisbon on 25 August he first had to renew his passport, but learned from the Hungarian consul where he could find several rebel leaders who were still based in Portugal. Koestler soon located Gil Robles, a prominent Nationalist politician, and Franco's brother Nicholas. They provided him with safe-conduct passes and a letter of introduction to General Queipo de Llano, the rebel commander of Seville. On 26 August Koestler set off. Thanks to what he knew about Nationalist brutality and the fate of certain journalists who had been apprehended on their territory, he was scared. He must also have been praying that none of the Nationalists had come across his 1934 book *Von Weissen Nächten und Roten Tagen*, since in the foreword to this he had declared that, soon after he took part in the Polar expedition, he 'ended his career as a bourgeois journalist', joined the 'Association of Proletarian-Revolutionary German Writers' and travelled to the USSR. During the journey he drank two bottles of wine to calm his nerves.[55]

He spent no more than twenty-four hours in Seville. Koestler first went to the Army Press Department, run by Captain Luis Bolin, who checked his credentials and provided him with an introduction to General Queipo de Llano. The General's audaciousness on the day of the insurrection had secured Seville for the rebels against overwhelming odds. However, his courage was matched by reactionary fanaticism and disregard for human life. He used the Seville radio station to make bloodcurdling broadcasts to the surrounding countryside and lived up to his words by ordering a string of executions and mass shootings. This terrifying man was lulled into a false sense of security by the presence of the 'friendly' journalist from Hungary and duly incriminated the rebels by referring to German and Italian support, as well as indulging in a rant which Koestler described as 'a perfect clinical demonstration in sexual pathology'.[56]

Koestler next headed for the hotel where, he was told, German pilots were staying. Once there, he identified several German-speakers wearing Spanish airforce uniforms. By eavesdropping on their conversation he was able to pick up details of which aircraft the Germans and Italians were supplying to Franco. However, he had overreached himself. A former Ullstein journalist who was also at the hotel recognised him and alerted the German pilots to the presence of a known anti-Fascist. Koestler tried to bluff it out, approaching his erstwhile colleague and insisting that he was in Seville for an English newspaper. An argument ensued until, by coincidence, Bolin appeared. Since he had personally approved of Koestler and had seen all his documents, he dogmatically ordered an end to the altercation. While the Germans remonstrated with Bolin, Koestler slipped away. He was in a taxi *en route* for Gibraltar by the time Bolin realised his error and a warrant for Koestler's arrest was issued in Seville.[57]

The article which he subsequently wrote for the *News Chronicle* justifiably made the paper's front page on 1 September 1936. It was a fine piece of reportage, rich in detail, incontrovertible and powerfully written. Koestler painted a hair-raising picture of Queipo de Llano and described the oppressive regime of the Falange in Seville. His vivid account of German airmen at the Hotel Cristina lounging in cane chairs, talking in Prussian-accented German and reading the *Deutsche Allgemeine Zeitung* was a crushing blow to those who denied the existence of direct Nazi aid to Franco.[58]

The article made his name known in England for the first time. It also turned him into a prime witness for the pro-Republican campaigners. Shortly afterwards he was invited back to London to testify to the Commission of Inquiry into Alleged Breaches of the Non-Intervention Agreement in Spain. The Commission, modelled on the investigation into the Reichstag fire, was another brainchild of Willi Münzenberg.[59] It was established and orchestrated, behind the scenes, by Otto Katz until he was banned by the Home Office from entering Britain. British intelligence were aware of the covert ties that bound Münzenberg and Katz to Moscow and were not in the least fooled by their public activities. Koestler, however, was free to shuttle between Paris and London. This allowed him to make friends and contacts in England and increased his value to Münzenberg.[60]

In mid–October 1936 Münzenberg sent Koestler on a second mission to Spain. This time he was instructed to scour the captured papers of Spanish politicians who were suspected of having conspired with the Fascist powers to bring about the rebellion. Once again Katz took care of the organisational details. He supplied Koestler with a false Spanish passport, money and made the travel arrangements. In Spain Koestler was provided by the Foreign Ministry with a car, a driver and an interpreter. For about three weeks he sat in Madrid and ploughed through the documents while rebel planes bombed the city and Franco's troops closed in around it. By the beginning of November he felt that he had got enough material to justify leaving. The atmosphere in the city was jittery and its fall was expected at any moment. Koestler had no wish to be there when the Fascists arrived.

He left Madrid in his official car accompanied by several airmen from the squadron raised by André Malraux. The car was loaded with suitcases full of documents, many in German, and he was anxious in case the militia units manning the ubiquitous roadblocks got the wrong idea about his activities: the airmen, one of whom was wounded, were his guarantee of safe conduct. This 'strange and burlesque' journey ended at Valencia whence he travelled on to Paris. Although the documents were hardly sensational, Katz made use of them in another propaganda effort published by Münzenberg, *The Nazi Conspiracy in Spain*. The mission had a dangerous legacy for Koestler: he felt guilty about leaving Madrid, when it seemed the city was about to fall, instead of joining in its defence. This guilt would later contribute to the almost suicidal act of defiance that led to his capture by Nationalist forces.[61]

Münzenberg now put Koestler to work on a fresh project. He was commissioned to use all the material he had obtained in his two previous visits to write an account of the origins of the civil war, the conspiratorial role of the Fascist states and the atrocities committed by the Nationalists. His relations with Willi and Otto were now close and he was doing valuable work for them. In order to write the book, Koestler moved into Katz's flat on rue Dombasle, in a quiet corner of south-west Paris. Unusually, Münzenberg visited him several times to supervise his progress. Once, after reading pages of the typescript, he shouted at Koestler that it was 'Too weak. Too objective. Hit them! Hit them hard!' Münzenberg wanted him to include more horrifying detail to 'wake up' world opinion. He was not choosy about where it came from and insisted that Koestler add some information that was not verifiable, as well as a portfolio of gruesome photographs.[62]

Koestler claimed to have felt queasy about this, although it is hard
to reconcile such fastidiousness with his *Von Weissen Nächten und
Roten Tagen* and his heavily biased article for the *News Chronicle*
which had, after all, been obtained by deception. And what else
could he have expected of a job for Willi Münzenberg? Regler
remembered that at the time of the *Brown Book* Münzenberg was
scarcely interested in truth for its own sake: 'He was not over
particular in the things he said; he believed that cynical lying must be
fought with equal cynicism. His books were hastily thrown together,
and where material was lacking he filled in the gaps from his own
profound knowledge of the enemy.'[63]

By autumn 1936 Münzenberg had good reasons for wanting results
at almost any cost. In October he was summoned to Moscow for a
grilling by the Central Committee of the Comintern and his
operation was subjected to a review by the Comintern International
Control Commission. His rivals and enemies in the KPD were
beginning to prevail over him. The trial of Zinoviev and Kamenev
was under way, and he sensed that the sand was running out for the
old Bolsheviks who were his friends and protectors in Moscow. It was
even touch and go whether he would get out of Russia alive. That he
did was largely because an appeal for further aid from Spain reached
Stalin at around this time, placing a premium on Münzenberg's work.
Nevertheless, Moscow had already dispatched to Paris Bohumil
Smeral, a Czech Communist, who was to be his 'co-worker' and,
ultimately, his nemesis. When Münzenberg returned he began to
hand over control of all his enterprises to Smeral. At the end of 1936
he retreated into a sanatorium, partly for reasons of health, partly to
write a book on propaganda and partly to get out of an increasingly
tense situation. Only a massive propaganda coup could restore his
position in Moscow, if it could be redeemed at all.[64]

In his memoirs Koestler doesn't mention Münzenberg's trip to
Moscow or his failing position. He attributes Willi's passion to a
belief in atrocity propaganda *per se* and an utter lack of scruples. This
is implicitly contrasted to his own flagging but persistent sense of
rectitude: he only caved in to Münzenberg's demands because,
whatever lies they told, the Nationalists were telling bigger and
worse ones. The truth is that by this time Münzenberg's Communist
ardour was weakening, while Koestler's seemed to be undergoing
one of its periodic revivals.

Koestler's book appeared in January 1937 in German as
Menschenopfer Unerhört and in French as *L'Espagne ensanglantée*. (A
heavily edited version was incorporated into the first part of his *Left*

Book Club publication, *Spanish Testament*, published in late 1937.
This omitted the gory photographs, much of the blatant anti-Fascist
propaganda and many of the rhetorical flourishes.) The French
edition was a critical and popular success. In October 1939 Simone
de Beauvoir told Sartre, who was then idling away his time in the
French army, that she took it to bed and found she 'couldn't put it
down. . . . It's an excellent book, without artistic pretensions, but
simple and agreeable in tone and incredibly moving.' She promised
to send Sartre a copy. Koestler was not allowed time to enjoy its
reception: in January 1937 he embarked on a third, disastrous trip to
Spain.[65]

V

In order to promote its case the Spanish government had created a
news agency, Agence Espagne. The agency was heavily controlled by
Communists: Otto Katz, for example, ran the Paris bureau. In
January 1937 Koestler was taken on to cover the war in southern
Spain. He combined this with another stint as a special correspondent
for the *News Chronicle*, which he had personally arranged. On 15
January 1937 he travelled to Spain in the company of Willy Forrest,
a fellow Communist who was also working for Agence Espagne and
the *News Chronicle*. In Valencia he met Mikhail Kolzov, the jovial,
roving *Pravda* correspondent whom he had first encountered in
Moscow in 1933. Kolzov made space for the two journalists on the
floor of his hotel room and did them another favour by warning
them that the trial of Radek and others was about to begin in
Moscow.[66]

Writing in a jaundiced spirit, Koestler later described Spain during
the Civil War as 'the rendezvous of the international Leftish
bohemia'. He had a taste of this Bohemia on the last night he spent
in Valencia when he and Kolzov went to a party attended by W. H.
Auden, who had recently arrived to begin a short spell as a stretcher
bearer for the British Ambulance Unit in Madrid.[67] Yet for all his
subsequent knowledge of the dilettantism and betrayal which
contaminated the war in Spain he could not prevent a sensation of
idealism from flooding back as he remembered that period. Like
most writers of the Left who threw themselves into the Spanish
cause, Koestler later found it nearly impossible to write about the
struggle with any kind of detachment. 'Spain caused the last twitch
of Europe's dying conscience,' he declaimed. It rallied the best and
the brightest in the defence of democracy, only for them to suffer

betrayal by the Communist Party acting at the behest of the Soviet Union. In retrospect 'the memories of those days are tainted with the knowledge of the cynical insincerity behind the façade'.

Nonetheless, much of the enthusiasm, especially that of the rank and file, was genuine. For a few 'pink intellectuals' it may have been a 'revolutionary junket', but he knew that for men like Kantorowicz, Regler, Kolzov, Malraux and Orwell it was fought in the best spirit for the highest of causes. Just as he recalled his Russian trip and his encounters with old Bolsheviks with mixed emotions, he could not screen out a genuine admiration for the men of the International Brigade and the people of Republican Spain. The fact that they were badly led, duped and deserted only highlighted their individual heroism.[68]

What turned Koestler decisively against Communism and the Soviet Union was less the *Realpolitik* and deception practised in Spain – he was used to that – than his *personal* experience of danger. Having gaily spoken about liquidating classes of people and the necessary sacrifice of the proletariat on this or that front, Koestler now connected revolutionary principles and rhetoric with flesh and blood. He realised the truth of Malraux's dictum, which he took as an epigram for his account of his Spanish prison experiences: *Une vie ne vaut rien – mais rien ne vaut une vie.* It is perturbing, and hard to accept in one who was so critical of others for their lack of imagination, that Koestler only realised that nothing, not even the most rationally compelling cause, was worth the sacrifice of a human life when it was *his* life that was at stake.

VI

On 26 January 1937 Koestler drove down the coast road from Valencia towards Malaga. He was accompanied by Gerda Grepp, a Norwegian journalist with a 'soft body and a soft figure' with whom he was having a routine transitory affair. They arrived in Malaga at nightfall on 28 January and proceeded to explore the front lines to the east and north of the strategically vital city. What they saw during the next week was dispiriting. The lines were manned primarily by anarchist militiamen whose bravery was rivalled only by their lack of discipline. Malaga was in a state of chaos, swamped by panicky refugees. Supplies were reaching the beleaguered town only sporadically, while it was clear that the Nationalist forces were preparing a massive assault, spearheaded by well-trained and well-equipped Italian mobile troops.[69]

The rebel offensive began on 4 February and was soon sweeping towards the outskirts of Malaga. On 6 February, Koestler sent Grepp back to Valencia in the car. She carried a message from him to the *News Chronicle* warning that, contrary to the report he had sent four days earlier, the town was about to fall. He urged the paper to warn the British Foreign Office to protect British citizens in the city. Koestler now moved from his hotel in central Malaga, which was under intermittent bombardment from the sea and the air, to the house of Sir Peter Chalmers-Mitchell, an expatriate Englishman who since 1934 had lived in a fine villa on the north-western outskirts of the city.[70]

He had met Chalmers-Mitchell thanks to a letter which he delivered to him on behalf of a friend at the *News Chronicle*. The two men took an instant liking to each other. Chalmers-Mitchell saw Koestler as 'a romantic young man and a very daring correspondent', while he, to Koestler, was clearly another father figure. Chalmers-Mitchell was born in 1864 in Dunfermline, the son of a puritanical Presbyterian minister and bookseller. He escaped from home to university, where he specialised in zoology. From 1887 to the First World War he holidayed in Germany and acquired such a mastery of the language that he translated works by Heine, Nietzsche and Otto Weininger. He also knew Spanish and Russian, and was fascinated by Mendel and the debate as to whether human and animal characteristics were acquired by inheritance or through environmental influences, something that intrigued Koestler. For many years he was Secretary of the Zoological Society, and was responsible for the creation of Whipsnade Zoo in 1931. In addition to all these activities, he had written leaders for *The Times* in the 1920s. He was politically liberal, but the events he was witnessing in Spain were driving him steadily leftwards.[71]

Koestler went to his villa because he hoped that the domicile of an Englishman, flying the Union flag, would afford him a measure of protection if the city fell. It was a sorry and ill-informed choice of refuge. On 22 October 1936 *The Times* had published a letter from Chalmers-Mitchell accusing the Nationalists of various atrocities. The letter had been drawn to the attention of Captain Luis Bolin. Bolin knew Sir Peter Chalmers-Mitchell lived in Malaga and was accompanying the advancing rebel forces with the intention of arresting him.[72]

The truth may have dawned on Koestler as he sat in a deck-chair on the terrace of his host's villa reading a copy of his newly published autobiography *My Fill of Days*. This contained a startling final chapter written in November 1936. According to Chalmers-Mitchell: 'Not-withstanding the grim deeds that have been done, I am sure that the Anarchists and Syndicalists of Malaga are fighting for the soul of the human race, for a possible future against greedy savages who are fighting, with the blessings of the Church, only in defence of their own unearned and undeserved privileges.'[73]

Such words easily qualified Chalmers-Mitchell as an enemy of the Nationalists, but he was determined to remain in Malaga. The British consul had already been evacuated and he hoped that his presence as a 'neutral' observer, protected by his British citizenship, might mitigate the slaughter that was sure to follow the fall of the city. Koestler stayed with him in the hope of getting a scoop and covering at first hand the sacking of a Republican stronghold captured by the rebels. However, on 8 February Koestler's resolve wavered. Malaga was in the grip of panic. During a visit to the Republican military headquarters he saw the commander fleeing. Colonel Alberto, the chief of staff, was in the process of abandoning his post too, and bundled Koestler into his car alongside members of his family. When the car reached the city limits, struggling through streams of refugees and fleeing troops, Koestler changed his mind and demanded to be let out. Alberto refused to stop, so Koestler opened a door and threw himself out. The car drove on and he walked back to Chalmers-Mitchell's villa.[74]

Why did he decide to stay? He told his host (who does not recall this episode in his memoirs) that he didn't want to abandon his typewriter, papers and other belongings. He felt bad about leaving the older man to his fate and added that, as he had run away from Madrid under the erroneous conviction that it would fall, he did not want to behave like a coward for a second time. It was possible he would be able to witness the occupation and, by getting his story out, ameliorate the consequences.[75]

Yet Koestler did not display much energy over the next few hours. According to Chalmers-Mitchell he spent most of the fall of Malaga in a deck-chair, reading. He seems to have been overcome by lethargy, which he later ascribed to a 'death wish'.[76] It was the same self-destructive pattern he exhibited when he burned his matriculation book, joined the Communist Party and failed to resist the threat to expose him at the Kochstrasse. Koestler was again drifting on to the rocks. However, on this occasion there were sharks in the water.

Chalmers-Mitchell was not simply trusting in the British flag to save him. While he had been outspokenly anti-Franco he had also protested against the killings perpetrated by Leftists in the early days of the Civil War and had acted courageously to help Spaniards fleeing the homicidal wrath of the anarchists when they took over Malaga. In particular, he had sheltered the wealthy, conservative family who lived in the neighbouring villa. The head of the family was Don Thomas Bolin, none other than the uncle of Captain Bolin. When Don Thomas had been imprisoned by the government authorities Chalmers-Mitchell had intervened to ensure his safety and improve the conditions under which he was being held. After Don Thomas was released the Englishman helped him and his family to escape from Spain via Gibraltar. Chalmers-Mitchell was banking on some sympathy for his correct behaviour and previous impartiality.[77]

On the morning of 8 February Koestler and Chalmers-Mitchell watched Italian troops move into Malaga from the north. Chalmers-Mitchell was cheered by the sight: the Italians were well led and disciplined. An Italian officer even came to the villa and, by permission, availed himself of the bathroom facilities. Then the Falangists and Spanish troops arrived and the shootings began. Nevertheless, Chalmers-Mitchell and Koestler stayed put. Chalmers-Mitchell even recalled: 'We had an excellent night.' Koestler's fatalistic passivity continued.

After breakfast the following day, he sat reading his host's memoirs on the terrace of the villa. This was the calm before the storm. When they observed the Italians remounting their trucks to continue their advance they realised that the occupation could turn even uglier. Koestler 'rather lost his nerve' and swigged from a brandy bottle to steady himself. At about 11 a.m. Don Thomas Bolin drove into the grounds of his house. It had been used as a field hospital by the Republican authorities and was severely damaged. Don Thomas was furious. He went to Chalmers-Mitchell's villa to recover some belongings and remonstrated with him for not doing more to protect his neighbour's property. Not long afterwards his nephew, Captain Bolin, arrived with two other officers. They had come to detain Chalmers-Mitchell but, just then, Koestler blundered into view.[78]

He attempted to bolt, but Bolin and the other officers had drawn pistols. Bolin vividly recalled the moment: 'a small-sized man was scurrying up the back stairs like a rabbit and I ordered him to stop. When he did so I recognised Arthur Koestler, who had disappeared the previous summer after presenting himself in Seville as a correspondent of the *News Chronicle*.' After that humiliation Bolin had sworn to kill Koestler if he had the chance. It looked as if his moment had arrived: 'Of the two, perhaps I was the more surprised, he the more frightened, and rightly so, for I was covering him with a pistol.'[79]

When Koestler had first arrived at the villa he suggested getting a revolver, but Chalmers-Mitchell knew that would jeopardise the neutrality of his house and refused. Koestler explained that he was a wanted man and was terrified by the thought of beatings: he needed the gun so he could shoot himself rather than fall into rebel hands. Ever solicitous, Chalmers-Mitchell provided Koestler with a syringe and soluble morphia tablets sufficient for a lethal dosage. Koestler secreted this equipment in his clothing, but had no time to make a suicide bid. In any case it looked as if he were about to be shot. He was probably saved by his English host, who reminded Bolin that he had done a favour for his uncle and that Koestler was his guest. At Bolin's orders Koestler's hands were bound with electric flex and he was pushed into a car with Chalmers-Mitchell. On its way into town the car passed improvised shooting squads and stopped once while Bolin got out to confer with other officers engaged in a casual massacre of captured Republicans. For a second nerve-racking moment Koestler thought he was going to be dragged up against a wall and shot.[80]

Instead, he was taken to Malaga police station, photographed and held under guard. Chalmers-Mitchell was escorted to a hotel and placed under house arrest. Bolin insisted on having lunch with him, but as soon as the Spanish officer had gone he again acted with impromptu good sense. He wrote a distress note to the American consul, a Mr Norton, and paid a boy who was passing by the hotel to deliver it.[81] Meanwhile, Koestler sat helplessly in the police station watching a stream of captured Republicans being brought in and beaten to death. In terror, he made a bid to kill himself before he was subjected to the same treatment. He persuaded his guards to let him go to the toilet in the hope of finding water to dissolve the morphine tablets. But the water was so foul he was unable to use it. A few hours later the syringe was discovered during a body search.

Koestler was not beaten. He was loaded on to a lorry and transferred to Malaga prison where, again, he thought he would be shot. This was one of the grimmest phases of his detention. Each night lists of men were read out before they were taken from their cells to be executed. Hugh Thomas, the historian of the Spanish Civil War, estimates that 4000 people were executed by the insurgents in the purging of Malaga, as reprisal for the 2400 killings while the government was in control.[82] Koestler was more fortunate: he was simply held there for four days until he was transferred to the Seville central prison. He was not to know it, but more than luck was working for him. Within hours of his capture efforts were being made to preserve his life and secure his release.

It was his good fortune that Malaga was a coastal city and relatively near Gibraltar. The British already had an interest in the port and were able to intervene there effectively by using naval forces. On 21 January 1937 the Royal Navy had evacuated the consul, Mr Clissold, and other British citizens. The situation in Malaga was monitored continuously thereafter. At the beginning of February the navy was contemplating a mission to land emergency supplies for the refugees in the city. On 9 February, the day after Malaga fell, HMS *Basilisk* sailed there from Gibraltar with Clissold aboard in order to ascertain whether supplies would be welcome. The ship's captain, Commander Dangerfield, and Clissold went ashore and met the Duke of Seville, the new Military Governor. At 9 p.m. the same day HMS *Basilisk* received a signal from the Commander in Chief, Home Fleet, Gibraltar, 'concerning Sir Peter Chalmers-Mitchell and Mr Koestler being in possible danger'.[83]

Incredibly, the British authorities knew about the threat to Chalmers-Mitchell and Koestler within hours of their detention. It is not clear how the information reached Gibraltar: it may have been via Gerda Grepp and the *News Chronicle* in London, or it could have been triggered by Chalmers-Mitchell's note to Norton, the American consul. Contrary to all Koestler thought at the time, and subsequently, his plight was not unknown or unrecognised. He was in serious trouble, but he had not been abandoned.

Dangerfield acted quickly and returned to shore to consult Clissold. It was too late to do anything that evening, but they set off again the next morning. Servants at Chalmers-Mitchell's house told them he had been taken away, so they went back into town to find him. At military headquarters a staff officer confirmed the preceding day's events, but not the Englishman's whereabouts. The officer described Chalmers-Mitchell as 'a flaming red', which boded ill. Dangerfield replied that 'Sir Peter was a British subject and his interests must be protected; that he was an old man and if he had possibly expressed himself indiscreetly, not too much importance should be attached to his utterances'. The officer retorted that Sir Peter's words cost thousands of lives, causing Dangerfield to note drily in his report: 'So far negotiations had not gone very well.'

Suddenly the Duke of Seville appeared at headquarters. Once appraised of the situation, he ordered that Chalmers-Mitchell be handed over as a gesture of goodwill to the Royal Navy. He would

not have to face a court martial and he would be allowed to leave
Spain on certain terms. Clissold and Dangerfield readily agreed. But
Sir Peter could not be found. A few hours later, and in complete
ignorance of these events, Koestler was taken from his cell and
escorted around Malaga prison in an effort to identify Chalmers-
Mitchell, who was, in fact, still in the Caleta Palace Hotel where
Bolin had left him. Norton fortuitously bumped into the naval party
in the street and guided them to Sir Peter. He was hurried out of the
city and by lunch time was in the wardroom of HMS *Basilisk*, being
entertained by the Captain.

Simultaneously, if rather half-heartedly, the navy was looking for
Koestler. Just before 11 a.m. HMS *Basilisk* signalled Gibraltar: 'No
trace of KOESTLER but believe British journalist name unknown
under arrest for espionage. Am investigating but from conversation
with Military, consider it most improbable that release of arrested
man can be effected as charges are regarded as well founded.'

The confusion about Koestler's identity and the speedy rescue of
Chalmers-Mitchell were probably decisive in saving his life. Initially
the information which Sir Peter supplied to the navy was unhelpful:
Dangerfield noted that 'As regards Mr Koestler we were informed by
Sir Peter that he was of Hungarian nationality. A signal containing
this information was sent.' The Home Fleet Command in its reply
directed Dangerfield 'to take no further action regarding this man.
His Hungarian nationality was later confirmed by Captain Bolin.
The opinion is that Koestler will be shot.' Dangerfield called off his
efforts to find Koestler on the afternoon of 10 February, but for
several crucial hours Bolin was under the impression that both his
captives had powerful protection. To have shot Koestler would have
been to risk an international incident. Meanwhile, Chalmers-
Mitchell was able to cable the *News Chronicle*, which was galvanised
into action. Just three days later the Foreign Office was receiving
enquiries from the Labour MP Reginald Sorenson about 'British
subjects' detained at Malaga. Viscount Cranbourne, Under Secretary
of State for Foreign Affairs, confirmed that a British subject had been
arrested and subsequently released. No mention was made of
Koestler, but in order to clarify events his name and his fate had been
registered by the Foreign Office.[84]

On 15 February 1937 the *News Chronicle* carried the story of
Koestler's capture prominently on its front page. The paper stated
that he had been condemned to death, whereupon strenuous intervention with Franco via diplomatic and press channels had secured
the suspension of the sentence. His future was 'uncertain', but

everything possible was being done to liberate him. The mention of Koestler's name was vital to prevent his 'disappearance'. Once the Nationalists were forced to confirm his detention it would be harder to murder him without repercussions. He didn't know it, but within a week of his arrest his life had been saved.

Koestler was held in Seville Central Prison from 13 February to 14 May 1937. For the first two months he was in solitary confinement and was not even allowed exercise. A three-week hunger strike later persuaded the prison authorities to allow him to mingle with other prisoners for an exercise period. On 19 February he was visited by a Falangist deputation which told him that powerful intercession had made the Nationalist regime reconsider his fate. The officials informed him that a helpful statement praising Franco's thoughtfulness would further ease his situation, but Koestler courageously refused to oblige them. The visit should have reassured him, but instead the conditional nature of the good news, with the implication that he would suffer if he did not co-operate, tortured him with doubts.[85]

VII

In *Spanish Testament*, written after his release, Koestler recorded some of the experiences of imprisonment: the volatility of his feelings, the therapeutic routines and mind games, the emotional 'sedatives' and 'stimulants' he perfected to maintain his sanity.

When, on 27 February, he obtained his first book from the prison library, the autobiography of John Stuart Mill in Spanish, he was euphoric. To his astonishment, the library was well stocked with European classics. (He was able to read de Maistre, Nerval, Sterne, R. L. Stevenson, Jules Verne and Tolstoy.) Seville Central Prison was, in fact, a humane and relatively comfortable institution.[86]

Koestler was an awkward prisoner, though. A brief hunger strike on 2 March secured him paper, a pencil, soap, a towel and a clean shirt. From then on he was able to keep a diary, in English, on which his subsequent account was based. A few days later he received a letter from Dorothea, cigarettes and money. On 11 March a note was tossed into his cell. It was from three imprisoned Republican militiamen. It told him that he would not be shot and begged him, when he got out, to tell the world about the plight of Franco's prisoners. On 5 April he began another hunger strike to reinforce letters to the governor demanding the right to exercise. His request was granted on 13 April. Paradoxically, the exercise periods heightened his agony. His four companions were all condemned men. Only one out of the group was executed, a young, illiterate Andalusian peasant, but his loss made the regular shootings tangible.[87]

On 21 and 28 April 1937 M. Coullbas, the British consul in Seville, to whom he had been sending letters, visited him. It was an uncomfortable encounter since Koestler was pretending to be the wronged liberal journalist, whereas the consul knew all about *L'Espagne ensanglantée*. Koestler made no mention of this incident in *Spanish Testament*, written while he was still posing as a hapless correspondent, but in *The Invisible Writing* he revealed the shame he felt as he evaded questions put to him by the consul about the blatant propaganda he had carried out against the Nationalists. Koestler was interrogated by Nationalist officials on 8 May, possibly so they could let him know what they knew about him. A further consular visit led him to expect a trial, but on 13 May he was asked to sign a declaration forswearing any 'meddling' in Spanish affairs and freed. He was flown to La Linea and the next day handed over to British officials at the border with Gibraltar.[88]

If Sir Peter Chalmers-Mitchell and the British Navy had saved his life, he owed his release to Otto Katz and Dorothea Koestler. News of Koestler's imprisonment reached Paris quickly and electrified Münzenberg's entourage. Sperber was so upset he was unable to sleep for several nights.[89] Dorothea asked Party officials to let her travel to London to orchestrate a campaign for his liberation. They agreed, but reluctantly. It was Katz who quietly provided the means for the rescue effort. He also planted stories in the press to keep Koestler's name in circulation and provoke the rebels to confirm that he was still alive. Recently discovered files in the former KGB 'Special Archive' in Moscow reveal how expertly and comprehensively Otto Katz and Dorothea set about saving Koestler.[90]

At first the campaign was directed by Katz and the Agence Espagne, which issued press releases and collected information via its branches in various countries. Katz even sent another journalist into Spain to help Koestler. According to Sheila Grant Duff, then a freelance journalist, Katz persuaded Edgar Mowrer, European correspondent of the *Chicago Daily News*, to dispatch her on a 'mission' for the Spanish government. In early February Mowrer told her to expect a briefing from a Spanish 'representative' in Paris. It turned out to be Katz. He asked her to go to Malaga to publicise the slaughter there and show how the port was being used to violate the arms blockade. "'There is one more thing I wish you to do", he said. "Arthur Koestler is in prison in Malaga. Try to get him out or at least go and see him and make a fuss so that he doesn't disappear.'" Katz made the travel arrangements and provided 'lots of money'. Duff reached Malaga and made contact with Norton, the American consul, but managed to do little more. The British consul told her, 'You would be extremely ill advised in your equivocal position to raise any sort of question about Koestler . . . It would do him no good and you considerable harm. Forget it.' When she returned to Paris, 'Mowrer and Simon [Katz] made no bones about their contemptuous disappointment.'[91]

There were obvious drawbacks to this *modus operandi* since the more the agency agitated on behalf of Koestler the more it seemed he was an enemy of the rebels. In order to establish Koestler's credentials as a 'liberal' journalist working for an English newspaper, the campaign was passed over to Dorothea. However, as the Moscow files show, she reported directly to her superiors in Paris.[92]

Dorothea went to London and based herself in a room at the Royal Hotel, Holborn. She built on the early work of the *News Chronicle* foreign news staff, who had been assiduously cabling various British and foreign officials demanding Koestler's release. Sir Walter Layton, the paper's owner, was an invaluable source of high-level political contacts. She fired off letters to dozens of Members of Parliament, peers and clerics. The formula was always the same: Koestler was a Hungarian journalist working for a liberal English newspaper who was falsely accused of espionage. Her tone was that of the tormented spouse. In her appeal to Eden, the Foreign Secretary, on 8 April 1937, she excused her forwardness by saying that the 'terrible uncertainty of my husband's fate has driven me to approach you personally to make this appeal on [*sic*] your humanity'. She also wrote to and met Vyvyan Adams, Victor Cazalet, Harold Nicolson, William Roberts, Eleanor Rathbone and several other MPs. A number of parliamentarians at her prompting asked questions about Koestler in the House of Commons, including Commander Fletcher (13 April) and Mr Mander (14 April). Others, like Winston Churchill and Harold Nicolson, wrote to the Foreign Office on Koestler's behalf.[93]

Dorothea Koestler also approached individuals and agencies who could help. She was informed that Lady Violet Bonham-Carter knew Count Grandi, the Italian liaison with the Nationalists, while Lady Astor reputedly had the ear of a member of the Spanish Royal family. She wrote to Lord Rothermere, the Archbishops of Westminster and York, the Quakers, the Red Cross and the London PEN Club. PEN persuaded H. G. Wells to send a cable to Franco pleading for

Koestler's life. Fellow journalists stepped in to assist: Willy Forrest arranged a deputation from the London branch of the National Union of Journalists to the Foreign Office. In addition, the International Association of Journalists, the Foreign Press Association and the Institute of Journalists sent cables to Franco and the British government. Well-known defenders of refugees were enlisted including Sylvia Pankhurst and the Duchess of Atholl. No effort was spared. Dorothea even mobilised contacts in Budapest, including Professor Vámbéry, and arranged for an appeal to go to the Hungarian legation at the Vatican.[94]

With the continuing help of the *News Chronicle*, which had its own motives and saw the case of Koestler as a way of blackening Franco, she mobilised public opinion. An early-day motion in the House of Commons garnered the names of fifty-eight MPs, of whom twenty-two were Tories whom she was particularly keen to involve in order to dispel the notion that Koestler was a left-wing agitator. Partly as a result of this intense campaign Sir Robert Vansittart, Permanent Under-Secretary at the Foreign Office, and Prime Minister Baldwin took a personal interest in the case. On 13 April, in reply to a question from Commander Fletcher, Eden said that even though Koestler was not a British subject the Foreign Office had asked its legation in Hendaye, the diplomatic base of the Nationalist regime, to make informal enquiries on his behalf. The Foreign Office received a response on 29 April 1937 confirming Koestler's location and well-being, but stating that his case was still under consideration. It was also reported that the British consul in Seville had been to see Koestler. Thanks to Katz's lobbying in Paris, even the French government offered to assist the efforts to have Koestler released.[95]

Sperber had considered Koestler's position to be all but hopeless and marvelled at the way Dorothea 'worked tirelessly in Paris and London for his release'. Harold Nicolson, a Conservative MP, recorded what it was like to be personally lobbied by her. In his diary for 21 April 1937 he wrote: 'Mrs Koestler, whose husband has disappeared in Spain, came to see me and sat upon the bench with tears pouring down her cheeks. The consul at Seville has been assured that Mr Koestler is "alive and well". If that were so, he would certainly have communicated with his wife, and I very much fear that he has been shot. I talked to Vansittart about it, and he promised to take the matter up tomorrow and insist on a reply.'[96]

It was an agonising time for Dorothea, whose zeal was more than comradely. Even making allowances for her need to pose as the loyal wife, her letters are emotionally charged. On 15 April 1937, after she had had no word from Koestler for over two months she wrote: 'In my heart I do not only hope but feel sure that our separation cannot last much longer and I am always thinking of the day when I shall have you back again and when I can give you all the love I feel for you.' After the British consul communicated the news that he had met Koestler her relief was palpable.[97]

Koestler was eventually released in an exchange agreement brokered by Dr Marcel Junod, the chief representative of the Red Cross in Spain. In May 1937 José Giral, the Spanish Foreign Minister, approached Junod with a list of twenty-one Republican prisoners in Seville. General Queipo de Llano was prepared to exchange them all for the wife of one of the rebels' leading airmen. However, Giral told Junod that 'I'm interested in one man. He's not a Spaniard, but he's a friend of the republic. His name is Koestler.' The deal was reduced to a one-for-one swap at the border at La Linea. Koestler was free.[98]

VIII

Koestler's release made the front page of the *News Chronicle* on 15 May 1937. According to the paper he said 'God Save the King' when he crossed on to British soil. But his essay in *The God That Failed* states that the first thing he did was send a cable to Münzenberg beginning with a line from Schiller, '"*Seid umschlungen, Millionen* = I embrace thee, ye millions." And, even more strange, I added the words, "I am cured of belly-aches" – "belly-ache" being our slang expression for qualms about the Party line.' On a rather more homely note, he also telegraphed his parents to let them know he was safe.[99]

He travelled to England on the cruiser HMS *Derbyshire*, arriving at Tilbury on 21 May. When he walked unsteadily down the gangway he was a celebrity, greeted by correspondents and photographers. Dorothea was also there. She embraced him with a fervour that was not just for the cameras.[100] While on the ship Koestler had already begun to write up his experiences for the *News Chronicle*, which paid £100 for the exclusive rights. They appeared in serial form daily, from 24 to 28 May 1937, and elicited an enormous reaction. Victor Gollancz commissioned Koestler to write an account of his experiences in Spain incorporating his book for Editions du Carrefour and adding the story of his imprisonment.[101]

Sir Walter Layton, chairman of the *News Chronicle*, put his summer house at Shepperton, by the Thames, at Koestler's disposal so that he could complete the book without distractions. In these ideal circumstances he was able to work fast, reshaping *L'Espagne ensanglantée* and his newspaper articles. He dictated from his prison diary in English to Dorothea who typed it up. She also typed numerous letters of thanks which he conscientiously sent to all those who had helped him while he was in prison. *Spanish Testament* was completed by mid-September 1937 and appeared as a Left Book Club choice at the end of 1937. The selection was made by the Club's literary panel, Victor Gollancz, the publisher, Harold Laski, the socialist academic, and John Strachey, a left-wing writer. It was a great success. To Koestler's immense relief, 'I was at long last launched on my course as a writer.'[102]

Spanish Testament is a classic of its kind. Despite protesting the inadequacy of language, Koestler manages to recall his experiences with terrifying precision, sucking the reader into his confined universe. It has lost none of its power today and has a ghastly familiarity in the light of more recent contributions to this appalling genre by Jacobo Timmerman, Natan Sharansky, Terry Waite, John McCarthy and Brian Keenan. However, Koestler rewrote his Spanish adventure several times with each version reflecting his altered circumstances and changed beliefs.[103]

By 1941 *L'Espagne ensanglantée* was an embarrassment to him. It had been partly embodied in *Spanish Testament*, but he sheared off the propagandistic account of the Spanish Civil War and negotiated with Allen Lane for the republication of just the second part, 'Dialogue with Death', as a separate book. *Dialogue with Death* was published in 1942 in the USA by Macmillan and in England by Penguin. There were many other, less noticeable but significant changes. The American Literary historian Murray Sperber ascribes the differences to three shifts in Koestler's self-perception between the autumn of 1936, when he composed *L'Espagne ensanglantée*, the summer of 1937, when he wrote *Spanish Testament*, and the years after 1938, when he was no longer a member of the Communist Party.

Sperber argues that *L'Espagne ensanglantée* reflects the writer's self-perception in orthodox Communist terms as an anonymous fighter in the anti-Fascist ranks whose subjective experiences count for little. By contrast, the opening of *Spanish Testament* is dominated by the personalised story of Koestler's first journey to Spain.[104] Sperber's argument has some force, but there is also a simple structural explanation for the change. The second half of *Spanish Testament* covers his imprisonment, which derived from his treacherous expedition to Seville. The encounter with Bolin in Malaga lacks force and meaning without the background of their first meeting in Seville.

Spanish Testament was also written for a different sort of audience. Instead of crude Marxist reductionism, although there is a good deal of that, Koestler plays up Popular Front themes that would appeal to liberal-minded English readers. So the war in Spain is rendered not as one between Communism and Fascism, but as a structural conflict rooted in land ownership, the role of the Church and the aristocracy. Rather than play to Continental revolutionary ardour, he wanted to make the Spanish Civil War something with which the English could identify. He actually compares the land reform programme of the progressive Spanish governments with the dissolution of the monasteries by Henry VIII. He cites Paine and Godwin as the thinkers who prepared the way for the Republican assault on the power of the Church. Fascism is represented not as decaying capitalism, but the spirit of the Middle Ages resisting the march of constitutional democracy.[105]

Still, as Sperber notes, *Spanish Testament* is full of tension. Is it objective reportage or propaganda? Is it an anonymous report from the 'workers' front' or one man's personal experiences? Both questions are rooted in the ideological mire in which Koestler found himself in 1936–7. For this reason, as well as for the purposes of combating Fascist lies, he is deeply concerned with the question of propaganda. Chapter six analyses Nationalist propaganda, while chapters seven and eight *are* propaganda. Koestler was always haunted by questions of integrity. His first career was as a journalist; his credibility rested on accuracy and verifiability. How could he have written such stuff?

The key to Koestler's attitude lies in a comment he made on the dangers of atrocity propaganda. 'The journalist who is determined to give proof of his objectivity often succumbs to the temptation of maintaining silence with regard to concrete facts, because these facts are in themselves so crude that he is afraid of appearing biased.' For him, objectivity did not exclude rubbing people's noses in horror even at the risk of reviving memories of the manufactured atrocity stories of the First World War. Nor did it mean equating both sides. Only the Nationalists launched aerial bombardments against largely civilian targets. Koestler described the air raids on the Spanish capital and concluded: 'Anyone who has lived through the hell of Madrid with his eyes, nerves, his heart, his stomach – and then pretends to be objective is a liar. If those who have at their command printing machines and printer's ink for the expression of their opinions, remain neutral and objective in the face of such bestiality, then Europe is lost.'[106]

In the author's foreword to *Spanish Testament*, Koestler acknowledge the tension between the tone of the historical chapters and the personal recollections. 'Nevertheless, I believe these chapters to be necessary. Without them the subjective experiences described in the second part would lack their background. In that second part I describe what I felt – but an essential – in some ways *the* essential part of this "Dialogue with Death" was my knowledge of the objective meaning of this war.'[107] In view of his treatment of 'objectivity', the starkness of the contrast between the two modes of reportage is greatly reduced. This is, in fact, a recognisable modern style of commited journalism in which the writer is actor and his emotional responses to what he witnesses are part of the story.

The real, subterranean tension between the objective and subjective modes are less about Koestler's objective relations to the Communist Party than his subjective relations to the proletariat as the agents of revolution and the individual's relationship with historical forces. Sperber writes, 'The successive Forewords point to Koestler's emerging individuality, and every change in the text underlines his new sense of self, as author, subject, political man, and psychological phenomenon.' In *Spanish Testament* he was torn between ideologically determined roles, for which he was a vessel. In 'Dialogue with Death' he wrote about personal experiences. In *Dialogue with Death* he emerged as 'the lone individual within an apocalyptic world'.[108]

There are many alterations between the 1937 and 1942 versions of 'Dialogue with Death', but these are not simply intended to 'emphasize his authorial character and/or produce a greater literary effect' as Murray Sperber argues. The changes are ideologically driven. For example, in *Spanish Testament* Koestler recalls his response to the voice of a prisoner in the Malaga prison singing the 'Internationale'. He was uplifted and imagined the rest of the prisoners standing like him, fist clenched in the Communist salute enjoying 'a rapturous feeling of brotherly love and oneness with the others'. The deletion of this passage from *Dialogue with Death* is not simply the elimination of 'sloppy sentiments', but the rejection of a certain kind of solidarity imagined and prescribed by the Party. In another passage that disappears from *Dialogue with Death*, Koestler writes: 'What matters is not what a man is, but what function the social system dictates that he shall fulfil.' Out goes a form of determinism derived from historical materialism.[109]

In *Dialogue with Death* Koestler confesses to feeling curiously homesick for the prison and the feeling of peace and freedom it engendered. He was nagged by the sensation that 'one has forgotten something in Cell No. 41'. In the original version he is more specific about what had been left behind. He recalls that during his captivity he would ask himself why was this happening to him: 'what palpable or secret meaning was behind it all? . . . It is the answer that has been forgotten; sometimes it seems to me as though I knew it all the time, as though a faint breath of knowledge had brushed by me; but it has vanished irrevocably.'[110]

A decade passed before Koestler 'revealed' more of what happened in the condemned cell, by which time it was extremely difficult any longer to separate occurrence from invention. In *The God That Failed*, he remarked, 'my hair had not greyed and my features had not changed and I had not developed religious mania; but I had made the acquaintance of a different kind of reality, which had profoundly altered my outlook and values; and altered them so profoundly and unconsciously that during the first days of freedom I was not even aware of it.' He recounts three distinct experiences in the cell: fear, pity and a third, 'a condition of mind usually referred to in terms borrowed from the vocabulary of mysticism which would present itself at unexpected moments and induce a state of inner peace which I have known neither before nor since'. His imprisonment taught him the pedestrian, but vital lesson that 'man is a reality, mankind an abstraction; that men cannot be treated as units in operations of political arithmetic because they behave like symbols for zero and the infinite, which dislocate all mathematical operations; that the end justifies the means only within very narrow limits; that ethics is not a function of social utility and that charity is not a petit-bourgeois sentiment, but the gravitational force which keeps civilisation in its orbit'.[111]

There is nothing mystical about this. These are practical themes which Koestler pursued with explosive force in his anti-Communist novel *Darkness at Noon* (1940). The character of his down-to-earth response in *The God That Failed* is confirmed by the impression of eyewitnesses that he was, indeed, unchanged. Malraux met him in Paris after his release and remarked with some disappointment: 'in the company of Marcel Arland, I met Arthur Koestler, freed from the Francoist prison cell where he had spent months under sentence of death. "It's always the same," Arland said to me after we left him. "One imagines they must be the bearers of a sort of revelation, and then they talk as if nothing had happened to them . . ."'[112]

Manès Sperber, an acute analyst of personalities, came to the same conclusion. While Koestler was in prison Sperber had tried to figure out why he had allowed himself to be captured. Sperber worked out that his friend, faced by doubts about Communism similar to those which plagued him, had fallen into the arms of the enemy rather than retreat and once again face all his dilemmas. 'Anyone who always keeps his face turned toward his enemy is spared the need to discover the weaknesses and pitiful failure of his own camp.' On this basis, Sperber realised that Koestler was in the same boat as he was and became deeply attached to him. They saw a great deal of each other after Koestler's release. But Sperber concluded: 'He had emerged from the death cell unchanged, and he had no new certainties, but he was resolved from then on not to settle for half-truths.'[113]

Sperber saw 'Dialogue with Death' as an act of therapy in which 'after vigorous self-examination, [Koestler] set down his experiences with uncompromising resoluteness, thus ridding himself of much inner distress'. As there was little which the two men concealed from each other and Sperber, who had grown up in an East European town dominated by Hassidism and wonder-rabbis, would of all his friends have been sympathetic to mystical ideas, it is hard to believe that Koestler had any such notions about his prison experience, at least at this stage of his life.[114]

In the light of such observations it is necessary to read sceptically Koestler's fourth version of his prison days, the account in *The Invisible Writing*. The ultimate fulfillment of the promise he had made to himself to write a transparent autobiography, this contains much additional material in the form of several 'confessions' and the experience is rendered very much in the terms of 'religious mania'. Because he was still posing as a bourgeois journalist when he wrote 'Dialogue with Death' he had not been able to explain the chief cause of the periodic serenity which overcame him in jail. The calm originated in a sense that unlike previous bouts of ill-fortune this time he was getting his just deserts: he had commited a breach of the law and moral decency in August 1936, when he tricked his way into Franco's lair, and now he was paying for it. The guilt complex which had tortured him was replaced by a feeling of equanimity. He even goes so far as to suggest that this was biological in origin, and develops a curious theory of justice that will be examined later.[115]

Nor was he able to mention in 'Dialogue with Death' an incident when he told a guard, half inadvertently, that he was 'no longer a Red'. Koestler squirmed at the thought of his 'unconscious craving to curry favour with the enemy', although it is characteristic of all prison narratives. He was also uncomfortable at the evidence it revealed of 'an unconscious tendency to betrayal'. This proclivity was, however, peculiar to him.[116]

In *The Invisible Writing* he unveiled his mystical experiences, the 'hours by the window', which seemingly had changed his life. According to this final account of the events in Malaga and Seville, the shock of his arrest, imprisonment and the repeated threat of death 'apparently had caused a loosening up and displacement of psychological strata close to rock bottom – a softening of resistances and rearrangement of structures which laid them temporarily open to that new type of experience'. This was revealed when he started scratching mathematical proofs on the wall of the cell. Euclid's proof that the quantity of prime numbers is infinite brought home to him in concrete terms the notion of infinity. 'Then I was floating on my back in a river of peace, under bridges of silence. It came from nowhere. There was no river and no I. The I had ceased to exist.' Koestler felt himself dissolve into the universe: 'for the first time the veil has fallen and one is in touch with "real reality", the hidden order of things, the X-ray texture of the world, normally obscured by layers of irrelevancy.' In this 'process of dissolution and limitless expansion which is sensed as the "oceanic feeling", as the draining of all tension, the absolute catharsis, the peace that passeth all understanding'.[117]

It is necessary to dwell on these passages at length because it was this experience which Koestler claimed altered his politics for ever and formed 'the groundwork for a change of personality'. His adherence to rationalism was shattered. Prison had 'filled me with a direct certainty that a higher order of reality existed, and that it alone invested experience with meaning'. This was the 'reality of the third order', the world to which access was gained only through extra-sensory perception.[118]

Yet however much the paranormal dominated the second half of Koestler's life, there is barely a hint of it in his behaviour or writings from 1937 to 1947. He did explore the 'oceanic feeling' in *Darkness at Noon*, but to radically different ends. In that novel the imprisoned commissar discovers through the 'oceanic feeling' his individual humanity in contradistinction to Party orthodoxy that the individual counted for nothing in the stream of history. This is the opposite of the dissolution of the self which Koestler later describes. In *The Invisible Writing*: 'the knowledge that it [the invisible text or the 'third order'] existed was sufficient to alter the texture of one's existence and make one's actions *conform to the text* [author's italics].' This is a form of determinism, but in *Darkness at Noon* the commissar is rebelling against all forms of inevitability.[119]

By the early 1950s, Koestler had jumbled up politics, ethics, psychology and the paranormal in an attempt to create a unified theory of existence. This resulted in a final, retrospective mystification of his prison experience. At the time it was much simpler: a blinding, elementary lesson that was shocking to record. To his credit, buried amid the mumbo-jumbo of the 'hours by the window', Koestler admits as much. 'Before my stay in Cell No 40, the words "prison" and "execution" had only brought to my mind some abstract cliché like Fascist Terror, or the Dialectics of Revolution. Now the same words had a different ring . . .'[120]

It took him thirty-three years to discover that all men are mortal, that they feel pain, that they bleed and that words can kill. He had been playing at revolution; others had been paying with their lives. Now the game was for real he didn't want to play any more.[121] Having experienced what it is to be disposable, the means to an end, Koestler was repelled by doctrines that held life worth nothing for the sake of realising a certain cause. He embarked on the search for a new politics and a new ethics, which did not render human suffering an acceptable means for the achievement of political goals.

His self-appointed task was made harder because he mistakenly lumped Communism together with all political and ethical thought founded on Enlightenment reasoning and, particularly, utilitarianism. As he ruefully confessed, 'It was easier to reject the utilitarian concept of ethics than to find a substitute for it.'[122] Because he rejected religion as unreason and saw reason as dangerous, he was condemned to an individual odyssey that led to science and then mysticism. In *The Invisible Writing* both approaches are backdated to his prison meditations.

IX

In September 1937, when Koestler completed *Spanish Testament*, he also wound up his relationship with Dorothea. 'All the circumstances were propitious; yet my neurotic inability to settle down with a partner for life again proved distressingly stronger than affection and gratitude.' Living in England was pleasant, except that he had to pretend he was not a Communist whereas he was actually still a Party member. Since he spoke at a number of fund-raising events on behalf of Republican Spain, putting his newfound celebrity to use for the cause, this was not merely an abstract problem. At a meeting in Manchester on 25 June 1937 he pronounced that 'There is a concrete body of help now for those who fight for the eternal ideas of liberalism, democracy and social justice', words which must have stuck in his throat in view of his real beliefs about liberalism. It must also have caused embarrassment when he met with Jewish and anti-Nazi exiles in London like Berthold Viertel, Robert Neumann and Hilda Spiel, who knew something of his Berlin background. The play-acting rubbed against his sense of integrity and he jumped at the chance to go back to Europe when the *News Chronicle* offered him an assignment as a special correspondent in the Balkans.[123]

On his arrival in Paris he was warmly greeted by Otto Katz, then debriefed by two Party officials in a café near the Place de la Bastille. His next stop was Switzerland, where he interviewed Thomas Mann. He had derived solace from Mann's writing while he had been in prison and wrote to him to tell him as much. But the interview went badly. Mann treated Koestler like a passing reporter, which he was, while Koestler behaved like an adolescent hungering for paternal approval. From Switzerland he journeyed to Belgrade to meet his real parents. It was a pathetic encounter. His father was ill with stomach cancer and looked like an old man. His mother was 'resolute, temperamental, caustic and irritable, as I had always known her'.[124]

On 20 September he travelled to Greece to write articles about the Metaxas dictatorship. Koestler was not in the right frame of mind to look dispassionately at another dim-witted, reactionary, authoritarian regime and his articles were so 'savage' that the *News Chronicle* spiked them. On 27 September 1937, however, the simmering unrest between Jews and Arabs in Palestine exploded into rioting and guerrilla warfare. He headed for his old stamping ground and spent six weeks in the country. Palestine was again to provide a turning point in his life.[125]

He had left Palestine in 1929 but he had never left the Jewish Question behind. Instead, he had entered the Communist Party in the belief that it offered an alternative solution to the Jewish predicament. 'During those eight years (1929–37) I had believed that the small and irksome Jewish question would eventually be solved, together with the Negro question, the Armenian question and all other questions, in the new global context of the socialist revolution. So I had left the old Promised Land for the new land of promise, and had found it an even more bitter disappointment. Now, on my way out of the Communist Party, I had come back.'[126]

Koestler was not returning to Zionism as a messianic movement destined to create a state that would inspire all mankind. He now understood that the Jewish Question required a limited, local initiative: a small state in which Jews could find sanctuary. He had learned the hard way that global universal Utopias are dangerous things. They demand the ironing out of all the kinks in nations, ethnic groups and individuals. They call for and seem to justify the most drastic measures with potentially unknowable human consequences; but the creation of a small state was something calculable. It might require draconian methods, even violence, but on a contained, regional, experimental and verifiable scale. Despite his bitter denunciations of utilitarian ethics he remarked, 'In this limited, resigned, and utilitarian sense, I was still a Zionist.'[127]

Koestler stayed in Palestine for six weeks. He saw old Zionist friends and more recent unhappy transplants from Germany. He also embarked on some serious investigative journalism. He interviewed Emir Abdullah, King of Jordan, about the prospects for resolving the Jewish–Arab conflict by a partition of Palestine, as a British Royal Commission had recently proposed. He also went after the Mufti of Jerusalem, leader of the hard-line Palestinian Arab Nationalists, whom the British had just forced into exile. The hunt took him to Beirut, where he scored a double scoop for the *News Chronicle* by locating the Mufti and uncovering Italian aid to the Palestinian Arab guerrillas. In between these adventures he reported on the bomb outrages perpetrated by Jewish and Arab extremists, and the hapless efforts of the British garrison to keep order. His last article for the paper, 'SOS for Palestine', was a plea for partition based on an incisive analysis of conditions in the country and a gloomy prediction that if Britain did not soon take action there would be bloody chaos.[128]

In the new year, 1938, Koestler travelled to England to undertake a lecture tour in connection with the publication of *Spanish Testament*. Now everything coalesced: his disillusionment with Communism, his discoveries in the prison cell and his passionate interest in the Jewish Question, which compelled him, as much as his experiences in Spain, to re-evaluate his political beliefs. The time had come to break with Communism and return to the pursuit of the old Promised Land.

Chapter 5
War, 1938–42

The years 1938 to 1942 were among the most creative and chaotic of Koestler's life. He wrote and published his first two novels, *The Gladiators* (1939) and his masterpiece *Darkness at Noon* (1940). He also produced a brilliant analysis of the fall of France in 1940, interwoven with the story of his personal experiences and escape from Nazi-dominated Europe. This book, *Scum of the Earth* (1941), had the added distinction of being the first that he wrote entirely in English. It marked yet another language shift, with all the profound effects on mental processes involved in translation from one language, political culture and artistic heritage to another. Throughout these writings he was trying to figure out where he belonged.

In April 1938, somewhat later than he made out in his memoirs, he finally left the Communist Party. Despite all that he had witnessed in Russia in 1932–3, and had subsequently learned about the country, he retained a deep loyalty to the Soviet Union, its people, their heroic efforts to modernise a relatively backward empire and the particular idea of revolution which animated this gigantic enterprise. His last illusions were destroyed by the Nazi–Soviet Pact in August 1939. From that point onwards he was doubly, or trebly, an exile: uprooted from the country of his birth and spurned by those he had adopted, he had broken with the Party, an international haven, and was now deserted by Russia. Where was his home?

This question was more than theoretical. When war broke out in September 1939 the French turned on foreigners in their midst. Koestler was interned twice. On the first occasion he was freed thanks to a strenuous campaign by friends and allies. The second time he took his fate in his own hands and escaped, living on the run from the French authorities and the invading Germans. He sought anonymity in the French Foreign Legion, eventually escaped to North Africa and from there made his way via Portugal to England. However, he was not given official permission to enter the country and arrived illegally, as a result of which he spent a further stretch in

prison. Once he was released, by dint of another campaign, he
enrolled in the Pioneer Corps of the British Army. Even though he
was now in uniform and subject to military discipline, Koestler continued to write and also engaged in political crusades. Jewish
preoccupations were to the fore. Despite being an alien he cam-
paigned for the rescue of refugees from German-occupied Europe in
1941–2 and monitored the Nazi persecution of the Jews.

   Jewish themes repeatedly emerge in his writing from this period.
Spartacus, the hero of *The Gladiators*, receives inspiration from a
prophetic Jew. *Scum of the Earth* is punctuated with references to the
role of anti-Semitism in the demoralisation of France and full of
observations on the singular plight of Jewish fugitives such as himself.
The central figure in *Darkness at Noon*, Nikolai Salmanovitch
Rubashov, *is* a Jew. But it was as an ex-Communist, someone who
had freed himself from the simultaneously reassuring and perilous
embrace of the Party at the expense of becoming an alien or outsider
in every sense, that Koestler at last achieved real fame and permanent
security as a writer.

I

After his Middle Eastern adventure and rediscovery of Zionism,
Koestler returned to France for a few weeks. In January 1938 he
travelled to England for a lecture tour to promote *Spanish Testament*.
The book had become a popular success and an effective propaganda
tool, as Münzenberg had hoped. According to the biographer of
Victor Gollancz, founder of the Left Book Club (LBC), 'Of the
books on the Civil War published by the LBC, the most influential
was Arthur Koestler's *Spanish Testament*, which came out in
December 1937 and was followed up in January by the author's
speaking tour to groups. Koestler's experiences as a prisoner of
Franco expecting imminent execution gave his book and his talks an
immediacy that added feverishness to the LBCs support for the
Popular Front forces.'[1]

   By now Koestler knew he was not a Communist, but had not
summoned the courage to break openly with the Party. He realised
it would mean adding homelessness to exile and obloquy to self-pity.
The lecture tour offered a device to break the impasse, a gentle way
of provoking his expulsion. At almost every one of the dozens of Left
Book Club meetings which he addressed a member of the audience
asked for his thoughts about the treatment of POUM – the
Trotskyist-dominated militia force that had had been broken up by

the Republican authorities at the behest of the Communists in 1937. Koestler answered that members of POUM might have been misguided in certain ways, but they were sincere anti-Fascists. This contradicted the Party line which denounced POUM as renegades who showed an independence of thinking alien to Communist practice. However, the English Communists merely expressed their disapproval by silence or argued with him politely and reasonably. The Party seemed willing to ignore his *faux pas* for the time being: England was a side-show. Nevertheless, Koestler felt relieved that he had recorded his dissent from the Party line. The Left Book Club was only a dress rehearsal for what he knew he had to do in the real political and ideological cockpit: the *émigré* German community of Paris.[2]

Events hastened his next move. In March 1938 the trial of Bukharin and other old Bolsheviks began in Moscow. Then Eva Weissberg arrived from the USSR bearing the incredible story of her own arrest, interrogation and imprisonment. Two years earlier she had been the object of fantastic accusations of sabotage and anti-Soviet espionage. She was arrested and held for eighteen months until representations by the Austrian consul secured her release. Even though Alex had separated from her in 1934 and knew that the penalty for supporting his ex-wife was almost inevitably to suffer the same fate, he had worked tirelessly to free her. Eva was eventually expelled from the USSR in September 1937; true to form, Alex Weissberg was arrested in March 1937 and was still in prison. Fired up by this further evidence of Communist perfidy, Koestler prepared for a talk on Spain to the Association of German Writers in Exile in April 1938.[3]

As a celebrity he attracted a large audience, mainly composed of German Communist refugees. Beforehand, the organisers asked him to stick to Party orthodoxy in his comments on Spain, but he refused. At the end of his talk he drew three provocative conclusions: that no individual or party was infallible; that it was wrong to persecute allies who took a different route to the same goal; and that Thomas Mann was correct when he declared: 'In the long run, a harmful truth is better than a useful lie.' His listeners understood exactly what he meant and immediately the meeting broke up he was cold-shouldered. To the Party he had instantly become a non-person; and just as quickly he was engulfed by loneliness. 'It was not a physical loneliness, for after the break with the Party I found more friends than I have had before. But individual friendships could never replace the knowledge that one belonged to an international brotherhood embracing the whole globe; nor the warming, reassuring feeling of a collective solidarity which gave to that huge, amorphous mass the coherence and intimacy of a small family.'[4]

Despite this the Party did not expel him, probably because it did not want a public breach with a famous survivor of Franco's jails. So in a mood of 'bridge burning' euphoria on 22 April 1938 he wrote a letter of resignation to the 'Writers Caucus' of the German Communist Party. The letter, which has only recently come to light in the former KGB 'Special Archive', is remarkably ambivalent. In it he promises not to join any oppositional group and pledges his loyalty to the Soviet Union which he regards 'as a decisively positive factor in the political balance of our time'. He begs his former comrades to regard him still as 'an ally'. Finally, he pleads for his breach to be kept secret to avoid embarrassing those who helped him in 1937 under he impression that he was not a Communist.[5]

It was followed by a much longer letter, sent a week later, explaining his motives. Koestler denounced the 'moral degeneration of the Party, which began long before 1933'. The Moscow Trials and the events in Spain forced Party members either to believe the unbelievable or abase their intellects. The 'Trotskyite–Nazi conspiracy . . . is gradually beginning to occupy for us the role *The Protocols of the Elders of Zion* occupies in the minds of the Nazis'. But the problem went deeper. The movement lacked a revolutionary ethics: Communists denounced bourgeois morality and utilitarianism, but had no adequate substitute. The only guide to practical action was that the end justified the means. Marxist theory had 'ossified' too. There 'is not a hint of an explanation in our theory for the laws that impel the masses' to act against their own 'objective class interests'. Koestler ended by reaffirming his loyalty to the USSR, but asserted that this could be combined with free inquiry and debate. 'I feel I am being suffocated by you, and I have the elementary need to breathe, to think, to write freely again, to dare to speak my mind.'[6] His profession of fealty to a country which he had seen at its worst is not the only odd facet of his 'breach' with Communism. Koestler broke with the Party at a rather late stage, long after his mentor Münzenberg, and remained on good terms with the 'apparat' for some time after that.

In *The God That Failed* Koestler asserted that Münzenberg 'broke with the Comintern in 1938, six months after myself'. Actually, Münzenberg had effectively broken with Moscow a year *earlier*. From January 1937 he deflected calls that he present himself in Moscow, at first pleading ill-health, then simply rejecting them. At a German Popular Front conference in Paris in April 1937 he condemned the mistakes the Party had made in the early 1930s, taking a barely veiled swipe at Stalin. Moscow then sent an emissary of the KPD to sequester the funds of the 'Münzenberg Trust', but Münzenberg refused to co-operate. In the summer he held talks with exiled liberal politicians and bourgeois figures such as the writer Leo Schwarzchild, the ex-Ullstein editor Georg Bernhard and the novelist Heinrich Mann about creating a new party. This would subsequently take shape as the Deutsche Freiheits Partei. In September 1937 his book *Propaganda als Waffe* appeared. It was a searing attack on the lies used by totalitarian regimes and could as easily be read as a critique of the techniques used by the Soviets or the Nazis. Sure enough, it was attacked in the exile German Communist press in November 1937. There are conflicting versions of precisely when Münzenberg was expelled from the German Communist Party, but it is most likely that the decision was taken in March 1938 although it was not published until May.[7]

Whichever date is selected as the moment that Münzenberg cut his ties with the Comintern, it is certain that by the time Koestler returned to Paris in September 1937 Münzenberg had lost his power base. Koestler recalls that 'Otto greeted me at the Gare du Nord, most incongruously and touchingly equipped with a huge bouquet of roses. We must have looked like a couple of gangsters out of an American film carrying a wreath at a funeral.' In effect, they were and it was Willi's funeral. Despite the fact that Katz was now acting as Münzenberg's undertaker, Koestler remained on good terms with him and continued to live in his old appartment on 10 rue Dombasle (where Walter Benjamin was a neighbour and fellow Saturday-night poker-player).[8]

Koestler's inexactitude regarding the timing of Münzenberg's departure from the Party signifies the intense difficulty he had in making his own break. The blurring of dates suggests that in retrospect he wished he had left earlier, pre-empting his mentor rather than trailing in his wake. What lies beyond doubt, however, is that during the first half of 1938 he was sawing through the ideological and emotional shackles that bound him to Communism. Perhaps the most important tool at his disposal was the novel about Spartacus, *The Gladiators*.

Thanks to the success of *Spanish Testament* he had negotiated a contract with Jonathan Cape to publish the novel in English. The advance of £125 enabled him to concentrate on the writing, even though he had to set aside some of the money to pay for the translation. It was an important turning point in his career for he was now able to think of himself primarily as a writer and 'writing as a purpose in itself'. The book provided the material means for his emancipation from writing as propaganda and the intellectual leverage he needed to free himself from the ideological compulsion.[9]

In *The Gladiators* Koestler makes the late Roman Republic resemble modern Europe. Its economic system is a parody of late capitalism, prone to all the same crises. A revolutionary situation develops when Spartacus, the leader of a group of runaway gladiators, forges an army out of rebellious slaves and discontented elements. A member of the Essenes, a Jewish sect, outlines to Spartacus a vision of society based on primitive Communism and he sets out to create the perfect society. Unfortunately, he falls victim to the 'law of detours'. As explained by the Essene, 'the worst curse of all is that he [man] must tread the evil road for the sake of the good and the right, that he must make detours and walk crookedly so that he may reach the straight goal.'

Using Spartacus, Koestler obliquely examined the dilemmas of the Bolsheviks in the years after 1917. Spartacus demands complete obedience from those who will follow him to the Utopian, egalitarian 'Sun City' he proposes to establish. But Spartacus is forced to make a series of compromises to preserve his Utopian community and is driven to ever more brutal measures to ensure internal discipline. The hoped-for rising of all the slaves of Rome, a metaphor for the world revolution, does not occur and Sun City, which is modelled on the kibbutz, remains isolated. In the end he wearies of leadership: he berates the masses for their lack of revolutionary discipline but refuses to bully them any longer. The rebel horde is defeated by the Romans whose commander, Crassus, tells Spartacus, 'you should have invented a new religion'. Spartacus dies in battle; his followers are crucified.[10]

The Gladiators is full of vividly drawn action and rich with characters. For a first novel it is an astonishing accomplishment. Admittedly it is replete with anachronisms, such as Roman houses equipped with 'fire escapes', even though Koestler laboured over the period detail. But none of this matters by comparison with the narrative drive and intense rumination on the dilemma of means and ends. The novel reflected a deep shift in Koestler's political thinking. In it he suggested that a revolution can only succeed if its leaders are ruthless and indoctrinate people with a new set of beliefs. Any humanity or toleration of dissent is fatal. Spartacus fails because he still has old-fashioned scruples and applies repression inconsistently, continuing to value human life over the cause he champions. This is

a chilling message which can be read in two ways, according to the reader's taste. In essence, however, it is a pessimistic, un–Marxist novel. Unlike his contemporaries, Ignazio Silone and André Malraux, socialist writers who had also been through a long involvement with the Communist Party, he saw little hope for spontaneous revolution amongst the people, and equally little hope that uncorruptable leaders would offer them decent direction.

During 1938 Koestler had contemporaneous experience of revolutionary ruthlessness at work. In the spring, having received Eva Weissberg's news about her husband, he mounted a campaign to help save Alex. He persuaded Frédéric Joliot-Curie and Jean Perrin, Nobel Prize winning physicists, to intercede with Stalin on Weissberg's behalf. He also saw Martin Ruhemann, an English-born scientist who had known Weissberg during a spell in Kharkov. Ruhemann refused to help because he was sure that Weissberg must have been a saboteur if that was what the charges said. Koestler was disgusted by this response: it was another demonstration of the Party's corrupting effect.[11]

The Gladiators was finished in July 1938. Over the summer, Koestler spent some time at Sanary-sur-Mer, a small resort on the French Mediterranean coast between Marseilles and Toulon, where the exiled German-Jewish writer Lion Feuchtwänger had lived since 1933. Feuchtwänger's home had become the meeting place for a circle of writers who were Communists or fellow travellers. Even though Koestler laboured under the stigma of a renegade, he was still welcome there. Alfred Kantorowicz remembers him visiting along with Heinrich Mann, Arnold Zweig, Ernst Toller, Ellen Wilkinson, the Labour MP, and Robert Neumann. He was frequently engaged in passionate argument with the other guests. Ludwig Marcuse recalled that Koestler would come to the house and make 'wild speeches' on the veranda in the presence of Kantorowicz and other stars of the Party.[12]

As soon as *The Gladiators* was completed he started work on the novel that was to emerge as *Darkness at Noon*. It began life entitled 'Watchman, What of the Night', later slightly improved as 'The Vicious Circle'. According to the publication proposal submitted to Jonathan Cape: 'the first volume of a trilogy on modern Russia, [it] opens with the arrest of the former People's Commissar, Rubashov on the charge of plotting against the state.' Koestler recorded that originally it was supposed to deal with some prisoners in a totalitarian country, under sentence of death, who re-evaluate their lives and realise that they are guilty of sacrificing men for an abstract ideal of

mankind.[13] If it was serendipitous that the title and precise content changed, it was nothing short of miraculous that the novel was ever finished and published. It was written in spite of the usual distractions that afflicted Koestler and some that were unprecedented. Its composition, which was stretched over nearly two years, was haunted by the events of the time, such as the Nazi–Soviet Pact, another spell of imprisonment and Koestler's beleaguered, pessimistic mood.

Manès Sperber has given an affecting portrait of Koestler in the last year before the war. 'Koestler and I were going on 32 and both of us were homeless in more than one sense and extremely sensitive, yet hardened to blows and deprivations, the dangerous allure of success and the inspirations of loneliness.' Although they disagreed on matters of taste and lifestyle, they concurred on the 'essential' things. 'Our friendship was like that of rock-climbers who are exposed to the same enticements and dangers and expect no less from each other than they do from themselves.' Both found comfort in their Jewish heritage. 'No matter how depressing the events of the day might be, the Jewish wit and gallows humour that each new day provoked determined the tone in which each of us expressed his fears and hopes. In fact, we felt more bitterness than is required to hate one's own life and all one's contemporaries, and yet we had a lot of fun when we were together and could often be heard laughing heartily.'[14]

In October 1938 Sperber and Koestler were drawn into Willi Münzenberg's last great publishing venture: a weekly anti-Fascist paper based on the principles of the Popular Front. Münzenberg acquired financial backing from the French Socialists and rented an apartment to serve as an editorial office. He recruited Koestler to act as co-editor and Ludwig Marcuse, the novelist, to edit a cultural section. Sperber became a consultant editor. In the early autumn Münzenberg's diminished circle of friends and supporters met regularly to hammer out a programme for the paper, christened hopefully *Die Zukunft* (The Future). The first issue appeared on 12 October 1938.[15]

Koestler writes rather dismissively that *Die Zukunft* was 'stillborn' and soon went stale. In fact, it continued until the fall of France in May 1940 and performed a multitude of important functions. It was a rallying point for disillusioned Communists and anti-Fascists of all hues. The paper was loosely tied to the Deutsche Freiheits Partei and together they represented one of the first attempts to create a progressive, anti-Stalinist and anti-Fascist politics for Europe.[16]

Typically, Koestler worked on it for only about three months, leaving before the end of 1938. He later said that he had been attracted to the project mainly because he wanted to fill the void left by his split from the Party, and he certainly seemed ill at ease, displeasingly glum one moment and engagingly euphoric the next. Marcuse remembered him as 'a melancholic who had enormous potential when he wanted to succeed'.[17] According to Sperber, Koestler resigned because the success of *Spanish Testament* 'made him decide to pursue a literary career and write only occasional articles and reports'. He wanted to concentrate 'on a novel that was intended to reveal the criminal and political background of the Moscow Trials'. Koestler was resentful that because of the paper he could write only at night.[18]

It was probably also through Münzenberg that around this time he met Paul Willert, the only son of Sir Arthur Willert, a former correspondent for *The Times* who moved into diplomacy via the News Department of the Foreign Office in 1920, remaining in the foreign service until 1935. Like his father, Paul Willert had been to Eton and Balliol where he became 'extremely left-wing'. He visited Berlin in the 1930s, encountering Willi Münzenberg and Otto Katz. From 1937 to 1939 he worked for Oxford University Press in Europe and America. Thanks to his eminent father and his Communist associations Willert was well placed to help left-wing German exiles. During 1938–9 he attended lunches which Münzenberg organised to cultivate important contacts. Willert was useful: he knew people at the British embassy in Paris and had access to journalists and politicians in Britain, including Harold Nicolson, MP. In a few months' time he would play a critical role in Koestler's life.[19]

In April 1939 there came another, familiar interruption to Koestler's writing. Jonathan Cape had accepted his proposal for the novel, but the advance ran out and he was forced to break off while he and Sperber worked together on a third sex book for the Aldors. For two months they and another exile, Fritz Kuenkel, concocted *L'Encyclopédie de la famille*, a vast tome exceeding 800 pages attributed to Drs A. Willy, A. Costler, R. Fisher and others. The revised English version was entitled *The Practice of Sex*. Like its predecessors, the book did very well and was translated into several languages. The first French edition was published in 1939 and was reprinted three times by February 1940, selling over 12,500 copies.[20] Like the other sex books with which Koestler was involved, it has been unjustly neglected.

The Practice of Sex began boldly by claiming that there was a crisis in erotic and family life due to 'systematic suppression by silence of the sexual instinct'. The book was dedicated to alleviating these woes by placing sex, love and the family in a correct scientific and historical perspective. The influence of its neo-Freudian, ex-Marxist (and mainly Jewish) authors was unmistakable, but they cleverly managed to blend earnest social psychology with soft pornography. A survey of sexual mores amongst 'primitive and other races' with the aim of establishing the 'natural forms' of sexual activity and human relations also allowed for much titillating detail. In order to supply the knowledge necessary for the achievement of a 'full sex life' the authors provided graphic chapters on women's anatomy and sexual development as well as po-faced studies of marriage in England, America and the USSR. By its mid-point the book became increasingly repetitive and ill-organised, although there was interesting and sensitive material on why marriages fail.[21]

Koestlerian preoccupations were evident throughout. The description of sexuality in France strikingly resembles the brothel passages in Koestler's autobiographical works of the 1950s. A section on 'Heredity and Eugenics' discussed Darwinian and Mendelian theories of evolution in terms and a style which recur in Koestler's later scientific writing. There is also an interesting Jewish thread running through it. In a section devoted to the erotic life of 'other races' there are comments on Jews and Judaism that prefigure much of Koestler's later writing on the subject and suggest not only that he authored these passages, but that certain attitudes were formed long before they are usually attributed to him. A closing chapter on 'Mixed Marriages' condemns Nazi racism and attacks the stigma attached to Jewishness.[22]

Sperber was grateful for the work on L'Encyclopédie de la famille since he, too, was desperately hard up and it was not uncongenial employment. He and Koestler were now inseparable and were often to be seen in the cafés of the Left Bank where the émigrés assembled, the one short, hair thinning and full of animated gestures, the other lanky, with a thick oily crop and nervy movements. They also met weekly with the great 1920s German writer Alfred Döblin, now an exile too. With him they thrashed out questions concerning Communism and the Jewish Question. Years later Koestler recalled: 'As I regarded Döblin as one of the most original and independent minds of the Left, I proposed that we should start a sort of seminar or Arbeitsgemeinschaft to clarify our outlook. I think the three of us met three or four times, but the project petered out as so many others among émigrés.' Unlike Koestler, in his memoirs Sperber added that

Döblin was, like them, a Jew and that anti-Semitism was one of the topics which interested him. At their informal 'seminar' they spent a great deal of time discussing the Jewish Question and Döblin's plan for a 'new Jewish movement'.[23]

Sperber did not get on well with all Koestler's friends. In the summer of 1939 Németh and his girlfriend turned up in Paris. By now Koestler was as close to Sperber as he had been to Németh in the old days. They discussed all their ideas and collaborated on money-making literary projects. But Sperber could not stand the sloppy, shabby and importunate Németh, whom he regarded as a lazy parasite. This was a recipe for constant friction until Koestler left Paris for the South of France in July 1939, accompanied by his new girlfriend, Daphne Hardy.[24]

Hardy was born in England in 1917, and grew up in Switzerland and Holland where her father worked at the Court of International Justice. Educated at the German Realgymnasium in the Hague and a French convent school, she was fluent in French and German. She studied sculpture at the Royal Academy School of Art and in 1938 won a scholarship to go to Paris. Friends in London gave her an introduction to Koestler and they quickly became attached to one another. She moved into his flat on 10 rue Dombasle, although in his accounts of the period Koestler pretended that she had her own place in the same building. He held out great hopes for this relationship. Hardy was not conventionally pretty but she had a lithe figure and sparkling eyes. She was intelligent company and a gifted artist. Although prone to insecurity, which meant that she was easily dominated, and occasional bouts of self-pity, most of the time she had a cheery disposition. It seemed as if he had at last found Helena.[25]

II

During August 1939 Koestler and Hardy rented a ramshackle villa near the village of Roquebilliere in the Alpes Maritimes. It was an idyllic location but the climate and the international situation grew oppressive. French troops were being called up and were massing close to the Italian border. When Koestler learned of the Russo-German pact on 22 August 1939 he realised that war was inevitable. The pact fatally undermined the faith in Russia that had nourished him for nearly a decade, and to which he clung even after his break with the Communist Party. He also knew that it doomed Europe to an apocalyptic conflict, which would settle his fate one way or the other. He was to be plunged into a war against Fascism, but for a cause that was hazy and hardly inspiring.[26]

To Koestler's irritation Hardy found events less of a distraction and set off for Switzerland to visit an art exhibition in Geneva. Koestler fretted in her absence, but made some progress with the novel. The passages in which Rubashov meditates on the betrayal of foreign comrades in order to defend the 'bastion' of communism, actually the national interest of the USSR, are imprinted with his reaction to the Russo-German pact. By the time Hardy returned the international crisis dictated that they make for Paris as quickly as possible. From there, Koestler intended to proceed to London and enlist in the British army. On 29 August they left the villa. Three days later, in Le Lavandu, they heard that Germany had invaded Poland. The homeward journey continued at a snail's pace. Their battered old car couldn't go very fast without overheating, while the roads were clogged with military traffic and panic-stricken city dwellers who anticipated imminent bombing raids.[27]

The constant delays had a fortuitous result. Almost overnight the mood in France had darkened. Fifth Column hysteria was intensified by the Russo-German pact, which added the Left to the forces of the Right as a possible source of subversion: the press spewed out anti-foreigner sentiment directed against the left-wing exiles. Anti-Fascist foreigners like Koestler were instantly suspect. Police raided his Paris apartment building on 2 September in search of 'aliens' and alleged subversives, but in his absence had to settle for carting off a sickly German-Jewish refugee doctor who occupied the neighbouring flat.[28]

Once back in Paris, Koestler presented himself at the local police station, relying on the fact that Hungary was a neutral country to protect him from detention. He was twice waved away and returned to his flat relieved, if rather puzzled. His encounter with the British consular authorities was less pleasing. A passport officer told him that his visa for entry to the UK had been cancelled, along with all other visas, on 4 September. Koestler insisted that he wanted to return in order to join the British army, but to no effect. He was instructed to apply for a new visa, which might take several weeks to come through. He briefly considered joining the French army, but he was not inclined to risk his life for a country that was locking up refugees and foreign anti-Fascists. Unwilling to sit passively, he asked a well-connected and friendly lawyer to enquire of the police and judicial authorities why he was a suspect. The lawyer told him that a right-wing clique in the government was hunting down political opponents and simultaneously appeasing Spain by arresting anti-

Fascists who had supported the Republicans. He advised Koestler to get to Britain as quickly as possible. The chances of this were slight. The British authorities were dragging their feet over the entry visa and the French would not let him leave the country.[29]

For a month Koestler waited for the inexorable return of the police, a packed bag ready for his departure. They finally appeared on 2 October when he was having his morning bath. Once the first shock had subsided Hardy set about organising provisions for Koestler's involuntary journey. She waved forlornly from the entrance to the building as he was led off to the police station. He was held there for several hours among a congerie of other 'suspects' before they were taken to the Salle Lepine, a lecture hall. The detainees spent three boring days in the hall and two uncomfortable nights in the building's coal cellar. Each day batches of prisoners were removed by the police. Finally the last contingent, including Koestler, was taken to a more permanent detention centre in the converted Roland Garros tennis stadium, near Auteuil. The conditions there were much worse, but the internees stayed long enough to improvise facilities and to develop some kind of collective spirit.[30]

Within a few days he was among a group of 500 men, including Gustav Regler and Hans Schultz, Münzenberg's former secretary, who were loaded on to a train heading south-west towards Le Vernet, an internment camp in the department of Ariège, near the Spanish border. Le Vernet had been established to hold Spanish Republicans who had fled into France when the Civil War ended: it had an odious reputation. Regler described the camp as 'a collection of ramshackle huts at the foot of the Pyrenees, without beds, without light, and without heating'. It was 'an eerie cemetery. The huts stood like great coffins on the plains.' When they arrived, the detainees 'lay on planks and were forgotten'. Koestler complained that facilities in the camp were so primitive that the inmates were reduced to living like Stone Age men.[31]

Having also recently left the Communist Party, Regler was bitter about being arrested along with dozens of genuine CP members, including the entire Central Committee of the exiled German Communist Party. But Regler had been a political commissar in Spain during the Civil War and his natural leadership qualities soon asserted themselves. He was elected spokesman for the 150 men in his block, which numbered many veterans of the International Brigade. Despite even his best efforts morale soon began to break down. These German exiles wanted to make war on Fascism, even if it meant fighting their countrymen. They felt useless and vulnerable held behind wire, hundreds of miles from the front line. 'There was constant repudiation and fighting among friends. Feelings were relieved by sheer baseness; it was a dysentery of the soul.' Regler dreaded the moment when he had to douse the lights in the hut, plunging the men into darkness and introspection. 'We sought to understand our time. No kind of evaluation could have withstood our grief at our imprisonment. For a time, everything seemed to us mere senseless chaos.'[32]

Koestler, who was in another hut (Quartier C, Barrack 24), was particularly demoralised. 'Internment in a concentration camp during a war is not in itself a pleasant experience. In my case it came too soon after imprisonment in a civil war.' Within a short time he had a physical and mental collapse. According to Regler Koestler 'lived withdrawn in his own hut'.[33]

In *Scum of the Earth*, written in England in 1941, Koestler describes the routine that was soon established in the camp. The internees had to perform manual labour, mainly road building and construction. They were forced to stand for hours while roll calls were taken at the start and conclusion of every day. As the weather deteriorated both the work and the parades became almost unbearable. The camp administration was 'run with that mixture of ignominy, corruption and *laissez-faire* so typical of the French administration'. French officers and guards relied on a system of trustees and elected block leaders. Few were as upright as Regler, who constantly fought for better conditions for the men in his barrack. Instead, Koestler had to deal with a string of petty, venal tyrants. To his acute eye it was a mark of how far civilisation had fallen that veterans of Franco's prisons or Nazi camps reacted with equanimity to these conditions.[34]

The Communists were, inevitably, the best organised and most disciplined group. Non- and ex-Communists also tried to organise, but with less success. Koestler, Regler and Leo Valiani, an Italian anti-Fascist, made an early attempt to resist the camp authorities and instil backbone into the non–aligned detainees. When it was announced that the men would have their hair shaven Regler drafted a petition of protest, while Koestler and Valiani drummed up support in the various huts. The petition was rejected by the camp commandant. This was not the end of the business. According to Regler, 'We had been herded like sheep to the shearing, and I remember that the humiliating nature of the proceedings was relieved only by the fact that Arthur Koestler, who was otherwise very reserved and furious about his arrest, had snatched the scissors from the barber before it was his turn, and in wild delight had cut great handfuls of hair from his splendid crop. "I've been wanting to do it ever since I was a child!" he cried, and then went quietly back to his place.'[35]

As soon as Koestler was sent to Le Vernet, Hardy made efforts to obtain his release but organisation was not her forté and she 'hadn't a clue how to set about this sort of thing.' In desperation she turned to Dorothea Koestler who loyally contributed her redoubtable skills and experience. The extent of their campaign is shown by the many letters and papers, which were confiscated by the French police in 1940 and ended up in the KGB's 'Special Archive'. On 10 October Hardy wrote to Jonathan Cape alerting Koestler's English publishers to his detention and begging for their help. She also enlisted the aid of the Duchess of Atholl who had written the introduction for the Left Book Club edition of *Spanish Testament*. Atholl, in turn wrote to Georges Mandel, a prominent radical politician, and a Jew, who became Minister of the Interior in 1940, assuring him that Koestler was anti-Nazi.[36]

In a demonstration of the affection he retained in the hearts of ex-girlfriends and ex-wives, Dorothea wrote to Anthony Eden and Sir Robert Vansittart, reminding them of the crucial part they had played in freeing Koestler from a Fascist jail in 1937. Her letters, however, were less than honest about Koestler's situation. She told Eden that the French must have misinterpreted the reasons for his incarceration in Spain and taken him to be a pro-Communist. She insisted that he had only had 'nominal relations with German Communist circles, which were finally and completely terminated over two years ago'. Dorothea warned that Koestler was ill and unlikely to survive a winter in a concentration camp, and implored Eden to intervene with the Hungarian embassy, which could establish that Koestler was a neutral. The use of English in these letters was superior to Dorothea's normal command of the language, which suggests that they were drafted by Daphne Hardy. It was an intimate collaboration.[37]

Hardy mobilised Koestler's colleagues and friends. Edgar Mowrer, the journalist, cabled Harold Nicolson urging him to act and telling him that Koestler had 'abjured Communist doctrine last year', a somewhat different line from that being spun to Eden. André Malraux offered the Ministère des affaires étrangères a personal guarantee on behalf of Koestler if he was freed, and completed one of the forms which were being used in the applications on behalf of hundreds of other internees. He also gave Hardy essential financial support. Jean Paulhan, editor of the prestigious *Nouvelle Revue française*, signalled his willingness to assist. At her request, Frédéric

Joliot-Curie signed a letter calling for Koestler's release. Hardy also wrote to Ferenc Aldor demanding that he send the final payment for the work on *L'Encyclopédie de la famille* to Koestler in Le Vernet so that he could use it to buy extra food and cigarettes. Meanwhile, in London, Rupert Hart-Davis at Cape was rallying PEN via Cecil Day Lewis and trying to get the *News Chronicle* interested in Koestler's arrest. David Scott, the paper's Paris correspondent, repeatedly questioned officials as to the reasons for Koestler's arrest.[38]

Paul Willert enlisted his parents on behalf of both Koestler and Regler, whom he also knew. Hardy combined forces with the wives of the Communists Gerhardt Eisler and Gustav Regler, and with Paul Willert, to procure food to be sent to the camp. Subsequently the internees were delighted to receive a goose accompanied by tins of dripping. Regler and Koestler shared their portion with their immediate circle, but Regler noted sardonically that Eisler, a KPD Central Committee member, hoarded his and ate alone.[39]

At the turn of the year winter closed in and conditions in Le Vernet worsened. Illness, suicide and madness claimed more prisoners each week. Because it was too cold to sit in the latrines, the men became constipated. Koestler's health and spirit weakened. For two weeks he was assigned to the latrine squad, unpleasant and heavy work pushing a trolley carrying barrels of waste to a nearby river. Only the intense comradeship of the camp maintained his resistance, an experience memorialised and celebrated in *Scum of the Earth*.[40]

The campaign to free Koestler finally bore fruit. The most influential helper was probably André Le Troquer, a Socialist deputy and lawyer who acted for the former Popular Front Prime Minister Léon Blum. At Hardy's behest Le Troquer made an intervention with the Ministère des affaires étrangères. The ministry responded with alacrity, although initially in non-committal fashion.[41] Few other internees could command such illustrious support and the weight of pressure on the authorities finally had effect. On 17 January 1940, with almost no advance notice, Koestler was discharged from Le Vernet.

III

A day later he was back in Paris where he celebrated by going on a 'drunken binge' and sleeping for twenty-four hours. But his position remained precarious. Officially he was under a deportation order, which could not be carried out due to wartime conditions. The Interior Ministry would only permit a short respite to the enforcement of the order, so each time the period of remission neared its end Koestler had to re-enter the bureaucratic maze to seek another extension or face detention. His indeterminate status confounded his attempts to volunteer for the French army or to serve as an ambulance driver for the Red Cross. Another request for a visa to travel to Britain and join the British army was refused.[42]

His anxiety was heightened when his flat was raided by the police on 12 March 1940. The officers made a terrible mess but he and Hardy could only watch as many of his papers and manuscripts were taken away. All attempts to find out why he was being harassed were rebuffed; any explanation was left to his ample imagination and persecutory fantasies. One evening he met Malraux who was about to depart for the front, announcing his readiness to die with the proletariat. There is a strong hint that Koestler envied him and felt his own macho self-image, a foible he shared with Malraux, was impugned by enforced passivity.[43] Despite everything Koestler kept working on *Darkness at Noon*. The first draft was wrtten in German, so Hardy translated it into English at a desk at one end of the flat with Koestler working over her initial translation, sitting on the bed or pacing around. It was finally sent off to his French publisher on 1 May 1940, an ironic date for what was destined to become one of the most significant literary attacks on Communism and the Soviet Union. Hardy retained one copy of the manuscript for the publication of the English edition. A fortnight later German armoured divisions broke through the French lines in the Ardennes and crossed the Meuse at Sedan.[44]

France was gripped by a Fifth Column mania: wave after wave of arrests decimated the immigrant and refugee communities. Those who had fled the Nazis were subjected to a double torture: apprehensive of detention by the French authorities and terrified of what would be in store for them if the Allies failed to stem the German advance. Koestler was in a frenzy. He discussed suicide methods with German *émigrés* and secured a supply of cyanide. Sperber recalled: 'At one of our last meetings Koestler gave me a white pill, to be used if a quick death was the only way out.' Even in the midst of this crisis Koestler did not forget his comrades still in the internment camps. He urged the PEN organisation in Paris to engineer the release of foreign anti-Nazi writers held in Le Vernet and elsewhere before the Germans reached them.[45]

The long-predicted police visit occurred on the morning of 22 May 1940, soon after German tanks had reached the French coast. Koestler was escorted to a converted sports stadium in a southern district of Paris and placed among dozens of 'enemy aliens', all in fact refugees who were as afraid of the Germans as were the French. He took with him a suitcase containing food, drink and the suicide pills. While he waited in the stadium he consumed a bottle of brandy and by the time he was called for interrogation he was drunk. Heedless of the consequences, he lied prodigally, asserting that he was a foreign journalist who had been mistakenly arrested. The interrogating officer was so impressed by his Hungarian passport, his press card and other papers that he didn't bother to check the facts with the policemen who had carried out the arrest. Koestler carried the bluff still further and insisted that he had to attend a vital press conference at the Ministry of Information that afternoon. The officer decided a mistake had been made and promised to look into it; meanwhile, Koestler was free to go.

For the moment he was in the clear, but he knew it would not be long before the authorities noted his absence. He went to the apartment of the writer and publisher Adrienne Monnier, where he was hidden for a night, before being passed on to another safe house, the French PEN Club, run by Henri Membre. While he was concealed Monnier went to Henry Hoppenot, a sympathetic official in the Foreign Ministry, and obtained a travel permit that would enable Koestler to leave Paris for Limoges. After a week in hiding, Koestler and Hardy (who had been staying with Andor Németh) made their escape.[46]

They arrived in Limoges on 3 June 1940 and stopped there for two weeks, watching France collapse before their eyes and taking stock of their predicament. All Koestler's endeavours to reach Great Britain had been rebuffed; he lacked the necessary papers to enter the United States. The international refugee organisations and PEN might eventually get him a passage out of France, but how long could he hang on if the Germans occupied the whole country? Even if the German advance was halted Koestler was still a fugitive in the eyes of the French police. He had to change his identity, get new papers and 'go underground'. The easiest way to do this was by joining the Foreign Legion. On 16 June 1940 Koestler went to the Limoges recruiting office and enlisted in the Légion étrangère as one Albert Dubert, a Swiss taxi-driver, claiming that he had lost his identity card. After a few cursory questions and a medical check he was given the papers necessary to establish his new identity. Despite orders to proceed to the Legion's depot at Angers, which was under German control, he and Hardy went south, intent only on staying ahead of the invaders.[47]

The saga of the following months was recorded by Koestler in cramped writing on the pages of a tiny diary. This later furnished the material for the final third of *Scum of the Earth*, but the printed version differs in several respects from the original notes. The order of events is rearranged to give them more dramatic colour. Characters are elaborated upon and several passages of an intimate nature are not reproduced. In particular, a number of encounters with women and some rather negative thoughts about Daphne Hardy are omitted. Otherwise, the powerful observations which made *Scum of the Earth* such a success when it appeared in 1941 were transcribed from the notes he had made at the time.[48]

On 17 June 1940, the day that Marshal Pétain formed a new government and ordered the French army to lay down its arms, Koestler and Hardy headed south. Such was the disruption of rail and road traffic that they got no further than the edge of Limoges. When night fell they took refuge in a wayside restaurant and slept on the tables. The following day they took a bus to Périgueux. On arrival, Koestler went to the Busseaux Barracks and presented himself as Légionnaire Dubert. While Hardy found a room with a local family, Koestler had his first taste of life in the military. It was initially an easy regimen. He spent the mornings hanging around the barracks or on labour duties and met with Hardy in the afternoons and evenings. Soldiers regularly disappeared in anticipation of demobilisation, but Koestler stayed on, hoping to be assigned to a depot in another town and given the necessary travel documents. On 21 June they learned that Périgueux would fall within the German Zone of Occupation. Koestler skipped over the barracks wall and joined Hardy. By a combination of lifts, lorry rides and buses, slipping through police and army roadblocks on the way, they reached Bordeaux two days later.[49]

Bordeaux, seat of the evacuated French government, was a scene of demoralisation and chaos. The British consul had departed and the last ships had left the port. From the quayside they rushed to the United States consulate, where they recognised Edgar Mowrer, the American journalist. He had a car and offered them a lift to Bayonne-Biarritz, where it might still be possible to get a boat to safety. Koestler and Hardy argued for several hours whether they should leave together or split up. He insisted that she leave him since his papers were useless. Hardy obstinately refused to abandon him, driving him to heights of frustration and provoking 'a sort of nervous breakdown'. Finally, they resolved to stick together and in the evening kept the rendezvous with Mowrer. All went well until they

reached Biarritz and drove into a military check-point. Mowrer and
Hardy passed inspection, but Koestler was hauled out of the car,
questioned and told he would be held pending investigation. Hardy
capitulated to circumstances and the car continued to Bayonne and,
with luck, a ship home. Koestler was taken to the local jail, where he
spent the night in the company of an inebriated French airforce
officer who had gone absent without leave.

In the morning Koestler was escorted by a policeman to the
military barracks at Bayonne, only to be dumped amid more chaos.
Thousands of uniformed men, many of them foreign volunteers,
clamoured at the docks for a place on non-existent boats. Alone and
in despair, Koestler left the port area and drifted through the town.
He thought of committing a petty crime that would get him locked
up for a few months out of sight of the Germans and knocked on the
door of a lawyer's house to ask his advice on the matter. The kindly
lawyer gave him some wine and warned him that he was more likely
to be shot for looting. That night he returned to the barracks
exhausted, his feet throbbing with pain from his new army boots. At
some point between 21 and 25 June, he records making a suicide
attempt by taking the potassium cyanide which he had been given in
Paris. It was 'no good' and he vomited it up. It was his third failed
suicide bid.

To adapt Oscar Wilde, to fail to kill oneself once is misfortune, to
fail to do so three times is suspicious. At this very time many other
exiles and émigrés managed it with distressing efficiency. The fact that
all the while Koestler kept a diary recording what he saw and
experienced must suggest that he had an eye to writing it up one day
and casts doubt on the seriousness of his intentions. His suicidal
endeavours may have been more like gestures of despair, calculated
to jolt him out of his despondency, for which purpose failure had to
be built into the attempt.

On 25 June the radio broadcast the terms of the armistice.
Bordeaux, Biarritz and Bayonne were all to fall within the German
occupied zone. At 3 p.m. the men in the barracks were assembled
and told they were being transferred to the unoccupied area. Koestler
was attached to an *ad hoc* unit which marched out of Bayonne about
three hours later. The Germans arrived soon afterwards. On the first
leg of the march the '22ième Compagnie de Passage' covered a mere
eight kilometres, but at least they were out of harm's way. They
marched for several days, lugging a miscellany of personal belongings
and military equipment. Each morning there were fewer men in the
company and fewer pieces of martial hardware. Koestler's feet were

now in bad shape and he sought relief whenever the column passed a pharmacy. Fortuitously, he met a sympathetic old couple who gave him a lift in their car as far as St Palais, a village adjacent to the demarcation line.

Koestler didn't wait to reach safety with his unit. He hobbled across the boundary between the occupied zone and the 'Free Zone', spending the night by himself in open fields. The next morning he set off eastwards, at first painfully on foot and, later, by lorry, in search of the others. For days he hitch-hiked through the foothills of the Pyrenees looking for his company, staying overnight at camps for soldiers separated from their commands. On 29 June he reached Audage. His feet were in such an appalling state that he found an infirmary where they could be treated. Somewhat restored, he bought toiletries, including a comb and toothbrush, and cleaned himself up. Since he was no longer capable of walking more than a few yards he took a bus to the next depot. On 1 July 1940, after more fruitless searching, he opted to stay at Susmiou, a picturesque hamlet near Navarreux, where about 120 assorted soldiers were billeted in farm buildings. This was to be his home for the next eight weeks.

He spent the first night in a barn with a representative collection of disgruntled soldiery. Over successive days he shuffled around the countryside in a pair of slippers lent him by a young Breton. In Castelnau he tracked down his unit and reacquainted himself with a priest he had met in Bayonne and marched beside on the first leg of the evacuation. On 4 July he limped to Navarreux and had his feet treated in the local hospital. Then he purchased a pair of espadrilles and whiled away some time in a café in the company of a young girl. A routine established itself: mornings were passed reading, sun-bathing and speculating whether Hardy had reached Britain. He listened to the radio, read what papers he could get his hands on and talked to the soldiers, soaking up their views on the war, politics and life in general. On several evenings he met German and Jewish refugees, including internees who had been released from the notorious internment camp at nearby Gurs. Their situation was even more desperate and the encounters, particularly with the women, were heart-breaking.

On Bastille Day, 14 July, he learned that Carl Einstein, a fellow writer, nephew of Albert Einstein and a veteran of the Spanish Civil War whom Koestler had met in Paris in 1939, had committed suicide. This was the pattern for a string of despairing *émigrés* and refugees, although only the most famous casualties would be reported at the time. Koestler's diary reveals that he too regularly descended into a suicidal melancholy. He was grateful for his conversations with the priest, which stirred his intellect and revived his combative spirit. But most of the time he was depressed and lonely. Self-recrimination, enforced idleness and a poor diet took its toll. He visited the infirmary again, but this time for mental as well as physical relief. When the priest got his demobilisation orders he handed Koestler the key to a hut in Castelnau which a local farmer permitted him to use for reading and writing. Koestler went there regularly, but spent most his time in the hut regretting Hardy's absence and falling into erotic reveries. His mood was not improved by the daily flood of fatuous decrees from the Vichy regime, the guileless propaganda in the press and on the radio, or the news that Vladimir Jabotinsky had died in New York. It seemed to Koestler as if he had been totally abandoned.

Orders for the demobilisation of alien volunteers arrived at Susmiou on 10 August 1940. Koestler was eventually directed to the Foreign Legion depot at Marseilles, which had always been his goal. After four days of travel, and with a huge sense of relief he reached the port. For the first time in five months he had a hot shower. He attended to his health and bought a pair of comfortable shoes. He was also able to buy newspapers and catch up with events, albeit filtered through the slanted Vichy French press. One of his first acts was to fire off cables to find out if Hardy was safe. It was not until 1 September 1940 that he received a message from her announcing that she had reached England some time ago.

While in Marseilles, Koestler bumped into a number of prominent German *émigrés*. They all carried stories of suicides and deaths among the refugee community. Sperber, who had reached Marseilles after serving in the French army, described the city in the summer of 1940 as 'a tragic drama that was staged like a vaudeville show'. On every corner refugees ran into acquaintances who were in a similarly parlous state. 'A completely unexpected encounter was with Arthur Koestler, and for an instant this was shattering as well as surprising. He was wearing the same Legionnaire's uniform that I had finally taken off the day before.' Koestler told Sperber that he had a scheme to get to Africa; it was 'very daring but prudent'. The quayside at Marseilles was the scene of innumerable poignant farewells. 'When we embraced at parting, I felt inexplicably sorry for him, and he probably feared the worst for me.' Kantorowicz also spotted Koestler, but characteristically thought it 'was not advisable to speak to him'.[50]

Amid the turmoil Koestler's life resumed a semblance of

conviviality: he began to have 'a lovely time'. During the day he was given nothing more to do than stand guard outside the depot or, because he was posing as a Swiss who therefore spoke German, run errands to the Germans now supervising the operations of the port. In the evenings he mixed with the large community of refugees, *émigrés* and relief workers from neutral countries who were based in Marseilles. He had an affair with a woman called Jacqueline. One evening he sat with Walter Benjamin in a bistro overlooking the Old Harbour. Benjamin told him of his plans to reach Spain by crossing the mountains. In case of failure, he had procured a supply of morphine or 'sedatives'. Since he had more than he needed he offered half to Koestler who gratefully accepted. Having been turned back at the border, Benjamin took his own life a few weeks later.[51]

Like all the refugees, Koestler's main concern was to get out of France as quickly as possible. He visited the American consulate and contacted various international refugee organisations. After a week of frustration he ran across a large group of escaped British prisoners of war who were interned at Fort St Jean. Since the American consulate proved 'hopeless', he joined their elicit escape scheme concocted with covert assistance from Varian Fry, an American who represented the New York-based Emergency Rescue Committee. Fry had previously worked as an editor in New York, but was recruited by the committee, which sent aid to refugee writers, artists and intellectuals. After he arrived in Marseilles in mid-August he also arranged the departure of prominent refugees. He listed Koestler and 'his wife' as one of his 'clients', although there are no details to indicate what this involved. However, Fry admitted later that he did co-operate with the British embassy in Lisbon to facilitate the escape of the British soldiers.[52]

Koestler obtained his discharge papers from the French military authorities at the end of August. On 3 September he and a party of fugitive British servicemen led by Lieutenants John Ray, John Hopkins and Ian McCallum, and Staff Sergeant Richard Newman, embarked on a ship bound for Oran. The voyage lasted four days. As they passed the coast of Spain, Koestler entertained the others with stories of his Spanish Civil War adventures.[53] On 6 September the party disembarked at Oran and proceeded to Morocco. Although there were difficulties at the frontier they were allowed to transfer to a military train and arrived in Casablanca on 7 September.

Koestler went immediately to the American consulate which was handling British interests. From there he was referred to E. E. Bullen, the local representative of Shell du Maroc, a subsidiary of the Anglo-

Dutch oil corporation. Bullen was actually a British diplomat on a covert mission. Formerly the British resident in Lisbon, he had been sent to Casablanca to organise an escape route for British servicemen who managed to reach North Africa. Once in Casablanca, he made contact with Baron Rüdiger von Etzdorf, an anti-Nazi German who was working for British intelligence and smuggling escaped POWs out of France. Bullen met Koestler in a café and set up a rendezvous with Etzdorf, whose cover-name was Ellerman. Bullen also arranged accommodation in a cheap pension for Koestler and the British servicemen, while 'Ellerman' worked out an escape plan to get them away from Vichy-controlled Morocco to more neutral territory.[54]

Two days later Koestler received a British Emergency Identity Certificate and within a week a visa. However, the next stage of his odyssey was via the covert route set up by British military intelligence.[55] At five in the morning on 14 September he clambered aboard the El Mar Azul, a small 'ignoble' boat, chartered by 'Ellerman' to carry over fifty escaped British troops to Lisbon. It was a long and unpleasant passage, and Koestler was seasick for much of the time. They finally reached Lisbon on 17 September.[56] When at last he was permitted to land he made straight for the Bar Anglais to celebrate. He was in a neutral country and relatively safe from German hands for the first time in four months. He could get English newspapers and send telegrams to London. Thanks to Macmillan, his publishers in the United States, he could take money from his accumulated royalties and was not even short of cash.

IV

Koestler's sojourn in Lisbon lasted for seven weeks. Despite all his efforts the British authorities seemed unwilling to let him re-enter the country, even to join the army. He found his enforced stay frustrating, but Lisbon was not without compensations. It was a comfortable exile, with plenty of bars, restaurants and hotels. The city was filled with refugees among whom he encountered Babette Gross, Münzenberg's wife and assistant. They met regularly to exchange stories about Berlin and Paris, Willi, his now scattered circle and the catastrophe that had overtaken their cause. On the occasion of their first meeting they talked until four in the morning. However, Koestler would not learn that Münzenberg was in fact dead, probably murdered by Stalin's agents, until he reached England weeks later.[57]

A typical day began with a visit to the British passport office or the military attaché. On some mornings he would be occupied sending telegrams to London or New York. These activities were followed by lunch, alone or in company. In the afternoons he read, slept or went for walks. Evenings were filled by seeing friends, going to the cinema or amorous adventures. Koestler spent a lot of time with Ellen Hill, a married American woman who was on her way to the United States. By mid-October their relationship had become stormy and his diary reported 'scenes'.[58] At the end of September Koestler heard of Walter Benjamin's suicide at Port Bou on the French–Spanish border. His death was an uncomfortable reminder that Fascist Portugal was no safe haven. In *The Invisible Writing* he claims that this information so depressed him that he attempted suicide yet again, but failed because of a 'weak stomach' that caused him to vomit up the poison. There is no mention of this in his diary, although there are indications that he redoubled his efforts to get to Britain. He saw 'Ellerman' a number of times and learned from him that the Home Office in London was obstructing his departure.[59]

He fired off telegrams to the *News Chronicle* and Hardy, and wrote to Macmillan in New York. Vernon Bartlett, MP, the foreign editor of the *News Chronicle*, urged Koestler to get in touch with David Scott, their local man, who would do what he could on the spot. In the meantime Bartlett took up Koestler's case in London. Walter Lucas, *The Times* correspondent in Lisbon, was also enlisted in his capacity as a member of the Unitarian service committee, one of a network devoted to assisting refugees.[60]

Notwithstanding Bartlett's efforts, the *News Chronicle* could neither secure Koestler a visa to enter Britain nor discover why he was being refused one. The paper passed his case on to Julian Layton, who was well known at the Home Office as an intermediary for Jewish refugees and exiles. Koestler meanwhile was frantic: the situation was 'hellish'. He felt a 'sudden craving for life in the USA – the first time – and betrayal of Daphne'. He was becoming increasingly resentful of Hardy, whose cables reached him only intermittently. By comparison with Dorothea Koestler she seemed to have let him down. This was rather unfair since Britain was experiencing major disruption due to the Blitz and Hardy was not always in London, near to post offices. But as days passed with no reply from her, Koestler became tetchy. At one point he wrote of their relationship in his diary '*la fin approche*'. He confided, 'Almost wish Daphne were dead – to be able to die in piece [*sic*], undisturbed.'[61]

With the help of Harry Donaldson, the American consul in Lisbon, he contacted the Exiled Writers Committee in New York (a

subsidiary body of the League of American Writers) and asked them
to sponsor his entry into the United States. Towards the end of
October he learned that the Committee of Publishers had advanced
$200 to purchase him a passage from Lisbon to New York and the
Exiled Writers Committee had submitted affidavits on his behalf to
the President's Advisory Committee on Refugees. The way to
America was all but clear.[62]

By the end of October 1940 Koestler could no longer contain his
impatience. Rejecting the option of going to neutral America in
favour of joining the British army, he planned to leave Portugal
illegally and throw himself on the mercy of the British authorities. At
least then he would be in a position to make his case directly. He
prepared for his illicit departure by writing to the British passport
control officer in Lisbon with a summary of his case to ensure that,
once he was discovered in Britain, he could show he had never
intended to slip into the country and remain there illegally.[63] He also
warned the British consul general in Lisbon, Sir Henry King, leaving
no doubt about his motives. He explained that all efforts to obtain an
entry visa, including appeals by the *News Chronicle* and his friend
Harold Nicolson, had failed. He attributed this to 'either a libellous
denunciation or some inevitable mistake'. He was therefore taking
the desperate step 'to have myself arrested on British soil in order to
have some means of defending and rehabilitating myself'. Since he
was a well-known anti-Fascist, who had twice been arrested for his
beliefs, it was unsafe to remain any longer in Portugal. While he was
happy to die for an ideal, he said, he refused to perish because of red
tape.[64]

In fact, Sir Henry was privy to Koestler's flight from Portugal and
the letter was part of an elaborate charade. Koestler arrived at Bristol
airport on board a BOAC plane on 6 November 1940. He had with
him one small suitcase containing personal effects and about $60 in
cash. On disembarking, he reported to the immigration officials and
was duly detained. He was taken under escort to London the next
day. (In a typically good-humoured and generous gesture, on his
release from internment six weeks later he sent the Bristol police two
shillings for cigarettes and thanked them for making the journey to
London so pleasant.) After two nights in Cannon Row police station
and a rather ludicrous interrogation by a hooded German ex-refugee,
he was transferred to Pentonville Prison. It was his third period of
confinement, without trial or fixed duration, in four years.[65]

Of course, this time the circumstances were hugely improved. On
learning of his arrival influential friends, including Vernon Bartlett,

Harold Nicolson, Harold Laski and Lady Atholl, wrote to the Home Office with assurances that Koestler was a trusted anti-Fascist who only wanted to volunteer for the British army. In view of his paranoia about the reasons for his exclusion from Britain, the most intriguing intercession came from inside Military Intelligence (Research), possibly from the rising Labour Party politician and future cabinet minister Richard Crossman. It was suggested in a letter that Koestler could offer valuable information on French trades union officials and left-wingers now working with the Vichy regime. The German Department of MI(R), run by the *Guardian*'s former Berlin correspondent F. A. Voigt, 'feel that they may also be able to make use of him'. The letter-writer was under the illusion, unless he was lying, that Koestler had never been more than 'in close touch with' the Communist Party: 'I doubt if he was ever a member.' He stated that, 'I am not prepared to say that he is 100% all right, but I cannot imagine that it would be possible for him to do any harm whatsoever and he might well be quite useful to us, but also to the Ministry of Information and other propaganda organisations.'[66]

The letters of intercession paid off. Koestler was released on 13 December 1940 and issued with alien's papers. In gratitude for the exertions on his behalf he had Cape send copies of *Darkness at Noon*, which had just come out, to Laski, Lady Atholl, Bartlett, Sir Peter Chalmers-Mitchell and Henry Wickham Steed, an ex-editor of *The Times* who had taken an interest in Koestler some time earlier. Laski modestly replied, 'You do not need to thank me. I am only ashamed that the trouble should have to happen to one who has done so much for democracy.'[67]

V

While he was in Pentonville *Darkness at Noon* appeared and was instantly well received. Praise for the novel flowed in from all quarters. Wickham Steed thought it was 'not far from being a masterpiece. It is the most devastating exposure of Stalinism that I have read.' John Strachey, the Left Book Club selector, remarked wickedly that it contained the best defence of Stalinism he had come across. Kingsley Martin, editor of the *New Statesman*, was no less impressed and asked Koestler to write for him.[68]

Darkness at Noon is one of those books that has ceased to be a work of literature and has instead become a monument. Read purely as a novel it is dark, static and obsessive It takes an effort to recapture the *frisson* it caused in readers when it was published, especially among the Communists and ex-Communists to whom it was addressed and for whom the issues it raised were more important than the artistry with which they were presented.

Much has been written about the novel. It has been seen as a historic milestone in the journey from the Pink Decade of the 1930s to the Cold War and a key text in the intellectual counter-attack against Communism. It has been read on a philosophical level as a debate about the 'dilemma of means and ends', the potentially destructive effect of universal Utopian ideologies that sweep aside the suffering of individuals for a greater good and a powerful assault on determinism, notably the crude Marxist theory of history. Finally, it has been taken as an historical curio, a reflection on the Moscow Trials of the 1930s.[69]

The most important fact about the novel is the one that is least remarked upon in critical studies: the central character, Nicolas Salmanovich Rubashov, is a Jew. In *The Invisible Writing* Koestler comments somewhat improbably and in a suspiciously offhand way: 'Incidentally, the second name, Salmanovich (Solomonson) made my hero a Jew, but neither did I notice this, nor has any reader ever pointed it out to me.' This is implausible for a number of reasons. It may be that Koestler really 'forgot' that Salman Rubashov (later Shazar) was the name of an editor of the Hebrew socialist daily *Davar* with which he had been familiar in Palestine in the 1920s. But could he have forgotten that of the three models for the character, Bukharin, Radek and Trotsky, two were Jewish?[70]

Finally, there is a great deal of Koestler in Rubashov: the novel is a fictionalised reworking of *Dialogue with Death*. Scenes in the cell and the prison are taken from Koestler's experiences in Seville. The references could not be stronger: in Seville he was in Cells 40 and 41: Rubashov is in Cell 404. Rubashov, like Koestler, is a deracinated Jew who has given up the messianism natural to Judaism, or any religious system of thought, only to find it in a materialist political philosophy.

Several critics writing on *Darkness at Noon* and Koestler's other novels have noted their Christian symbolism, but Rubashov's most explicit religious references are to Jewish tradition.[71] At the end he wonders about the fate of the revolution: 'What happened to these masses, to this people? For forty years it had been driven through the desert, with threats and promises, with imaginary terrors and imaginary rewards. But where was the Promised Land?' Just before his execution he compares himself with Moses, who 'had not been allowed to enter the land of promise either'.[72] At one level *Darkness at Noon* is a perceptive examination of the attraction which Marxism exerted on many Jews between the 1880s and 1940s. While the novel and the lure of Marxism cannot be reduced to ethnicity, it would be perverse to ignore the specific identity of both the chief character and the author, who together constitute a case study in the phenomenal and ultimately tragic relationship between the Jews and Communism.[73]

Although the book deals with Koestler's general problem with Communism, its trigger was the series of Moscow Trials of 1936–8. He wanted to explain why hardened old Bolsheviks like Bukharin confessed in captivity to crimes they could not possibly have committed, and repeated these falsehoods during the show trials, incriminating themselves and others in what appeared to be a wholly craven fashion. Manès Sperber, one of the first to read the finished manuscript, recalled, 'For years Arthur and I had been discussing the question that concerned and even obsessed us: why did the defendants in the Moscow trials . . . confess to imaginary crimes instead of turning the tables on their accusers in these public trials and sharply attacking them, and thus Stalin as well?' [74]

Koestler deduced that the logic of their own political philosophy, with which he believed he was familiar, compelled the old Bolsheviks to act thus as a 'last service' to the revolution.[75] Sperber concurred at the time, but was doubtful that it would be possible to convey this to ordinary readers. 'During the many months in which Koestler was working on his book we had carried on many discussions about his plan, in particular the difficulty of convincingly presenting this absurdity even to those who were trying to shield themselves from the truth. And now the finished manuscript was lying before me one afternoon. I immediately began to read it and I did not put it down until I had read the last page. It was almost dawn.' Sperber was convinced that Koestler had succeeded in penetrating the mystery and presenting it in such a way that neutral readers would be convinced of the 'confession theory'.[76]

Unfortunately, the most authoritative account of the trials refutes this interpretation. Stephen Cohen, Bukharin's acclaimed biographer, comments: 'Owing to Koestler's powerful art, this image of Bukharin–Rubashov as repentant Bolshevik and morally bankrupt intellectual prevailed for two generations. In fact, however, as some understood at the time and as others came to see, Bukharin did not really confess to the criminal charges at all.' In the courtroom he actually turned around the charges against him. Bukharin mocked his own confession, but pleaded guilty to the accusation that he had opposed Stalin – which was precisely the message he wanted to leave behind him.[77]

Darkness at Noon is more Koestler's confession than Bukharin's. It is his attempt to understand how he had been suborned by the logic of the revolution and how he had betrayed men for the sake of mankind: most obviously 'Nadeshda' in Baku, but also all those who had been lured into Communism by his propaganda. The novel's wide and enduring resonance is partly due to the mistaken identity of the protagonist (as Bukharin, rather than Koestler) and the belief that it could explain the show trials. Its initial powerful appeal, rooted in a specific period, was to tens of thousands of ex-Communists who wanted their disillusion explained and their transgression forgiven. Koestler offers such a powerful case for the revolution that no ex-Communist could feel ashamed of his or her youthful idealism. Yet he also exposes the amorality of the Communist Party and the Soviet Union, thus justifying and pardoning those who turned their back on them. Anti-Communists, of course, absorbed only the latter and revelled in the compelling refutation of revolutionary doctrine.

Darkness at Noon tells the story of Rubashov, an old revolutionary and veteran of Fascist jails who is arrested for treason on the orders of the authoritarian figure who controls the Party and the state. While he knows he is innocent of the charges against him, he cannot quell the suspicion that: 'The Party can never be mistaken . . . The Party is the embodiment of the revolutionary idea in history . . . History knows her way. She makes no mistakes.' Yet, he reflects in prison, the more the Party tried to build the Utopia which reason and the logic of history dictated was possible and necessary, the more repression was needed. Loyal Party members became schooled in deception and murder.[78]

In his 'diary', one of Koestler's favourite literary devices, Rubashov explores the 'dilemma of means and ends'. He once believed that revolutionary ethics had replaced bourgeois liberal notions of 'fair play' and that a useful lie might serve mankind better than the truth; but his faith was shaken. Doubt was connected with the discovery of the self: the 'I' which was rendered a 'grammatical fiction' in materialist theory. He began to reflect critically on the betrayals he had committed for the sake of the cause. At that time 'he had not enough imagination to picture the details of an execution'. Now that he could connect himself, the 'I', with the suffering of others, his deeds appalled him.[79]

His first interrogator, Ivanov, another old revolutionary, tells him that revolutionaries cannot afford the bourgeois luxury of sentiment and pity. 'Most great revolutionaries fell before this temptation, from Spartacus to Danton and Dostoyevsky . . . The principle that the end justifies the means is and remains the only rule of political ethics.' However, alone in his cell Rubashov concludes that history is not a science, that human beings are not predictable. If the future cannot be predetermined it is wrong to justify terror because it is in accord with the 'laws of history'. Gletkin, a younger and rougher interrogator, nevertheless traps Rubashov by getting him to interpret his thoughts and actions according to the revolutionary ethics to which he was once bound and which he still cannot deny. Condemned by his own words he agrees to sign a confession and is even convinced to incriminate the 'opposition' as the 'last service the Party will ask of you'.[80]

In his cell awaiting death Rubashov experiences the 'oceanic feeling', the sense of himself as a human being, a part of humanity and perhaps something larger. It seemed to him that 'for forty years he had been running amuck – the running amuck of pure reason'. What could supplant revolutionary logic? Rubashov/Koestler speculates that it might be like a new religion or movement that would combine 'economic fatality *and* the "oceanic sense"', in which 'only purity of means can justify the ends'. It would forge individuals into a new collectivity that would 'develop a consciousness and an individuality of its own, with an "oceanic feeling" increased a millionfold, in unlimited yet self-contained space'. Moments later, Rubashov is executed.[81]

Darkness at Noon is a *tour de force*. Once Koestler began it, the novel virtually wrote itself. It spoke with searing passion to cohorts of Communists and ex-Communists in the 1940s and 1950s, but since Communism collapsed so precipitately, and left so little behind except ruins and the memory of pain, it is hard to recall the hold that the ideology exerted over millions of people, the shock when its dark underside was exposed and the liberating results of Koestler's book. Forty years later Michael Foot recalled its effect on him in words that may stand for a whole generation: 'Who will ever forget the first moment he read *Darkness at Noon*? For socialists especially, the experience was indelible. I can recall reading it right through one night, horror-struck, over-powered, enthralled. If this was the true revelation of what had happened at the great Stalin show trials, and it was hard to see how a single theoretical dent could be made in it, a terrifying shaft of darkness was cast over the future no less than the past.'[82]

The novel was regarded as a potent anti-Communist weapon from the 1940s to the 1970s when, alongside Orwell's *Animal Farm* and *1984*, it was a set text in schools in the USA and Britain. It was hated and feared by the Communist Party which did its utmost to refute the text and discredit the author, something in which Koestler gloried. Like the greatest political novels it rapidly passed from literature into the realm of concrete action. It became a weapon in the arsenal of the Cold War and now stands as a monument to that conflict.

VI

On the strength of *Darkness at Noon* Koestler approached Victor Gollancz with a proposal for a personal account of the fall of France and his escape to England. It was immediately accepted for the Left Book Club and Koestler obtained an agreement from Gollancz for the book to be published simultaneously by Jonathan Cape. He began work on it as soon as he left prison.[83]

On his release, he moved in with Daphne Hardy at 26a Bute Street, South Kensington. She had visited Koestler in prison, but it was such a painful experience for both of them that he once asked her not to return. For many weeks each had thought the other dead; to meet divided from one another by wire and glass added insult to injury. Although they subsequently lived together for several months, their relationship never recovered from the traumas in France and the months of separation. As soon as Koestler moved to Bute Street they started quarrelling. The virtues which had once attracted him to her now became vices. Her carefree, Bohemian and slightly irresponsible ways and lack of concern for domestic niceties, which were fine in Paris and the South of France, became irksome to him in their cramped London quarters. Koestler criticised her for alleged 'vices of laziness, schlampig-ness [slovenliness], casualness etc'. Hardy, who was trying to combine sculpting with a full-time job, naturally resented this. She would sink into rancorous moods before exploding with rage. The separation enjoined by Koestler's military service dealt a further blow to their tottering relationship.[84]

True to his word, Koestler presented himself to the Alien Recruitment Office on the Euston Road soon after his departure from Pentonville and volunteered for service in the British army.[85] At the time, the army did not have the equipment for battalions of foreign-born volunteers who were of low priority and he was told to return in two months' time. This enabled him to work on *Scum of the Earth*, banging away on a rented typewriter and living off the five pounds a week advance from Cape. It was intended to last for twelve weeks and Koestler needed all that time. But in mid-February the army decided it needed him. Jonathan Cape appealed to the recruiting office to defer Koestler's call-up for another two weeks. This was accomplished without demur. Koestler was astonished at the casual handling of the matter, but grateful for the extra time since the writing did not come easily.[86]

It was the first book he had written from scratch in English and it was composed during the worst of the Blitz. It also had to be vetted. When each instalment was completed he sent it to Jonathan Cape who, in turn, sent a copy to Harold Nicolson at the Ministry of Information to make sure that it contained nothing that would aid or comfort the enemy. Nicolson found it 'admirable stuff'. Like *Darkness at Noon* it benefited from Daphne Hardy's attention to grammar and vocabulary. Indeed, without her ministrations it is hard to see how it could have been such a *succès d'estime*.[87]

By the end of February he had a typescript of 250 pages and was ready to begin polishing it. He sent Nicolson the final draft on 1 April, just a fortnight before he was due for call-up. Nicolson disagreed with Koestler's pessimism about France and gently requested the deletion of a passage illustrating the depth of French hostility to Britain. With that minor change the book was cleared. Gollancz was pleased with the finished product and made it a Left Book Club choice to coincide with the publication by Cape on 30 May. Paul Willert was deputised to correct the proofs of *Scum of the Earth* if Koestler was prevented from doing so by his army service.[88]

Scum of the Earth blends reportage and autobiography. It covers the period from the Nazi-Soviet Pact to Koestler's internment in 1939, his arrest and detention in Le Vernet, the fall of France, his wanderings around southern France and escape. Koestler brilliantly dissects the mood of the French public and the sources of their demoralisation, including the pervasive xenophobia and anti-Semitism. He excoriates the theory and tactics of the Communist Party, accusing it of being out of touch with real people, such as the soldiers he marched alongside in the catastrophic days of May–June 1940. 'In three weeks here I have learned more about mass psychology than in seven years of Communist busybodiness. Good God! In what an imaginary world we have lived. Have to start quite afresh – all of us.'[89] The portrayal of Le Vernet includes a devastating insight into the plight of International Brigaders: 'Ten years of constant defeat had reduced them to what they were; and their fate

merely exemplified what had happened to all of us, the European
Left. They had done nothing but put into practice what we had
preached and believed; that had been admired and worshipped, and
thrown on the rubbish heap like a sackful of rotten potatoes, to
putrefy.'[90]

Scum of the Earth is remarkable, bursting conventional genres, rich
in analysis and prediction. It perfects the unique style of combined
reportage, diary and political commentary that Koestler had tried out
in *Spanish Testament*. If *Darkness at Noon* signalled his arrival as a
novelist of the first rank, *Scum of the Earth* confirms his place among
the greatest journalists of the century.

Ever economical with his literary products, and keen for their
potential to be maximised while he was a name, Koestler also
proposed to Gollancz to publish the second half of *Spanish Testament*
as a separate book. If the LBC didn't want to do it he asked Gollancz
to release it to Penguin. With Gollancz's permission Penguin
accepted the proposal at the start of April, although various delays
and Koestler's service in the Pioneer Corps prevented *Dialogue with
Death* from appearing until February 1942.[91]

Meanwhile, *Darkness at Noon* was taking America by storm.
During February Koestler had pressed Cape rather irritably to speed
up the book's publication by Macmillan in the USA in order to
capitalise upon its *succès d'estime* in Britain. At the end of March he
was delighted to learn that it had been selected as a Book of the
Month Club choice, guaranteeing a large sale and healthy royalties.[92]
Such success lifted Koestler far above the other exiles and refugees in
London, although they continued to play a major part in his life. He
received many letters from less well-off Continentals imploring him
for assistance, which he dutifully passed on to his political and literary
contacts.[93]

In January 1941 the publisher Freddie Warburg had suggested that
Koestler contribute a study of the Gestapo to the 'Searchlight' series
which George Orwell and Tosco Fyvel, the Jewish writer and
journalist, were co-editing. Koestler met Fyvel and lunched with
Orwell in mid-February, but counter-suggested a book on the way
ordinary people in Europe viewed their countries. Orwell approved
the project and a contract was issued, but Koestler's service in the
Pioneer Corps made it impossible to complete.[94] On 15 April 1941,
at No. 8 Recruiting Office, Euston Road, Arthur Koestler took the
oath as a member of His Majesty's armed forces. Three days later he
jokingly wrote to Tosco Fyvel: 'Now at last I can relax, mainly by
peeling for Victory.' But military life was not going to be a lark. The

eleven months he was to spend in the army turned into an agony of frustration that culminated in another nervous collapse.[95]

VII

Koestler's first posting was to No. 3 Training Centre, Pioneer Corps, Ilfracombe in Devon. Barely a month passed before he was moaning bitterly to Hardy, 'I am working now eight hours a day in the bloody open air and it is really no fun.' Inoculations made him feel ill and he had no chance to recover. 'We are living in a terrible rush and strain, heavy work from 6 a.m. to 5 p.m. and afterwards still drill; I have not left the camp since I arrived and barely manage to find the time to read a newspaper; and at night there is firewatching.' He proposed to endure it for another two weeks and, if there was no improvement, try to find a way out.[96]

In May he joined 251 Company, Pioneer Corps, at Shirehampton near Bristol. The hard manual labour combined with news of the German invasion of Russia was debilitating. He wrote to Willert: 'Since it began I live in a sort of daze, and there is nobody with whom I could discuss it and try to get some order into my thoughts.' He had not totally surrendered his idealistic aspirations for the revolution. 'Whether the Soviets are victorious or defeated, Stalin and his bureaucracy will disappear. The great question is, what will come after? In the first case – perhaps the rebirth of all our hopes and not only hope but fulfilment. In the second case some sort of Asiatic Soviet Republic will probably survive east of the Urals . . .' John Strachey, who heard from Gollancz that Koestler was unhappy in the Pioneer Corps, was just as desperate to discuss the new world situation, although in his view the change was '*potentially* for the better'. By mid-August it was hard to be optimistic. Each day Koestler read about familiar Soviet cities falling to the Germans, often in the wake of devastating battles.[97]

Strachey had been greatly affected by *Darkness at Noon*. According to his biographer, Hugh Thomas, the novel and the Communist Party's anti-war line before June 1941, 'completed Strachey's political re-education'. He was now an RAF adjutant with 87 Fighter Squadron, stationed near Bath, and one of those whom Koestler went to for company while he was posted to the West Country. Strachey recalled the impression which Koestler made during a visit to his RAF base: 'There entered the rumpled, battle-dressed figure of Private Koestler of the Pioneer Corps, surely one of the oddest men ever to dig a British latrine.'[98] In fact, Koestler and the other men in 251 Pioneer Company had been excavating pools in which oil would be poured ready for burning to divert German bombers attacking Bristol. Many years later, in a lecture to the British Academy, he recalled that the men were so eager to help the war effort that they asked for the tea-break to be abolished, to the consternation of the British NCOs and officers.[99]

During the summer Koestler started lecturing for the Army Educational Corps. He gave talks on 'Vichy France', 'The history of the Fifth Column' and 'The war on the Eastern Front' to British troops in the neighbourhood of his new posting, Oakley Farm Camp near Cheltenham, Gloucestershire. The lectures were tiring, but his encounters with British servicemen were instructive. He found the troops 'shockingly ignorant of real Nazism'. He told Willert that 'I find again and again by this contact with British soldiers how totally ignorant they are about mass-feeling. If we survive this war we all should sit down modestly on our arses for 2 or 3 years and shut up and learn the ABC of what human thinking, feeling, the laws which govern their actions and inactions are really like. We have all lived more or less in a phantom world.'[100]

Koestler's commanding officer adapted uneasily to running a company filled with European coffee-house types. He refused to allow Koestler to lecture without specific permission and reserved the right not to give it. Nor was he prepared to relax the usual camp regimen in his favour. This meant that he put in several hours of fatigues in the morning and was often exhausted when the time came to give the talks. Koestler could not simply apply for a transfer to the Education Corps since it did not accept aliens.[101]

He began to pull strings to get out of the Pioneer Corps. When *Scum of the Earth* was reviewed in *Horizon* by Major Bonamy Dobrée, a pre-war academic employed in the Ministry of Information (MOI), he wrote to him explaining his difficulties and asking if Dobrée would write to his CO in support of his work for the Education Corps. He confessed: 'I'm rather at the end of my tether.' Towards the end of October he reported to Guy Chapman, husband of the writer Margaret Storm Jameson, who was also attached to the MOI, that after five months' lecturing he had been sent back to digging. It seemed impossible to get official sanction for his lecturing work except on an *ad hoc* basis.[102]

Was Koestler really so badly treated in the Pioneer Corps? True, it would have been better for all concerned if he had never been stuck there, but once in he was permitted a great deal of latitude. During his eleven months in the army he was granted at least two substantial leave periods, not to mention weekend passes which enabled him to stop over in London or stay with friends in their country houses. While he was based at Cheltenham he had 'no lack of social life', seeing Strachey, Michael Sadleir and Cecil Day Lewis, who lived in the Cotswolds. He was first granted a five-day leave in early September to enable him to speak at a PEN congress in London. It took a bit of lobbying on his behalf by Storm Jameson and Guy Chapman, but in the end the army recognised the importance of his participation. The furlough allowed him time to dine with Stephen Spender, Fyvel and Robert Neumann, the *émigré* German novelist.[103]

Koestler quickly became a member of several overlapping social, literary and political groups. Through Gollancz and the LBC he had met Strachey and Laski. Through Warburg he met Fyvel and Orwell. He met Cyril Connolly, the editor of the new and hugely influential literary magazine *Horizon*, soon after the publication of *Scum of the Earth*. They quickly became friends. Koestler was invited to contribute to *Horizon* and introduced to Connolly's circle. Even while Koestler was in the Pioneer Corps, Connolly arranged a party for him at which he met the journalist and future newspaper proprietor David Astor, the poets Stephen Spender and Louis MacNeice, the writer Philip Toynbee and other *Horizon* contributors. In 1974 Koestler remembered that the '*Horizon* crowd was a very cosy one'. He told Iain Hamilton that 'I couldn't say I was an insider in the clique. I was, of course, a strange bird on the periphery but I felt at home.' He was always grateful to Connolly because he 'took me under his wing'.[104]

Via Laski and Strachey he met the Labour politicians who founded *Tribune*: George Russell Strauss, Michael Foot and Nye Bevan. Foot took him on to write a column for the *Evening Standard*, which led him into contact with Frank Owen and eventually with Lord Beaverbrook himself. He met Lord Victor Rothschild via John Strachey and in due course Koestler became close to Victor's sister, Miriam. She added a second branch of the Rothschild dynasty to his collection of acquaintances by introducing him to Guy de Rothschild, her cousin. Guy's wife Alix was from an old Hungarian Jewish family, which aided the bonding process. This connection would later lead him back into Zionist politics. Paul Willert introduced Koestler to Freddie Ayer, with whom he had been at Eton and Oxford. Ayer had 'read and admired' *Scum of the Earth* and *Darkness at Noon*, although he soon found Koestler's pronouncements on philosophy rather irritating.[105]

Most of those who met Koestler at this time recall a tremendously vital, attractive and even glamorous figure who breathed commitment. Their first encounter was imprinted in Astor's memory: Koestler was 'dressed in a battle dress with his hair cut short, sort of army length, in a collection of writers in the home of Cyril Connolly . . . and here was this figure, standing out in contrast to all the others who had not got their hair cut short and were not in uniform'.[106]

Yet Koestler grew restless with the constraints imposed on him by the army. He complained about 'mental deformation by cockeyed values'. He now felt guilty reading philosophy in the morning, but at ease sweeping corridors. His exasperation increased when he damaged his hand in an accident during a work detail on 20 September. Nursing his injury back at camp his thoughts yet again turned to suicide. 'Why not?' he asked his diary–notebook. There is no explicit reply, only the suggestive comment: 'Like a postman killed before able to deliver the contents of his bag.' Koestler, as usual, toyed with suicide, but was held back by a supervening consciousness of his mission and his own importance.[107]

Separation from Hardy created more discomfort. While he was stationed near Ilfracombe, she arranged to stay in Totnes and tried to find lodgings for him nearby. Since it was difficult for an unmarried couple to take a room in a boarding house these fleeting rendezvous, so hard to organise for both of them, were especially frustrating. When Koestler was posted to Shirehampton Hardy was transferred to Buckinghamshire. He encouraged her to get a job with the BBC in London, but she was eventually posted to Oxford. Visits to her were awkward because she lived in a house dominated by a fearsome landlady. An attempt to make room for Koestler to stay over during a leave weekend in early June only provoked a row.[108]

Hardy was angry that Koestler wrote to her infrequently, but her irritation turned to guilt when she learned how badly he was faring. She gallantly promised that next time she had leave she would travel from Oxford to wherever he was stationed. They managed to see each other in London in June, August and November 1941, but Koestler was in town more often than that. Hardy felt she was becoming an incidental part of his very busy London schedules. After one blazing argument he wrote to Cyril Connolly, 'I am sorry Daphne got hysterics in the taxi when I saw you last time, it was not serious, only a legitimate protest against my alcoholic talkativeness.'[109]

Hardy's sense of injustice and the quarrels were not simply hysterics. He owed the title of *Darkness at Noon* and much of its literary success to her. She was still collaborating with him on his writing and at least one dispute flared up because, as he later explained, 'I made her work too hard on polishing an essay I had written'. Hardy read, commented upon and improved his English, making sure it was elegant as well as intelligible. However, while Koestler mentioned this assistance to friends such as Paul Willert, apart from her translation of *Darkness at Noon* she never received public credit. It was little consolation that he referred to her sometimes as 'my fiancée' or 'my wife': he took her for granted and that rankled.[110]

Despite the inconveniences of army life Koestler remained astonishingly productive and assiduous at 'networking'. At the beginning of May he sent off *Dialogue with Death* with corrections and production notes. During stop-overs in London in the summer he saw Crossman and Neumann, and spent a weekend with Gollancz at his country home in Brimpton. The PEN congress in London on 11 September provided the opportunity to see Jonathan Cape, Storm Jameson, Tosco Fyvel, Cyril Connolly and E. M. Forster, with whom he was soon on friendly terms.[111] In October Koestler also started broadcasting for the BBC Home Service. His first radio performance was in a scripted discussion, but a few weeks later he was invited to write and present his own material. He was soon being granted special leaves to broadcast. His scripts, such as 'Europe in Revolt', transmitted on the Home Service in mid-1942, usually dealt with events on the Continent. His gutteral accent, as well as his background, gave these broadcasts an authenticity and authority much sought after by the BBC.[112]

Due to the bombing of their printer, Cape were not able to meet the deadline for publication of *Scum of the Earth* in May 1941, so the Left Book Club edition appeared first and with rather less of a fanfare than Gollancz had hoped. The Cape edition arrived in September and was an immediate hit.[113] It further heightened Koestler's celebrity status. George Russell Strauss, the left-wing millionaire and Labour MP, invited him to stay at his London house when he was next in town and asked him to contribute to the first weekly issue of *Tribune*. Laski, who was sent a complimentary copy of the book, which he dubbed a 'historic document', invited Koestler to dinner. Koestler was diligent about turning such contacts to good use and soon asked Laski to write references on Hardy's behalf when she applied for a job at the LSE.[114]

The book turned Koestler into a hero figure for all the *émigrés*, exiles and refugees who had experienced flight and internment either on the Continent or in Britain. From September 1941 onwards, letters flooded in from members of the Pioneer Corps, erstwhile comrades and even family members who had lost track of him. On Christmas Eve, Koestler heard from Leo Valiani, Mario in *Scum of the Earth*. Writing under the name Leo Weiczen, he told Koestler that he had reached French Morocco and thence travelled to Mexico. He asked Koestler to help him join the British army and also requested money so that he could continue writing a book on Croce. Typically, Koestler did his utmost to help.[115]

Koestler's Pioneer Corps blues were temporarily lifted by a week's leave in London between 30 October and 6 November, into which he fitted a prodigious number of social engagements and meetings. He stayed at the house in Drayton Gardens, off the Fulham Road, which Cyril Connolly rented from Celia and Mamaine Paget. Peter Quennell, the writer, lived on the top storey. Koestler found the place in rather a mess when he arrived and 'made some order' before launching into twenty telephone calls before dinner. The next morning was also heavily devoted to the phone. He dined with Stephen Spender and the Connollys and then went to a party attended by Count Károlyi, the ex-Hungarian premier, David Astor, Arthur Calder-Marshall, a writer now at the MOI, Quennell, the poet Louis MacNeice and the painter Augustus John. Over the next days he saw Orwell, Neumann and Fyvel, and had meetings at Cape. Another day he dined with the co-editors of *Tribune*, George Russell Strauss and Aneurin Bevan, who he thought was 'a nice boy but a tipler [*sic*]'. In the course of the week Koestler lunched or dined at the Reform Club, the Travellers, the Dorchester and David Astor's home.[116]

Pleasure was not the only reason for this exhausting schedule. He wrote in his diary on his return that he was 'back from eventful leave, crusaide [*sic*] for Virgin Island settlement'. Koestler had developed a scheme for extricating some of the 80–100,000 internees and stateless aliens in France, of whom 45,000 were in internment camps. Most of these were Jews and the remainder left-wing exiles or former members of the International Brigades, all of whom were in peril. Many had already been sent to Germany, committed suicide to avoid repatriation or been transferred to labour camps in French North Africa. Yet rescue from Vichy France was still possible. His plan was for the United States to offer to intern the aliens on territory under its control, possibly the Virgin Islands, for the duration of the war.[117]

With this in mind he contacted Eleanor Rathbone, who had been stirred to action about Le Vernet after she read *Scum of the Earth*, Harold Laski, David Astor, Sir Edward Hulton, proprietor of *Picture Post*, and the secretaries of the main refugee organisations in London.

During his stay in town he saw Rathbone, Lady Asquith, Lady Cripps and Astor several times. The most important meetings were with G. Kuhlman, the Deputy High Commissioner for Refugees, and John Winant, the United States ambassador. The critical objective was to persuade the Americans to take up the plan. To publicise it Astor asked Koestler to write an 800-word article for the *Observer* on the position of political refugees in Vichy France. Koestler also drew up a lengthy memorandum detailing the scale of the refugee problem there, the threat the refugees faced and the possible solution. Astor subsequently presented the memo to Winant, who seemed amenable. Afterwards Koestler, Astor and Rathbone had a 'victory tea' to celebrate.[118]

Koestler was buoyed up by the meetings, but he was driven frantic by the restrictions he faced once back in camp. He told Astor that 'I feel cut off and buried alive while burning to carry on with this thing. Last thing I heard was that the Nazis are sending German Jews to camps in Poland which are even more horrible than the French camps.' The celebrations were anyway premature. Winant passed the matter on to an embassy official, Lewis Einstein, who displayed little interest or energy. Then the entry of the United States into the war altered everything. Rathbone told Koestler on 12 December that the scheme's chances of success were ruined. Soon afterwards Koestler's health broke down.[119]

His collapse can be attributed to the failure of the refugee scheme coming on top of the cumulative frustration of army life. In order to get some privacy for his writing he had taken up residence in a room that served as the 'Company's library-plus-sports-stores-room, surrounded by boxing gloves, cricket-bats, old volumes of *Punch* and a Jewish holy shrine containing two Thora-rols [*sic*] wrapped in gold and velvet'. These rather unusual quarters were far from ideal. During November relations with his superiors deteriorated. The quartermaster confined him to barracks for two weeks over a petty incident involving the distribution of tickets for a dance. This meant that he would miss a PEN conference in London. This decision was only reversed after PEN officials intervened with the War Office. It was little wonder that he willingly signed the *Horizon* manifesto 'Why Not War Writers', which Connolly had concocted in an attempt to persuade the government to support writers, as well as artists, and to help aliens like Koestler get out of stupid Pioneer Corps jobs.[120]

During November he had discussed an idea for a propaganda film with Arthur Calder-Marshall, who was at the MOI film unit, and pleaded with him to ask the War Office Public Relations Office to secure him leave so that he could work on it. Even better, he suggested that Calder-Marshall arrange for his transfer. Koestler concluded his letter tersely 'this is an SOS'. He managed to write an outline – despite the fatigues, digging and lecturing – which was sufficiently promising for Calder-Marshall to offer him ten pounds for a rough treatment. Calder-Marshall also tried to help Koestler get some time off so that he could do research in libraries and write in peace, but the next thing he knew was that Koestler was in hospital.[121]

It is not clear exactly what happened. He told Michael Károlyi that he had suffered 'a nervous breakdown'. In a letter to Neumann he said: 'I was brought in with rather melodramatic nervous collapse . . . I feel pretty rotten.' He informed Sir Herbert Read that 'I have been in hospital after a nervous breakdown – the first I have ever had. It must have been accumulating for years.' The medical notes for his discharge from Mill Hill Emergency Hospital specify a carefully controlled diet of milk, rusks, eggs, cream, olive oil and orange juice. The drugs prescribed are sodium citrate, atrophine mixture and magnesium trisilicate. Rather hopefully he was advised not to smoke.[122] The treatment suggests that Koestler had a stomach complaint, possibly ulcers, brought on by tension.

Messages of sympathy poured in to the emergency hospital in Cheltenham to which he was first sent. Hardy was terribly worried about him, but could not visit at once. By letter she advised him to adopt her philosophy and 'be passive', though she knew he wouldn't agree. George Russell Strauss sent best wishes from himself and Nye Bevan, and told Koestler not to worry about an overdue article for *Tribune*. Astor expressed his concern and Calder-Marshall sent a box of chocolates. Kingsley Martin wrote soothingly, 'Don't forget that you have masses of friends in this country and that we treasure you as one of the people we are most proud to know and whose books we believe will last.'[123] More practically, Calder-Marshall made a final push on Koestler's behalf. He discussed his case with Sir Arthur Willert, Paul Willert's father, who was head of the MOI Office for Southern Region. He also asked Louis MacNeice to put Koestler's name forward for the BBC European Service. One promising avenue seemed to be getting Koestler work on propaganda films so Basil Wright, at the MOI Film Unit, put in a request for his release.[124]

On Christmas Eve 1941 Koestler was transferred to Mill Hill Emergency Hospital for convalescence. Things were looking up.

Connolly had called him the day before to say that the War Office had agreed to second Koestler for propaganda work: only a technical blunder had delayed his discharge. But Koestler was in no rush. He told Hardy that the hospital was 'so efficiently run you would think it is in a different country'. He was well fed and cared for; several of the doctors had read his books and fussed over their famous patient. He rose at 7 a.m., bathed, breakfasted, then did light gym for an hour. He had a siesta after lunch and was allowed to work in a room put aside specially for his use. In the evenings he attended lectures on such useful subjects as car engines and electronics. It was, in short, 'a near miracle – an eldorado-island in the midst of general army-muddle'.[125]

At the end of December Koestler went for an interview at the MOI where Calder-Marshall and Richard Crossman, then with the Political Warfare Executive, were pressing for his immediate release from the Pioneers. He was discharged from medical supervision in early February and took up temporary residence at 102a Drayton Gardens, Chelsea. On 10 March 1942 he was formally discharged from the British army for 'ceasing to fulfil army physical requirements'. His discharge notice recorded that Private Koestler had been 'A good soldier during his period of service'.[126]

Chapter 6
Holocaust, 1942–4

In the spring of 1942 London was awash with foreigners: members of exiled governments, the survivors of half-a-dozen defeated armies who had regrouped in Britain, as well as thousands of refugees. Life during and after the Blitz was intense. People took each day as it came, retreating into pubs, clubs and cellars when night came and with it the threat of bombing. English and aliens, workers and intelligentsia, men and women mingled with unaccustomed freedom in sweaty, smoky and alcoholic bolt-holes. Robert Hewison has remarked that for the first and last time London had a Bohemian quarter in the streets of Fitzrovia and Soho. The Ministry of Information (MOI) and the BBC, which framed this zone, were crammed with intellectuals and writers busy harnessing creative figures to the war effort. It would have been hard to design an environment more suited to Arthur Koestler's talents and temperament.[1]

He began working for the MOI Film Unit and branched out into propaganda work for the BBC. Soon he was also writing for the *Evening Standard* and the *Observer*. He maintained his involvement in PEN and turned out several important essays for *Horizon*. His social life became frenetic, accelerated by and accelerating the collapse of his relationship with Daphne Hardy. He had one affair after another. His friendships were closely related to his evolving political outlook. He drew away from pained ex-Communists, such as John Strachey, and moved towards socialists in the mould of Michael Foot, whose projection of the future was untrammelled by a sense of guilt about the past. Dissatisfied with their pragmatism, he then drifted in the direction of Utopian and mystical visions formulated by characters such as Raymond Postgate and Olaf Stapledon.

At the same time, a chill sense of reality underpinned his propaganda work, journalism, essay writing and fiction. He continued to campaign for Jewish refugees and political fugitives in Europe and was one of the few who grasped the scale of the tragedy being enacted across the English Channel. It was against this background that he began work on *Arrival and Departure* (1943). In November 1942 Koestler met Jan Karski, an envoy for the Polish underground who conveyed to the West an eyewitness account of conditions in the Warsaw ghetto and the deportation of Jews to the death camps. Unlike many others, Koestler was easily convinced that Karski was telling the truth. The appalling information about the Nazi extermination programme is etched into *Arrival and Departure*, which is almost the only work of fiction published in Britain during the war, or even *after* the war,[2] to register the catastrophe.

Koestler described it as 'the third novel of a trilogy on ends and means' following on from *The Gladiators* and *Darkness at Noon*: 'its central theme is the conflict between morality and expediency' treated at the level of individual psychology. While he was working on it he broke off to write a major essay on the related subjects of myth and heroism. However, like its predecessors, the novel is inexplicable if it is detached from his continuous preoccupation with Jewish questions and his own Jewishness. Throughout the spring of 1944 he wrestled with a sequel to *Arrival and Departure*. This work was permeated by his awareness of the Jewish fate and reflected his concurrent activism in the Jewish cause.

In September 1943 he entered the circle of London-based activists assisting Chaim Weizmann, President of the World Zionist Organisation. In March 1944 their work was overtaken by the German occupation of Hungary, which unleashed a new phase of the 'Final Solution'. For several months, Koestler's life was overshadowed by the news of the deportations of Jews from Hungary, where his mother and her family still lived, and the puny attempts by Jews in the free world to delay or halt the transports to Auschwitz-Birkenau. In July 1944 he could not withstand the horror and frustration any longer: he suffered a breakdown and left London for a country retreat.

Echoing his behaviour in 1933, he resurrected and rewrote *Twilight Bar* as a form of therapy. He then produced the four interlocked pieces which comprise the final chapters of *The Yogi and The Commissar* (1945). These epochal essays included a relentlessly documented attack on the Soviet Union and Communism. They also set out the first sustained statement of his developed political and social thought. In autumn 1944 he decided to write a novel set in Palestine, developing his interest in Jewish issues further than anything he had yet written. The impetus for this re-evaluation of his Jewishness lies in the events of 1942–4.

I

When he was discharged back into civilian life Koestler temporarily
moved in to Cyril Connolly's maisonette at 102a Drayton Gardens,
Chelsea. The fortnight he spent there was unhappy. Lys Lubbock
was living with Connolly and they shared quarters with his friend
Peter Quennell. There was not much room for another highly strung
literary type. Connolly, who was at the height of his influence, was
immensely kind to him and Koestler never forgot this generosity, but
his affection for Connolly wore thin.[3]

Although he respected their literary work, he despised the politics
and behaviour of the 'pink generation', the left-leaning English
writers of the 1930s. His contempt often focused on their sexual
mores. 'English intellectuals', he confided to his diary–notebook,
'need 5–10 years to get over their public school complex, if ever they
get over it.' He transcribed a scurrilous story told by Philip Toynbee
about Spender allegedly going to Spain during the Civil War in hot
pursuit of a boyfriend. The story-teller fared no better: 'Again and
again horror-stricken about morbidity of this pink generation.
Unable to digest prep-school and public school [experience] before
30. At 30 some (C.C.) manage to find the bridge to para–normal sex,
majority not; and even minority remains para-normal. T[oynbee]
scratches at table his balls and then smells his fingers – at every meal.'[4]

Effete behaviour drew out the worst of Koestler's macho
character, perhaps because he was beset by doubts about his own
sexuality and agonised over a 'bisexual' streak in his make-up. That
he was defensive towards any suggestion of effeminacy is shown by
his reaction to the notorious 'hair-net' incident that occurred during
his stay at Drayton Gardens. One morning Quennell ran into
Koestler who was *en route* to the bathroom wearing a hair-net on his
head. This sight left Quennell temporarily flummoxed, but he later
regaled friends with the tale and it caused widespread amusement.
Inevitably, word of this got back to Koestler who was mightily
offended. He protested that Central European males often used a
hair-net while bathing and shaving. Quennell was forced to
apologise, explaining to him that 'never did I state or imply that you
slept in a hair-net. I merely described the rather alarming impression
made on me, at a period of my life when I usually woke up with a
hangover, by the early-morning apparition of a foreign man of genius
rushing hair-netted towards his bath. I take your word for it that it is
proper attire at that time of day for "any civilized continental". It is
also a fact that, from the hidebound anglo-saxon point of view, the

hair-net is still a slightly comical garment.'[5]

Despite the laboured irony and self-deprecation there is more than a hint of prejudice in his apologia. Quennell's sense of Englishness here and elsewhere in his writings was often defined against 'foreigners', frequently in stereotypical and racist terms. Nor was Connolly immune to jocose excursions at the expense of those unfortunate enough not to be English (or in his case Anglo-Irish). He loved to make fun of his friends behind their backs. According to Clive Fisher, one of Connolly's biographers, Koestler 'was a favourite butt, his tendency to arrive at cocktail parties uniformed and close-cropped a declaration of anti-fascist zeal which was cruelly undermined by his impotent travails in the Pioneer Corps'. Connolly 'found such urgency irresistibly comic and was fond of jokes about Koestler's Sergeant Major and his new vulnerability to nervous breakdowns'. David Astor remembered Connolly's cruel impersonations of Koestler 'delivered in a gutteral and imprecise mid-European accent when the conflict in the North African theatre was dominating the headlines: "Who shall command ze dezzert? Wavell, Orvell or Fyvel?" '[6]

To Astor Koestler was a tonic after the incestuous London literary crowd, 'the embodiment of an uncompromised, unafraid, international idealism'. He 'seemed to radiate a heightened liveliness and sense of reality'. Koestler's cosmopolitanism, volcanic energy and genuine anti-Fascism must have made him an uncomfortable house guest for such louche, posturing, ineffectual under-achievers as Quennell and Connolly, and it is little surprise that Koestler soon moved out. Yet even such a sympathetic observer as Astor noted the incongruity between what he represented and the way he looked: 'This small, passionate man, with his excruciating accent, his self-mockery, and his devotion to his friends in Europe', the 'Scum of the Earth'. Guy de Rothschild, who was put up by Koestler when he was in London in 1944 and served breakfast in bed by him, remembered 'A small man with a receding forehead, thick, black hair slicked back, and a nervous twitching face . . . not very imposing at first sight'.[7]

After the 'Connolly interlude' he moved into a flat in Chelsea Cloisters which he shared with Daphne Hardy. Clad in a new suit bought at Simpsons he launched himself into propaganda work with the MOI Film Unit under the direction of Sylvester Gates and Arthur Calder-Marshall. Initially he developed an idea for the propaganda film series 'Into Battle'. It dealt with aliens serving in the British armed forces and had a long pedigree. In spring 1941, while he was in 251 Company, Pioneer Corps, Koestler had drafted a proposal for a Penguin Special called 'Regiment With No Traditions' that would present a 'collective account' of the origins, activities and achievements of an aliens unit. Originally he suggested that he co-author it with Major McKay, his company commander, in collaboration with the members of the unit. The book would not only inform the public about the work of aliens in the army, but explain how and why they had come to Britain as exiles and refugees from Fascism. The project never came to fruition and McKay ended up as the chief obstacle to Koestler's literary endeavours rather than their midwife.[8]

A year later he resuscitated the draft in the form of a film outline entitled 'Those Who Escaped', 'to feature the life of a unit of the British Army consisting entirely of foreigners'. It would help the public to understand how the people of occupied Europe were '100 million allies' and counter Nazi propaganda about the 'New Order'. The stories of the men in the unit would bring home to the audience the actuality of Nazi rule, the urgency of liberating Europe and realisation of the goals set out in the Atlantic Charter. It would also flatter the English by letting them see themselves as a bastion of liberty around whom exiles and fugitives rallied, thus inducing a more positive view of aliens in the process. The 'plot' was simple. It was based on an incident witnessed by Koestler when a meeting was arranged between a Pioneer Corps unit and a nearby Home Guard unit. In the course of explaining their life histories to the Englishmen the aliens radically changed the way they were perceived. For the purposes of the film Koestler proposed that the CO of a Pioneer Company interview six of his men for such an encounter as a device to elicit their stories. These would then be developed more exhaustively. The group would include a Czech, an Austrian, a Pole, a Frenchman, a German socialist and an Armenian. Unlike the Penguin Special proposal, no Jewish cases were to be used in the film. However, Koestler recommended using his old Pioneer Corps unit and added: 'From the political angle it is worth considering whether (a) one of the six typical people should be a Spaniard and (b) whether one of them should be a Jew.'[9]

His caution about the inclusion of a Jewish figure was understandable, given the reluctance of the Political Warfare Executive and the MOI, as well as the BBC, to draw attention to the specific fate of the Jews under the Nazis. There is no evidence that he remonstrated over this point, but his recommendation was apparently accepted since the filmed version, called *Lift Your Head Comrade*, eventually focused on Central European exiles and refugees in the

Pioneer Corps, of whom several were implicitly identified as Jewish. The film begins with the Regimental Sergeant Major asking one Sergeant Rosenberg to 'call this bloody roll'. The roster quickly reveals that Rosenberg is not the only Jew. The Commanding Officer who delivers the narration refers to the men as 'German and Austrian anti-Fascists' who volunteered for service having suffered 'racial and political persecution' in their own countries. This was as close as official British propaganda at this time came to speaking about the persecution of Jews.[10]

'To them', the narrator continues, 'the war started in 1933 when Hitler came to power. They have gone through the hardest trials man can endure for his convictions. And their loyalty to our course [*sic*] is absolute.' The narration by the CO has a slightly patronising effect, mediating between the English audience and the foreigners, and actually reinforcing their otherness. The men are shown taking tea-breaks (which most actually resented as a waste of time) and playing football to demonstrate their acculturation. The cheery affirmation that 'they are great football fans' leaves the distinct impression that although Europeans had been playing soccer for decades they were just now absorbing the benevolent influence of English culture. The apologetic tone only disappears when it deals with the Nazis, concentration camps and anti-Fascism. The peroration is classic Koestler: 'Every shot these men fire is a shot against the ghosts of their past. At last these men are on the right side of the barbed wire.'[11]

Koestler's script drew on his own insecurities and an accurate perception of how foreigners were regarded by the English, which was a justifiable cause for nervousness among aliens. In a private letter to a member of the Rothschild family he explained that one aim of the film was to counter the intense anti-Semitism in wartime Britain by showing that, contrary to popular belief, not all foreign Jews were black-marketeers.[12]

Although he wanted to use 251 Company, practicalities meant that the film was shot near Weymouth where the men of 74 Pioneer Company were erecting coastal emplacements and having weapons training. It was directed by Basil Wright, who concluded the day's shooting with pink gins in a hotel on the sea front. When it was finally released it enjoyed considerable success and was one of the few British propaganda films to be repeatedly and widely screened in the United States.[13] The *News Chronicle* considered that it told the story of Central European exiled anti-Fascists 'quietly and well'. Joan Lester, reviewing it for *Reynolds News*, called it 'invigorating'. It convinced the audience of the 'indestructability of the human spirit'. Only the *Spectator* noted that the bulk of the pioneers were Jewish. The film gave the 'dreadful details' of their persecution and represented 'a timely reminder of the original causes of the war, and . . . good propaganda for our attitude towards at least some "enemy" aliens'.[14]

At the same time that he was working on the film he was writing a thirty-minute radio play for the BBC Home Service called *Protective Custody*. The play, in two acts, is set in a concentration camp in 1938: it, too, has a Jewish dimension. A visit to a camp by journalists provides the pretext for a ghastly picaresque through the Nazi terror system. They encounter three inmates who represent a cross-section of those persecuted by the Nazis: a Jew, a trade unionist and a Bible student. The Jew, named Liebkind, is depicted as weak and pitiful. He asks the trade unionist, called Brandt, 'What makes *you* so strong?' Brandt replies, 'Hope . . . Fraternity . . . And hatred.' The Jew then enunciates the stereotypical view of all Jews as passive sufferers: 'My people can't hate. They have beaten us so much that they have beaten even hatred out of us.' Fired by Brandt's example, Liebkind tries to hate and manages it by recalling the Pesach (Passover) service. As he staggers along a path carrying a load of stone from the camp quarry he counts each painful step and mutters to himself: 'Hate them. Try to hate them. Hate them. And all the water in the river was turned into blood. 120 steps and the fish died. And the river stank. 110. And frogs came upon them and swarms of flies. 100. And all their cattle died . . .' Here Koestler adapts the story of the Ten Plagues as told in the Hebrew Bible and the Haggadah, the saga of the Jewish exodus from Egypt which is recited in almost every Jewish home during Passover. As the play was written during April and broadcast on 7 May 1942 its composition straddled the Passover festival and it is not fanciful to assume that Koestler either dredged up memories of Passover from childhood or was aware of the Passover celebrations among the Jews in wartime London.

The BBC announcer prefaced the broadcast with the words: 'This play has been written by Arthur Koestler, who, because of his anti-Fascist convictions spent the major part of his last years in the prisons and concentration camps of various European countries as Hitler's night gradually descended upon them.' It might have been rather more accurate to have acknowledged the influence which Koestler's Jewish identity almost certainly had on his appreciation of Nazi repression.[15]

Koestler followed up the success of *Protective Custody* with two scripts for a series of BBC Home Service broadcasts, called *The Black*

Gallery, which dissected the character of leading Nazis. His first effort dealt with Julius Streicher and was broadcast on 11 June 1942. It focused on Streicher's propaganda techniques and his treatment of the Jews in Nuremberg, the city over which he held sway as Gauleiter. The second play presented Koestler with a set of technical and aesthetic problems. The subject was Heydrich, the cold and brutal head of the SS Main Office and the Reich Protector of Bohemia-Moravia. Koestler found his character so repulsive and his actions so appalling that he could barely explain them to himself, let alone an audience that was largely ignorant of Nazi practices. He adopted an unusual and not wholly effective tactic of bringing Sherlock Holmes and Watson back to life and setting them on the trail of Heydrich. This was a clever device for presenting his murderous career, but in the end Holmes and Watson give up trying to explain this monster and admit defeat. The two genres of documentary and English detective story mixed unhappily.[16]

The difficulty of making the English understand Fascism and the reality of what was happening in Nazi-occupied Europe never ceased to perplex Koestler. Connolly's mocking stance towards his 'urgency' was merely symptomatic of a national malaise. Koestler returned to this myopia and lack of empathy time and again. In another 1942 broadcast he tackled it head on. The occasion was a review for the Home Service of an exhibition in the Charing Cross underground station on resistance. Koestler began, 'The trouble with being a contemporary in times like this is that reality beats imagination at every step. Try as one may we are unable to form a comprehensive idea of what is going on day by day and night by night in continental Europe. For an educated Englishman it is almost easier to imagine conditions of life under King Canute on this island than conditions of life in, say, contemporary Poland.' The statistics of those who perished due to Nazi oppression, including the victims of 'mobile gas vans', were meaningless. In an attempt to bring home to his audience what the figures really meant he pointed out that people trapped under the swastika died every minute, and that his broadcast had already been under way for ninety seconds. His review concluded ambiguously. The MOI exhibition used understatement rather than 'horror stuff' and perhaps this was 'just as well' for those stopping for a few minutes on their way home from work. On the other hand, he mused, maybe it would be better to administer to them a 'wholesome shock'.[17]

Alongside his broadcasts he laboured on the essay that emerged famously into light as "The Yogi and The Commissar" in *Horizon* in

June 1942. 'Trying to write essay "Yogi and Commissar" – torture myself, doesn't come off. Fed up and miserable.'[18] But the finished product justified the agonies. Koestler had burnished the political argument of *Darkness at Noon*: shorn of belletrist devices it became an ideological scimitar cutting through the popular wartime cant about Communism and the Soviet Union.

Koestler passed 'all possible attitudes to life' through a 'sociological spectroscope' revealing a band of ideological positions ranging from that of the Commissar to that of the Yogi. The Commissar saw human society as a mechanism that could be analysed rationally and adjusted appropriately. But change, in the form of revolution, could only come from without. Since it would solve all social problems at a stroke, it justified the use of any means. The Yogi was sensitive to the complexity of human life and more cautious about the possibility of changing society in predictable ways. Yogis placed the emphasis on the means used to accomplish modifications and preferred evolutionary, non-violent methods.

However, both were prone to disaster. The Commissar was likely to be driven by the logic of revolutionary thinking to ever greater atrocities. Yogism in practice turned into quiescence and subservience. Consequently, most political activists, and entire generations, oscillated between these two poles, eventually becoming paralysed. Commissars fared best because they 'completely severed relations with the subconscious', living in a state of constant pubescent excitation until some shock to their system reintroduced them to their subconscious and their sense of connectedness with humanity at large – the 'oceanic feeling'.

Koestler ended by examining the effects of disillusionment on the 'pink generation'. As a result of the 'serial defeats of the left' it had become 'allergic to rationalism, the shallow optimism, the ruthless logic, the arrogant self-assurance, the Promethean attitude of the nineteenth century'. Instead it was attracted by 'mysticism, romanticism, the irrational ethical values'. He foresaw that a new spirit, as yet indistinct, would emerge from this reaction to the failure of Marxism.[19]

Although it was clearly a personal *cri de coeur*, Koestler's analysis resonated among a swathe of disappointed ex-Communists. The potency of the argument lay in the demolition of Communist Prometheanism rather than the hint of a new, undefined (and possibly undefinable) ideology. Several decades later, however, its impact is hard to grasp. Koestler's methodology was deeply flawed. While claiming to reject Commissar-like materialism, he used a scientific model which presupposed that human society has finite possibilities and can be analysed definitively, using conceptual instruments in the way a scientist uses physical ones. This is the very materialist fallacy he condemned in Marxism. He then compounded his heuristic gaffe by dismissing all nuanced political positions and simply asserting that in essence there are only two choices about how to resolve social questions. 'You can argue with post-war planners, Fabians, Quakers, Liberals and Philanthropists. But the argument will lead you nowhere, for the real issue remains between the Yogi and the Commissar, between the fundamental conceptions of Change from Within and Change from Without.'[20]

Yet practical politics, even in moments of great crisis, is rarely about such absolutes. At the depth of the slump, when British politicians considered slashing public expenditure, they did not think in terms of 'Change from Within or Change from Without'. Koestler wrongly accused the Left of ignorance about the masses and mass psychology. Lenin's slogan in 1917, 'Bread Peace Land', was a brilliant response to the longings of the peasants and workers in Russia. The doctrine of class conflict mobilised visceral feelings of envy and resentment. Social democrats throughout Europe had tried and were trying to balance mass feelings of social injustice with the socio-economic fine-tuning which is the diurnal task of politicians: compromise was possible. Koestler may have been stuck in political adolescence, but the political fixers whom he disparaged were guilty of no more than a wariness born of maturity.

'The Yogi and The Commissar' engendered extensive debate in political circles, but it was only one point on Koestler's own agenda. He had not abandoned the refugee scheme or forgotten those whom it was intended to succour. In June 1942 he wrote two powerful articles about Le Vernet and the pitiful 'scum of the earth' for the *Evening Standard*. The articles were commissioned through the agency of Michael Foot, a feature writer on the paper since 1940. They had first met while Koestler was still in uniform, whereupon Foot 'fell immediately, swooning victim to his wit, charm and inordinate capacity for alcohol'. In mid-1942 he commissioned Koestler to write a column in which 'typical' characters to be found on the London Underground reflected on the war. The articles 'made a great stir' according to Foot, though not necessarily of the right kind. 'Within weeks he had ruptured my relations with pro-prietor, management, and, as they alleged, a considerable portion of the reading public.' 'The Idle Thoughts of Sidney Sound (Your Neighbour on the Underground)' depicted a harassed, petty-minded commuter whose thoughts flit from one subject to another, giving little more weight to developments on the Eastern Front than to an attractive female air-raid warden of his acquaintance. They were probably intended to deliver a 'wholesome shock' to people who Koestler assumed were all complacent, but they gave the impression of condescension and mistakenly exaggerated the ignorance of ordinary people. The newspaper's business manager objected to the 'erotic' reveries too. Only a few appeared and the experiment was not repeated.[21]

In October 1942 Koestler published in the *Observer* an interesting attempt to explain Hitler's political appeal. 'The Great Crank' marked the early fruits of his association with David Astor, who had editorial say over the centre pages of the paper from early 1942 and proceeded to bring in a string of new writers, many of them with European backgrounds, such as Isaac Deutscher, and others who were ex-Communists, such as John Strachey.[22]

The success of *Darkness at Noon* in the United States also led to openings in the American press, which was always to be a lucrative outlet. Foremost amongst these was the influential *New York Times*. In January 1943 the *New York Times* published his article 'Knights in Rusty Armour' based on notes he made in the summer of 1942 about the attitudes of British soldiery. He had observed the discontent created by wasteful and arrogant officers, an echo of the demoralisation he had witnessed in the French army, which he called 'browning off'. He also identified a pervasive anxiety about post-war employment prospects and an absence of any idea what the war was being fought for: the troops had no inkling of Dachau or Lidice and no positive values to motivate them. He explained to American readers that this defensive ideology made it crucial to formulate clear war aims with a social component.[23] The article, with its social democratic underpinning, also reflected his changing political outlook.

II

Koestler's political evolution was registered in the shifting constellation of his friendships. As soon as he was out of the army he lunched or dined or had drinks or some combination of the three with men and women friends almost every day. The list includes his old Left Book Club contacts Gollancz, Laski and Strachey; the Labour politicians Patrick Gordon Walker, Richard Crossman and George Russell Strauss, all of whom were engaged in war work, Michael

Foot and Eleanor Rathbone; journalists, writers and literary figures including Rebecca West, the editor John Lehmann, Rex Warner, Calder-Marshall and Lovat Dickson; Hungarian *émigrés* and exiles such as Michael Polanyi and Count Károlyi; Victor and Miriam Rothschild, and Guy de Rothschild; Paul Willert, who was stationed away from London with RAF Bomber Command, and a number of women apart from Daphne Hardy. Guy de Rothschild introduced Koestler to Isaiah Berlin, although he seemed rather overawed by Berlin and 'remained stubbornly silent' when they met for the first time.[24]

It is not clear when or how he met Crossman, but the contact may have been made via Willi Münzenberg or through the Political Warfare Executive. Crossman visited Germany many times in the 1930s and got to know Münzenberg. He even stayed in his Berlin flat in 1930–1. Anthony Howard, Crossman's biographer, suggests that Koestler had had a relationship with Zita Baker who became Crossman's partner in 1934 and his wife in 1937. However, it is hard to see quite how they could have come across one another before the war. Crossman had succeeded Michael Foot as a cub-writer at the *New Statesman* in 1937 and also knew Gollancz. Foot, who was pro-Republican Spain, pro-Zionist and pro-refugee, was associated with Ellen Wilkinson and was well aware of Koestler's activity on all these counts. Koestler met George Russell Strauss, the Jewish millionaire socialist MP who bankrolled *Tribune*, Nye Bevan and Patrick Gordon Walker as a result of his friendship with Foot.[25]

During 1942 he mixed frequently with the cohort of rising Labour left-wingers. His admiration for Bevan in particular grew after seeing him perform in the House of Commons: 'Aneurin brilliant . . . Isn't the victim of hootch', a rather cheeky observation in view of his own weakness for the bottle. These political friendships had important reciprocal effects. While he was in the army hospital in Gloucestershire and through his Army Education Corps lecturing, Koestler had encountered working-class Englishmen and learned something about their conditions of life prior to military service. He was shocked by the inadequacies of their education and the extent of the poverty, bad housing and poor working conditions to which they testified. His indignation was channelled by the left-wing Labourites, who helped to reshape his perception of social democracy. From being an ex-Communist he became 'a fervent Labour Party supporter, a fervent Social Democrat'.[26]

Koestler's political re-education was fostered by regular encounters and correspondence with Michael Polanyi. Polanyi was born in

Budapest in 1891 to a ferociously intellectual Jewish, middle-class family. He studied medicine but his passion was for science and he eventually taught chemistry at universities in Hungary and Germany. In 1933 he obtained a chair at Manchester University and migrated to England. As a youth he had been active in the Galileo Circle, a left-liberal and mainly Jewish discussion group in Budapest, and he returned to political thought in the 1940s. Polanyi was an early critic of the USSR and centralised control of the economy. He excoriated Marxism since it disguised Utopian, messianic aspirations as scientific fact.[27] If Koestler was vital to Foot and Crossman for inoculating their socialism against the Soviet bacillus, and helping to wean former Communists like Strachey and fellow travellers such as Laski off Communism, the influence of Polanyi on his own thought cannot be underestimated. 'Misi', as he was affectionately known, was a sounding board and a touchstone for Koestler.

Meanwhile his relationship with Daphne Hardy staggered on. In the spring of 1942, while she was in Oxford and Koestler in London, they attempted to meet each weekend, but it was an unequal arrangement. She complained: 'The problem of my being here and you in London with all its various difficulties is nagging at me non-stop, and I can't concentrate on my work, and I am getting quite hysterical.' She was unable to do any sculpting due to his demands on her free time. 'I am always expected to adapt myself to your working so I don't see why it shouldn't be the other way around for a change.' She sensed that he was slipping away from her: 'I can't help having a suspicion that you can't be bothered to try, because the present arrangement seems to you fairly satisfactory.' Although Koestler recommended Hardy to Crossman and others, no London job was forthcoming. Isolated in Oxford, aware that Koestler was living the high life in London and seeing other women, Hardy's letters became increasingly tetchy. She wished he would come to Oxford for a weekend in December 1942, but added: 'perhaps it would be better in imagination than it would be in reality; it would probably rain, and the room would be horrid, and we wouldn't find anywhere to eat, and we would quarrel because I would be in an unrelaxed state in which everything would seem wrong to me.'[28]

The unremitting work schedule, furious socialising and tension with Hardy took their toll on Koestler's health. In August he went to see Dr Egon Plesch, a fellow Hungarian, who treated him for a stomach complaint. Plesch instructed him to avoid alcohol, eat more moderately, rest before and after meals, and cut down on smoking. From this it is easy to deduce the kind of life-style Koestler had been leading. He continued to see doctors for several months and told Michael Polanyi that he was suffering from a duodenal ulcer.[29]

Exile life and letters also made claims on his time. He corresponded regularly with Weiczen/Valiani, who now petitioned for his assistance with the publication of a book on Italian philosophy. Despite exhausting battles with the exchange control authorities, Koestler used his American publisher to send him money. He complained to Erika Mann, in California, 'you see it drives me simply mad that some of my comrades who mean more to me than anything else urgently need my help, and I have the means to help, but no legal possibility.'[30]

Nor did Koestler forget his wife. When he reached Lisbon he had established contact with her mother, Elizabeth Ascher, who lived in London. She cabled him that Dorothea was destitute and living in Mirepoix, Ariège, in southern France and appealed to Koestler to do what he could to help her. He used the contacts he had made with the Unitarian relief network and Walter Lucas, but could only establish that Dorothea was apparently still in occupied France.[31] On 19 January 1941 Elizabeth Ascher received a plaintive cable from her daughter: 'Fatigue. Plus Argent. Ni Passport.' Using PEN in London and his US publisher Koestler sent money to Lisbon in anticipation of Dorothea's escape from France. But his plan to get her to Portugal and thence to the USA came to grief because it was discovered that, since their separation, his estranged wife was unable to travel on his documents. She lingered on in Marseilles, eking out a living in the employment of the American Aid Committee.[32]

His US publisher finally obtained a Cuban visa for her, a costly business paid for out of Koestler's American royalties. This got him into trouble with the Board of Trade when it was discovered through the postal censor that part of his US income was being used without being first repatriated and taxed. By early November 1941 Dorothea had the necessary papers and a passage booked on a ship from Marseilles, but shortly before she was due to leave she had a serious fall and broke several bones. For a number of weeks she was laid up and over subsequent months had to undergo two operations. She missed the boat and the visa expired. The whole exhausting process had to be started again.[33]

By the summer of 1942 stateless Jews such as Dorothea Koestler were being rounded up in France and deported to 'the East'. Koestler pleaded with Harold Nicolson to intercede with Osbert Peake MP, Parliamentary Private Secretary to Herbert Morrison, to get his wife a permit to enter the UK. Meanwhile, the Relief Committee of the

Friends Service Council and Eleanor Rathbone secured a transit visa
for Dorothea to go to Portugal. It was too late: in November the
Germans occupied the Free Zone and all chances of extricating
Dorothea faded.[34] Her plight brought Koestler face to face with the
Nazis' assault on Europe's Jews. For the next two years this was to
dominate his life.

III

At the end of the year Koestler and Hardy moved from Chelsea
Cloisters into a cosy terraced house in Tryon Street, a quiet, narrow
passage running off the King's Road. Here he continued to work on
his third novel, *Arrival and Departure*, which since the previous
summer had been written increasingly under the influence of news
emanating from Europe about the extermination of the Jews. The
details about the 'Final Solution' which reached London in the
summer of 1942 affected him dramatically. In June and July 1942 the
Bund, the Jewish socialist party of Poland, and the World Jewish
Congress, publicised reports that the Jews in Poland were being
murdered *en masse* by means of poison gas at specially constructed
death camps. In August 1942 survivors of the exterminations at
Chelmno, in Poland, sent graphic eyewitness reports to the West
detailing the use of gas vans in the mass killing. Koestler kept a thick
file of press clippings on the fate of the Jews in Nazi-occupied
Europe. He attended one of the first public protests against the Nazi
atrocities, a mass meeting organised by the Labour Party at Caxton
Hall on 2 September 1942.[35] The reports, especially those of
August–September 1942, were incorporated almost verbatim into
the novel.

In November he met Jan Karski (Kowielski), a member of the
Polish underground who had been asked by the Jewish leadership of
the Warsaw ghetto to report to the Government-in-Exile on the
plight of Jews in the ghetto and the mass murders at Belzec
extermination camp. Once Karski reached the West he tried to alert
governments and opinion formers to the fate of the Jews in Poland.
Whereas some writers whom he met in England, such as H. G.
Wells, were sceptical or hostile, Koestler believed him at once. Over
thirty years later he recalled Karski as 'a very modest, unassuming,
very tall, rather aristocratic Pole'. For his part the visitor was
intimidated when they first met and suspected that Koestler 'had
access to Military Intelligence'. Indeed, Koestler had been asked by
MI5 to 'vet his reliability', but found him 'quite convincing'.[36]

He introduced Karski to Gollancz and Rathbone, who were equally impressed. Rathbone later told Koestler that 'the BBC were anxious to broadcast an account of those horrors, mainly to Germany and the Balkan countries'. As Karski had by this time left for America on the second stage of his mission, Koestler sent the BBC European Service 'a draft protocol' based on his story. It was a frightful assignment: Koestler was afraid that the audience would simply not appreciate what it was hearing. He told a correspondent: 'I tried to make out a proper script, but it just doesn't come off. I have done too much of this sort of thing, and I am paralysed by the feeling that the facts are so horrible that nobody will believe them.' When *Jewish Massacre* was transmitted in June 1943 it was ascribed to Karski, but was essentially written by Koestler. He also read it over the air, his accent lending the text even greater authenticity. In fact, Karski's report bore little relation to the actual killing process at Belzec, which he had not witnessed personally. The account which Koestler published in *Horizon* and *Arrival and Departure* was much closer to the truth, as it was known at the time. This was based more on information provided by the Bund and the World Jewish Congress than Karski's recollections.[37]

Throughout 1943 informants fed Koestler details about events in occupied Europe. In July he attended a meeting organised in London by Polish Jews to commemorate the Warsaw ghetto uprising. He contributed to a broadcast about the uprising which was used by several of the BBC overseas services. He also lent his name to Rathbone's National Committee for Rescue from Nazi Terror.[38] He suggested to Herman Ould, the chairman of PEN in London, that it run a series of meetings with eyewitnesses to the persecutions in Europe, but the project foundered. He also hatched another rescue scheme for Jewish refugees, which he presented to several refugee agencies. This time he proposed that the British and the United Nations should approach the Germans to allow women and children out, grant them travel documents and provide facilities for them, in exchange for detained German civilians. Sadly, the plan did not get very far. Individual Jews might come up with ingenious, even practical rescue plans such as these, but the Allied governments obdurately refused to take them seriously.[39]

IV

The text of the novel *Arrival and Departure* absorbed another extraordinary wartime episode: the story of Richard Hillary. Hillary was an Australian-born Royal Air Force pilot whose 1942 book *The Last Enemy* won instant success as the voice of 'The Few', the small band of young RAF fighter pilots who at a fearful cost kept the *Luftwaffe* at bay during the summer of 1940 and thereby helped stave off a German invasion. Hillary's editor at Macmillan, Lovat Dickson, introduced him to Koestler in the hope that he could assist the young airman's literary development.[40]

The two men had a lot in common despite the differences in age and background. Before the war Hillary had spent several weeks in Budapest. Like Koestler he had experienced the 'oceanic feeling' after he was shot down in a dogfight over the English Channel in September 1940. The proximity of death administered a 'psychological shock' to his belief system too. It caused Hillary to question his motives for fighting and to challenge his rationalistic, egocentric personal philosophy. *The Last Enemy* charts his conversion to a belief in the war as a 'crusade for humanity' against 'Evil'. Whereas he once approached life and death in a spirit of wry detachment, he now accepted the limits of rationality and drifted into a quasi-mystical acceptance of his fate. During 1942 Koestler got to know his young friend intimately, perhaps uncomfortably so. Hillary supplied the character of Andrew in *Arrival and Departure*, the scarred and psychologically tortured fighter pilot. Like Hillary the novel's hero comes to see himself as the herald of a new, undefined ideology and a new kind of man.[41]

Despite his appalling injuries Hillary insisted on returning to active service. He was killed on 8 January 1943 when the plane he was flying on a night-time exercise was involved in an accident. Lovat Dickson proposed a commemorative volume and brought Koestler together with Eric Linklater, the writer and journalist, and Phyllis Bottome, the Adlerian psychoanalytical writer, who had both known Hillary. Koestler was also invited to join members of the Hillary family, Lovat Dickson and Linklater on a management committee to run a trust in his memory. Koestler attended a couple of its meetings and offered many practical suggestions before losing interest in it. The memorial volume was one of the trust's projects, but Koestler preferred to publish his tribute as 'The Birth of a Myth' in *Horizon* in April 1943.[42]

It was built around the letters which Hillary wrote to Koestler and to other friends, but it was more than a tribute to one pilot. It delved into the question of why young men fight wars even when they lose their faith in the cause, or any cause. The correspondence was a record of Hillary's tortured search for a reason to die, since he knew that his life chances were slight once he returned to combat. Young men of Hillary's generation – he was twenty-three when he was killed – distrusted the 'big words and slogans'. After the betrayals of the 1930s – appeasement, Spain, Munich and the alliance between the democracies and totalitarian Russia – they winced at the mention of patriotism, glory or 'making the world safe for democracy'. Hillary could find no rationale; he only had an 'instinct' or gut feeling that it was the right thing to do. At best he fought out of a sense of 'fellowship' with his comrades in arms.[43]

Yet Hillary wanted a better explanation than that and continued to search for it in *The Last Enemy* and in his letters. Koestler concluded that he was driven by a nostalgia for an era of certainty; he personified the *mal du siècle* which had infected several generations since 1900. Men like Hillary, and by extension Koestler, were 'in search of a redeeming emotion; of a credo, neither sentimental, vulgar nor archaic, whose words one could say without embarrassment or shame. When all isms became meaningless and the world an alley of crooked query marks, then indeed a man's longing for the Holy Grail may become so strong that he flies like a moth into the flame.'[44]

Koestler's identification with Hillary is emphasised when he discusses the young man as a writer. Although his promise was unfulfilled he represented the new breed of author whose work would supplant the tired 'bourgeois novel'. This new type was typically an airman, revolutionary or adventurer: 'men who live the dangerous life; with a new operative technique of observation, a curious alfresco introspection and an even more curious trend of contemplation, even mysticism, born in the dead centre of the hurricane.' Men like Malraux, who had experienced life in its tragic and its trivial modes and saw that art was produced at their point of intersection. Men like Arthur Koestler. Koestler's description of Hillary can equally be applied to himself: he was 'sick with nostalgia of something to fight for, which as yet is not. It is the myth of the crusader without a cross, and of desperate crusaders in search of a cross.' The new cause, possibly a new religion, had still to make itself known. The end of *Arrival and Departure* makes exactly the same point.[45]

For all the debunking, Hillary paradoxically achieved his apotheosis in Koestler's essay and subsequent novel. The piece certainly struck a chord with *Horizon* readers who voted it their favourite article in 1943. It is equally curious that Koestler declined to write much about his actual relationship with Hillary or draw further on their exchange of letters. Koestler seems to have been uneasy about the degree of

emotional proximity between them. When declining to write anything more personal he explained to Hillary's father, 'the role of the
father confessor ['and wonder rabbi', crossed out] for young officers
would not be fitting'. This reticence seems more a product of his
insecurities as a Jew and a foreigner than the result of solicitude for
Hillary, who was never less than frank in his published and unpublished writing.[46]

After finishing 'The Birth of a Myth' Koestler set out on a ten-day
army lecture tour. He found these excursions tiring but informative.
He 'went around the most God-forsaken units. Anti-aircraft
companies in the Thames Estuary . . . Mobile laundry units and so
on.' Through them, he recalled in 1974, 'I got a real feel for the
English working classes'. He also had to spend some time writing
propaganda leaflets for the Political Warfare Executive, possibly at
the invitation of Richard Crossman.[47]

When he returned to Tryon Street he put the finishing touches to
Arrival and Departure. By mid-April 1943 the first draft was completed
and three months later the novel was dispatched to the publisher.
Koestler then moved on to researching and writing several substantial
and hugely influential essays. 'The French Flu', which appeared in
Tribune in November 1943, was a swingeing attack on English
writers who indulged in uncritical adulation of their Gallic counterparts. It was prompted by a special issue of *Horizon* inspired by
Connolly's nostalgia for all things French (mainly pre-war cuisine).
Koestler penetrated beyond this jejune infatuation to expose the
dodgy ethical message of three pillars of contemporary French letters:
Gide, Louis Aragon and Vercors. Gide's crime was a certain
effeteness, but his sin was that he had been a fellow traveller and
approved of Aragon, a paid-up Party member. Vercors, a hero of the
resistance, got a pasting for more mysterious reasons. Koestler found
the plot of his underground novel unlikely and compared the punishment of a 'decent' German, which it depicted, with the imprisonment of German anti-Fascists in 1939 and 1940. This is a curious
reading of the novel, to say the least, and may have been motivated
by the desire *pour épater L'Horizon* since it was one of Connolly's
choices for the magazine the previous month.[48]

In 'The Fraternity of Pessimists', published in the *New York Times
Magazine* in November 1943, he extrapolated from some of the
themes in his essay on Hillary and in *Arrival and Departure*. To the
question 'Why fight the war?' he answered famously: 'we are
fighting against a total lie in the name of a half truth.' He could give
reasons for defeating Hitler: Nazism had to be extirpated because 'by

proclaiming that might is right it reduces Civil Law to the Law of the Jungle, and by proclaiming that race is all reduces Sociology to Zoology'. But it was harder to identify the rationale for defending capitalism and liberal democracy which had performed so miserably in the 1930s. What else was there? Koestler complained that the 'horizontal' bonds that knitted mankind into national and inter-national associations with unifying ideologies had collapsed, and until new structures were evolved there would be no cause for which to fight. Change might only come as a result of 'an irresistible global mood, a spring-tide like early Christianity or the Renaissance', a new era that would supplant the spiritually desiccated age of reason, ascend to a 'higher historical level' and 're-establish the disturbed balance between rational and spiritual values'. In the absence of this messianic gear-shift he concluded by identifying with the 'short-term pessimists' who despaired at current events but saw a glimmer of hope: 'They will not aim at immediate radical solutions, because they know that their own instruments are polluted. They will watch with open eyes and without sectarian blinkers, for the first signs of the new horizontal movement' and create 'oases' in the desert of the 'interregnum'.[49]

Koestler's essay chimed with the confusion of ex-Communists and disillusioned idealists who knew what they were against but not what they were for. Yet it was a peculiar analysis. The reasons he gave for defeating Nazism were idiosyncratic: few men went to war to defend 'civil law', let alone sociology. By contrast he omitted the obvious point that the Nazis were a criminal regime conducting genocide. It seems as if he deliberately wanted to blur the positive reasons for fighting by showing that no side had a monopoly of right. As to the future, he is vague about which social group will regenerate society or which countries will take the lead. At one point he even speculates that it will be Britain since, in an era in which societies were careering out of control, without 'ethical brakes', a slow moving, conservative country had many advantages. A *less* likely place for a renaissance based on a harmonious interaction between 'rational and spiritual values' would have been hard to find.

During the late spring and summer he also embarked on his investigation of the intelligentsia that would appear as an essay in *Horizon* in March 1944. And he worked on the follow-up to 'The Yogi and The Commissar', a major enquiry into the history and politics of the USSR which required extensive research. For this he relied on a number of helpers who read Russian or were familiar with Soviet politics, including the exiled Polish-Jewish socialist

Lucjan Blit.[50] In the course of this work Koestler refined his political philosophy. But, although his social and political writing was full of excellent analysis and critique, it was short on detail or positive policy. There is a sense of desperation about the current state of the world and a frustrating inability to see a way to improve it. The source of that desperation was not hard to detect. For a Jew, the world had become a threatening, alien place.

In October *Horizon* published 'Mixed Transport', the chapter of *Arrival and Departure* that incorporated a description of the mass murder of Jews in Poland. It sharply divided opinion. The well-informed Lucjan Blit told Koestler that 'Few words either spoken or written are still capable of moving me. But what you wrote moved me deeply.' Phyllis Bottome said, 'I am very glad you are writing this. We forget if we are not nailed to it. That Europe is a torture chamber a few miles away! This will nail us. I also think it will decrease anti-Semitism except among the few determinedly mad.' However, several correspondents to *Horizon*, including Alex Comfort and Osbert Sitwell, protested that the story was atrocity propaganda. Sitwell wrote indignantly, 'Is that rigmarole of Koestler's intended as fact or fiction?' He prophesied that in ten years' time such information would be revealed as no more accurate than the lies manufactured to blacken the Germans in the First World War.[51]

Koestler was stung into a reply. He demanded to know why members of the intelligentsia who would never dream of challenging a controversial statement about a literary subject happily questioned something as grave as the mass murder of Jews. 'There is no excuse for you – for it is your duty to know and to be haunted by your knowledge. As long as you don't feel, against reason and independently of reason, ashamed to be alive while others are put to death; not guilty, sick, humiliated because you were spared, you will remain what you are, an accomplice by omission.' Connolly was unhappy with this tirade. Peter Watson, the magazine's backer and manager, passed on the marked proofs of Koestler's letter with the message that Connolly 'wants to know if you could tone it down a bit as it presupposes that every 'doubter' is a culture snob which is not necessarily true. This of course does not excuse the incredulity shown.'[52]

However, Koestler did not let matters rest there. He wrote a blistering article, 'On Disbelieving Atrocities', for the *New York Times Magazine* in January 1944. It was a remarkably perceptive explanation of why people found it possible and necessary to deny horrifying evidence. He repeated the famous observation, first made in 'Mixed Transport', that 'Statistics don't bleed': lacklustre imagination compounded by time, physical distance and sheer numbers dull the knowledge of terrible things. And he confessed that 'all this is becoming a mania with me'. He sent the article to Connolly and told him that if he thought it was convincing he should pass it on to Osbert Sitwell, whom it might do some good.[53]

V

Arrival and Departure appeared in November 1943. If *Darkness at Noon* fictionalised Koestler's experiences from 1932 to 1938, the new novel was powered by his continuing odyssey from 1938 to 1942, especially his spell in North Africa and Portugal, and his vacillation over whether to go to the USA or to Britain. The central character, Peter Slavek, is a hero of the anti-Fascist resistance from a country 'somewhere between the Danube and the Balkans'. Many years later Koestler revealed that he was loosely modelled on the Hungarian poet Endre Havas, whom Koestler knew in wartime London. However, there was a lot of Koestler, too, in the guise of Peter Slavek.[54]

At the start of the novel Slavek has escaped from occupied Europe to 'Neutralia', a barely disguised Portugal. Like Koestler, for weeks he is prevented from reaching England to enlist in the army. In the interim he has an affair with a vacuous girl called Odette who represents the temptations of hedonism. But when he tries to follow her to America his leg becomes paralysed. He is rescued by Dr Sonia Bolger, a psychoanalyst. Bolger mocks his heroism, attributing his urge to save the world to an unconscious desire to make amends for childhood transgressions. In the course of analysing him back to health she proves that real and imagined guilt feelings, rather than convictions, are what drive him. Each incident of betrayal she uncovers echoes a guilt-producing act in Koestler's life. Slavek, too, learns that his revolutionary slogans engender death and destruction in the real world.[55]

Some critics have noted that *Arrival and Departure* is full of Christian imagery. Indeed, there is a sense in which all Koestlerian heroes – Spartacus, Rubashov, Slavek – are Christ-figures who must die to redeem mankind. However, Jewish themes are almost as prevalent in this as in his other novels. Slavek suffers from guilt for the childhood offence of mistakenly eating his pet rabbit called 'Jerusalem'. The traumatic incident is revealed by a dream in which he hears the words, 'If I forget thee O Jerusalem, may my right hand forget her cunning.' Slavek is acutely conscious of the special predicament of the Jews.

Amongst the first people he meets in Neutralia are elderly Jewish refugees. He is tormented by the fate of the 'Useless Jews' from the mixed transport whom he saw killed in gas vans.[56]

Koestler endows Slavek with a sensibility appropriate to a Jew. He is momentarily shaken by a Nazi agent who attempts to win him over to the Third Reich, until the agent defends Nazi biological politics: 'We have started to breed a new species of homo sapiens. We are weeding out its streaks of bad heredity.' The Jews, the Gypsies, the insane were being liquidated: 'we are turning the whole Continent into a biological laboratory.'[57] Few other commentators had dissected the modernist and the reactionary elements of the Nazi dystopia with such acuity. Koestler's Jewishness gave him a vantage point from which to make sense of the Nazi enterprise that set him apart from any other novelist writing in England during the war.

It is only after meeting a disfigured British airman, based on Hillary, that Slavek finally decides not to go to America. Thanks to this encounter he realises that he is fated to be a 'crusader without a cross'. Psychoanalysis might reveal that the well-springs of action lie in childhood, but it made no difference.[58] Indeed, the novel offers no clear reason for Slavek's return to the fray. Before he sets off on a lethal mission into occupied Europe he explains to Odette: 'Already the philosophies and great political movements of the last centuries are irretrievably buried under the wreckage. All attempts to revive them are futile. And salvation will not come by an improved laboratory formula. The age of quantitative measurements is drawing to a close.' What will replace them? 'I think a new god is about to be born. . . . Don't try to divine his message or the form of his cult – this will be after our time. The mystics of today are as trite as the political reformers. For we are the last descendants of Renaissance-Man, the end and not the beginning . . .' As he parachutes into enemy territory he has no motives or aspirations other than the hope that his gesture will hasten 'that event'.[59]

George Orwell put his finger on the problem with this novel in an essay on Koestler written in September 1944. Koestler's experiences in the USSR and the Communist Party had resulted in a conviction that revolution is inexorably violent and destructive, with only a chance of redemptive success for the survivors. His encounters with ordinary folk, recorded in *Scum of the Earth*, had destroyed any faith he had in the spontaneous goodwill and good sense of the people. By the time of *Arrival and Departure* Koestler had moved to an 'anti-revolutionary' position. The novel was really a 'tract purporting to show that revolutionary creeds are rationalisations of neurotic impulses'. Orwell retorted: well, so what, as long as the neurotic is on the right side in the struggle to save humanity. All the same, he is bothered that someone with Koestler's knowledge of Europe is unable to find plenty of reasons, negative as well as positive, for wishing to scourge Nazism. He attributes Koestler's inability to find positive reasons to his lack of any vision for the future. 'To take a rational political decision one must have a picture of the future. At present Koestler seems to have none.' His dream of Utopia is cancelled out by the ugly realities of attempts to make the revolution. Orwell chided Koestler for the 'quasi-mystical' outlook to which he was consequently driven. It resulted from 'the very great difficulty, once one had abandoned orthodox religious belief, of accepting life on earth as inherently miserable, and on the other hand, from the realization that to make life liveable is a much bigger problem than it recently seemed'. Koestler wanted happiness for himself and mankind; he wanted perfection in an earthly paradise. But, Orwell admonished, the real choice is not between Utopia and totalitarianism, but between lesser evils. The aim of socialism, 'is not to make the world perfect but to make it better. All revolutions are failures, but they are not all the same failure.'[60]

Orwell used his review to issue a caveat to revolution: politics cannot deliver human happiness. All attempts to do so since 1789 had, in fact, led to misery. Such an impossible goal would lead to disillusionment and ultimately a reactionary posture. But Koestler took Orwell's gentle chiding that he was in thrall to 'hedonism' as a critique of his life-style. This stung him: he returned to it over and over in later years. Why should he be an ascetic like Orwell? What was wrong with wanting some fun in life? His 1944 play, *Twilight Bar*, a rewritten version of *Bar du Soleil*, was an implicit riposte to Orwell. In it, the world is threatened with destruction by aliens because there is so much unhappiness. It can be saved only by hedonists, who understand that life can only be justified if everyone has a good time.[61]

Most other reviewers were more positive, even though the book did not enjoy the success of its precursor. The *Times Literary Supplement* called it a 'striving, impassioned and at times profound novel' although it was also a 'difficult and imperfectly resolved fable'. Michael Foot, in the *Evening Standard*, dubbed Koestler 'the greatest foreign novelist since Joseph Conrad paid us the compliment of writing in the English tongue'. The young Saul Bellow raved about it in the *New York Times Book Review*. 'Whatever single criticisms may be made of him, Arthur Koestler is one of the very few living novelists who attacks the most difficult and troubling issues of private and political morality, and who, having voiced serious questions, never tries to satisfy the reader with ready made evasions.' The *New Yorker* declared that 'The war has thrown up one first-class imaginative writer . . . Koestler has a vision deeper than that of any other writer.' Storm Jameson told Koestler it was the best novel she had read since *Darkness at Noon*. 'If my small store of novels worth keeping has to be reduced to two, it will be these two,' she wrote to him. Paul Rotha, the film-maker, gushed: 'Jesus, what difficult ground you are treading on, and how much I admire your courage in so doing. From book to book you progress further in searching out the key to the tangle of the individual.'[62]

VI

Between February and June 1944 Koestler laboured over a sequel to *Arrival and Departure*, although his notebooks show that he was rarely able to work for more than three or four days in a row. In April he devoted only five days to the new novel. This was partly due to political and social distractions, but also because he was carrying on research for the follow-up to 'The Yogi and The Commissar' and writing other essays. A further reason may have been that the material was simply too difficult. 'Arrival and Departure II' is rooted in the 'Final Solution' and revolves around the failure of the Allies to rescue Jews from the Nazi genocide.

It opens with Peter Slavek landing by parachute in an unidentified Central European country in occupied Europe. He makes a rendezvous with a priest, Father Zlatko, who is in the underground. Zlatko also happens to be hiding two Jewish children, Rachel and Davidka, who were placed in his charge by a Jewish merchant during one of the round-ups. Through them, Slavek learns more about the Nazi occupation, the isolation of the Jews (the 'cursed race') and the deportations to the death camps. In the pages of the manuscript which cover this material the reader is given a precise description of how the Nazi policies of dispossession and ghettoisation were enforced and how the Jews, afflicted with the 'smell of doom', reacted.[63]

After accomplishing his mission to destroy a military target, Slavek returns to England (dubbed 'Lotusland'). Brushing aside the congratulations heaped on him by his commanding officer, 'Major Apple', Slavek asks to be allowed to organise a rescue mission to save the two Jewish children and also set up an escape route to help more

Jews flee. Slavek's plan is to use the same route by which he made his escape, then send the Jews on to America or Palestine. The Major is 'vexed' by this notion. His response reads like a verbatim report of actual Jewish delegations to the Foreign Office at this very time: ' "but my dear fellow", the Major began to look really alarmed. "Surely you must see that this has nothing to do with us. I respect your feelings and all that but surely you can't expect the Service to turn into an organisation of masses. There are millions and millions of cases like those few . . . if we started using our limited and precarious channels for philanthropic purposes . . . after all, we have a war on our hands." ' Slavek is sent 'on leave'. On one draft Koestler scribbled: 'They don't believe in atrocities – last war – Belgium.' This is clearly a reference to Sitwell's abuse.[64]

In notes for the unfinished novel Koestler proposed that Slavek go on a wild goose chase through Whitehall in pursuit of a rescue mission, while Rachel escapes – only to die when one of the boats carrying 'illegal' Jewish immigrants to Palestine sinks *en route*.[65] The connection with actual events and Koestler's own experiences could not be closer: these passages were written between 11 May and 8 June 1944, when Koestler was enmeshed in the real-life drama surrounding the deportation of Hungarian Jews to Auschwitz and the frustration of rescue plans put to the Allies by Jewish bodies.

Perhaps because it was so painful to reflect on the futility of rescue efforts Koestler found it easier to address general political and ideological problems. Essays on these themes rolled off his typewriter. In March 1944 he published 'The Intelligentsia' in *Horizon*. Here he set out to explain where the 'independent thinking' stratum of society came from, what its function and its limitations were. In effect, he applied to intellectuals the same analysis he had used on revolutionaries in *Arrival and Departure*. Independent thinking was the product of social and psychological frustration. All intellectuals were prone to neurosis because 'To think and behave independently puts one automatically into opposition to the majority whose thinking and behaviour is dependent on traditional patterns: and to belong to a minority is in itself a neurosis forming situation.' By virtue of being detached observers, commentators, critics or dissidents, intellectuals are burdened with guilt feelings: 'there never was an intelligentsia without a guilt complex.' Finally, he speculated on the fate of the intelligentsia once the collapse of the 'revolutionary movement' had deprived it of its historical partner. Its residual task was 'to save *some* of the values of democracy and humanism or to lose them all; and to prevent this happening one has to cling more than

ever to the ragged banner of "independent thinking" '.[66] This modest
conclusion confounds Orwell's suggestion that Koestler was totally
incapable of appreciating meliorative strategies in politics.

In 'The Reader's Dilemma', which appeared in *Tribune* in April
1944, he addressed himself to a related problem: 'the tragic barrier
which separate the progressive intelligentsia from the educated
working-class'. The article was an imaginary response to a letter from
a soldier asking for advice about which reviews to read and which
reviewers to trust. Koestler drew on his Army Education lecturing to
construct a member of a typical audience: 'the reliable and serious
reader', a man who left school aged sixteen, had left-wing politics
and aspired to better himself culturally. Such people were alienated
by the tone of highbrow writing and frustrated by its closed circle of
allusion and reference. Koestler urged the 'reader' not to hate the
intelligentsia: all that separated him from them was duration of
education, which was itself a function of wealth and a result of the
class society. Writers should not write down to the 'masses' in order
to communicate, but instead try to create a more egalitarian society.
'But that is a political, not a literary task. It is, I believe, the main and
ultimate task of socialism.'

VII

In April 1943 Koestler struck up a friendship with Olaf Stapledon,
the author of several pioneering science-fiction books that, although
they seem unbearably turgid today, were acclaimed when they first
appeared. Reviewers often bracketed him with H. G. Wells, who
admired his work. Stapledon was essentially a late-Victorian writer
haunted by the 'death of God' and man's consequent loneliness in a
vast, causeless and meaningless cosmos. In his fiction Stapledon
envisaged two options for mankind: either becoming god-like and
creating paradise on earth (or other planets) or capitulating to despair
and descending into an orgy of hedonism resulting in madness and
self-destruction. In books such as *Last and First Men* (1930), which
attracted great attention and launched him as a professional writer,
Odd John (1935) and *The Starmaker* (1937) he suggested that man
could attain an harmonious existence by merging individual
personality into the life of the community at a psychic level. This
notion was informed in equal parts by mysticism and by a crude
understanding of Communism.[67]

Stapledon saw man as divided between higher and base instincts and
framed his political thought within this conception of human nature.

His analysis was reflected in the title of his personal manifesto *Saints and Revolutionaries* (1939). The saint 'feels that unless he first learns to know himself in relation to the universe or in relation to what he calls his God, and unless he thereby gains self-mastery, he can neither know what is truly desirable nor have the strength to live in service of his fellows'. The revolutionary 'feels that to worry about his own soul is selfish . . . he seeks to understand society . . . in order that . . . he may be an effective instrument of the historical forces which, he believes, are pressing towards a far-reaching social change.'[68]

There are evidently very strong, and until now unrecognised, echoes of Stapeldon's ideas in Koestler's polarity between the Yogi and the Commissar. Stapledon, too, rejected the 'crude materialism' of science which promised to answer the riddles of existence. Instead he proposed that man strive towards an 'ecstasy of acceptance' – rather like Koestler's 'oceanic feeling' – through which mankind could become reconciled to its fate and cease striving futilely, and destructively, to overcome it. He certainly saw an analogue between his dichotomy in *Saints and Revolutionaries* and Koestler's dyad of yogis and commissars. The fact that they met frequently during 1943–4 increases the suspicion that Stapledon had a substantial impact on Koestler. Stapledon provides an unnoticed link in the chain of influences that led to *The Yogi and The Commissar*, as well as Koestler's post-war efforts to reconcile psychology and the biological sciences with politics.[69]

During the autumn of 1943 Stapledon proposed that they collaborate on a volume to be edited by Raymond Postgate, an ex-editor of *Tribune*, that would set out an agenda for a post-war politics. At one point it seemed as if John Strachey would join the project, but it collapsed for want of a publisher. They also explored the possibility of an anthology of science-fiction writing, but it too was stillborn. Koestler went on seeing Stapledon for another year and read several of his books. Eventually he seems to have tired of him as a crank, but his writing around this time and later bears unmistakable traces of Stapledon's thinking.[70]

VIII

Throughout May and June 1944 Koestler collected more material for 'The Yogi and The Commissar Part 2'. He instructed Margaret Dewar, his chief researcher, that he intended to write 'merely a well documented essay of 10–15,000 words, in which facts should merely serve as the illustration for what I believe to be the general trend away from socialism in the USSR. But the few facts and quotes must of course be waterproof.'[71] He made little solid progress with the project until the late summer. The war in Europe and the war within himself left him no peace of mind. Notwithstanding his doctor's orders, and more medical tests for his stomach pains early in 1943, he continued to combine a frenetic social life with political and literary figures by night and hard pounding at the typewriter by day. Among those he saw most regularly were his literary agent A. D. Peters, Connolly, Crossman, Gordon Walker, Laski, Gollancz, Kingsley Martin, E. M. Forster, Kenneth Clark, Storm Jameson, Alexander Korda, Miriam Rothschild and Chaim Weizmann.[72]

His relationships followed a depressingly familiar pattern. Evenings spent over drinks or a dinner with friends routinely culminated in booze-fuelled arguments. Evidence of an exception proving the rule is a letter he wrote to Strachey in January 1943: 'what fun to spend a whole evening in wise talk without quarrelling.' Although *Horizon* published some of his best work in 1943–4, Koestler's relations with Connolly deteriorated and he became openly critical of the way the magazine was directed. Connolly protested: 'There is no doubt that we are very necessary to each other at least you are to me and not as a catalyst but as an oxygen tent.' Despite his gratitude to Connolly, once Koestler was established as a writer he paid less heed to his erstwhile mentor.[73]

In the first half of 1944 London life acquired a particular weariness. The 'Little Blitz' of February–March 1944 reintroduced an element of precariousness into everyday existence, but without the leavening provided in 1940–1 by the sense of heroic isolation. People were exhausted, nervy and unwilling to accept danger now that the end of the war was in sight. On 6 March the windows of Koestler's house were blown out. 'While raids last', he later wrote, 'moderately scared; in between almost looking forward to it – like a drug. And even while it lasts fear so repressed that after effect stronger than co-effect – fear only conscious during dive of a plane and of bomb.'[74]

Koestler's disenchantment was mirrored by increasingly frenzied, ill-tempered socialising and an inability to work. The two, as ever, interacted viciously with one another. He became an *habitué* of several well-known clubs, including the Frisco, Cloisters and the Gargoyle. He lunched and dined regularly with Crossman, Connolly, the Willerts, the publisher Hamish Hamilton and David Astor, along with their lovers, mistresses and wives.[75]

He had numerous women friends. Almost as soon as he was out of the army Koestler began sleeping around. Despite the progressive advice on technique that he dished out in the encyclopaedias of sex, Koestler's sexual politics (and practices) were of their time. To him, heterosexuality was the norm, men were dominant partners and women were submissive. He ascribed feelings of 'physical repulsion' to Slavek when he discovered that Sonia Bolgar and Odette were lovers and characterised the sexually aggressive Bolgar as an 'Amazon' and a 'carnivorous flower'. Her thighs reminded Slavek of 'insect-eating flowers which close over their victims to stun and devour them'.[76]

He treated marriage as a farce and argued that anyone with an ounce of psychological knowledge would never insist on such a convention, although there must be a suspicion that this advanced, 'radical' attitude was really the justification for a predatory attitude towards women.[77] In *Arrival and Departure* Slavek's seduction of Odette veers into nothing less than rape, but she is forgiving and even titillated by the assault. Mocking Slavek's romantic ardour she comments that 'love-making is only rape by mutual consent'.[78] Too often Koestler did not confine such violent and bizarre ideas to the pages of his novels.

Some of the women Koestler slept with were gushing debs enamoured of the European intellectual and man of the world. One, known only as Annette, sent him the following note: 'I woke up this morning with an acute feeling of loss and emptiness, for a moment I couldn't think why? and then I remembered that you were the reason and I felt very miserable.' She was 'besotted' and felt it a privilege to share 'a little of your life and thoughts'. She was glad to give him 'pity' after all he'd endured in his life. Koestler had evidently worked hard on this conquest: 'I long to admit that one side of me, in the usual illogical female way, sees the force of your argument in persuading me to see you again.'[79]

Others were less pliant. Marie, a friend of Daphne Hardy, left a scorching note after a one-night stand that sounds more like date rape:

Perhaps I should have written earlier to thank you for the splendid opportunity you gave me of knowing the kind of person you really are. May I say that I was not impressed but hope I gave good value for the meal I so unsuspectingly accepted. Certainly the price paid for being such a fool was very high, but not being accustomed to the ways of such brilliant foreign gentlemen as yourself it never dawned on me that your invitation to your flat to rest and have tea was anything but genuine and disinterested. Perhaps your intellec-

tual acrobatics were sufficient compensation to other women for
such poor treatment, but for myself I am much more impressed by
those stupid unintelligent men and women who with their flesh
and blood keep the Nazis from you, and who make the sacrifice,
so that you can have the women, drink etcetera so essential for
your great brain. . . . I doubt if anything on earth could shatter
your conceit and self-importance, so I won't waste any more
paper.[80]

During 1943–4 Koestler frequently saw Miriam Rothschild to
discuss science and Jewish issues. Her father, Charles Rothschild, had
married Roszika von Wertheimstein, who came from an aristocratic
Hungarian-Jewish family. She had been educated as a zoologist, but
during the war worked at the cypher station at Bletchley Park.
Miriam Rothschild was unconventional, brilliant and vivacious and
they got on well. It was, she recalled, 'a very platonic friendship. He
liked my writing.' Their exchanges commingled science with a
cerebral eroticism. She wrote to him in June 1943, while she was
unwell, 'Even in my feverish state I am fully aware that physio-
logically speaking it is not possible to generalize from bird to man.
Nevertheless I am rash enough to compare some aspects of their
behaviour. Thus it appears to me that sea-gulls a) deliberately *tease*
one another b) derive some sort of satisfaction from doing so.' She
ruminated on the 'symbolic display of dominance' among such birds.
In the same letter she noted that she had seen foxgloves on her way
home from the train station: 'phallic emblems I suppose'.[81]

Koestler's circle expanded and contracted rapidly. He met Graham
Greene at a dinner with David Cecil and Rose Macaulay, and discussed Catholicism with him at a follow-up lunch some weeks later.
On Greene he pronounced, 'His Catholicism is with lots of grani
salis.' But he made use of Greene's Catholic contacts for researching
his novel and communicated with Father d'Arcy, Greene's grey
eminence. He also met Isaiah Berlin, whom he deemed 'rather
unpleasant, oily'. The antagonism was mutual. According to Miriam
Rothschild, Berlin regarded Koestler as merely 'iconoclastic, almost
a nihilist'. Koestler was painfully aware that he lacked Berlin's
humour, charm and repartee. Later their respective attitude towards
Jewishness would emerge as a more profound cleavage.[82]

Even his closest friendships were increasingly bedevilled by alcohol
and fractiousness. He dined and quarrelled with Egon Plesch, who
pointed out that Koestler was getting dependent on drink, which was
causing him a renewed bout of stomach trouble. One day, lunch

with Paul Willert at the Ritz was followed by drinks with Plesch and other friends and 'in the end Bordeaux-like nervous breakdown'. He even managed to quarrel with the usually imperturbable A. D. Peters, his literary agent. An evening in Leatherhead with Beaverbrook turned into a drunken, although enjoyable, rampage. A dinner with Astor necessitated the subsequent pledge that in future 'I will do my best to behave myself'. He wrote to Lovat Dickson after a night out together, 'I hope the slight contretemps at the Gargoyle did not cause you too much distress.' It was followed a week later by an evening with the Crossmans and 'unpleasantness with Sonia [Brownell]'. The following day he was chez Lady Rumbold, 'but was so depressed broke up whole evening'. At the end of May he met Hemingway at a party which he tersely summed up as 'drunkenness, row, unpleasant'.[83]

Political allegiances as well as friendships fluctuated. Koestler became troubled by the insouciance of the British Left towards Russia while the Red Army was occupying tracts of East Central Europe. Gollancz, he noted, 'Sees Russian danger clearly. But Laski, Strachey, my God! . . .Their attitude the exact replica of Tory's [*sic*] to Hitler.' Yet he was frustrated that no one came up with an alternative to what the Left had on offer. Laski was the target for his most colourful invective: 'the pickled prophet continues to display his tape-worm rhetorics in the "New Statesman".'[84]

At the start of 1944 he and Hardy moved into 1 Kensington Palace Gardens, the mansion home of George Russell Strauss, which functioned as a refuge for displaced *Tribune* writers and Labour MPs. He worked up a film treatment on racism for the MOI. There were a number of PEN meetings, including one in May to which he gave the paper on 'The Intelligentsia'.[85] He delivered a large number of lectures in the spring, including several for the army in mid-February 1944 and an appearance on the army Brains Trust soon after D-Day. He also contributed to the preparatory programme for workers being sent overseas by the Jewish Committee for Relief Abroad. These speaking engagements took him all over the country and were draining. By the end of May he was refusing invitations to speak. He told a correspondent: 'I am trying to sort out my ideas about certain things and I find all this public talking doesn't lead anywhere except the cheapest sort of gratified vanity which I loathe.'[86]

To add to his myriad obligations, during the mini-Blitz he applied to be a volunteer fireman. He did this in order to 'appease guilt feelings' but learning to drive a three-ton lorry was actually 'enormous fun'. He passed his driving test on 20 March and was assigned to the Western Auxiliary Ambulance Station, Phillimore Terrace, Kensington. The experience of ferrying sick and dying people to hospital was grim: his first case was an old, senile and incontinent man with bronchitis.[87]

These distractions were symptomatic of an unsettled state of mind. In early March he started to complain about a 'work block'. It was worsened by his stomach trouble and turned into a 'terrible depression. Is it St[alinist] atmosphere, D[aphne], the tummy? What is objective what subjective. Oh Christ.' In desperation he let Dr Bluth 'the devil in person', who supplied opium to the novelist Anna Kavan and artistic patron Peter Watson, suggest a cure for his writer's block. 'Shall we', he mused, 'make a pact with Mephisto? For five "Darkness at Noons" I'd do it. But my petit-bourgeois common sense rebels.' He was so 'utterly miserable and unable to work' that he asked Phyllis Bottome to recommend an Adlerian psychoanalyst and does appear to have had some sessions with Plesch — 'Jewish horse commonsense with dash of charlatanism'. In his diary–notebook he tried to work through his anxiety on his own: 'Don't try to imitate what you admire. Don't distrust what you write if it comes easy. Don't try to do the impossible; don't think its [sic] better because its [sic] harder. Don't try to catch up with wasted time. Kill the bureaucrat in you.'[88]

But he could not settle into a steady routine and suffered 'internal turmoil' while awaiting the Second Front. In April 1944 he explored the possibility of going abroad to do relief work for the United Nations Relief and Rehabilitation Administration, and after the invasion lunched with David Scott of the *News Chronicle* to discuss becoming a war correspondent. He was also waylaid by negotiations for the American sale of *Arrival and Departure* and a film deal with Alexander Korda, the Hungarian-born film mogul. The 'work crisis' reached its nadir in late May and early June. It broke with the beginning of Operation Overlord on 6 June 1944: 'Invasion started one day after saw Dr Bluth to get drugs to make me work. Since it started everything better.'[89]

The intemperate socialising continued nevertheless. After a week-end in the country with Connolly he wrote, 'Cyril disgusting. First evening snobbish, unpleasant . . . Next day very pleasant. Got "genius" mark in psychology book. Cyril galled.' Their relations were not helped when Connolly sent him a scrounging note asking for a loan of twenty pounds, 'as you used to do at Drayton Gardens'. A dinner with Korda at Claridge's left Koestler 'totally drunk'. He blacked out and had to ask Mary Dunn, a friend, what happened next. A dinner with Henry Green was merely 'unpleasant'. The thought of Hardy depressed him and he looked for ways out of their relationship. In March 1944 they had a row, following which she conveniently took up with another man. Koestler remarked in his diary: 'leaving time approaches . . . it leaves me cold, rather relieved, but can't fathom what's really going on within me; she was, I thought, the real and lasting thing but neurosis keeps butting[?] in.' When Hardy announced that she was moving in with her new boyfriend Koestler merely observed, 'tension makes all couples break up'. But, a month later, he was less sanguine about the dénouement of their six-year liaison. In a 'list of miseries' which he compiled on 3 June 1944, at the nadir of a depression, he included as no. 13, 'Collapse of lebens-plan (Daphne)'.[90]

To make his life even more complicated, Koestler was hiding two Polish Jewish soldiers who, along with dozens of their comrades, had deserted from Polish army units based in Scotland. Anti-Jewish feeling was rife among the Free Poles, some of whom were ethnic Germans captured in *Wehrmacht* uniform in North Africa and Italy, but assigned as replacements to the Polish forces under British command. The two Polish Jewish servicemen had first gone to Tom Driberg's home and had been passed on to Koestler while Driberg carried on a political campaign to obtain an amnesty for them. Koestler approached his contacts to take the men, whom he referred to as his 'patients', off his hands, but without success. He apologised to Victor Gollancz for accosting him after a meeting because 'I was trying to get the help of anyone I could think of'. He told Gollancz: 'Meanwhile I have some hopes that a solution will be found for our patients this week.' In spite of efforts to get them 'boarded out', at the end of April the two Poles were still with him. The situation was desperate since several other Jewish 'deserters' had been court-martialled and given stiff prison sentences. Another week passed with no relief. At last, at the end of June, he reported: 'Bill and Tom both dispatched to hospital after staged suicide, the cock and bull story [concocted] with A Calder Marshall.'[91]

Just when one problem ended another arose. In June he got sucked into the vortex of Anna Kavan's distressed life. Having tried to help her, he apparently triggered a crisis by observing that her writing had a 'neurotic character'. A few weeks later she made her fifth attempt at suicide. To cap it all, on 26 June a V-1 rocket-bomb landed near his house, which was badly damaged in the blast. In mid-July he finally fled London and took refuge at the Strauss's country house in Slaugham, Sussex. 'Feel re-born in solitude,' he wrote. 'Can't

understand how had been able to carry on with that party-snobbery-
life for over a year (though conscious at the time that it was dissipation
and wrong, snobbism, Connolly values, and yet went on and on).'[92]

IX

There was another reason for the sense of release which he felt, for
July marked the end of a prolonged and agonising drama in which
the course of the war, the fate of the Jews and his own family interests
were interwoven. In September 1943 Koestler was introduced to
Chaim Weizmann, the president of the World Zionist Organisation,
probably through Miriam or Guy de Rothschild.[93] Within a few
weeks of their first conversation he was drawn back into the world
of Zionist politics, this time at the highest level. Even though he had
not lived in Palestine since 1929, Koestler never renounced his
Palestinian nationality which he had gained while there. In January
1943 he actually set about renewing his Palestinian passport.[94] His
motivation was partly pragmatic, but opting for Palestinian citizenship at such a time was hardly a neutral gesture. His involvement in
Zionist affairs during 1944–9 showed that he was still driven by his
earliest ideological and personal inclination to identify as a Jew in a
modern, secular and national sense. His shared destiny with other
Jews was brought home by the events which followed the German
occupation of Hungary in March 1944.

Koestler saw Weizmann almost monthly. Despite their political
differences, which would grow wider as time passed, David Astor
recalled that Koestler looked on Weizmann as 'the finest kind of
Jewish patriarch'. He also conferred with Moshe Shertok,
Weizmann's right-hand man. Through them he became a member
of the Anglo-Palestine Committee, which met under the chairmanship of Israel Sieff, the millionaire director of Marks & Spencer. The
group included at various times Sieff, his brother-in-law Simon
Marks, Guy de Rothschild, the journalist Frank Owen, Kingsley
Martin, Michael Foot, David Astor and Frank Pakenham, then a
rising Labour politician. The meetings were also sometimes attended
by Weizmann and Shertok.[95] After a few weeks Koestler was so fired
up over Palestine that he made 'hectic efforts' to go there to write up
the story of the illegal immigrants running the British blockade. At
the beginning of 1944 he asked Michael Polanyi to help him get a
commission from either the *Guardian* or *The Times* to visit Palestine
as a journalist.[96]

The German occupation of Hungary on 19 March 1944 interrupted the deliberations of the Committee. 'What a misery to be in a minority,' he wrote in his diary–notebook on 22 March. The Nazis rapidly proceeded to expropriate, ghettoise and round up the Jews on Hungarian territory. In May they started deporting them to Auschwitz-Birkenau: Koestler was sure that his mother and members of his family were about to be murdered.[97]

He had last had news of Adele in August 1942, via the Red Cross and a relative, Michael Stricker, who lived in New York. Koestler learned that his father had died earlier in the war, of natural causes, and that his mother was living with her sister. He managed to get a letter to Adele explaining that he could not send financial help during wartime, but that any support from members of the family who were living in neutral countries would be repaid. He promised to bring her to England as soon as he could. Another message reached him via Stricker in February 1944; after that there was a ghastly silence. With his mother's fate 'gnawing' at him, Koestler tried to get her a Palestine immigration certificate which offered a slender chance that the Nazis would not deport her to a death camp. Francis (Ferenc) Aldor, his cousin who was now also in England, begged him to get Palestine certificates for his sister Margit and her two children. 'Please do anything to get these children out from Hitler Hell.' Aldor's sister and her children perished in Auschwitz and it seemed certain that Koestler's mother had suffered the same end. He received condolence letters from Fenner Brockway, MP, and Harold Laski, who remarked: 'You're lucky: you can hate.'[98]

The Palestine group continued to meet in May and June and Koestler continued to see Weizmann, but all business was overwhelmed by the crisis in Hungary. Thanks to his involvement with Weizmann and Shertok, Koestler became privy to Adolf Eichmann's extraordinary offer to exchange Jews for trucks and goods. On 10 June he reported that he had lunch with Weizmann who 'says that Hungarian Zionist leader Brand arrived Istanbul in Gestapo plane with Nazi offer to let 800,000 Hungarian Jews go to Iberian Peninsula if allies deliver 10,000 lorries, tea, coffee etc. Shertok went to negotiate – i.e. to temporise. First batch 2,000 Jews gassed in Osswetchian [*sic*] Mother . . .' Koestler was even vouchsafed a copy of the top secret notes of the conversation between Brand and Shertok in Aleppo, where Brand had been detained by the British.[99]

Eichmann's offer was treated with extreme caution by the Allies, who suspected correctly that it was a device to lure them into negotations that would alarm the Russians. The British also feared that if the offer were genuine any Jews allowed to leave Hungary would want to enter Palestine. British officials consequently did their best to frustrate the rescue scheme. The apparent lack of official or public concern as Hungarian Jewry was slaughtered embittered Koestler. 'One more funereal lunch with Weizmann,' he wrote on 8 July. 'So far 400,000 Jews deported from Hungary, 100,000 killed. Eden charmingly indignant. Not one paper-headline for 5 million Jews. But for 50 British Officers — what a ballyhoo.' Meanwhile, the Brand negotiations were leaked to the press and the rescue scheme collapsed amid recriminations between the Foreign Office and the Jewish Agency.[100]

Koestler also played an active but little known role in the evolution of the plan for bombing Auschwitz-Birkenau. He recorded on 11 July that he had 'Lunch with Shertok and John [Strachey]. Worked out the case for bombing the death camps, made drafts sent it to John . . .' The proposal was taken to the Allied governments, but its progress was blocked in spite of receiving Churchill's personal endorsement.[101]

The strain was too much: in early July he succumbed to another breakdown.

> Yesterday crisis came to a head. As usually, the climacteric took a smooth form: in the bath. Sunday morning had the usual guilt attack, and this time decided (with effort) . . . not to touch alcohol, not to accept invitations, not to go to west end restaurants for three months. This should not be self-punishment or masochism as Plesch would have it, but a form of mourning . . . The obsolescence of mourning-rites are a sign of degeneration . . .There is no excuse for leading a merry west end life while my people are slaughtered by the thousands per day, mama among them. To prevent my making money out of it, am sending cheque for £100 to Weizmann — 13 times about £2 per week.

In fact, the deportations were halted by the Hungarian premier Admiral Horthy at about this time.[102]

Koestler was left to reflect on his personal tragedy.

> As a child, the idea that mother should die, seemed a cosmic catastrophe; I prayed not to survive her. According to JTA [Jewish Telegraphic Agency] report Jews deported to Oswiecim die by new gas manufactured in Hamburg, thrown into death-chamber by SS-men wearing gas-masks; the victims (c. 1,000 at a time) are stripped naked under the pretext of having shower — it takes approximately 3 minutes. Or if sick, phenol injections over heart.

– So that is how mama died, or is dying, in this minute, or shall die, – I have tried, all day, to analyse what's going on now . . .

Once again he played with the notion of suicide, but 'I am deprived of the desire to die, feeling all those unwritten books in me, and not knowing whether I can write at all'. In fact, he was more worried about his latest amour. 'I feel horror, but no emotion. It is too remote. Can't penetrate with any awareness . . . I wish I could crack; but my automatic controls function all too well.'[103]

The Anglo-Palestine Committee reassembled in July to hear Michael Foot address the implications of the massacre of Hungarian Jewry. Shertok provided details of the Brand negotiations which Koestler described as 'grand guignol – horrifying beyond words'. They decided that the Allied nations must be pressed to offer protection to the Jews still alive in Hungary. But they also came up with the wild idea that Koestler should himself go to Budapest with G. Kuhlman, from the High Commission for Refugees. Needless to say, nothing came of this suicidal proposition, but it says a lot about Koestler's state of mind that it was even conceivable. He, Gollancz, Foot and Shertok persisted for a few more days until the deportations were suspended. Koestler then retreated into the country to Strauss's house at Slaugham.[104]

While there, Koestler learned exactly how the Brand negotiations had been exposed and the rescue plan foiled. 'A week ago would have gone off my head; now sad, but calm.' He was still tormented by the thought of his mother's supposed death, although he was as much racked by his apparent numbness of feeling as by her fate. 'Am I stone?' he asked himself. 'Has it [his mother complex] burned itself out in my childhood?' Then, around 25 August 1944, he received a telegram informing him that his mother was alive. 'Was happier about it than I expected. So after six weeks, drunk again, moderately, when M[amaine] was here . . . At last, thanks to false alarms about mother and this retreat, at last pattern of the life I should leave [*sic*] begins to emerge . . .'[105]

Koestler saw his exeat from London society as similar to other radical breaks in his life: his departure for Palestine, his entry into the Communist Party, his trip to Russia, his mission to Spain, the debacle in Malaga, the adventures of 1939–40 and his ending of relations with, first, his wife Dorothea, then Daphne Hardy. He wrote in his diary–notebook, 'am away from alcohol, parties, Mermaid. A succession of jumps into cold water, of self-destruction; suicide symbols as Plesch would call it . . .' The reference to Mamaine/Mermaid, however, signified a new chapter in his life.[106]

X

Mermaid was Mamaine Paget, his latest girlfriend. She, and her twin sister Celia, were born in September 1916 into a family of minor gentry in East Suffolk. Their mother was over forty when she became pregnant with the twins and died a week after bearing them. Her husband, a vicar's son who was grave at the best of times, never recovered from this loss. Aged fifty at the time, he was a remote and depressive figure. The twins were raised by a nanny until they were eleven and were sent to a boarding-school. A year later their father voluntarily entered a private mental hospital and died not long afterwards.

They were taken in by his equally unstable brother, Major-General Jack Paget, who lived near Richmond Park in London. Paget was a British Israelite, a follower of Madam Blavatsky (inventor of theosophism) and dabbled in the occult. He also believed in reincarnation and was convinced for a time that his youngest daughter was a re-embodiment of William Pitt. After a few months he decreed that the twins attend a totally unsuitable boarding-school in Essex. They were removed from there after appeals to their legal guardian and dispatched to a no less ineffectual finishing school in Switzerland. In 1937 they were presented at court and launched into London society. For two years they did little except learn the piano and mingle with artists and writers, notably the Sitwells, Cyril Connolly, Peter Quennell and Dick Wyndham, with whom Mamaine had a relationship. When the twins came of age they left their uncle's dour and oppressive mansion and, on the eve of the war, took a studio in Drayton Gardens, Chelsea.[107]

Mamaine Paget first encountered Koestler at a party thrown by Cyril Connolly in January 1944. She was then working at the Ministry of Economic Warfare and Koestler asked her to supply him with information on government attitudes to the supply of exit visas to refugees in occupied Europe. They did not hit it off particularly well. After another meeting at a party for Paul Willert in early March 1944 he described her as 'unpleasant as always'. At that time he had already nicknamed her Mermaid. Contrary to the lore of the sea, it was not she who lured him into her embrace. On 25 May he recorded in his diary for the previous Saturday: 'dinner and uneasy seduction of Mermaid'. It was not a felicitous moment to enter Koestler's complicated emotional world. He was in tumult due to events in Hungary and still not reconciled to the end of his relationship with Hardy. A few days later he listed in his diary–notebook the following 'miseries':

1. Incest barrier	sex
2. Devaluation of partners	,,
3. Lack of self confidence (sense of failure)	work
4. Guilt	social
5. Dissipation (party obsession)	,,
6. Lack of concentration (gedankenflecht) except if brain enflamed	,,
7. Devaluation of friends – snobbery	,,
8. Hunt for father image (loneliness)	,,
9. Lack of personality	,,
10. Impatience (to finish work) greed (to immediately obtain anything coveted)	work
11. Vanity, jealousy, vulnerability (hypersensitiveness)	social
12. Drink, sentimentality, rudeness, vulgarity	,,
13. Collapse of lebens-plan (Daphne)	,,
14. Lack of aesthetic quality	work
15. Bi-sexual streak	sex
16. Mental fatigue.	

The compilation of such a list was an impressive act of self-knowledge. But it also indicates what Mamaine Paget was taking on, not least because Koestler failed to act on any of the insights that he had about himself.[108]

They dined together on 7 June, but the evening ended in a row. Next day she wrote to him, 'Sorry I was so beastly last night, it was because I felt so depressed and enervei [sic] not because I hate you or anything like that.' They were soon passionately reconciled; Koestler recalled in his diary, 'M – after crisis and capitulation lovely.' Towards the end of June he spent his first night in her bed; it was 'almost perfect'. Initially it seems that Paget was the moody partner. After a weekend with him she wrote: 'I am sorry I was so bloody when I first arrived but I did improve didn't I?' As with his other relationships he adopted a tutelary role, the wise owl instructing a younger woman in the ways of the world and the mind. She told him she had stopped worrying about her 'irresponsible behaviour and [my] bad character. All due to the sage A.K.' Yet it was not long before the 'sage A.K.' was dubbed 'a shit' because of a letter he wrote to her probably pointing out some alleged defect in her character. 'I didn't hate you before I got it but I certainly do now, blast you . . . For gods [sic] sake go back to Sussex and stay there.'[109]

When Koestler resolved to give up drink and dining out due to the unbearable contradiction between social life and the tragedy of the Jews, he determined to leave Paget as well. He went to a party with her, decreeing silently that it would be the last such outing for three months. Afterwards they walked in Hyde Park and sat by the Round Pond in the early hours. Paget was shaken by his announcement, but to sit with her underneath a full moon was 'ecstasy'. Next day he reflected: 'All yesterday felt very elevated, in spite of some complications. One is Mamaine: the whole affair was based on dining and sleeping, a lets-have-a-pleasant-time liaison, and that couldn't last under austerity conditions.' He chastised himself for using his 'genuine suffering and self-deprivation' to win sympathy. They dined at her flat the same night, however, and made love 'standing in front of [the] mirror' only to discover that she had forgotten to draw the black-out curtain. Afterwards Paget pardoned him for leaving her: 'Please don't think you behaved badly to me, I think just the opposite . . .You did give me a lot of pleasure and we might have been very happy together, and it certainly isn't your fault that we can't now. I shall miss you very much.'[110]

In fact, they missed each other painfully. Even as he was working on the plan for the bombing of Auschwitz, Koestler was 'Waiting for Mamaine. She alone upsets newly-won tranquility.' On 11 July they had dinner in a 'dingy little restaurant in Church Street'. The food was horrible, but they enjoyed it and 'for the first time I felt something like intimacy with her'. Paget told him 'she had booked her evenings until next Monday . . . I felt, and I told her very quietly, that, as I am going to spend all my evenings alone, it would destroy my peace of mind to have to count the days until I was going to see her. She then offered in a shy, english way, to spend all her evenings with me. Doing that, I said, would be a honeymoon and not mourning. There are, as far as I can see, two motives in it: masochism and genuine concern for my peace of mind. . . . Then came the little incident which made me fall in love with her – out of pity.' After the pretence of resistance she tugged her hair over her eyes, pouted, said she needed a haircut, raised her 'swimming eyes' to him and announced: 'You are the limit!' She kissed him and they made love. From then on he was on tenterhooks, waiting for her to telephone, send him photographs and letters, or visit. He fell in love with her as an adolescent would, but was sufficiently self-aware to know it would not work in the long term. 'Restless. Waiting for photographs, a word or call from Mamaine. Damm this . . . she fears to disturb me. Or . . . hates me? Not to know her reaction to my letter is the new torture. And yet, and yet, I know against my feeling, that after a fortnight of living together I would have only one desire left, to be alone.'[111]

Despite his efforts to lead a monastic life in Slaugham he could not stop thinking about her. At first he claimed to have 'practically forgotten Mermaid' but after little more than a month in the country he asked himself: 'When will all these storms in a tea cup cease?' Not so soon and not so easily: the 'tentacles of the hydra of nostalgia fasten now on Daphne, now on Mermaid, or Dorte [Dorothea]: the glue is pity. At other times it may be desire. The whole thing is called falling in love.' Tokens of affection passed back and forth between them and eventually she visited him for the weekend. He, in turn, stayed with her when he went to town towards the end of August. But with his customary ambivalence he already dreaded spending longer in her company. She certainly had come to accept quarrels as part of the routine of being one of Koestler's consorts. In a letter she speculated whether they might spend time together 'in the movies, or drinking, or fighting, or something?'[112]

While recuperating in Slaugham, Koestler did some of his best work of the year. He completed the play *Twilight Bar* in six weeks and broke the back of the long essay on the deformation of socialism in the USSR. From mid-July he was 'back on the wagon', working steadily for the whole day and 'happier than for a long time'. On 22 July he noted: 'Peace lasts, play progresses . . .' Three days later he had almost finished the third act and started on the 'ever postponed Russian essay'. He wrote ten pages in one-and-a-half days: 'My bones ache from writing 12 hours per day . . . can't sleep, got dyorrhoe [*sic*], and this is happiness.' Needless to say, he was still plagued by self-doubt: 'I wonder how long this self-congratulatory mood will last. Working like a trooper.' In fact, the oasis of peace was invaded by visitors on bank holiday weekend which 'though pleasant, broke down systems of last fortnight'. He was able to move on to act four of the play, 'But it is not the same sacred fever'. He soon had to return to London.[113]

Koestler's next rural retreat was Bwlch Ocyn, in North Wales near Blaenau Ffestiniog, Merioneth. He had probably learned about the place through Michael Polanyi, who regularly holidayed in the region, or Robert Neumann, who rented a farmhouse there. Once installed, he reflected: 'Of other people I hardly hear. Such lots of acquaintances and such few friends. They all seem institutions to dine and drink with, if you cut them out they look like furniture in an empty restaurant.' In fact, Paget stayed with him for part of the time. *Twilight Bar* was finished on 15 August and the book of essays, *The Yogi and The Commissar*, was falling into place. This productivity cast a harsh light on his former life-style. He resolved, rather hopefully, to live in the country during the week and the city at weekends, travelling one month each year. 'Decided on seclusion, work, austerity – and no more phoney Greek balance, harmony etc. There is no harmony for creativeness of my constitutional type.' This seems to be a reference to Orwell's criticism of Koestler for his 'hedonism', and an admission that Orwell was correct.[114]

XI

Most of the pieces in *The Yogi and The Commissar* had appeared in various magazines and journals in 1941–4. The element that was new, and which caused most controversy, came in the last part of the book in four interconnected essays on the Soviet Union, Communism and alternatives to both. The final one sketched out Koestler's ambitious bid to construct a new political and ethical system founded on scientific proofs. He took immense pains over these essays and they form the keystone of his later political beliefs as well as his 'scientific' work.

In 'The Anatomy of a Myth', Koestler laid out his social-psychological theory of political belief. Fascism prevailed over socialism in the 1930s because it appealed to the instinctual need for faith and used archetypal images of good versus evil. Communists had fared better than socialists because they were able to make the Soviet Union into a mythic object: Russia was transmuted into paradise and the Soviet era turned into the 'Golden Age'. The myth of the Soviet Union took on the character of a religious belief, internally coherent and immune to logic. The only way to cope with this illusion was a campaign of attrition to prise myth apart from reality and 'the emergence of a new creed of equal emotional power and in better harmony with reality'.[115]

The next essay, 'Soviet Myth and Reality', began the attritional process. The Red Army's role in the war was heroic, but, Koestler argued, this did not justify the iniquitous political system it was serving. In any case, he suggested that the Russian war effort was motivated by self-preservation and nationalism rather than a love of Communism. He attacked the benign presentation of the USSR in the Western press and presented the carefully researched evidence of famine, inequality and illegality. This catalogue of failure was also intended to show that the revolution had gone awry, that it was impossible to use violence and police terror with any assured outcome and, hence, to justify obnoxious means by a much-desired end. Koestler concluded that, ultimately, the 'reason for its failure was the arid nineteenth-century materialism of its doctrine. It had to fall back on the old opiates because it did not recognise man's need for spiritual nourishment.'[116]

'The End of an Illusion' examined the USSR in an international framework. Koestler put forward the extremely unfashionable argument that Soviet foreign policy ran along the same expansionist lines as its Tsarist predecessor. Indeed, without a public opinion to worry about or any 'ethical ballast' it was almost totally unconstrained. Only Britain and the United States working together could thwart Soviet expansionism in the Middle East, the Mediterranean and Europe. Consequently it was vital to find an alternative popular ideology to Communism and wean the Left off its potentially treacherous attachment to the USSR. The Red menace could only be resisted by a reanimated commitment to human rights and a revivified social democracy, creating a mass base for opposition to the Soviet Union. Koestler ended with a call for something akin to, but not necessarily the same as, socialism.[117]

These essays were as bold as they were far-sighted. They were composed in London, Slaugham and North Wales during 1943–4 in isolation from research institutes or scholars, at a moment when the Soviet Union was routinely depicted in a heroic light and long before George Kennan or Winston Churchill warned against a Cold War.

In 'The Yogi and The Commissar II', Koestler attempted nothing less than the formulation of a unified theory of physics, biology, psychology, ethics and politics that implicitly answered the need for a new ideology. He began with the hoary debate over free will and determinism. In his view the argument was structured by a false antithesis: determinism or destiny as expressed in the form of religious belief, historical materialism or biology was rooted in human instinct. Humans want the reassurance that they do not exist in a random universe, that life has a purpose. The explanation for life can take various guises at different stages of human development, such as the belief in gods or Marxism. Paradoxically, the more mankind learned about the world, especially cause and effect, the more notions of pure freedom receded. Thus, increasing scientific knowledge set up a tension in which 'the mind is driven to deny its own experience of freedom'. The struggle is visceral. 'The conflict between freedom and determinism is a conflict between two instinctual beliefs, experienced in alteration and with equal intensity.'[118]

Koestler next looked at the expression of the conflict between free will and determinism in primitive religion, Christianity and the Enlightenment. In the modern era free will was subordinated to new iron laws of psychology or biology. Correct social behaviour was no longer governed by fear of God; instead, it was regulated by ethical canons that were based on scientific formulae such as the utilitarian equation that good was the greatest happiness for the greatest number. This had profound political implications. Whereas believers in religion, the 'saints', could 'explain' the universe and offer comfort to men by cloaking them under a mantle of divine omnipotence, social scientists and 'commissars' could explain things but could not offer any reassurance that anyone or anything was looking after mankind's interests.[119]

However, at the close of the nineteenth century scientific determinism went into crisis. In physics it appeared that the stuff of life was not subject to laws; metaphysics and physics converged in their forlorn attempts to explain the workings of the universe. Scientists reverted increasingly to a hierarchical explanation reminiscent of religious thinking: they hypothesised that the conduct of matter or life forms was determined by a higher level of 'organisation' of which they were a part, although at their own level they had 'freedom', which was in turn greater than that of the preceding level.[120]

Koestler went on to apply this theory to the working of the brain. He then elaborated a 'principle of Levels of Organisation' to explain how all fundamental change occurred in the form of a transition from vertical to horizontal planes. He was insistent on the need to avoid 'reductionism': explaining happenings on one level by reference to the one below. This had a baleful effect on ethics in particular. Reducing behaviour to psychological or biological determinants resulted in a form of relativism in which to explain was to pardon. Biological determinism, in the form of racialism or social Darwinism, engendered Nazism and Fascism. The worst ethical consequence of reductionism was utilitarianism and the subordination of means to ends. Human behaviour could not be quantified and predicted: it was an imponderable, like infinity, that confounded any formulae.[121]

He ended by invoking the merits of 'contemplation' and seeking change from 'within' while not going too far in the direction of the Yogi. The alternative was unclear, but he asserted that there was a chance for a new system of thought and practice to emerge. Science had been humbled: 'its aggressiveness is beginning to change into the modesty of achievement. The two-dimensional plane of nineteenth-century mechanism is gaining depth and height by the erection of the new hierarchy of levels, and the validity of the "vertical" approach is beginning to be recognised again.' This created an opportunity to achieve a synthesis by which 'while thinking and acting on the horizontal plane of our existence, we yet remain consistently aware of the vertical dimension. To attain this awareness without losing the other is perhaps the most necessary and most difficult task that our race ever faced.'[122]

Much of the scientific argumentation and evidence in the essay was contentious. But it would be missing the point to focus on this aspect of the tract. It was really a political manifesto. Koestler left the reader in no doubt of this in his closing peroration which begins with the tumult in science and ends with the question of which is the best form of society and political organisation. 'The crisis in explanation has found its most violent expression in the ethical crisis and its political projection. Its root is the paradox of the individual whole which has to function as a social part; and again of social wholes – classes and nations – which have to be integrated into a whole of a higher order.'[123]

This was the most concise and accessible expression of Koestler's unified theory. It contains in a nutshell the argument of *Insight and Outlook*, the massive, nearly indigestible, treatise he wrote in 1946–7 and rewrote for a new edition fifteen years later. All his 'scientific' work of the 1950s to the 1970s was derived from this essay, and was an attempt either to underpin his social theory and political philosophy or to disrupt scientific notions that challenged the pillars on which his nostrums rested. For Koestler science was politics by other means. But the 'law of detours' led him in directions he could not have anticipated and eventually consumed all his energies. The political philosopher disappeared into a quagmire of science. This was not necessarily because Koestler wanted to become a scientific thinker and writer; his much trumpeted abjuration of politics and his embrace of science should not be taken at face value.

In order to validate his political beliefs by science he had to aver that his scientific work was conducted purely for its own sake: otherwise it would be dismissed as the predetermined search for answers in the service of politics. In truth, this is what it was, but Koestler was so successful in making his audience believe that he had renounced politics that his real mission was increasingly overlooked. Of course, thanks to his unified theory he could genuinely claim that he was giving up politics; but, as 'The Yogi and The Commissar II' shows, his scientific and political thinking were one.

XII

Koestler's retreat came to an end in mid-September 1944, although his return to town was little more than a stop-over. At the beginning of July he had determined to visit Palestine to collect material for the sequel to *Arrival and Departure*. This was an interestingly perverse choice of destination since those of the London beau monde who could do so, including Connolly, were heading for liberated Paris. Koestler had plenty of illustrious contacts in France such as Guy de Rothschild and the publisher Robert Calmann-Lévy, whom he saw in the late summer and autumn of 1944. However, he 'decided go Palestinewards', the telegraphic language hinting at the journalistic side of the mission. He had another reason for avoiding France: 'My feelings about France and the things to come in Europe are [such that] I am looking forward to the armistice celebrations with the horror of facing a lonely Christmas.'[124]

The liberation of France allowed the surviving refugees to surface. In the autumn there was a flood of news from Sperber and his estranged wife Dorothea, who were both safe. Once the Allies invaded southern France, he leaped into action bombarding Elizabeth Ascher with letters and cables, and arranging for Dorothea to come to England. She preferred to stay in France and moved to Paris, where Guy de Rothschild tracked her down and offered her assistance. Recovering from ill-health, and apparently still traumatised by the years underground, she now used the name Nicole and behaved with an obsessive secrecy. Koestler offered her a divorce if she wanted one, but lied about his personal circumstances. 'Personally,' he told her, 'I am in no great hurry as I have no intention to re-marry – and nobody to whom to . . . Daphne and I are great friends, mais c'est tout. I thought these [sic] news will in some feminine way cause you some satisfaction and cheer your heart. Anyway, I am going to remain a bachelor for the rest of my middle-aged days.'[125]

He spent the last three months of 1944 in London. He negotiated with *The Times* and the *Guardian* to act as a special correspondent on the Palestine situation. Lovat Dickson was instructed to send the proofs of *The Yogi and The Commissar* to Palestine, where he could correct them, and he gave Peters the power of attorney for the sale of *Twilight Bar*. He was keen for both to appear at roughly the same time since he saw them as complementary. One of his final acts before he left was to purchase a five-year lease on a farmhouse at Bwlch Ocyn in North Wales from James Wylie, its avuncular owner, who was at the time resident in Morocco. But the very last was parting from Mamaine Paget. It was a painful moment since they had seen each other often during the autumn, frequently going for drinks at the Prospect of Whitby on the Thames. 'It was bloody awful when you went away,' she wrote, 'you were so incredibly sweet to me and made me so very happy, that is why I was so miserable when you left.'[126]

Chapter 7

Palestine, France and Science, 1945–7

The shattering events of 1942–4 turned Koestler back on his Jewish roots. 'From 1942, when the mass-extermination of European Jews began, until the consolidation of the Jewish State in 1948, Palestine became once more my main preoccupation.' During 1945–7 he spent half a year in Palestine and wrote *Thieves in the Night* (1946), a fictionalised account of the struggle for a Jewish state. He also wrote 'several pamphlets, countless articles, made speeches, and sat on committees – all the time pleading the case of partition [of Palestine], as the only means to end the horror and save those who could still be saved'.

In December 1944 he set out for Palestine to research his Zionist novel. Chaim Weizmann hoped to use Koestler as a bridge to the Jewish terrorists who had launched an insurrection against British rule, but instead of persuading the terrorists to abjure violence Koestler found himself taking their side. A reinvigorated belief in Zionism led him to modify his critique of political philosophies in which ends justify means. Instead, he was driven to 'explain and defend the cause of the Jewish terrorists'. His reborn Zionism also prevented him from consummating his relationship with his newly adopted homeland: he spurned the possibility of British nationality while the Jewish world was virtually at war with Britain.[1]

Throughout 1946–7 he was a highly visible advocate of the Jewish national cause, boldly risking hostility from the British public. Mamaine Paget's letters to her sister Celia show that Palestine was so important to him that news of the events there had a direct effect on his mood. However, Koestler continued to develop his wider political thinking. The response to *The Yogi and The Commissar* encouraged his belief that the moment was right for refounding political life in the light of post-war realities. George Orwell seemed to be moving in the same direction and for a while they jointly explored the prospects for a new political movement.

A key to Koestler's political thinking may be found in his renewed passion for science. Once he had completed his novel about Zionism, he started telling friends that he was working on a book about psychology. This project occupied him throughout 1947. Superficially it was about human creativity, the mechanisms of the brain and evolution. At another level it was an ambitious attempt to establish the basis for a new political philosophy.

I

Guy de Rothschild, who saw Koestler frequently during 1943–4, recalled: 'He was above all preoccupied, tormented even, by the nightmarish fate of the Jews.' He had a dream in which he witnessed atrocities, but could not stop them because no one would heed his alarums. Koestler's obsession with the slaughter of the Jews powered his decision to write a novel dealing with the Jewish tragedy in the twentieth century. His letters and diaries reveal that as early as January 1944 he wanted to go to Palestine to research a sequel to *Arrival and Departure*.[2] Palestine was the arena in which the drama of the Jews was now being played out. It was there that refugees from Nazism fled, only to run up against British naval pickets deployed to prevent them finding a haven in the Jewish National Home. It was there that Jews were building a new society, dismantling the economic, social, political and psychological structures conditioned by centuries of existence in the Diaspora. A new kind of Jew was emerging, determined to break with traditional Jewish responses to oppression. At another level Koestler embarked on the novel to expiate some of the guilt he felt at being alive while most of his family, or so he believed, and millions of other Jews had died. He explained to Mamaine Paget: 'If it comes off . . . I shall perhaps get rid of some of my surplus guilt feelings and get absolution for some of my sins.'[3]

Koestler planned to collect material and write as much as possible *in situ*. But the Zionist leadership in London saw his expedition as an opportunity to contact Jewish extremists in Palestine, using him as an intermediary. In January 1944 the Irgun, the Zionist underground group led by Menachem Begin, Jabotinsky's successor as leader of the Zionist Revisionists, declared war on the British empire and resolved to drive the British out of Palestine. A second underground group, Lehi (also known as the Stern Gang), launched a ferocious terrorist campaign. Their sanguinary efforts culminated in November 1944 in the assassination of Lord Moyne, the Colonial Secretary and friend of Winston Churchill. British opinion was outraged and Churchill's ardour for the Zionist cause was irreparably damaged. Weizmann knew that Koestler had once been close to Jabotinsky and therefore had good credentials with the leaders of the underground. He asked him to track down Begin, who was in hiding, and try to persuade him to suspend terrorist operations against the British.[4]

Subsequently Koestler claimed: 'my purpose was to write a book and the secondary or primary [sic] purpose was this very loose arrangement with Weizmann . . . to talk some sense to the Irgun.' This rather inflated the significance of his mission: the Zionist leadership had more reliable envoys and Koestler's trip was not given top priority by the Jewish Agency or the British authorities. Jewish officials in London authorised him to tell the Colonial Office that he was commissioned to help Weizmann, but they did not indicate any special task, least of all one that would have won support from the British government. So Koestler travelled to Palestine by sea, not by plane, setting out on 20 December 1944 and not arriving in Port Said until 8 January 1945. He covered the last stretch overland.[5]

Even without this cloak-and-dagger element the trip was an indication of Koestler's absorption in Jewish affairs. At a time when many members of the *Horizon* crowd were rushing to liberated Paris to re-establish European links and satisfy Continental appetites, Koestler demonstratively headed for the new Jewish homeland. At a crucial moment in the history of Europe and in Koestler's own life he chose to act as a Jew.

He plunged into the social and political scene from the moment he arrived. On his first night in Jerusalem he attended a party thrown by Gershon Agronsky, proprietor and editor of the *Palestine Post*. (The *Post* handled Koestler's mail until he found a flat.) Over the next few weeks he met a series of Jewish political leaders, notably Moshe Shertok, Teddy Kollek and David Remez, chairman of the Vaad Leumi (the Jewish national council of Palestine). He lunched with Lord Gort, the High Commissioner, and consulted a range of past and current British officials, such as Norman Bentwich, the attorney-general for Palestine from 1920–31, and Eric Mills, the serving commissioner for migration and statistics. He saw local intellectuals, like the British-born writer Edwin Samuel, Kafka's amanuensis Max Brod, the refugee German author Arnold Zweig and some with underground connections, such as Joseph Nedava. In early February he dined twice with Weizmann in Rehovot. In conscientious pursuit of all points of view, he saw Dr Husayn Fakhri al-Khalidi, a former mayor of Jerusalem and a guiding light of the moderate Palestinian Arab opposition to Zionism.[6]

Koestler's fame was such that the *Palestine Post* announced his arrival in its society column. This precipitated a whirlwind of re-unions with old acquaintances from Budapest, Vienna, Berlin, Paris and his earlier stay in Palestine. After a fortnight he told Paget that his brain was 'in a kind of marmalate [*sic*] state what with receptions, parties (Jewish, English and even Arab) and hundreds of old friends turning up after twenty years'. Koestler also made journeys to see his 1920s Ullstein patron von Weisl in Gedera and the Weinshalls in Haifa. He celebrated Passover with Israel Sieff, Guy de Rothschild and Teddy Kollek at Kibbutz Ein Gev, where Kollek lived.[7]

During the first month Koestler covered a lot of ground, visiting places that would furnish the landscape of the novel. He worked in the Zionist archives in Tel Aviv, visited an Arab college, and the kibbutzim at Givat Brenner, Kfar David and Ein Hashofet. The latter was a bastion of Hashomer Hatzair, a far-left Zionist party that was aligned with the Soviet Union. Koestler enjoyed several days of hos-pitality at the kibbutz, arguing ceaselessly with its highly politicised membership. He admired their commitment as much as he despaired of their political judgement and bade them an affectionate farewell before he left Palestine: 'May you prosper and flourish in the Hebrew socialist tradition – and shed . . . your sectarianism [and] your infantile allegiances to Uncle Joe.'[8]

At the other extreme of the political spectrum he obtained the desired meeting with Begin. It took some time to arrange since Begin's lieutenants opposed any rendezvous with a person from outside their underground circle. Begin finally overruled them because he was interested in Koestler 'as a man who likes looking into the inside of things'. The encounter was full of black comedy. Koestler was picked up from his Jerusalem flat just after a senior British police officer, whom he met for drinks, had left. He was spirited from there to Begin's hide-out in Tel Aviv in a succession of different cars before being led into a totally darkened room.

Begin, who was going under the *nom de guerre* of Israel Sassover and was disguised with a beard, could not risk being seen. He had been told by his intelligence officers that Koestler was frequently in the company of British officials so, even though he did not suspect the commission from Weizmann, he was not convinced that the author was merely conducting research.

They fenced verbally while chain-smoking. Each time Koestler wanted to light a cigarette one of Begin's bodyguards leaped forward to strike the match and shield the light. Begin formed the view that Koestler's amazing feats of inhalation were actually intended to illuminate the room and give him a chance to see his interlocutor. Afterwards, the Irgun was convinced that Koestler had come as a police spy and believed he had reported to the British authorities that Begin had undergone plastic surgery to hide his appearance. In fact, Koestler had no wish to identify the underground leader. He wanted only to persuade Begin that some elements on the British political scene, notably the left wing of the Labour Party, were pro-Zionist and could be trusted. Weizmann also wanted to know if the Zionist underground would be placated by an offer to permit limited Jewish immigration over a ten-year period after which a Jewish state might be created in part of Palestine. It was a waste of time: Begin dismissed any idea of negotiating with or trusting the British. Koestler left the meeting chastened and turned his attention fully to the novel.[9]

The foetal Jewish State revived Koestler's ingrained ambivalence about the Jews and his own Jewishness. He told Paget that he was 'sinfully happy' in Jerusalem, a town which 'acts like a drug'. It was a place of 'such incredible tragic beauty that every time I look down from my balcony I go all soft and shakey [*sic*] inside'. He was so enraptured that he 'toyed with the idea of perhaps settling here; after a month I find that I love this country more than I ever thought – the incredible beauty of the landscape more than anything else'. On the other hand he was afraid of being sucked into the narrow, introverted intellectual life. 'The people here are so obsessed with their own tragedy and the problems of the country that Europe becomes very remote.' He also feared that his English, 'a very tender plant', would suffer if he stayed.[10]

Yet Palestine fascinated him. 'The problems of a continent concentrated on one country,' he wrote to Daphne Hardy. 'Scrap [*sic*] a human being and out come all the archytypal [*sic*] conflicts – racial, religious, social, ethical – which in Europe one gets in a thin diluted state.' The country was 'over-spiced, over-salted, over-heated'. His visits to Jewish settlements and Arab villages left his sympathies so sharply divided that he described his thinking as schizophrenic. The prospect of putting it all into a book was daunting, but he was 'thriving in a kind of a dream'.[11]

By mid-February he had completed his field work. He rented a roof flat in the attractive suburb of Talpiot in Jerusalem, one of his haunts in the 1920s, and settled down to sketch the first draft. His routine was to sunbathe and sleep during the hotter parts of the day and to work at night when it was cool. He commenced the evening shift with a glass of arak at 7.30 p.m., had dinner and half a bottle of wine, followed by coffee and brandy. His domestic needs were taken care of by a char lady. Once he started writing he went out little during the day. 'This of course is great happyness [sic] as long as it lasts and the book gets on,' he told Hardy. 'I work with the usual intensity of my working spells, hardly see any people, cook my meals myself and am very happy, having written about half of the first volume.' He believed it was 'doubtless one of the best things I have ever done; and I pray I should be able to keep it up to the end'. He anticipated finishing the first draft by July, although he regarded it as merely the 'first volume' of a trilogy. He told Harold Rubinstein, his solicitor: 'I am choking on material and it carries me on and on.'[12]

Life was very pleasant when compared with the austere conditions at home. He told one correspondent back in England: 'I am typing this during a week-end visit to Tel Aviv on the beach, having had a swim and getting ready for a breakfast consisting of two boiled eggs, tomato-and-olive salad, goats cheese, marmalade and grape-fruit juice.' Although he informed Paget in early June that he was still pursuing what was for him a Spartan regime and 'only living for my book' this did not preclude affairs with a number of women.[13]

When he had left Britain their relationship was unresolved. Paget wrote him letters that swung between longing and wariness. 'I miss you like hell, darling. I don't think I have really laughed properly since you went away.' She negotiated on his behalf to rent a farmhouse at Bwlch Ocyn, but announced that she did not plan to move in with him when he returned. 'I would like to live with you if you weren't such a Branch Street kid, but anyway I will come to stay with you perhaps and cook you lovely post-war meals.' She told him that she wanted to get a job abroad so that she would not be in London when he got back, but begged to know how long he would be away and enquired if he had got himself a Jewish girl-friend. 'Have you got an *affreuse* [frightful] *juive*? I hope she is very *affreuse* if so.' In March she looked into getting a Ministry of Information job in Palestine and sent Koestler photographs so that he wouldn't forget her looks. A month later the prospect receded and she fell into a depression: she needed 'dope' to sleep and sat in bed, late, writing to him with news about the reception of *The Yogi and The Commissar* and London literary gossip.[14]

Koestler was no less equivocal. He told Paget that he missed her badly, but joshed her about her ex-boyfriend, the journalist Richard Wyndham. Wyndham was in the Middle East for the *Sunday Times* and formed a drinking partnership with Koestler, who could not resist goading him with references to Paget: 'We get on quite well about you and less well of course about politics.' Wyndham saw things differently and wrote an aggrieved letter to Paget about Koestler's behaviour. 'You might be a bit more considerate,' she reproached him. 'You know that if I met Daphne I would rather cut my tongue out than say anything about you which might possibly depress her.' Regardless, Koestler told Paget that he expected her to move into the Welsh house with him in 'a kind of common enterprise'. If she did develop a rival affection he joked that he would kidnap her and carry her off to Bwlch Ocyn.[15]

In June he asked her if she was being faithful to him and admitted, 'I am only having a utility affair for week-ends – a boring but necessary evil.' The 'utility affair' was a twenty-three-year-old Czechoslovakian-born Jewish refugee named Anny, who was working for the British administration. The 'necessary evil' for her included an abortion after Koestler had left Palestine.[16] Anny was young, naïve and nervous, which was typical of so many of his girl-friends. When with her he accentuated his age, posing as a benign uncle figure as well as lover. Koestler inducted her into *la dolce vita*; infidelity was part of his sophistication. However, there were rough moments, too, and Anny was the victim of Koestler's anger more than once. She later reflected that 'those six months were on the whole happy ones for me – and if bits of them were miserable – why the happiness by far outweighed the miserable ones. There were days when you were neither beastly nor bad nor mean – but kind, understanding and loving. It is true it never lasted long, but while it did I felt it was good to be alive.'[17]

Back in London, Paget was busy mingling with the literary beau monde: Connolly, Strachey, Spender, Clive Bell, Kingsley Martin and Humphrey Slater among others. She told Koestler that 'I have been unfaithful to you a certain amount, rather unenthusiastically, and now I have quite a sweet boyfriend (he is 28 but looks 18 – progress isn't it?). So that is allright (nobody comes within a million miles of you, of course) . . .' Koestler's most serious competition came from the American writer Edmund Wilson who was Paget's for the taking. Wilson met her in London in April 1945, on the first leg of a long trip through liberated Europe on behalf of the *New Yorker* magazine. He asked her to accompany him to Italy, but she demurred. Despite her avowal of loyalty to Koestler, Wilson continued to send her impassioned letters: 'I miss you and have been thinking about you almost all the time since I left London this morning . . . Please don't fall in love with anyone else before I see you again.' In May he formally proposed marriage and even informed her that he had asked his estranged wife, the novelist Mary McCarthy, for a divorce.[18]

Wilson hastened back to London to see her again and resumed his futile courtship. Paget told him: 'I don't think I can marry you or indeed do anything to make our relationship fit any conventional pattern, if it doesn't do so anyway. I don't think you know me very well either.' But Wilson may have known her better than she thought. He and Koestler were similar types in many ways and her dalliance with Wilson illuminates her relationship with Koestler. Wilson, too, was worldly, linguistically gifted and had eclectic interests. He, too, was a philanderer who felt no need to constrain his sexual appetite. In Paget he saw a vulnerable, neurotic but perceptive person: 'always wound-up and . . . physically rather frail'. As it did for Koestler, her fragility appealed to his protective, macho instinct; but unlike Koestler he appears to have taken Paget more seriously and valued her intelligence. For years afterwards he wrote to her about his interests in an unpatronising way that was foreign to his erstwhile rival's dealings with women.[19]

Paget resisted Wilson's blandishments, the promise of longed-for travel and the presents he showered on her. In June she wrote to Koestler: 'Please come back in September, I can't go on much longer without any advice from my Uncle Nyuszi [Hungarian pet-name for Koestler].' To leave him in no doubt how she felt, the following month she told him that she had 'walked out' on her latest boyfriend and set about renting a room for Koestler. With the mixture of excitement and apprehension that Koestler inspired in women she asked: 'Where shall we have dinner? I am trying to think of a place where we can have a good meal without it being the sort of place where we might quarrel but can't.'[20]

By this time Koestler had begun to miss both England and Paget. He had earlier told Daphne Hardy: 'Looking at England from a distance of a thousand miles and 8 weeks absence, I feel a solid and already faintly nostalgic affection for the country and the people – I feel I have taken root there as nowhere else during my previous wanderings; I feel no homesickness for Paris or Vienna or even Budapest, but for London I do.' When Paget informed him that she had not got the Palestine job, he said how disappointed he was not to be able to show her the sights, but commiserated: 'This country is only bearable for people who have very strong emotional ties with it – otherwise the climate is hell and the provincialism of life would bore you to death.' Palestine was 'for married people with children, bridge, hobbies or political passions. I love it and feel rooted in it – but then my case is different.' He joked that 'Colonial life is not made for single-girls; and you are not made to marry a colonial'.[21]

Towards the end of July, having finished the first draft of the novel, Koestler prepared to leave. This time he got authorisation to travel by air on 'urgent press affairs'. Anny drove him to the airport on 6 August, the day the atomic bomb was dropped on Hiroshima. He stayed in London for a fortnight, at a flat arranged by Paget, writing two articles for *The Times*. Although they were couched in Olympian prose, they stirred up a controversy by calling for partition and immediate Jewish statehood.[22]

His stand won plaudits from right-wing Zionists, but Weizmann and his followers were less than impressed. Instead of winning Begin over to their point of view, it seemed as if Koestler had met the underground and been converted by them.[23]

II

Once he was in London, Koestler picked things up with Paget. Over dinner at Scott's restaurant he went so far as to discuss marriage, but both drew back. She noted in her diary on 12 August: 'A. said he would like to marry me but (a) cyclical neurosis (b) refused to have children. I said I would like to too but refused not to have children.' It could not be said against Koestler that he ever disguised the terms of a relationship he wanted with a woman: their interests and desires were firmly subordinated to his own. Paget was prepared to accept such a deal at this stage of her life, but she told Wilson that unless she could have children marriage with Koestler was out of the question.[24]

While Koestler finished his articles for *The Times* Paget organised the move from London to Bwlch Ocyn and supervised work on the house. After a last round of meetings in London he travelled to North Wales and began the long process of settling in. Despite an agreement with Jim Wylie to renovate the building there was much left to do. He complained bitterly that neither the garage nor the drive had been completed, so that their car had to be quartered a long walk from the house. The interior still needed painting and finishing, but every job was tortuous due to the shortage of labour. Although Paget did her best to relieve Koestler of these chores they preyed on his mind. The move set a pattern that was to be repeated *ad nauseam* for the rest of Koestler's nomadic life.[25]

Koestler worked in the small study that opened off the main living room. Its compact size was a virtue since the farmhouse was ill-equipped with heating and soon turned into an ice-box. Paget had a room for herself situated between the dining room and the kitchen, but in the bitter winters of 1945–6 and 1946–7, the kitchen and Koestler's room, heated with a paraffin stove, were frequently the only ones in which it was bearable to sit. Nevertheless, he hammered away at the novel. He dubbed the farmhouse his 'hermitage' and told the film-maker and fellow Hungarian Alexander Korda that he was leading a 'sober, hard-working naturalists life'. Developments in Palestine, he told Orwell, spurred him on.[26]

The Labour Party, which had come to power in August 1945, was formally committed to a pro-Zionist policy. Once in office, however, this changed. Prime Minister Clement Attlee and Ernest Bevin, the Foreign Secretary, rejected Zionist demands for immediate large-scale immigration by survivors of the Holocaust into Palestine. However, the new American President, Harry Truman, announced his support for the resumption of immigration and the Zionist underground stepped up its attacks on British targets in Palestine. Relations between even the moderate Weizmann and the British government cooled to sub-zero temperatures; Britain and the Jews were on the brink of armed conflict.[27]

Victor Gollancz was alarmed by the growing crisis. He pleaded with Koestler to come to London to meet Weizmann, who was due to address a major gathering of Labour MPs. Koestler was unwilling to leave Bwlch Ocyn, but spoke to Gollancz on the telephone from the Oakley Arms, a nearby public house and hotel (the farmhouse did not yet have a phone) and drew up an extraordinary six-page *aide mèmoire* for Gollancz to pass on to the Zionist leader. He recommended that Gollancz submit the paper as if it were his own since Koestler's articles in *The Times* had diminished any influence he might have had with Weizmann. 'My relations with him have become slightly strained mainly because I reproached him with political quietism and our deplorable shortcomings in the field of propaganda and Public Relations. Besides – and I would say, mainly – Weiczman [*sic*] still resents, perhaps unconsciously, my friendship with the late Jabotinsky.'

Koestler began with the 'mentality of the audience', since all his political advocacy stressed the psychological dimension. Labour MPs would feel torn between a desire to help the Jews and a fear of doing an injustice to the Arabs. They would also hesitate before taking any action that might validate accusations that the Labour government was responsible for the dissolution of the empire. Zionists first had to admit that the establishment of a Jewish state in Palestine would involve an injustice to the Arab inhabitants, but one that was insignificant compared with the injustices suffered by the Jews. Second, they had to make people understand that anti–Semitism would not end and that a Jewish state was therefore essential: 'It is not a question of whether the Jews want to be a separate race or not, but the fact is that the pressure of the social environment forces them to be one.' Anti-Semitism in America and pogroms in Eastern Europe since the liberation proved that. Nor was there an alternative to partitioning Palestine into two ethnic states. The Arabs were stuck in the fourteenth century and were unable to coexist with the Jews, a twentieth-century people.

Finally, he scorned the attempt of mainstream Zionists to reassure the British that a Jewish state would not imply the end of empire. Sentimental slogans for or against the empire cut no ice: it was better to address issues of self-interest. Due to the British evacuation from Egypt, the strategic value of Palestine to the British was bound to be enhanced. It would be in British interests to have a strong, friendly Jewish Palestine whereas appeasing the Arabs had been shown not to work.

Koestler mocked Weizmann's predilection for arguments based on legal and moral grounds, and defended the Revisionists who had been denounced as 'Fascists' merely for advocating a policy of *Realpolitik*. 'For God's sake do try to make the old man see that if he wants action in our favour involving trouble with the Arabs he must drive home the political advantages of such action.' Taking a last swipe at Weizmann he concluded: 'We have really such an overwhelming case that it is idiotic to base our claims on Bergen Belsen or Abraham's interview with God alone.'

And yet Koestler's line was not so different from Weizmann's. Moreover, he added a hair-raising proposal that rather undermined his ridicule of Weizmann's emotive speechifying: 'There is one very favourable circumstance for us – horrible as it may seem to say so – the Belsen trial and its appeal to public imagination.' He suggested to Gollancz that he organise a march of Jews, preferably ex-soldiers who would make a good impression with their military bearing, from Whitechapel to Whitehall coinciding with a demonstration of Jews outside the British embassy in New York (*sic*). 'One should not be afraid of using a little imagination – e.g. the carrying of barbed wire fences or some other concentration camp and horror symbols.' He even thought it might be good if there were clashes with the police so that a few Jews were hospitalised. 'Ten Jews injured in London hospitals appeal more to the imagination than one million dead in Poland . . .'[28]

There are few more vivid examples of Koestler's commitment to Zionism or his familiarity with the techniques of political agitation, learned at the feet of Willi Münzenberg. His references to 'us' and 'we' in the document proclaim a complete identification with the Jews. However, he avoided diluting his energy any further and instead concentrated on his novel – where many of the ideas in the *aide mémoire* appear in a different form. Koestler informed a Palestinian correspondent: 'All this bitterness [about British policy] goes into the novel I am writing.'[29]

Thieves in the Night is set in Palestine during the years 1937 to 1939, although it cleverly recounts a much larger slice of Jewish history. The novel opens with the foundation of a new Jewish settlement in Galilee and then traces the fortunes of a cluster of individuals present at that moment. Each figure has a didactic function, but Koestler manages to infuse his cast with enough vivacity to prevent the novel declining into a homily. Its pace and interest owe much to the central character, Joseph, who is clearly entrusted with Koestler's own agenda.

Joseph is an intellectual with a tendency towards self-analysis, self-dramatisation and self-loathing. He is English-born and although his father was Jewish he had no attachment to the Jews until an 'Incident' made him aware that others would consider him a Jew despite all his protestations otherwise. He had an affair with an English woman of Fascist and anti-Semitic sympathies who was appalled to discover that her naked lover was circumcised and hence probably a Jew. Rejected by Gentile society, Joseph resolves to throw in his lot with the Jewish people.[30]

Through Joseph the reader learns about the history of Zionism and the Jews, Jewish society in Palestine and the conflict between the Jews, the British and the Arabs. Since many of the ideas, and even entire phrases, attributed to Joseph recur in Koestler's factual accounts of Zionism, notably *Promise and Fulfilment*, it is safe to read them as fictionalised versions of Koestler's own convictions: to all intents and purposes, Joseph is Koestler. The character has been described as a classic portrait of 'Jewish self-hatred'. This is true only in so far as the entire Zionist enterprise may be described as an act of 'Jewish self-hatred'. Joseph merely restates in a more concentrated and vulgar form the views of Theodor Herzl, Max Nordau, Vladimir Jabotinsky, Chaim Weizmann and David Ben-Gurion, all of whom held Diaspora Jewry in greater or lesser degrees of contempt and believed that a Jewish state would transform the Jews, purging them of the worst defects of character acquired during years of exile and subordination.[31]

The narrative swiftly summarises the origins of the pioneer movement and the kibbutzim. The pioneers had imbibed the Bible, Marx and Herzl; they 'regarded themselves as the spiritual heirs of the Essenes', perhaps a reference back to the Essene of *The Gladiators*. Their fanaticism was also a symptom of exile. 'The exiled have nothing to hang on to except doctrines and convictions; hence they fight over ideas like dogs over bones. The others call it politely our semitic intensity.'[32] Here, as throughout the novel, Joseph generalises wildly about 'the Jews', often veering into the language of race and using some blatant anti-Semitic tropes. He looks at the settlers and feels 'revulsion against this assembly of thick, curved noses, fleshy lips and liquid eyes', which resemble the 'masks of archaic reptiles . . . It was no good denying to himself that he disliked them, and that he hated even more the streak of the over-ripe race in himself.' Elsewhere, however, he considers that the Jews are merely humanity writ large: 'no species would be complete without its Jews: they are the exposed nerve, an extreme condition of life.'[33]

Joseph is ill at ease with any kind of Jew. He surveys the Sabras (indigenous Jews) and immigrants alike with a jaded eye. 'Their parents were the most cosmopolitan race of the earth – they are provincial and chauvinistic. Their parents were sensitive bundles of nerves with awkward bodies – *their* nerves are whip-cords and their bodies those of a horde of Hebrew Tarzans.'[34] Like its main character, *Thieves in the Night* is beset by contradictions. One of the most glaring is that Joseph presents a brilliant exposition of the corrupting effect of exile, a condition to which any Diaspora minority might fall prey, but then proceeds to deride the supposed corrective: the creation of a Jewish nation-state followed by the ingathering of the exiles.

In his diary (a familiar literary device in Koestler's novels) Joseph sets out the Zionist analysis. Thanks to centuries of dispersion, persecution and segregation 'the Jews' had developed habits of ostentation and vulgarity, and neuroses ranging from exaggerated ratiocination to their 'mixture of arrogance and cringing'. 'Jewry is a sick race; its disease is homelessness; and can only be cured by abolishing its homelessness. I became a socialist because I hated the poor; and I became a Hebrew because I hated the Yid.'[35] While the closing sentence is not a pretty one, its sentiments were by no means unique among Jews and Zionists at that time. What sets Koestler apart from his Zionist mentor Jabotinsky and co-workers such as Kollek, is his dissatisfaction with the Jewish achievement in Palestine. Nor were many Zionist publicists comfortable relapsing into racial discourse so soon after the Nazi era. Koestler messily blurs an environmentalist explanation of alleged Jewish traits into a racial one resting on inherited characteristics.

It seems as if Koestler cannot make up his mind whether he believes that 'Jewish' characteristics are inherited biologically or induced by natural selection in the context of environment and, therefore, amenable to change. However, there is one clue to what he really thought at this stage of his life, a point of view with profound consequences. Mid-way through the novel, Joseph visits the tomb of a Jewish patriarch dating from the biblical era. Standing before it he muses: 'Inside my testicles there are some complicated but stable groups of molecules which were handed down to me from him with their pattern unchanged.'[36] If he truly believed this, Koestler was trapped as a Jew. This explains the intensity with which he writes about Jews and Zionism in *Thieves in the Night* and in later works on the same theme. Arguably, his subsequent interest in psychology and genetics was overdetermined by this half-acknowledged racial fundamentalism.

Koestler was, and remained, a Zionist, but he was always a highly ambivalent Jew. He credited Judaism with preserving the unity of the Jews during the centuries of exile and keeping alive the idea of Zionism, but he dismissed its value in the modern era. It was a 'world petrified into symbols and make-believe'. Hebrew culture was an oxymoron: 'It has no records, no memories, hardly any trace of what happened to mankind since the destruction of the Temple.' Koestler, who confessed that his Hebrew vocabulary was that of 'an educated hotel porter', was hardly in a position to make such sweeping judgements on Jewish culture. They were more a reflection of prejudice and his ambivalence about his own Jewish identity.[37]

While working on *Thieves in the Night*, he was asked by the East End Jewish writer Willy Goldman to contribute to an anthology of modern stories by young Jewish writers in England. Goldman confessed that he was not sure if Koestler was actually Jewish, but if so he was 'the best living Jewish writer'. Koestler demurred: 'being a Zionist, I don't quite see the point of an anthology of this kind. I believe that the term "Jewish" should be reserved for the Hebrew Nation in Palestine, and that all those who do not opt for it should stop regarding themselves as a separate community.' This was, in a nutshell, his position for the next thirty years. But Goldman was a thoughtful and tenacious correspondent. He immediately pointed out the weakness in Koestler's argument. Goldman didn't want to go to Palestine, but the world said that he was a Jew none the less and while they did he was not inclined to hide the fact. If a Jew didn't believe in God or the 'chosen race', and refused to abjure the fact of his birth, what was he to do? 'It's hard to believe you're an orthodox Zionist who's gone to Palestine and thinks the world has seen nothing like it,' Goldman commented.[38]

Koestler was trapped by his peculiar, contradictory and reductive analysis of Jewishness. At times he treated it as an ersatz national identity, which could be shed at will in the Diaspora. Judaism would ultimately wither in Israel so that Jewishness would become a mere badge of nationality. But he also referred to the Jews as a 'race', distinguished by a 'hereditary substance' which transmitted Jewish characteristics down the generations.

Another contradiction was not so much within the novel as between its message and all that Koestler had written up to then about the dilemma of means and ends. One of the personalities at the founding of the new kibbutz is Bauman, a tough ex-socialist from Vienna and a veteran of the Spanish Civil War. Bauman is an officer of the Haganah, the underground militia loyal to the mainstream Zionist movement. He proclaims that the Arabs will be compelled to accept the Jewish presence in Palestine only by force of arms and expresses impatience with the European-born intellectuals among the ranks of the pioneers who agonise over the Jewish–Arab conflict. 'We cannot afford to see the other man's point', he snarls. Simeon, a settler who is drifting into the ranks of the extremist underground, shares Bauman's conviction: 'We have to counter terror by terror for purely logical reasons.'[39]

As the members of the new settlement endure a rain of blows Bauman and Simeon try to convince Joseph that the flow of history renders personal choices irrelevant. Uncannily echoing Gletkin in *Darkness at Noon*, Simeon tells him: 'Each of our acts goes on record. It is weighed on objective scales and not on the individual balance.'[40] Bauman persuades Joseph that 'the moment had come for us to stop redeeming the world, and to start redeeming ourselves. We can't wait until socialism solves all racial problems. That will perhaps happen one day, but long before that day we shall have been exterminated.' They had entered a 'political ice age', with its own logic: 'We have to use violence and deception, to save others from violence and deception.' Joseph's moral system crumbles. He is 'too weary to argue about Ends and Means – for that is what the question boiled down to'. With insouciance, the hard-won argument of *Darkness at Noon* is apparently jettisoned.[41]

Thieves in the Night thus marks a serious qualification of Koestler's earlier political thinking. He now felt compelled to justify the use of violent means for political ends, albeit ones that were calculable and limited. History did, after all, have its own logic.[42] Joseph's argument differed only by degree from the Communist line that violent revolution was justified to improve the lot of the masses and that a police state was necessary to protect those gains.

These were difficult questions to which Koestler would return again and again in his writing career. But in the New Year of 1946 he did not have time to resolve such conundrums. *Thieves in the Night* was a political act; with news of events in Palestine inciting him he slaved over drafts of the novel. He wrote the first versions in longhand and then dictated from his almost illegible screed to Paget, who typed the first draft; he then worked on the rough typescript until it was ready to be retyped. In early January 1946 they were working solidly throughout the day in Koestler's room, accomplishing twenty-five pages by dinner time. Paget, who played an unsung role improving Koestler's English, found the pace tiring, but it had the advantage of keeping her in the one warm room in the house and she was excused from cooking elaborate meals, which she found even more tedious. In February 1946 the corrected typescript was sent to the printers. A month later he worked over the proofs, which required a lot of fact-checking with British Zionists, but by then he had already moved on to his next book.[43]

III

During the autumn and winter months of 1945–6 Koestler and Paget were not exclusively occupied with the novel. Almost as soon as they were installed at Bwlch Ocyn visitors began to arrive: they included Daphne Hardy and her partner Henri Henrion, Tom Hopkinson, the left-wing editor of *Picture Post*, Michael Polanyi, the Hungarian-born scientist teaching at Manchester Victoria University, and Lys Lubbock, Cyril Connolly's partner. George Orwell and his son Richard stayed for Christmas. These guests created a lot of work for Paget, upset Koestler's routine and consumed hard-to-obtain provisions, but they also brought food, warm clothes and supplies for the house. Paget welcomed them, too, because they liberated her from servicing Koestler's writing.[44]

The visits often had a political complexion. *The Yogi and The*

Commissar had appeared while Koestler was in Palestine so he had missed the initial reaction. Once his novel approached completion he turned his mind to effecting the ideas set out in his wartime essays. But who were his allies now? As expected *The Yogi and The Commissar* was panned, sometimes libellously, by Communists and many hard-left socialists.[45] The range of positive responses, from right-wingers to independent socialists, such as Basil Liddell Hart, Connolly, Malraux and George Orwell, only illustrated the protean interpretations to which it was open. Even Conservatives and far-right figures like Sir Ronald Storrs, a founder of the Atlanticist 'London International Group', and Commander Stephen King-Hall, a reactionary former Independent National MP (1939–44), courted him.[46] Koestler was himself unsure of how it would be percieved. He told Guy de Rothschild to send his greetings to Malraux, 'though I don't know whether he regards me as friend or foe'. In fact, Malraux was following a political trajectory not dissimilar to Koestler's and he embraced the book wholeheartedly.[47]

Koestler's anti-Stalinism also harmonised with Orwell's thinking. Soon after his return to London in August he invited Orwell to Wales but Orwell declined, explaining that he had a seventeen-month-old adopted child whom he was caring for alone since the death of his wife. But he very much wanted to meet. Koestler repeated the invitation and went out of his way to accommodate Orwell's family needs: 'This house is quite comfortable and as there are two women about you could bring your little boy or do as you like without interference.' He proffered Christmas as a suitable time.[48]

Orwell accepted and travelled to Bwlch Ocyn with his son, Richard, for the festive season. Domestic arrangements were helped by the presence of Celia Kirwan (later Goodman), Mamaine's twin sister. Orwell and Kirwan had travelled up together and hit it off. But the reunion with Koestler was initially strained. Koestler admired and liked Orwell, but felt he had to work hard on the friendship. In 1974 he recalled that Orwell was 'Rather intimidating. Rather cold, a real Burma Sergeant. It took a long time before we became friends.' The two men also disagreed about Palestine and Zionism, and decided to avoid the topic. Initially, however, their relations were endangered by a caustic review of *Twilight Bar*, which Orwell had just written. Koestler was extremely sensitive to criticism and expected his friends not to execute too harsh a judgement on his products, at least not in print. Yet Orwell had performed 'a sort of hatchet job' on the play. Neither man mentioned it when Koestler picked up Orwell and

Richard at Llandudno station, but for very different reasons. Koestler was too angry to talk, while Orwell thought nothing of it. Eventually Koestler realised that Orwell's silence was due to indifference rather than tact and blurted out: 'It was a bloody review you wrote wasn't it?' Orwell barely registered an emotional response and simply replied: 'Yes. It's a bad play, isn't it.' Few of Koestler's other friends could have got away with such a blunt appraisal, but he was so awed by Orwell's integrity that he was silenced. In his heart of hearts he knew it *was* a poor piece of work.[49]

During their stay Orwell and Kirwan developed a rapport which Koestler encouraged. In fact, Orwell was so smitten by Celia Kirwan that he proposed to her soon after they were back in London. She turned him down. In other respects, too, the visit did not go as smoothly as Koestler had hoped. He complained to Tom Hopkinson: 'We have George Orwell and his 19 month old son which is turning the house upside down . . . This is written in a stolen moment of quiet in the general upheaval with the baby howling and having just broken a wine glass.'[50]

Despite these distractions Orwell and Koestler worked on a programme for a political movement that would realise some of their ideas. The vehicle was to be a revived League for the Rights of Man, dedicated to the promotion and defence of human rights, especially freedom of thought. The manifesto was to be sent to one hundred leading personalities around the world for their endorsement. It began by stating that since the end of the war there had been an alarming increase in mutual suspicion and tension between the Western powers and the USSR. This tension resulted from the different and conflicting political structures amongst the victor nations which, if allowed to develop unchecked, would lead to decades of instability. However, a *modus vivendi* could be found if efforts were made to decrease the level of international distrust by a process of 'psychological disarmament'. 'Psychological armament' was defined as the extent to which a government prevented the free exchange of information and ideas with the outside world. Disarmament would involve dismantling obstacles to the circulation of ideas.

They proposed that Britain set the ball rolling by seeking the free distribution of British newspapers, books etc. to the public in the USSR on a reciprocal basis. In addition, Reuters and Tass would compile factual daily summaries of the world news for distribution throughout the respective blocs. Broadcasting across frontiers would not be interfered with. Citizens of each bloc would be encouraged to travel freely and holiday in the territory of the other. Since such a proposition would be met with opposition, it should be given a high priority by the Big Four at the UN and acceptance of 'psychological disarmament' should be made a precondition of political, economic or financial concessions.[51]

Koestler attempted to popularise this strategy in an article for the *New York Times* published on 10 March 1946.[52] It never caught on with either politicians or the public, but it contained a kernel of sense which was finally vindicated in the age of satellite TV, video and audio tapes, faxes and PCs. Freedom of information was lethal to totalitarian regimes: the inexorable pressure of technology would have the solvent effect on the structures of power in the Soviet bloc which Koestler envisaged forty years earlier.

After his return to London Orwell typed up the draft petition and arranged to have lunch with Tom Hopkinson and Barbara Ward, assistant editor of *The Economist*, to discuss it. Koestler was charged with making an approach to Bertrand Russell, who lived nearby at Llan Festiniog. It was a smart move. According to Freddie Ayer, 'Koestler and Russell got on well together, finding a bond at that time in their common hostility to Russia.' Paget told Wilson that Russell thought the only way to stop Russia was for America to have the atomic bomb: 'K fully agrees.'[53]

The draft petition met with Russell's approval, but he deemed that the international situation had deteriorated too far for the course of action it proposed to be effective. Koestler reported to Orwell that 'he fully agrees with our aims but not the method of approach' because 'war will be on us soon'. Instead, Russell suggested that they convene a small conference of experts on the Far East, Middle East, Eastern Europe, America, science and propaganda to work out a political programme. He offered to read a paper, but declined any organisational role. Likewise, he would support a revitalised League, but would only join it as a figurehead. Koestler proposed taking up Russell's idea and using it to launch an organisation on the lines that he and Orwell envisaged.[54]

During January and February copies of the petition were circulated to the writer Rupert Crawshay-Williams, Michael Polanyi and Michael Foot, who suggested constructive modifications. Foot was particularly enthusiastic, having become very 'anti-bolshevist'.[55] Everything seemed on course for a gathering in North Wales during Easter (19–23 April 1946). Koestler booked rooms for the participants, who now also included Manès Sperber. He asked Sperber to persuade Malraux to come, telling him: 'The concrete purpose will be to lay the foundations of a new, broader and more modern League for the Rights of Man, with the primary aim of coordinating those at present isolated movements, people and groups from America to Hungary, which have a common outlook. . . .' He intended that Rodney Phillips, the wealthy Australian-born patron of the new (and short-lived) magazine *Polemic*, edited by Humphrey Slater, would provide the finance for the meeting. Celia Kirwan was an editorial assistant on *Polemic* and acted as a go-between.[56]

However, in mid-March the project fell apart. Orwell was ill and planning to move to Jura. More seriously, Humphrey Slater, an ex-Communist and veteran of the International Brigade, took fright at the prospect of involving *Polemic* in an anti-Soviet event and scared Phillips off. After a meeting with Orwell, Kirwan and Freddie Ayer in London he wrote to Koestler demanding that the magazine's name be kept out of the programme. Koestler was furious since the conference depended on Phillips's support. In a letter to Kirwan, he called Slater an 'ass' and derided any fears that the meeting would threaten *Polemic*. But with a mixture of 'anger and relief' he had to concede that it could not go ahead. He did not give up completely: he suggested to Orwell that new financial backing for the League might come from Sir Edward Hulton or Victor Gollancz. But the project needed someone who was 'business-minded' and based in London to take it in hand.[57]

Russell remained the lynchpin of any appeal to the public. Paget noted sarcastically in her diary on 14 April 1946 that 'K. has hatched a new plot to save the world from the Russians: Russell agreed to it. So we . . . drafted a petition about it.' It was a short-lived, prickly collaboration. Koestler characterised Russell as 'impish, waspish, donnish, and for a champion of so many humanitarian causes from Pacifism to Free Love, strangely lacking in warmth'. But Russell seemed interested at first and summoned Koestler and Paget to dinner at the Oakley Arms which, according to Paget, 'we both thought very flattering'.[58]

This cosiness was not to last. A week later Patricia 'Peter' Russell, Bertrand's wife, came to dinner at Bwlch Ocyn while Bertrand was away in Cambridge. According to Paget she 'immediately had a blazing row with Arthur, as a result of which she left in a huff after five minutes'. The ostensible reason was that Peter Russell had brought with her certain amendments to the petition, which Koestler found unacceptable and so difficult to credit to Bertrand Russell that he accused her of acting on her own initiative. The deeper cause was that Koestler could not take clever women seriously and did not give the amendments the consideration he would have done if they had come directly from Bertrand Russell. The damage was compounded when Russell accidentally received a draft of the petition with a covering note intended for Gollancz. This said, *inter alia*, that he had agreed to its contents, whereas Peter had passed on his rejection of the suggestion that the Western powers should offer territory to the USSR in return for 'psychological disarmament'. Russell was 'amazed' to find that Koestler could not accept his wife as his representative and protested that co-operation was impossible. He demanded an apology.[59]

Koestler remained convinced that Peter Russell had acted alone and in a spirit of malice, but expressed his regrets at having caused offence to either of them. He desperately tried to keep Russell on board, pleading with him not to let a personal misunderstanding wreck their project: '[I] would be distressed to think that this should be the end of a political and personal contact which I value and cherish.' He then addressed Russell's reservations. Russell advocated attacking Communism through assorted publications, but Koestler maintained that a cultural campaign needed organisation. 'It is my conviction that the so-called intellectuals have to try to influence the politicians by concerted action, as a chorus and not as solo voices.' He made a few concessions, but was less pliable about 'psychological disarmament': this was the 'crux' of the project.[60]

The quarrel degenerated into an unseemly exchange over who said what to whom. More significantly, Russell dug in his heels over the petition. 'I do not think that psychological disarmament could be made part of a bargain against territorial concessions, since the latter would be irrevocable and the former not.' Russell was ill-disposed towards further co-operation: 'The difficulty that you and I have had in reaching agreement has brought me back to my earlier opinion, that men who are writers do better work as individuals than by collaborating in groups.' Why didn't Koestler just write a manifesto and publish it by himself and await the response? Koestler could not take this course. As one of Willi Münzenberg's last and most loyal disciples he knew the value of manifestos and petitions that were launched by big names who would impress the public and bring lesser stars in their wake. Without Russell's backing the League was doomed.[61]

The plan limped on. He and Orwell revised the petition again and circulated it to Gollancz and King-Hamilton. Initially, Gollancz bubbled with enthusiasm: 'I am tremendously in favour of your new League for the Rights of Man,' he told Koestler. It seemed as if he

would assume responsibility for its organisational side, but he soon
cooled. Like Russell, he had qualms over 'psychological disarmament' and, anyway, proved too busy to push it further.[62] The project
did not die entirely. The petition which Koestler hammered out
with Orwell was one tributary that flowed into the Congress for
Cultural Freedom, which met in Berlin in 1950.

Nor was the friendship between Koestler and Bertrand Russell
completely terminated. It was briefly and ill-advisedly called back
into life when Russell asked Paget if she and Arthur would like to
meet for dinner at the Portmeirion Hotel. She accepted, athough she
remarked to her sister that 'had it been Arthur he would probably
have said, yes on condition that you take back everything you ever
said . . .' Having once again become 'palsie-walsies' they gathered at
Portmeirion. It was a mistake. 'Peter provoked Arthur so much that
half way through he went off and was discovered later haranguing
about women with Jim [Wylie] . . .' Meanwhile, Russell flirted with
Paget until she performed her customary duty of dragging the
inebriated Koestler home from the bar.[63]

Several years later Paget told Koestler that she had learned another
reason why Russell took against him. 'It is, of course, mainly because
Peter told him that you had made love to her!' Paget was inclined to
dismiss the story as invented by Russell to justify his own infidelities.
Koestler immediately slapped it down: 'As you know my taste and
allergies there is no need to go into the Peter story.' He was lying:
Koestler was named as a co-respondent in Russell's divorce
proceedings.[64]

IV

For Mamaine Paget, life with Arthur in Bwlch Ocyn had started
hopefully. Soon after arriving she wrote to her sister Celia: 'Relations
with K. could not be better, and he has made several encouraging
remarks such as that he has never lived so well with anybody else, and
that he can't see what can go wrong with our ménage.' However,
the pathos in this remark betrays an awareness that Koestler's moods
could quickly turn black. She was not even certain that she would
remain with him. 'Nobody could be more surprised at these
developments in my life than I,' she told Edmund Wilson, 'nor do I
suppose them to be very lasting.' She complained to Wilson, now
back in the United States, that Koestler 'firmly refuses to have
children, for reasons with which I entirely sympathise . . . so there
seems no chance of getting married and no point in doing so'. This

rekindled Wilson's hopes that he could entice her to America. He reiterated his love for her and observed: 'You don't sound as if you thought that you and Koestler had much of a future together. . . .' Paget quickly put him right: 'I am living with Koestler and hope to go on doing so, so I am not in a position to have any sort of serious relationship with anybody else, and I can't imagine having an un-serious one with you.' Later she explained: 'I never meant to give the impression that I didn't want to go on with Koestler – it was just caution and pessimism.'[65]

The more perceptive visitors to Bwlch Ocyn sensed something uneasy about the 'ménage'. After Daphne Hardy and her partner Henri Henrion stayed there in October 1945 she wrote:

> I was going to scold you for behaving so stupidly, as I thought when you invited us. I had a revelation and saw you as many others have probably seen you all along, as quarrelsome, ill-behaved, self-centred and boring – and thought to myself 'Good Lord, is that how he really is, all this time and I didn't see it?' But on thinking over, I remembered that for one thing you were drunk – much more drunkenly-behaved in fact than I remember ever seeing you – maudlin, almost; for another thing I was probably viewing the proceedings with a somewhat jaundiced eye in fact. Not that I take back any of the adjectives, but I can't feel irritated about it.
>
> Anyway, I'm glad that I made the acquaintance of your new domesticity [*sic*] – chiefly because it reduces at last an unknown bogey to the level of a common-or-garden girl (more garden, than common, of course). I must say I think she behaves very nicely – a wonderful calm and slight aloofness, however disquietening your behaviour. None of the governessy nagging, such as I could not refrain from. Still I hope she does tell you a few home truths occasionally, as otherwise I don't see what's to prevent you developing your mild megalomania to a horrid size – especially in your present splendid isolation.[66]

This magnificently bitchy letter projects a shaft of light into Bwlch Ocyn. Miraculously it did not destroy their friendship, perhaps because Daphne, his companion during the crisis days of May–June 1940, remained one of the few women from whom Koestler would take criticism.[67]

By the new year, Mamaine Paget was ready for a holiday. She told Celia: 'Life has been very pleasant lately except for an awful spell of highbrow social life with Polanyi, the Crawshays and Bertrand

Russell.' Polanyi, who often vacationed at the Oakley Arms, spent several evenings with Koestler. Paget found him excruciatingly boring: 'Koestler had endless conversations about the weight of various particles. What with this, a clash of semantics, more physics, and emergent vitalism with Russell, a discussion with the latter on politics came as a great relief to my weary brain.' Although Edmund Wilson, among others, considered Paget bright and witty, Koestler was so overbearing that he reduced her to pathos: 'my inferiority complex about my ignorance and general dumbness is worse than ever.' In another insight about conditions in the Koestler household, she added: 'No major rows since you were here; things seem to be looking up.'[68]

She gratefully seized the chance of a trip to Switzerland where she looked forward to a rest from cleaning and typing and listening to abstruse conversation. She also hoped that the climate would improve her health: Paget was asthmatic, and the cold, damp farmhouse in wet North Wales had a deteriorating effect on her condition. She travelled to Zurich and stayed for a month at Wengen and Gstaad, where the mountain air worked its magic and her asthma improved. Her feelings about Koestler benefited too. 'I am blissfully happy but I do miss you, especially in bed at night it is sad not to have a mumbling Nyuszi curled up beside me.' She wrote to Wilson that

> really things do seem to be working out much better than I had foreseen, and it does look to me as though we will be permanent. At any rate I am very happy with Koestler and I think he is too. He is not altogether easy to live with, because he has a violent and emotional temperament which carries him to extremes in both directions; but he is never mean or selfish and never boring. Also he is really fond of me and looks after me wonderfully. So you see I don't think of marrying anybody else and don't suppose I ever shall. It's funny, I never expected to be able to live with Arthur for five minutes, but I find I can. I certainly find it very difficult to live without him. I don't know if I could possibly manage that.[69]

Koestler accompanied Paget to London and stayed in town for several days to work in libraries, buy books and socialise. He saw Michael Foot, 'with whom I became great friends again – he has become very anti-Bolshie and full of enthusiasm for the League idea', before returning to Bwlch Ocyn with Lys Lubbock and Cyril Connolly. After his guests had left the weather closed in and he settled down to an 'orgie [sic] of being alone and working'.[70]

Shortly before Paget's return he left Wales again and stayed in London, where he recorded a broadcast for the BBC in a hugely popular series called *The Challenge of Our Time*, which attracted audiences of three to five million listeners. It sought to clarify values in the wake of the war and remedy 'the lack of synthesis in modern thinking and in particular the wide gulf between the scientific and the humanistic approaches to life' by giving a platform to a range of social thinkers, writers and scientists including J. D. Bernal, Michael Polanyi and J. B. S. Haldane. Koestler's talk on 'The Modern World and the Soul of Man' opened the series and was one of the most popular. According to him the current political crisis posed to humankind an unresolvable ethical dilemma: whether to risk moral erosion by expediency or destruction through seeking impossible compromise. Progress depended on 'an admixture of ruthlessness'. But the end only justified the means 'within very narrow limits'. The crucial task was to calibrate the mixture to the needs of the times, not Utopian plans. He concluded: 'I am not sure whether what the philosophers call ethical absolutes exist, but I am sure that we have to act as if they existed. Ethics must be freed from its utilitarian chains, words and deeds must again be judged on their own merits and not as mere makeshifts to serve distant and nebulous aims.'[71]

This talk, and the other lectures, included a good deal of hostility between Koestler and the fellow-travelling scientists Bernal and Haldane, the latter commenting that Koestler had indulged in 'utter nonsense' and stated the moral dilemma 'as wrongly as was possible'. Even Crawshay-Williams, who wrote the conclusion to the publication based on the lectures, conceded that Koestler had polarised the debate unnecessarily. Koestler was more worried by how he sounded. Mamaine Paget noted that he 'was horrified by what he calls his strong German accent'. Public speaking was, indeed, torture for him and he loathed his alien cadences.[72]

Paget meanwhile travelled to Lausanne and Geneva until dwindling resources forced her to return. Koestler collected her in London and by mid-March they were back in Wales working on the book about 'psychology' which would subsequently be published as *Insight and Outlook*. When the weather improved they walked up Snowdon, although Koestler's age was beginning to show and according to Paget he 'could hardly make it'. Their relations were fragile, as always. She told her sister Celia: 'Imagine, we haven't had the slightest row since before you were here. It is like that, one has bad spells and good spells.' Koestler tried his hand making Austrian-style noodles, but such jolly interludes were rare. 'Everything is going well except for the

mountains of correspondence Arthur gets which I have to answer . . .
It is [a] stinking bore. It makes us both frightfully bad-tempered.' A
few weeks later she protested to Celia: 'K. has been in an absolutely
fiendish temper, so life has been hardly worth living.' Koestler
expected her to toil as his secretary and housekeeper. Sometimes these
roles clashed: he would get tetchy when Paget's house cleaning or
cooking caused too much noise. But he gaily invited friends to stay,
then became irritated when the preparations and entertainment
disturbed his work. 'I begged K. just for once to desist from his
nagging on the subject. But has he done so? Not for one minute.'[73]

To add to Paget's burdens, in July Koestler's mother Adele arrived
in Wales to convalesce from her wartime experiences. After the
Germans had moved into Hungary and the deportations started
Koestler managed to get Palestine immigration certificates from the
Jewish Agency for his mother and her sister's family, but for five
months no word reached the outside world about her fate. Then, on
23 October 1944, Koestler was informed by Francis (Ferenc) Aldor
that his wife (Adele's niece) had got a cable to him and included the
information that Koestler's mother was safe. However, her sister
Rosa, her other niece Margit and her family had all been deported
and murdered.[74] There followed the siege of Budapest by the Red
Army and the Russian occupation, during which Koestler heard
nothing more from Adele and assumed that she had been killed. But
Adele was alive. She had been forced into the Budapest ghetto on 18
December 1944, but survived the bombardments and raids by the
anti-Semitic Fascist Arrow Cross gangs.[75]

In July the Jewish Refugee Committee in London passed on a
message to Koestler from his mother informing him that she was well,
but desperately in need of financial help. Koestler used a businessman
operating in Hungary and members of the British mission in Budapest
to get news to and from Adele, and set in motion the diplomatic
machinery to bring her to England. He wrote to her: 'Only a little
more patience, dearest, and we shall be united again. Don't let yourself go; everything depends on one's own will. My books have been
fairly successful here and in America and I shall be able to give you all
the comfort which you have so bitterly missed.' In the meantime, he
sent her tea and chocolates, which she ecstatically received. Ever the
proud mother, she also asked him to send copies of his books.[76]

Getting interim aid to Adele and arranging for her permanent
settlement in England was a drawn-out and tedious business due to
exchange controls and diplomatic rules, and Koestler fretted that his
mother might become the target for Russian reprisals against him. In

November 1945 Hungarians in Britain learned that under a new scheme announced by the Home Secretary they would be able to bring to the country 'distressed relatives'. Koestler's mother was eligible for the programme and his hopes for an early rescue soared. Once he had given a guarantee for her maintenance, in December 1945 he told her to apply for a visa to travel to England. Not content to let things work through the normal channels, he pleaded with Michael Foot to intercede to speed up the process. It was 'the usual story: she is the only survivor of her family which has been gassed at Auschwitz, is 76 and undernourished and her only means of support are the monthly 30 pounds which I am allowed to send her through the FO.' Foot contacted the Home Secretary personally and thought that it was such a strong case there could be little delay. He was wrong.[77]

The problem lay in Hungary where Adele was having difficulty getting a passport, a Soviet exit visa and medical proof that she was able to fly to Vienna. Koestler turned to an old friend, Paul Ignotus, who was working for the Hungarian diplomatic service, to see if he could accelerate the exit process. Koestler was afraid that his mother would suffer due to his anti-Soviet stance, but Ignotus was amused to find that Adele was so proud of her son that she did not disguise who she was. When she made a rendezvous with Ignotus she came up to him and loudly announced, 'Ich bin die Mutter von Arthur Koestler.'[78]

In mid-April Adele obtained the passport, but was still short of the Soviet visa. By this time her health was deteriorating. When the exit visa was finally granted in July, Koestler wrote to Dr Plesch asking him to arrange a medical examination and any necessary treatment. 'So at last my conscience is appeased and now the problem starts, what to do with her.' As Adele couldn't live with him in a freezing cold farmhouse in Wales he wrote to Dr Berliner, an old family friend, who ran a home for refugees in Ashtead, Surrey, asking if he could recommend a nursing home preferably 'with continentals of her age'. Adele Koestler left Budapest on 11 July 1946. She flew to Vienna and took the train to London, finally arriving on 24 July. Two days later she travelled to Wales and stayed in Port Madoc while she had medical tests in Bangor. In August she moved into a boarding house in Swiss Cottage run by former German refugees. In response to her nagging Koestler paid off her debts to family and friends in Budapest and dutifully supplied her with cigarettes as well as copies of his books. But he visited her infrequently and always with a sense of dread.[79]

There was other unfinished personal business left over from the war: his wife Dorothea. She was in Paris, living in Paul Willert's flat, unemployed and in poor health. Koestler asked Guy de Rothschild to help her find work, but she did herself no favours with her odd behaviour. When she wrote to Koestler she insisted on using her underground name 'Nicole' and refused to give him her address. Koestler was alarmed by the depressed tone of her letters and the demands for money. Willert and Rothschild advanced her small sums on his behalf and by February 1947, with their help, she had settled down to a new job and a new boyfriend. She had no objection to a divorce, but wanted to cite abandonment as the grounds, as if to reprove Koestler for leaving Paris without her in 1940.[80]

Other calls on his resources came from old comrades and friends among the exiles. Leo Valiani, aka Weiczen or 'Mario' in *Scum of the Earth*, had escaped from Europe to Mexico in 1940–1, where he married Eva Tay, whom Koestler had known as a child in Budapest. Valiani returned to Italy to work with the resistance in 1943–5, emerging as a hero of the liberation. He subsequently embarked on a successful career as a writer and politician. Koestler did his best to find English publishers for Valiani's accounts of the liberation of northern Italy and his philosophical works.[81] In May 1946 Alexander Weissberg, now going under the name Cybulski, turned up in Sweden as a business agent of the post-war Polish government. Koestler was delighted to have news of him and immediately offered help. Through him, Weissberg obtained a generous advance on the book he planned to write about his experiences as a prisoner of Stalin and Hitler. The two men were reunited in November 1946 when Weissberg managed to visit Britain.[82]

V

From March until June 1946 Koestler concentrated on science. When Orwell asked if he would like to succeed him as a reviewer for the *Manchester Evening News*, Koestler declined. 'The eight regular guineas are tempting, but for once I shall let puritanism get the upper hand over hedonism (dig), and try to finish the book in austerity.' Orwell also offered him the work he had been doing for the *Observer*. On this Koestler was less decisive: 'I am in two minds. I don't want to do only journalism; on the other hand, being buried in my psychology book I am beginning to feel that I am getting donnish and losing contact with political reality.' In the end he decided to risk donnishness.[83]

It turned very cold and there were few distractions. While Koestler wrote, Paget tackled the secretarial work. When the weather and Koestler allowed, she took the day off and walked in the countryside or along the coast. Or they went out together to exercise Koestler's latest dogs, named after characters in *Thieves in the Night*, Joseph and Dina. They did not entertain visitors until early April, when Guy de Rothschild, Freddie Ayer and Celia Kirwan provided welcome relief from psychology and physiology. Paget noted in her diary: 'Everything went well, the weather was good, K. good-tempered, food edible.' Two days later, Freddie and Celia, Mamaine and Arthur dined with the Russells. Koestler's mood improved once he was stuck into *Insight and Outlook*. He told Anny, his ex-girl-friend from Palestine: 'This long stretch of quiet work got most of the jumpiness and quarrelsomeness out of me at least for the time being, and I have settled down to become a dull middle-aged and respectable homme de lettres.'[84]

In May Paget fell ill and went to stay with Lady Julia Mount in London. Otherwise Koestler's tranquillity was only disturbed by the attentions of Roger Stephané, a left-wing French journalist, who specialised in luring celebrities into conversation, then publishing the exchanges as 'interviews'. Koestler resisted all political entanglements.[85] During the summer months, however, the routine of work began to crack. The Palestine emergency deepened and he felt compelled to go to London on Zionist business. Not unconnected with this, a stream of vistors began to arrive at Bwlch Ocyn.

The Zionist movement was demanding that the Jewish survivors of Nazi persecution who could not or did not want to return to their homes should be allowed to emigrate to Palestine. Tens of thousands of Jews in Displaced Persons (DP) camps clamoured to leave Europe. The pitiful spectacle presented by this remnant stirred public opinion in the United States, especially among American Jews. Faced by congressional and presidential elections, American politicians became fervent Zionists and opponents of British imperialism. Pressure built up on the new British Labour government to allow Jews to enter Palestine. But Attlee and Bevin resolutely opposed unrestricted immigration and rejected Zionist demands for the partition of Palestine and the creation of a Jewish state.[86]

In an attempt to buy time and appease his transatlantic critics, in October 1945 Attlee announced the establishment of an Anglo-American Committee of Inquiry to investigate the plight of Jews in Europe and options for solving it. Richard Crossman, a freshly elected left-wing Labour MP, was Bevin's choice for one of the four

British members to work on the Committee. When he was appointed Crossman shared the predominant British view that the Jews were a religious group and deserved equal rights in their country of domicile. However, as he heard the arguments of Zionists in Washington his mind changed and he became pro-partition. His conversion was confirmed when he toured the DP camps in Germany, followed by several weeks in Cairo and Jerusalem. Crossman believed that Bevin had promised to accept the report of the Inquiry if it were unanimous. To achieve this he stopped arguing for the principle of partition and merely called for the admission into Palestine of 100,000 Jewish DPs. However, after the Inquiry had concluded its work and published its report in April 1946 Bevin remained obdurate.[87]

Crossman felt betrayed and proceeded to organise a campaign to overturn official government policy. He found several willing allies in Labour's ranks, including Gollancz and Michael Foot, now acting editor of *Tribune*. While Crossman denounced Bevin in the *New Statesman*, Foot lambasted the Foreign Secretary in *Tribune*; Koestler's influence on their thinking was decisive. They argued that partition was politically inevitable and morally irrefutable. It was futile to try to suppress the Jewish underground armies and isolate the Jewish Agency since they articulated the overwhelming feeling of the Jews in Palestine and world-wide. By denying Jews the right to immigrate to their designated 'National Home' the British were only breeding terrorism.[88]

The coalescence between their positions led to an extraordinary collaborative venture. In June 1946, as American and Jewish pressure built up on the British government, Koestler told Crossman: 'Gollancz wants to start an all-out campaign for the transfer of the 100,000.' He was keen to secure their participation and suggested that Crossman and his wife come to stay to discuss what they could do. The result was a pamphlet entitled *A Palestine Munich*, a searing attack on the policy which Attlee and Bevin were implementing in the Middle East.[89]

Crossman and Foot wrote the first part of the pamphlet chronicling in painful detail the commitments to the creation of a Jewish 'National Home' made by Labour Party leaders, including several members of the current cabinet, and successive Labour Party conferences. Koestler dashed off a summary on the effects of British policy since 1939 and the case for partition, cannibalising the notes he made in Palestine in 1945 and his articles for *The Times*. He exposed the traditional pro-Arab Foreign Office arguments as bankrupt and counter-productive, and reiterated his view that British policy was responsible for terrorism. The pamphlet concluded that the only morally just and expedient policy was partition. Authorship was attributed to Crossman and Foot, but Koestler received twenty-five per cent of the royalties from Gollancz, who published it. Even so, this probably undervalued the extent of his contribution.[90]

London was now a centre of Zionist diplomatic operations. Koestler had the idea of distributing one hundred paper-bound copies of *Thieves in the Night,* which was due for publication in October 1946, to key MPs and opinion leaders. He asked Crossman what he thought of this since 'I would do it only if I were convinced that it could do some good'. Crossman advised against: 'It would give everyone who read it, and who had predetermined views, excellent quotations to prove his case. It would give everyone who really wanted to understand an understanding. If it were published normally, I should say "Thank God". I am more dubious about one hundred copies being sent out in advance.'[91]

Koestler's mood was darkened by the Palestine imbroglio. Mamaine reported to Celia that he avoided discussing Palestine since 'it depresses him so much to think about it'. However, the Crossmans came to stay for a week in August and Koestler's temper improved while Dick was available for argument and chess. Teddy Kollek also briefly joined them and was coached by Koestler before addressing an important meeting of MPs at the Palace of Westminster. The visitors created extra headaches for Paget: 'they have anti-social meals like tea which take hours, especially when one has to make coffee at the same time for Arthur.' Koestler couldn't understand why she had to do so much cooking, which distracted him from his work and her from her normal duties. Fortunately, Zita Crossman pitched in when it came to plucking chickens and skinning rabbits. They loved staying with Koestler. Afterwards, they told Paget that they could not 'understand why people say he is difficult and quarrelsome'. They were soon to find out.[92]

Meanwhile critical responses to *Thieves in the Night* began to appear. Cyril Connolly read it in one sitting and by the end felt that at last he knew something about the Palestine situation. He was less positive about the literary qualities of the novel: the first part was 'magnificent', but then the narrative lost momentum. He was also uncomfortable with the message. 'I view with grave alarm your adherence to the terrorist mystique in the last chapters.' He protested that if Koestler applied his own criteria of means/ends 'they are entirely wrong and that to conspire to kill people for the highest nationalistic motive is still murder'. Koestler avoided a political debate with Connolly, but acknowledged that 'as far as the artistic aspect is concerned I believe, with some resignation, that your opinion is by and large correct'.[93]

Crossman was unstinting in his praise. 'You are one of the few people who has got inside the Jews, the Arabs, and the British administrators . . . and . . . has the literary skill to express it. Like all good writers you are an anarchist in the sense that you are so truthful that your book doesn't fit into any party line . . .' Teddy Kollek was less fulsome. 'Not a kind book at all,' he told Koestler. 'We poor Zionist officials get it properly in the neck, but I must confess that in spite of that it was a great joy to read it.' Ben-Gurion wanted the translation rights for Am Oved, the house publisher for the main socialist Zionist party, but Koestler had promised them to the right-wing Eri Jabotinsky.[94]

Guy de Rothschild told him that Isaiah Berlin, Randolph Churchill, Victor Gollancz and Alistair Forbes had all read the book and been impressed by it. Yet they, like Rothschild, took exception to the 'Incident' in which Joseph's Gentile mistress is alarmed by his circumcision. 'Such an episode could indeed easily take place in Central Europe and even in France, but in an Anglo-Saxon country it is out of the question.' Many other critics and correspondents took issue with the emphasis which Koestler placed on circumcision. Eric Mills noted this too, but concentrated his fire on the depiction of the British Mandatory officials: 'All of us can be caricatured,' he complained. 'I do not think you will be loved for this book.' Edwin Samuel, to whom Koestler also sent a copy, found it 'witty, malicious and, in places, memorable'. Margaret Storm Jameson was 'enormously impressed'. She was convinced by Koestler's argument that the Jewish situation simply exemplified a dimension of human existence: to her this made *Thieves in the Night* as universal as *Darkness at Noon*.[95]

One of Koestler's toughest critics was Daphne Hardy. She mercilessly attacked his use of English and recommended that he get help with his prose. There was an element of vanity in this suggestion since she had translated the acclaimed *Darkness at Noon*, but the manuscripts of his novel, not to mention his diaries, suggest that he indeed remained in need of linguistic guidance. Her main critique was reserved for the politics of the novel. Hardy knew *Darkness at Noon* inside out. She accused Koestler of reneging on the principles it set out: 'I can't see why you don't have the courage of your convictions about the end *not* justifying the means; it doesn't become any the less true because you feel vicarious conscience pangs at the thought of other people suffering . . . Anyhow the terrorist tactics seem to me more likely to increase Jewish suffering than reduce it, however long a period you take into consideration, by arousing mutual hatred between Jews and British, and anti-Semitism among ordinary people here.'[96]

Koestler was stung into a long and careful reply which conveyed the essence of the riposte he had made to every critic who accused him of back-tracking on the most important point of his political philosophy.

> I agree with most of your literary criticism of *Thieves*, but the political question is another matter. I never said that the end doesn't justify violence under any circumstances (you can look it up in the Yogi [*sic*] if you like) but that the problem is partly a quantitative one (proportion of sacrifice to aim) and partly one of the historical constellation. If one accepted the total Yogi attitude, one would have to reject all revolutionary movements including the French, the Russian, all the maquis etc – or describe them as 'fascist'. Whether the terrorists have done more harm than good is a consideration on a quite different, utilitarian plane. On the whole I think that acts of sabotage with due preliminary warning, passive and active resistance against the prevention of immigration, and even retaliation for floggings may be historically justified, whereas indiscriminate assassination cannot be justified either on ethical or utilitarian grounds.[97]

It is true that Koestler never claimed to be a pacifist, but Hardy was not accusing him of failing to live up to such standards. His self-defence exposes the extent to which he was still in thrall to a materialist conception of history and morality. 'History' justified violence: the precise scale of violence was a utilitarian calculation. Rubashov had rejected just such equations because the human element rendered them incalculable and, above all, he challenged the notion that human life could be taken in the name of abstract, historical forces. It was a breathtaking volte-face.

Thieves in the Night sold 20,000 copies in Britain, which was good in the circumstances, but created a sensation when it appeared in the United States: 50,000 were sold in the first week of publication. Begin's propagandists in America used it shamelessly as a pro-Irgun tract. There were even rumours in the USA and Palestine that Koestler was about to undertake a tour on behalf of the right-wing Zionist underground. The book was so potent that Kollek proposed smuggling copies into Palestine. The plan for it to be sent to British MPs was dropped, but it was subsequently read by the members of the United Nations Special Commission on Palestine, which eventually recommended partition and the creation of a Jewish state to the UN General Assembly. Koestler later learned that the chairman and several members of the Commission had found the novel most illuminating. It was one of his proudest achievements.[98]

VI

The Palestine emergency in the summer of 1946 put paid to the long stretch of isolation, constructive work and, with it, peace of mind. Koestler made more trips to London to give talks and attend meetings. Kollek and Crossman kept him up to date with events in Westminster, while he put Kollek in touch with politicians like Randolph Churchill, who he thought would find his point of view useful.[99] Often he cabled Paget at the last minute to warn her that he was returning with a crowd of chums. These 'invasions' caused trouble for her and usually ended up annoying Koestler too. Since visitors involved cars and drinking, they frequently led to automobile crashes. In August Koestler drove Paul Willert's car into a ditch and damaged the front axle.[100]

Notwithstanding his disenchantment with British policy on Palestine, he resolved to seek British nationality. He told John Strachey, now the Minister for Food, that as he was nearing the age of forty-one he felt it was time to become 'normal'. As 'one of my oldest friends in this country', he told him, 'if I am to become a British citizen I would like to do so in style and have a member of the Government among my sponsors.' Strachey was only too glad to oblige, as were George Russell Strauss, Michael Foot, Nye Bevan and Sylvester Gates. In early September he formally applied to the Foreign Office for a certificate of naturalisation.[101]

During the summer Koestler also toyed with the idea of going to Palestine to give lectures at the Hebrew University. Instead, when the time came for a break from psychology, he decided to visit Paris. There were several reasons for this excursion. A French version of *Twilight Bar* (*Bar du Soleil*) was being staged by Jean Vilar at the Theatre de Clichy in Paris in October and Koestler wanted some say in the production. A visit would also allow him to restore his ties with old friends, especially Manès Sperber. He had unfinished business, too, from 1940, including the recovery of abandoned manuscripts. Pre-eminently, however, he wanted to relish the success of the French translation of *Darkness at Noon* (*Le Zéro et l'Infini*). Koestler regarded France as the front-line of the war against Soviet influence. The huge sales of the book were a reflection of, and contribution to, anti-Communism. His celebrity might also provide a basis for rallying French intellectuals such as André Malraux in support of the League.[102]

Le Zéro et l'Infini had appeared at a crucial juncture in French politics. In elections to the constituent assembly in October 1945 the Communists had emerged as the largest party, with twenty-six per cent of the vote. In the subsequent debate over a new French constitution it pressed for a unicameral legislature that it could dominate thanks to its commanding electoral position. In the run-up to the referendum on the constitution, to be held on 5 May 1946, both sides engaged in intense propaganda. *Le Zéro et l'Infini* was promoted by conservatives and socialists as proof of the iniquity of Communism, while pro-Communist publicists attacked it remorselessly. Sales spiralled upwards: by April 1946 it had sold around 70,000 copies. When the Communists lost their bid for a single-chamber legislature, several commentators, including François Mauriac and Sperber, attributed the defeat partly to the influence of the novel. This delighted Koestler. He wrote to Guy de Rothschild: 'The results of the referendum were the happiest political news for a long time. Vive la France.' Now he wanted to enjoy what he considered to be an almost personal triumph. By mid-August 1946 sales had reached 200,000 and Koestler was also keen to spend some of the massive royalties he was earning in a country where food and other luxuries were not rationed.[103]

He prepared for the trip with a sense of anticipation and foreboding. He confided to Leo Valiani that his success in France seemed to have come too late: it was 'somehow too cheap to get real fun out of it'. His mood was not improved by the trouble he had obtaining travel documents. As a former refugee – one of the 'scum of the earth' – he had 'an archytypal [*sic*] neurosis' about visas and passports, and suspected that the problems were due to a 'dossier' in the hands of the secret services of either France or Britain. A few days before Mamaine and Arthur left for London they had dinner with the novelist Richard Hughes and his wife, who lived on the coast near Portmeirion. Mamaine told Celia that Koestler got so drunk that 'on the way home along the sand . . . he kept falling down; once he walked off a wall where he thought there were some steps and there weren't; then he disappeared into a hole, and shortly afterwards was seen up to his waist in the sea.'[104]

On 1 October Koestler made the channel crossing and was immediately re-enchanted by France. The dock workers all looked like the film star Jean Gabin. Even the ruins of recently fought-over towns looked 'picturesque'. Yet the romance was tainted by an awareness of past and future perils. Many coins still bore the head of Marshal Pétain; the dockers were probably all pro-Communist. For the duration of his visit Koestler was suspended uneasily between personal history and current politics.[105]

The first days passed in 'a kind of alcoholic whirlwind'. He had meetings with Jean Vilar, members of the cast and the play's financial backers, although it was soon clear to him that he should never have agreed to the production: the play was doomed. Years later he reflected that 'vanity got the upper hand over critical judgment'. Nevertheless he worked with the actors almost daily and rewrote part of the play at their suggestion. Much of this was accomplished over lunch, particularly with the female players. Friends claimed as much time as the theatre. After he had checked into a suite in the grand, but rather gloomy, Hotel Montalembert, Guy and Alix de Rothschild formally welcomed him to Paris with a dinner at one of the city's finest restaurants, an 'orgie', as he described it in his diary. Afterwards they went to the Sheherazade, a nightclub owned by a White Russian where glasses were smashed in ritual toasts. The night culminated with oysters at a bistro. He saw them several more times, but before long he advised Paget that he was 'bored by Alix and Guy'. He also found his old companion Paul Willert and his wife Brenda, who were in Paris at that time, tiresome.[106]

As a major literary figure he was invited to dinner at the British embassy and introduced to the new arbiters of French culture such as Maurice Merleau-Ponty. His eminence strained relations with old friends, few of whom had prospered as he had done. Manès Sperber was now working for the French occupation authorities in Germany supervising propaganda work. It was ill-paid and Koestler had little sympathy for a job that involved propaganda and censorship.[107]

The Holocaust had sharpened Sperber's sense of Jewish identity, too, and accentuated his nostalgia for the world of East European Jewry, which the Nazis had destroyed. But to Koestler this made him seem increasingly 'rabbinical'. That did not stop him seeking Sperber's help for his crippling depression. Sperber was a disciple of Adler and even though Koestler was hostile to all branches of Freudianism, he was ready to try anything. He spent hours 'pouring out his soul' to Sperber, as in the old days. When the attempted 'psychoanalysis' failed Koestler blamed Sperber claiming that he 'lost

[his] grip after 20 minutes'. It must have been a strange kind of analytical session, though, with Koestler's dependence on Sperber juxtaposed against the wild divergence of their fortunes. By the end of the visit Koestler found Sperber clingy and 'painful'.[108]

Sperber was in good shape compared with Andor Németh. He and his wife had survived the occupation, but were now penniless. When Németh spotted that *Twilight Bar* was about to go into production he saw a chance of easy money since he had translated the play in Budapest in 1933 and Koestler had then conceded co-authorship to him. He pestered Koestler for a meeting and they saw each other for a rushed and 'sordid lunch'. Németh asked if Koestler could provide him with enough money to work for a stretch on a new book; otherwise he would have to take his chances and return to Hungary. Koestler reluctantly agreed and arranged for the money to be transferred to him. Németh took the cash and returned to Budapest anyway: it was a pathetic ending to a friendship.[109]

After a week in Paris, Koestler wrote to Paget: 'The first three days were heaven, but then I got rather depressed. To be a lion is only fun for a very short time, or if one is younger, or if one's vanities are of a simpler nature.' He had cancelled a press conference, a reception and now refused interviews. 'The real trouble is that my friends of the old scum crowd are partly dead, and with those who are still here I can't recapture the old contact and warmth. I have so much looked forward to seeing Sperber, Németh and two or three others again – but it is all rather ghastly. They live in greater misery than ever and I have become an arrivist [*sic*] for them. That kills everything. I have always comforted myself when feeling lonely that these people are in the background to fall back upon, and now I feel more cut off than ever.'[110]

His encounters with Malraux were more successful. The two men had known each other slightly in the 1930s, so there were fewer memories to betray and their respective successes enabled them to meet as equals. Both were writers and men of action who had thrown themselves into the Spanish Civil War. Both had been men of the Left, although Malraux was too independent-minded actually to join the Communist Party. Both were disillusioned with the Soviet Union and by 1945 perceived it as the greatest threat to Western Europe. Malraux had thrown in his lot with de Gaulle during the General's brief tenure as head of government leading a multi-party coalition from November 1945 to January 1946. At roughly the time that Koestler was in Paris, he was busy with the formation of the Rassemblement du peuple français (RPF), intended as a vehicle for the General's bid for power. Malraux hoped the RPF would occupy a middle position between anti-Communism and pro-Americanism, the two poles of post-war French politics. To this extent his political project was similar to Koestler's. Koestler looked to Malraux as the key to his attempt to relaunch the League for the Rights of Man in France and to rally intellectuals against Communism.[111]

They first had a 'long, explosive, intensive dinner' at Malraux's large art-deco home in the suburb of Boulogne-Billancourt, then regularly saw each other until the day Koestler left. He was tremendously impressed by Malraux, whose capacity to write on art and literature while also engaging in political activism approximated to Koestler's personal ambition. Paget thought that he was 'rather in love with him'. With Malraux, Koestler was 'unusually humble and hardly able to get a word in edgeways'. To be fair, it was not unusual for Malraux to silence his interlocutors: he spoke at a furious pace, rarely ending a sentence and punctuating his orations with a repertoire of sniffs, coughs and tics. Koestler confessed to Paget that in order to avoid utter exhaustion he would deliberately stop paying attention while Malraux was indulging in a long anecdote and would occasionally even allow himself to nod off.[112]

Koestler worried that he was too old to make new friends, fearing that there was not enough time to amass the hinterland of shared experiences that bound people together. For a moment he thought that Albert Camus would prove the exception. They discovered much in common. Camus, like Malraux, had a distinguished record in the Resistance, but was also growing uncomfortable with his erstwhile Communist allies. Like Koestler, he had been a Party member, if only briefly, before the war and was currently searching for a new political philosophy that would translate the ideals of the Resistance into a peace-time context. His wartime novel *L'Etranger* and his philosophical essay *Le Mythe de Sisyphe* brought him fame and displayed a breadth of talent that placed him alongside Malraux and Koestler.[113]

He found Camus 'charming', with the looks of 'a young Apollo'. They shared an 'easy camaraderie' based on similar tastes, which included boozing and 'running after women'. One evening when they met at the Café de Flore, Camus even tried to pick up a girl for Koestler. But Koestler sensed 'a slight streak in Camus' character which prevented him from entering into deeper human relations'. Two weeks after first meeting they quarrelled, although a letter from Camus smoothed things over. A few days afterwards they went out to dinner and proceeded on to an 'unpleasant nigger bar' where they got drunk. He had another high-octane encounter with Camus in the company of Jean-Paul Sartre and Simone de Beauvoir which turned into a drunken riot at the Sheherazade night-club. According to Jean Cau, Sartre's amanuensis: 'One night, Camus and he, pissed, proposed a challenge. Who could cross the place St Michel the fastest on all-fours? Koestler won the race but Camus accused him of getting up slightly before the end. They hit each other. It was a feeble scrap, but Camus got a poke in the eye.'[114]

Thanks to the hunger for new ideas Sartre, much to his own surprise, had become a world figure. His play *Huis Clos* (*No Exit*), the philosophical essay *Existentialism and Humanism* and his founding role in the new journal *Les Temps modernes* established him as a major thinker. Like most intellectual visitors to Paris, Koestler made his way to St Germain des Près, where Sartre and his partner Simone de Beauvoir did their writing and where they held court. Koestler's recollections of his whirlwind alliance with Sartre and de Beauvoir are coloured by the ugly rows that as quickly drove them apart. This may explain his 1970s description of Sartre as a 'malevolent goblin or gargoyle' and his slighting portrayal of de Beauvoir as 'a planet shining with reflected light'. But he never disguised the excitement and admiration that propelled his journey to the Left Bank. 'I admired both of them as novelists and playwrights, though not as philosophers.' While politically distant, 'there was a warmth of feeling and affection between us which had all the makings of a genuine friendship'. For a time he believed that they would replace his pre-1939 comrades. It was not to be.[115]

After much vacillation, Koestler decided that Paget should join him in Paris. She arrived on 17 October and was immediately swept off on a tour of his old haunts, cafés and bals musettes, ending up with oysters and wine at 4.30 a.m. Her diary is a wonderful source of information about the rest of the visit. It also exposes the tension between her physical frailty and his gargantuan appetite. Koestler whirled on and on, like the maniacal little boy in Budapest who never knew when to stop, barely cognisant of his playmates' exhaustion.[116]

Koestler first caught up with Sartre on 18 October at the subterranean bar of the Pont-Royal Hotel, which Sartre and de Beauvoir had taken to using after the Café de Flore became too well known as their haunt. They met again two days later at the Deux Magots, with the addition of Mamaine Paget, Teddy and Tamar Kollek, Sylvester and Pauline Gates, and Leo Valiani, who had come to Paris for two days to see Koestler. It was not a good mix. In the evening, after a 'dreadful dinner' with Sperber, Koestler and Paget met Sartre and de Beauvoir alone for more serious discussions. In his diary he recorded that Sartre 'agrees that moral question the decisive one, prepared to drop "neant"-side; agrees Ends and Means. Seems to be moving rapidly from URS [Soviet Union]'. Astonishingly, he was convinced that he had persuaded Sartre to jettison his most important philosophical work, *L'Etre et le Neant*, and adopt Koestler's political outlook.[117]

In the afternoon of 29 October, Sartre, Camus, Sperber and Koestler met at Malraux's flat. This was the climax of Koestler's political mission. Sperber put the case for reviving the League for the Rights of Man and adopting an essentially anti-Communist position. Koestler tried out his own anti-Soviet arguments. But there was no substantive agreement in the ensuing discussion. Malraux and Sartre clashed repeatedly over the 'historical role of the proletariat', to which Sartre was increasingly attached. 'He and Sartre like cat and mouse,' Koestler noted, whereas Malraux was 'quite friendly'. This was not quite how Camus perceived the outcome. He recorded in his journal that Malraux doubted whether Koestler's plan would win mass support, while Sartre refused to be involved in any denunciation of political morality that was confined to the USSR. He remained unswayed by Koestler's rhetoric that they would be 'traitors before history' if they failed to 'denounce what was to be denounced'. Camus refused to commit himself either.[118]

A few days later, Koestler, Sartre, de Beauvoir and Camus joined up for a boisterous evening. The party began at an Algerian bistro and moved on to a dance hall. Paget danced with Koestler for the first time, and judged from this and his clumsy *pas de deux* with de Beauvoir that neither had enjoyed much experience on the ballroom floor. The well-oiled group moved on to the Sheherazade, despite Sartre's protestations that it was not their sort of place. After a few vodkas, however, 'they all started to enjoy it no end'. Koestler seems to have been least cheerful of the revellers at this point and was reduced to melancholy by a combination of alcohol and wandering violinists 'playing soulful Russian music'. By the early hours only Paget and Camus were at all sober, although sobriety did not prevent him flirting with her. They prised Koestler away from the night-club, but he then insisted on dragging them to Chez Victor, a bistro in Les Halles, which he used to frequent when he was a journalist. Here they drank onion soup, which Koestler swore was a great pick-me-up. But they also consumed oysters and drank more wine.

According to Paget: 'By that time Sartre was simply roaring drunk, and awfully sweet and funny. He kept pouring pepper and salt into paper napkins, folding them up small and stuffing them into his pocket.' Koestler recalled that 'Simone cried like a crocodile'. He did not let up about politics: 'For two hours Sartre offers "unconditional friendship", I stuck to conditions.' But Sartre had more immediate problems on his mind: he was due to give an important talk at UNESCO the following day. Some time around eight in the morning the party finally broke up. Koestler then meandered around the waking streets, weeping with nostalgia 'about [the] lost paradise'. It took Paget a while to steer him back to the Montalembert. They slept most of the day.[119]

Unfortunately for Sartre, he did not have that luxury. He had to swallow a handful of pills to rid himself of the hangover and generate enough energy to get through his presentation. It was a turning point in their relations and for 'the family' of Sartre as a whole. Simone de Beauvoir, who monitored Sartre's health, wondered if he could stand such extreme self-abuse and began to see Koestler as a bad influence. She was, in any case, becoming disenchanted with their visitor from England. If Koestler's relations with Sartre and Camus had been stormy, his encounter with de Beauvoir was tempestuous. This collision of great minds and greater egos was immortalised in the third volume of her memoirs, *Force of Circumstance* (1964), and her roman-à-clef *The Mandarins* (1954).[120]

De Beauvoir's version irritated Koestler and he was at pains to counter the 'sadly distorted echo' of their relations as presented in her writings. He attributed the 'caricature' of him mainly to 'intellectual jealousy'. Rather pompously, he suggested: 'She resented Sartre's repeated offers of "unconditional friendship" and such influence as my anti-Stalinist arguments and experiences might have on him – particularly as they only saw people who belonged to, or sympathised with, the French Communist party and Stalin's Russia. Simone's own influence on Sartre aimed in the opposite direction, towards the extreme left.' She made Koestler think of 'the *tricoteuses* – the worthy housewives who sat knitting through the murderous sessions of the revolutionary tribunals'.[121] In fact, she was the least political of the duo and was doing her best to restrain Sartre from immersing himself in politics at the expense of his writing. She distrusted the Left far more than he did, and between 1945 and 1947 both of them were at the receiving end of vituperation from the Communist Party.

There is more truth in his comment: 'There were some private reasons for Simone de Beauvoir's later hostility towards me which are too trivial to go into.' This is a cryptic reference to their brief affair, an entanglement which in later years he wanted to play down. Contrary to the impression he later gave of de Beauvoir as a stern Jacobin, when they first met he found her 'qiet [*sic*] and intelligent'. Paget recalled that she and Koestler 'both got on like a house on fire with Simone de Beauvoir'. De Beauvoir had read *Spanish Testament* years earlier and commended it to Sartre. On Christmas night in 1944, Camus had lent her *Darkness at Noon* which she had devoured in one sitting. When Cyril Connolly saw her in Paris in 1945 she 'was pleased to learn that Koestler enjoyed Sartre's books'. By May 1945 she was also familiar with *The Yogi and The Commissar* and distanced herself from attacks on the book in *Les Temps modernes*. She never criticised Koestler's work for its assault on Stalinism.[122]

A year after she first met Koestler, she described him to her American lover, Nelson Algren, as 'a strange, interesting man; sometimes when he is drunk, he is very conceited and he feels a kind of martyr, and he takes himself so seriously it is awful'. But he could also be 'very sincere, simple and friendly'. Even though she wrote bitterly about him in *Force of Circumstance*, de Beauvoir refused to hide the thrill of their first encounter. Koestler was a 'tumultuous newcomer' who brought fresh air into the claustrophobic intellectual circles of the Left Bank. She recalled the very first meeting at the Pont-Royal when he 'accosted Sartre with pleasing simplicity: "Hello, I'm Koestler."' However, she and Sartre found his pre-occupation with science tiresome. They were 'a bit embarrassed by his self-taught pedantry' and the 'doctrinaire self-assurance and the scientism he had retained from his rather mediocre Marxist training'. Koestler made their toes curl by constantly referring to his own publications, violating their own 'cool' approach to work. 'Success had gone to his head; he was vain and full of self-importance. But he was also full of warmth, life and curiosity; the passion with which he argued was unflagging; he was always ready, at any hour of the day or night, to talk about any subject under the sun. He was generous with his time, with himself, and also with his money; he had no taste for ostentation, but when one went out with him he always wanted to pay for everything and never counted the cost.' The sharp-eyed de Beauvoir noted other characteristics. Koestler 'disliked young people: he felt excluded from their future, and any exclusion seemed to him a condemnation. Touchy, tormented, greedy for human warmth, but cut off from others by his personal obsessions . . .' This was an incisive portrait and it is not surprising that it got under Koestler's skin.[123]

The attention he payed her belied his later claim that she reminded him of a '*tricoteuse*'. He sought her out in the bar of the Pont-Royal and tried to impress her by criticising Sartre's ideas. She told her biographer, Deirdre Bair, that 'he never knew when to stop. Always pushing, pushing, pushing – arguing until I agreed with everything he said, just to shut him up.' There was no mistaking his intentions. 'One night I got so drunk I let him come home with me. We slept together. It wasn't any good. It didn't mean anything. He was too drunk, so was I. It never happened again. Only that night was real, the rest is how I loathed him. I really detested him, that arrogant fool.' In fact the loathing only came later and was more to do with accumulated political differences. She told Algren in September 1947 that 'it was rather strange because we were attracted to each other, but in [*sic*] the same time there were "political discrepancies"'. She was chiefly alienated by his demand that she be more anti-Communist and his constant 'challenging'.[124]

Koestler preferred to draw a veil over the incident. But in his 1946 Paris diary he records that, on the evening of 23 October, after Paget retired, he stayed out: 'With Simone and Sartre; sleep there.' Writing in the early hours of the next morning Mamaine told Celia that after an uproarious reunion with Hans Schultz, she and Koestler had gone to the Pont-Royal bar, where she had left him with de Beauvoir and some others: 'but I can't sleep and K. shows no sign of coming in, which worries me rather as he must be terribly drunk by now (3 am).' Not only was he drunk; he was also unfaithful.[125]

In the 1980s de Beauvoir recalled this night with disgust. Yet her reconstruction of the 'seduction' and its aftermath in *The Mandarins*, in which Koestler appears in the guise of the character Scriassine, is nuanced and remarkably sympathetic towards Koestler. There is no doubt about the correlation between the two figures. In *Force of Circumstance* she describes Koestler's 'almost feminine smile'. In *The Mandarins* Scriassine has a 'thin, almost feminine smile'. Scriassine had 'prominent cheekbones' and 'fiery eyes': 'It wasn't at all the face of a Frenchman.' Indeed, Scriassine deployed a 'Slavic charm'. Like Koestler, Scriassine disliked having young people around him. The political fit is exact: Scriassine is a fanatical anti-Communist who 'saw red whenever anyone mentioned Russia to him'. De Beauvoir instinctively linked Scriassine/Koestler's politics to deracination. 'To him Russia was the enemy nation, and he did not have any great love for the United States. There wasn't any place on earth where he really felt at home.' She brilliantly connected his dislocation and insecure identity to his personality. Scriassine too 'had fled his country, and they had called him a traitor. That probably was the reason for his immense vanity: since he had no homeland, no one to stand up for him but himself, he needed always to reassure himself that somewhere in the world his name meant something.'[126]

In *The Mandarins* Scriassine represents the ex-Communist, anti-Soviet lobby which pressed Sartre to adopt either a pro-American stance or a neutralist, 'Third Force' position. But he chiefly provides a way for de Beauvoir to work through the experience of being seduced by Koestler. Her fictionalised account of their entanglement gives a clue to Koestler's successes, and failures, with women.

Anna, the character who is a vessel for de Beauvoir, admired Scriassine's writing which was 'an impassioned testimony'. There was much in what he said that made sense to her: his combination of brilliance and megalomania is authentic Koestler. Anna reflected: 'It's difficult to engage in a discussion with someone who, while talking of the world and of others, talks constantly of himself.'[127] And yet she is drawn by his energy and freshness as well as flattered by his attention: Scriassine was 'a very good listener'. Anna was moved by his compassion. They discussed psychoanalysis and Scriassine announced that: 'There's only one sickness that really amounts to anything – being yourself, just you.' At this 'an almost unbearable sincerity suddenly softened his face, and I was deeply touched by the confiding sadness in his voice'.[128]

Scriassine asks her whether she'd sleep with a man she liked and her own logic, and her boredom, lead her to say yes. But she is taken aback by his brisk, matter-of-fact way of proceeding: 'I hate a lot of beating about the bush. Paying court to a woman is degrading for both oneself and for the woman. I don't suppose you go for all that sentimental nonsense either.' Once she consents Anna feels a chill descend over them: 'There was a lot of hate in his eyes and I was ashamed to have let myself be taken in by the mirage of casual pleasure.' For just long enough while they are making love 'a conquering tenderness appeared in his face, a childlike tenderness, and I had pity as much for him as for myself. Both of us were equally lost, equally disillusioned.'[129]

Several days after their one-night stand Koestler recorded in his diary: 'two nighmare hours with Simone'. In the novel, Anna and Scriassine meet again the next day. They agreed that the night was not to be repeated. She is shocked when he admits that he was hostile, because 'We're not on the same side. I mean politically.' Anna saw the sadistic side of Scriassine, the illusion that 'loneliness can be cured by force'.[130]

Nothing Koestler wrote about himself, or anyone else for that matter, is as perceptive as this fictionalised portrayal. The undisguised affection warrants the accuracy of the criticism: the egoism, mono-mania, arrogance and sexism, his 'childish vanity', his 'overbearing enthusiasm' and his tendency to believe that 'it was manful to impose his whims on others'.[131]

The Paris jaunt displayed Koestler at his worst: opinionated, quarrelsome, snobbish and unfaithful. It was a sign of what success would do to him. The contrast was all the sharper because he was surrounded by people and places that reminded him of his earlier persona. He went to his old flat and, surprisingly, recovered some lost manuscripts. A contact in the Ministry of the Interior obtained the 'dossier' which the French secret service and police had compiled on him, which included details of the expulsion order made out against him six years earlier. The day before he left he paid a nostalgic visit to the Bourse where he had worked in 1929–30. The place was full of ghosts.

Typically, he combined serious work with socialising and drink-ing. He had several meetings with Edmond Charlot, who published a special French edition of *Scum of the Earth*, and the Calmann-Lévy brothers who brought out the French translation of *Darkness at Noon*. He assiduously counselled senior staff of the American embassy about the political situation, especially Norris Chipman. And he made contact with past and present figures in the political world, such as Léon Blum and Raymond Aron, who would provide the raw material for articles. But over lunch, dinner or drinks he could turn into a drunken, lecherous and touchy bore. One night he indulged in a spot of debauchery telegraphically recorded in his diary: 'later go off alone to Carrefour Bd Edgar Quinet, entertain two tarts one fat other thin to chicken and assiette anglaise, two pimps quarrel beat each other blood washed up with monkey-speed, try to be vicious dont [*sic*] succeed, home depressed.'

It was fitting that the visit should have a slightly tawdry conclusion. When he checked out of the hotel on 3 November he found he did not have enough French currency to pay the bill. Camus had to help him out. After a last round of drinks he left by train for the coast.

Paget stayed on and embarked on a brief but intense affair with Koestler's new friend. After four days on her own Camus told her, 'I can't leave you', and proposed that they 'run off' to southern France. She met up with him in Avignon and they spent a passionate week together. This was extraordinary conduct for people who constantly talked about friendship and loyalty, though Paget didn't deceive Camus about where her chief allegiance lay. When she left Paris he wrote to her acknowledging, 'I cannot tear you away from that other heart which, nevertheless, you do not find good.' Nor did she hide the affair from Koestler, although when she told him he 'exploded'.[132] Conventional morality seems to have had little purchase in these circles. In the short term their infidelities did not undermine their relationship and Koestler stayed on amicable terms with Camus.

VII

On his way back to North Wales Koestler paused in London for a few days, then travelled to Birmingham to see a rare British performance of *Twilight Bar*. He returned to London and stayed there for about three weeks, working in libraries and seeing friends. 'Ma' and the Berliners were upset that he had come back from Paris without any gifts for them so, in typical fashion, he improvised a lie and told them that Paget would be bringing the presents. He then instructed her to purchase pâté de foie gras, eau de cologne and a dressing gown for 'ma' and some 'hair pomade' for Mr Berliner.[133]

Instead of immediately getting back to work on his book he had to spend several days on the first of a series of articles for the left-wing New York journal *Partisan Review*, which had come his way thanks to Orwell. Koestler's agreeing to take on the 'London Letter', which Orwell had written during the war years, was not a casual gesture. He was thinking increasingly of a move to the USA: the *Partisan Review* provided an apt platform for broadcasting his views and his reputation to a like-minded American audience. It was also a perfect space for applying his theories to British and European politics. To Orwell's irritation, he used the 'Letter' to deliver excoriating commentaries on the conduct of the Labour government and disconsolate meditations on social democracy in general. Orwell complained to Philip Rahv, the editor of *Partisan Review*, about Koestler 'squealing at petty discomforts like petrol rationing that don't touch the mass of people'.[134]

The first article landed like a grenade in a symposium on the future of socialism in the magazine's November 1946 issue. Koestler damned the Labour government for pursuing correct fiscal policies and 'levelling down' in the pursuit of social equality at the expense of electoral popularity. It was inadequate for the government to defend its conduct by referring blandly to the persistence of the old ruling class and external economic circumstances. He wanted it to use some flair in presenting its policies and mobilising opinion:

otherwise it would be like the failure of Weimar democracy all over again. He reiterated the need for socialism to have a psychological dimension: 'socialism minus emotional appeal, structural changes in economy without functional changes in mass consciousness, must always lead to a dead end of one sort or another.' The Labour government was doing nothing to change the 'mental climate of the country'. He did not advocate a full-blooded revolution; indeed, he understood that reformism fitted Britain perfectly. But the Labourites made the error of 'equating gradualism with dullness'. Unless they captured the popular imagination, the Tories or the far left would capture power.[135]

One must feel some sympathy with Orwell. Koestler rattled on about the failure of social democrats to mobilise the masses, when the Attlee government had been swept to power on a tidal wave of idealism. Even after its support began to ebb away due to the persistence of rationing, adverse economic circumstances and the effects of the terrible winter of 1946–7, the Labour government commanded fierce loyalty. It lost seats in the General Election of 1950, but its vote actually rose. As so often in his political commentaries, Koestler was right, but for the wrong reasons.

On 11 November he wrote to Paget that when he finally arrived back at Bwlch Ocyn he found three hundred items of mail waiting for him which could only be cleared with the assistance of a temporary secretary. Dick Crossman came to stay for a few days, discussing Palestine, playing chess and arguing about politics. Then Koestler got back into his science book and tried not to be distracted by events in Britain, France or Palestine.[136] But he could not remain politically mute. In January 1947 he published an article in the *New York Times* condemning left-wing neutralism and anti-Americanism in France. It created an uproar when it was republished in *Carrefour*, an anti-Soviet French political weekly. Sperber admonished him that if he wanted to assemble a coalition of independent left-wingers and socialists it would not help to ridicule the neutralist position. Sitting in North Wales, he was not sensitive to the damaging effects of his tirades in the right-wing press.[137]

Paget returned to Bwlch Ocyn in mid-January 1947, to appalling weather and domestic drudgery. When she wasn't driving on treacherously icy roads to Bangor to shop for fresh food, or doing Koestler's correspondence, she was reading psychology textbooks. The worst winter in post-war British history struck Bwlch Ocyn severely. Roads were blocked by snow drifts; fuel in the house ran out; supplies of fish, meat, fruit and vegetables soon followed. Water in the pipes froze solid, leaving the toilet next to Koestler's study the only source. The oil-fired cooker stopped working so that water and food had to be heated on a primus stove. On 18 March a gale blew in one of the large windows in the main room. In the snow-covered fields outside they could see lambs and sheep starving and freezing to death. Like many people in Britain during this hideous winter they were thrilled to get a food parcel from one of Koestler's relatives by marriage who lived in the United States.[138]

The extreme weather stopped Koestler working, but created an emergency atmosphere, an *ersatz-abenteuer*, which he relished. All of his macho instincts came to the fore; Mamaine told Celia he was 'sweeter than ever, he never gets cross'. He fussed over her, worrying about her health and patching together ailing domestic appliances. 'I now see that his constant niceness creates an atmosphere of mutual affection and helpfulness which is what makes us both happy. . . .' But just as the weather improved, Koestler's disposition took a turn for the worse. During the bitter cold he and Paget consoled themselves thinking of where to take their next holiday, but couldn't agree on a country. This dissension shaded into the question of where they would move once the lease of the farmhouse expired. A letter by Paget illustrates the intersection of politics and place in Koestler's thinking:

> K. is more and more keen on going to America as soon as possible, and talks about it nearly every day. Thus, last night we had one of our long arguments about and around this subject, starting as usual with K. running down the English, going on as usual with me pointing out the horrors of American Capitalism and the dangers of having de Gaulle in France . . . then K. pointing out on the other hand the difference between the dictatorships from Stalin through Hitler, Mussolini and Franco, to Kemel [Ataturk] and Salazar and finally de Gaulle, who he believes is more or less safeguarded from becoming very rabid by his character . . . The upshot of these arguments always is, that living in Europe means living in France or Italy, and in both countries there is the dilemma between Communism and the opposite, and so on.

She maintained that since Europe as they knew it would probably not last much longer they should enjoy it while they had the chance. However, she was conscious that Koestler's English was liable to go into decline if he lived on the Continent and this troubled her.[139]

Koestler's incurable restlessness made Paget feel wretched. He talked about going to Palestine in the autumn or to America and rejected her plea to holiday in Italy on the grounds that he was too old to learn Italian. She feared that once they were in the USA she would never have the chance to see Italy again. Paget pleaded with him to stay in England and to satisfy his wanderlust by making regular visits to the Continent. He retorted that he was 'fed up with living in England' and feared that 'the Communists might come to power in France within the next 18 months' and so poison British politics. In late March he announced that he wanted to apply for travel documents to go to the USA when the lease ran out. Paget wrote to her sister in a spirit of resignation: 'Well, we'll see, it is all very gloomy, isn't it.'[140]

She was ground down by psychology, which she attempted to master to please Koestler. To Celia she confided: 'You have no idea how boring most of the latter is.' In March, once the rail-lines and roads were cleared, their social life picked up, but visitations always entailed drinking bouts, the effects of which went beyond a mere hangover. Mamaine regaled Celia with the story of an overnight stay by Kollek: 'he and K. just went on drinking Armagnac which Teddy had brought. Consequently K. had a bad attack of anxiety neurosis the next day; and of course it was a perfectly dreadful day . . .' When Koestler got into a mood he was unbearable. She complained that 'K. has been in a bad temper for about a week, but is improving now. Anyway, I take his outbursts much more philosophically than I used to. He got furious the other evening because he wanted to go to Oakley and I didn't seem enthusiastic.' Paget hated going to the pub where Koestler got steadily drunk while droning on to people she found boring; she preferred to sit at home listening to music on the radio and reading. She understood that after a day spent writing he wanted to get out for a welcome drink, but that didn't make it easier for her.[141]

In May Koestler and Paget made a brief recreational trip to France, although it was not much of a respite for either of them. Paget told Wilson that Koestler 'nearly drove us both into (a) a lunatic asylum and (b) the divorce courts. There is nothing worse than going to a place with someone whose youth was spent there and who has been hankering for it ever since.' They stayed at the Barbizon in Paris, lunched with Sartre and visited Chantilly. They also saw Malraux, who was now up to his neck in the RPF, the success of which rather alarmed Koestler. As a right-wing nationalist movement inspired by an ex-general it could not fail to ring alarm bells, no matter how hard Malraux tried to reassure him.[142]

Despite the break, once he was back in Wales he couldn't get down to work. This was partly because his mother came to stay. Mamaine told Celia: 'Poor K. is in despair, his brain is simply not functioning at all, and he still can't get back into his work; it's over two months since he was working properly so you can imagine the state he's in, and how impossible he is.' In the teeth of Koestler's opposition Paget had ordered an upright piano during her last visit to London, but once it was installed in Bwlch Ocyn she couldn't practise for fear of annoying him.[143]

The book made little progress. Koestler was distracted by another trip to London and work on a further *Partisan Review* article. This was a scorching attack on the neutralism and anti-Americanism of left-wing Labour MPs. Characteristically, it was less an analysis of foreign policy debates in the Labour Party than an exposition of his theories about political neurosis and the capacity for self-delusion. The comparison between the late 1930s and the late 1940s showed how Koestler was becoming stuck in a time warp. If he had paid more attention to the substance of the arguments he might have seen that the threat posed by the Soviet Union existed in a very different diplomatic and military context from the dangers of Fascism a decade earlier.[144]

Paget now became seriously concerned about his state of mind. 'Arthur is still depressed and morose. I always have doubts about his ultimate sanity when he is like this. This mood seems to have lasted a long time – nearly three months, I should think.' However, he was beginning to settle down to a routine of working in the afternoon from 4 p.m. to 7.30 p.m. The book was making 'slow and steady progress'. He benefited from a visit by Michael Polanyi, although for Paget it meant more cooking and more boredom. Koestler talked with him about extra-sensory perception and religion, which at least amused her. 'For believe it or not, K. has only one interest: mysticism. He also believes in miracles.' Paget couldn't take this latest development seriously. 'K. is feverishly reading about Yoga. Of course he is greatly disappointed.'[145]

Stuck together in the farmhouse, surrounded by psychology text-books, visited occasionally by academics or politicos, their relations were under terrific strain. Mamaine told Celia that Koestler 'has not yet recovered his normal interest in life, and yesterday complained that he hadn't been able to experience real rapture about anything for over a year . . . He complained that he seems to get little or no stimulation from people. He bewailed the collapse of all his heroes, and said how awful it was to have nobody to look up to.' Paget's perkiness was wearing perilously thin: 'I fear for myself, living with K. – his cynicism and pessimism are so overwhelming, and besides he has such a *mauvais caractère* he brings out all mine; I mean, we are both getting awfully bad-tempered.'[146]

One of the most curious guests at Bwlch Ocyn was Anton Ciliga, a Yugoslav ex-Communist who was doing the circuit of anti-Soviet publicists. Even in his retreat Koestler continued to assist anti-Communist exiles, referring those with exposés of Stalinism to various publishers. Others with more sensitive information were steered to members of the American 'diplomatic' service. Ciliga, who was one of those who had benefited from Koestler's advice, arrived with almost no luggage, and ate and talked without pause. Koestler was impressed with what he had to say and tried to help him find a publisher for his work, later even financing it himself. He passed Ciliga on to Camus, who responded with a humorous note. '*CILIGA m'a dit que tu travaillais comme un boeuf de labour, on attend le résultat, avec impatience.*'[147]

By the end of May Koestler had cheered up. A fortnight of steady work moved the book on significantly. He had reached a section about the psychology of jokes, which was conducive to good humour. On balmy afternoons he would stroll around the farmhouse reciting anecdotes and shaggy dog stories to himself, or trying them out on Paget. Then, just when he was making progress, Palestine erupted again. He was still thinking of a trip there in November to research the sequel to *Thieves in the Night* and to give some lectures at the Hebrew University, when, instead, Palestine came to him. Koestler was bombarded with appeals to join protests against the Royal Navy's interception and detention of the *Exodus*, a boat carrying 'illegal' immigrants to Haifa. At the end of July the hanging of two British sergeants in Palestine, an atrocity carried out by the Irgun which he supported, provoked riots against the Jews in Britain. Although no one was injured in the violence over the August bank holiday weekend, Jewish-owned property was damaged, synagogues were vandalised and Jewish cemeteries were desecrated.[148]

Politicians and the press were shocked by these 'pogroms' on British streets. The *New Statesman* was especially vocal in its admonitions. Koestler could not remain silent. He contributed a powerful article entitled 'Letter to a Parent of a British Soldier in Palestine', which attempted to explain to the British public why there was terrorism there. It cogently summarised the Jewish case and reminded readers of what the Jews had just been through. 'If, instead of Smith, your name was Shmulewitz, it might have happened to you.' The violence should be blamed on the Labour government's policy of blocking partition and restricting Jewish immigration, not the Jews. 'Political terrorism has not been invented by them; it is as old as injustice and oppression, which is its cause.' The article made such an immense impact that Koestler could not handle all the letters that poured in to the *New Statesman*. Many readers wrote in saying that they now understood what drove the Jews in Palestine and why hostility to them was wrong-headed. Gollancz was so impressed that he wanted to republish the article as a pamphlet.[149]

The events in Palestine and their repercussions in England confirmed Koestler's awareness of anti-Semitism. It seemed to him the paramount reason for securing a Jewish state as soon as possible. He wrote to F. A. Voigt at the *Manchester Guardian*:

> What you say about Palestine is unfortunately mostly true. It is already a Levantine, provincial and rather nasty little country. It will become even more Levantinized if and when partition comes about and the Sephardi Jews from the surrounding Arab countries flock in under pressure. I nevertheless believe that a Jewish dwarf state is an absolute necessity. The sharpening of the conflict with Russia will inevitably increase anti-Semitism everywhere, particularly in the United States, and Palestine will remain the only alternative to a new wave of persecution. So, without illusions, and despite my allergies against the Namiers and Glucksteins, I am prepared to fight tooth and nail for this solution. It is only a lesser evil and a palliative . . .

However, there was a price to pay for this boldness. Koestler feared that he had burned his boats again. He told Camus that thanks to his outspoken views on the USSR and Palestine he was becoming 'more and more of a leper' in England. Soon afterwards he began to make urgent enquiries about his naturalisation: would the Home Office allow him to retain his Palestinian citizenship? He was told that this would not be possible since the Home Office would treat his application as 'half-hearted'. Faced by the choice between becoming British and retaining his membership of the Jewish polity, Koestler temporarily suspended his naturalisation application.[150]

Several years later he explained: 'I felt unable to take the oath of allegiance at a time when Englishmen and Jews were virtually at war.'[151] But this was not the whole story. Koestler was driven by the logic of his Zionist ideology and his own analysis of Jewish identity to seek Palestinian citizenship as his certification of Jewishness. If the

Jews were not a race and he was not a believing Jew, the only way he could still be Jewish would be by membership of the Jewish state. His bid for dual-citizenship shows that he clung tenaciously to his Jewish roots and wanted to be 'a Jew', albeit on his own peculiar terms.

During September Koestler worked ferociously on the book. After successive ten-hour stretches, Paget reported that they were both 'quite gaga'. Their goal was to get it ready for typing by 20 September; then they would go to Paris for a break. She ought to have looked forward to this, but she had been scalded by the last visit. 'In Paris I shan't be free for one second to see any friends whom he doesn't feel like seeing, so I look forward to the trip with quite a lot of apprehension; still it is better than nothing.' They spent the final days of September in London where Koestler saw A. D. Peters, Crossman, the dentist and bought a gramophone for Bwlch Ocyn. Then they set off to France.[152]

They arrived when the country was in the throes of another political crisis. In November 1946 the French Communist Party had won the largest number of seats in the legislature and was confirmed as a major player in the 'tripartite' government: a Communist was even appointed to the Ministry of Defence. But in the spring of 1947 the government swung determinedly towards an Atlanticist orientation and began to crack down on Communists inside and outside the government. In April the RPF was launched, with Malraux as its main orator. Over the following months the Communist ministers resigned from the government amid a wave of strikes. It appeared as if the Gaullists and the Communists were squaring up to each other. On 19 October 1947 the RPF won nearly forty per cent of the vote in the municipal elections, signifying its arrival as a political force. During the autumn the police again clashed with strikers. The government summoned reservists in an atmosphere of incipient civil war. There were fears of an attempted coup by the Gaullists and full-scale insurrection by the Communists.[153]

Koestler and Paget were in Paris from 29 September until 16 October. They met Guy and Alix de Rothschild, visited Calmann-Lévy and dined with Malraux and Sperber. Malraux got drunk on vodka and was consequently even more incomprehensible than usual. However, he also gave rare insights into the political crisis when he spoke about his 'gamble' on de Gaulle. Rather frighteningly, he admitted that he was not wholly convinced that if the General launched a bid for power it would not degenerate into a dictatorship.[154]

They saw Camus and had dinner at his flat in the rue de Buci with Suzanne Labiche, his secretary, Celia Kirwan, who was now living in Paris, Sartre, de Beauvoir, Harold Kaplan, an American journalist working for the US Information Service, and his wife. Koestler soon got into his oratorical stride and began to irritate the other guests. He 'started talking about the "iron curtain" which has separated the French intellectuals from Anglo-Saxon culture since 1939, and said what a pity it was that, through no fault of their own, they were ignorant of all the latest developments in e.g. psychology, biology, neurology . . . semantics.' Paget observed that Sartre and Camus 'expressed polite regret at their ignorance, but didn't sound very worried about it'. After much alcohol had been consumed the conversation turned to politics. Sartre disliked Kaplan who was, unsurprisingly given his official role, vociferously anti-Communist. After Kaplan had gone, Sartre vilified him in the most extraordinary and insulting terms. In the unpublished version of her diary, Paget recorded that 'First he said that Kappy's vie sexuelle was such as to make Sartre think that Kappy was a salaud. We said, "What's that got to do with it?" and Sartre said "la vie sexuelle fait partie de l'homme".' But that was just for openers. The inebriated Sartre continued that Kaplan was 'anti-semitic and anti-negro and anti-liberty'. Koestler had met Kaplan in 1946 and liked him a lot. He was part of the US embassy staff with whom he did a good deal of business, some of a semi-covert nature. When he heard him spoken of in this way he 'let fly at Sartre and said who are you to talk about liberty, when for years you've run a magazine which was *communisant*, and thus condoned the deportation of millions of people from the Baltic States and so on?' Sartre was startled by this reproach and the party mood turned icy. Koestler and Paget soon left, muttering, 'We are now enemies.' De Beauvoir 'had no regrets at all' about this turn of events. She recounted to Algren that Koestler had spoiled the evening by being serious and humourless.[155]

Koestler was anguished by the row. After an autopsy, aided rather ineffectually by Paget since neither could recall clearly how it all began, he wrote a note of apology to Sartre. Sartre was glad that Koestler had taken the initiative to repair matters and replied immediately. He explained that he didn't like Kaplan and was annoyed with Koestler for having engineered his presence. After Kaplan went he got bored with the conversation and this provoked his onslaught. He realised it was wrong since Kaplan was Koestler's friend and guest. However, he didn't treat the row too gravely: 'There exists no profound reason whatsoever for such a quarrel [*brouille*] between us; quite to the contrary I am very fond of you and you yourself must be aware of this.' At the same time Sartre acknowledged that 'there is a certain fairly fundamental difference between us, which guarantees that we will be exasperated by each other, but which to my mind cannot prevent us from being friends'. The difference was that Koestler had been a Communist, a member of a movement in which individuality was subordinated and psychology was an irrelevancy, an experience that had marked him. Sartre, by contrast, was a product of bourgeois, individualistic culture and habitually separated a person from his or her beliefs or party. In a socially and politically divided society disagreements were inevitable; but this should not interfere with friendship.[156]

Sartre had made a fascinating observation about the other man. Whereas Koestler claimed that 'I did believe, and still believe, that friendship can transcend politics', in fact he did expect a high level of concurrence with his views among those whom he considered his friends. As much as he asserted that he ruled out friendship only with those who espoused totalitarian views, he actually rowed over politics with a variety of people of non-totalitarian opinions.

Over the next few days Koestler drank and ate with Camus, Sperber and Father Raymond-Léopold Bruckberger, a Dominican monk and writer who had ministered to the maquis and who was a friend of Camus, Calmann-Lévy and Raymond Aron. Paget recalled that he 'did a lot of catalysing and started a sort of marriage bureau for the "atomised" homme de bonne volonté of the Left, who he thought ought to be made to get together'. He dined with Guy de Rothschild, Aron and the American foreign policy sage Walter Lippmann. Throughout these meetings he pressed his anti-Communist views, especially on Camus. With Lippmann, Koestler became positively apocalyptic: 'if war is inevitable should one make a preventive war, and if not why not? He said that personally he was convinced it was inevitable, but wouldn't advocate a preventative war because of the chance that one might be wrong.'[157]

Such bellicose views were not unique, but on the centre-left they were rare and soon got Koestler into trouble with his erstwhile comrades. Slowly but surely he was turning into a Cold Warrior. Simone de Beauvoir told Nelson Algren that Koestler's anti-Communism was beginning to grate on her and Sartre. Before leaving he stunned the pair by declaring that he was '100% Gaullist', which in their eyes was tantamount to admitting sympathy with Fascism. She later recalled that 'Koestler was never politically honest, because his anti-Communism made him irrational, maybe even insane. We could find no common peaceful accord with him in any-thing.' However de Beauvoir was seeing Koestler through ever more jaundiced eyes, not least because he made a pass at her again even though Paget was present. They parted on frosty terms.[158]

Back in Bwlch Ocyn he vented his fury on Sartre, de Beauvoir and other Left Bank intellectuals whom he regarded as Stalin's Fifth Column in France. The result was 'Les Temps héroïques', a scabarous, thinly fictionalised account of French intellectual life which he gave to Celia Kirwan, who had joined the staff of *Occident*, a Paris-based magazine, where it appeared in March 1948. The malice and crudity of this article, written before Sartre and de Beauvoir publicly broke with Koestler, should be borne in mind when evaluating his claim that *they* caused the rupture.[159]

Written in French, it is set in a Paris ravaged and poverty-stricken after the 'second liberation', i.e. a Soviet occupation. De Beauvoir appears as Sinaida Bovarovna at the publishing house Gallimardov which boasts among its recent output such tomes as *Memoirs of an Infantryman 1939–41* by Maurice Thorez, the Communist leader, who was in reality opposed to the war with Nazi Germany until Hitler ordered the invasion of Russia in June 1941. Sartre's journal *Les Temps modernes* is transmuted into *Les Temps héroïques*, with a front-page article by M. Pontife (Merleau-Ponty), 'proving' that objective truth is a bourgeois illusion. De Beauvoir is depicted as a frigid woman of letters who schizophrenically places 'sensations and emotions, in the category of Things Not To Be Spoken About' while engaging in blood-curdling revolutionary rhetoric. The literary office which Bovarovna visits, modelled on the Gallimard office, is now a centre of propaganda and censorship, where the more senior figures such as the 'stakhanovite-poet Arogan' (Louis Aragon) sit at the front row of desks and eat bread and cheese while the lower-ranking staff make do with herrings at the back of the room. Bovarovna works on a course in 'dialectical language', the redefinition of words, which openly draws on Orwell's *Animal Farm* and anticipates his 'Newspeak'. Thus democracy becomes 'the unanimous expression of the unified will of the united people'. Liberty becomes 'the right to vote for the unanimous list of the unanimous people'. History is rendered as 'the past which is fluid, elastic and determined by present necessities'. And so forth. After hearing a talk by Professor Ilya Ehrentour (Ehrenburg), the censor leaves for a drink and peruses the Soviet-controlled papers which, *inter alia*, announce the elimination of the 'jackal Malraux, Francoist agent' and 'Camus, agent of the Vatican' condemned by Bovarovna's Committee for Vigilance over Liberty and the Press.[160]

The ferocity of this attack may have owed something to the foul mood induced by work on the final draft of the science book, finally entitled *Insight and Outlook*, which Koestler and Paget laboured on until the end of the year. This was always a bad time for Koestler: stranded between projects, but condemned to do finicky work on a text that always looked unsatisfactory in his perfectionist's eyes. The long-suffering Paget told her sister Celia: 'I am afraid he is starting a period of very bad temper, but perhaps it will blow over. I just try to shut my eyes and ears and withdraw into my shell. I feel pretty dismal . . .' In mid-November Koestler sent the revised typescript to Connolly as a 'guinea pig'. A month later they completed the changes to the final version and sent it to the publisher. Paget's sense of release was not a whit less than Koestler's. She made her feelings about the book clear by composing a very funny lampoon of Koestler's turgid style of scientific prose, which she inserted into a letter to Celia.[161]

VIII

Insight and Outlook is rich in ideas and references, stimulating and frustrating at the same time, and held together by an ego of vast proportions. It needed huge self-confidence to publish a work so full of lofty assumptions, empirical holes, unfounded hypotheses and apologias for the absence of supporting data. But however much psychologists, psychiatrists, neurologists, biologists, physicists and chemists may feast like vultures on the detail, it is irrelevant whether the evidence or argumentation is objectively right or wrong (where this can even be ascertained).

It is essentially a political tract and cannot be divorced from Koestler's politics any more than John Locke's *An Essay Concerning Human Understanding* or Hume's *Treatise of Human Nature* can be sundered from their political philosophy. Koestler makes this explicit in the subtitle, 'An Inquiry into the Common Foundations of Science, Art and Social Ethics', and in the first paragraph of the opening page. The book is, first, an attempt 'to present a unifying theory of humour, art and discovery' and, second, a bid 'to show the possibility of a system of ethics which is neither utilitarian nor dogmatic, but derived from the same integrative tendency in the evolutionary process to which the creative activities of art and discovery are traced'.[162]

The polarity he draws between preceding ethical systems is fundamental to understanding his enterprise. Nineteenth-century

utilitarianism had eventuated in Marxism and the logical principle
that the end justifies the means. Morality was reduced to a mathematical formula in which the death of thousands could be justified for
the sake of improving the lives of millions. Liberal humanism, and
religion, might assert that human life was sacred and that people had
natural rights, but ultimately these notions could be dismissed as mere
dogma. *Insight and Outlook* is one of the first political texts of the
Cold War which seeks to refound ethics and politics on an objective,
scientific basis, free of the relativism inflicted upon a divided world.
The belief that science could have such a function reveals that
Koestler was actually as much of a materialist as the nineteenth-
century thinkers whom he denounced.

Koestler began with a theory of laughter since, he asserted,
laughter was a physical reflex that registered a brain function and,
hence, offered a window into the working of the mind.[163] He
hurried on to prove that his analysis validated his theory of
'bisociation'. This was the notion that patterns of thought and
behaviour are organised into diverse 'operative fields'. The
simultaneous occurrence of a process in two 'operative fields' was
'bisociation'. Although he insisted that 'operative fields' had a
neurological basis, he confessed that he could not yet provide any
scientific validation for this theory. Unfortunately for the credibility
of the book, this was held over until volume two — which never
appeared as such. The absence of such data became more glaring
when Koestler went on to explain the workings of the brain by
extrapolating from his theory of humour.[164]

Part Two moved from laughter to crying and from the neurological to the biological. His examination of crying revealed its
association with passivity, a sense of integration and, associated with
this, self-transcendence. Whereas laughter is a manifestation of 'self-
assertive' tendencies, crying expressed 'self-transcending emotions'.
In a chapter on the 'biological foundations of integrative and self-
assertive tendencies', Koestler set out his evolutionary and developmental theory. He argued that all organic matter existed in sets
arranged hierarchically according to the complexity of their form
and function. At each level there was a tension between the
integrative or self-assertive tendencies of each part of a whole unit.
Changes in the environment of an organism led to 'excitation' and
destabilisation which could only be resolved through regression to a
lower or earlier stage of development. Thereby it established a
'regenerative equilibrium' on the bases of which further progress
was possible.[165]

Koestler saw no problem in applying the same processes that occurred in organic matter to humanity. The scope of his ambition was made explicit in a chapter on the behaviour of 'social wholes'. 'Sooner or later biology and sociology, which at present have but few points of contact, will appear as branches, or rather levels, of one discipline.' The social organisation of tribal units, for example, was comparable to the functioning of primitive cell colonies: 'social organisation is a direct continuation of biological organisation.' In human society, the 'integrative tendency' was manifested in institutions such as common law and customs. History was merely a record of social organisms adjusting to their environment and seeking to protect or enhance the means to reproduce themselves. But humanity had entered a phase when social development was gravely out of kilter with changes in the man-made environment. Totalitarianism was one form of 'faulty integration' in social terms.[166]

Koestler then turned to infant psychology to show how sophisticated societies became faulty. The infant began with a feeling of oneness with its environment, but the 'protoplasmic' consciousness which engendered harmony was replaced by a differentiated one, and conflict ensued. He attributed this to the flawed socialisation process: 'as human society, and our present civilisation in particular, are still in a transitional para–normal condition, the self-assertive tendencies of the growing individual are developed one-sidedly without adequate development of the integrative counter forces. The protoplasmic consciousness of primitive participation wanes with maturation, as it must; but no cosmic consciousness takes its place as a higher form of self-transcendence, except in a few contemplative sages, artists, and poets.' In modern societies education encouraged self-assertion, competition and the suppression of affection: 'The whole structure of our competitive society collaborates to frustrate the integrative tendencies of the individual, to thwart his potentialities of self-transcendence through cosmic consciousness, social consciousness, and other channels.'[167]

Koestler did not define 'cosmic consciousness', but in the following chapter he related transcendental consciousness to ethics. He argued that ethical clashes occurred when there was conflict between modes of social integration. In a conflicted society ethics could not solve social problems because all options for achieving harmony were necessarily partial. In well-adjusted societies, however, 'the ethical imperative is identical with the "integrative gradient," and is in need of neither utilitarian nor theological props.'[168]

Koestler gave only the vaguest notion of what such a 'well-adjusted society' might be like. The closest he came to a blueprint is this passage:

> In a balanced society, that is, a civilisation slowly evolving under fairly stable environmental conditions, we would find a continuous scale of integrative values with contemplation and competition as the opposite poles, and the various shades of integrated social behaviour between them. Nearest the top or contemplative pole of the hierarchy would range love of humanity in general, that is, the permeation of all social relations with the oceanic feeling; while art and scientific research would serve as different modes of its expression with a varying admixture of competitive impulses. Lower down the scale we would find the successive forms of integration in the successive sub-wholes of the hierarchy – the state, profession, parish, family – each with a stronger possessive and competitive factor, until we finally reached the other pole, purely selfish competition. An ideal society would form a continuous hierarchy from some kind of global federation down to the lowest sub-whole, the family (though not necessarily of the present monogamous and rigid type). In such a society individual stresses and conflicts would still occur, but they would be conflicts of relative 'right' against relative 'wrong' on one integrative gradient, and not ethical conflicts in the sense defined in the previous chapter, that is, conflicting social integrations of 'right' against 'right.'[169]

It is hard to think of this in concrete terms, let alone to distinguish conflicts between absolutely or relatively different prescriptions for right conduct. One reason for the vagueness is that all conflict is resolved on a psychic level.

The chapter on forms of self-transcendence culminated with a section on ESP, in which he asserted that the work of J. B. Rhine had put study of the paranormal on a 'scientifically solid footing' and justified the hypothesis that a 'collective mind' might exist or might be ushered into existence. The 'collective mind', not dissimilar to the form of communion fostered through meditation by mystical Eastern religions, would be the ultimate expression of the integrative tendencies and would provide the ligaments of a perfect society.[170] Koestler's Utopia now began to emerge and the connections between psychology, biology and ethics clarified, as did the role of parapsychology, a keystone in the architecture of his political thought, regardless of any scientific merit it might have. His 'scientific' agenda for the next thirty years is inscribed in these chapters of *Insight and Outlook*.

The last part of the book was devoted to uncovering the creative urge. With grinding throughness Koestler applied his theory of bisociation to exploration, scientific discovery, the visual and plastic arts, film, creative writing and even to rhythm and metre in music, poetry and fiction writing. As an analysis of archetypal literary forms the penultimate chapter was a *tour de force*, but its sparkling quality threw into relief the confused material which had preceded it and overshadowed the final attempt to draw all the threads together.[171]

Insight and Outlook sputters to an unsatisfactory conclusion. It is clear from the agony it caused while he was writing it that he was aware of its flaws. He was, however, unable or unwilling to sort out the incoherences. To make matters worse, the proofs were delivered to him in Israel in the summer of 1948 while he was on a journalistic assignment. He had no facilities to check facts, locate page references for footnotes or supply an index. Throughout the book, reference was made to an impending second volume, that would contain vital supporting data, which never appeared. A book that laid claim to being a scientific treatise of revolutionary import had all the appearance of sloppy amateurism. It was duly massacred by scientists who had the grim duty of reviewing it when it finally appeared in 1949.[172]

IX

The book had a crushing effect on Paget as well as Koestler. She had worked on it with him every day for months from 9 a.m. to 1 p.m. From 3 p.m. until 6 p.m. she either dealt with mail or worked alone on aspects of the book. Between that and shopping, cooking, cleaning, walking and feeding the dogs she had little time of her own. She seemed to have surrendered independent thought. She told Celia: 'As I have no desires, at any rate any concrete ones, I don't think much and am having a rest from my usual mental and moral struggles.' Often Koestler dictatorially insisted on going to the Oakley Arms in the evenings to relax over a game of poker or several drinks. Paget found these excursions tedious and was resentful that she had little time to read or play her beloved piano. She complained to Celia: 'I know full well that K. would never spend one single evening with friends of mine who bored *him* – but one doesn't apply the same standards to men as to oneself, does one. And I think quite rightly, for I believe there is a justice of quite another kind beneath the apparent injustice of the lives of women with men, in that the latter always do what they want and never do what they don't want.' The contrast between this account of their unequal relations and the ethical aspects of the book they were working on is painful. Paget was worn down. 'I *am* awfully gloomy because I am so worried about my future life with K. which I am determined to make a success of if it's humanly possible.'[173]

They had ferocious rows. In November she reported to Celia: 'we had a great shouting match and I threw a saucepan full of mashed potatoes at a wall, but for one thing I disapprove of this sort of thing, and secondly it wears one out and gives one a headache.' Somehow, she managed to write that she was 'getting on quite well with K., really' and to downplay his moods. But she betrayed her true feelings and the state of affairs between the two of them by adding: 'I do have moments of feeling quite gay and happy, but they are usually soon hit on the head by some new row from K.' Paget seemed prepared to find endless excuses for Koestler's boorish and violent behaviour. After one dinner with friends when he got drunk: 'The end of the evening was like the end of all evenings when K. is present, namely a struggle between me, on behalf of myself and the rest of the company, and K., on behalf of himself, in which I try to persuade him to go home and he refuses.' By the end of December she was at her wits' end.[174]

The atmosphere at Bwlch Ocyn then brightened. This was partly because *Insight and Outlook* was nearing completion and they could look forward to a well-earned holiday, but also because of the situation in Palestine. During November the United Nations debated the future of the territory. Koestler followed the news very closely and prepared for a visit if and when the UN declared the creation of a Jewish state. Mamaine informed Celia on 2 December: 'Life has changed for the better, as you can imagine, since the UN agreed on Partition in Palestine.' Koestler took the day off work and toasted the Jewish state with a string of whiskies.[175]

Insight and Outlook was packed and posted on 18 December 1947. They celebrated with a dinner accompanied by a bottle of 1916 claret. Koestler was now on tenterhooks about its reception. He 'simply can't wait to know whether his book will turn out to be good or mostly balls – it is such a gamble for him, as he has spent two years on it and will probably spend another two on the second volume. But I do feel that it is a wonderful book, even if parts of it do turn out to be wrong.'[176]

The jolly mood continued over the Christmas holidays. The

Crossmans came to stay and Koestler decided not to go to Palestine at once. Instead, he took up an offer from David Astor to write several pieces on France and Italy for the *Observer* and arranged to use this as the basis for a long vacation. Paget was pleased since she realised now that the only way Koestler would actually relax 'on holiday' was if he had a job to do at the same time. Otherwise he got tense and morose, 'feeling he was just sitting about eating and drinking while people were starving and cutting each other's throats'.[177]

Chapter 8

France, America and Israel, 1947–9

Since the collapse of the Soviet Union it is hard to grasp the sense of menace it posed to democrats in Western Europe during the Cold War or the unsettling effect Communism had on domestic politics by appearing to encourage subversion. In the late 1940s and early 1950s Koestler was in apocalyptic mood. All he saw in France and Italy tended to confirm his belief that without serious remedial action Europe was doomed to fall under Soviet domination. His anti-Communism led him closer to the Gaullists in France and the Atlanticists in Britain, and made him increasingly interested in the United States as the only source of effective resistance to the USSR or, in the worst case, potential refuge. His pro-Americanism as much as his anti-Communism set him apart from most European intellectuals on the Left and fractured many of his friendships. A long, exhausting trip to the USA, however, brought new more ideologically amenable companions.

As Koestler's politics modified he wavered between settling in Europe and the USA. To remain in Europe entailed 'saving' Europe from Communism. To do that he needed to help create a viable political alternative. So throughout 1948–9 he engaged in frantic work at the interface between political activism and the formation of political ideology. This dilemma would not have been necessary had Koestler decided to live in Israel, which might not have seemed unreasonable for a stateless Jew with fervent Zionist beliefs. Much later he admitted that in 1948, when he visited the newly created state, he came close to moving there permanently. He confessed that 'The ostensible reason for the journey was to act as a war correspondent . . . But my personal motives were more confused. I was vaguely hoping to be able to make some positive contribution to the reborn nation's struggle for survival.' He and Paget 'even, half-seriously, discussed the possibility of settling in the Promised Land if some creative opportunity for being useful offered itself'.[1]

However, his encounter with the Jewish state was a disaster. The consequences are registered most obviously in *Promise and Fulfilment* (1949), the book which came out of his six-month stay in the country. In this factual account of the struggle for Israel, the Jews and Zionism are treated with ambivalence at best and hostility at worst. Much of *Promise and Fulfilment* recurs in his later autobiographical works, projected backwards in time. It is impossible to understand what he says about his Jewish origins, Judaism or Zionism in *Arrow in the Blue* and *The Invisible Writing* without taking into account the effects of his 1948 visit. The views he then developed on Jewish questions are either attributed in essence to the young Koestler, or summoned up to expose his youthful naïveté as if there had never been alternatives to the eventual outcome of his life's journey.

Once Koestler had decisively rejected the realisation of his Jewish identity through Zionism he deliberately cultivated a cosmopolitan, de-Judaised image in his autobiographical writing. The break with Jewishness and Zionism, which is flagged at the end of *Promise and Fulfilment*, began a process of repression that inflected all his subsequent activities. Koestler moved restlessly from place to place and subject to subject; his personal life was equally unstable. At odds with his origins, uneasy with himself and unable to settle because with no clear identity it was not clear where he belonged, he was condemned to a nomadic life-style. Homelessness became his domicile, and his politics were the politics of location and dislocation.

I

After the Christmas break Paget and Koestler set off for France again. They first travelled to London and spent several days seeing friends. Koestler paid a dutiful visit to his mother and refreshed his political contacts. They arrived in Paris at midnight on 7 January and stayed until the end of the month. The mood there was tense. Political strikes led by the CGT (the Communist-controlled trades union movement) had rumbled on all through the autumn. Riots, leading to clashes between Communists and the police, had occurred in Paris and Marseilles. France seemed to be polarising into two antagonistic blocs. Although the centrist government, led by Robert Schuman, had broken the strike movement in mid-December, the situation remained precarious. During the new year the Communists led a new series of anti-American actions.[2]

The conduct of the French Communist Party and the CGT convinced Koestler that either a coup or a civil war was bound to occur in France, probably heralding a Russian invasion and thereby triggering the Third World War. His customarily frenetic socialising was consequently tinged with even more hysteria than usual.[3]

Malraux was now running the propaganda office of the RPF and was de Gaulle's chief cheerleader. Koestler visited him at his office on the boulevard des Capucines but was perturbed by what he found. The RPF was a right-wing anti-Communist coalition that included the flotsam and jetsam of the Vichy regime, as well as non-Communist former resistance fighters who were motivated primarily by patriotism. As its meetings were regularly attacked by Communists it evolved a self-defence corps that looked dangerously like a Fascist militia. Even Malraux was nervous about where it was headed and asked Koestler to help raise money from his wealthy French contacts to reinforce the moderate wing of the movement. Koestler was by this time sufficiently Gaullist himself to ask Guy de Rothschild if he could help. He also worried that if he told the truth in his *Observer* articles he would alienate those on the left with whom he still had credibility. Malraux had given up trying to persuade him and other leftists that de Gaulle was anything more than a man on a white horse: a strong leader who would put the Communists in their place. Koestler, who was more than ever impressed with Malraux after seeing him speak at an RPF rally, accepted this as a necessary but lesser evil.[4]

Politics inexorably impinged on relations with Sartre and de Beauvoir, already strained by Koestler's merciless satire in *Occident*, and aggravated by his demand that their friendship should entail ideological concurrence. Matters were further complicated because Sartre seemed bent on seducing Paget. De Beauvoir later recounted the effect of this combustible mixing of politics and personalities during an evening out:

> As a joke, Sartre was making love to Mamaine, though so outrageously one could scarcely have said he was being indiscreet, and we were all far too drunk for it to be offensive. Suddenly, Koestler threw a glass at Sartre's head and it smashed against the wall. We brought the evening to a close; Koestler didn't want to go home, and then found he'd lost his wallet and had to stay behind in the club; Sartre was staggering about on the sidewalk and laughing helplessly when Koestler finally decided to climb back up the stairway on all fours. He wanted to continue the quarrel with Sartre. 'Come on, let's go home!' said Camus, laying a friendly hand on his shoulder; Koestler shrugged the hand off and hit Camus, who then tried to hurl himself on his aggressor; we kept

them apart. Leaving Koestler in his wife's hands, we all got into Camus' car; he too was suitably soused in vodka and champagne and his eyes began to fill with tears: 'He was my friend. And he hit me!'

Once everyone had sobered up a period of anxious reflection began. Camus and de Beauvoir agreed that they could not go on drinking like that and hope to accomplish any work.[5]

Relations with Sartre were not easily repaired. Koestler had annoyed him personally, and on the most sensitive issue, by getting at him through de Beauvoir. She was in the bar of the Pont-Royal with a friend one evening when Koestler rolled in from a party with a well-lubricated vociferous Gaullist whom he had met. Koestler ungraciously interrupted de Beauvoir's conversation and added insult to injury by referring to her as 'Sartre's woman'. The Gaullist blow-hard then called Sartre a 'clown' and claimed, absurdly, that Sartre had offered his support to the RPF. While the RPF man told obvious lies about Sartre, Koestler just stood grinning. De Beauvoir, who knew how dangerous such a story could be in the political tinder-box of Paris, got up with her friend and left the bar. Sartre was furious when she told him what had happened. He protested to Paget, whom he saw alone for lunch the next day, that if Koestler was prepared to defend his friend Kaplan against abuse, why was he silent when his friend Sartre was defamed? Paget relayed the story to Koestler, who hurried off to patch things up. He did not succeed. De Beauvoir informed Algren: 'We met Koestler this evening [20 January] and told him in a half-pleasant, half-unpleasant way very unpleasant things; he looked very childish and treacherous, and in the whole [*sic*] he seems to me a very corrupted man.'[6]

Koestler fulfilled the French segment of his assignment for the *Observer* by rattling off two contentious articles on the political crisis. He attributed the unrest to the persistence of a peasantry on the one hand and the power of the organised, Communist-led proletariat on the other. Since the fate of France was vital to the well-being of Europe he urged that it be enfolded within a European plan of reconstruction – the nascent Marshall Aid Plan. His derision towards the Third Force option and his comments about Gaullism aroused controversy in France when the pieces were republished in French. Koestler even had to argue with the foreign news staff of the *Observer* (and Crossman), who preferred to think that a left-wing alternative to de Gaulle was viable.[7]

Paget put up with all the politicking and the drunken

confrontations, but she was 'depressed and longing for Italy'. The only benefit of Koestler quarrelling with others was that he got on better with her. With the articles done they set off by car for Italy on 23 January, meandering southwards via Fontainebleau and Châtillon, through Burgundy, to Lyons and thence to Avignon, Aix and Nice. *En route* they ate voluptuously and bought quantities of wine. Koestler observed the countryside and the people minutely, spotting black marketeers at work and noting the influence of Communists in municipal politics. He realised how much and how little had changed since 1940: 'Undigested hangover of the resistance and the grand mensonge [big lie]'. They drove along the Riviera and crossed into Italy, making their first stop in Genoa. From there they travelled down the coast, passing sombrely through a string of war-battered towns and resorts, before turning inland to Pisa. They reached Florence at the beginning of February.[8]

Now the holiday began to go off the rails. 'Unfortunately,' Paget told her sister Celia Kirwan, 'K. loathes Florence, so we have not had a nice time here.' They dined with the art historian Bernard Berenson in Fiesole and Paget took a wicked delight in hearing Koestler get the names of painters muddled up so that what he said was 'quite unintelligible'. From Florence they drove via Arezzo, Perugia and Assisi to Rome. There Koestler met Leo Valiani and the left-wing but non-Communist writers Ignazio Silone and Carlo Levi. These meetings were not idle get-togethers. Koestler was actively soliciting material for a book of essays by ex-Communists, which he had hatched with Crossman the previous Christmas. Although Koestler had proclaimed to Paget that he 'loathed' Italy, he seemed happy enough spending time with writers and politicians whose company she found stifling. She soon yearned to escape from Rome.[9]

On 20 February they returned to Florence and over the next four days wound their way through northern Italy. Despite the cold weather and snow, 'K. insisted on our trying to get over the pass between Florence and Bologna without chains . . . Of course we soon got stuck.' Their car blocked the narrow road and had to be towed out by local farmers. Somehow, no one remembered to remove the tow rope and in the course of descending the pass the rope wrapped around the axle and snagged the brakes. The car slithered perilously round the last remaining hairpin bends and limped into Bologna. Parma followed, then Milan, which was 'hell' for Paget probably because Silone, whom she found dull beyond words, lived there. In Milan Paget entrained for Trieste, where she was to stay with Bob Joyce, an American diplomat, and his wife Jane.

Koestler crossed the Alps via the Simplon Pass and reached Paris after a 'Nightmare journey . . . in drunken swaying car'.[10]

He remained in Paris for a week writing up his travel notes into a further article for the *Observer*. The result was pretty grim. He juxtaposed the art of the Renaissance with the artlessness of the Communists who dominated town after town. It was as if two opposed civilisations were in collision, with the old one doomed. The 'only revolutionary alternative is Balkanisation of the West and the Police State'. He dismissed the socialist advocates of a Third Force, asserting that society in Europe was too polarised. There was no longer a middle ground, only a strip of no-man's-land running through a battlefield. He also nailed his flag to the Gaullist mast by contributing an article to Malraux's new weekly, *Le Rassemblement*. Koestler considered it essential to make a stand against the Communists and the Soviets, even if that meant working with the Americans or the Gaullists. The rift with Sartre and de Beauvoir was now gaping.[11]

When he had arrived in Paris the city was again gripped by war fever. A week earlier the Communists had staged a coup in Prague. Norris Chipman and other officials in the US embassy were in a panicky state. Chipman reputedly said: 'Let's drop the bloody things on Baku and have finished with it.' Malraux appeared to Koestler 'much calmer now that apocalypse truly at hand'. By contrast, Sartre was 'unable to understand my pessimism about *fin du monde*' and expressed certainty that he and de Beauvoir would be intellectual leaders in France in twenty years' time. Koestler derided their confidence and flayed the new Third Force movement with which they were involved, the Rassemblement démocratique révolutionnaire (RDR). Its manifesto, which Sartre and de Beauvoir had signed, condemned capitalist democracy simultaneously with 'the limitation of Communism to its Stalinist form'. To his mind this was hardly a slogan to rally the people in the defence of Europe against the Red Army.[12]

De Beauvoir saw Koestler again after he had arrived back from Italy, 'tired and lonely'. He 'had an awful hangover and was scared to death by what had just happened in Czechoslovakia, so scared that he felt sure if there is a war, American people will put him in a concentration camp first if Russians don't shoot him'. He was convinced that before long the Communists would sweep to power in France and Italy. It was a terrifying prospect for a man with his political record, but de Beauvoir interpreted his apprehension as springing from another source. 'I suspect when Koestler pretends he is so remorseful because he was *once* a Communist, it means in fact he is remorseful *not to be* any longer a Communist, because now they are going to win and he wishes to be on the winning side.'[13]

In her memoirs she elaborated: 'Excluded from such a future himself, he intended to forbid it to all his contemporaries: the very mechanisms of thought would be overthrown. He believed in telepathy; it was a means of communication due to develop in a way that would defy all expectations.' De Beauvoir perceived that Koestler's yearning to belong was an ingredient of both his Communism and his anti-Communism, and underlay his fantastic, Utopian vision of a civilisation based on expanded consciousness. More immediately, 'his "catastrophism" expressed itself in headaches, fits of lethargy and black moods'.[14]

The sense of impending doom had engulfed London, too. Dick Crossman and Frank Pakenham told him that there was a '25% chance of war this year'. During the day he felt exhausted, but he was tormented by sleepless nights. Even light relief playing croquet with the Crossmans didn't mitigate his gloom. If anything it was worsened by a visit to his mother followed by dinner with John Strachey and Paul Willert. He found Strachey 'more complacent than ever'. A sense of what he could expect if the Red Army did roll to the English Channel was conveyed by Alex Weissberg, who was in London. Koestler arranged for him to dine with Astor and both men were transfixed by Weissberg's hair-raising tales of life in the gulag.[15]

II

Koestler's mood was aggravated by uncertainty about his plans for a trip to America, a project which had been gestating for a long time. In March 1946 George Orwell mentioned that he had been approached by Francis Henson of the International Relief and Rescue Committee (IRRC), which had been formed in 1933 by American liberals, leftists and trades unionists to help the victims of Nazism and, from the 1940s, those fleeing totalitarianism. He was enthusiastic about this group and advised Koestler to make contact with them. The IRRC soon invited Koestler to make a speaking tour of the United States, which would create links between like-minded European and American intellectuals, and raise funds for its work 'to aid the cadres of freedom loving men and women who have thus far survived, and are in the forefront of the fight for freedom'. However, he had great trouble getting a visa to enter the United States and had to ask friends such as Crossman and Chipman to help.

The problem, of course, was that he had been a member of the Communist Party.[16]

Koestler's FBI file reveals that his covert aid to counter-espionage and Chipman's influence were probably decisive factors in securing his entry into the United States. In early March the US embassy in Paris informed the State Department in Washington that Koestler had been invited to the USA by the IRRC. The cable stated that he had once been a member of the Communist Party, but had broken with it and that 'his recent book "Darkness at Noon" had been very effective in combating the spread of Communism particularly in France . . .' In view of this the State Department informed the Attorney General that it 'considered the entry of Mr Koestler into the US as highly desirable in the national interest'. The Immigration and Naturalisation Service called on J. Edgar Hoover for the advice of his agency and received an extensive dossier covering Koestler's life and activities. This was compiled largely by the CIA and documented with reasonable accuracy Koestler's relations with Münzenberg, his subsequent split with the Party and his anti-Communism.[17]

Eventually the visa came through and after hectic last-minute preparations Koestler embarked on the *Queen Mary* on 12 March. The voyage was uneventful. He was disappointed to find the ship full of trades union officials and more 'Lyons Corner House' than luxury. At first he worked in his cabin, afflicted by the 'usual lost-dog feeling about being alone on board'. Then he discovered 'lots of people', such as the publisher Edward Knopf and film-director George Cukor. In the evenings he saw several films, including *Crossfire*, which exposed anti-Semitism in post-war America. 'Alas,' he commented, 'if only the problem were as simple as that.' By the third day of the trip he was suffering headaches and depression. The crossing, with its abundance of time and drink and little else to occupy him, sent Koestler into a self-indulgent, reflective and self-pitying spiral. 'Off the waggon [*sic*] to-morrow – it's time, too. On the other hand don't want to become enslaved again to alcoholic schizophrenia . . . Living in Wales alone enables one truly to enjoy the sun: living in the celtic twilight of the consciousness of death alone enables one truly to appreciate the pleasures of life. Saint, artist, chronicler, hedonist? Fouthy-three [*sic*], and still in search of one's leitmotif.'[18]

The first ten days of Koestler's stay in America, which he spent in New York, were no help in clarifying his *raison d'être*. They passed in a kaleidoscopic frenzy of press conferences, lunches, dinners, parties and quarrels. He was met at the quayside by James (Jim) Putnam, his US publisher, and Sheba Strunsky of the IRRC. The very same afternoon he addressed a press conference, the first of many. A running sore during his visit was the intrusiveness and ignorance of American journalists. Then again, he was not the ideal interviewee, throwing out one poor hack who confessed that he had never heard his name before. In an attempt to shield him from the worst, Putnam and Strunsky acted as his 'bodyguards', shepherding him around as much as possible. The writer Elizabeth Hardwick, whom he met over dinner on the first night, befriended him and took him on a tour of Manhattan sights. But Koestler's days were so long and so varied that for a lot of time he was on his own – and a loose cannon. He regularly had dinner with friends, followed by drinks, then a party that might lead to more drinks at someone's apartment until the early hours of the morning.[19]

During his stay in New York he mingled with several clusters of intellectuals. Via the *Partisan Review* he met Philip Rahv, Daniel Bell, Delmore Schwartz, Lionel Trilling and Sidney Hook. James Burnham, whose book *The Managerial Revolution* had a huge influence on his thinking during the war, was also there and they inaugurated a long, stimulating association. At a party given by the socialist *New Leader* he encountered Max Eastman, David Dubinsky, Eugene Lyons and Dwight MacDonald. He met Theodor Dallin, a Russian exile and one of the first Sovietologists. Putnam introduced him to a clutch of writers including James T. Farrell and John Hersey, who at that time was working on one of the first novels to be set against the background of the 'Final Solution'. He chatted with Dorothy Thompson at a cocktail party and saw Mary McCarthy for lunch. Just before he left New York for Washington, he had lunch with W. H. Auden and dined with Edmund Wilson and John Dos Passos, whom he had last seen in London during the Blitz.

He had a great deal of personal and public business to get through, too. New York was home to members of his extended family, exiles from Europe and Palestinians. While there he saw Eva Tay, Louis Fischer, Judy Weinshall and Jupp Füllenbach, Willi Münzenberg's former chauffeur. He also met Eri Jabotinsky and Peter Bergson (aka Hillel Kook), one of Begin's lieutenants in the United States. But his main business was political and some of it was covert. On 20 March he saw General 'Wild' Bill Donovan, the director of the wartime Office of Strategic Services, which was reconstructed as the Central Intelligence Agency by the Truman administration in 1947. The rendezvous took place at Donovan's apartment on Riverside Drive. Koestler told him about his ideas for psychological warfare and came away impressed by his 'first-rate brain'. A few days later, Donovan

ostentatiously graced the stage of Koestler's first major public engagement, a speech in Carnegie Hall arranged as a fund-raiser and
propaganda event by the IRRC.

Koestler had begun writing his speech on the day of his arrival, but
was hindered by the poor quality of his secretarial assistance, social
calls and a series of typical upheavals. No sooner was he installed at
the Ambassador Hotel than he demanded to move to a flat,
relocating to a place on Fifth Avenue. He got through three
secretaries in as many days. While the first was to his eyes distinguished by 'virginal boney-nosed [*sic*] innocence' the second was
'charming' and soon became the object of his close attention. They
went out socially a couple of times before her marital problems
started to bore him. On 25 March, the day before his big speech, he
cancelled a series of press meetings and worked alone in his room.
Even so, when he finally took to the stage, backed by representatives
of the exiles whom the IRRC helped, he decided to speak
extempore from rough notes.

His talk was broadly addressed to left-wing and progressive circles
in the United States, and was structured around the 'seven fallacies'
which he thought bedevilled the ability of leftists and liberals in their
fight against Communism and encouraged them to advocate the
appeasement of Soviet Russia or neutrality between the two blocs.
To make his point, and to bring it home to an American audience,
he used as his paradigm the figure of George Babbitt, the eponymous
anti-hero of Sinclair Lewis's brilliant 1922 novel who, in the midst of
a mid-life crisis, is temporarily seduced from solid American values
by the lure of Bohemian ways and superficial radicalism.

To be left-wing, Koestler advised, did not necessarily entail being
pro-Soviet since the USSR was no longer really a socialist country.
Nor should left-wingers believe that because capitalism had problems
and Western societies were flawed, they had no moral right to
oppose Soviet expansion. The USSR represented a greater evil than
that present in the Deep South of the United States or disfiguring any
of America's authoritarian allies. By the same logic, because there
were lynchings in Alabama in 1941 the USA should not have fought
Hitler. Nor did it make sense to condemn both blocs equally (the
Third Force position), since Russia was far more oppressive than any
capitalist country. His fourth fallacy was the 'anti-anti-attitude'. This
raised a big laugh from the audience, but Koestler was in deadly
earnest. The mere fact that the reactionary press, Senator Joe
McCarthy and vile regimes in Greece or China were anti-Soviet did
not make the Soviet Union any better. Two and two make four even

if a violent reactionary agrees with the arithmetic. Koestler then tackled the residue of affection for Russia due to its heroic role in the war, pointing out that Stalin would show no mercy to the West just because they had been allied against Nazism. His sixth fallacy was the dilemma of dirty hands, which was basically a repeat of his second point. He ended with 'the confusion between short-term and long-term aims'. Social democracy and reform had not yet triumphed in the West, but this did not rule out anti-Communism in the meantime. At the climax of his oration Koestler urged his audience to remain committed to Europe and not to repeat the isolationism of the 1930s: 'For there will either be a Pax Americana in the world or there will be no pax. Never has such a burden and such a responsibility been borne by any single nation in history. It is the more unfair to you as yours is an adolescent civilisation, with adolescent enthusiasms and adolescent pimples. The task of the progressive intelligentsia of your country is to help the rest of the nation to face its enormous responsibilities. It is time for the American liberal to grow up.'[20]

This was a prophetic utterance to make in 1948. It was also a brave one to issue before such an audience, in the context of an appeal to the left-wing intelligentsia. Although Koestler underestimated the autonomy of social democratic governments within the Western alliance, making Pax Americana sound more like the American Empire, he was right that in the medium term the American military umbrella was fundamental to the balance of forces in Europe.

The speech was more successful than Koestler had any right to expect in the circumstances. He was physically and mentally drained after several days of hectic socialising and non-stop talking. He had had only a few hours of quiet to prepare the speech and was thrown off his stride at the last minute when he was confronted in the wings of the hall by Vera, his childhood sweetheart from Budapest. Once he was on stage the microphone failed, so he ended up speaking from the edge of the platform, sitting on a table and swinging his legs in the air. In spite of all these pitfalls, the speech was warmly received by the capacity audience and won approving comment in the press the next day. Afterwards, Putnam took him and a bevy of admiring women to the 21 Club, but he was too tired to enjoy the company and soon headed back to his hotel.

He next travelled by train to Washington. There were the routine meetings with the press, but less socialising since he knew fewer people in the capital. One evening he even had time to go to the cinema, where he saw Elia Kazan's *Gentleman's Agreement*, another film on the theme of anti-Semitism in America. Naturally, he met more politicians and officials in Washington. On his second day he lunched with ex-Ambassador William Bullitt and members of the State Department. He met Norris Chipman for drinks with the chief adviser to the European Division. He also saw the head of the 'Visa-Immigration Bureau, security and counter-espionage or god knows what' to discuss the 'mystery' of his visa. In the evening on 31 March he gave another public address and went to bed soon after dinner, 'exhausted but content'. He took the following morning off and did a tour of art galleries. Later in the day he saw Supreme Court Justice Felix Frankfurter, one of the great Jewish figures of the New Deal. It was a disappointing encounter. Frankfurter looked to Koestler like a 'Jewish Truman' and had 'nothing to suggest, of course'.[21]

Koestler wrote to Paget giving some of his impressions of America and his trip. 'It's a kind of delectable nightmare. Five times a day I am telling myself that this is the country where I want to be forever and five times a day that I would rather be dead than live here.' In his diary he embroidered his ambivalent feelings. New York rather disappointed him. It lacked the 'robot uniformity' he had anticipated, perhaps with Fritz Lang's film *Metropolis* in mind. Instead, he found 'untidiness and improvisation' everywhere. He complained to an interviewer for the *New Yorker* that 'Nothing functions. The hot water is cold. The elevator bells do not ring. Messages are not delivered.' He was keenly aware of the extremities of poverty and wealth. After a lonely meal in a diner, where he had a hamburger for the first time, he noted: 'To be poor in this country means suicide as the only balanced, reasonable attitude.'[22]

What impression did Koestler make on the Americans? The *New Yorker* described him as 'a small, tense, restless man in his middle forties with brown hair, blue eyes, and a pleasant German-Hungarian accent; a chain smoker; and a frequent taker of aspirin'. *P.M.*, a left-wing paper, also remarked on his diminutive stature (by American standards), but added that he had 'rather heavy hips'. When he spoke it was with a 'voice tense and gestures chopping'. The *Chicago Tribune* described him as a 'dynamic man, wiry, quick with ready answers'. Since he had brown hair and blue eyes in one paper and black hair and grey eyes in another the veracity of these reports is open to doubt. But they all conveyed his intensity, nervousness and driving intellect. They also noted that he constantly smoked, drank coffee and chewed aspirins in unhealthy quantities.[23]

On the next leg of his journey he flew from New York to Los Angeles. During the flight he was impressed by the sheer size and diversity of the United States. In his diary he gave an excited, lyrical description of the changing landscape, a kind of prose rarely seen in his published work and reminiscent of his youthful journalism. Indeed, the flight reminded him of his Zeppelin journey.

Like the wave of Central Europeans who preceded him to Hollywood, Koestler found the place fascinating and repellent. He was depressed by the parochialism of the film world which, at that time, was obsessed with the House of Representatives un-American Activities Committee investigations to the exclusion of anything happening across the Atlantic. He gave the obligatory press conference and met a host of local politicians and trades union organisers. At a dinner given by the Knopfs he saw Deborah Kerr, Olivia de Havilland and Danny Kaye, but nothing impressed him more than the quantity and quality of the food and wine. On 6 April he worked for several hours and made a speech at the Los Angeles Philharmonia Hall. Drinks afterwards went on till 3 a.m. He never got to bed before dawn and only kept going by taking Benzedrine pills. On one extraordinary day he lunched with Aldous Huxley and Geoffrey Heard, before being 'whisked off' to meet Louis B. Mayer, the film mogul. Mayer, he observed, 'looks quite incredible: a para-human face modelled of shit'. Throughout his visit he was particularly sensitive to the presence of Jews and noted that 'Jews in USA look much more Jewish than elsewhere'. By the morning of Friday, 9 April he was 'half dead'. He only recovered after a long sleep in the car taking him north to San Francisco, but he was soon sufficiently awake to admire the scenery on the coastal road and the profusion of wildlife. He arrived in San Francisco the next day

He began with some sightseeing, then visited Stanford University. This was followed by yet another press conference and 'some much needed sleep'. Macmillan had arranged a 'literary reception' for him at a big bookshop, but he left after less than an hour. Instead, he drove off with a fellow called Mark Hopkins, with whom he got very, very drunk. Hopkins was sick over him in the car and they ended up in a flat with some young women students. The mixture of alcohol, Benzedrine and aspirins was taking its toll on Koestler and he was unable to sleep that night. The next morning he had one of his 'nervous breakdowns' and phoned Sheba Strunsky to call off the rest of the trip. He cabled the IRRC to cancel his remaining engagements and bring forward his return journey. After several phone calls, however, he agreed to go to Chicago and speak there, but he insisted that the organisers make the pre-publicity 'dignified and non-controversial' to avoid the strenuous confrontations with

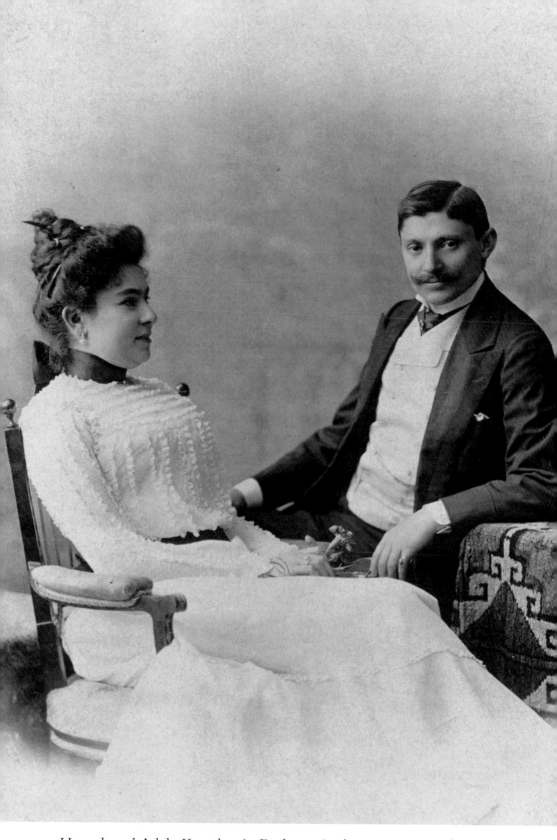

Henryk and Adele Koestler, in Budapest in the 1890s, soon after
their marriage.

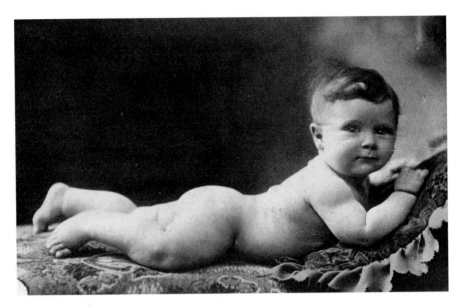

Baby Arthur, 1906.

Henryk, Authur and Adele Koestler on holiday on the Dalmatian
Coast, 1911.

At school in Baden bei Wien, 1919. Koestler is on the far left.

Koestler as a student in Vienna, where he became a keen Zionist, 1922.

Koestler in Palestine, working as a journalist for the Ullstein Press, c. 1928.

On the *Graf Zeppelin* polar expedition, 1931.

Koestler in the early 1930s in his sporty Fiat,
later used by his Communist Party militia
friends.

Koestler with Langston Hughes (second from left)
in Central Asia, 1932.

Dorothea Ascher, c. 1936.

Koestler, hands bound and under arrest, in Spain, 1937.

Koestler greeted by the press on his arrival in Britain after his Spanish imprisonment.

The many faces of
Private Koestler,
Britain, 1941.

Koestler at the founding of a 'tower and stockade settlement' during his 1945 trip to Palestine to research *Thieves in the Night*.

Jan 28, 1945   Ein Hashofet

At Kibbutz Ein Hashofet in 1945, where he spent several days
arguing with highly politicised, pro-Soviet Kibbutzniks.

Mamaine and dog in
Palestine, 1948.

Daphne Hardy in North
Wales, 1946.

Mamaine and Koestler at Verte Rive, 1950. Verte Rive's damp
proximity to the Seine made it hell for asthmatic Mamaine.

Dick Crossman in an unusual position, with Cynthia,
Paul Winkler (in beret), Koestler (with champagne), Bertaux
and Zita. Verte Rive, 1949.

With Melvin Lasky at the Congress for Cultural Freedom,
Berlin, 1950.

Amongst scientific luminaries including Claude Lévi-Strauss,
Sir Herbert Butterfield and Professor Stephen Toulmin,
Washington, 1965.

Michael Polanyi and Cynthia, Alpbach, 1960s.

The Alpbach Symposium, 1968: Koestler is speaking while Cynthia
operates the tape-recorder.

At the 1979 Koestler Award ceremony, with Sir Hugh Casson,
Joyce Grenfell and the head of B.P. House.

Following page: Koestler in aggressive posture, c. 1980.

the press which he had endured across the continent. He gave his speech in San Francisco, then flew to Salt Lake City rather than hang around for the IRRC to arrange a sleeping compartment on a train to Chicago.[24]

The detour to Salt Lake City was a mistake. He was so dependent on alcohol that he paid a cab driver to take him across the teetotal city, to the very worst districts, in search of a bottle of whisky. He saw the sights, including the Mormon Temple, but was keener to get beyond the city limits where he thought he could track down some booze. On 16 April he flew into Chicago, where he stayed for just two days. His speech went well and he had time for a tour of the rail yards, stock yards and slaughterhouses. In the evening he went with his local IRRC host to two strip joints and a night-club in the Afro-American section of town. The L and L Club impressed him the most: 'where hottest strip-tease ever seen, with naked girl performing mock-coitus with male, dangling breasts and buttocks (like apples and melons) before middle-aged clients' eyes.'

Koestler stayed in New York from 18 April to 9 May, with only short trips to Boston and Princeton. For several days he worked up an article for *Life* magazine bringing together the content of his speeches. He saw Burnham regularly to discuss various political projects. He also negotiated about the filming of *Darkness at Noon*, but rejected the best offer, worth £50,000, because he considered that the subject of the Moscow Trials was now too distant. On 23 April he went to Boston to make another speech for the IRRC and attend a dinner at the invitation of the young up-and-coming Harvard historian Arthur Schlesinger Jr. His IRRC contact was a Jewish woman whom he immediately disliked: the 'most unpleasant type of Israelite'. But the dinner with I. A. Richards and Gaetano Salvemini was a great success and his spirits rose. The next day his speech went well and he was able to relish the calmer atmosphere of Boston. Before he left, he saw Edmund Wilson.

During the last fortnight in New York, Koestler continued to socialise relentlessly and fitted in spurts of work on articles and the American edition of *Insight and Outlook*, which James Putnam was bringing out for Macmillan. He lunched with Henry and Clare Luce, pillars of the American liberal establishment, rowed with Cyrus Sulzberger, and had numerous drunken soirées with Putnam, who was drowning personal sorrows in whisky and wine at the university bar almost every evening. He visited Princeton and stayed overnight, seeing a computing machine and discussing psychology. On 3 May he was invited to cocktails with the *émigré* German novelist Erich

Maria Remarque and Dos Passos. He also saw an indefinite number of women and confided to his diary that they were like Californian fruit, 'pleasant to the eye, but juiceless, tasteless'.

Koestler's farewell to America took on operatic proportions. It began with a shopping spree and continued with a bar crawl through Harlem until he and his companions reached 'the real thing, no whites, excellent floor show'. He was so interested in the district that he returned the next day with a social worker, when it appeared rather more poverty-stricken and derelict. He was inebriated almost every night, going from dinner to drinks to clubs, until the eve of his departure, when he didn't actually get to bed until 9 a.m. It was wholly fitting that he was accompanied to the airport by James Putnam, with a bottle of bourbon passing back and forth between them. Before he left he cabled Paget with details of his flight, told her that he had lost fifteen pounds and joked: 'Otherwise all well. May be running for President.'[25]

Koestler returned to England with a host of plans for living and working in America although, throughout his visit, Palestine kept bursting into the news. He was unable to take part in an emergency conference on the Middle East convened by a group of senators in Washington, but recorded that he felt a 'tortured conscience'. Eri Jabotinsky went to see him several times to discuss tactics for this gathering and one of his last acts was to write to him with advice. When he arrived back in London he was more unsettled than ever, with plans for America and urges towards Palestine competing in his head.[26]

III

While Koestler was in America Paget had been in Italy restoring her health and her spirits. She wrote to him that 'this kind of holiday does completely get me out of my fits of melancholia and introspection from which after a few months in rainy Blaenau I begin to suffer'. However, she understood that Koestler's trip to America posed a threat to her reborn happiness. She foresaw that he would want to live there, a prospect which she found unappealing. Mixing self-effacement with loyalty she told him: 'I suppose we should move to the States soon if you are determined not to stay in England. We might as well go to California, or wherever you want.' Perhaps the increased possibility of marriage to Koestler was a form of compensation. While in Paris in March, he had seen a divorce lawyer to begin the proceedings to annul his marriage to Dorothea. *En route* to

England Paget saw the man to check on progress. On 4 May she recrossed the Channel in the company of Camus and his wife, with whom she had met up in Italy.[27]

Koestler spent a few days in London and made an obligatory visit to his mother. The drive back to Wales was marred by his usual misadventures with wheeled vehicles: the car windscreen shattered and he drove for hours into the teeth of cold wind and drizzle. Koestler was always miserable after returning to England from an adventure abroad and this did nothing to help. Paget, of course, bore the brunt of his ill-disposition. 'It was pretty grim when K. arrived back in the worst possible mood. He was tired and crotchety . . . So I had to sit back and wait till he recovered . . . but it took a week, during which I despaired once again of ever being able to stick it out.' His revival followed a period of relaxation, catching up on letters and, more important, good news about Palestine. A boost for Zionism was always a tonic for Koestler, so he was buoyed up by the news that Israel had been recognised by the United States.

Paget, on the other hand, descended deeper into gloom: 'Wales is more awful than ever.' She had fierce arguments with Koestler, often triggered when he criticised her for an alleged lack of domestic skills. When he complained that she had left a pile of books on a chair for three days, she just burst out laughing at the triviality of his concerns and, one suspects, what they implied about the way he regarded her. She confided to her sister that 'it is exactly this kind of thing which will get us down in the long run'. Koestler's behaviour towards her was haughty and bullying with regard to everything from the correct arrangements of the furniture in their house to the country in which they would live. She felt crushed by his unilateral decision that they would move to America. 'We are migrating to the States, I mean emigrating, early next year, if I still find I can stick the prospect by then.'[28]

The news from Israel and the decision to go to the USA lifted Koestler out of his black temper. An improvement in the weather helped, as did the dictaphone purchased in New York which enabled him to spurt through the pile of mail that awaited his return. After just a fortnight in Bwlch Ocyn they travelled to London. It was their adieu to Wales and the abrupt end of another phase in Koestler's life.[29]

Palestine was, yet again, the spur for a sudden move. The situation in the nascent Jewish state had never been far from Koestler's mind all through 1947. In October he told Kollek that he was intending to go there with Paget. At the end of the year he informed the journalist

Tosco Fyvel that he felt impelled 'to do more than discuss'. While in Europe, Koestler had made enquiries about travelling to Palestine and was frustrated to find that his old Palestinian citizenship was no longer valid. This was a double blow since it was also his passport to secular Jewishness. He railed against the 'impossibility of being a Palestinian', which to his way of thinking meant being a Jew as much as a citizen of the new country.[30]

He was finally pitched into action when Arab armies and irregular forces moved into the territory allotted to Israel by the United Nations on the day after the Jewish state declared its independence (15 May 1948). He felt that his place was among his fellow Jews in the Jewish state he had longed and worked for since his student days and his apprenticeship in Zionism under Vladimir Jabotinsky. Quite simply, as Celia Kirwan recalled, 'Arthur felt he ought to be there'.[31]

Koestler's own interpretation of his motives for going to Israel was more confused. He hoped 'to make some positive contribution to the reborn nation's struggle for survival'. Yet he also 'half-seriously, discussed the possibility of settling in the Promised Land'.[32] In May 1948 Koestler stood again on the cusp of an existential decision. If he could not be a Palestinian/Jew outside Israel, the only way to affirm a Jewish identity was to go there. His decision to do so, whatever the public pretexts, indicates how at that moment his Jewishness was central to his sense of self. The outcome of the visit would be critical in determining his identity and, consequently, his place in the world for the rest of his life.

In London he busied himself getting the travel documents he needed for the trip and arranging commissions with newspapers, to finance the expedition and give it an external rationale. He wrote to Jim Wylie telling him: 'I am leaving this country for good.' Wylie could dispose of Bwlch Ocyn from June and sell all the furniture and fittings except for Paget's piano, some paintings and a few other items of sentimental value. Ever the shrewd businessman, he suggested a minimum price for the radiogram, heater, oil cooker, electric fires and lighting. Rather confusingly, he instructed his accountant, who was concerned with the change in his tax status, that he was going on a journalistic assignment for sixth months, then to the USA, 'where I have been offered a lecturer's job at Harvard University and where I shall take up residence'.[33]

IV

Because Britain had not yet recognised Israel and there were no consular or immigration officials in London, Paget and Koestler flew to Paris at the end of May to begin their journey officially. He was terribly proud that his visa was only the seventh issued by the Paris representatives of the new state. They travelled on a plane chartered by the Jewish Agency in the company of, among others, the Revisionist Zionist activist Samuel Merlin and the artist Mané Katz. The itinerary, via Italy, Greece and Cyprus, was wearisome while the landing at Haifa was tense, since enemy fire was anticipated. It reminded Koestler of flights into Barcelona during the Spanish Civil War. In fact, his memories of Spain run through the diary of his stay in Israel and to a great extent they structured, indeed distorted, his interpretation of events there. Shortly before he left the country he sent David Ben-Gurion, the Israeli Prime Minister, a copy of *Spanish Testament* with a covering note recommending that he read the chapter that 'reflects the atmosphere of the Spanish Civil War' since it had 'some resemblance' to events in Israel.[34]

Much of his Palestine diary, nearly 200 typed pages, was regurgitated in the book *Promise and Fulfilment*, which he wrote on the strength of his stay. In style and structure it is reminiscent of *Scum of the Earth* and *Spanish Testament*, with discursive and analytical sections framing a personal account based on a diary. However, like the preceding mixtures of reportage and autobiography, the diary of his Israel trip was used for raw material and to give an atmosphere of *vérité*. The unpublished manuscript is peppered with observations and incidents that were never allowed into the light of day. It reveals, above all, that the trip turned into a disaster which forever coloured his attitude towards Zionism, Israel and the Jews.[35]

The visit began propitiously. The childish pleasure of the immigration officials at Lydda Airport when they handled the diplomatic documents issued by the fledgling nation delighted him. For the first few days he and Paget stayed in Haifa interviewing wounded soldiers about the early battles of the war and meeting old friends, including Abraham Weinshall, who had been among those Jews arrested by the British in the brief clampdown in June–July 1946. The stories from the front are movingly recapitulated in the book. On 6 June they drove to Tel Aviv along the coast road, past abandoned Arab villages and columns of cheering Israeli soldiers in trucks. In the provisional seat of government Koestler encountered the emerging bureaucracy and things started to turn sour.[36]

He was irritated by the government information office, which accredited foreign journalists and shepherded them around. He bridled at its version of events, especially concerning the tension between the Irgun, the militia of the Revisionists, the Haganah, which was under the control of the Labour Party, and the Palmach, an elite strike-force closely linked to the radical-socialist wing of the Zionist labour movement. The government apparatus was controlled by the Labour Party, which did its best to blacken the Irgun, blaming them for past and present atrocities such as the blowing up of the King David Hotel and the massacre at the Arab village of Deir Yassin. From his informants Koestler learned that the Irgun and the Haganah were actually co-operating at the time that both outrages occurred.

The internal propaganda war reminded him of Spain and he got 'rather furious' with the government spokesman. 'The Irgunists are certainly fanatics, but without fanatics one can't wage a war of liberation against such overwhelming odds.' His good will and enthusiasm carried him along for a while. He wrote in his diary: 'Resolution: effort to be understanding: sympathetic and not to lose patience.' But he relished drinking with Alexis Ladas, a representative of the UN, because 'already after a few days in this country it is a relief to have dinner with a non-Jew – like a glass of water after a salty dish'. His early unease was making itself evident in the dispatches he sent off to London, which were distinguished by a critical, even querulous, tone towards the new state.[37]

Koestler's arrival attracted a lot of attention in the Palestine press, not least because of *Thieves in the Night*. He was besieged by old friends, journalists and politicians, most of whom wanted to dispute with him. He was irritated by the lack of *sang-froid* among the Tel Aviv Jews, who clung grimly to the black-out and trembled at the thought of air raids. Among the civil population the 'conception of civic responsibility seems to be almost entirely lacking', he noted angrily. After a number of rows with the staff of the hotel where they were staying, Koestler and Paget moved to a flat overlooking Tel Aviv's beach. But the 'general lack of feeling for form, dignity, beauty, gets one down terribly'. He looked on the inhabitants with a jaundiced eye. After he had referred to 'dismal fat middle-aged Jewesses' in a restaurant Paget reproached him for anti-Semitism. He countered that she would not complain if he said the room was full of 'drab, horsy English country women'. Paget pointed out that this rather missed the point, since there had not been 2,000 years of prejudice against horsy English women.[38]

Koestler's meetings with high-ranking members of the new government did nothing to assuage his hostility. He bemoaned Shertok's table manners, although this was hardly as worrying as the foreign minister's refusal to rule out ties between Israel and the Soviet

Union. Koestler was dismayed at the paralysis inflicted on the government by the need to satisfy all parties in the coalition. For one thing, this prevented the creation of a ministry of information, which he thought was needed urgently. Matters were made worse when the Political Department of the Jewish Agency objected to his meetings with Irgun personnel. At his own initiative Koestler was seeing them, and members of the even more extreme break-away Lehi group, in order to obtain material and, unofficially, to mediate between them and the government. He interpreted the resulting strictures through the optic of his experiences in Spain in 1937–8, when the Communist-dominated government suppressed the Trotskyite and anarchist militias, and, rather fantastically, imagined that his life might be in danger if the 'apparatchiks' of the Jewish Agency got their way.[39]

On 18 June 1948 a letter by Koestler protesting about the government public relations apparatus appeared in the *Palestine Post*. It was followed by one in his support signed by a phalanx of foreign correspondents. The effect of his intervention was further to poison his relations with the government and the Jewish press, which now started to attack him almost daily. He was accused of being an American agent and was lambasted in a *Palestine Post* editorial for criticising the government's campaign against the Irgun.[40]

For five days he travelled around central Israel, visiting a POW camp and making a dramatic night journey to the 'Burma Road', the improvised route built through the hills into Jerusalem to break the siege of the city by the British-officered Arab Legion. The evidence of the 'Pontius Pilate' attitude of the British in the six months between the announcement of their decision to leave Palestine and their final departure angered him intensely.[41]

The noise and bustle of Tel Aviv were driving Paget and Koestler to despair, but a trip to Kibbutz Ein HaShofet offered scant relief. Ein HaShofet was the model for Gan Tamar in *Thieves in the Night*, but the far-left kibbutzniks reproached him for his depiction of their settlement and denounced what they saw as his glorification of the Irgun. Koestler retorted that their Marxist interpretation of events had been proved totally wrong. When he and Paget went into the communal dining hall, 'None of my old friends or any other kibbutznik joined our table.' He sneered at almost everything he saw, such as the 'futile and white-towerish' children's house, and the pair left 'as soon as decently possible'. By contrast, at Kibbutz Gal Ed, the protoptype for Ezra's Tower in *Thieves in the Night*, he was cheered to the rafters.[42]

In the course of their tour of towns and battlefields in the north, Koestler and Paget crossed the Sea of Galilee by night to visit a Jewish settlement soon after it had repulsed a Syrian attack. The mixture of beautiful scenery and the debris of war made a 'macabre impression' on Paget. But Koestler was forming a very different idea of the war. It seemed to him a grotesque shadow play. The Israelis claimed to have defeated an invasion by five Arab armies, but actually the incursions had limited objectives and were uncoordinated. He had learned from Shertok that King Abdullah of Jordan had even concluded a secret agreement with the Israelis and the British not to push the Arab Legion beyond a certain point. The Arab powers were more interested in fighting each other for the spoils of war and clashed with the Israelis only when there was no alternative. Meanwhile, the Israeli authorities smuggled in arms, but attacked the Irgun for doing the very same. 'What my eyes fell upon was corruption and the smell of death.'

His disenchantment was focused by the *Altelena* affair which occurred two days before they returned to Tel Aviv. On 21 June, Ben-Gurion ordered government forces to fire on a ship carrying arms and volunteers to the Irgun. Koestler was outraged at what seemed like a repetition of the events in Barcelona in 1937 and immediately set about documenting the affray. The smoking hulk of the *Altelena* was clearly visible from the balcony of his hotel as a constant reminder of these bloody events. Like any good journalist, he tracked down participants in the drama and soon cabled to London a powerful dispatch documenting the incident.[43]

Several of Koestler's Revisionist contacts, including Bergson and Merlin, had been jailed after the *Altelena* fighting. His view of the clash was tainted by intense meetings with the imprisoned men, along with Menachem Begin and Max Seligman, a prominent lawyer who was acting for them. His diary reveals all the prejudices that in a more sculpted form enter his reportage and *Promise and Fulfilment*. He became convinced that the Labour movement was striving to create 'under the guise of socialism, a totalitarian party-regime'. His contact with Revisionists and his articles drew bitter attacks in the Labour-dominated Israeli press, which accused him variously of being an American agent and pro-Irgun. The *Palestine Post* once carried a front-page article headlined 'Koestler Against Israel' to which he replied with a furious letter to the editor. Actually Koestler looked on the Revisionists with a fairly dispassionate eye. In his diary he marvelled at their political naïveté and commented: 'Begin is a romantic Pole who has taught his people how to die but not how to live on the political plane.'[44]

The press attacks further jaundiced Koestler's views of the new state: 'A totalitarian Lilliput is no less totalitarian for the smallness of its people. The venom and defamation . . . the philosophy of the useful lie . . . are all common to Nazism, Stalinism, Haganahism.' He repeated his views in his articles for the *Manchester Guardian*, which provoked further denunciations by the Israeli press and government spokesmen.[45]

Tel Aviv continued to get him and Paget down. He found it 'more loathsome than ever'. More than once he slept most of the day and rose only to get plastered at night. As usual when he was tetchy, Koestler was also bullying. Paget, who felt 'very demoralized', desperately wanted to see the newly arrived American journalist Cyrus Sulzberger, whom she knew from Paris and liked. But Koestler disliked him and she knew it was no good asking him if they could meet. At the beginning of July Koestler got mild dysentery, so Paget travelled to Jerusalem on her own to collect material for him. This caused the journalist Jon Kimche to remark mischieviously that she did much of the 'leg work' for Koestler's articles. In fact, even while Paget was in Jerusalem, he was gathering information on the Israeli party system. Paget saw many friends and enjoyed the time she spent away from Koestler, but she was still depressed and resentful that he would not allow her to meet Sulzberger.[46]

Koestler then got involved in a typically quixotic and convoluted business. He and Paget were driven to distraction by the noise in their apartment and wanted to rent a flat on Bograshov Street from an aged Czech lady called Rose Trumer, who was planning to return to Europe to see her surviving relatives. However, she was prevented from leaving by the visa authority. Koestler was drawn into her struggle and financed legal aid for her case. This brought him into close contact with the judiciary and more government officials. The result was both farcical and corrosive. After briefing a lawyer he commented: 'This systematic corruption of the legal and political life is not a result of muddle but of an ingrained disrespect for legality and straightforward "gentile" methods.' Paget reported: 'K. rants on night and day about Palestine politicians to everyone until I nearly go mad.'[47]

Koestler was so miserable he couldn't work. He felt cut off from the outside world 'and at the same time being an outsider here makes us both very depressed . . . All my old friends without exception have turned into cranks, monomaniacs or fanatics, one year of this existence would be enough to do the same to us.' He read Josephus

– on the Jewish war against Rome, a text about betrayal that was as influential on his thinking as the Spanish Civil War – and felt like Job.[48]

His comments about Jews became vicious. In the midst of the imbroglio over the flat, he wrote: 'All this, or most of it, is disappearing with the next generation. But it should be on record what centuries of ghetto and persecution made out of the East European Jewish lower classes, otherwise all explanations of anti-Semitism would be one-sided.' He opined: 'the women of Israel's statesmen are all insupportable hystericals; their table manners and conversations are on the level of the Cracow ghetto; they don't drink, they don't relax, they aren't human.'[49]

On 15 July he presented his ideas on the Latinisation of the Hebrew alphabet to the Rotary Club and was jeered for his trouble. There were further attacks on him in the press. Into the midst of this hot, sweaty, torpid world landed the proofs of *Insight and Outlook*. For the last half of July he toiled over these in the most unfavourable circumstances, cut off from libraries or his stock of reference works. There were even a few air raids. But Koestler's absorption in the task enabled Paget to sneak away and meet Sulzberger as she had so wished. When she was with Koestler they rowed constantly.[50]

During August, Koestler conscientiously amassed material for the book. The research prompted renewed introspection about Zionism and the Jews. He confessed to

Marvelling at the fool I had been a year before . . . That this Palestine revisiting would be a waste, now I see how necessary it was to the asymptotic process of growing up. Jabotinsky, Revisionism, Irgun, was still an undigested lump in my stomach. When I touched upon these subjects I descended from maturity to adolescent emotion. It remained a raw and bitter enclave in this hard and bitter strive [*sic*] for maturity. It was necessary to go through the tunnel to be able to emerge from it, to assimilate this lost religion of unreasoning loyalty. After a consummated illusion, omni homine triste sunt [*sic*].[51]

Paget could no longer stand the country, the heat or Koestler and left for a holiday in Cyprus. In her absence he descended into 'the throes of Palestine-depression, well-remembered from former sojourns. Combined effect of August heat with its unnerving, tummy-undoing consequences, and of isolation, hostility, loneliness.' He looked forward to seeing Kollek, who had returned from a diplomatic mission abroad, but their meeting turned into an almighty quarrel: 'I made the mistake of not trying to hide my disappointment and letting go pent-up emotions with a friend.' Kollek 'started by saying that he had re-read *Thieves in the Night* and had found that I had no real love for this country and its people, no sympathy for a single character in the book . . . either I felt I belonged to Israel for better or for worse, or I did not.' Koestler responded that Kollek had spoken 'injustice and truth mixed, how much truth, I know unfortunately more than Teddy'.

This was a turning-point. He reproached Kollek for 'forgetting that I had burned my bridges in England, came here to help, and was rejected by the same clique which makes life hell for him'. His journey to Israel was more than a journalistic assignment or the gift of assistance. Koestler saw himself cutting his ties with England, his country of adoption, and aligning his sense of being a Jew with his place of residence. But Israel had made him feel unwanted and a stranger. It demanded more than he was willing to give. Whereas Kollek was prepared to weather the political attacks and manic atmosphere, Koestler was not. Having decided to surrender the Israeli/Jewish option, he was cursed to seek an identity and a home somewhere else, as yet undefined.[52]

On 5 September, Koestler celebrated his forty-third birthday and, as so often on this annual occasion, he was depressed. The event is interesting for the company he chose to keep. It was marked the next day by a reception at Samuel Merlin's flat and attended by a bunch of Irgun fighters and Revisionist politicians. A few days later Paget got back from Cyprus feeling much better. But Koestler was in a foul mood. They went to Haifa where he got 'FRIGHTFULLY drunk' at the home of an acquaintance. Paget 'abandoned' him on the street and he ended up sleeping rough. In the morning he was found on some scrubland by a Carmelite monk who took him to the monastery where he recovered from the previous night's binge.[53]

During the rest of September he was occupied researching and writing newspaper articles which were, in turn, to provide the basis for his book. This work only deepened his disillusionment, since it brought him face to face with Israel's leading politicians. Koestler met Ben-Gurion on 13 September. It was a strenuous, argumentative, but fascinating encounter. Koestler described the Israeli Prime Minister as having a 'Judeo-Slavonic face', a 'patriarchal look', and declared him full of 'paternally despotic authority'. First they discussed Israel's international position: Koestler pressed Ben-Gurion to denounce Russia and assert a pro-American policy. Ben-Gurion insisted on a neutralist stance and ridiculed the notion that anyone could suspect Israel of turning pro-Soviet: that reflected a lack of understanding of the Jews. To Ben-Gurion, he recorded, 'I am not really a Jew and haven't got the feelings of one'.

The discussion then turned to Koestler and his writing. Ben-Gurion had read most of Koestler's novels, but protested that *Thieves in the Night* was so erroneous that it undermined his trust in the veracity of *Darkness at Noon*. Koestler 'with great modesty' refused to be drawn into a debate over the literary merits of his opus and dragged the conversation back to Russia. He refused to believe Ben-Gurion, who scoffed at the idea of Israel adopting a pro-Russian posture, although Ben-Gurion was being entirely honest and Koestler was leading him in a most unprofessional way for a journalist. After Ben-Gurion conceded that perhaps a clear statement of Israel's international outlook would help, they moved on to Israeli culture and the future of the country. 'Was it', Koestler asked, 'to be Levantine or Western, or Orthodoxy [*sic*]?' If the latter, this meant a regression to 'the first century AD'. Ben-Gurion retorted 'that I was not a Jew and had no notion what Jewish tradition meant'. He launched an attack on Koestler's assertion in his most recent *Guardian* article that there was a '2000 year gap in Jewish history' between the Bible and the recrudescent state. The two men grappled over the dynamics of national culture, with Ben-Gurion asserting that the Jewish cultural creativity praised by Koestler was the work of an élite only. European culture would anyway percolate into Israeli society once books were translated into Hebrew. Koestler asserted that this would never happen, and that unless the Hebrew alphabet was Latinised the country would be cut off from Western culture and science.

Koestler next challenged Ben-Gurion over the influence of the orthodox politicians, who were members of the governing coalition, and the rabbinate. Ben-Gurion brushed aside Koestler's strictures on the enforcement of the Sabbath laws and returned to the attack on Koestler's books. Even though he conceded that it was fabulous propaganda in America, Ben-Gurion accused *Thieves in the Night* of being untrue and mired in ignorance. When Koestler protested that he had lived for 'for years' in the country, Ben-Gurion whipped back that he didn't know the language. Koestler then continued the conversation in his best Hebrew, which was not good enough for the Prime Minister, who asserted that you had to be able to read and write Hebrew in order to appreciate Jewish culture. Ben-Gurion was no more sympathetic to his pleas to embrace the Revisionists in a national government. The conversation left Koestler more pessimistic than ever for the prospects of democracy in Israel. But what affected him personally was the treatment meted out to him by the patriarchal Premier.

His private record of the meeting is as important for what it shows about Koestler as about Ben-Gurion. He wrote bitterly that Ben-Gurion 'treated me . . . as a stranger and goi [*sic*]'. In other words, Koestler longed to be regarded as a Jew, one of Ben-Gurion's own people, enfolded in the national community of Jews and given a home. Despite his sniffiness towards Hebrew, his rampant prejudice against all sorts of Jews, and his endless reservations about the Israeli state and society, he had a deep, almost desperate yearning to be accepted as a Jew and to belong to the Jews. It was his sense of rejection that coloured the tone of his articles about Israel. This set in motion a vicious cycle of counter-attack and increased alienation. The rest of his stay only deepened his estrangement.[54]

Four days after his talk with Ben-Gurion, Jewish terrorists assassinated Count Bernadotte, the UN representative in the Middle East. Koestler went directly to Moshe Shertok, who had impressed him in an interview on 14 September, and outlined a public relations campaign to minimise the damage to Israel's standing. This was highly unusual conduct for a journalist, since at the same time he was reporting on the murder and the government's response. To underline his invidious position he was soon embroiled in a public controversy over the UN's subsequent clash with Shertok.[55]

The last weeks that Koestler and Paget spent in Israel were marked by grim farce. On the evening following the murder of Bernadotte, Koestler took Paget to a café patronised by Lehi to test the mood. The young gunmen averred that the only good non-Jew was a dead one, reinforcing Koestler's impression that Israel was no longer the place for him and Paget. Another night thieves tried to steal their new jeep from outside their block of flats, only to be foiled by Paget, who summoned help by standing on the balcony and shouting out the Hebrew title of Koestler's novel *Thieves in the Night*. According to Paget, Koestler was at odds with the whole country, 'depressed and melancholic'. He complained that 'The only thing that keeps us going here are these excitements. Otherwise we are utterly depressed, stale and demoralized.' The only relief was a canoeing expedition.[56]

Their thoughts were locked on to their departure, although given their lack of agreement over where to go next this heightened the tension between them as much as it offered the promise of release. Paget was deputed to make the travel arrangements and obtain the papers, only to find this was complicated by Koestler's unresolved status as an ex-Hungarian, ex-Palestinian temporarily domiciled in Britain who was intending to live in France and/or the United States. The strain between them, aggravated by the visa problems, sparked a 'major row'. It was followed by a 'spectacular' quarrel on the eve of her departure to France. The effect of this bitter fight showed in a letter to her sister in which Paget wrote: 'We will spend a couple of months in France before going to America or wherever we go, separately or together as the case may be.'[57]

Koestler rushed around researching and writing articles, and assembling material for his book. He was alternately drunk or buzzing with the effects of Benzedrine tablets and saw everything in a negative light. To compound his fractious mental state his jeep was commandeered at gunpoint by soldiers from the 89th battalion of the Israeli Army, under the command of none other than Moshe Dayan. Koestler was humiliated and stormed into a police station to make a complaint. The policemen were unhelpful and an argument ensued – 'some idiot implied that I was a fascist' – whereupon Koestler lost his temper and 'went for him' with his fists flying. The 'idiot' turned out to be a high-ranking officer of the Israeli Air Force.[58]

By mid-October he could not stick it any longer and drove to Haifa to fix his departure. He felt 'anxiety, depression, constant palpitations', although given his intake of alcohol and drugs this is hardly surprising. It was, perhaps, not the best state of mind in which to engage in serious reflections on religion and history. On his penultimate day in the country, which happened to be the Day of Atonement, he wrote: 'The Jews are a much sicker race than we all thought. Dispersed among the gentiles, their sickness was latent, they had to keep a hold on themselves; now they let go and the accumulated psychic pus is threatening to flood the new state.'

He left Israel on 14 October 1948, never to return. Koestler's involvement with the Jewish people, Zionism and Israel ended amidst a welter of mutual recrimination, exaggerated criticism, mis-understanding, mishaps and farce. The consequences were not to become clear for some time, but in effect he was unhinged from one stable element in his life. His whole sense of being was shaken by his unsuccessful confrontation with the very entity that was supposed to resolve all the contradictions in his identity and his place in the world. Yet, at the same time, the failure of his Zionism exaggerated the quirks of his situation and personality that had made it so needful to begin with. Having turned his back on Israel, Koestler was once again the Wandering Jew.

V

Despite pleas from Crossman to return to Britain permanently, Koestler vacillated. He reactivated his application for British nationality, but he and Paget temporarily settled in France. When his naturalisation was confirmed on 3 December 1948 he was residing in Chartrettes, near Fontainebleau, at the country residence of Paul Winkler, the Hungarian-French press magnate who owned Opera Mundi. Here he worked on the Palestine book and made only one fleeting trip to London, probably to swear the oath of allegiance on 7 January 1949. Crossman was hounding Koestler for his contribution to the book of anti-Communist essays, but Koestler felt compelled to finish his study of Zionism and Israel first. He begged Crossman to give him time 'as I don't want to interrupt the beautiful train of my thoughts'.[59]

From the moment he started writing on Israel, he found it 'heavy uphill work'. The challenge was 'to keep out all resentment, to avoid the other extreme, to avoid judicious middle-position, to dig through layers of emotion and acquired conviction to the core of truth'. But as it neared completion he was able to reassure Abraham Weinshall that 'he need not worry about the contents; with distance and perspective regained I have reverted to solid patriotism'. Paget took an important role in its genesis, policing against bias. 'I constantly press for the exclusion of too vehement or propagandistic arguments.' It was hard going for both of them. Paget found the work which Koestler compelled her to do 'rather tedious' and 'torture'. But at least the surroundings in which they lived and worked were pleasant and there were staff to deal with domestic chores that otherwise would have devolved on to her. As always when he was stuck into writing, Koestler calmed down and was easy to live with. Even so, she chafed at the lack of free time. After two months of this regimen, she 'made a beautiful strike notice for K. in cardboard covered with blue paper and with the following slogan stuck on in large letters of pink and white paper: more CARROT less STICK'.[60]

In between chapters they went house-hunting along the Seine valley. Koestler's motives for settling in one country over another were never simply personal or psychological. As a rule, he followed his royalties. In France the income from his books had been piling up. Not only did this make it viable to live there, but it gave him an incentive to invest in a property to protect his earnings against inflation. An estate agent showed them Verte Rive, 'a hideous villa built in the French 1920s style' at Fontaine le Port on the river opposite the forest of Fontainebleau. Koestler was besotted with the house the moment he saw it and looked forward to the opportunities it offered for canoeing and water sports. He completely ignored Paget's interests. She suffered from asthma and even found Chartrettes too damp for comfort. It was so bad that in early January 1949 she thought it would be necessary to go to London for treatment and a change of environment. For her a riverside villa was poison. But, undeterred by any thoughts of her health, he made an offer which was accepted early in 1949.[61]

From time to time, Koestler saw Camus and Malraux, or went to Paris on business. Otherwise, for most of the last quarter of 1948 he was sober and assiduous. He and Paget spent Christmas in France and at the beginning of February moved into Verte Rive. A few days later, Koestler reported: 'Finished Palestine book — and with the whole problem.'[62]

Promise and Fulfilment: Palestine 1917–1949 was one of the first and remains one of the liveliest, if not the most reliable, accounts of Israel's origins and early development. It typically combines several elements of Koestler's technique and reflects his general philosophy as well as his particular concern with Zionism, Israel and the Jews. He wanted to illustrate the role of psychological forces in history, which he felt were neglected in most liberal or Marxist historiography. And he believed that although Israel was a very special case, the country nevertheless illustrated the problems of humanity in microcosm. Thus he hoped his book would have a universal significance.

At the outset, Koestler was keen to establish that the Jews were not a race and that Israel was not unrepresentative of human experience as a whole. Israel showed 'basic archetypes of human conflict and experience'. Yet he persistently referred to the 'Jewish race' and attributed an essential quality to their experience that was tantamount to a complete acceptance of stereotyped racial thinking.[63]

This ambiguity was partly a marketing strategy to ensure that the book was not read just by Jews, but it had a deeper meaning. If the Jews were a 'race', then Koestler was ineluctably a Jew. But if they were an unusual product of time and place, then he could efface his Jewishness. However, Koestler was too steeped in eugenics and Mendelian science to make that leap. Although he apparently eschewed racial thinking he persisted in listing 'Jewish' characteristics as if they were natural and inherited genetically. The constant slippage between his environmentalist approach and his use of racial stereotypes betrayed a genuine conviction that, as Joseph remarked in *Thieves in the Night*, through their semen the Jewish patriarchs transmitted Jewishness down the ages.

In the first part of the book Koestler told the story of the Balfour Declaration, Jewish settlement in Palestine and Arab responses. This was more or less straight history, with the stress on the 'irrational forces and emotive bias in history'. His version of British policy in 1917 and thereafter was structured by his notion that there are two planes of existence: the tragic and the trivial. Lloyd George made the pledge to the Jews in 1917 during a war, while elevated to the 'tragic' or romantic plane of history. But it had to be enforced in peacetime by mundane officials with rather more trivial preoccupations. Koestler then charted the ensuing conflict over the land between Jews and Arabs, lamenting that the Jews failed to explain their insuperable moral and practical case to the Arabs.[64]

He deftly sketched Britain's pragmatic retreat from the Mandate, the struggles over Jewish immigration and the radicalisation of Jewish opinion against the background of Nazi terror in Europe. In a powerful chapter he drew on his research and his personal experience to catalogue the fate of the ships carrying 'illegal' immigrants to Palestine. Koestler went to great pains to account for the rise of Jewish terrorism, setting it against the backdrop of the Holocaust.[65]

In a breathless, and rather one-sided, manner he ran through the diplomatic and political battles of 1945–7, emphasising the role of subjective and irrational factors. After a brief history of the underground struggle against the British and the war of independence, he summed up the reasons for this bloody outcome to a Utopian dream. He argued that at several turning-points a compromise solution based on the partition of Palestine would have been possible. Koestler, who was usually so keen on dichotomies, surprisingly displays the hallmarks of the pragmatist.[66]

In the second book, Koestler built on extracts from his diaries to give a 'close-up' of the war of independence. Contrary to the widespread belief that the war was a struggle of Israel, like David, against the Goliath of the massed Arab states, he described 'a phoney war of small and hopelessly inefficient bands of Levantine mercenaries skirmishing against improvised Jewish home-guard units, with a great amount of bragging and bombast on both sides'. Koestler also went against the grain in his microscopic analysis of the *Altelena* affair which included an impassioned defence of the Irgun and Jewish terrorism.[67]

The third section, called 'Perspective', was adapted from his *Guardian* articles on Israel's political structure, society and culture. He praised the experiment in collectivist economics under the management of the Histadrut, the Jewish trades union federation, but his accounts of Mapai, the Israeli Labour Party, and Mapam, its Marxist partner, were distorted by his prejudices and propaganda objectives. He suggested that Mapai, the party which Ben–Gurion led, testified to the 'ghetto heritage of suspicion, intolerance and self-righteousness'. Mapam was the product of a recent merger of two Marxist-socialist Zionist parties that were pro-Soviet. Yet Koestler was so eager to assuage British and American fears that Israel would tilt towards the Soviet bloc that he misrepresented the party's pro-Moscow orientation. His bias was most evident in the sympathetic treatment of the right-wing Zionist parties. Other political groupings got short shrift, including the religious party, even though it had won twelve per cent of the vote in the recent elections.[68]

Koestler's prejudices ran riot in the chapters on culture and religion in Israel. He denigrated Yiddish and mocked the revival of Hebrew. He reiterated his contempt for the social mores of the new society, belittling everything from urban architecture to modes of dress. Israel's chief merit was exercising a 'curious biological alteration' on the Jews born within its boundaries. Sabras, native-born Jews, might be 'unerotic', provincial and chauvinistic, but at least they didn't look 'Jewish'.[69]

His treatment of religion was withering. Rabbinical Judaism was described as 'sterile brain acrobatics'. Jewish religious observance amounted to 'the art of cheating the Lord'. It was 'mental corruption in matters divine'. Most significantly, he described Judaism as 'a perpetuum mobile for generating anti-Semitism'. By preserving Jewish differences and setting them apart, it laid the basis for antipathies towards the Jews. The major purpose of Zionism, and a Jewish state, was to end this anomalous status and break the vicious circle of Jewish apartness and anti-Semitism.[70]

Koestler opined that in five to ten years religion would decline in influence and that 'within a generation or two Israel will have become an entirely "un-Jewish" country'.[71] This might seem a curious conclusion for a book about Zionism, written by an ardent Zionist, but like many Zionists of his era, Koestler saw the Jewish state as a device to transform the Jews into a people just like any other. Not to take this opportunity would be a fateful error.

In the Epilogue, Koestler argued that the creation of Israel had fulfilled the historic mission of the Jewish religion. 'With the creation of Israel, Judaism had lost its rationale; if the mystic yearning for the return to Palestine is eliminated from the Jewish faith, its very foundations and essence will have gone'. Every Jew faced an historic choice 'between becoming a citizen of the Hebrew nation and renouncing any conscious or implicit claim to nationhood'. The choice could not be avoided. Anti-Semitism was on the rise, but it was caused chiefly by the persistence of Jewish difference and would worsen if Jews in the Diaspora clung to an outmoded identity. Judaism 'implies membership of a definite race and potential nation . . . The "Englishman of Jewish faith" is a contradiction in terms. His faith compels him to regard himself as one with a different past and future from the Gentile. He sets himself apart and invites being set apart. His subjective conviction creates the objective fact that he is not an English Jew, but a Jew living in England.'[72]

The were no longer good reasons for maintaining Judaism in the Diaspora. Few Jews believed in its tenets, so their insistence on remaining a separate people must rest on inertia or sentimentality. In either case, they risked incurring obloquy and dooming their children, if raised as Jews, to a similar fate. Once it was an act of cowardice to renounce Judaism, but now Jews could make an honest choice between emigration to Israel and ceasing to be Jewish. The latter did not mean surrendering Jewish values since these had been absorbed into the mainstream of Western civilisation. Koestler ended with an appeal to his Jewish readers, although he never once throughout the book described himself as a fellow Jew: 'These conclusions, reached by one who has been a supporter of the Zionist Movement for a quarter-century, while his cultural allegiance belonged to Western Europe, are mainly addressed to others in a similar situation.' The Jews were responsible for anti-Semitism by virtue of persisting in their Jewishness. 'Now that the mission of the Wandering Jew is completed, he must . . . cease to be an accomplice in his own destruction. If not for his sake, then for that of his children and his children's children. The fumes of the death chambers still linger over Europe; there must be an end to every calvary'.[73]

This was an extraordinary prescription. In effect, Koestler was blaming the victims of Nazi persecution for their appalling fate. He saw nothing in Judaism or the Jewish heritage that was worth preserving and reduced the Jewish religion to a vehicle for Zionism. Although he hit some targets, notably the dilemma of dual loyalty facing Diaspora Jews after the establishment of Israel, much of his argument was ill-informed and ill-judged. His version of Judaism was nonsensical, ignoring centuries of distinctive legal, ethical and philosophical thought as well as cultural creativity. Judaism does have a national dimension, but it also has a universal message. There is nothing racial in the notion of the 'Chosen People'. Anyone can become a Jew if he or she converts to Judaism according to Jewish law. Endogamy, marriage within the faith group, is prevalent among all religions and can hardly be equated with racialism. Judaism has both inclusive and exclusive aspects, but the main thrust of Jewish thought has been to reconcile the practice of being 'a Jew at home and a gentile on the streets': in other words, to integrate without losing core Jewish beliefs and values. It is a moot point whether Judaism obliges Jews to move to the Jewish state. The ultra-orthodox certainly believe that only the Messiah will restore the Jewish people to Zion: they regard the secular state of Israel as an abomination.

In other respects, however, he was articulating classic Zionist beliefs in the mould of Leo Pinsker, Max Nordau, Theodor Herzl and his hero Vladimir Jabotinsky. These Zionist ideologues regarded anti-Semitism as a fact of life, a disease that could not be ameliorated by education or cured by progress. The only solution for the Jews was evacuation from the Diaspora or auto-eradication. Like Koestler they saw little of value in the Jewish heritage worth transporting to a new Jewish state. Its function would be to end anti-Semitism, 'normalise' the Jewish condition by removing the quirks bred in the Diaspora and, in effect, make the Jews like everybody else. In his assertion that Israel would see the withering of Judaism, while it also enabled Jews in the Diaspora to erase their particularity, he was being a good Zionist.

However, the dilemmas of his own life revealed that the stark dichotomy posed by classic Zionism was a false one. For the harder Koestler tried not to be a Jew, the more he accentuated what it was that set him apart. In the second half of his life the suppression of Jewishness was a conscious act that coloured everything else he was or did. The attempt to flee Judaism was the quintessential act of the modern Jew: it was, itself, a badge of identity.

Chapter 9

Cold Warrior, 1949–52

In 1949 Koestler's life entered a long period of turbulence. He moved into a house in France, but two years later purchased another home in the United States. His work veered between writing fiction, *The Age of Longing* (1951), his fourth novel, and autobiography, his essay in *The God That Failed* (1950). Almost the only constant theme was his implacable anti-Communism. This had a fundamental effect on the way he constructed his autobiography for *The God That Failed*, establishing a pattern that was to be followed in the two subsequent volumes of memoirs.

Koestler was on the front line of the Cold War in these years. *The God That Failed* was explicitly conceived as anti-Communist propaganda. In the introduction to the volume Dick Crossman piously stated that when he dreamed it up with Koestler, 'We were not in the least interested in either swelling the flood of anti-Communist propaganda . . .' Twenty-five years later Koestler admitted: 'That of course was precisely what we were interested in, but for a Labour MP in those days it just wouldn't do to say so in as many words.'[1] The rest of Koestler's autobiographical oeuvre dating from this era followed the trajectory marked out by *The God That Failed*: trimming the story of his life to fit into a political framework.

His anti-Communism led to his involvement in the Congress for Cultural Freedom, the defiant gathering of intellectuals in West Berlin at the first peak of the Cold War. Koestler was one of the moving forces behind the Congress, probably its best performer and one of those who tried to institutionalise its achievements. Verte Rive, his home outside Paris, became a nodal point for anti-Communist writers and activists. In France, Britain and the USA he met with government officials and members of the security services who were engaged in espionage and counter-espionage against the USSR. His violently held convictions led to the disruption of a number of friendships, notably with Sartre, and a spectacular public altercation with Dick Crossman.

Politics and personality continued to frustrate his ability to settle in any one place. Koestler feared that a third world war would soon devastate Continental Europe, if it did not succumb more quietly to Communist subversion. For a man with his political record it would be suicidal to remain in France. Yet he felt at odds with Britain and found American culture uncongenial. For a while he owned houses in all three countries. Each move to a new home involved tortured legal and financial transactions, and created a burden of management that he was reluctant to accept. As if it were not bad enough having to contend with immigration controls and exchange regulations, in 1951 Koestler also embarked on a complex and ultimately fruitless legal case against the American playright who dramatised *Darkness at Noon*.

His personal life reached a crescendo of chaos and fractiousness. In 1949 Mamaine fell ill. While she was hospitalised he started an affair with his secretary, Cynthia Jefferies. Soon after that he began a relationship with Janine Graetz, a wealthy and beautiful woman in the film business. In April 1950 Mamaine and Koestler married, although for long stretches afterwards they lived separate lives, partly because Koestler was hard to live with and partly because he chose homes in places that made her ill. They separated in August 1951. This volatility naturally infected his work. For much of the time it was not clear to him what he should be doing. When his writing went badly Koestler became depressed, drank to excess, quarrelled, brawled and smashed up one car after another. It was extraordinary that he remained so productive.

I

Early in February 1949 Koestler and Paget made a brief trip to London to resume contact with friends and to visit his mother. They enjoyed the usual round of lunches, dinners and nights at the Gargoyle with Eric Strauss, a psychologist, Daphne and her husband, and Connolly. Koestler met Strachey and Crossman, but was now less than impressed by them. After watching Crossman give a 'usual half-cock act' in a Parliamentary debate on German rearmament he ruminated that democracy was, 'after all, also only a lesser evil'.[2] Around this time there appeared the first reviews of *Insight and Outlook*, which had just been published in America, a few months ahead of its UK publication date. Koestler was shocked by the negative reception accorded his *magnum opus*. *Time*, for example, crushingly reported that 'his one per cent of inspiration demands ninety-nine per cent of his reader's perspiration'. While Paget made a depressing excursion to Bwlch Ocyn, to wind up their tenancy of the farm, Koestler went back to Paris to find solace with old pals. He saw Camus, Malraux, Vallon and Margarete Buber-Neumann, with Sperber 'popping up with wise talk and moderate drinking'. He also had business with Robert Calmann-Lévy and spent some of his huge French royalties on a brand new Citroën – a sleek, black model of which he was extremely proud.[3]

He met de Beauvoir, who was with Sartre, for the last time on 15 February. According to a letter she sent to Algren soon afterwards he seemed untouched by their previous, frosty encounter when the two had been as off-putting as possible without being downright rude. This time they left no doubt about where they stood. Koestler invited them to Verte Rive for the weekend, but they declined; he then suggested an evening out, but they again said no; finally, he suggested meeting for lunch, to no avail. De Beauvoir and Sartre 'explained to Koestler that we could have nothing to do with somebody who was Malraux's friend and de Gaulle's supporter. So he was rather angry and looked beaten and I enjoyed it very much.'[4]

In her memoirs she embroidered the scene. According to de Beauvoir, Koestler asked: ' "When are we going to see each other?" Sartre got out his notebook, then changed his mind. "We haven't got anything to say to each other any more." "But we're not going to quarrel over our political opinions" said Koestler, with an inconsistency that left us temporarily speechless. Sartre put his notebook back in his pocket. "When people's opinions are so different, how can they even go to a film together?" And that was how things remained between us.'[5]

Koestler's version of the rupture differs. In his recollections Sartre told him that there could be 'no more friendship because Malraux's friends can't be his friends'. The ostensible reason was that Malraux had allegedly attempted to force Gallimard, the publishing house, to jettison *Les Temps modernes,* which Sartre edited. Koestler was incredulous and attributed the break to more obvious political differences, aggravated by what he perceived as de Beauvoir's malice towards him. But a few days later at a dinner with the Sperbers he had the chance to question Malraux about these claims. To his distress, Malraux admitted that they were essentially correct. The result was a row which Koestler attempted to patch up, explaining that 'this happened a couple of days after Sartre, whom personally I like very much, had broken off "diplomatic relations" with me on account of my solidarising myself with you'. Koestler was now gravely disillusioned with Malraux and the entire Gaullist project.[6]

While Koestler was politicking, Paget was engaged in the practical business of furnishing Verte Rive. It was a spacious house but had been neglected. The ground floor comprised a large sitting room leading into the dining room, which was equipped with a gaudily designed bar. Koestler's study was on the first floor, looking out over the river and towards the forest. Nearby were Paget's study, their bedroom and two guest rooms. Although every room still required furniture and redecoration, they moved in on 27 February. In a typically generous and ill-calculated gesture Koestler invited Margarete Buber-Neumann to stay the day after their installation. She was the first of many guests, the care of whom usually fell at Paget's feet.[7]

She was immediately swamped by difficulties: the septic tank leaked, the water pump was noisy and there was no telephone. Koestler was soon depressed by these inconveniences and racked by doubt whether the purchase had been a good idea. Paget tried to put on a brave face and cheer him along. 'Poor chap, I feel sorry for him and try to tell him all will be well when we get some carpets, but I'm not sure that it will.' Weeks passed before the furniture and carpets arrived; in the meantime every footstep she took echoed around the house, disturbing Koestler who had not even got bookshelves in his study. Next, the staff proved to be a headache. The cook, Madame Grandin, was a sour-faced woman whose meals were as bad as they were late.[8]

The settling-in process stopped Koestler getting down to work. Not the least of his worries was unpacking his private library of 2000 books, which had been shipped from Wales. Just then the proofs of *Promise and Fulfilment* arrived, followed by the publisher, Jim Putnam, who was not at all happy with the book. As a result, Koestler was 'madly irritable'. Paget observed that he was 'having a really serious crisis about his writing, he has quite lost confidence in himself. It is too awful and I don't know what to do . . .'[9]

Suddenly, in the middle of March, she fell ill. A cold led to an asthma attack, which the local doctor treated with novocaine. She suffered a severe allergic reaction and nearly died. After recovering from the worst effects she had to stay in bed for days, leaving Koestler in charge of the house in addition to dealing with doctors and pharmacists. Her condition worsened. In April she was transferred to a hospital in Paris where she remained for nearly a month. She returned to Verte Rive in early May, but did not improve. She lay in bed in a converted ground-floor room most of the day, attended to by Koestler, and watching him work in between. Paradoxically, she took comfort from this situation: it seemed as if her illness was drawing them closer together. They talked about 'things one can't usually say to anybody at all and with a wonderful understanding between us'. But a month later her health deteriorated so much that Koestler had her flown to London and installed in a nursing home. She did not come back until August 1949.[10]

Koestler tried hard to be considerate while Paget was unwell, but her plight was a distraction and evidently irritated him. In June, while she was in a nursing home in England, she recalled 'those mornings when I used to sit, hardly able to keep my eyes open, failing lamentably to concentrate on anything, and getting on your nerves.' Now she was gone he was able to concentrate on his writing: reworking the galleys of *Promise and Fulfilment* and completing the autobiographical essay he had promised Dick Crossman and the publisher Hamish Hamilton in the winter of 1947–8. First he hacked away at the diary passages in the Palestine book, removing the more personal observations and ironing out inconsistencies of tone. At Putnam's insistence he added to the chapters on the contemporary political and cultural scene. An entire chapter that Jascha Weinshall had provided had been excised long ago and he now felt duty bound to translate it for *Horizon*. None of this was pleasant work and he joked to Jim Putnam that since his editorial visit he had been rereading the Book of Job.[11]

He proceeded on to his life story and had completed it by early June. Once the first draft was handwritten, he needed a secretary to type it so that he could make revisions and produce a final draft. To lighten his load he called on the assistance of Daphne Woodward. She came to Verte Rive several times in May to do secretarial chores and labour over the proofs. But perhaps her most important function was to obtain a permanent secretary for Koestler. She placed an advert in the Paris edition of the *New York Herald Tribune* and took charge of vetting the applicants. One of these was a pretty twenty-one-year-old South African woman called Cynthia Jefferies, who had previously worked for the South African Association of Arts. Jefferies was about Koestler's height, with fair hair, slim but robustly built. She had travelled to France with her mother in January 1948 to study French and had already obtained a secretarial job in Paris. As this was boring work she applied for the position as part-time secretary to 'an author'. She was interviewed by Woodward about three weeks later.[12]

Shortly afterwards she was summoned to meet Koestler at the

Montalembert. After a brusque exchange he suggested that she go with him to Verte Rive the following day so that he could examine her *in situ*. In fact, the visit consisted of little more than an encounter with Daphne (Hardy) Henrion, accompanied by her husband, a ride in a rowing boat and a picnic. Koestler liked the look of her and she was hired.[13]

Like many of the women with whom Koestler became entangled Jefferies hadn't had an easy life and she bore the scars. Her father had committed suicide when she was ten and she was raised by her mother. Although she was capable of independent judgement and developed a sardonic view of life, as a young woman her self-esteem was hardly buoyant. Koestler thought she would suit his requirements by virtue of her 'unobtrusiveness, almost [of] self-effacement'. For her part he fulfilled a deep need for a father figure. She was certainly attracted to him and speculated on 'what he would be like in bed' even as he was driving her to Verte Rive. She would not have to wait long to find out.[14]

With the end of his autobiographical essay in sight Koestler started considering his next venture and opted to resume volume two of *Insight and Outlook*. The notes he had made over previous years had been deposited in A. D. Peters's office, but now he needed them they could not be located. He endured a 'nightmarish week' while Margaret 'Stevie' Stephens searched high and low for the bundle of papers. The package was eventually located in an office safe and transported to Verte Rive. Having recovered his notes, Koestler sweated over them for a few weeks before giving up. 'After a hopeless struggle I had to shelve volume II "for the time being".' Consequently, he was 'left freewheeling in a vacuum'. He began a play, planned out a new novel, sunbathed and went out on the river in a sailing boat he had bought a few weeks earlier.[15]

Back in England Paget was slowly recovering. When she left France she had weighed barely more than six stone. She told Edmund Wilson, 'I looked like something out of Belsen and was almost a gibbering maniac with nervous strain.' Careful treatment and sensitive visitors, including her sister Celia, Eric Strauss and Cyril Connolly, aided her physical and mental recuperation.[16] She now began to suspect that her ailments were not simply a result of her asthma, or the humid climate at Fontaine le Port, and sought psychiatric advice. These reflections naturally extended to her life with Koestler and his behaviour. While her letters to him are frequently self-lacerating, they also show flashes of anger and herald a tougher approach to their relationship.

On 3 June she told him: 'If only we could find somebody to do for your mind what Dr Deller is doing for my body, all our troubles would be over.' Distance from Koestler enabled her to question his approach to the world: 'I feel I have been taking for granted certain things, ways of looking at things, or systems, which I had either worked out for myself or got from you, and that one can't really take anything for granted for long without being guilty of the sin of intellectual arrogance. . . .' Paget struggled to assert her personality against Koestler's: her optimism, emotionality and *joie de vivre* against his pessimism, ultra-rationalism and depression. 'You see I believe, and I know you do too, that brains alone don't get one anywhere except in minor matters like politics and diplomacy . . .' This self-assertion was agonisingly difficult because Koestler was adept at persuading people that he was always right, particularly his women friends whose youth, lack of education or weak character left them prone to falling in with his world view. Her friends were an antidote to Koestler's insistence that she was merely neurotic: 'I have noticed that my friends who've known me for a long time all seem to think I am moderately sane.' Indeed, she turned the tables and reported that Eric Strauss would like to 'diagnose' him: 'Perhaps it wouldn't be a bad idea.'[17]

The irregularity of Koestler's letters to her, and their content, were hardly reassuring. In mid-July she sent him a stiff note: 'I have quite lost my former confidence in your understanding – that's the trouble. But I suppose its only because you have been depressed. Let me know when it's over; I do hope for your sake as well as mine that it will be soon.' She relented the next day. Her forbearance is remarkable given that since she had been flown to London Koestler had not travelled to see her once, had written only erratically and had laced his letters with unhelpful advice.

Paget considered going to France in early June, but felt too weak to take on the combined responsibilities of Verte Rive and Koestler. She was also worried that the damp air was bad for her and was now less willing to concede to Koestler's preferences for domestic architecture and landscape. Instead, she opted to recuperate at a small hotel in Theydon Bois, in Essex. When she toyed with returning in mid-July Koestler put her off, saying that she should not move until she was stronger. He was having fun at Verte Rive and she was evidently still too unwell. So she spent some time in Stokke, Wiltshire, with Robin and Lady Mary Campbell. Finally, in early August, her doctor sanctioned the journey to Fontaine le Port, even though she was still 'a bit nervy'. He wrote to Koestler personally to warn him that Mamaine should be allowed to take it easy.[18]

Koestler had finally settled down to work on a new novel and at last was more relaxed. He told Eric Strauss, 'when work is in progress, neurosis is in regress'. He was also entertained by a succession of visitors: Manès Sperber, Stephen Spender, Pierre Bertaux, head of the Sûreté nationale, Louis Vallon, a Gaullist government official, and Hamish 'Jamie' Hamilton. In July Dick and Zita Crossman, Michael Foot and Jill Craigie came to stay. They were joined by Sperber and Cynthia for the weekend. Everyone had fun, according to Koestler, 'except for Zita, who seems to be really a bore when abroad . . . The first evening she started knitting and only stopped it reluctantly after I told her that it was the one thing I really could not bear.' They ate on the sun-drenched terrace, sailed and swam, and walked in the forest arguing about politics. Afterwards Crossman thanked him profusely: 'They were wonderful days – gastronomically, sportively and plain enjoyable.'[19]

However, Koestler was ill-rewarded by his guests. The Crossmans noted the warmth between him and his secretary and, being inveterate gossips, soon spread the rumour that they were having an affair. Paget was initially spared these tales since she left London for Verte Rive in August 1949. They only caught up with her after she went back in October for further medical treatment. Ironically, the Crossmans arrived for a second stay at Verte Rive at almost the same time that she returned to England.

Cynthia Jefferies, who observed Mamaine's reunification with Koestler, noted that she was painfully thin and easily tired. In fact, she weighed just six stone and seven pounds. Paget's worries about the returning were quickly vindicated. She informed Celia: 'this climate has got me back to where I was before my illness, there is no doubt that it is a lousy climate for me.' She was immediately plunged back into household chores; the house was a 'mess' and new staff had to be found when Madame Grandin left because she was afraid Koestler's villa would become a target for a Communist terror group. Paget was soon travelling regularly to and from Paris to shop for decorative material. She supervised the curtain maker and the decorators who were hanging wallpaper, and interviewed several applicants for the posts of cook, housekeeper and gardener. By the start of September she had lost four pounds. In despair she wrote to Celia: '. . . for the time being I have to spend most of my working hours coping with them and other household problems; and the only thing to do is not to imagine that one is ever going to have time for anything else.' The presence of workmen 'reduced K. to a near breakdown' with the inevitable effect that he turned on her.[20]

At first they got on well. Paget, who had genuinely missed Koestler, was delighted to be back and enjoyed sailing with him in his new boat. He was 'on fine form'. But then she made a fatal error of sanctioning a visit to the house by Bill Curtis. 'When I told K. he went quite mad with fury and struck me a stunning blow on the head.' She wisely chose not to respond in kind, which would have been 'useless and highly dangerous'. This was, she told Celia, 'only' the third time that Koestler had beaten her: 'three times too many, of course, but considering how berserk he goes, surprisingly few'.[21]

Paget now longed to get away 'and have some time off from thinking about housekeeping and servants'. She left for London on 6 October, for a check-up. While there, she attended the poignant wedding of Sonia Brownell and George Orwell in University College Hospital. Soon after her return to Verte Rive things started to go wrong again. The new staff, a Polish couple, got wind of Koestler's unpopularity with the Communist Party and fled. But the visitors continued to arrive: the Prince and Princess of Hesse (who were Paget's friends), Bertaux and Sperber. Koestler was deep into his new novel and was so desperate to keep up the momentum that he suggested they move to Paris and spend the winter in a hotel or flat. The staff problem made him despondent about France in general and he talked increasingly of going to America, which Paget viewed with foreboding.[22]

Mamaine again went to see her doctor in early November. It was while she was in London on this visit that word reached her about Koestler and Jefferies. 'There's not much gossip worth writing,' she told him in a letter, 'except a story about US, which is going around, to the effect that you are very keen on your secretary, but want to marry me nevertheless though you intend to leave me afterwards, and I have come over to discuss this situation with Celia! The Crossmans are as far as I can make out the originators of this story, but I haven't seen them since I heard it to find out how and why they did originate it; apologies to Cynthia for her name being taken in vain.' Koestler retorted: 'I can't really believe the Crossmans put out incredible rumours about the secretary – sounds rather like Paul Willert or Barley [Barley Alison: a friend who worked at the British embassy] . . . As for Cynthia. I don't think anybody likely to believe anybody else to take her seriously.' Koestler did not deny the truth of the charge: he merely disputed its origins and slighted Jefferies.[23]

Mamaine's doctor performed a bronchoscopy and once she had

recovered she enquired cautiously whether it would be a good idea to come back to Verte Rive or whether it would suit Koestler better for her to wait until the Crossmans had ended a planned Christmas visit. She got the green light and returned to France, bringing Adele in tow. Koestler met them in Paris and treated his mother to oysters and white wine. Once her visit was over he tried to get back to work, but problems continued to dog Verte Rive, distracting him and making him bad-tempered. Because it proved impossible to keep staff and Paget wanted to go to Austria to convalesce, he planned to evacuate to Paris for several weeks. He told Alex Weissberg that he was 'fed up with having to run the home by myself'. Koestler simply couldn't function for any length of time without domestic help.[24]

The year ended badly. He drove to Paris on 23 December to rent a room for the weeks that Paget would be away. Late in the afternoon she received a call from the police telling her not to worry if Koestler was unable to return for some time. She immediately rang Pierre Bertaux and Louis Vallon, who started contacting friends in the Paris police. It transpired that after Koestler had done his Christmas shopping he started drinking heavily and was inebriated by the time he began to drive home in the early hours. He got as far as the suburb of Charenton when, unable to remain conscious, he slewed the car on to the hard shoulder, slumped across the passenger seat and passed out. In the morning two policemen came across the car and found him half in, half out. They carried him to the Charenton police station and placed him in a cell. Koestler groggily demanded to phone Paget to assure her that nothing too serious had happened to him, but was denied permission. He then hit one of the police officers. In the ensuing scuffle he took several punches to the face and came off much the worst.[25]

Bertaux was able to effect his release and Koestler was transferred to Verte Rive in a sorry state. He swore never to touch alcohol again, although his notion of abstinence was rather loose. Paget commented that he was willing to 'ration himself to three brandies an evening at most'. Even so she looked on the fracas as useful: 'I really do think this has done the trick, so I am glad it happened, because he has been drinking too much again lately.'[26]

The Charenton affair had serious repercussions: striking a police-man in France in 1949 was not a laughing matter. Koestler was summoned to appear before a Tribunal correctionnel, which had the power to impose a fine or a prison sentence. Inevitably, the press got hold of the story and were merciless, especially the Communist papers. One headline ran 'Yogi hits Commissaire'. The story was then picked up by several European, British and American papers. Over the following week, Koestler and his lawyer cooked up a tale which they hoped would get him off the hook: he had gone to Paris to buy toys for children, drank a bit too much and responsibly pulled over when he realised he was unable to drive safely. When he was hauled out of the car by the police and taken to the cell he had a flash-back to his imprisonment in Fascist Spain and lashed out in confusion.

The anticipated court appearance cast a shadow over the new year and disturbed Koestler's concentration. On 26 January 1950 he confided to his diary: 'For last month have lived intermittent nightmare . . . of Charenton affair.' But Paget was partly right in one respect: for nearly two months he was on the wagon and working hard at the novel. When the date for the hearing was set for 1 March he called Paget back from her Austrian convalescence to lend moral support. 'It will be an unpleasant half hour, with photographers, reporters etc., and afterwards we will offer ourselves an exceptionally good champagne lunch.' As unlikely as his story was, in combination with string-pulling, it worked; Koestler was relieved to get off with a hefty fine.[27]

II

The first work Koestler completed at Verte Rive was his contribution to *The God That Failed*. The idea for a book of essays by ex-Communists and fellow travellers about their conversion and disillusionment, tentatively entitled 'Lost Illusions', had germinated during the winter of 1947–8 when the Crossmans stayed at Bwlch Ocyn. On his trips to France in the spring of 1948, Koestler approached Malraux and Silone to solicit contributions. Crossmann was keen to secure Richard Wright, the Mississippi-born black writer who achieved fame with *Native Boy*, but Koestler considered that 'he is neither sufficiently first class nor sufficiently reliable politically to be admitted into this most illustrious company'. The 'company' continued to fluctuate, for a time including Camus as a replacement for Malraux, Franz Borkenau and, at one point, Hemingway. It eventually comprised: Koestler, Ignazio Silone, André Gide, Richard Wright, Louis Fischer and Stephen Spender. But Koestler's piece, which Crossman and Hamish Hamilton deemed the most important, was held up by his stay in Palestine and the writing of *Promise and Fulfilment*.[28]

Once finished, it satisfied all Crossman's aspirations. Both men had been involved in the black arts and knew that the most convincing propaganda was that which appeared personal and confessional, disarming theoretical retorts by reducing politics to individual psychology. Koestler's was a masterpiece in miniature and rightly led the volume.

He began with a socio–psychological theory of revolutionary faith: it was a blend of mankind's archaic yearning for Utopia and an individual's revolt against his or her environment, a neurosis that was socially engendered. His childhood guilt when his family was well-off and his rage against the injustices of society when their fortunes fell would have been of no social importance were it not for the crisis years of 1914–19 when his fate was generalised and his inner feelings found legitimate external expression. While events were exposing the superficiality of bourgeois values, replacing civility with the struggle for existence, Marx and Freud liberated him 'from the rusty chains with which a pre-1914 middle-class childhood had cluttered one's mind'.[29]

Koestler gave the impression that his response to the post-war upheavals segued neatly into his decision to join the Communist Party in December 1931. His years as a student Zionist and his stay in Palestine were compressed into the sentence: 'For the last five years I had been working for the Ullstein chain of newspapers – first as a foreign correspondent in Palestine and the Middle East, then in Paris.' The object of this deception was to construct the Koestlers as a 'typical Continental middle-class family' and his own life story as a 'case-history [like] thousands of other members of the intelligenstia and the middle classes of my generation'.[30]

He recalled his excitement at studying Marxism while the Nazis mounted their bid for power: 'something had clicked in my brain which shook me like a mental explosion'. Suddenly the world seemed to make sense and all doubts and conflicts were resolved. Then he gave an account of his years in the Communist Party. Koestler laid bare the thought mechanics which insulated recruits from external criticism or inner conflicts: 'once you had assimilated the technique you were no longer disturbed by the facts; they automatically took on the proper colour and fell into their proper place. Both morally and logically, the Party was infallible.'[31]

Throughout his anlysis Koestler employed his notion of political neuroses. Political behaviour, he argued, resembled stages of personal growth and sexual development. Communist propaganda was logical and effective at a rational and an emotive level, but it had a particular appeal to a certain type of personality. Conversion to Communism worked because it was self-willed: he was 'one of those half-virgins of the Revolution who could be had by the S.S.S. [Silent Soviet Services], body and soul for the asking'. The Comintern 'carried on a white slave trade whose victims were young idealists flirting with violence'. He submitted to 'intellectual self-castration'.[32] There is always a strong sexual current running through Koestler's metaphors, not least because he conceptualised personality and politics in quasi-psychoanalytic terms.

Koestler groped for a plausible explanation of why he and others held faith with Communism for so long. He claimed to have been uneasy with the mind-control exercised by the Party as early as 1932 and 'shocked' by what he witnessed in Russia. But his faith persisted because he believed in the 'necessary lie' and because of his anti-Fascism. Like many others he hoped that the Party could be reformed from within; to leave would be to lose any influence and to exist alone, without meaning to one's life. Finally he summarised his plunge into the Spanish Civil War and the transformative experience of his imprisonment in Seville. He explained how, even then, he retained a faith in the USSR until the Molotov–Ribbentrop pact marked the end of his 'addiction to the Soviet myth'.

In his introduction, Crossman explained that the book was intended 'to study the state of mind of the Communist convert and the atmosphere of the period – from 1917 to 1939 – when conversion was so common'. When they first bruited the project he had agreed with Koestler that since 'ex-Communists are the only people who know what it's all about' they should have pride of place in the anthology.[33] Koestler's contribution was a vindication of this proposition; but it was more than that. It was the source of his claim to be useful and influential in political terms. Over the next few years, Koestler would trade on his insider's knowledge of the Communist apparatus and the USSR. This was greatly exaggerated, but even discounting poetic licence and self-inflation it was not inconsiderable. It was particularly important to him in framing his appeal to the American public and government officials at a time when he was thinking of leaving Europe. He knew the difficulties faced by Communists and ex-Communists in the United States: *The God That Failed* was his entry ticket into McCarthyite America.

The erasure of his Jewish identity was a necessary price to pay for being useful to American anti-Communists. It is striking that the biographical details for both Koestler and Fischer omit the fact that they are Jewish. Fischer, who was born in Philadelphia, mentions that his parents were of Russian origin and often spoke to him about the pogroms they had suffered, but never explicitly admits to being a Jew.[34]

It was always a myth that Bolshevism owed anything to Judaism or that Jews were behind the Russian Revolution, but it was certainly true that Jews, as an ethnic group, were disproportionately involved in left-wing movements in Europe and the USA before and after 1917 as compared with other national or ethnic minorities. There were solid reasons for this: the impoverishment of the mass of Jews and the discrimination they faced in the Tsarist empire; the discomforts of the newly settled and proletarianised Jews in the slums of Berlin, Paris, East London, the Lower East Side of New York and cognate districts in other US cities; the association of anti-Semitism with the far right and conservatives in the 1920s.[35] The last point was still highly relevant in the 1940s. Koestler was aware of the anti-Semitism in the United States and the common assumption that Jews had a predisposition towards Communism. He and Fischer may have felt it tactful to suppress their Jewishness to avoid confirming the myth of Jewish Communism. It would certainly have reduced their utility to anti-Communists if they had given the impression that their political trajectory had also been a specifically ethnic one. In order to carry weight, they had to claim to speak for an entire generation around the world.

There is no evidence that it was Crossman's intention to whitewash the religious and ethnic origins of his Jewish contributors. But he displayed an almost incredible ingenuousness towards Koestler and Fischer, telling the former: 'Funnily enough, all of you are Christians, though you certainly are a permanent heretic, or possibly Anti-Christ himself.'[36] But the two 'Christians', Koestler and Fischer, may have been cannier than Crossman. Purged of any excuses attributable to ethnic background, their contributions seemed to explain a universal proclivity to favour Communism.

The God That Failed appealed to millions of readers of all types and had the desired propaganda effect. The variety of those it touched may be extrapolated from some of the fan mail sent to Koestler after the book appeared. This included praise from Malcolm Muggeridge, who like Koestler had sojourned in Moscow in the early 1930s; the Hungarian writer George Schöpflin, who identified with Koestler's writing and confessed that it 'contributed in no small part to my bitter decision' to break with the CP; and the young Arnold Wesker, who reported that having read the book he felt driven to leave the Young Communist League.[37]

The warmth of the reception for his essay made up for the rough treatment of *Insight and Outlook* in the summer of 1949. That book had respectable sales for a quasi-scientific, quasi-philosophical treatise, 3000 in the UK and 1500 abroad by early 1950, but in the United States it sank with barely a trace, selling about 8000 copies. It was the last thing Koestler's American admirers expected or wanted from him. The reviews in Britain were mostly hostile and it met a disdainful silence from specialists. Michael Oakshott in the *Spectator* sniffed that 'Mr Koestler is not enough of a philosopher to write on aesthetics or ethics with any great confidence'. The book was marred by a 'certain portentousness'. Herbert Read for the *Observer* dismissed Koestler's prescriptions as 'cosmic hedonism'. A. J. Ayer in the *New Statesman* protested that much of the argument was unsupported by proof and in his attempts to cover everything Koestler had worked to death the basic concept of bissociation. By (rare) contrast, Alex Comfort in the *Jewish Chronicle* deemed it 'monumental' with the 'solidity of a standard work'.[38]

This negative reception had a devastating effect on Koestler's confidence. When he returned to the project in spring 1950 he asked Eric Strauss if he would collaborate with him. He hoped that this would save him having to revise the text of the 300-page manuscript and give it greater scientific legitimacy. Strauss demurred and tactfully suggested that even if a second volume were called for, Koestler might not be the best person to write it.[39]

Promise and Fulfilment was much more successful, although it enjoyed a wildly different reception in Britain from that in the United States. In Britain the general public was sick of Palestine and the Jews. The reviews were polarised on political lines: the left-of-centre *New Statesman* and *Guardian* were congratulatory, whereas the *Spectator*, *The Economist* and the Tory newspapers were savage. To Koestler's irritation, even the *Observer* was caustic. By November it had sold only 5000 copies. In America, by contrast, it won near-universal praise and sold well in the first months of publication. It was a best-seller in Palestine, where 9000 copies were sold despite the tiny and impecunious population.[40]

Koestler was convinced that *Insight and Outlook* had done badly in Britain and America because it was poorly marketed by Macmillan. The publishing house became a *bête noire*. He was further irritated by what he saw as delays to the publication of *Promise and Fulfilment* and developed an antipathy towards Lovat Dickson, his editor in Britain. In the summer he started to complain to A. D. Peters about the way he felt he was being treated and agitated for a change of publisher. Peters had been through this before with Cape and tried to soothe Koestler. But by the autumn he was on the warpath, demanding that Peters prevent Macmillan from publishing *The Gladiators* in the USA. Since his experience with *The God That Failed*, he had become enamoured of Jamie Hamilton and wanted to transfer to his imprint. He proposed to offer Hamilton the first volume of his autobiography, but Peters warned him not to mix friends with publishers and urged him to go with Collins. Despite a last minute intervention by Harold Macmillan, Koestler prevailed. Macmillan remained his US publisher, but arrangements were made gradually to transfer the rights in his existing books to Collins and Hamish Hamilton.[41]

III

For the first eight weeks of 1950 Koestler was alone at Verte Rive or in Paris, while Paget was on holiday in Austria. His anxiety about his appearance before the Tribunal had the salutary effect of curbing his drinking and he made solid progress with the new novel. He also laboured on the French translation of *The God That Failed* and the German version of *The Yogi and the Commissar*. He loathed this work, but considered it essential since he always found translators unsatisfactory. Neither project was particularly lucrative, but he told Paget that 'in the end it pays – morally I mean'. Money was, in fact, becoming a problem for them both. The cost of living in France was high and Paget was constantly taken aback by their domestic expenditure. When she was in Austria her funds began to run low and she had to resort to Koestler and his pals for supplements. Better than expected sales of *Promise and Fulfilment* in Holland in March 1950 saved them from serious embarrassment.[42]

Financial anxiety obliged Koestler to curb his spending on marginal items such as magazine subscriptions, although he continued to order streams of books from Edward Bumpus in London. He also interspersed work on the novel with some journalism and looked seriously at writing a film-script. In February 1950 he wrote for the *New York Times Magazine* an explosive article on ex-Communists, focused on the controversial role of Whittaker Chambers in the trial and conviction of Alger Hiss.[43] This piece forms part of the prologue to Koestler's participation in the Congress for Cultural Freedom.

Koestler wrote a fine obituary of George Orwell, who died on 21 January 1950. He had been in touch with Orwell intermittently since leaving Bwlch Ocyn. In August 1949 he tried to persuade him to give *1984* to Calmann-Lévy for publication in France: 'Just at present it is politically very important that *1984* should get a mass circulation in France. It is a glorious book.' He was delighted when Orwell married Sonia Brownell, wickedly praising him for rescuing her from the Connolly 'crowd'. Although Paget had reported on Orwell's deteriorating health, his death was nevertheless a shock. When David Astor asked him to write an obituary he seized the chance to 'get it out of my system'.

It was an incisive portrait of Orwell, a fascinating reflection of Koestler's relationship with him and a mirror of Koestler's own foibles. He lauded Orwell for his rigid principles and withering honesty. His writing was the only worthwhile product of the 'pink generation' and would survive because Orwell had never succumbed to the illusion of Soviet Communism. But the eulogy was double-edged. Koestler observed that by virtue of his scruples Orwell could be hurtful towards those closest to him. As a writer, critic and political commentator he was harder on himself and his friends than on the distant masses whose cause he espoused. No doubt Koestler had in mind Orwell's critique of his 'hedonism' and the scathing review he wrote of *Twilight Bar*. It was easier for Koestler to praise Orwell's 'savage vision of *1984*', his anti-totalitarian polemic, than to acknowledge his persistent faith in democratic socialism. The obituary ended with an ungenerous meditation on Orwell's love of humanity and his belief in progress: it was 'this quaint belief which guided the rebel's progress and made him so very lovable though he did not know it'. Ostensibly, Koestler paid tribute to a great rebel in the cause of truth; in reality he was mocking the idealism which had driven Orwell to a premature death. It was a cruelly ambivalent memorial, but somehow Astor, Sonia Orwell and others saw only the glowing approbation. She wrote to Koestler: 'I thought your piece on George was so good and I was so glad you did it as everyone else – above all Pritchett – wrote such depressing nonsense.'[44]

During the spring Joel Carmichael, later to become a distinguished historian of the Russian Revolution, corresponded with Koestler about a film version of *Darkness at Noon*. Koestler also discussed film projects with Paul Graetz, the Leipzig-born head of a production company, Transcontinental Films. Graetz formed the company in France after he fled from the Nazis in 1933 and won acclaim for a series of 'art films', which he produced in Hollywood and Europe. At first he was interested in filming *Arrival and Departure*, but this proved unviable when his pro-Communist scriptwriter objected to the book's message. This of course infuriated Koestler and confirmed his view that French culture was becoming corrupt. Graetz then

considered making a film with Koestler about Freud. He visited
Verte Rive on 1 April 1950, bringing with him his wife Janine. The
date and the encounter were inauspicious: some time afterwards
Koestler and Janine Graetz began a roller-coaster affair that lasted for
several years.[45]

His relations with Mamaine followed their customary bumpy
course. She had travelled to Germany on 2 January 1950 and
convalesced in Garmisch until mid-February. Soon after her return
they took a short trip along the Loire valley with the Willerts and the
Winklers. For a while she was very happy. Cynthia Jefferies relieved
her of most secretarial burdens and she was free to wander in the
forest of Fontainebleau bird-spotting, to go rowing or potter in the
garden. There were many visitors to Verte Rive whom she found
congenial: Wolfgang von Weisl, the Sperbers, Vita Sackville-West,
Sonia Orwell and Stephen Spender. Until mid-April Koestler
managed to avoid the bottle and this helped to stabilise his behaviour.
The only shadow on Paget's horizon was his propensity for
apocalyptic political prognoses, which had an unsettling effect on his
thoughts about where to live. At the start of March she recorded that
Koestler was convinced war would come 'probably autumn 1951 or
soon after, so he would rather go to the States'.[46]

But there were mitigating factors. Since October 1947 he had been
clearing the way to marriage so that Paget's deepest wish for a
permanent relationship was about to be granted. By July 1949
Dorothea and Koestler had reached an amicable financial agreement
as a basis for annulling their marriage: he gave her a lump sum of
£500 and £200 to cover the 'expenses' of the divorce. It was a lot of
money, but Koestler assured Mamaine that 'it is worth it'. Paget
hoped that they would marry in October 1949, while her German
friends were in France, but this proved impossible: the divorce was
not made effective until 15 December. Jefferies was then deputed to
obtain the papers for the remarriage of her employer (and sometime
lover). Paget personally arranged the venue, the British Consulate in
Paris, and the date, 15 April 1950.[47]

The marriage ceremony was intended to be small-scale and confidential. It turned into a drunken rout. In mid-morning the civil
ceremony was witnessed by the Winklers. It was followed by
champagne, then lunch. In the afternoon the happy couple met up
with Jefferies and Stephen Spender (who had visited Verte Rive the
previous day) at the Café de Flore. Arthur Calder-Marshall was also
there and while they were all having more drinks, one of Koestler's
ex-Party comrades chanced to enter. By this time 'K. was fairly

plastered'. He and his comrade reminisced in a sentimental vein about the old days 'much to everybody else's embarrassment and boredom', but Mamaine took advantage of Spender's presence and chatted happily with him. Suddenly, Koestler got into a furious argument with a couple at a neighbouring table, who stormed out in disgust. When calm was restored the wedding party had dinner and set off for a night-club where Koestler drank still more. Late in the night he decided it was time to drive to another club and staggered towards the car. Mamaine remonstrated, causing Koestler to storm off. They found him in the black Citroën, whereupon he announced that he was going back to Verte Rive. Mamaine refused to be driven by him, but he refused to let her take the wheel. Finally, he screeched away into the night, leaving his newly minted wife, secretary and wedding guests standing in the middle of St Germain des Près. Mamaine took refuge on a sofa in Spender's flat, with Cynthia Jefferies as chaperone. The next day he joked, 'I've always wanted to spend a night with you, it's too bad it was your wedding night.'[48]

This explosion of drunken, boorish behaviour had not come out of the blue; Mamaine explained to Celia: 'K. is at present having one of his "mad fits".' Koestler was beset by 'That summer 1939 feeling'. He was convinced that France was overrun by black-marketeers and political opportunists, and wanted to leave. Work was again going badly: he was depressed by the demise of plans to film *Darkness at Noon* and 'between books', having nearly finished the novel.

Meanwhile Verte Rive was a magnet for visitors, a source of endless irritation and a drain on his resources. On 11 April he wrote in his diary: 'Decide to get out to USA in good and earnest. Europe *foutu*.' Rather unhelpfully, in view of this decision, at a farewell dinner for Norris Chipman of the US embassy, he got stinking drunk and ended the evening by ranting that American liberals did not understand Europe and its problems. He was so inebriated he could drive no further than the Bois de Boulogne and slept in the car. This time he was far away from prying commissaires.[49]

Information about Koestler's conduct on his marriage day reached the press, which caused much unhappiness at Verte Rive. When Daphne heard the news she sent him an acid letter: 'I can't help feeling Mamaine is more to be admired than envied.' As on previous occasions, the shock of his behaviour led to a fortnight of abstinence. He congratulated himself: 'can now read after dinner with concentration; before, was always in slight euphoric haze and couldn't remember a word of what read the next day.' He boasted to Camus that he drank only mineral water (except on Saturday, when he allowed himself wine) and was canoeing daily to stay svelte.[50]

In May Mamaine was again in London for treatment. This time Koestler accompanied her. He was notoriously squeamish and her sinus operation shook him so much that he was 'sick all afternoon'. But in the evening he managed to make drinks at the Ritz and dinner with Julian Amery to discuss the forthcoming Congress for Cultural Freedom.[51]

Preparations for the rally preoccupied Koestler throughout the next few weeks. A stream of anti-Communist friends passed through Verte Rive; urgent planning meetings were held with Raymond Aron, James Burnham, Pierre Bertaux, Ignazio Silone and Melvin Lasky. However, to his wife's delight, he still found time to go on a short holiday to Alsace at the beginning of June. 'Besides,' she told Celia, 'K. is now on good form and he and I at least didn't quarrel and always wanted to do the same things.'[52] Koestler was on the eve of his greatest political triumph and, as always before such leaps of activism, he was enveloped by a kind of serenity.

IV

Since his short-lived collaboration with Münzenberg on Die Zukunft in 1938–9 Koestler, like other ex-Communists, had been searching for a political and ideological home. In Britain during the war he had found congenial company among left-wing Labour politicians and journalists. But he quickly tired of the practical questions that engrossed career politicians like Foot and Crossman, and tended to regard pragmatism as a form of opportunism. Consequently he gravitated towards independent leftists such as Orwell and less easily classifiable liberal free-thinkers such as Olaf Stapledon and Bertrand Russell, who seemed to offer the promise of a magic formula that would solve social and political dilemmas at a stroke.

Koestler and Orwell had tried to assemble an élite corps of intellectuals who shared their outlook in order to trigger the formation of a larger international movement to recast politics, but the scheme foundered. In the meantime The Yogi and The Commissar had made him into a standard-bearer for left-of-centre anti-Communism and he was inundated with manuscripts and ideas from men and women who had travelled a similar path. Among others he was able to help Anton Ciliga, Suzanne Labin and Alex Weissberg. All three had been victims of Stalinism; their analysis of Soviet Russia from the inside and their personal histories, validated by years in the service of the

Comintern, were appalling indictments of the regime and an inspiration to resist it. Weissberg was perhaps the most extraordinary personality and the one to whom Koestler was closest.

Weissberg had been arrested in Kharkov in March 1937. Three years later he was handed over to the Gestapo under a secret clause of the Molotov-Ribbentrop pact. He finally escaped from the Gestapo and survived underground in Poland thanks to the help of a Polish woman, whom he subsequently married and whose name he took. After the liberation he set up in business as Alexander Cybulski and began travelling all over Eastern Europe. Weissberg made contact with Koestler shortly after the war and used the cover of his business to move between the Eastern and Western blocs. In 1949 he gave dramatic testimony in the libel case which David Rousset fought against *Les Lettres françaises* (which denied the existence of the gulag). Three years later he published a vivid account of his experiences in the Soviet and Nazi camps, *The Conspiracy of Silence*.[53]

Koestler encouraged Weissberg to begin the chronicle, but was constantly frustrated by his procrastination. In a torrent of long, discursive letters written from hotels in Poland, Sweden and Germany, Weissberg reported his progress and discussed thorny questions. Periodically he sent Koestler chunks of the book to read, but it needed hard work to turn it into a readable, marketable product. Nor was Weissberg the easiest man to deal with: they almost fell out when Koestler endorsed the cuts to the final draft recommended by Jamie Hamilton in August 1951. By this time Hamilton was as tired of Weissberg as was Koestler, who had the added burden of writing an introduction to the book without offending the author, his ex-wife and other mutual friends. However, Weissberg was such a charming and eccentric figure that he usually mollified even those he irritated most. Paget found him delightful company when he stayed at Verte Rive in September 1949.[54]

He was only one of a number of visitors with a similar political pedigree at Verte Rive during 1949, including Margarete Buber-Neumann, Anton Ciliga, Manès Sperber and André Malraux. In March, Koestler broached with Malraux the possibility of an 'international summer-school university', which would take up the ideas mooted in Bwlch Ocyn years earlier. He tried to rope in James Burnham, who had just arrived in France, saying that 'it is high time we did something to save the world'. T. S. Eliot was another of his targets. The planned conclave depended on the good offices of Denis de Rougemont, an aristocratic Swiss writer of pre-war fame, with a track record of anti-Nazi work, who ran the European Centre for

Culture. When he pulled out the project folded; but the preparatory discussions brought together many of those who were to collaborate in the Berlin Congress the following year.[55]

As the Cold War deepened Koestler was whipped into a fury by the behaviour of European intellectuals. In July 1949 he noted bitterly in his diary–notebook: 'Shaw on his 93rd birthday calls Stalin "mainstay of peace". Clowning through three quarters of a century, never tiring of it, still the naughty–naughty little boy. The most over-estimated writer of this and probably of all time.' In the same month he used a review of Manès Sperber's novel, *Et le buisson devint cendre* (*The Burned Bramble*), in *Le Figaro littéraire* for a ferocious assault on the French intelligentsia. Sperber's book was based on his experiences working for the Comintern in the 1930s. Nothing had changed according to Koestler: most French intellectuals still took Soviet propaganda at face value, not understanding that 'extreme Left' now signified totalitarianism and that 'peace congresses' were a cover for warlike intentions. They were the 'semi-virgins of totalitarian flirtations . . . Won't you learn from our experience, you clever little flirts of St Germain des Près? Yes and No, they whisper. With them it is always Yes and No – or rather "Oh no, please don't." They neither want the Russians nor the Atlantic pact. Neither capitulation nor self-defence. Neither life nor death. They are only happy doing a pirouette on the tightrope over the No Man's Land suspended between heaven and earth. And they will never understand that under Stalin and Thorez there will be no pirouettes, no neutrality and No Man's Land.'[56]

Koestler willingly assisted the counter-subversion operations of Western governments and intelligence agencies. In several confidential conversations he urged American embassy officials in Paris to support French intellectuals who were prepared to accuse the USSR of crimes against humanity despite the inevitable consequence of being tarred as 'rightist'. The British Foreign Office asked permission to translate and distribute his autobiographical essay in *The God That Failed* in the British Zone of Germany and Canadian National Intelligence sought him out for a chat about the 'ideological side of our Intelligence Directorate'.[57] He was, therefore, primed when he received notice about a planned gathering in Berlin of intellectuals committed to the cause of liberty.

The counter-attack was long overdue. Riding on the crest of its wartime popularity the USSR had launched a wave of propaganda at the West. The leading events in this campaign were the German Writers Congress in East Berlin in October 1947, the Cultural Conference for Peace in Wrocław in September 1948, the International Peace Conference in New York in March 1949 and the Peace Congress in Paris the following month. Each gathering was graced by culture heroes such as Picasso, Chaplin, Paul Robeson and Howard Fast. The unanimously adopted resolutions proclaimed that the peace-loving Soviet peoples had no ill intention towards the Western democracies, but that American 'imperialism' threatened to enslave the world and had to be resisted.[58]

The Soviet 'peace offensive' went almost unchallenged, but here and there counter-demonstrations occurred. In Berlin, in October 1947, Melvin Lasky, an employee of the American Office of Military Government, launched a powerful attack on the pro-Communist writers. Sidney Hook, a brilliant New York academic, organised a rally in the name of Americans for Intellectual Freedom as a spoiling operation at the time of the pro-Soviet peace conference in Manhattan. David Rousset, a camp survivor, staged an 'International Day of Resistance to Dictatorship and War' to coincide with the April 1949 Paris peace congress. Rousset obtained support from Ignazio Silone and Carlo Levi, as well as Burnham and Hook – all of whom would later be tapped by Lasky when he became responsible for organising the largest and most effective riposte.[59]

Lasky, whose parents were East European Jews, was born and educated in New York. He associated with several anti-Fascist and anti-Stalinist student groups in the late 1930s and wrote for the left-wing but anti-Communist *New Leader* magazine. During the war he served with the US army as an official historian and stayed on in Berlin when he was demobilised. After his retort to the Writers Congress he was invited to edit a monthly magazine as part of the official American re-education programme in Germany. *Der Monat* first appeared in October 1948: one of the contributors was Arthur Koestler.[60]

In March 1949 Lasky broached to Ruth Fischer and Franz Borkenau, respectively refugees from Stalinism and Nazism, the idea for a Soviet-style congress in the cause of democracy to be held in Berlin. It was an audacious proposal. Berlin, subdivided into Allied and Soviet zones of occupation, was isolated one hundred miles behind the 'iron curtain'. In June 1948 Stalin had signified his hostility towards Allied policy in Western Germany by instituting a blockade of West Berlin: the city was only kept alive by a costly air lift. This was the perfect backdrop for a gesture of defiance. Lasky turned the office of *Der Monat* into the administrative centre of the Congress and obtained funding from American government agencies, including the recently created CIA, which already had a station in the city.

He and his co-organisers called on like-minded individuals throughout Western Europe and the USA to join them in Berlin in June 1950. The invitees included Sidney Hook and James Burnham from America. Hook was a New York Jew who struggled out of the slums to embark on a successful university career as a philosopher. He became a Communist in the 1920s and for a spell did research in Moscow. In 1932, however, he became disenchanted with Communist Party methods in the US and helped to form a breakaway group. He organised a counter-trial during the Moscow show trials and in 1939 helped form the Committee for Cultural Freedom to aid opponents of Nazism and Stalinism. Burnham had started as an academic Marxist, but made the transition to anti-Communism in the course of revealing that the techniques of state capitalism in the USSR were not much different from 'monopoly capitalism' in the West. This was the substance of his hugely influential book *The Managerial Revolution* (1942), which had a profound impact on Koestler.[61]

Lasky had mentioned to Koestler the possibility of a visit to Berlin when he wrote to him on matters connected with *Der Monat* in July 1949. Next Koestler heard from Ruth Fischer, who asked him to help win support for the Congress from sympathetic ex-Communists. Lasky later sent Koestler an outline of the project and asked him to suggest names for the membership of its national organising committees. The Congress grabbed Koestler's imagination and he threw himself into the preparations. During May and June 1950, Verte Rive was virtually an antechamber for the Berlin gathering.[62]

Koestler was quickly sucked into organisational matters for which he was least well-suited. When Raymond Aron and James Burnham came to dinner on 4 May, he was worried that the Congress already seemed chaotic and 'riddled with the usual jealousies'. So, Mamaine noted, 'K set to work to organise it'. On the eve of the opening he wrote angrily: 'The Berlin Congress . . . is driving me crazy. The organisers phantastically [*sic*] inefficient.' Lasky, who was closely in tune with Koestler politically, was certainly keen to use him, but mainly as an orator. He asked him to take a prominent role in the inaugural session, since he doubted whether the existing line-up of speakers, Silone, Alfred Weber and Jules Romains, was strong enough. While still fretting about practical arrangements, Koestler worked on his speeches and drafted a manifesto on intellectual freedom for the Congress to adopt as its closing gesture.

As the Congress approached he grew excited and tense: it was just like the old days. He slipped easily into a conspiratorial frame of mind and several times met Pierre Bertaux to discuss his personal security. This was not melodrama. On the eve of the opening, Soviet-backed North Korean forces invaded South Korea, triggering a military intervention by the United States under the mantle of the United Nations. It looked as if the Third World War might indeed be about to begin and the espionage services on both sides went into a higher gear. Without any hint of mock heroics, before he left Verte Rive he tidied away his papers and told Cynthia Jefferies what to do if he never came back.[63]

Mamaine and Koestler travelled from Paris to Frankfurt on an overnight train. They were accompanied as far as the French border by a policeman assigned to them by Bertaux. By coincidence they bumped into Sartre, who was on his way to a conference in Germany. Koestler, who still harboured warm feelings for him, suggested they join forces for a picnic supper. He thought Sartre looked in poor shape and felt smug – unjustifiably, perhaps – when Sartre confessed that he and de Beauvoir had quarrelled with most of their old friends. It was the last time they met. Koestler and Mamaine arrived in Frankfurt on the morning of 23 June, embarked on a plane to Berlin and checked into the Hotel am Steinplatz just after midday.[64]

While Mamaine went for a stroll along the Kurfurstendamm with James Burnham's wife, Koestler dived into a conclave with Burnham and Lasky. These two were barely on speaking terms due to a row over the inclusion among the Congress delegates of a suspected Vlasovite – the term for Russians who had followed the turncoat Soviet General Vlasov and collaborated with the Nazis during the war. This would be only one of several personality clashes that would threaten to disrupt the Congress. In the evening they dined with Silone, a potentially awkward encounter since Koestler and Silone had little affection for each other. Indeed, in March Koestler threatened not to attend if Silone was invited. Their mutual antagonism compounded a bitter divergence over strategy.[65]

The differences between the two men were based on background and personal history, as well as temperament, and represent the dilemma at the heart of the Congress and the fate of ex-Communists in general. Silone was born into a peasant community in the Abruzzi in 1900. Destined for the priesthood, the poor peasant boy's road to a decent education, he was expelled from his seminary for opposing

Italy's participation in the Great War. He then earned a living as a journalist for the left-wing press and organised the socialist youth movement. In 1921 the Italian Socialist Party fragmented and he joined with those who went over to the Italian Communist Party. This was the heroic era of Bolshevism and a time of epic conflict in Italy. Silone was absorbed by the struggle to improve the lot of the peasantry and to withstand the advance of the Fascist Party and its blackshirted 'squadristi' who were doing the thuggish work of the big landowners. The Communist Party became his 'family, school, church, barracks'.

He later served the Comintern in Spain and Moscow, but the closer he got to the Kremlin the less enamoured he was of what he saw. He was shocked by the suppression of free debate and the manipulation of the Party apparatus during Stalin's struggle against Trotsky in 1926–7. Silone realised that he was witnessing 'a new version of the inhuman reality against which in declaring ourselves socialists, we had rebelled'. In 1931, after a period of deliberate passivity, he provoked his expulsion from the Party by refusing to denounce Trotsky. Life outside its ranks was almost unbearable. He was sustained only by his essential socialist beliefs and a faith in the intrinsic goodness of man, which took on a religious quality. He explored his experiences and searched for a new politics in a series of novels written as an exile in Switzerland, most notably in *Fontamara* (1933).

Silone had briefly entered politics in post-liberation Italy and helped split the socialists in 1949 by campaigning against co-operation with the Communists. Yet at the Congress he consistently took a more moderate line than Koestler and his allies. He was less dismissive of socialist parties and social democracy than Koestler, and more rigidly opposed to working with the Right. Whereas Koestler wanted the Congress to be aggressive, to take the ideological war to the enemy and challenge neutralism head-on, Silone favoured 'spiritual resistance' to Communism. The two men personified the split that ran through the Berlin meeting.[66]

On Sunday, 24 June, Mamaine and Koestler went on a tour of Berlin. Their driver and guide was also the bodyguard assigned to them by the mayor of Berlin, Ernst Reuter, who had officially con-voked the Congress and who was ultimately responsible for the security of his visitors. It was a mournful excursion: most of the places where Koestler had lived or worked had been destroyed by bombing or were inaccessible in the Eastern zone. They had lunch with Lasky and Burnham, took another spin around the town, then returned for drinks with two of the English contingent – Freddie Ayer and Hugh Trevor-Roper. Ayer and Koestler had friends in common, notably Paul Willert and Cyril Connolly, and Ayer had stayed at Bwlch Ocyn while he paid court to Bertrand Russell. This did nothing to prevent them disagreeing over politics and it may not be coincidental that immediately after this encounter Koestler persuaded Hook, Burnham, Irving Brown, the delegate from the American Federation of Labour and a source of funding for the event, and Lasky 'to constitute [an] unofficial steering committee which [sic] to meet every night for a night-cap'.[67]

Despite a late night at the bar with Arthur Schlesinger Jr and Sol Levitas, editor of *New Leader* and a former Menshevik who had been imprisoned by the Bolsheviks before emigrating from Russia, Koestler was up bright and early the next morning. (Hook recalled that no matter how late he went to sleep, or in whatever condition, Koestler was always the first to appear at the Congress 'house keeping committee' which assembled at 7 a.m. each day.) Then he and Mamaine worked frantically on his speech for the opening session, which had to be written, translated and typed in German and English.[68]

In the afternoon the Congress was formally inaugurated by Ernst Reuter in the Titania Palast. The massed ranks of the Berlin Philharmonic played the overture to Beethoven's *Fidelio* and the speeches began. It was a warm day; the audience of several hundred sweated through addresses by Silone, Romaine, Hook, Josef Czapski, a Polish exile and survivor of the gulag, Panayotis Kanellopoulous, a Greek delegate, Alfred Weber, a distinguished anti-Nazi German economist, and Haakon Lie, a Norwegian social democrat and former resistance fighter. Koestler's oration was the most popular and with good reason. By the time he got up to speak he was in his shirt-sleeves and looked like a man getting down to business. He laced his speech with homely references to the gospels, Beethoven and German student songs which reassured, flattered and titillated his listeners. Striking a populist and anti-intellectual pose, Koestler poured ridicule on thinkers like Sartre and Mann, who agonised over the preservation of their neutrality and supposed integrity, when forced to choose between Communism and anti-Communism.

There were times, he began, when men could legitimately refuse to see the world in black and white and search instead for a compromise: the 'neither-nor' approach. But there were dire moments when St Matthew's advice was more pertinent: 'Let your communication be, Yea yea, Nay nay.' In the current crisis the choice was stark: 'either-or', yes or no to totalitarianism. Even a simple man knew the correct answer; only the intellectuals prevaricated. 'Faced with destiny's challenge, they act like clever imbeciles and preach neutrality towards the bubonic plague. Mostly they are the victims of a professional disease: the intellectual's estrangement from reality.' Melding science and politics in a fashion that would be his trademark, Koestler asserted that the more radical choice was in fact rooted in human biology. The brain was a calculating machine and self-preservation dictated it respond on the 'either-or' principle. He ended by appealing to the waverers to abandon their detachment.[69]

Not surprisingly, some of the more intellectually fastidious observers were disconcerted by Koestler's argument and demotic style. Hook understood him to be saying that there were many options once one made the choice between totalitarianism and democracy, but other listeners believed that Koestler was demanding they align with all anti-Communist forces, in one camp, regardless of their various orientations. Franco Lombardi accused him of thinking like a totalitarian, while Trevor-Roper and Ayer bridled at 'the hysterical atmosphere in which the Congress was held, orchestrated as it was by revengeful ex-Communists, *imprimis* Koestler'.[70]

The programme favoured the radicals. After dinner, when the Burnhams and Koestlers got together again, they drove to the suburb of Wannsee to a reception thrown by Reuter. Here they met members of the underground who smuggled anti-Communist propaganda into the Russian zone and helped people escape to the West. The work of these 'scarlet pimpernels' appealed to Koestler and Burnham. They did not show any discomfort with the nomenclature adopted by these covert teams: *Kampfgruppen*, a term only recently employed to describe battlegroups of the *Wehrmacht* panzer divisions and Waffen-SS. On the contrary, Koestler was having a wonderful time. He moved around in a state of euphoria which he denied had anything to do with the copious amounts of alcohol he was consuming. Back at the hotel he closeted himself at the bar with Brown, Burnham, Hook and Lasky to plot the morrow's events. They spent some time arguing with Professor Hans Thirring, an Austrian scientist, and persuaded him to scrap a ritual statement of the Soviet peace line to which, as a fellow traveller, he was an adherent.[71]

Thirring's dramatic gesture was not the only high point of the second day. In the session on 'Science and Totalitarianism' Alfred Weber announced his resignation from the Deutsche Akademie because it sent birthday greetings to Stalin. An East German student rose from the audience, described the repressive mood in the Eastern sector and defected on the spot. Koestler continued to live on the 'plane of destiny' with a visit to the headquarters of a *Kampfgruppe*. He was 'much impressed'. The activists had files on thousands of Communists and their victims in the Eastern zone, and had compiled statistics on the eighty per cent mortality rate in the concentration camps run by the Soviets. Koestler thought the figures 'fair and rather on the conservative side'. Reinforced by this evidence of totalitarian methods, he drove to Lasky's house for the 'night-cap meeting'. For hours he argued for the need to draft a manifesto to close the Conference. He eventually succeeded, but did not return home until 4 a.m.

Mamaine, who had spent the day in the Soviet sector, was beginning to tire of the pace and had gone to bed early with a sore throat. Not so Koestler: he was up again after just a few hours' sleep. He spent the morning working on the manifesto and finished a draft, including translations, by 1 p.m. There was little time to rest before he had to deliver a paper to the panel on 'Defence of Peace and Freedom' along with André Philip, Lie and Burnham. It was a stormy meeting. Burnham drove up the temperature by ridiculing neutralism and the notion that Europe could avoid taking sides in a conflict between Russia and America. He appalled many delegates by defending America's development of the atomic bomb and justifying its potential use.

Koestler's paper, 'The False Dilemma', addressed the problem of European attitudes from a different angle. He analysed the meaning of the terms 'Left' and 'Right', showing how they had strayed far from their original significance when they came into being at the time of the French Revolution. 'Extreme Left' now described a totalitarian movement. Because leftists and liberals had been duped into defending Soviet tyranny, the struggle against 'terror and despotism' had been taken up by the 'Right': 'Christian democrats in Italy, the Gaullists in France, by Senator McCarthy and his associates in the USA.' He performed a similar exegesis on the meanings of socialism and capitalism. Socialism was meant to entail internationalism, yet in the USSR 'cosmopolitanism' was a pejorative word. The Labour government in Britain was the least enthusiastic of any European government for the idea of European unity. The non-socialist governments of France, Italy and Germany displayed the greatest zeal for international integration, while the USA had given up a portion of national sovereignty to make the United Nations and NATO a real force.

Socialism was also a social and economic doctrine, but socialist Britain and the capitalist USA were each as free as the other, while the USSR and Fascist Spain were unfree, despite their opposed economic systems. He cited the work of James Burnham to show that state capitalism in Russia gave workers no more control over their factories than was the case for workers in the West, while the ownership of publicly quoted companies was diffuse. The extent to which nationalisation of the means of production and distribution enhanced the power of the individual depended on the political system and the extent of democracy. 'The alternative is no longer nationalisation or private economy in the abstract; the real problem is to find the proper balance of state ownership, control, planning and free enterprise'

Anticipating the 'end of ideology', Koestler explained that the terms of political debate no longer corresponded to reality. He was not against socialism or for capitalism: the apposition was becoming meaningless. Thus the anguish of liberals and neutralist intellectuals was a false dilemma. It might ultimately be resolved by sheer inanition after years of stalemate, or the defeat of the West, or the evolution of a new form of consciousness. He hinted at the latter outcome. The 'terrible pressure' of tyranny against freedom would be a 'biological stimulus as it were, which will release the new mutation of human consciousness; and that its content might be a new spiritual awareness, born of anguish and suffering, of the full meaning of freedom'.[72]

Koestler's mystical conclusion, encapsulating the biological politics of *Insight and Outlook*, did nothing to allay the fury of his audience which, as Hook recalled, was 'rapidly growing restive'. One after another, social democratic politicians stood up to criticise his cavalier denunciation of centre-left politics and his seeming inability to differentiate between European welfare states and the unfettered free-market capitalism in North America. One speaker accused him of still thinking like a Communist, in dialectical terms. Franz Borkenau clumsily came to Koestler's defence by arguing that Europeans should be grateful that America was prepared to defend South Korea by force. Such an endorsement of American military action was anathema to many delegates. When David Rousset dissociated himself from Borkenau's comments he triggered shouts of 'hear, hear' and table-thumping by Ayer and Trevor-Roper.

In fact, as Sidney Hook later showed, Koestler's paper was informed by a keen sense of the difference between various non-totalitarian political systems. But he was a victim of his own rhetoric:

'Partly because Koestler's formulations were literary rather than pointedly political, he was taken to task for oversimplification.' The asperity of his delivery was another problem: 'Koestler was capable of reciting the truths of the multiplication table in a way to make some people indignant with him.'[73]

In the evening Koestler sat through one act of *Fidelio* before the caucus reconvened to discuss the institutional follow-up to the Congress. The next morning he attended another organisational meeting, only to find disorder reigning. It took two hours to get agreement to the formation of an 'editorial committee' to approve his draft of the manifesto and the closing resolution of the Congress. Koestler was appointed chairman and from 11 a.m. until 1 p.m. he wrangled over the wording with Ayer and Trevor-Roper, who were also on the committee.

Ayer later bragged: 'In alliance with Hugh Trevor-Roper, I was myself an obstructive element at the first meeting of the Congress for Cultural Freedom . . .' They had come to the Congress in a less than reverential spirit. In blind disregard of the Berlin airlift Ayer remarked that 'The choice of venue seemed to me strange but I was glad of a free visit to Berlin . . .' Once there, according to Ayer, both men were embarrassed by their lack of preparation and agitated by the strident political atmosphere. Their moment finally came when the committee met to draft the resolution 'to which Hugh and I, with one or two followers, raised what were mainly mischievous objections'. In particular they refused to accept a clause that 'totalitarians have no right to membership in the republic of free spirits'. When the disputed clause was discussed in the plenum and attracted more widespread opposition, Koestler agreed to drop it. Burnham was outraged, but Hook praised Koestler's willingness to sacrifice a cherished point for the sake of unanimity. He 'kept his biting words in check even when he was baited by garrulous fools and spitefully clever Englishmen. More than any of us Koestler was prepared to compromise on every issue, except one of principle, to preserve harmony.'[74]

The climax of the Congress was a mass rally in the Funkturm Garden attended by 15,000 Berliners. Eight rather dull speeches, delivered beneath a blazing sky, culminated in the presentation of the manifesto by Koestler. This was his moment: he had drafted it with Sperber weeks earlier and pushed it through the Congress committees. It pronounced his cherished beliefs and carried forward many of the ideas worked over in the meetings with Orwell in North Wales in 1945–6.

The first of the fourteen points, framed in the style of the American Declaration of Independence, proclaimed: 'We hold it to be self-evident that intellectual freedom is one of the inalienable rights of man.' No single political philosophy, economic theory, creed, nation, class or race could claim infallibility and hence justify intolerance. Freedom, the 'right to say "no"', and peace were inseparable, since totalitarian regimes that were unconstrained by popular control threatened international stability. 'We hold that the theory and practice of the totalitarian state are the greatest challenge which man has been called on to meet in the course of civilised history . . . indifference or neutrality in the face of such a challenge amounts to a betrayal of mankind.' But that did not preclude the search for answers to the problems of society: indeed, it was a 'positive obligation'.[75] Koestler concluded the recitation by declaiming: '*Die Freiheit hat die Offensive ergriffen.*' The crowd went wild, cheering and applauding this defiant slogan. At that moment it was truly Koestler's Congress.

From high passion events sank to low farce. Koestler, Hook, Lasky and some others went to the Hotel am Zoo in response to an invitation from Professor Havemann, a leading scientist from the Eastern zone. They were ambushed there by East German newsmen and it became evident that the invitation was a set-up designed to give Havemann a chance to denounce the Congress. But Havemann ludicrously insisted that it was not he who had initiated the encounter, and required that he and his colleague address only an equal number of Congress participants. Koestler played his part in the charade with a wide grin. The meeting broke up after an hour when the East Germans said they were hungry. They rejected Lasky's fraternal offer of sandwiches and did not return later, as promised. It was the last of any 'dialogue' across the ideological divide.[76]

The day ended with a party at a hotel by the Wannsee. Mamaine caught the festive mood when she commented: 'The whole of this congress is in a way rather like one long party, at which one is always having drinks and meals with various groups of people, mostly old friends, with real parties thrown in at intervals.' They slept late the next day, Friday, and had a leisurely morning going to the Zoo with Margarete Buber-Neumann. But Koestler returned to politics at lunch-time, joining with Hook, Schlesinger and the former Menshevik Solomon Schwartz to meet a Vlasovite Russian. Koestler advised the Russian to keep his politics to himself when seeking allies against the common enemy, which was wise in view of his collaboration with the Nazis, but surprising given Koestler's principles. Then

Koestler went to the Free University to meet some students and found time to see the publishers Suhrkamp, who were keen to organise a rendezvous with Brecht. Koestler declined the invitation since it would have been held *in camera*.[77]

The whole time that the Congress had been in progress, Koestler and Lasky had been repulsing press and radio attacks from the East. The assault began the moment Koestler arrived in Berlin, with an attack by the East German literary figure Gerhard Eisler, who called the participants 'literary monkeys' and American police spies. Koestler had known Eisler in the 1930s and immediately arranged a radio interview in which he replied in kind: 'Are you by any chance listening Gerhard? Do you remember when we were together in the concentration camp of Le Vernet in France, in 1940? We were carrying shitbags to the latrines and you asked me what I would do once freed, and I said "I'll join the army to fight National Socialism." You laughed in my face and said "You are a hopeless petit bourgeois romantic." I suppose you have changed your opinion again, and will do it once more. But what you said about our Congress shows that you are still trembling, you poor dogs, as soon as the word freedom is being pronounced.'[78]

In France the Communist *L'Observateur* on 6 July dubbed the Congress the KKK – Koestler's cultural congress – with obvious reference to the Ku Klux Klan, and condemned 'la violence Koestlerienne'. On 8 July *L'Humanité* published a map showing Fontaine le Port, with the implication that good Communists should proceed to Koestler's home to barrack him or worse. Jefferies and the staff were terrified by these imprecations. Once he was back in Verte Rive Koestler gave instructions to his colleagues to write to him via the US embassy in Paris, since the local postal workers were Communists.[79]

Koestler expected this response from the pro-Communist press, but he was less prepared to deal with the attacks on him and the Congress in liberal newspapers in Britain and the USA, mainly orchestrated by Trevor-Roper in the *Manchester Guardian* and *The Economist*.

On 28 June, the *Guardian*'s 'own correspondent' reported with breath-taking naïveté: 'What was presumably intended to be a series of productive discussions between the members of the intelligentsia lapsed this morning [27 June] into a catalogue of personal declamations against Communism.' It praised the British delegation for trying 'to interrupt the flow of prepared denunciations of Communist dragooning of scientific inquiry'. And it lauded Trevor-

Roper for his 'impartial examination of the methods and aims of free inquiry'. Two weeks later, Trevor-Roper published a signed article in the paper attacking the Congress. He objected in a slightly ridiculous tone of wronged innocence that it had turned out to be a 'political demonstration' whereas it had not been advertised as such. Koestler was largely to blame for this: 'his theme throughout was constant, if unconstructive.' He and Burnham sundered the delegates into Cold War hawks and European moderates, and there was a danger that these two would force the moderates into the Communist camp because they insisted that the only effective anti-Communism was on the Right, which offered people little in the way of social justice. Trevor-Roper concluded haughtily and self-righteously: 'I am confirmed in my view that a more satisfactory solution will be offered by those who have never swallowed, and therefore never needed to re-vomit, that obscurantist doctrinal rubbish whose residue can never be fully discharged from the system.'

The *New Statesman*'s observer, Peter de Mendelssohn, sneered: 'how could the assembly shout and think at the same time?' He suggested that Lasky's lofty purpose had been frustrated, first, by the atmosphere created after the invasion of South Korea and, second, by Koestler. In words that almost exactly matched the *Guardian* reports, he accused Koestler and Burnham of hijacking a genteel assembly of thinkers. 'It was all brushed aside by Koestler's effective dialectical over-simplifications. Speaking with skilful demagogic artistry, he claimed that the time for discussion was past and the nature of freedom had to be established "by the rule of thumb". What was required were not definitions as "you don't argue in the front-line" – but the formation of the Western intelligentsia into a *Kampfgruppe*, a fighting squad unequivocally pledged to saying Yes and No – nothing else.' According to the *New Statesman*, Koestler 'finally proceeded to clear away what is now to him no more than a rubbish heap of antiquated political and social conceptions in the Western world, in order to establish a "United Front" of anti-Communists. His argument was a dialectical tour de force.' Koestler and Burnham were guilty of a 'nihilistic brand of non-conformism'. But at least they had bowed to the British delegates who objected to the 'out-lawry' of totalitarian ideology. 'Once again Voltaire had prevailed.'[80]

The pace slackened once the formal events were completed. On 1 July Mamaine again toured the Eastern sector. In the evening they dined at Lasky's home with Burnham, François Bondy, Ignazio Silone and their wives. It was rather a dull gathering, 'though K. did his best to make it go by drinking a considerable amount of wine'. Under the influence of the wine Koestler started berating Silone for his unfriendliness. 'Silone was obviously very bored by this, but made some kind of friendly answer, which however did not satisfy K. as he was too drunk to understand it . . .' Koestler's boorishness did not end once they left the party: he kept Mamaine up until three-thirty in the morning moaning about the supposed coolness of Silone, Burnham and just about everyone else. The next day, in spite of a majestic hangover, he addressed a *Kampfgruppe* and was well received. It was his last engagement in Berlin: they flew out at 6 p.m. The Congress for Cultural Freedom was over.[81]

V

Koestler was not to know it, but as Peter Coleman, a chronicler of the Congress movement, has noted: 'If Berlin was a triumph for Arthur Koestler, it was also the climax of his swan song.' No institutional mechanisms had been created to perpetuate its work. An unwieldy international committee of twenty-five leading figures associated with the Congress was called into being, but active direction of the movement devolved on to a self-appointed temporary executive committee comprising Lasky, Silone, Brown, Rousset, Koestler and Carlo Schmid, a social democrat. Its composition placed Koestler in a minority concerning the future direction of the Congress. Several members even regarded him as a liability. An informal steering committee was also set up that included François Bondy, the editor of the Zurich weekly *Die Weltwoche*, Brown, Burnham and Denis de Rougemont.[82]

From Verte Rive, Koestler bombarded Burnham and Lasky with ideas for further activity and complaints about the lack of progress. He wanted the movement to be established on a constitutional footing with bureaux in Berlin and Paris which would, respectively, conduct propaganda work in the East and the West. It should immediately begin to publish attacks on neutralism and educate public opinion in the democracies, while encouraging covert propaganda operations in the Soviet bloc. But he was increasingly isolated as the less militant wing of the CCF strengthened its grip and he began to suspect that he was not being kept properly informed of what was being planned. Although Bondy was a protégé of Burnham, he turned out to hold diametrically opposed views and his advancement alarmed Koestler. On the other hand the impression of Koestler as a wild man was compounded in late July after he addressed a meeting of the Anglo-American Press Association in Paris. He had been invited to describe the broad aims of the CCF, but the reports focused on his interest in covert work and made him out to be a rabid hawk.[83]

Notwithstanding these internal tensions, some practical progress was made. The CCF obtained a Paris office and set about establishing national branches. Koestler worked with Sperber to set up the French branch, tentatively called Les Amis de la Liberté. Together they laboured over a pamphlet setting out the ideals and programme of the CCF, writing and rewriting it to anticipate the questions the movement would face.

The pamphlet, *Que veulent les Amis de la Liberté?*, described its aims as 'survival', since only the spread of freedom and democracy would prevent war. To break the 'hypnotic power' of Communism, Koestler and Sperber demolished the 'dirty hands' argument against active anti-Communism in familiar style. They defended co-operation with right-wing anti-Communists and countries like Fascist Spain on the grounds that Soviet totalitarianism was far worse. The lessons of 1939–40 showed that divisions over long-term goals within the anti-totalitarian camp could have catastrophic results. Nor were neutrality or passivity an option: every Communist and fellow traveller was a potential fifth columnist. They concluded by admitting that they had 'no panaceas' to the social questions of the day. However, even in the absence of a fresh ideology to counteract Communism, 'To the totalitarian threat and its fanatical creed we oppose an absolute and unconditional NO. But our Yes to the civilisation which we are defending leaves full scope for nuances, divergent opinions, social theories and experiments.'

This modest finale underlines the degree to which Koestler was aware of the varied political options in the free world, despite his tendency to polarise when speaking on his feet and his impatience for the arduous business of working through the democratic process. In another sign of pragmatism he and Sperber deleted from earlier drafts an inflammatory discussion of whether the potential 'Fifth Column' should be banned outright. They also dropped a very clumsy defence of nuclear arms made on the grounds that if 'the atomic bomb is a horrible weapon. So are flame throwers.' It was perhaps just as well that such careless sentiments were excised.[84]

By early August little else had been done and Koestler was getting agitated. Mamaine reported that: 'K. has been in a great state about the Congress ever since Berlin, i.e. for the last six weeks or so. He hardly sleeps at night and thinks about the work all the time. It is an obsession with him. For one thing he feels he alone is capable of running it; but of course nobody believes K's willingness to work at it is not dictated by some ulterior motive.' A meeting of the executive in Paris confirmed his fears about Bondy, whom he regarded as 'politically biased and incapable'. On 18 August, a few days after the meeting of the committee, he abruptly informed him that having 'had a slight nervous breakdown' he intended to resign 'on grounds of health'.[85]

As usual, there was a welter of conflicting explanations for Koestler's sudden departure. Two days before his resignation he had driven to Paris for a meeting and ended up staying overnight at Aron's flat having got extremely drunk and suffered a 'nervous breakdown'. Afterwards he told Sperber: 'The nervous strain was too much and I had to resign from the Congress for reasons of health. I am really very run down.' But, just prior to telling Bondy that he was 'ill', he threatened to resign over an invitation to Sartre, de Beauvoir and Thomas Mann to attend an event sponsored by the Congress. He also complained that his pamphlet had been rewritten without his consent and then lost by the Paris office. He was piqued over the rejection of several of his pet schemes, such as taking thousands of Frenchmen to the USA each year and channelling help to writers who fled the Soviet bloc. And he could not stand working with the pacifist-minded Silone, or his alternate on the executive, Nicolas Chiaromonte, who disparaged all forms of militancy. There were other, generic reasons which may be surmised from his prior engagement in political activism. Koestler was ill-equipped for organisational work: he was the worst combination of a perfectionist and a worrier. The result was exhausting for him and those close to him. Mamaine noted in her diary that he would resign from the CCF committee 'giving grounds of health', not *because* he was ill. There is no evidence of any real malaise. Koestler was certainly in need of a holiday, but the 'nervous breakdown' was probably just a pretext.[86] The most likely reason is that Koestler was too much of a loner to persist in any institutional framework. His active involvement with the Congress had lasted just over four months. In every respect this was consistent with the pattern of his association with the Zionist Revisionist movement, the Communist Party, the Münzenberg apparatus, INFA and even the Pioneer Corps.

He clearly felt bad about this dénouement. After his return to Verte Rive he had written proudly to Burnham: 'I have a feeling we started something in Berlin which is going to turn out bigger than any of us realized at the time.' When he told him he was resigning he defensively listed everything he had accomplished. On the day of his resignation he also told Brown that he planned to turn over ten per cent of the royalties from the dramatisation of *Darkness at Noon* to a fund for refugee intellectuals. Burnham later pleaded with him that his departure 'would be close to the symbolic liquidation of the Congress. You were the most prominent participant in the Berlin proceedings, and the destiny of the Congress is closely bound to you.' Koestler was persuaded not to break entirely with the Congress and he remained associated with it for several months longer.[87]

By the time the CCF was established on a firm basis and fully staffed, Koestler had left Europe. He had played a decisive role in the genesis of the Congress and the success of the Berlin assembly, although his influence on its subsequent direction was almost nil and, as much as he might try, he could not claim credit for the string of cultural and political accomplishments attributable to it. For the next decade it was responsible for initiating and supporting a range of influential magazines, including *Encounter* and *Preuves*, and organising a host of path-breaking scientific and cultural conferences. In 1967, however, the CCF was shaken by the revelation that the entire operation was covertly funded by the CIA and that its Executive Director, Mike Josselson, had been a CIA employee since he joined the Congress in 1950. Many leftists and liberals who had been content to work with and within the CCF were outraged: Stephen Spender, one of the editors of *Encounter*, resigned in protest. The movement and its publications never recovered.[88]

Koestler viewed the 'scandal' with wry detachment. Thanks to his State Department friends he had known for certain since 1951 that the Congress was receiving CIA money. At a dinner with leading officials from the CIA and the State Department in Washington in April 1951, his friend Bob Joyce 'revealed unexpected familiarity with Congress in which he and W[isner] play an invisible directing part'. Joyce had transferred from the US Foreign Service to the Office of Strategic Services in 1943 and ended the war as head of the OSS station in Switzerland. From there he returned to America to take a role in the formation of the CIA, successor organisation to the OSS. Frank Wisner had also served in the OSS and was an architect of America's Cold War strategy. He had played a key role recruiting anti-Soviet East Europeans into the service of US counter-espionage activity. Norris Chipman, another friend from the US Foreign Service whom Koestler had got to know well while he was serving in the Paris embassy in the late 1940s, confirmed this information in 1954.[89]

He had suspected as much from the outset. In 1972 he told John Dittberner, an American researcher: 'I knew from the beginning that there was American government money behind the Congress for Cultural Freedom and had no objection to this as long as there were no strings attached.' The likely source of the finance did not bother him. In the context of the Cold War during the early 1950s counter-intelligence work in most guises was deemed necessary and acceptable. There were worse causes for the US government to spend its money on. Even so, twenty years later he was not entirely truthful about his knowledge of CIA funding and his initial suspicions. He assured Dittberner that: 'I did not know until the scandal broke that the government agency in question was the CIA. My reaction to the disclosure was that it had been a clumsy and bungling way of channelling funds . . .' He claimed that he would have preferred the CCF to adopt fiscal transparency and that he resigned partly due to the murkiness surrounding Brown's channelling of funds from American trade unions into the CCF and, indeed, there is some evidence of this in his correspondence at that time. Koestler jokingly pointed out to Dittberner that due to his royalty arrangement he was not a 'beneficiary but a contributor to the CCF' and hence, in a manner of speaking, had actually subsidised the CIA. But there was nothing in this to worry Koestler the Cold Warrior: on the contrary, it was a source of ironic pride.[90]

VI

Koestler's 'breakdown' in August was typical of the turning-points in his life. The Congress had put him under great strain. In addition to the work and anxiety it generated, he was putting the finishing touches to his latest novel, *The Age of Longing*. Nor was there much peace at Verte Rive, with visits by members of the steering committee, Celia Kirwan and his mother, who came to stay for ten days at the end of July. He also entertained Sidney Kingsley, an American playwright, who had obtained the rights to dramatise *Darkness at Noon*. These encounters were particularly depressing.

He had expected to have a large part in writing the script, but Kingsley was intent on turning out a 'lowbrow' play with mass appeal and saw no place for collaboration. Koestler became worried that the American would 'spoil' his finest work and began obsessively to fret that he had been wrong to approve the arrangement. He kept Mamaine up till the early hours rehearsing the arguments for and against the dramatisation. The next day he set off to Paris to confront

Kingsley: this, drink and more trouble with his car contributed to his collapse.[91]

Nor could he settle where to live. He talked endlessly with Mamaine about the problem and in late July even thought of spending part of each year in Berlin. Mamaine was horrified at the prospect of their nomadic life going on and reminded him that he could not keep lugging 2000 books around indefinitely. She was very tired and had been ill again. In the days before he finally snapped, Koestler was even more boorish than usual. One evening, while the Kingsleys were visiting, they had followed up dinner by listening to German and Russian Communist songs. When he finally joined Mamaine in bed he 'insisted on going on singing, with me, the Volga Boatmen and other Russian songs till about 3 a.m.' A few days later, she told Kirwan, he again kept her up till the early hours, 'though I am very exhausted and am not well now'.

The catharsis on 17–18 August was associated with another mishap with his car: Koestler was coming to regard automobiles almost as oracles. He had driven to Paris on 15 August to see Kingsley in the evening. The next morning the car developed a flat tyre and in the course of driving it around in search of a garage he damaged the wheel. He rang Mamaine to say that he would stay overnight in Paris, but in the evening Raymond Aron called her to report that Koestler was at his flat, lying drunk on the sofa. Aron drove him back to Verte Rive that night. Mamaine recalled that when he had sobered up he explained: 'his pattern when drunk is one of self-annihilation: he has fantasies about hanging himself, and tends to do suicidal things like hitting police *commissaires* or (in this case) having a car accident.' It was at such points that his 'guardian angel' intervened to reveal the correct path.

So, in one convulsive day Koestler resolved to go on the wagon again, dissociate himself from the stage version of *Darkness at Noon* and donate his share of the royalties to helping political refugees, resign from the CCF executive, and go on holiday with Mamaine (once the car was fixed). He also suggested, to her joy, that they should move to London. Shortly afterwards he summed up the crisis: 'Emerging from one of the major periodic shocks which determine the pattern of my life. Novel finished; Berlin triumph and resignation; Kingsley (dramatization of *Darkness at Noon*) major disappointment; summer 1939 feeling. All this combines in first *very bad* attack of DT three days ago. Resolved not to intervene in French politics; to dedicate 10 per cent of my income and all proceeds of 'Darkness' drama to refugees from East; to leave France this winter.'[92]

A week later, Mamaine and Koestler set out for a long and well-deserved vacation. They drove south, visiting Limoges, Sarlat, Pau, Susmiou, and Navarreux – the places Koestler had passed through in 1940. From Lescun they proceeded via Lourdes to Montauban and the Massif Central, where they went walking. Mamaine was relieved to have escaped the lethal air of Fontaine le Port, but soon went down with 'mild dysentery', which made Koestler 'very cross' with her. Meanwhile, he started to enjoy himself and insisted that they climb the highest peaks in the Puy-de-Dôme. His bad behaviour did not vanish: he got drunk several times, argued with nearly every restaurateur and hotelier they had dealings with along their route and declaimed against the 'decay of France'. On 3 September Mamaine felt too ill and tired to continue, so they returned to Verte Rive, where they were greeted by a holidaying Michael Polanyi.[93]

They stayed only a short while. Mamaine soon left for London and Koestler moved on to Paris. She was on her own in England for nearly two weeks, seeing old friends and bird-watching in the country. Her ambivalence towards Koestler was now so extreme that she felt liberated to be away from him. She confided to her diary that: 'separation of a week or so and freedom of life alone makes me realise what a strain it almost always is being with him, because of his violent and often unpredictable behaviour, constant changes of mood and never-failing desire to make people do something different from what they want to do . . .'[94]

Their tour did not persuade Koestler of the charms of Europe. Despite everything he had said to Mamaine, on 6 September he visited the American consulate in Paris to obtain a visa for the United States, where he intended to go in search of a new home instead of England.

On 18 September he arrived in London. As if to confirm that nothing had changed about either his attitude to England or his character, he had a terrible public row with Dick Crossman before he had even unpacked. Crossman had arranged a private dinner at the House of Commons attended by John Strachey, Arthur Schlesinger Jr, Raymond Aron and their wives. The discussion turned to the Labour Party's half-hearted attitude towards European integration. Crossman and Strachey defended the government's stand-offish position, and were berated by Koestler and Aron, who argued that pan-European institutions and identity were necessary to motivate people to defend Europe against the Soviet threat. Crossman retorted that the Americans would defend Europe: Britain's responsibilties lay in Asia. Koestler then 'reproached the Labour Party for having done nothing to counteract communist influence in Europe and US, leaving the job to capitalist USA, and backing pro-Soviet [Italian Socialist leader] Nenni . . .' Crossman, who was rather drunk, seems to have been confused about which Italian socialist faction the Labour Party had in fact supported and accused Koestler of uttering 'A bloody anti-British lie'. After Koestler had got Crossman to confirm this phrase he walked out, taking Mamaine with him.

According to Mamaine Koestler justified his behaviour by saying: 'he couldn't stand Dick's frivolous attitude to politics, his irresponsible articles in the *New Statesman*, and his support of what K. considers a suicidal line of isolation'. But she had a shrewder perception of what lay beneath the explosion: 'I have witnessed so many outbursts from K. that I couldn't help feeling that the real reason was neither Dick's abuse nor his frivolous attitude . . . but some sort of sub-conscious urge not to have any friends.' It was all very well to crow over Sartre's break-ups, but the list of friendships which had been ruptured by Koestler in recent years was no less impressive. Moreover, he had displayed 'outbursts of rage' at a string of dinner parties. Significantly the *casus belli* was often the same. In April, at a dinner for Norris Chipman, 'he lost his temper completely and shouted that he couldn't stand the unreal and frivolous attitude of the left any longer'.[95]

While a pattern may be apparent, this does not mean that Koestler was entirely culpable for the bust-up. Dick Crossman was quick to write him a contrite note: 'Let me first apologise for my ill-manners, even less pardonable since I was your guest. It was my fault that the dinner broke up as it did and it probably wouldn't have, if both of us had been on the cider wagon . . . My feeling for you is based not on compatibility of views but on incompatibility!!! I want to test my ideas against the toughest opposition – and survive. You provide the opposition, and I still hope that this is a basis for a genuine friendship. After all it *was* a good discussion last Monday, and I believe you too learnt something from it.'

Strachey, perhaps with a touch of mischief-making, assured Koestler that 'Dick left you very little option to do what you did. What an old Prussian he is!' Strachey did not conceal that he, too, differed from Koestler on the question of European unity, but reiterated that he was in favour of active defence against the USSR and apologised for any part he had played in the débâcle.

Zita Crossman did her best to heal the breach. 'I cannot bear to lose a friend and particularly the idea of losing you left an aching void. I didn't sleep all night. You are quite right about you and Dick being better apart during the present political weather, but it is only with bitter disappointment that I admit this.' Crossman put a nail in the coffin of their friendship by publishing an article in the *New Statesman* on 16 December 1950 that included a gratuitous swipe at his old sparring partner. 'British Labour', he opined, 'is not prepared to adopt the anti-Marxist dogmatism of ex-Communists such as James Burnham and Arthur Koestler . . . when they turn Marx upside down and "prove" the inevitability of war and the inherent impossibility of Communist and non-Communist states existing alongside one another.'[96]

Given that this message was implicit in the essay by Koestler which Crossman had brought to the world in *The God That Failed*, it is impossible not to sympathise with his grievance about Crossman's opportunism. Anthony Howard is unsparing about Crossman's inconsistency, which at this period in his career was even more pronounced than usual. Even so, Koestler was strangely blind to the reality of British foreign policy which, under Foreign Secretary Bevin's guidance, was staunchly anti-Communist even if it was cool on European unity. Crossman's antics could have been treated as the ravings of an impotent backbencher. To take them so seriously indicated a lack of perspective and an emotive undercurrent. Koestler was not able to control his feelings on matters that touched him deeply, especially if they intertwined with personalities. Mamaine was probably right.

The bitter exchanges continued in public and in private. In the midst of a controversy between Crossman and Sidney Hook in April 1951, Koestler wrote to Hook that 'your letter to Dick Crossman ought to make mincemeat of him, if a politician made of synthetic rubber could be made mincement of'. But Zita was overjoyed when Koestler returned to England from the United States in 1952 and anticipated a reunion. It was not to be: she died soon after. Koestler then wrote a moving condolence letter to Crossman to which he responded: 'Your telegram gave me the sort of pleasure which you can get very occasionally, on such an occasion as this.' There was a measure of reconciliation, but they were never to be close again.[97]

VII

Koestler's pretext for going to the United States was to help promote *The Age of Longing* and to see the dramatisation of *Darkness at Noon*. Another motive was to find a place to live for part of the year so that he could experience life on both sides of the Atlantic and obtain a bifocal view of world affairs. The decision had been maturing for years. It was finally triggered by the Congress experience and his second disillusionment with France during their holiday. 'The feeling of corruption and decay in France became unbearable,' Koestler noted, '3,000 kilometres with Mamaine – and were almost everywhere cheated and treated with hostility.' Once the choice was made, the difficulties of getting a visa due to his background in the CP confirmed his belief that he had to go there to close that chapter of his life.[98]

After an enjoyable flight to New York, which again revived memories of the Zeppelin expedition, he moved into a room in Jim Putnam's flat and entered the whirl of Manhattan literary life. The first week was a 'frightful rush': he wrote two newspaper articles, reviewed Bertrand Russell's latest book and started correcting the proofs of the novel. He also resumed 'saving the world', as he termed his activity for the CCF.[99]

On 8 October he published in the *New York Times* a long article proposing the formation of a European 'Legion of Liberty', which he hoped would spark a political campaign. In the piece he maintained that Europeans had to play a part in ensuring their own security, but could not strengthen their societies and deter Communist infiltration just by promoting social welfare and justice. Nor was there time to devise a new ideology that would rally intellectuals and masses alike. Europe needed unity, but formal alliances and supernational organisations would not command mass loyalty. The only way of achieving this would be the creation of a European army. Even this would take time, so he proposed the immediate formation of 'an élite force, within the framework of the Atlantic Pact', consisting of volunteers from the eleven Western European states. Much of the article was devoted to details such as the common language to be used and the type of unit organisation, for which information he had consulted members of the US military. The main benefit of the unit would be psychological: it would be 'the catalytic agent for a truly integrated European Army, and thus the pioneer of a United Europe'. The article reinforced the perception of Koestler as a dangerous hawk with a taste for armchair generalship.[100]

After three weeks he began to weary of the hectic social round. Through Putnam and Macmillan Koestler had a ready-made circle, although he was not always complimentary about his dinner companions. When Nora Beloff took scant interest in his Legion of Liberty he dubbed her a 'grade 14 fellow-traveller'. Vladimir Nabokov, whom he saw in the company of Saul Bellow, was a 'prize bore'. He also met Dos Passos, Aldous Huxley and Patricia Highsmith. Much of his social time was spent in the company of New York Jews, whom he detested: 'wonder why there is not more anti-Semitism in USA', he scribbled in his diary–notebook. Conditions in Putnam's flat began to get him down. Like many New York apartments it was overheated: Koestler complained to Mamaine that it resembled a 'steambath'.[101]

He was also beginning to tire of politicking: 'my 7-year rush of world-saving is beginning to wear thin.' Koestler wore himself out hustling support for his pet Cold War initiatives: the CCF, his own Fund for Intellectual Freedom (FFIF), which was intended to benefit refugee writers, and the Legion of Liberty. He saw Aldous Huxley, Dos Passos, James Farrell and contacted Hemingway, John Hersey, Norman Mailer and Graham Greene to interest them in the FFIF. In addition he appeared as guest of honour at a party for the CCF, at which the luminaries included the bridge guru Ely Culbertson, the writer Alfred Kazin and the social historian Lewis Mumford.[102]

For the weekend of 28 October he escaped the hurly-burly of Manhattan and stayed with friends who lived in rural Pennsylvania. They suggested going to a real estate auction for fun and almost before he knew what he was doing Koestler had acquired an island in the Delaware River at a cost of $41,000. He explained excitedly to Mamaine that: 'We are proprietors of a steel bridge of 250 feet length with an island attached to it and accommodation for 2800 chickens on the island, also 112 acres of woodland, kukurcz [*sic*] fields and pasture. Also a rather lovely 1824 Pennsylvania farm-house. . . . Lest you think I have gone off my head let me explain that this was the most reasonable and inspired transaction of my life.' The price of Island Farm was almost exactly the sum of his dollar royalties that Macmillan were holding for him on account, currency that he could not hold as a British subject and which he did not want to convert into sterling. He reassured her that the house was 'neither flashy Hollywood nor dingy Bwlchocy'. Despite the presence of sheep, ducks and bees, and the need for staff, he claimed: 'It doesn't tie us down in the least as no maintenance is required.'[103]

Koestler purchased Island Farm almost in a dreamlike state; the act revealed graphically many of his deepest fantasies. He disliked the 'openness' of American country houses, which were rarely surrounded by hedges or fences: they left him feeling 'exposed'. He had always wanted an island, to be 'ruler of an island kingdom'. In his *Hermes Agenda* pocket book he noted 'Treasure Island bought'. It was as if he were acting out a childhood fantasy of independence, self-sufficiency and absolute dominance. Much later he admitted that it was a 'rather crazy venture'.[104] The farm was a massive headache and needed constant attention, not to mention capital for running costs. While Koestler was attracted yet again to a riverside location, the atmosphere was totally unsuitable for his asthmatic wife. In the late spring and summer it became unbearbly hot and humid: much of it was actually marshland. Island Farm was an act of gross self-indulgence, the gesture of an irresponsible, thoughtless and greedy little boy inside a grown man.

Mamaine's response was pained. She tried to be jolly, but only succeeded in sounding transparently English-stiff-upper-lip: 'It is wonderful and you are the cleverest fellow in the world.' Then came the 'buts'. 'What I want to know is, where oh where are we going to live in the future? and will the place we live in have the sort of outhouses where I can put a piano? Will we have a wonderful working room for you? Are we likely to live in a place which will not cause me to be ill all the time? But no of course not — only the Seine is that sort of place I think.'[105]

She had been very happy living in London without Koestler. Much later, when she looked back on the time she had been apart from him, she reflected that those 'three months were among the most pleasant I have ever spent'. She had resumed the piano, which she loved, and saw friends whom Koestler did not approve of and with whom she had consequently lost touch. While she protested that he did not make her unhappy and described him as her 'prop', the inference of her letters was clear. 'I am so happy here and have established for myself such an agreeable way of life, that I am reluctant to move into the uncertainty of New York.' A new note of assertiveness entered her letters while they were apart. She reiterated that she did not want to move to America before she was ready and was determined never to go back to Verte Rive, to spend six months each year 'feeling like death, which is what I always have and always will do there. I'm sorry about it; and I only hope that you've decided really to give up living in France because otherwise I don't see quite how we'll get around this difficulty.'

Mamaine grew less tolerant of his silences and the lack of detail about his activities. After the news about Island Farm she chided him that 'it is hell having simply no idea what you are doing or where you are or anything'. A few days later (while a letter from Koestler was in the post to her) she complained: 'As far as I'm concerned you are floating about in a void.' After a visit to France to deal with matters at Verte Rive (which was being let) and collect some papers for

Koestler she pointedly wondered what she was doing with a house outside Paris and a husband in Pennsylvania.[106]

In a burst of cheery, mollifying letters Koestler did his best to calm her fears. Energised by his coup, he moved out of Putnam's flat into a room in the Hotel Duane and set to work on the proofs of *Age of Longing*. Once this job was completed he worked fitfully on a volume provisionally entitled 'Essays of Despair', which would include revised versions of his CCF addresses and a piece on 'political neuroses'. In early November he went to Washington to resolve his immigration status and see his friends Roy Murphy and Bob Joyce at the State Department. He learned that to get a residential permit would require an act of Congress, which would take several months, so he planned to prolong his stay in America until March 1951 and issued orders to Mamaine to arrange the letting of Verte Rive for a further period. He also paid a visit to the notorious American ex-Communist Whittaker Chambers and met the head of US overseas propaganda. It was only the first of many such meetings.[107]

Neither he nor Mamaine displayed much enthusiasm for a reunion. In mid-November he told her that he had acquired the services of a maid so there was no need for her to rush over as 'I don't need you in a technical hausfrau sense'. They agreed that she would come to New York just after Christmas and they would move together to Island Farm. So it was that Mamaine arrived in America full of foreboding. She observed that Koestler had 'got much fatter' and was alarmed to find that he was drinking heavily again. 'I find him a bit of a strain after these months of freedom,' she told Kirwan, 'but I dare say things will turn out all-right.' They did not. After they moved into Island Farm on 8 January 1951 all the usual settling-in problems arose.[108]

Island Farm was a large, attractive, wood-boarded house. Koestler occupied a suite of rooms on the third floor, with his own bedroom, bathroom and study with a window overlooking his domain. On the second floor were the master bedroom and several guest rooms plus bathrooms. The ground floor comprised a large living room which opened on to a veranda on three sides. The house was constructed on an incline, which allowed for a semi-basement comprising a dining room and kitchen. Abutting the main structure was a self-contained house for staff. There were also assorted barns and outhouses.[109]

It had been modernised throughout, but the living quarters had to be furnished, redecorated and maintained. However, because Koestler had impulsively sunk all his capital into the purchase they were short of money. Mamaine scoured second-hand shops for crockery, utensils and 'antique' furniture. Since they could only afford a cleaner three times a week, she was burdened with the upkeep of the house, too. She reported it was a 'hell of a job to keep it moderately clean and do the cooking, washing up, laundry, ironing, mending and all K's correspondence, as well as buying the basic furniture etc.' Koestler didn't make her life any easier by his inability to take care of himself. She could not take time off to visit friends in New York because 'as we have no servants I can't leave K. alone very often for very long'. Freezing cold weather made things worse. Koestler's mood rapidly went sour and he made life 'a considerable strain' for Mamaine. In despair she, too, started hitting the bottle.[110]

Less than four weeks into their new life on the island he exploded in one of his periodic bouts of domestic violence. Agnes Knicker-bocker, who ran the FFIF, had joined them for dinner when Koestler 'suddenly worked himself up into a rage and stampeded about knock-ing things over . . . Agnes and I spent the rest of the evening mopping up wine, whiskey, brandy, blood, glass and china; K. also broke a couple of chairs and a lamp, and almost broke his foot kicking at things . . . There was no apparent reason for his outburst . . . '[111]

A sullen peace descended on Island Farm. For a week Mamaine barely exchanged a word with Koestler: 'he is too bad-tempered, and I too bored and fed up with him.' Although a char arrived to rescue Mamaine from some of the drudgery, the relief came too late for her health. In the second week of February she became ill and fell into a serious depression — the first since she had parted from Koestler in France. 'I feel empty and can't see why I am alive,' she lamented to Kirwan. A few days later she had a serious attack of bronchitis. This had been brewing for some time. At first she had tried to believe that the island's climate would be kind to her, turning a blind eye to evidence that the place was very swampy. The cold, damp winter air eventually removed any doubts about the effect it would have.[112]

Twenty-five years later Koestler could still not admit to the cause of Mamaine's condition or take responsibility for his part in her suffering. Reflecting on her 'asthma attack' he wrote: 'This had happened with distressing repetitiveness each time we moved to a new house.' Perhaps it was the strain of moving, he mused, 'or else there was some psychosomatic devilry at work, for though Mamaine loved travelling, the only place where she really wanted to live was London'. In fact, Mamaine loved northern Italy, southern Germany, Austria and Switzerland, where the mountains offered a healthy environment for an asthmatic. He knew she was sensitive to a damp climate when he bought Island Farm, but he preferred to blame her for getting ill. Perversely, Koestler did eventually build a home in the Austrian mountains – after Mamaine was dead.[113]

Life on the island ground to a halt. For Koestler the interruption came at a bad moment. He had finished working on the French and German translations of *The Age of Longing* and was anxiously awaiting the reviews of the US and British editions. Money worries were pressing on him, but he could not decide in which direction to go next. He started uncertainly on the first volume of an auto-biographical novel, but after experimenting with the genre opted for a conventional format. He reasoned that no one would believe a character like Münzenberg really existed if he cropped up in a work of fiction and the historical background would inevitably play second fiddle to the psychological development of the main character. Koestler wanted his life story 'to be focused on the political events of my time'.[114]

In desperation, he wrote to Cynthia Jefferies inviting her to Island Farm to work as his secretary. He could offer no salary, only room and board, but he reckoned that if he dictated the first draft of the autobiography it would take only two months to complete. Jefferies was bowled over by the summons. She had been stricken when Koestler went to America and never settled down to another job. She had moved to London and found work with Sidney Bernstein, the film and television magnate, but was not happy. Once she received the call from America she waited only as long as it took to obtain a visa: ten days. Koestler met her at Newark airport, looking all-American in a leather wind-breaker. The black Citroën had given way to a large black Cadillac.[115]

Once Jefferies was installed, work on the autobiography resumed, Koestler relaxed and Mamaine's health picked up. Koestler began with his 'family saga' and got into his stride quickly. His technique was to dictate for two hours every morning and afternoon, while Jefferies sat 'curled up' in an armchair hanging on his every word. By March 1951 he had written 40,000 words in this way and had taken the story up to his adolescence.[116]

In March 1951 *The Age of Longing* appeared. A lot was riding on it and Koestler monitored its progress in the lists of best-selling books. Yet he refused all radio and television interviews to promote it.[117] This was possibly because he was afraid that his guttural accent would reveal too clearly the alien character of the author and deter US readers. The book was a political act, a Cold War novel *par excellence*

– the work of the CCF carried on by other means. It was designed
to influence public opinion and government officials in the USA, in
much the same way that *Thieves in the Night* had helped to shape both
popular and official opinion about the Palestine crisis. Since it contained several American characters and reflected on the relationship
between the Old World and the New, its reception would have
important ramifications for his future in America.

Koestler had begun working on the novel in summer 1949, after
several false starts, and finished it in the spring of 1950. The plot had
come from an editor at Macmillan who mused on the possibilities of
a Romeo and Juliet style love story between a Russian spy and an
American woman. In Koestler's hands, however, the story lost any
light or romantic touch. It became a ponderous 'novel of ideas' set
against the background of a world teetering on the edge of atomic
war, populated by thinly camouflaged versions of Malraux, Sperber
and Sartre, orchestrated around a series of set pieces in which the
chief characters pontificated in a more or less entertaining fashion.
Sandwiched uneasily in the middle was a fantasy of Europe after an
atomic show-down: the novel was suffused by an apocalyptic
spirit.[118]

The Age of Longing is essentially about faith and the loss of faith, and
more generally about the conflict between the West, which has become decadent, and the Soviet bloc, which retains its vitality thanks
to the resilience of Communist belief. The two main characters who
personify this opposition are Hydie, who is American-born and
English-educated, and Fedya, a Russian of Armenian origin, who has
grown up under Bolshevism.[119] The action takes place over a few
days in Paris. Hydie is there with her father, a Colonel attached to
the American embassy, who is preparing lists of Frenchmen to be
evacuated to the USA when the Red Army rolls over France.
Through him she meets a trio of pessimistic ex-Leftists of the Pink
Decade. The first, Julien Delattre, is a limping veteran of the Spanish
Civil War with a touch of Camus and Malraux. Count Boris is a
lachrymose, philosophical East European who lost his family to the
Nazis and whose reputation for being 'nasty and quarrelsome' suggests Koestler himself. Professor Vardi is a Viennese Jewish
intellectual whose 'rabbinical pathos' and taste for sweet vermouth
identify him as Manès Sperber.[120]

These three represent different responses to exile and homelessness, both physical and spiritual, and Koestler is at his best describing
their plight. All meet a miserable end except Delattre, who prepares
a resistance cell to challenge the Soviet occupation when it comes,

even though he knows the struggle will be hopeless.[121] Julien Delattre puts into words Koestler's fundamental analysis of what he saw as the crisis afflicting Western Europe in the late 1940s. Secularisation and rationalism had cut people off from belief in God or the afterlife. Society had become the new deity and mankind the plaything of secular ideologies. 'The only, the one and only hope of preventing this is the emergence of a new transcendental faith which would deflect people's energies from the "social field" to the cosmic field – which would re-establish direct transactions between man and the universe and would act as a brake on the motors of expediency. In other words: the emergence of a new religion, of a cosmic loyalty with a doctrine acceptable to twentieth century man.'[122]

The philosophising on Koestler's favourite themes is broken up by several action sequences. Delattre takes Hydie to a 'Rally for Peace and Progress' which gives Koestler the opportunity to parody the peace congresses addressed by Paul Robeson, Lord Haldane and Jean-Paul Sartre, who appears in the guise of Professor Pontieux, the apostle of 'neo-nihilism'. Hydie and Fedya have an affair until she learns that he is preparing lists of prominent Frenchmen to be liquidated. Inspired by the saints with whom she had been infatuated in her convent schooldays, she sets out to assassinate him, but succeeds only in shooting him in 'the loin'. This suggests that she had in some way neutered his potency, but the novel ends as the invasion of the West begins.[123]

The Age of Longing set out to create a mood of ennui and doom. Whereas Chekhov could do this with humour and pathos, Koestler's jokes are as flat as his characters. The novel feels contrived and disastrously ill-judged, for all the craftsmanship poured into it. In the 1970s, Koestler defended its unfounded pessimism by claiming that it 'was intended as a warning and not a prophecy'.[124] But even his warning was too shrill and wide of the mark. He entirely failed to see the real moves towards European integration and common defence that would ultimately stymie Soviet expansionism. His prescription for a new religion was a hostage to fortune. It looks even more far-fetched when juxtaposed against the evolving network of mundane commercial and diplomatic agreements that would eventually lead to NATO, the West European Union and the European Economic Community. Koestler wanted a single panacea to the crisis of post-war European politics: he had no patience with politics itself. The quotidian success of the politicians left his 'warnings' sounding terribly pompous and hollow.

The novel had unfortunate personal ramifications. Sperber was deeply hurt by the character of Vardi and contrasted his fate in the

novel with that of St Hilaire, a resistance hero who resembles
Malraux. Koestler protested that Vardi was in fact modelled on a
student he had known in Vienna, but Mamaine confessed otherwise.
Malraux, in turn, was offended by the character of St Hilaire.
Koestler agreed there were some 'Malrauxesque elements in the
composite picture of St Hilaire', but tried to persuade his friend that
everyone found him the most attractive figure in the book.[125]

The Age of Longing received mixed reviews in Britain and the US.
Crossman was uncomplimentary in the New Statesman, proclaiming
haughtily (and somewhat inconsistently in view of his role in The
God That Failed) that 'Ex-Communism is a sterile state of mind'. He
complained that Koestler gave the best lines to the devil (Fedya), but
that even he was hardly more than a stereotype. The psychologist
Emanuel Miller, writing in the Jewish Chronicle, regretted that aside
from some perceptive characterisation it was a novel of ideas in
which speeches were constantly 'rising to the level of the banal'.
Tatler readers were warned that, although well-told, 'the story itself
is drowned in dialectics'. But the sales were healthy enough and for
a while it was number four in the US best-seller lists. It even
outstripped From Here to Eternity.[126]

Jefferies's arrival, progress with his writing and the success of the
novel cheered Koestler, but it was a temporary improvement. Once
again his refusal to quit dabbling in politics upset his precarious
equilibrium. At the end of January he had protested to the CCF
executive about the direction in which it was moving. A meeting
with Irving Brown at Island Farm only made him more pessimistic
about its fortunes. He warned Burnham, whom he openly blamed
for the appointment of Bondy and Rougemont, that unless there
were reforms he would cut all ties with the movement. This was no
mean threat. Koestler was probably the best-known figure in the
Congress: he was a star attraction at a meeting of the American
Committee of the CCF at the Waldorf Astoria in late March and the
key speaker at a rally for the CCF at Freedom House the following
May. Senator Hubert Humphrey, a rising Democrat, was so
impressed by Koestler that he read one of his articles ('We Put
Freedom First') into the Congressional Record. But the arrangements
for the proposed 1951 Paris Congress were the last straw. Koestler
was disgusted that what had been founded as a political force had
turned into an 'effete' arts movement. At the end of July he wrote to
Nicholas Nabokov, the Congress Secretary General and prime
mover of the Paris event, resigning from the international executive
committee. He bitterly told Sperber: 'I did not withdraw from this

movement. I was made to withdraw in a gentle and effective way.'[127]

Koestler meanwhile constructed a new cross to bear. In November the Fund for Intellectual Freedom was officially inaugurated. Its aim was to provide for exile and *émigré* writers the kind of support that was so cripplingly absent to the refugee literati of Koestler's generation. His idea was for successful writers to fund it by contributing a portion of their royalties, a sort of self-imposed tax. But he found it hard to persuade his fellow authors to contribute.[128] A full-time (unpaid) general secretary/case worker, Agnes Knickerbocker, was appointed but she was overwhelmed by the amount of work it generated. After the initial blaze of publicity the FFIF was inundated by requests from writers in Europe, mainly East Europeans resident in the US zone of Germany, for grants and loans to allow them time to complete novels or just purchase typewriter ribbons. The Nobel Prize winner Czeslaw Milosz was only one of those whom Koestler helped.[129]

The Fund caused just as many rows with his new friends as his previous bouts of activism had with old ones. An early supporter in America was the highly successful novelist and screenwriter Budd Schulberg, who lived near Island Farm. Koestler hoped that Schulberg would pull in Irwin Shaw and Norman Mailer, who would have been valuable props for the Fund's work. They met frequently, until an ugly altercation in March 1951. Schulberg was worried that very little information was vouchsafed to the supporters of the FFIF. He was, too, unsure about its aims and wondered whether it should not also assist the victims of racism in the US. Koestler would have none of this. Mamaine recorded a 'catastrophic' evening with the Schulbergs during which Koestler was 'very aggressive and trying to bully Budd'. Schulberg retorted by accusing Koestler of running the Fund on 'totalitarian' lines. Koestler's response typified his inability to work in any organisation, even one he had set up and virtually controlled himself. 'The moment I feel that there is an "opposition", a factional struggle, a split and so on,' he wrote to Schulberg, 'I shall resign and continue financial support by sending cheques directly to the recipients in Europe.' By April he was looking for a way out of his FFIF responsibilities and set in motion the process by which its work was eventually handed over to PEN.[130]

Underlying the row with Schulberg was a deeper split. Schulberg reproached Koestler with underestimating the threat posed by McCarthy and 'McCarthyism' in America. At the very least, McCarthy's attempt to purge American society of 'Communists' was driving liberals towards sympathy with the 'persecuted' Communist Party. Koestler needed to look harder at American society: it was the opposition to McCarthy that made America a strong, vibrant democracy.[131] Schulberg, like Crossman, had been exposed to Koestler's anti-Communism, but underestimated the full extent to which he had drifted to the right. He was not to know that this had taken him into murky company, including that of Senator Joe McCarthy himself.

In Paris, Koestler had developed close ties with US Foreign Service officials like Norris Chipman, Roy Murphy, Bob Joyce and the ambassador 'Chip' Bohlen. The line between them and the CIA was non-existent: many, like Joyce, had worked for Bill Donovan's Office of Strategic Services, the forerunner of the CIA, during the war and made the transition to its successor organisation when it was set up in 1947. Another of his State Department contacts dealt with potentially useful ex-Communists who needed a recommendation from an established ex-Communist like Koestler to help get them into the United States. In a correspondence with Koestler about Hans Schultz (one of the 'ex-boys'), Münzenberg's one-time aide, this official signed himself 'Your scout master'. During his 1948 American tour, Koestler had met other high-ranking officials. Once he was installed in Island Farm, he deepened these ties. During a visit to Washington in November, Roy Murphy introduced him to Theodore Kaghan, who ran American overseas propaganda. He assisted Bertram Wolfe, the Sovietologist and future historian of the Russian Revolution, to set up an 'ideological unit' within the State Department.

He finally met several of the key players in the CIA in Washington in April 1951, when he was invited to dinner at the home of Frank Wisner. Wisner controlled covert operations against the USSR and took a keen interest in refugees, exiles, émigrés and defectors with inside knowledge of the Soviet imperium. He was, reckoned Koestler, 'supposed to "get an impression"' of his Hungarian guest, who had been in the CP and the USSR in the 1930s. It must have been a positive one, since during the dinner Koestler was let into the dark secret at the heart of the CCF. At a subsequent dinner arranged by Bob Joyce, Wisner was again present, this time along with Charles Thayer. Wisner and Thayer stand alongside Chips Bohlen, Allen Dulles and George Kennan as the architects of US Cold War policy towards the USSR.[132]

These meetings were of importance to Koestler in their own right, but they were also instrumental. In January 1951, lawyers in New

York acting on his behalf set in motion a complicated and rarely used legislative device to lift the legal bar on the permanent residence in the USA of a former member of the Communist Party: Koestler's bill was only the fourth of its kind. It was sponsored in the House of Representatives by none other than Richard Nixon, who was then achieving fame as a Communist-hunter working at the side of Senator McCarthy. Bob Morris, Koestler's lawyer, urged him to supply Nixon and Senator Owen Brewster, who was responsible for the bill in the upper house, with all possible evidence of his anti-Communist credentials. In these circles a word from Koestler's CIA and State Department chums was worth its weight in gold.[133]

The bill turned into a nightmarishly prolonged exercise which trapped Koestler and Mamaine in America long after they wanted to return to Europe. It was also an expensive affair, which involved a form of lobbying and sycophancy that Koestler found corrupt and demeaning. He was uncomfortable with the insularity and ignorance of American politicians and felt uneasy about McCarthy, if only because his antics confirmed the prejudices of European intellectuals who erred on the side of anti-Americanism. However, when he tried to explain this to Senator Brewster he was rudely brushed aside. On 17 April he had an unscheduled lunch with McCarthy, 'to whom I talked about Europe versus Asia'. This was just one rite of passage on a day in Washington that included appearances before the Senate Judiciary Committee and a string of senators considering his case. His experience of American law-making and his encounters with American politicians contributed to his disenchantment with the New World. The bill did not pass through both Houses of Congress until July and did not pass into law until 8 August 1951, by which time Koestler was fed up with America and had decided not to live there after all.[134]

On top of his money troubles, the work on Island Farm, the FFIF and the bill, Koestler created another mammoth source of disturbance and anxiety. In 1949, he had agreed that Sidney Kingsley be given the rights to dramatise *Darkness at Noon*. By the end of the year he had developed misgivings and sought to recover a measure of control over the drama, particularly the 'ideological line'. In August 1950 he had tried to confront Kingsley, but was ignominiously rebuffed. To rub it in, the published version of the play attributed authorship solely to Kingsley, albeit with the acknowledgement that it was 'based on a novel by Arthur Koestler'.[135]

Koestler tried to divorce himself from the dramatised version by donating all his royalties to the FFIF, but this ploy irritated Kingsley because it made his play seem 'political'. In January 1951, after seeing the stage version, he instructed his lawyers and agent to prevent Kingsley producing the play in Europe, where he feared it could actually do damage. In July Kingsley retaliated with his own legal action and attempted finally to remove any control over the play from Koestler. This wrangling tortured Koestler and kept him awake at nights.[136]

Thanks to these cumulative pressures tempers were severely frayed at Island Farm. Mamaine and Koestler longed to escape to Europe for the spring and summer, but were stuck due to the passage of the bill. Their relations slipped another few notches. In mid–March domestic discord erupted again: 'K. and I had a really major row in the course of which we decided to separate, and then decided not to − at least K. thought we had decided not to, but I didn't realize this till the next day.' This row cleared the air, but took its toll on Mamaine: 'God, how many more of these scenes will I have to go through and how will the whole thing end?' Early in April she fell ill again and had to be treated with penicillin. Koestler also felt unwell, with symptoms of an ulcer, which made him more irritable.

Now his ire was directed at Cynthia Jefferies. With the advent of spring she was afflicted by terrible hay fever, which she tried to keep at bay by taking antihistamine tablets. At night the hay fever kept her awake and the lack of sleep combined with the effect of the tablets made her drowsy. The result was that she occasionally nodded off during dictation or made errors. When this happened Koestler would lash out at her. Paradoxically, his bursts of fury against Jefferies cemented an alliance between the two women.[137]

In April all three left for a 'holiday'. First they stayed in Washington, where Koestler insisted on seeing all his political and intellectual pals, leaving Mamaine no free time. From there they went to Boston which, by comparison, Mamaine found 'great fun'. Arthur Schlesinger Jr threw a party with more convivial company, including Thornton Wilder and Mary McCarthy. But Mamaine's chest complaint was getting worse, and on the way back to Island Farm she went to Johns Hopkins University Hospital in Baltimore to get some treatment. Its cost underlined the parlous state of their finances. When the medical bill arrived Koestler had to plead for the payments to be spread over several months. Mamaine told Celia that to live decently in America Koestler 'would have to produce a best-seller every year'. Economy was one cause of their impatience to leave for Europe.[138]

Mamaine took a wicked delight in his discomfort. She reported to

Kirwan that 'The pressure of this godforsaken country is getting him down, and more particularly such institutions as the best seller list . . .' In April she crowed: 'I am happy to say that he is getting absolutely fed up with being in America and is pining to come to Europe.' One incident more than almost any other alarmed him. Al Hart, his editor at Macmillan following the departure of Jim Putnam, gave a strong hint that Koestler should write a book designed to ingratiate himself with Americans. He said over a dinner at Island Farm that 'in view of K's present position here, and the ambivalent attitude of the critics and writers to him, it would probably be a good thing for him to write a novel about an American theme, in which his attitude to "this country and its problems" would be stated.'[139]

The fact that Koestler never published any extensive reflections on America is all the more significant in the light of this exchange. His copious notes on the subject offer a clue why not. Koestler could not decide whether he loved America or hated it. Such ambivalence was not unusual and it had never prevented him writing about other countries. However, the things he disliked about the country ran against the very grain of the American ethos. From the first days on the island when he engaged with an America beyond hotels and service apartments, he found it inefficient as a society and uncongenial to the individual. The breakages and delays in moving into Island Farm were 'staggering'. Technology was self-defeating: the cars were fast, but there was so much traffic in the cities they could only crawl along. The only comparison was Russia. 'Both countries have one thing in common: utter frustration of the individual, enslavement there by the state, here by a totally mechanised and stereotyped culture-pattern.' The materialism of American urban culture made him nostalgic for Europe. 'The rich are in this country really revolting. In Europe they have a tradition – here just money, ostentation, the crudest, inhuman, neurotic patterns and snobbery.'

With his talent for identifying and cataloguing that which bothered him Koestler railed against radio noise, overheated restaurants, tasteless food, false politeness, the 'unreality' of American city-scapes, and teenagers who spent hours driving around in large cars. The lists were endless: 'Iced drinks; overheated rooms, noise, tons of newsprint to leaf through every day to get two columns of reading matter; miles and miles of concrete annihilating the landscape; the mail-chutes on every floor; the badly organised subways . . .' America, he mused in the shadow of de Tocqueville, was more of a pioneer country than its inhabitants realised. 'It extroverts even the visitor – in the last four weeks I have become much more heartier, louder, more self-assured. Shyness, as a virtue, restraint as a form, are invalidated . . .' There was no true friendship or social coherence: no one listened to anyone else. There was no flow of conversation, only monologues.

In public, Koestler admitted only to his unease with the commercialisation of literature. He told the *New York Times* on 1 April 1951: 'the social climate in this country has made the creation of art into an essentially competitive business.' This corroded readers and writers. Authors could only think in terms of instant appeal; reviewers promoted books on the grounds of their likely popularity; readers expected immediate gratification.[140]

In private, he excoriated American culture as 'civilization in a cul de sac'. France was in decay, England was a case of 'complete strangulation and stubborn, suicidal isolation', but America was 'heading for a dead end'. Children were raised into a form of autism, unable to make contact with other humans. It was a 'contactless society' populated by automatons. He couldn't decide whether the crime and corruption was a sign of 'adolescence or decay'. It resembled Rome in the latter stages of the Empire: 'a similarly soulless, politically corrupt, everybody-for-himself civilization'. The United States was like the Roman Empire, but without the leaven of Greek culture. While he recognised the good will, idealism and energy in the US, he told Storm Jameson that the fate of the world 'depends today on the most naive and inexperienced people'. He came to loathe New York's Jewish intellectuals, dismissing the guests at a party given by Sol Levitas as 'an assembly of anti-semitic caricatures' and proclaimed that he was 'allergic to American Liberals'.[141]

In this jaded mood, Koestler revived the debate over where to live and for a while speculated on the merits of Bermuda. Mamaine greeted this with exasperation: 'Isn't it extraordinary how quickly he can change his whole idea of where and how he wants to live. But I don't worry, for whatever we do we never do it for long, and I really don't care particularly what it is, so long as it keeps him happy and isn't bad for his work.' May and June slipped by in a reasonably stable fashion, with Koestler working steadily on the autobiography, side-trips and vistors coming to stay. Koestler had more motor accidents, and once even managed to hit a police car. He made friends with the brilliant Hungarian-Jewish-born quantum-mathematician John von Neumann, and entertained the novelist Cornelius Ryan, who was to move into Island Farm while the Koestlers were in Europe. On 27 June 1951, to their immense relief, they left New York for London.

On arrival, Mamaine commented simply: 'Everything wonderful after America.'[142]

VIII

They stayed for a week in London with Jamie Hamilton. Koestler saw his literary agent and his publishers on business. They took out Adele, went to the Festival of Britain and shopped. On 3 July Koestler travelled to Paris. Mamaine followed with Adele, who stayed at Verte Rive for ten days. Mamaine then accompanied Koestler's mother back to London and remained there for a month. More visitors until late July prevented Koestler making much progress with the autobiography. He also got tied up in more red tape thanks to a hare-brained scheme to take Anna and Maxime Mouette, the cook/housekeeper and gardener at Verte Rive, back to Island Farm. The sultry weather, anxiety about the Kingsley case and problems transferring his royalties from one country to another stopped him from sleeping. But in the last week of the month he made a breakthrough and completed over forty pages of the book, reaching the point at which he turned twenty-five.[143]

Mamaine was very cool about the prospect of shipping the ménage from Verte Rive to Island Farm and warned Koestler against returning too soon since the heat and chores would stop him working. She had her own reasons for not wanting to move again: she felt harassed, worried and depressed. She had been to a doctor who diagnosed a bad liver, a gall-bladder problem and high cholesterol. She had 'latent jaundice' and felt washed out. Mamaine was coming to the end of her tether. She asked Koestler when he was going to make up his mind where to live 'instead of drifting along like this? . . . I would like to stay on here [London] as long as possible, as there is so much more that I can do here than would be the case in France, and I am extremely happy here considering, and NEED this holiday badly if I am not to go quite off my head. Still I don't want to leave you alone if it is very inconvenient for you.'[144]

On 14 August Mamaine travelled to France for a show-down. Koestler met her in Paris and drove her to Verte Rive in a foul mood. She was jumpy and looked terrible, but he did nothing to make her feel more positive. The next day she told Koestler she was leaving him. He was momentarily stunned and reacted passively. Together they broke the news to Jefferies, who had arrived a week earlier and was staying at the house. It was all very civilised. But the next day, as he was driving Mamaine through the Forest of Fontainebleau on a last trip to one of her favourite places, he got into a tussle with her and smashed up the car, ruining any semblance of a harmonious parting. After she had left Paris he set off on a binge, landed in the ill-omened Sheherazade and drank so much he ended up vomiting in the street.[145]

The following Sunday Koestler wrote a long, obsessive analysis of the break-up of the marriage and his current situation. 'The great crisis. Everything smashed up: our marriage; the two houses here and in the USA which I cannot run alone; Maxime and Anna towards whom I assumed grave responsibilities; Cynthia, whom I cannot have permanently around if I am alone.' To add to his misery, President Eisenhower had refused to sign his bill (although this would not prevent it becoming law). He no longer felt welcome in America. The concatenation of disasters was the 'language of destiny' speaking to him. It was no use fighting. 'I felt the coming of a spiritual crisis for a long time and have done half consciously everything to bring it to a head. Mamaine is only part of it — the relatively easier part to explain.' He knew why he had cooled towards Mamaine: the so-called 'incest barrier'. This was his term for the loss of sexual desire for a woman once she became familiar, like a mother. He could not do anything about it. He suspected that she was the best woman he would ever meet, but was not prepared to battle for their relationship. 'The real alternative was . . . to shoulder the burden of ultimate loneliness to settle for good on the tragic plane; to obey to [sic] the apparent unreason of what I feel to be my destiny.' The car crash had crystallised his thinking: it was time to shed the responsibilities: the properties, dogs, wife, secretary, retainers which 'eat me up . . . externalised me, diffused all my energies, with no time, energy, concentration left for the essential — the dialogue with destiny; with my work'.

It was the manifestation of 'the masochistic, smash-up — suicide pattern'. Because of the guilt feelings inculcated in childhood he could not allow himself to be happy, enjoy company or maintain a stable relationship. He had to wreck everything. Then, to his surprise, when he received news that the bill had become law he cheered up and all his anxieties lifted. The 'real' cause of the crisis became clear to him. It was 'visa-archetype' neurosis: 'even now, I don't really know myself, don't know the true causes of miseries.' Yet he stuck by his resolutions to discard worldly trappings and fall back on his work.[146] Needless to say, he did not succeed. Koestler could be perceptive, but his tendency to render everything abstract and mysterious ultimately frustrated any concrete reform of his behaviour. Understanding was not pardoning, but it became a substitute for anything else.

In a manner resembling the convulsion which occurred at Verte Rive almost exactly a year earlier Koestler took a series of swift decisions. He resolved not to take Maxim and Anna to Pennsylvania, but as compensation for the upheaval he had caused them he lent them money to build their own home in France. He coolly told Mamaine that he had instructed A. D. Peters to supply her with the funds she needed to set up her own home in London. They could arrange the divorce in due course: he had no objection to ending the marriage. He told Peters: 'I am now going to simplify my life,' although to most people what he proposed was a recipe for a headache. He intended to lease Island Farm, keep Verte Rive as a summer home and live somewhere quiet in either England or America.[147]

A few days later Peters, who added the role of father confessor to that of literary agent, flew to France to console and counsel Koestler. Peters helped him to arrive at a series of financially and morally sound arrangements. In an exchange of businesslike letters, Koestler informed Mamaine that he would buy her a house, retaining it himself as an investment. She, meanwhile, agreed to go to Verte Rive when he was not there and retrieve her possessions.[148]

Koestler's morale recovered quickly, with the aid of Jefferies's presence, some steady work and vigorous sculling on the river. Cynthia Jefferies filled Mamaine's shoes with an alacrity that grates against their real affection for each other. Before he left France, on 14 September, Koestler set off with her for a four-day sailing holiday on the Loire. Afterwards he recorded: 'strange revelation at the end: still uncertain about the result.' It was abundantly clear that Jefferies was devoted to Koestler body and soul, and would happily replace Mamaine as his full-time lover and help-mate, should he wish. However, Koestler initially returned to America alone.[149]

Getting there provoked an ugly scene at the American consulate in Paris. Despite the passage of the bill lifting from him the restrictions on entry to the USA normally applied to members and ex-members of the Communist Party, two peculiarly zealous officials insisted that they would not issue him with a visa on the ground that since arriving in France he might have rejoined the CP. Koestler appealed to the chargé d'affaires and eventually the officials were forced to comply with the spirit of the law. But Koestler, who was always agitated when dealing with passport and visa matters, became completely obsessed with the case and demanded an apology from the consul. An ignominious and petty correspondence ensued and, not surprisingly, the consular officials found a host of trivial regulations with which to dog Koestler's progress. He was forced to leave France without a visa and obtain the papers from the more friendly and compliant consulate in London. Koestler erected the spat into an issue of great principle: if this was how he was treated, what would be the fate of those less fortunate who had as much 'experience' to offer the United States? Once in America, he referred the case to Congress, where it was pursued half-heartedly. Thanks to Sam White, the *Evening Standard*'s Paris correspondent, the fracas made the newspapers and added to the growing image of Koestler as one of the awkward brigade.[150]

On 26 September, Koestler found himself back at Island Farm: 'little man in a big house,' he noted with a hint of self-pity. For the next two months he lived a 'hermit's life', slogging away at the autobiography, with only a few visitors and trips to Washington to break the drudgery. It was hard going, made worse by hot and stormy weather, illness, worry over his action against Kingsley and the search for a tenant for Island Farm.

Koestler developed kidney stones and had such pain that he took morphine for relief. This eased the discomfort, but left him in a stupor and gave him terrible headaches when the drug wore off. He wrote mournfully to Mamaine: 'Darling, middle-age is setting in in earnest. I had a ten-day attack of kidney-stones; most of the time either in mad pain or under morphia.' He concluded that the ailment was psychosomatic. At Verte Rive he had given Sidney Kingsley the nickname Kidney. Once he developed kidney stones, the circle was completed to his satisfaction, even though he had suffered from pains which he described as an ulcer long before the pun was made. He endured his discomfort alone, apart from his dog Miss Nellie. Equipped with a vacuum cleaner he did his best to keep the house clean; he made his own meals, usually a sandwich lunch, and dined out with friends on most evenings. By November his energy and enthusiasm for the memoir was ebbing. He found the last chapters boring, so it was with relief that he finished the first draft just before Thanksgiving. He celebrated by getting plastered with his festival host, Rube Barkin. During December he started typing up the autobiography. This phase took three months, since the first draft was a mess and needed a lot of revising, but he was unable to do much work in December or in the following January due to social and legal diversions.[151]

Left to his own devices, and possibly influenced by his autobiographical ruminations, he engaged in prolonged introspection. 'I seem to have become unfit for a normal life through prison experiences. . . . My desire to live alone is due a) to my desire for freedom, greed for adventures, for escaping from stale household of my own, b) of stale married life c) the longing to live on the tragic plane.' He ducked responsibility for the fate of his marriage: 'Mamaine broke up our household. I saw in it the language of destiny: seize the occasion if it is offered to you, if you miss the chance you have failed. But I feel increasingly that to live alone – in the country at least – is beyond my powers . . . I am made to live permanently on the tragic plane. . . . But if not alone the only choices are *to live in town – or marry again.*' If he could not admit his role in Mamaine's departure he did at least acknowledge the problems with Island Farm: 'the climate is depressing, no congenial neighbours, farming enormous headache. In favour of it: uniqueness. However, from June to September inclusive uninhabitable.' He concluded that 'Solitude on the tragic plane turned out to be another mirage'. He would have to marry some time, and settle down. But not in America. That country 'with its mechanised bruit . . . mass produced sex . . . psychoanalytic supermarket is no country for you. If Europe must perish, perish with it.'[152]

At the end of October Island Farm was leased for three years and Koestler planned to move out in the new year. The choice of where to go now pressed on him. He listed the key factors: Anglo-Saxon language; 'imaginary obligations', such as 'Connolly; mountains and bracing climate; congenial neighbours, *not* snobs'; a new land or one freighted with history. His ability to make a rational decision was not helped by his propensity to rely on the 'language of destiny . . . Now only know that the invisible writing exists, and that to obey the few admonitions of the Alchemists Rosary is all I can do.'[153]

Koestler's destiny took a fateful turn as he embarked on a long, fraught relationship with Janine Graetz. He had first met her at Verte Rive in spring 1950. She was young, glamorous, cosmopolitan and independent, having developed a career in film production alongside her husband Paul Graetz. Initially their friendship was mediated through dogs. Janine, like Koestler, was a great dog lover and he gave her a puppy ominously called Romeo. They met occasionally during 1951 in France and America. It is not clear when they started having an affair; he was almost certainly seeing her in Paris during the summer of 1951. By the autumn they were meeting openly in New York and she was introduced to several of Koestler's American friends. She stayed with him on Island Farm over several weekends at the end of the year. Perversely, Koestler wrote to Mamaine at exactly this time saying how much he missed her. His feelings for her were no doubt genuine, but no more worthy for that. It was part of the pattern: longing for a woman he had maltreated while she was compliantly his, as soon as she made herself unavailable to him.[154]

His litigation against Kingsley also entered a decisive phase after his legal advisers recommended that he go to arbitration. In July Koestler had instructed his lawyers to seek to prevent Kingsley producing the play in Europe unless he made changes to the script. He argued: 'Its inaccuracies when dealing with the language and atmosphere of Communist Parties in Europe would lead to a debacle and that a failure of the play in France and Italy would mean not only a personal loss of prestige for both authors, but would also be a political defeat in the propaganda war against Communists and fellow-travellers.' To suppport his case he asked Mamaine to go to France and persuade his anti-Communist friends to supply affidavits to the effect that Kingsley's drama would be counter-productive. Mamaine unselfishly did his bidding, just as Dorothea and Daphne had run campaigns on his behalf when their relationships with him were virtually over. She contacted Cyrus Sulzberger, Sperber, Camus, Aron and Rousset, not all of whom could see what the fuss was about. But Rousset and Aron were prepared to testify that parts of the play were crude and would appear silly to European audiences. These interventions did little good.[155]

As if the litigation were not enough of a distraction, on top of it Koestler had lodged an appeal with the Bank of England to enable him to avoid the inconvenience and expense of transferring all his royalties to England even if he wanted to invest them and live off them abroad. It was hardly surprising that he couldn't concentrate on his writing. In January he went to see a psychotherapist to seek help for his depression and to see if he could assist him to recall more incidents from his past for use in his autobiography. He was also having serious trouble with alcohol: he had got blind drunk over the Christmas holidays and consumed a bottle of whisky by himself on New Year's Eve. As a result he suffered from hangovers, guilt and mild DTs.[156]

The arbitration dragged on until mid-February. Despite personal appearances by Burnham, Arthur Schlesinger Jr, Father Bruckberger and Edgar Mowrer the court ruled that if Koestler had been content to waive control over the play in the United States there were no special grounds for making an exception in the case of Europe. He was forced to concede control over it to Kingsley. After the ruling

Koestler got cathartically drunk with Bruckberger. He claimed that the 'squalor and grotesqueness' of the whole business had neutralised his emotional investment and he walked away from it. The litigation had cost $5000, but since he had donated his royalties to the FFIF, the Fund covered the legal costs.[157]

With the case out of the way he could return to polishing his memoirs and packing up the island. Father Bruckberger helped him out by staying on the farm and cooking him meals. Rather less conventionally he also said a mass for Koestler. Janine Graetz made a couple of visits, although these were less conducive to work and involved him in yet another road accident. On 3 March 1952 he moved out of Island Farm. His mood was a mixture of exaltation and exhaustion. He wrote to Mamaine: 'the island is liquidated, the law suit is lost, the book is finished and I am washed out.' For a while he stayed with Putnam, and then moved into the Hotel St Moritz on Manhattan. It was there that he worked on the proofs of his memoirs, using the redoubtable New York Public Library to check facts. At this stage the book still had a provisional title 'Memoirs of a Tightrope Walker', but Jamie Hamilton and his American publishers were understandably unhappy with that. It was finally entitled *Arrow in the Blue*.[158]

Far from being a conventionally organised memoir, the book was informed by Koestler's emerging belief in the hidden 'language of destiny'. Cars were one bizarre channel through which destiny spoke to him. The connection between fate and automobiles is to be found prominently in the second volume, but the origins are clear in his diary–notebook from this period. Recalling the weeks up to mid-March, he catalogued a series of car accidents. On 28 February he cut across the path of a truck and nearly ended up dead; the next day he accidentally rammed Janine Graetz's stationary car; the same afternoon she was caught by the police for speeding; and the following morning he collided with another vehicle in a snowstorm. On 10 March he drove to Yale University and almost caused a pile-up by stopping suddenly on the road. 'But what does it all mean?' he asked plaintively.[159] The obvious answer is that he was an appalling driver who was often drunk while at the wheel. But Koestler was never one to see the obvious when a vast, self-serving and utterly unprovable cosmic theory could be manoeuvred into place to obscure it while at the same time meeting some dramatic need in his life.

Koestler stayed at Yale for five days, from 10 to 14 March, giving seminars on Marxism and literature to graduates and undergraduates, and meeting the Fellows. The visit had been organised by Charles

Sawyer, the University President, and met a longstanding desire of
Koestler to sample academic life. He found Yale 'delightful' and a
contrast to the 'malice' and 'snobbery' he had met in Oxford. The
students were less well informed than their English counterparts, but
had more imagination.[160] American universities would continue to
lure Koestler with their large fees, fawning students and majestic
facilities; but his attraction to America was terminated. His last weeks
in the United States were spent in a series of long, alcoholic farewells,
short flings with various women, and work on the proofs of *Arrow in
the Blue*. When the finishing touches were put to the galleys he sent
them to A. D. Peters with the recommendation that if any of his
other authors fancied their hand at the genre he could recommend a
good title: 'An Empty Life in three volumes'. He left New York for
Paris on 14 April 1952.[161]

Chapter 10
'My harem is beginning to wear me out', 1952–5

From 1952 to 1955 Koestler composed the autobiographical works for which he is celebrated and which remain among the best of this century: *Arrow in the Blue* (1952) and *The Invisible Writing* (1954). At the end of the period he assembled a volume of essays, *The Trail of the Dinosaur* (1955), that drew together his political commentaries and prescriptions from the previous decade. In the preface, however, he announced his withdrawal from active politics. In this series of books he described the origins and development of one Arthur Koestler, then turned his back on that person ostensibly to become another version.

The process of self-analysis and self-transcendence appeared impressively smooth and seamless. It concealed, however, on one side a mass of discrepancies and ruptures and, on the other, strong continuities. The Koestler whom Koestler portrayed was only partly the 'real' Koestler; the Koestler who was doing the writing and projecting a contemporaneous persona was, equally, not the 'real' one. Both author and subject were to a crucial extent fictive creations. Koestler gave a coherence to his past life that it lacked and wrote with Olympian detachment as one who had resolved all the crises of life, an impression utterly at odds with his day-to-day existence.

For Koestler autobiography was doubly instrumental. When he set out to write his life story he intended to chronicle the century. His experiences were to typify those of the generation born into the optimism and prosperity of the 1900s, only to see that world wrecked by the First World War and blighted by the twin evils of Communism and Fascism. He was indeed a witness to these cataclysmic events, but a very particular one, and in order to make his point of view representative he had to tailor his story to fit his interpretation of events (and vice versa). As well as testifying to history, Koestler wanted to draw lessons from it and so help to shape the future. He dedicated his life to the Cold War both in the sense of his activism *and* of his 'life' as the version offered to the public in his autobiographical writing.

In contrast to the world-weary and mature tone of his memoirs, his personal life reached a crescendo of chaos and fractiousness. He had numerous short and sometimes brutal affairs in which he seemed criminally unable to distinguish between seduction and rape, as well as a number of longer-term relationships with women friends whom he dubbed his 'harem'. His life verged on a Feydeau farce as ex-wives, future wives, mistresses, ex-lovers and prostitutes whizzed in and out of his embrace with bewildering velocity, until the deceit and sexual athletics wearied him. Despite repeated efforts to 'simplify his life', Koestler continued to acquire properties and mistresses as quickly as he divested himself of them.

Mamaine died in June 1954, when Koestler was in Ischia in the company of one of the women with whom he had betrayed her. Her death set off an orgy of introspection, middle-aged braggadocio, promiscuity and despair. In August 1955, after he had completed the last volume of autobiography and the volume of essays, he turned to an entirely new project and a new 'crusade' – against capital punishment. At the same moment he invited Cynthia Jefferies back into his life. On the eve of his fiftieth birthday the Arthur Koestler recognisable in the second half of his life emerged from the chrysalis of the mid-term crisis, but this Koestler was actually far more like the young Koestler than the authorial personality of the autobiographies.

Koestler had succeeded in remaking himself as a character in the story of the twentieth century. This Koestler would become a politicial and literary icon. The 'real' Koestler was always somewhere, someone else; a person with many other beliefs, habits and attributes that were only hinted at or entirely suppressed. Among these was his Jewishness. His failure to integrate all the parts of his personality and his past in either his writing or his life may account for the permanent sense of unease, and the questing for identity and belonging that afflicted his politics, as well as his relationships, with chronic instability.

I

When Koestler left America he told Mamaine that he intended to go to Paris first in order to check some of the facts in *Arrow in the Blue* against his files at Verte Rive, then 'settle down in London for a quiet couple of months'. In fact, he spent 15 to 21 April on 'very enjoyable holidays' with Janine Graetz before arriving in London and his time there was anything but quiet. He restored contact with old friends, notably Cyril Connolly, Jamie Hamilton, Humphrey Slater, Daphne

(Hardy) Henrion ('retired to smug domesticity, with two awful children . . . but still as neurotic as before') and Paul Willert; made peace with his political sparring partners, Crossman, Strachey and Foot; and explored the rising generation of Labour MPs, including Anthony Crosland and Barbara Castle. Jefferies had returned to London in September 1951 and held various odd jobs while Koestler was at Island Farm. The moment he was back she eagerly resumed part-time secretarial work for him. In the early evenings she went to the service flat he took at Athenaeum Court, Piccadilly, and helped deal with correspondence or type up the memoirs.[1]

Koestler embarked on a 'Second honeymoon with England' and rediscovered the country he had spurned in 1948:

> It really is the last solid country in the world – relatively, of course. Yet the problem of acclimatization remains. Paradoxically, the country which has become the approximation of home to me, is also the country where I am least known as a writer, am permanently snubbed as a foreigner and 'not quite quite'. This I feel more intensely than before. Before I regarded myself more or less as a visitor, and was not naturalized – which, funnily enough, counts just as the legal act of marriage does. So have decided to go to a phoneticist, and entirely decided to learn to write English.[2]

Much of his time was spent looking for a new place to live. He concentrated on Chelsea and Kensington, his old hunting ground, and only tentatively ventured further afield to Regent's Park and Hampstead. Koestler never liked the cosmopolitan districts of north London, where most Central Europeans preferred to settle. Instead he gravitated towards west London, where he was an odd man out, but where he felt he had to prove himself if he were to 'acclimatize' and avoid life in an *émigré* ghetto. Mamaine had moved into her new home in Eaton Mews and they met regularly. Her house-warming party gave Koestler a chance to bury the hatchet with Freddie Ayer. Notwithstanding his affair with Graetz, Koestler dined out, had drinks and slept with a succession of women friends almost every day. Several accompanied him on his house-hunting expeditions.[3]

It was on one of these outings that Koestler raped Jill Craigie, the wife of his friend Michael Foot, MP. On 4 May he rang up excitedly announcing that he had decided to settle in England and wanted to go to 'an English pub'.[4] Craigie explained that Foot was away on a 'Brains Trust' but Koestler was insistent and since she recalled his wonderful hospitality at Verte Rive a few summers ago felt she could not refuse. He arrived in his rented car and she gave him a 'Jill Craigie tour of Hampstead', pointing out the homes and pubs inhabited and frequented by local celebrities. They went to several pubs and Koestler drank in each one, although Craigie stuck to ginger beer. His behaviour was quite proper until he demanded that she make him lunch at her place. Craigie objected that she had no food at home (she had been working on a film) and countered that a roast beef lunch would be more fitting. He would not take no for an answer and bullied her into making him an omelette. After the meal Koestler helped to wash up. When the last plate was done and Craigie set down the dish cloth he 'suddenly grasped my hair, he pulled me down and banged my head on the floor. A lot.'

Craigie thought he had gone mad. They had 'the most terrible, terrible fight' as she struggled back to full consciousness and tried to resist him. He was 'very, very violent', but she was young and healthy and managed to work herself free and rush out of the house. Once outside she sat on the steps, her clothes torn, and wondered what to do. She had no money. Her nearest friends, Jenny Lee and Nye Bevan, were away in Nye's constituency. Hampstead police station was nearby, but she was scared that such a recourse would lead to awful publicity for her and Michael. She would be accusing a world-famous novelist of rape; they had been on a pub crawl and she had admitted him into her home by herself. It did not look good. So she waited in the hope that Koestler would calm down and emerge on his own accord. He did not and she went back inside, expecting to find him come to his senses. 'And so I took a chance and went back, which was rather stupid of me. And it started all over again: very, very violent, mostly pulling hair.' He even placed his hands on her throat and she feared that he would murder her. 'In the end I was overborne. I was terribly tired and weakened. There's a limit to how much strength one has and he was a very strong man. And that was it.'

Koestler showed no contrition afterwards. As he left he merely gave her a side glance and said: 'I thought you always had a bit of a yen for me.' Craigie had done nothing to give such an impression and during their outing together he had not indicated that he was attracted to her. The assault had come without any warning; but the practised manner in which it was executed made Craigie think it was of a 'pattern'. Indeed, there is evidence that he had raped before. One of his wartime 'conquests' had fired off a bitterly reproachful note to him that testified to an experience not dissimilar to that endured by

Jill Craigie. Dick Crossman later told Foot and Craigie that Koestler 'was a hell of a raper; Zita had a terrible time with him'. Koestler had beaten and raped women before; over the next few years it would be almost a hallmark of his conduct.[5]

On 28 May Koestler made an offer on a three-storey Georgian town house on a corner of Montpelier Square in Kensington, number 8. This part of London had been settled by Huguenot refugees, although it had long since lost any Continental character and was decidedly upper-class English. Koestler was determined to make his home among the English and invested the purchase with great significance: 'got a country and a house again'.[6]

He spent June and July at Fontaine le Port divesting himself of Verte Rive. His disillusionment with France and his French friends was complete. After a lunch with Malraux he lamented: 'another fallen idol . . . For once listened to all he said; half of it or more was sheer, flat nonsense, interspersed with paranoid boasting.' Poor Malraux seemed out of his depth when forced to discuss science: he had 'one thing in common with Sartre and Camus and these [sic] are that they are twenty years behind the times . . .' Old friends like Guy and Alix de Rothschild had lost their allure, too. After a dinner with them he wrote meanly that Alix was 'bitter and dull as ever', while he dismissed Guy as 'deaf'. Even more unkindly, after this socialising with Jewish friends he reflected: 'one of the irrational factors in anti-Semitism may be instinctual aesthetic revulsion.'[7]

He also started writing the second volume of his autobiography, but in mid-June work was interrupted by a crisis with Graetz. He had seen her fairly often since arriving in France and someone who spotted them together informed Paul Graetz. And so 'the squalid storm broke' followed by 'complex negotiations and measures'. These undisclosed 'measures' had restored the *status quo* by the start of July and he enjoyed a further productive spell. The fine weather and outdoor activities helped maintain his equilibrium. Now approaching his forty-eighth birthday, Koestler was beginning to show signs of middle-aged spread, fostered by his constant drinking and dining-out habits. As a countermeasure he went on the wagon again, dieted, swam and canoed regularly. At the end of the month Verte Rive was sold, leading to a flurry of activity that again distracted him from writing. This time he was more sanguine about the reasons: 'God, I am glad to be rid of house, Maxim, Anna et tout.' He drove back to London on 6 August, sleeping in his car during the crossing on account of being 'rather tight'. The subsequent journey to Montpelier Square was as comic as it was perilous, with trunks and suitcases toppling off the wildly veering car as Koestler manoeuvred blearily through heavy rain on the road to London.[8]

Koestler now set about renovating his latest house. The work took a month and stopped him making progress with the memoir. His peace of mind was not assisted by his crowded sex life. Graetz regularly visited London and helped him choose furniture and fabrics. In her absence he fluctuated between nights with Jefferies or various other women – his 'harem' – called (discreetly) Christine, Felicity, Priscilla, Moira, Barbara. His attitude towards them may be gauged from an 'inventory' he compiled in September 1952: Christine, 'since married, decided to go straight but did it rather non-gracefully (resentment for not meeting the dark man with the Koestler millions before committing herself); Felicity – Bovary complexes (grace au dieu [sic]); Prisc (hopeless . . .); Moira . . . [illegible]; Janine – demain; Cynthia – toujours là; Barbara . . .' In October he was reacquainted with Janetta Jackson, a beautiful, intelligent woman who had been one of Connolly's lovers in the late 1930s and a member of his wartime circle. She now lived across Montpelier Square. One evening they 'went off drinking till 5 a.m.' while she told him about her unhappy marriage to the wealthy industrial physicist Derek Jackson. Once notorious for her informal style of dress, to the discerning Koestler Jackson now appeared rather 'Harrodsy'. But that did not forestall the onset of yet another romantic entanglement.[9]

It is hard to generalise about the women of Koestler's 'harem', but there does appear to be a common strand between some of those who can be identified. They were almost always younger than Koestler and usually combined independence of spirit with vulnerability. Some 'damage' in childhood or youth had led them to pose as resilient, whereas in fact they were insecure and emotionally dependent. Jefferies, who became something of an expert in this respect, observed that they were 'mostly feminine and sylph-like, some with a masculine trait, bossy and clever. All shared one thing: at some point in their lives they had been scarred by sorrow, and it showed.' When he was younger he knocked around with women who were as fiercely independent as he was, but in later life he seems to have spurned relationships with those who could have been considered his intellectual equals. His girlfriends, lovers and wives were all bright and talented, but they always felt intellectually overshadowed by him. In Koestler's own words: 'I always picked one type: beautiful Cinderellas, infantile and inhibited, prone to be subdued by bullying.'[10]

The cast, locations and character of Koestler's frenzied social life resembled the war years. He went to a 'legless party' thrown by the novelist Henry Green (Yorke), got 'legless' a few days later with Dylan Thomas, was roaringly drunk with Philip Toynbee and not appreciably more sober following cocktails with his wife and Connolly the day after that. On 16 September he dined with Strachey, whom he now regarded with a mixture of revulsion and contempt. It is hard to judge from the elliptical record of this evening what Koestler found most off-putting about him: 'mentioned casually that still masturbates, as he did all his life, imagining himself in the female position . . . As usual I paid for dinner.' One difference from the 1940s was that Koestler now had a car and inevitably he was soon involved in a serious accident. He wrote in his diary–notebook after Mamaine's cocktail party: 'nearly killed myself driving home by running headlong into a lorry.' He woke with a 'terrible hangover' and next day opted for an 'austere dinner' with a girlfriend.[11]

Koestler was fully aware of the drift in his life. 'It seems that for a while, I am living as perhaps never before in the present, not in past or future; for how long? When broke up with Mamaine I felt that I was destined to live on the tragic plane, all alone; now swung to the opposite extreme. For how long?' He wanted to settle down to work, but his house and 'harem' were a constant diversion. 'When oh when, am I going to change back from the life of Decoration to the life of the Spirit?' Judging from the volume of entries in his diary–notebook, he was as obsessed with sex and 'romance' as any adolescent. On 20 October he noted 'Janine back again; Cynthia *en crise*', Barbara 'threatening next Thursday', Priscilla 'unhappy because neglected', while 'Janetta gives me a sign' and so is the 'only desirable one'. A few days after this entry Graetz moved into 8 Montpelier Square, probably the cause of Jefferies's distress. But she was constantly travelling back and forth between London, New York and Rome and, in her absence, he formed new attachments, of which the most serious was with a pretty young woman called Lena. His feelings for Graetz ebbed and he got irritated over the delay her peregrinations had caused to the refurbishment of the house.[12]

II

In September 1952 *Arrow in the Blue* was published in Britain and America, to mixed notices. The headline of Peter Quennell's nasty review in the *Daily Mail* summed up its inherent problem: 'Clown, Careerist, Philosopher'. The piece so annoyed Koestler that he wanted to sue, but his lawyer, Harold Rubinstein, sagely advised him to tarry until he could return the favour in a review of a book by Quennell. The far more sensitive and sympathetic reading by Stephen Spender also noted that the book continually changed key. It honestly reflected Koestler's restless personality and changing allegiances, but: 'His danger is to make a heroic virtue out of the changeability which has made him a public success.' The ruthless analysis was alienating: the book was held together by a theory of existence, sketched on the opening pages, which rendered each episode more of a laboratory test, with Koestler as the guinea pig, than a chapter of picaresque. Orville Prescott, writing in the *New York Times*, was more blunt: 'it is hagridden by theories . . . Mr Koestler can't consider anything . . . without trying to explain, to dissect, and to find a secret reason.'[13]

The autobiography began with an overpowering impression of determinism. Koestler's stated intention to represent his life as symbolic of the century compounded the sense of an individual at the mercy of great, anonymous forces.[14] The avowed candour of the intimate and personal chapters was more superficial than real. Koestler humorously described his home life and revealed that 'from my ninth year onward we led a gypsy life', moving from one boarding house and hotel to another. This may well explain the style of life that he compulsively followed in adulthood, yet there is no sense in what he writes that the book was composed under not dissimilar circumstances.[15]

The revelations about his childhood are intended as a counterpoint to the mature man. Koestler explained how his mother, abetted by nannies and governesses, imbued him with 'guilt, fear and loneliness'. It was this which accounted for his 'chronic inability to terminate an evening once it is properly started' and a 'tendency on the rare occasions when I go to a party, to get drunk and make a fool of myself'. However, he claimed that 'As the years wore on, my life gradually fell into a pattern, oscillating, like a pendulum, between periods of complete isolation and shorter bursts of hectic gregariousness.' He eventually found a satisfactory balance between asceticism and excess.[16] Contrary to his self-declared efforts to emulate Rousseau's *Confessions*, this can only be described as autobiography as wishful thinking.

Writing of his education and intellectual development, Koestler explained his fascination with the 'paradox of infinity and eternity' which begot the title of the book. In the absence of religious faith his 'thirst for the absolute' drew him to science and a string of ideologues or 'shamans' who claimed to have the key to enlightenment.[17] But how could this explain his serial attraction to utterly opposed doctrines such as right-wing Zionism and Communism? Again, this was only half the truth.

Koestler described himself at the age of sixteen as self-conscious and guilt-ridden, with no sense of who he was. Nor had this changed much in adulthood: 'Shyness and insecurity have remained my silent companions to this day. I have never outgrown, merely overgrown, them by a chatty, sociable, synthetic personality which I despise.'[18] There is something both disarming and disturbing about this admission. Koestler was indeed an eternal adolescent, but he seems to have been content with knowledge of this and deployed it as both a badge of identity and an alibi. His relentless self-analysis procured sympathy and then excused his bad conduct when the aggressive grown man turned on those, mainly women, who tried to comfort the vulnerable little boy.

Much the brightest writing covers his student days in Vienna and his wandering in Palestine, although the account of these years suffers from his determination to marginalise his Jewish identity and his recently aggravated ambivalence towards Jews, Zionism and Israel. From Zionism he turns to an analysis of his split personality, the 'simultaneous urges to become an apprentice-Yogi and a pocket Commissar'. The line he draws between the two is questionable and there is a strong sense of teleology in his interpretation of youthful incidents, as if a concept is being imposed on events to make sense of them.[19] Anyway, Koestler never could separate action from contemplation as neatly as he suggests. He might have been physically at ease when working on books but they were always tools to achieve some other end.

Throughout the memoir Koestler's handling of time is remarkable. The reader could be forgiven for thinking that Koestler's life was an epic, but on closer examination none of the phases through which it passes last for more than two years. The period of Koestler's destitution and vagabondage, including several months in Cairo and Berlin, lasted from April 1926 to September 1927; he returned to Berlin from Palestine as an Ullstein correspondent and remained in Jerusalem for nineteen months; he was based in Paris from June 1929 to July 1930, when he was reassigned to Berlin. Koestler manages to make it seem as if he had always been doing what he was doing at any one time, rather than flitting from one thing to another. His treatment of duration, the variation of pace, is masterly and warrants the attention of an Einstein: time slowed whenever it encountered Koestler and accelerated the further away he was.

The chapters on his life as a journalist in Paris and Berlin are a superb melding of reminiscence and historical reconstruction. But the confessional passages on sex reek of self-justification. His search for the ideal and his 'incest taboo', which meant that once he was familiar with a woman it was impossible to continue a sexual relationship, appear, to his satisfaction, to exonerate him of the charge of promiscuity, the emotional damage perpetrated in the course of adultery and the cruelty of deception.[20] Koestler seems as completely insensitive to the feelings of women in these one-sided entanglements as he does when writing about the plight of humiliated wives in the Parisian brothels.[21] This is hardly surprising in view of the pleasure he took in creating such scenes himself. At Verte Rive, Island Farm and Montpelier Square he wittingly engineered situations in which wives and mistresses, mistresses and lovers, routinely collided.

The penultimate chapters of the book which deal with his conversion to Communism are the tithe he paid to the Cold Warriors in Washington. They merely extended his essay in *The God That Failed*, elaborating the psychological impulses to join the Party. One added piece of information was the role that car trouble played in his conversion.[22] This is another indication of teleology at work in the composition of the autobiography: it was only between writing *The God That Failed* and completing *Arrow in the Blue* that he had developed the bizarre notion that the 'language of destiny' spoke to him through car accidents.

Nothing reveals more starkly the gap between the mature and worldly-wise narrator of *Arrow in the Blue* and the reality of its author than the closing weeks of 1953. The year ended chaotically for Koestler on every front. He put the second volume of autobiography aside to write a play on a Freudian theme. *The Fall of Doctor Icarus* is a curiosity in the catalogue of attempts to dramatise psychoanalysis and not without merits. But it overreaches itself trying to depict a Freudian relationship between Dr Icarus, an analyst, and his son, as well as the clinical relationship between analyst and client. Some of the dialogue is crisp, but much of it didactic and wooden. It has a strong autobiographical tang, as if Koestler could not totally emancipate himself from the memoir. After six weeks of intensive work he decided the play was 'no good'.[23]

In the days before Christmas he went to a string of parties and was regularly drunk. He embarked on a brutally short affair with a woman called Phyllis, whom he described as 'a hysterical South African publicity-career girl'. After seeing her almost daily, including at Christmas, he recorded in his pocketbook: 'more hysterics; insupportable – schluss, exit Phyllis.' On 28 December he had another car accident, this time with more serious consequences. After a boozy lunch and a row with his girlfriend he proceeded to Hampstead for a dinner party at the Lousadas, friends who had invited him to meet Alec Guinness. On the way home he ran over a traffic island in Hammersmith and got into a furious argument with the police who arrived to deal with the ensuing mess. He ended up with a summons to appear in court. As he noted, 'the pendulum isn't settling down yet.'[24]

He reverted to the autobiography in the new year and bashed away until, by March 1953, he had reached the section on his trip to the USSR. By this stage it had became a dreary task, since he was largely recapitulating ground covered in previous books. He asked a psychiatrist called Dr Gould to psychoanalyse him in combination with the use of Pentothal, a 'truth drug', which he hoped would give access to hidden memories. It was 'a total flop', although Koestler did not give up and had a further session, this time employing a stronger dose.[25]

Circumstances conspired to distract him. In November 1952 he was transfixed by the Prague trials. These trials were part of a series triggered by Stalin whose chief object was to mobilise popular anti-Semitism, dressed up as anti-Zionism, in order to eliminate a whole generation of Communist Party leaders. In Prague the main victim was Rudolf Slansky, deposed head of the Czech Communist Party. One of those who testified against him was André Simone, better known as Otto Katz, who had returned to Czechoslovakia in 1946 to serve the Party. His 'evidence' contributed to the wholly fictitious case against Slansky, but in the process Katz incriminated himself. The climax of his confession seemed deliberately to echo Rubashov's closing speech at his trial in *Darkness at Noon*, as if he were sending a forlorn message to the West. These tragic convulsions within the Soviet imperium gained added poignancy when it was announced, in March 1953, that Stalin was dead. In many excited letters and conversations with fellow ex-Communists, Koestler ruminated on the implications and predicted either world war or the early collapse of the USSR.[26]

Then, for several weeks, he and Jefferies were in a panic when she suspected that she was pregnant. She visited two doctors, one of whom was a discreet Hungarian friend of Koestler's, but no abortion was necessary. Graetz flew into and out of London, though the flush of the romance was wearing off and Koestler's feelings for her alternated between 'sympathy and exaggerated boredom'. His other women friends were a mixed blessing. 'Yesterday I slept with Pris, day before with Janine; tonight probably with Lena. Each of them very desirable and impressive to others. Yet instead of privileged lucky-dog feeling, only guilt, bad conscience, shame. Only the forbidden enjoyed; when permitted, misery, impotent; i.e. only entitled to enjoyment when this paid for by guilt. Don't I lead an enviable life? So everybody would say. But all of it poisoned by the guilt-curse laid on by ma – But can't ever get my own back on her.'[27]

What is interesting about this plaint is Koestler's assumption that a life of promiscuity and deception is normal and should be pleasurable, were it not for the inconvenience of a bad conscience. It may be deemed incongruous, at the least, that a man who was so keen on defining and underpinning moral behaviour should attribute ethical conduct in human relationships to a 'curse' laid on him by his mother.

When he was not sorting out personal crises, the good weather subverted his concentration: 'Can't work: too much spring.' He was out almost every night. On 19 April he had another car accident, 'rolling absent-mindedly at 10 mph around Hyde Park Corner'. Graetz's semi-permanent presence in Montpelier Square had predictable results. To him she became, 'increasingly aggressive – from Devil to Deep Sea'. He began to suffer from a prostate complaint and after she left attributed it to her. 'Prostate trouble gone with Janine; potency increased three fold; obviously protest of prostate against coitus as duty.' He regarded the periods when she was away as 'great relief'. Meanwhile he was 'plodding' on with the book. The parts on the poet Attila Jozsef were mildly stimulating and led to a welcome friendship with fellow Hungarian George Mikes, who helped him to translate Jozsef's poems. As he approached his account of the exile in France, he began writing to the surviving members of Münzenberg's circle to confirm his memories. He told Babette Gross: 'I feel that it is in our common interest that every word that I put down should be dead right.'[28].

There were various visitors to London: Manès Sperber, Abraham Weinshall and Melvin Lasky. Unfortunately they did not mix well with his women friends. Lena made an evening with Lasky particularly uncomfortable and provoked the bitter reflection: 'the insoluble dilemma: either the Sperbers and Mels unconvivial company, or the Janines and Paulines – good company, intellectual stimulus zero. The two don't mix; it is a matter of choice. But the intellectuals after three meetings also become uninspiring . . .'[29]

At the end of May the coronation of Elizabeth II occasioned renewed introspection about his place in English society. Sperber had berated him for 'being too assimilated to England and its snobbery'. Koestler retorted with a defence of the English upper classes, whom he deemed 'endearing' because 'naive not blasé'. He appreciated the English for what he saw as their decency, their love of furniture and pets, and their hospitality (in contradistinction to the French). He liked the 'moderate' landscapes in England and the way the country was declining with 'grace'. Its upper classes supplied the intellectuals whereas in France the aristocracy was completely decayed. Finally, he thought 'British snobbery differs from e.g. American because climbing into a different stratum impossible. It is rather a snobbery of standards . . .' Yet, for all his eloquence against Sperber, another displaced *mitteleuropean* Jew, he could not talk himself into feeling at ease in England. Surveying the square bathed in spring light, he mused it was 'all I hoped for . . . Yet I shall always remain the stranger in the square.' His sense of being an outsider was brought home by the coronation. In private he mocked the pomp and festivities, the charladies 'goggling at the Woolworth edition of a fairy princess', and exuded relief when it was all over; but this was as much because he felt excluded as from any distaste for the spectacle. He was the only resident in the square not to display flags and buntings: 'partly lazyness, partly exaggerated delicacy . . .'[30]

Throughout May, June and July he laboured over *The Invisible Writing*. He contacted other former comrades-in-arms and helpers from 1938–9, including Harold Nicolson, Lord Farringdon and Willy Forrest. He again sought the help of Mikes, this time to deal with his account of Andor Németh. Two key sequences were completed in these months, both written in a trance-like state: his record of the weird interlude in Como in 1938 and his imprisonment in Spain. Meanwhile, he continued to go out almost every evening, meeting A. J. P. Taylor, Frank Pakenham, Anthony Hobson and Auden. His conversations with Pakenham related to a flirtation with Catholicism. For a time he saw the famed priest to the literati, Father d'Arcy, although he would have found it hard to reconcile Catholic values with his life-style. No matter the number of his sleeping partners he found the time and energy to begin new 'romances'. But he conceded after an 'unforgettable' threesome that 'my harem is beginning to wear me out'. He was now enjoying the company of five women. Graetz was the least in favour. He looked on her with 'boredom and pity' until she bought a yacht and for a while it looked as if the sea air would revive their relationship.[31]

Koestler seemed indifferent to the effect these affairs had on Jefferies, although her dog-like devotion to him was blazingly obvious. His passion for Graetz, as contrasted to his coolness towards her, made Jefferies suicidally depressed. In December 1952 she became involved with another man, and decided to marry and move with him to the United States. Koestler was perhaps more aware of her unhealthy admiration for him than he let on because he seemed keen for her to get married and move out of his life. Once she was gone, however, he had pangs of a familiar syndrome. He recorded in his diary: 'Cynthia left 30 July [1953] – unexpectedly depressed at losing her. Partly because exceptionally sweet – cheerful, naive, pretty, devoted; and, also, because it is a breaking apart of another bit of my life.' He also noted ominously that Jefferies's husband was in analysis. In fact, he turned out to be deeply troubled. His mental instability led to the collapse of their marriage after just one year, although Jefferies's undimmed ardour towards her former employer could not have helped. She kept Koestler informed of the fluctuations in her marital state and never hid her true feelings. 'I also hope you are missing me a little,' she wrote just a short time after arriving in New York. 'I miss you terribly and would come rushing back to London as soon as I could if I didn't realise how hopeless the situation would be.'[32]

In August Koestler had a seasonal spasm of self-analysis: 'Have at last the courage to be yourself. They all wrote the same kind of stuff all their lives – Henry James, even Tolstoi [sic]. Nobody writes your kind of stuff – Silone and Malraux have stopped, Orwell and Serge are dead, the Continental who had my experiences can't write. Take pains over your style but don't get obsessed with it.' He added: 'remain true to promiscuity too, so long as the going is good. Though actually women no longer represent the hope for "perfect union and understanding", only a drug. These short (even shorter) flickers of violent fallings-in-love are surely only a kind of emotional masturbation.'[33] There is a disturbing tone of self-aggrandisement in these notes to himself. The insight into his affairs with women shows a laudable degree of self-understanding, but it seems to have had no weight when set against his sexual hunger and predatory behaviour.

III

After a marathon writing session which had begun at the start of the year, in mid-September Koestler finished the first draft of *The Invisible Writing*. It left him 'exhausted as never before in life'. As a reward he took off to Ischia for a month with Graetz. Once on this beautiful and peaceful island he staged a 'miraculous recovery'. They went sailing, hill walking and swimming. Acting 'on the spur of the moment' he bought a house on the island: Casa Aquedanto. This was the second island retreat he had purchased and his third 'home', a pattern which suggests a subconscious drive to own land and property, although every time he did so his 'nomadic' instinct bridled and he was soon on the move again. At first sight it looked like an idyllic *pied-à-terre*: a small farmhouse on a hillside facing the sea, surrounded by vines and fig trees. But the house had no modern conveniences, not even a toilet or a bathroom. It was also perilously remote.[34]

He returned to London on 10 October, to begin one of the most disturbed, and disturbing, years of his life. For three months he worked at great speed revising the draft of *The Invisible Writing*. By the start of January 1954 it was completed, on schedule, and handed over to Hamish Hamilton.[35] The last lap of a book and the period after it was finished were always dangerous for Koestler, leaving him deflated and lost for a new subject. He tended to throw himself into political crusades or affairs as a distraction from his sense of emptiness and depression: 1954 was to be no exception.

Throughout November and December he added to and subtracted from his circle of female friends. He got into a 'stupid and harrowing predicament' with Joan Redgrove ('new conquest, nice deb', he noted in his diary on 6 August); and 'new entanglement' with June Osborne (described by Barbara Skelton when younger as having 'the slightly bandy legs and wrestler's arms of a champion horse-woman') that was 'fraught with danger'. He was also seeing Pauline Gates, in circumstances that suggest this, too, was an affair, although her husband, Sylvester Gates, had been a close friend since the 1940s. Graetz was 'coming and going; and the rest of the harem unstable and boring'. He did detect some 'redeeming factors: one week had lunch with five ex–Mrs Koestlers: Daorte [Dorothea], Daphne, Mamaine, etc. That's loyalty tout de même'. His concept of loyalty was obviously highly fluid. One of the few women successfully to repulse his attentions was Jocelyn Rickards, Freddie Ayer's semi-detached partner, whom he met at a party just before Christmas. This prompted him to minute in his diary: 'when will you ever learn?' Not for a while. He spent Christmas Day with friends, including Janetta Jackson, and clutched at her to save him from loneliness and a perennial depression.[36]

At the beginning of the year he wrote: 'Janine left, having finished her job here for good; this, plus finishing book very depressing. Suddenly found harem disappeared: Lena in Sweden, Moira and Prisc have new lovers; with June ended. Luckily, in panic of loneliness, Janetta turned up, sweet, weather beaten, and abandoned.' Thus began 'a month of hell and heaven with Janetta'.

She had met Koestler intermittently during the previous year. Koestler had taken her and Freddie Ayer to see the football international in November 1953 when Hungary beat England. In the interim she had been struggling to re-establish her life after the end of her marriage with Derek Jackson. On first encounters Janetta seemed waif-like and vulnerable: this was part of her attraction to men. But her appearance was deceptive: she was also strong-willed and blazingly independent. To Jackson 'Koestler was fascinating . . . I loved his company — but he was frightening; very demanding'. Their relationship was tempestuous from the start: Koestler's diary for January 1954 alternates between rows and reconciliations. After much toing and froing across the square they travelled to Cornwall and toured for ten days despite freezing weather. On a boat trip Koestler consumed enormous quantities of fresh oysters, which he flavoured with a lemon he carried around in his pocket. He bragged to his diary about his 'miraculous' rejuvenation, thanks to which he was able to discard his reading glasses and enjoy a 'potency increased to an average frequency of two per day'. The sex may have stepped up a gear, but Jackson's elusive spirit began to bother him.[37]

Afraid 'of being alone in London, half a mile from Janetta, and unable to work — not because I love her so, but because her casualness continues to hurt me', he decided to divert himself by going to Vienna to research the background for a potential new novel. He had become acquainted with Nicholas (later Sir) 'Nicko' Henderson, the First Secretary at the British Embassy in Vienna, and now wrote to him for advice. In particular he wanted reassurance about the threat of kidnapping by Soviet agents, since the city was still under great power supervision. Henderson allayed his fears and offered him hospitality at his home. But instead of using the trip to escape Jackson he arranged for her to take a side trip from a skiing holiday in Austria and accompany him. He flew to Vienna on 7 February; she joined him a week later.

It was the first time Koestler had been back to Vienna. Janetta Jackson recalled that 'it was very exciting. He saw lots of old friends, drank and talked a lot.' It was 'like a star going back; he adored that'. However, in order to continue their tour of Austria they had to take a train through the Soviet zone. While it was in transit two young

Red Army soldiers rode in the carriage. Their appearance was enough to provoke Koestler, who was a little drunk, to a macho display. With much huffing and puffing he worked himself into a lather over these scruffy representatives of Soviet tyranny and threatened to pick a fight with them. When Janetta tried to calm things by saying that they were just ignorant conscripts, Koestler told her that she understood nothing. In the end she had physically to restrain him: 'it was frightening.' Koestler must have been a handful for the Hendersons, too, since his letter of thanks for all their hospitality included a humorous assurance that next time he visited Vienna he would stay at the Hotel Sacher.[38]

Soon after he returned to London, Janine Graetz arrived. This time her husband was with her, so she and Koestler could only spend the days together. After she had gone his obsession with Janetta grew out of control. Koestler was compulsively introspective and, equally compulsively, had to write about his feelings. His notebooks give a blow-by-blow record of the affair, his emotions and his attempt to understand what was happening inside himself. He wrote in his diary: 'only excited when rejected, really or in imagination.' The pattern was repeating with Jackson: 'When jealousy or insecurity – libido awakened, incest barrier falls.' Except that it was nothing so high-falutin as that: rather it was 'a sort of trapped feeling, a snobbish "I might do better" – "is that all" – "there must be something more perfect" complex'. For all his self-awareness, he now behaved like a pimpled teenager. 'Am tense all these days, again, mounting tension, pain, obsession, simply unbearable. . . .' He couldn't concentrate on the proofs of *The Invisible Writing*, which had just arrived. Instead, he wrote endless letters to Jackson (who lived five minutes walk away), set deadlines for return letters or phone calls and drank and drank. The affair became a battle of wills. He refused to believe that Jackson was simply tired of him and attributed malign impulses to her. He was sure she thought she had the 'upper hand' because she knew Janine Graetz was in Paris and he was determined to settle the relationship, but on his terms.[39]

Days passed in the wake of the Viennese excursion without any message from her. They finally met 'by chance' outside Harrods. Koestler reproached her and she retorted that she had believed Graetz was with him. They had a row; they made up. A few days later, after a period of silence from Jackson, they met and had another row. Then Graetz arrived for a weekend at the Dorchester and 'saved' him. As soon as she had flown out again he went to see Jackson. They had another row and this time he struck her. Koestler apologised over the phone and, somehow, they resumed cordial relations. A few days later the cycle repeated itself. He spent 1 April composing a seven-page letter, delivering it by hand and pacing the house awaiting a reply, aching with 'loss and the defeat'. The tension was so great that eventually he rang a prostitute 'and had a sort of lovely evening'. Koestler unrealistically considered enlisting Mamaine's sister, Celia Goodman (previously Kirwan), as a go-between in the struggle but felt that at last he had 'regained upper hand'. Contact was re-established, they had dinner, he devoured three dozen oysters and slept with Jackson. A few days later he invited her to join him on a holiday in France. She declined. There were more letters and deadlines, but Jackson held firm. On 6 April he left for a long holiday, temporarily baffled.[40]

None of these goings-on would be worth recording, were it not for the light they shed on Koestler as against the persona which he was contemporaneously projecting to the world in his autobiographical oeuvre: the adamantine opponent of tyranny, the lofty moralist above party and country whose misspent youth had seared ethical conduct into his soul, the scourge of hypocrisy and duplicity, the ruthlessly frank and self-aware savant. He was certainly self-aware: in June, amid a torrid affair, he scrawled in his notebook: 'all this only pseudo-love, really, hurt ego. How different the whole pattern would have been had I met her in middle of a book and if Janine had not had to leave.' The gulf between his self-knowledge and his actual conduct indicates a capacity for self-deception that arguably vitiates any claim to either insight or scruples. If Koestler could not be honest with himself and do the right thing, he was on distinctly shaky ground when preaching sincerity and virtue to others.

It is true that Koestler had a clearly defined and well-advertised approach to sex and family life. Women knew where they stood with him: on shaky ground. But however sincerely held Koestler's personal morality was, it was only personal, and unsurprisingly it was convenient mainly for him. It did not absolve him or those he inveigled into affairs from following social conventions. He entered into adulterous liaisons and played the game by engaging in systematic deceit. It is hard to say whether Koestler's knack for duplicity was a cause or an effect of his political gyrations, but dissembling to himself and others was second nature. His 'autobiography' was perhaps his most stupendous act of deception.

IV

Koestler set off for Ischia, his holiday destination, intending to rendezvous with his American pal Jack Newsom, his wife and Janine Graetz. On 8 April he arrived in Paris for a week and did the round of old friends: the Vallons, Sperber and Winkler. He saw Graetz and had a terrible row with her. The next day they made up and, perhaps to celebrate, he purchased a landscape by Courbet.[41] He then drove down to Chamonix and spent several days walking in the French Alps. The mountain air helped to dispel his obsession with Janetta Jackson and his displeasure with Graetz. Further aid was provided by a lovely young Milanese student called Paola, whom he picked up on his first night in Chamonix. This accomplishment put him in a 'very boastful mood'. But it was followed by angst as he continued on to Milan unsure whether she would respond to his cabled requests to meet again. She agreed, long enough for 'sad adieux', before he took the road southwards. In Rome he was joined by Graetz and they journeyed together to Ischia, arriving on 25 April.[42]

The next day Koestler heard that Newsom had died of a heart attack on the ship carrying him to his longed-for retirement. This shocking news augmented Koestler's bad mood. He was furious to discover that the house he had bought was uninhabitable: the workmen whom Graetz was supposed to have engaged had done little or nothing. She and Koestler had to stay nearby, while he marshalled new builders, not his favourite pursuit. Needless to say, he was unable to do any sort of work. They both left the island, Koestler to help arrange Newsom's funeral and Graetz to go back to the Via Appia Antica, in Rome, where she lived. He returned to Ischia alone and passed a few enjoyable days sightseeing, sailing and canoeing. Graetz continued to come and go, never staying more than three or four days. The weather was sultry and the work on the house proceeded at a snail's pace. Despite cheery and stimulating dinners with W. H. Auden ('More sex-obsessed and ridden than anybody I know') and Robin Maugham, who lived on the island for part of each year, he sank into a suicidally black depression.[43]

On 2 June he received a cable informing him that Mamaine was dead. He was poleaxed. They had met frequently over the preceding two years and remained very fond of each other. There was no reconciliation, but Koestler did acknowledge that he had behaved atrociously towards her. Ruminating by himself at Island Farm during autumn 1952, he admitted that he had not been the easiest of partners: 'I must really have made life rather insupportable for you, and feel sorry and guilty about it.' Apart from an initial chilliness, the separation was handled in a very civilised fashion on both sides. He behaved impeccably in organising through his solicitor, Anthony

Lousada, ample provision for his wife's material needs.

She quickly built a new life and got a job working for Verschoyle, the art publisher. She, too, confessed to some regrets and admitted to missing Koestler. But poor health continued to dog her. When Koestler saw her on his return from America he was 'helpless with pity'. By the time Lousada set in motion their legal separation at the end of 1953 her health was failing. In April 1954 she seemed to Koestler to be 'only half alive'. A short while after he made this observation, she had an asthma attack and was taken into St Pancras Hospital for eight days. Mamaine turned to him for support, but he had evaporated: 'God I longed for you in my lowest moments – but didn't even know where you were.' Yet the old dynamic of their relationship was so ingrained that she followed this letter with one full of remorse for bothering him. She put on a brave face and described how she was 'racing around the room in a wheelchair'.[44]

Koestler wrote to her from Ischia three days later under the impression that she was about to convalesce in Garmisch. Indeed, Mamaine sent him a letter the same day saying that she hoped to be home soon. But two weeks later she had another attack and was rushed to University College Hospital. This time she was unconscious for forty-eight hours and came to in a state of utter terror. She managed to write to Koestler begging for a word from him: 'Sweetie I *am* sorry to do nothing but write you depressing letters, please don't be worried about me. . . . I just would like a *LETTER* from you, though I know you hate writing and what a big demand it is.' She signed it, 'Love darling Sweetie, and alles Gute von Deiner immergetreuen . . .' Koestler replied on 19 May, saying how 'ghastly disappointing' it was that she was back in hospital but suggesting that it was for the best if the doctors could find a permanent cure, which was only a matter of time. He chatted about seeing Maugham, his problems with his novel and the publication date of *The Invisible Writing*. Mamaine Koestler died of a heart attack soon after the letter arrived. She was thirty-seven years old.[45]

Arthur Goodman, Mamaine's brother-in-law, held up the funeral while Koestler rushed back to London. On 4 June he went to the undertakers to say 'Goodbye to my darling'. The service was attended by many of their mutual friends, including Sonia Orwell and Janetta Jackson. His tanned and healthy appearance was in rude contrast to the depressed mood of the spectators at the interment ceremony. This and his delayed arrival created bitterness towards him among Mamaine's closest companions. Janetta Jackson remembered that 'Not one single one of the people at the funeral spoke to him except me . . . They were blaming him; they'd decided he'd killed her.' When he had the chance Koestler reproached the doctors who had been caring for her, accusing them of not alerting him to the seriousness of her condition. But his crucial absence was always held against him by some, although never by Celia Goodman, who remained his staunchest defender.[46]

For the rest of the summer Koestler meditated on Mamaine's death and where it left him. He returned to Ischia and moved into the 'desolate house' that now gave him no pleasure. Graetz flitted in and out; when she was there they quarrelled ceaselessly. At one point he 'felt so exasperated with Janine that had to take an injection of anti-kidney stone (first time in life) and slept most of day'. This was a relationship that needed doses of morphia to keep it on track. After two fruitless days spent working on an essay about snobbery and a gruesomely bad stab at a novel set on Ischia he gave up any semblance of writing. His only solace was physical exertion: walking, swimming, canoeing and sailing. Some relief was provided by visitors who came to dine or to stay: Auden, Leo Valiani and the Lousada family. He insisted on piling the Lousadas aboard the yacht and personally piloting them around the Bay of Naples, leading expeditions ashore to Ravello and Pompeii. What was supposed to be a restful holiday for them was turned into a distraction for Koestler and they began to protest against his 'mad-hatter's pace'. Paola paid a visit, too. He brought her together with Graetz in one of his French-brothel exercises. Not surprisingly, it was a 'hateful' experience. On 20 July, Koestler and Graetz together left Ischia for the last time.[47]

He spent four days in Rome sightseeing and 'car-nursing'. Like him, the black Citroën was now showing its age and the wear and tear to which it had been subjected. His mood had not improved and he was haunted by Mamaine. 'Here I am,' he wrote, 'with a car in Rome, free to go everywhere, with only technical financial worries, an enviable mistress . . . a young Italian beauty in love with me and miserable like a dog.' The money difficulties were related to complicated, unresolved transactions with Graetz, as a result of which he accused her of irresponsibility. But this was nothing compared with his guilt feelings over Mamaine and his work (or non-work) anxiety. 'I have – poor rich man – in women and houses – nowhere to go. Three houses, umpteen mistresses, car, yacht – it is grotesque and pathetic. Yet the problems of the "rich", though the poor think they are pseudo-problems and would gladly swap – are just as real . . . In fact the rich commit more suicides (I suppose) than the poor. Still, once I am back to work, I shall get more balanced again.

But what work? This is the real crisis, the root of everything.' He could not decide whether he should or could continue writing fiction and thrashed around for both a genre and a subject.

His irritation with Graetz burgeoned, fastening on to trivial misdemeanours. When she was fifty minutes late for their departure from Rome her tardiness 'spoiled the journey' for Koestler and put him in such an evil temper that he was 'unable to speak' until after dinner and a lot of drinks in Ferrara. Their paths diverged in Verona on 26 July. This location, resonant of *Romeo and Juliet*, was a curious, inverted echo of the role played by Romeo (the dog) in their earliest flirtations. After two bottles of wine, Graetz went back to Rome and Koestler drove northwards through the night into the Dolomites and a rendezvous with an old German chum called Korman, who owned a hotel situated between Bolzano and the Brenner Pass. As soon as he arrived he got drunk with Korman 'and some dumb blond.'[48]

From late July until mid-August he stayed at Korman's. He read, tried to write and walked, although mountain ascents were getting harder and harder. For a while the physical exertion calmed him and he made some progress reworking the Ischia story. Before long, however, bad habits reasserted themselves. He began to fret obsessively about what he perceived as Graetz's casual attitude to financial arrangements: her silence gnawed at him. He picked up a student at the top of Mount Marmolada and indulged in a passionate three-day affair. The only counterweight to his depression was the news that Island Farm had been sold for a substantial profit. This induced the same sensation as when he received his first food parcel during his incarceration in Spain. Mostly he bumped along in a slough of loneliness, self-pity, self-recrimination and self-flagellation. He was 'physically a wreck . . . impotent as a novelist . . . too bored to write essays'. He had let himself be 'seduced by luxury, comfort and being spoilt'. His affair with Graetz rested on opulence and pampering: 'I have never had such a long affair with somebody of so little value for all her sweetness.' With a shudder he realised that Orwell was right when he identified hedonism as Koestler's greatest flaw: 'The chink in Koestler's armour was this time gaping wide.' In another uncanny echo of Orwell he recalled the 'one intelligent remark' made by Graetz: 'You are kind and self-sacrificing to people who are indifferent to you, but if you accept to live with somebody, you become inhuman to them as to yourself, and torture them as you torture yourself.'[49]

With that singular combination of perception and paralysis, he shrewdly reassessed his relations with women: 'I can neither live alone, nor with somebody. It is true, I always picked one type: from Helga to Eva to Daphne and Mamaine and Janine and Janetta: beautiful cinderellas, infantile and inhibited, prone to be subdued by bullying. But this realization doesn't solve the problem.' In an alcoholic scrawl, night after night, he poured out his demons and dilemmas, searching for the 'middle way' and a reading of the 'invisible writing'. What did the auguries mean? What was he supposed to do with his life? How was he supposed to live? He made various resolutions to change his life-style: to work on ESP seriously and decode the 'language of destiny', to form a stable relationship, to mourn Mamaine properly. He decided to qualify the amount of travelling he did and to end his 'retreats' since neither proved to be especially productive. But as hard as he might try he could not break his habits of drinking and womanising even while he was 'on retreat'. He contacted a woman called Marietta and set up an assignation in Innsbruck. 'Just had notice that M will call at 7 p.m.,' he wrote on the eve of his departure, 'Heart pumping like an adolescent – quite literally. At 49! Can hardly write.'[50]

From the Dolomites he drove to Milan, where he saw Valiani and his Italian publishers. He then spent several days in Maggiore in the company of Sperber and Erich Maria Remarque. Remarque was as moody and fond of the bottle as he was and they got plastered in the local night-clubs several nights in succession. Koestler smashed up his car and had to wait days for it to be restored to running order. On 28 August he took to the road again, reaching Paris two days later. He arrived back at Montpelier Square at the beginning of September.[51]

V

In Milan people recognised Koestler and came up to him in bank queues to ask for his autograph. In London his marginality was confirmed by the critical response to *The Invisible Writing*, which appeared, after some delays, in August. These were partly attributable to Cyril Connolly, who threatened to sue over a passage in the manuscript version accusing him of 'slatternly habits and being hopeless about money'. This was actually mild stuff compared with what Koestler really thought of him. To Orwell he had denounced the 'steady, stultifying effect' of the Connolly circus. In May 1952, he described Connolly's cottage as 'sunk in the usual Cyrilian filth (the bathtub simply unbelievable). He has that need of building himself a nest of faeces.' During this visit he charged that in conversation Connolly attacked him like an 'envious fish-wife' and casually left him to pay the lunch bill 'presumably on some private counter-theory that the world owes him a living'. Koestler had good cause to despise Connolly. Their private lives may have been equally as selfish and reckless, but Connolly's indolence and general uselessness high-light the most admirable qualities of Koestler as a campaigner and activist. His campaigns may have been spasmodic, but at least he was striving to have an effect on the world beyond his private appetites. A world without Koestler would have been noticeably different; but there would have been little difference to a world without Connolly. Knowing that he was a better writer and more productive, he was infuriated by Connolly's snooty review, especially since he had praised the book in private.[52]

Aside from Connolly's snide remarks, *The Invisible Writing* was received with greater warmth than even *Arrow in the Blue*. Reviewers noted that Koestler had erected a monument not only to his life but to the first half of the century. And, as Stephen Spender observed, the man seemed to emerge more clearly. He thought that in the second volume Koestler had succeeded in asserting his individual identity against the universal experiences of his generation. 'At heart Koestler seems to me a religious man in search of penitence, homesick for a communion of saints.' However, too often pride blinded him to obvious character faults and might still confound his quest. The *New Statesman* treated him as an extreme, not a typical, case and declared: 'We refuse to take him seriously.' Raymond Mortimer in the *Sunday Times* was so dismissive of the book's message that Koestler was driven to write to the paper in protest.[53]

The Invisible Writing remains one of the most extraordinary autobiographical works of the century. If it is not wholly successful as either literature or memoir this may be because it carries too great a weight. It was first and foremost a political act: to explain the allure of Communism, to expose the myth of the Soviet Union and the malevolent influence of the fellow travellers, and to inoculate future generations against the appeal of Marxist revolutionary theory. To achieve this Koestler had, again, to show how ordinary he was, how his fate was that of millions and could befall many more in the future. For this reason he railed against his critics, particularly those in England such as Raymond Mortimer, who had dismissed the experiences recounted in his 1940s writing as aberrational. 'The awareness that the first thirty-five years of my life were a typical sample of our times and the chronicler's urge to preserve the sample, were my main reason for writing these memoirs.' Throughout the book he juxtaposes the 1930s with the 1950s, maintaining that the defenders of the USSR were as blind to the atrocities of Stalin as the world was to the fate of the Jews under Nazi persecution. He quotes his 1943 essay 'On Disbelieving Atrocities' to explain the mentality of the fellow travellers and the critics who preferred to dismiss his jeremiads.[54]

It is also a very personal gesture: a statement of Koestler's emerging belief in the existence of a parallel universe which determines the known one and to which a privileged few, possessing a higher form of consciousness, may have access. In this sense, as some reviewers noted, it was hardly a 'typical case history'. On the contrary, the book is a case study of Koestler's theory of 'serial coincidences' revealing 'the language of destiny'. This notion is spelled out in great detail in the chapter 'House by the Lake', a gothic episode which Koestler wrote in one dreamlike session.[55] He also works his new theory into his account of his imprisonment in Seville. This now becomes a 'spiritual crisis and turning point' as well as a political juncture. Each man is deemed responsible for the lives of his fellows, but not just for abstract ethical reasons: humans are all of the same cosmic 'substance'. Political ideologies are unjustified in using murder as a means to an end not just because this is wrong *per se*, but because they are only a partial truth. In the cell, he claims, he realised that there are eternal truths, independent of political doctrines, and that 'a higher order of reality existed, that alone invested existence with meaning'. This was the parallel universe accessible only through the paranormal: it alone made sense of the mundane.[56]

Most remarkably, Koestler sets himself up as one of the few able to comprehend the 'language of destiny'. He attributes a subtle logic to the apparently random, destructive and abrupt transformations of his life. His crazy, impulsive gestures were carried out in obedience to 'the commandments of the invisible text, revealed for a split second to the inner self'. He was the embodiment of the combined saint–revolutionary who would show the way to a new moral and political order.[57]

The more mundane purpose of the book is to expose Communism and the USSR. He does this with a thoroughness that must have pleased his friends in the State Department and the CIA. The passages on his conversion, his activism in the Red block, the methods of indoctrination and the duplicity of the Soviet authorities when they sent him around the USSR read like a textbook for a course in anti-Communism. Even so, in the passages on Central Asia Koestler's infatuation with progress and the revolution are barely suppressed and old Bolsheviks bestride the narrative like Titans. Similarly, the brilliant chapters on Willi Münzenberg and his court uneasily blend exposé with adulation. Münzenberg emerges less as the man who set out to subvert the West than a flawed and tragic hero.[58]

Co-existing with this historical and political narrative there is the saga of his personal development, narrated in the tone of 'benevolent irony' he perfected in the first volume. On the surface he delivers a chain of breath-taking revelations about his promiscuity, psychological foibles and self-absorption. They are all of questionable veracity. Sex was his 'only pursuit exempt from guilt', a statement baldly contradicted by all his private reflections on the subject.[59] He records his self-pity and suicidal feelings after his first novel was savaged by Party comrades and comments that it was 'the only prolonged period in my life when I abandoned myself to that vice'.[60] But even as he was writing those words he was fluctuating between elation and despair. In an explanation of his pattern of political activism he observes: 'I began to accept that I was a person of the obsessive type. Blessed or cursed with a surplus of nervous energy which demanded excessive outlets, I had to be obsessed with some task if I was not to be obsessed with myself.' This is perceptive and very true. But it is followed by a passage that must have taken aback all those who knew him well: 'Gradually these manic bursts of activity, followed by morbid depressions, levelled out into a relatively stable working discipline which keeps me chained to my desk all the year round for eight or nine hours a day.'[61] There is no need to make further comment on this flagrant act of deception except to wonder if it was also self-deception.

Much of the book recycles material from his earlier autobiographical works, but it remains a stunning panorama of the pre-war decade: the USSR under Stalin, the international Communist movement, the anti-Fascist struggle, the lives of the exiles and refugees, the Spanish Civil War and even Zionism. After retracing the subject matter of Scum of the Earth, adding more details about his flight from France, Koestler finally breaks new ground in the Epilogue, which sets out his explanation for settling in England. Initially he came to the UK to continue the war against Fascism, but he decided to stay for a variety of other reasons. He felt comfortable in the English language, and had begun to think like an Anglo-Saxon. He grew to appreciate the 'human climate' of the country, which acted as 'a kind of Davos for internally bruised veterans of the totalitarian age'. There was less aggression in English society: the people lived 'closer to the text of the invisible writing than any other'. This is a very peculiar compliment, implying a national aptitude for paranormal communication. It was perhaps intended to counterbalance his next reason, which was that England was subsiding gracefully and he seemed 'only to flourish in a climate of decline'. This more than compensated for the fact that he was less well known in England than elsewhere and read only by highbrows. The marginalisation of the intellectual, especially of the foreign-born variety, was the price paid for the sanity and stability of English society.[62]

Koestler ends by confessing that he finds it hard to reconcile all the contradictory aspects of his character. It is left to the reader to do that. If there is any resolution to be found, he suggests, it will be by judging him 'against the background of his time, by taking into account both the historian's and the psychologist's approach. It was my aim throughout this autobiography not to withhold from the reader any clue, however embarrassing, that is relevant to the solution.'[63] But Koestler withholds the greatest clue of all: that he had barely changed. If the man remained the boy, then the passage of time and the currents of history were less than relevant. The real message of *The Invisible Writing*, which actually subverts it as an historical text, is that in Koestler's highly individual case pathology prevailed over politics. For all his attempts to construct his life as representative, shaped by the currents of the era, another more plausible interpretation emerges, which suggests that Koestler's odyssey was less driven by political ideologies or social forces and more by his own quirks of character. While his choices certainly were not random, the ease with which he moved from one allegiance, locality and relationship to another spoke more about his own egocentricity and congenital restlessness than the process of enchantment and disillusion.

VI

Koestler's life in London soon returned to what passed as normality for him. He bustled around the house restoring it to order and went through two charladies in a week. He began work on the volume of essays he had been mooting for half a year, resumed dining out and sleeping around. On 5 September he marked his forty-ninth birthday with a party and went out to dinner with the novelist Henry Green and his wife. He bought a new car, collected it on 13 September and 'bruised' it five days later. He had a much more serious accident in November, following a mellifluous dinner with Connolly, whom he had never stopped seeing despite their wariness of each other. After little more than two weeks back he was 'on the wagon' again. He had what he described as 'occasional meetings and sleepings with Janetta, but now unimportant as her pathetic preciousness rather repellent and boring'. And he started a risky affair with a 'Park Lane acquaintance'. Janine Graetz visited in September–October, the first time they had seen each other since the end of August when Graetz made a 'staggering disclosure' to Koestler. It was the news that she was pregnant. Although he complained that she was 'aggressive and unpleasant' their encounter was 'less painful than expected. Fortunately for him, her husband assumed the child to be his own and she managed to remain within her extremely comfortable milieu.[64]

After this shock he commenced what he called, rather misleadingly as it turned out, 'the great discarding'. Proclaiming that the 'phase of greed' was over, he set about rationalising his affairs, as he had tried to do in the summer Mamaine left him. But for all the 'absolutely final' rows with Graetz and Jackson he continued to see them both, while adding a level-headed young woman called Gillian Richardson to his roster of female company. Richardson, who worked in publishing, was 'completely middle-class' and imported a temporary stability into his life. She didn't drink and lived simply. At first he was somewhat nonplussed by this behaviour: 'how difficult it is to adjust to her standards having been accustomed to upper-class [women] and allied bitches, drunks and nymphos.' Not much time elapsed before he was 'hovering between boredom and commitment'. Boredom won out, 'less because of middle-class homeliness than lack of temperament. No charm, no intelligence, no culture, no books, no temper (except sexual) – what remains?' Notwithstanding this private disparagement, he went on seeing her almost every other day well into 1955. 'Very bored with sweet Gill, but also fed up with affairs. Desperately looking for something really stable – yet knowing how these attempts ended in the past.' Instead, it became a 'utility affair' in accord with a rather different outlook: 'Don't look for female redeemer. Solution must be found between god and you and your work. The female element merely a stabilizer (not even a catalyzer), a sedative.'[65]

Koestler's sexual opportunism could go to astonishing lengths. In July 1954 he received a fan letter from Senika Taskiranel, a strikingly pretty young Turkish woman who worked at the UN in New York. Recapitulating a passage from *Arrow in the Blue* about the tall, unattractive *grandes dames* who 'rush at him' at parties, she described herself as twenty-five years old and five foot three inches tall, and offered to rush at Koestler, if he wished. Three months later she visited England and he slept with her. On her way back to New York she wrote to him, 'since you touched me I consider my body sacred . . . I won't let anyone get close to me until I see you again.' There is no record that she ever did.[66]

So the merry-go-round kept turning. In the run-up to Christmas 1954, he was seeing Richardson, a new friend called Felicity, and June, an old flame. He simply could not spend an evening alone at home. He installed loudspeakers in the sitting room as an enticement to remain safely indoors listening to music, but to no avail. Having secured the services of a Viennese cook earlier in the year, he also entertained extensively at home. He threw a cocktail party to which he invited, among others, George Weidenfeld, Nigel Davenport, Sir Edward Hulton, Sir Martyn Beckett the architect, and Lady Pakenham. He met Isaiah Berlin (whom he found 'frivolous and super-donnish'), Laurence van der Post and the Hungarian pianist Louis Kentner. The year ended as had many a previous one, with 'complications' within his female circle.[67]

Graetz spent part of the winter in the Swiss mountains, where she was visited by a friend of Koestler who brought back first-hand accounts of her condition. In February he flew to Paris to see her for a day. On 13 April 1955 she gave birth to a baby girl, whom she named Christine. Koestler did not see mother or child until the following August, when they came to London over the Bank Holiday weekend. He saw his daughter only fleetingly, but the visit left him 'very shaken'. Graetz 'looked so lovely and sad; thought we would start again; unable to understand why I insisted on her staying at the Dorchester. Isabelle Christine looks really a darling. Am I missing my last chance here?' He gave no sign of this to Graetz. Cynthia Jefferies was then temporarily installed at Montpelier Square and when Graetz visited the house Jefferies accompanied Koestler to make up his favoured triangular situation. The situation that had obtained when Graetz visited Verte Rive was thus reversed. The turn-round of fortunes was galling to her and Jefferies noted her discomfiture, not without a feeling of glee.[68]

Yet the urge to settle preyed on him. In January 1955 he met the novelist Elizabeth Jane Howard at a party thrown by Moira Verschoyle. Even though he was still seeing Richardson they started going out. Jefferies, who met her much later, considered her a suitable match for Koestler. He was certainly very serious about Howard and on St Valentine's Day 1955 proposed to her. Four days later he noted in his pocketbook 'Jane, crisis'.[69] Like all his relationships this one was marked by extreme fluctuations. Howard, who quickly sensed that he was a difficult man, wisely parried his offer of marriage and instead proposed that they try living together.

This was just as well since, as Howard recalled, after about eight weeks it was clear that the arrangement was 'not a success and we had to stop'. Although he was 'a very loveable man' Howard quickly discovered the other side of Koestler's personality: he was 'very temperamental, very highly strung'. They quarrelled spectacularly. Once, in the course of 'a violent row' she threw a water jug at him; another time she found she could calm him down by stuffing salami in his mouth. Part of the problem was that despite his legendary capacity for booze, he couldn't take drink. She also learned that he was 'a natural bully', especially towards women; he simply couldn't treat them as his equal.

One evening in the course of a canoeing holiday during the early summer, they were making love when Howard 'insisted he should use a form of birth control. He said "No, no, it's a safe time." I was so beaten down by being bullied in his canoe all day that I just gave up.' The inevitable happened and Howard became pregnant. But having caused the situation Koestler behaved appallingly. When she told him that she was pregnant he went into 'a state of panic'. The 'idea of having children was anathema to him'. Despite Koestler's experience in these matters, Howard arranged the abortion and went through the whole process more or less on her own. When she was ejected from the nursing home after the operation she called him from her flat because she had no milk or food and was too weak to go shopping. He came over but made it clear he wanted to be somewhere else. Instead of showing much sympathy he brusquely told her 'you'll get over it'. Fortunately a relative of Howard's turned up to care for her. 'Koestler was terribly relieved' and left.[70] However, eventually they became friends again, and remained on good terms until his death.

In her 1965 novel *After Julius* Howard did in a sense record her disappointment with Koestler and the circumstances of her abortion. At a party one of the chief characters, a woman called Cressy, is attracted to an older man who is 'very intelligent and concerned with the state of the world'. They start seeing each other and he asks Cressy to marry him, but she is unsure and suggests that they cohabit for a few months. 'He liked to run everything' and one night brushes aside her pleas to use a contraceptive. His subsequent behaviour is cruel. 'This man was supposed to have loved me: he wrote books about people and ideology — he was regarded as a pioneer, a humanitarian, someone of great integrity who cared what happened in society – a responsible and courageous man – one in a million. And yet there I was pregnant, honestly because he bullied me about knowing better, and all he wanted was to be shot of the situation – never mind what happened to me in the process.'[71] Howard incisively related the public persona to the private life and showed how the one undermined the other.

VII

Between these amours, altercations and emergencies, Koestler managed to work fairly steadily on translations of the auto-biographies, prefaces for new editions of *Scum of the Earth* and *Spanish Testament*, and the volume of essays. By November he had finished the essay on snobbery and began a piece about the Jewish Question, which he nicknamed his 'Jew-essay'. By the New Year the essays were packed up and ready to go, now under the collective title *The Trail of the Dinosaur.*[72]

The public make-over of Arthur Koestler was completed with the publication of this volume. In the preface he informed readers that the book was a sequel to *The Yogi and the Commissar*, and a vindication of his then 'pessimistic forecasts'. But he was not concerned to score political points: the politics of the 1940s were meaningless in an age of mass destruction in which old ideological labels merely disguised the real threats to humanity. The survival of the human race dictated that new, 'more vital questions' needed to be addressed. So the book was 'a farewell to arms': 'I have said all I had to say on these questions which had obsessed me, in various ways, for the best part of a quarter-century. Now the errors are atoned for, the bitter passion has burnt itself out; Cassandra has gone hoarse, and is due for a vocational change.'[73]

The first eight essays were political commentaries published between 1947 and 1950, which have already been dealt with. The central section contained a miscellany of articles and talks on broadly cultural themes. 'The Future of the Novel', which first appeared in John Lehmann's *New Writing and Daylight* in September 1946, distilled elements of the chapter on literature in *Insight and Outlook*.[74] In 'The Boredom of Fantasy', a BBC Home Service Broadcast in May 1953, he argued that science fiction articulated the hopes and fears of the atomic age. He lightly broached a favourite theory, which he would explore at length in the 1970s, that 'the human race may be a biological misfit doomed to extinction' and that a sense of this led to the booming interest in stories about life on other planets.[75]

He also included a story which he had first published in a contro-versial issue of *Collier's Magazine* in October 1951, which speculated on the causes and effects of the Third World War. Koestler's contribution was 'The Shadow of a Tree', an imagined journey through 'liberated Russia' recovering from the effects of a devastating conflict in 1961. It is a fascinating curio because many of its hypotheses were vindicated after 1989, but without the need for a war. In his premonition Communist society collapsed because it was rotten from within, its citizens the victims of an artificially preserved illusion that could not withstand an open challenge by capitalist democracy. The first free elections since 1917 led to an 'exuberant honeymoon with democracy' characterised by an efflorescence of batty parties of the kind which have been seen recently in Pushkin Square, Moscow.

Two substantial essays, 'An Anatomy of Snobbery' and 'Judah at the Crossroads', were composed specially for the book, although the latter was in essence an extended version of the Epilogue to *Promise and Fulfilment*. The former had been haunting him for years. It offered an analysis of snobbery, based on his pet theory of bisociation, the collision of two inappropriate sets of values, such as the aesthetic worth of a painting and its marketability. This could only occur in an age when there were many competing sets of values. So snobbery is 'a reflection of the spiritual crisis and moral and intellectual chaos which accompanies it. In the absence of any firm standards of values, it is inevitable that the wrong scale should be applied to the wrong object.'[76]

'Judah at the Crossroads', which had provisionally been entitled 'The Conversion of the Jews', cannibalised parts of his major writings on Palestine and an interview he gave to the *Jewish Chronicle* on his Jewishness in 1952. Koestler repeated his assertion that Judaism is not simply a denomination: 'The Jewish faith is nationally and racially self-segregating.' The effect of Jewish apartness is to create anti-Semitism. But the establishment of the State of Israel rendered this quixotic creed cum identity redundant, since it had persisted solely in order to transmit the Zionist urge. Koestler could see no intrinsic value in either Jewish orthodoxy, the reformed versions of Judaism or, least of all, the secularised 'Jewish values' to which most Jews adhered. Orthodoxy was dying out; the other versions of Jewish belief were so attenuated that they were not worth preserving if the cost was the continuation of Jew-hatred. The neurosis induced by the life of a persecuted minority might produce a superabundance of geniuses, but if the price was anti-Semitism it was not worth paying.

Jews should seek actively to assimilate or, if they really valued Jewish uniqueness, migrate to Israel and become citizens of the Hebrew nation.[77]

In the process of writing the piece he consulted Isaiah Berlin, who had published a series of articles in the *Jewish Chronicle* on the Jewish predicament in modern times, in which *inter alia* he had criticised Koestler's stance. 'Your attack was the only one which could serve as a basis for serious discussion and I would like to go back to it as a starting point for the present essay. I shall, of course, send you an advance copy and if you feel moved to answer, we can have some more fun.' He invited Berlin to dinner to thrash things out and to sample the unusual skills of his Irish cook 'who makes Polish borscht'.

Berlin rose to the challenge. In a carefully drafted response he agreed that they had much in common with regard to the inevitability of assimilation. But they differed in one significant and illuminating way: 'you demand tidiness and order, whereas I am daily becoming more and more obscurantist and cling to Kant's proposition "Out of the crooked timber of humanity no straight thing was ever made".' The 'crooked timber' shouldn't be forced to be straight, especially not if that meant doing violence to cherished beliefs and venerable traditions. He accused Koestler of sharing the totalitarian impulse towards tidiness and uniformity: why shouldn't Jews be allowed to be different? He put his finger on Koestler's propensity to blame the Jews for anti-Semitism, to blame the victims for their own persecution. He also rejected the sweeping assertion that Jewish culture and tradition were worthless: even if they were objectively archaic, Jews still had a subjective right to preserve them. Koestler would have no truck with this. In an ad hominem conclusion, he accused Berlin of being the sort of liberal who labelled an opponent a totalitarian if he forced him to make hard decisions.[78]

The final section comprised mainly the orations and publications connected with the CCF. It also included 'A Guide to Political Neuroses', which had first appeared in *Encounter* in November 1953. The 'Guide' brought together the psychoanalytical metaphors for varieties of political behaviour that he had used in his essays on French intellectuals and more generally elsewhere. Superficially he offered an analysis for certain forms of public conduct, but in reality he was only attaching provocative labels to them. It was clever, but shallow.[79]

The last essay, the title piece, was an extended statement of his conviction that the rate of technological progress and the spiritual evolution of mankind were out of kilter and threatening the human species with mass destruction. Action was urgently needed to secure the survival of mankind, but it could not come from politicians, who were locked into the quotidian round, or saints who were too aloof to get their hands dirty. Despite his apocalyptic prognosis, surprisingly, Koestler declared himself against nuclear disarmament. The real issue was which ideology would eventually prevail, or which new doctrine would emerge to render the political stand of the two opposed power blocs irrelevant. He reiterated his familiar argument that the era of rationalism, which had superseded that of religious faith, was now ending, but that nothing had appeared to take its place. The only hope lay in the evolution of a new creed: 'Is it really too much to ask and hope for a religion whose content is perennial but not archaic, which provides ethical guidance, teaches the lost art of contemplation, and restores contact with the supernatural without requiring reason to abdicate?' The alternatives were stark: 'We shall either destroy ourselves or take off to the stars.'[80]

The interconnecting themes of science and faith, and the search for a new belief system, were to dominate Koestler's life for the next thirty years. Although he claimed to have left politics behind, these themes were absolutely rooted in political dilemmas. The dilemmas may have been overly apocalyptic and even phoney, the results of overworked analogies rather than empirical research, but they found an echo with millions of readers around the world. It was no accident that a secularised Jew, faithless and displaced, who had experienced the terror of absolutist ideologies, should lead this quest for identity, belonging and enduring ethical values.

VIII

As the volume of essays summing up and saying farewell to his life as a political activist neared completion, Koestler resolved that his next project would be a biography of the seventeenth-century astronomer Kepler. He had been thinking of doing this for two decades, but when Kepler's name cropped up in a conversation with Isaiah Berlin, Koestler interpreted this happenstance as the 'language of destiny' speaking to him. He was delighted with his initial research on the Kepler project since he saw a lot of himself in his new subject. But, as usual, he would not give himself a straight run at it. He was torn away by a lecture in Berlin, although this also gave him the chance to do some research in the Stuttgart library. When he returned to

England he jumped into a campaign against capital punishment and before long he was writing two books at the same time: one on the history of science and the other on hanging. To bring some order to this chaos he summoned Cynthia Jefferies's help.[81]

By autumn 1953 Jefferies's marriage was in ruins; it was annulled the following year on grounds of her husband's 'mental incapacity'. She subsequently found work with the bridge entrepreneur and apostle of internationalism Ely Culbertson, but begged Koestler to re-employ her. Despite an occasional boyfriend she was marking time. Her letters to Koestler are flirtatious and supplicatory: there is also a hint of the sado-masochistic bond between the vulnerable young woman and tough man of the world: she routinely signed her letters to him 'your old slave'. She wrote to him loyally after Mamaine's death: 'I knew you would blame yourself – more than you should, I think. No I do not deny that you nagged her a lot. But you were also very good and sweet, and loving and you mustn't forget that side. In other words, don't magnify your quarrels.' As if to absolve him further, Jefferies reminded Koestler: 'You said in London about eighteen months ago that there was a streak of self-torture in both girls.'[82]

Koestler had kept Jefferies up to date with his progress. Once he was back in London after his cataclysmic Italian sortie and desperately casting around for a source of stability in his life, he made his most explicit overture to her: 'When is your planned visit to London supposed to take place? Your succession is still vacant.' From this point his letters regularly enquired when she would be coming to Europe. But Jefferies now sounded more ambivalent. She had a new boyfriend and signed off her letters 'your affectionate semi-ex-slave'. All the same, she made it clear that she was prepared to resume her former place in his life. In February 1955 Koestler told her that he was starting a book on Kepler and joked that since it would take two years and not make much money he needed to marry a rich Brazilian widow. Jefferies retorted that what he needed was her. It so happened that at the same time her relationship was breaking up. (Her boyfriend turned out to be 'very complicated, moody and broody'; they often rowed. Jefferies clearly homed in on difficult men.)[83] The resumption of this relationship was another turning-point in Koestler's life. With a false start and some prolonged separations, he was to form his last and most stable partnership. Its inauguration completed the remaking of Arthur Koestler: how deep this went only time would tell.

Chapter 11
Hanging and Science, 1955–60

In the preface to *The Trail of the Dinosaur* Koestler announced his turn from the *vita activa* to the *vita contemplativa*. However, even as he prepared a major work on the history of science he violated his own self-denying ordinance and launched a campaign for the abolition of capital punishment in England. It was a classic Koestlerian crusade: initiated with a noble purpose it was soon marred by quarrels between its author and his no less volatile collaborators. After just a few frenetic months he resigned. Nevertheless, the campaign continued to distract him and, true to form, led him into a convoluted legal battle. In addition to numerous newspaper articles he wrote *Reflections on Hanging* (1956) to propagate the abolitionist message. The book on science, *The Sleepwalkers* (1959), with which he intended to inaugurate his new career, was not finished until spring 1958.

During 1958–9 he made a long tour through India and Japan in pursuit of the elusive religious creed that might nurture social calm and give men access to the 'language of destiny'. The disappointing results were set forth in *The Lotus and the Robot* (1960). The study of Eastern religion and the history of Western science were not as unrelated as they might seem at first sight. *The Sleepwalkers* was the first of a trilogy of scientific works including *The Act of Creation* (1964) and *The Ghost in the Machine* (1967), 'which attempted a scientific analysis of the creativity and pathology of mankind'.[1] By 'pathology' Koestler meant the 'predicament of man', which was, of course, the subject of political thought. Rather than breaking new ground he had returned to the agenda set out in *Insight and Outlook* a decade earlier.

If Koestler had not abandoned politics, but merely changed his approach, nor had he managed to shake off his disturbed life-style. For several weeks in mid-1955 Cynthia Jefferies worked at his side. This arrangement commenced as a temporary expedient, but when she returned to New York she left a vacuum that was quickly and chaotically filled by other women. These affairs reached a brutal climax in the autumn and led Koestler to another breakdown. Sobered by his own violence, he recalled Jefferies from America. From that point she functioned as his permanent secretary, lover, companion, hostess and cook, although at Koestler's insistence she continued to live apart from him. This odd arrangement seemed the only one he could endure.

He did not grow any more sedentary, either. In the summer of 1956 he leased the Lacket, a country house in Wiltshire. Later that year he bought Long Barn, a seventeenth-century farmhouse in Kent, and moved out of Montpelier Square entirely. In the meantime he began the construction of a summer home in the small town of Alpbach in the Austrian Tyrol.

I

In the preface to *Reflections on Hanging* Koestler explained to readers that as someone who had been sentenced to death, but reprieved, each time he heard that a person had been executed he was deeply affected. 'I shall never achieve peace of mind until hanging is abolished.' In June 1953 he had cabled the American President pleading with him to reprieve Julius and Ethel Rosenberg, two Communists found guilty of espionage, even though they represented all that he loathed. He noted bitterly that the Christie trial succeeded the coronation as the latest public spectacle in London. Yet the mood in Britain was swinging against mandatory capital punishment for the crime of murder: several tragic cases in the early 1950s, notably the fate of Derek Bentley and Ruth Ellis, had highlighted the inadequacy of a penal code that did not recognise or take full account of hereditary or psychological factors, or 'crimes of passion'. It was therefore not on a whim that he wrote in his diary on 14 July 1955, 'capital punishment crusade started'.[2]

Initially he hoped to continue work on the book about the sixteenth–seventeenth-century astronomer Johannes Kepler which he had begun to research in the spring. Then in mid-July he wrote to Jefferies, who was in France on holiday with her mother, asking for her help on a second project. She readily abandoned both holiday and mother and in a few days was installed at Montpelier Square taking dictation about the 'Bloody Code'.[3] Koestler spoke with Victor Gollancz soon after, probably to offer him a pamphlet against hanging. Having slept on the idea he suggested to him that it would be preferable to organise a campaign at once, perhaps under the leadership of the Anglican priest Canon John Collins.[4]

The approach to Gollancz was inspired, although not without risks. The two men had seen little of each other since the war years, partly because Koestler found Gollancz intensely irritating. C. H. Rolph, the veteran journalist who collaborated with Koestler on anti-hanging propaganda, recalled that 'he hated Gollancz with all his heart and soul ("I loathed Victor")' because he was 'the Jew who forgave for what he had not endured', probably a reference to Gollancz's post-war polemics in favour of magnanimity towards the German people. Both men had become bullying egomaniacs who could accept little in the way of opposition or disagreement. They both had volcanic tempers. Beneath the carapace of smooth reason they seethed with emotion.[5]

Nevertheless, Gollancz was a superb organiser and at his offices in Henrietta Street had the necessary infrastructure. Within a few weeks he had set up the National Campaign for the Abolition of Capital Punishment (NCACP). It had an executive blending activists of long standing on this issue, establishment figures and publicists including Canon Collins, Gerald Gardiner, a Quaker and a QC, Christopher Hollis, a Conservative MP, Reginald Paget, a Labour MP, Frank Owen and Koestler. Peggy Duff, a long-time associate of Gollancz, acted as secretary. For a while Jefferies helped out, too. Gollancz, who chaired the executive, insisted that his wife also join the committee. Koestler was unhappy about this, since the move was obviously designed to bolster Gollancz's authority, but he backed down from a confrontation for the sake of harmony and to get the campaign going. It was not an auspicious start.[6]

The committee planned to mount an information and propaganda blitzkrieg in support of contemporaneous moves by the Labour MP Sidney Silverman, who had introduced a bill into the House of Commons for the abolition of hanging. (Silverman was omitted from the committee because he and Gollancz could not abide each other.) It was a campaign of which Willi Münzenberg would have been proud. The media, public figures and MPs were to be sent information about the case against hanging. A rally was to be held at Central Hall in November. Meanwhile, the committee and its local branches set about holding smaller meetings and lobbying MPs. Koestler was to contribute his book on hanging while Gerald Gardiner was working on another one. Gollancz, as always once he was fired up, dashed off his own pamphlet.[7]

From the start the committee was divided over tactics. Koestler favoured the most radical action, such as shopkeeper strikes, but failed to press home his arguments. His uncharacteristic reticence was partly due to a consciousness of his status as a 'relative newcomer' in England. He consistently eschewed a public-speaking role because he believed English people would react badly to being told how to behave by a 'foreigner'. Instead he worked demonically to finish *Reflections on Hanging*. It was completed on 3 October and he expected to see it in print very shortly, but to his great frustration Gollancz delayed publication for several months. In that time, he wrote and published his own polemic, *Capital Punishment: The Heart of the Matter*. This presented the case from a 'religious and moral' point of view, which Koestler believed was irrelevant and ineffectual.[8]

In the clash with Gollancz personality was important, but so was policy. Koestler's approach was typical of his political and polemical technique. While he set out to achieve a high moral end, he avoided woolly appeals to ethics and instead combined attention to the 'psychological' factors in decision-making with the claims of expediency. His book was powerfully written, with a constant reiteration of shocking but well-authenticated cases of barbarity. Reading it, one can imagine the ghost of Willy Münzenberg shouting in his ear: 'Hit them, hit them hard!'

Reflections on Hanging begins soberly with an historical account of capital punishment in England and the attempts to abolish it. Koestler established that its persistence rested less on proven effectiveness than on tradition and inertia. This historical analysis was intended to demystify hanging and to show how barbaric it really was. In Koestler's thinking this section was an exercise in 'psychological disarmament'. Historians might quibble over his interpretation of the origins of the 'Bloody Code', but Koestler's aim was to prove that English penal legislation was a human construct instigated to meet a social crisis at a certain juncture in the country's history, and not part of the natural order. He was extremely rude about judges. They were 'ignorant of the forces of heredity and social environment, hostile to any psychological explanation, [had] no faith in humanity [and] frightened men'. Citing their stated fear that if hanging were abolished murderers would roam the land and all values would collapse, he concluded that they were in the grip of an 'anxiety hysteria'. It is little surprise that he dreaded his appearances before the magistracy as a consequence of his abysmal driving.[9]

Turning from the 'psychological' to the pragmatic, he demonstrated with a wealth of statistics that the arguments for hanging were simply wrong. Capital punishment did not act as a deterrent since few murders were premeditated; in the countries in which capital punishment had been abolished, crime rates had not soared. By contrast, Part Two of the book is a curious and rather bemusing excursus into the question of free will and determinism. It illustrates another of his preoccupations, although perhaps not in the best of places.

Koestler held that the retention of hanging was predicated on a fallacious notion of free will or 'criminal responsibility'. This doctrine was crystallised in the so-called 'M'Naghten Rules' which insisted that whereas any other crime admitted of mitigating circumstances due to diminished responsibility, murder did not. Koestler maintained that such an idea of free will was impossible to sustain logically or ethically. It denied all inherited characteristics or the influence of environment. The problem of this argument was that he seemed to be taking a highly deterministic, even behaviourist view of human conduct. In a personal footnote he explained that: 'I think that free will is a fantastic notion, but also that man is a fantastic creature. I believe in the unprovable existence of a factor x, an order of reality beyond physical causation, about whose nature only a negative statement is possible; namely that in its domain the present is *not* determined by the past.' Creation is unfolding continuously according to some inner logic. 'If that be so, the experience of freedom, the possibility of making a choice which is *influenced but not strictly determined* by heredity and environment, would be the subjective reflection of an objective process negating time and injecting moral responsibility into the amoral edifice of nature.'[10] This passage gives an insight into his confused state of thinking and his need to escape from complete fatalism by means of a vapid supernatural explanation of the universe.

The rest of the book was rather less otiose. He boldly argued that hanging was really a form of primitive vengeance which was utterly unacceptable even if one believed in either determinism or free will. He hammered home his case by showing how capital punishment was inherently vulnerable to error. The laws of probability, for example, showed that even if juries were ninety-five per cent certain of a murderer's guilt, this still meant that one in twenty of those hanged would be hanged in error. To persist with an irrevocable sentence presupposed infallibility, a faculty which was denied to mortals.[11]

He was convinced that if the public knew these facts the support for hanging would evaporate. For all his belief in the irrational and 'psychological factors' in politics, Koestler continued to uphold a notion of public sanity, an Enlightenment conviction that reason was a force for good in public affairs.[12] His campaign against capital punishment was also an extension of his belief that social and political systems could be adjusted to contain humanity's destructive nature. This alone makes sense of the concluding lines of the book, where he suggests that the survival of mankind depended on the abolition of hanging. The gallows were a 'symbol of that tendency in mankind which drives it towards moral self-destruction'; ending their use would be a stage in mastery of the 'fur-clad little man in us'.[13] This crusade was at one with his earlier spasms of 'world-saving'. And, like them, it soon turned into farce.

On 10 November the NCACP convened a mass rally in Central Hall. The venue was packed to capacity and hundreds of people crowded into overflow halls. The meeting was addressed by a galaxy of speakers, including the television personality Gilbert Harding, Lord Pakenham, Montgomery Hyde, MP, and J. B. Priestley. Koestler sat on the platform bathed in reflected glory as Gollancz, in his opening address, praised him for initiating the movement. However, the show of unity did not extend beyond the platform. Behind the scenes Koestler was fuming about the delayed publication of *Reflections on Hanging* and openly accusing Gollancz of foul play so that he could get his own pamphlet out first. Gollancz, however, had not unreasonably insisted that Koestler make extensive corrections and changes to avoid libelling certain judges. During the second half of October Koestler had to grit his teeth and rewrite several sections. Those portions of it that were published in the *Observer*, however, gave an immense boost to the movement. David Astor, the editor, was heart and soul behind the campaign and heaped tributes on Koestler for his part in it.[14]

But Koestler was less confident than his bellicose prose would suggest. He had an idea for a series of articles in the paper, each by a famous writer, on a current murder case or aspect of the question. However, he was as reluctant to lead the series as he was to speak in public or broadcast on the radio about hanging. J. B. Priestley, a man who knew Little England better than most, empathised with his reluctance. 'I think he is right,' he told Astor. Advocacy of the abolitionist cause by a foreigner would grate on the public. He hastened to assure Astor that he meant nothing personal by echoing this mild xenophobia: 'I fancy Koestler imagines that I dislike him personally. But while I may have some reservations about some of the things he has written, in fact I have no feelings against him personally. I don't know him.' In the end Priestley failed either to deliver an article by his own hand or to bring in half a dozen other writers. Instead, Koestler offered to write a series of pieces by himself under the *nom de plume* of 'Vigil'.[15]

The *Observer* supplied Koestler with trial transcripts, press association reports and a pass to the House of Commons press gallery. In addition to rebutting the government's defence of capital punishment he sought to expose the barbarity of hanging. One of his most powerful weapons was a Home Office document from 1925, which instructed law officers to conceal from the public any distressing aspects of a hanging. This citation was picked up by supporters of the government who accused Koestler of misquoting the document and violating official confidentiality. He was threatened with contempt of Parliament — a serious charge. Astor and the paper stood by him and it became a typically convoluted business. In the end it was proven that the document had been in the public domain for many years, but that the original version had been slightly altered. Koestler was not to know this because the amended version was, indeed, secret. On 15 March 1956, Lord Mancroft, the Under Secretary of State at the Home Office who had levelled the accusation of a breach of confidentiality, formally apologised to Koestler and the *Observer*.[16]

Astor took immense pride in the role which Koestler and the *Observer* played in the campaign. After the victorious second reading of the private member's bill sponsored by Sidney Silverman, he told Koestler that the 'success was yours more than anyone else's'. He added: 'your "hanging" journalism — the book extracts, the Vigil pieces, and your handling of the attacks — have contributed something of real value to this country and to this newspaper. It is the episode that most deserves to be recorded in the history of this paper since I've been here. I'm very proud of being associated with what you've done.'[17]

By this time Koestler had actually broken with the NCACP. During November and December 1955 he had worked tirelessly, lobbying and writing. He even defied his terror of public speaking to address the Cambridge University Conservative Association. But in February his simmering resentment against Gollancz began to get the better of him. At an NCACP executive he threatened to resign unless Gollancz agreed to support a long-term campaign. He also demanded weekly meetings of the executive to co-ordinate and stimulate activities. Gollancz reluctantly agreed to raise funds for a prolonged campaign, but dug in his heels on the other matters and made it an issue of confidence in his chairmanship. He got his way.

Gollancz, whose span of commitment was even shorter than Koestler's, was loosing interest in the fight. When Silverman's bill passed its second reading on 14 February Gollancz bustled out of the Houses of Parliament in the company of his aides, issuing orders left and right to wind up the campaign. Koestler, however, foresaw that the battle was by no means won: the bill was bound to meet stiff resistance in the Lords. He accosted Gollancz and upbraided him for acting so high-handedly. The two men then stood eye-to-eye raging at each other to the astonishment of passers-by and the embarrassment of their respective friends and supporters. Koestler did not let the matter rest: he returned to the attack at a stormy meeting of the executive on 21 February at which Frank Owen resigned in protest against Gollancz's conduct.[18]

It was clear that the NCACP was not big enough for two such gigantic egos. In mid-March Koestler made it plain to Gollancz that he could no longer sit on the executive while Gollancz was chairman. It was a personal matter between the two men, but he added that he was also disappointed by the methods Gollancz imposed on the campaign and his reluctance to accept that it would be necessary to keep up the pressure on Parliament. Gollancz offered a compromise, but undermined his conciliatory stand by telling Koestler that he was being 'totally unreasonable'. After just four and a half months on the executive, Koestler resigned.[19] This phase of activism had followed exactly the same pattern as all those that preceded it, most recently the Congress for Cultural Freedom.

He did not stop being involved in abolitionist work, but by early May 1956 he was sick and tired of hanging and longed to get back to his work on the history of science. He even went on holiday with Jefferies although the bill was due to get its third reading. In July, as he had predicted, the House of Lords tossed it out. Koestler engaged in a flurry of correspondence with Gardiner, now leading the NCACP, and Astor, but refused to re-enter the fray.[20]

The anti-hanging crusade mirrored Koestler's role in the CCF in other ways. Just as he left the CCF and set up, with his own money, the Fund for Intellectual Freedom, so Koestler entered into the world of penal reform and prisoner care on his own terms and relying on his own resources. In 1959 he opened negotiations with the Home Office to set up an annual award for the best piece of creative work by an inmate of an English prison. Initially he went to C. H. Rolph to act as an intermediary, since he feared that he was *persona non grata* with the authorities. Rolph accompanied him to the Home Office and helped to calm him after a typically bureaucratic encounter. Astor also lent a hand. Eventually, a committee of eight was set up to administer the £400 of prize money which Koestler

provided. The committee included: Koestler, A. D. Peters, Cynthia
Jefferies, Hugh Klare (of the Howard League), John Grigg and his
wife. Peters chaired and acted as a trustee of what became the
Koestler Awards Trust. At various times the judges included Henry
Green, J. B. Priestley, V. S. Pritchett, Philip Toynbee, Sir Kenneth
Clark and Sir Arthur Bliss. By 1981 the Trust, now chaired by Sir
Hugh Casson, had made 4000 awards to prisoners and nurtured
talents that would otherwise have gone to waste.[21]

Koestler's abhorrence of hanging was utterly consistent, unlike
many of his other enthusiasms. In 1960 Israeli agents kidnapped Adolf
Eichmann from Argentina and brought him to Israel to stand trial for
his part in the Holocaust. Jascha Weinshall hoped that the trial would
lure Koestler to Israel, but although he followed it closely in the
newspapers he did not take the bait. He only became animated when
the death sentence was passed on Eichmann by the Israeli court. He
wrote to a colleague: 'I thought from the beginning the whole
Eichmann affair was utterly deplorable. It would have been a
different matter if, after kidnapping him the Israeli Government had
handed him over to Bonn or to the jurisdiction of an International
Court.' Now the Israelis had to reap the bad publicity the sentence
engendered: 'Repressed sadism, ambivalence, guilt-aggression are in
full-bloom. A few friends are trying to organise a petition to Ben-
Gurion at least not to hang Eichmann, but I am sceptical.'[22]

Koestler hoped that the NCACP network might do something.
He wrote to Gerald Gardiner and even called on Gollancz to see if
they could work up a petition. He suggested rather ambitiously that
the NCACP might use a forthcoming rally in the Albert Hall to send
a message to Ben-Gurion, the Israeli Prime Minister: 'It would
demonstrate the campaign's sincerity. It would also do something to
counteract the unfavourable impression that the Eichmann Trial is
making in various ways.' Gollancz, however, was reluctant to get
involved: it was a 'complex' question and he doubted whether any
prominent Jews or rabbis would support a petition. Koestler's initial
scepticism was well founded. 'No luck though,' Jefferies noted in her
diary, 'because it would be difficult to find Jews to sign it.'[23]

II

Jefferies worked by Koestler's side on the hanging book literally day
and night. During the morning in the hot attic study she took
dictation while he paced the room; later she typed up his drafts; in the
afternoon she accompanied him to pubs, where he got into arguments

with publicans; she took more dictation in the evening – always a 'fertile' time for Koestler – and several times jotted down the words he cried out in his sleep as he lay next to her in bed. He was true to his word about canoeing, though, and they had several trips on the River Wey. They went to Cambridge to see Celia Goodman, too, and Jefferies 'discovered' how drunk Koestler could get. He was so inebriated on the drive back to London that they had to abandon the journey and spend the night in a seedy hotel. Jefferies also witnessed more of his operations with women. While she was staying in London that summer Paola visted, as did Janine Graetz. In the latter case Jefferies had the dubious pleasure of turning the tables on an old rival, taking part in one of Koestler's orchestrated French-brothel scenes. She was having such a wonderful time that she delayed her return to New York by ten days to help him finish the first draft of *Reflections*. Shortly before Koestler's fiftieth birthday the time came for another 'sad adieu'. On parting she insisted rather weakly that she had a life in America, which she would not give up that easily, but promised to return if he needed her. She even offered to pay her fare back to London.[24]

As soon as Jefferies had gone Koestler fell into a depression. His birthday pitched him into such a foul mood that he burned all the cards and messages he received. When George Mikes sent him a jolly note to mark the occasion, he snarled back: 'Wait until the same happens to you.' As if to defy the passing years he got involved in several more affairs with women. One of these unfortunates was a woman about half his age, whom he nicknamed 'Kikuyu' because she had been born in Kenya. In anticipation of meetings with her he experienced all the thrills of adolescence and behaved not much better than a teenager. He roughly ejected Robin Maugham from his house in the midst of a drunken soirée for allegedly 'flirting' with his girl-friend. In October, during a visit to Oxford, she incurred his wrath by straying off one night. When she returned to their hotel room he 'half murdered her'. Later in his diary he recalled being 'half crazed' and 'beating her up terribly'. This violent climax marked another 'breakdown' and turning-point. Chastened by his appalling conduct, he resolved to concentrate on his work and to recall Jefferies. On 7 November he cabled her asking if she would return to work for him. Despite financial obligations in New York, she immediately replied that she was preparing to leave. 'I am overwhelmed. What can all this be about?? It sounds so exciting . . . I have spent a night in the clouds – I didn't even sleep.' She would soon find out. Koestler paid off her debts and bought her a ticket to Europe.[25]

But Koestler did not surrender to middle age (and Jefferies) with grace or dignity. Having summoned her, he set off for France to see Sperber and visit Maxime and Anna. He also intended to stay with Paola, who now had a flat in Paris. On the ferry he picked up a woman and slept with her during a stopover on the road to Paris. Later she rejoined him for another gruesome triangular encounter, this time with an ex-girlfriend named Gill. Not unsurprisingly, in view of these goings-on, he had a major fight with Paola. Promiscuity on this scale and at this velocity ceased once Jefferies arrived in London on 22 November.[26]

Their relationship was not a conventional one, however, and it left Koestler plenty of latitude for sleeping around. Jefferies moved into a furnished flat in Thurloe Place, not far from Koestler's house, which she dubbed 'Bachelor Fortress'. It was a peculiar arrangement: on most evenings, even if they dined together, she returned to the flat. But it seemed to function well. He looked for a Jungian analyst, as if finally admitting that he needed external help to control his sudden mood swings and violent temper, although the year ended with the usual alcohol-sodden round of parties and a seasonal brush with the police for drunken driving. He and Jefferies spent Christmas with Celia and Arthur Goodman, establishing a routine that would persist for several years. In his reflections for the new year he noted: 'I am now committed to moderation. But moderation must be moderate, i.e. admit occasional excess, otherwise moderation becomes excessive.'[27]

III

Although Koestler had revised *Reflections on Hanging* and sent it off at the end of October 1955, the first months of 1956 were dominated by more writing on the subject. Between January and April he published several articles as 'Vigil' and a substantial piece on the outcome of the free vote on abolition in the House of Commons on 19 February 1956.[28] He did not get back to the history of science until March. Then there were more disturbances, mainly connected with his women friends. Paola briefly visited London, which was pleasant enough. His relations with Graetz, however, had been reduced to a cash nexus and there was much correspondence with his solicitor to sort out the financial loose ends of their liaison. Rather more seriously, in the middle of the month it became apparent that Jefferies was pregnant.

Koestler was happy to tolerate other people's children for short periods, mainly in holiday situations, and took a benevolent interest in the offspring of close friends like Celia Goodman. But he certainly didn't want any of his own. He had made it clear to Mamaine that he regarded children as an unwanted burden and many years later he told an old girlfriend: 'I have always preferred dogs to bambinos.' So Cynthia Jefferies, like Anny and Elizabeth Jane Howard before her, had an abortion. Since abortion was illegal in England at the time, in his diary Koestler referred to Jefferies suffering from 'food poisoning'. In fact, she had to endure something far worse than that. She went to a place 'north of Hyde Park' where she was ushered into a makeshift operating theatre and 'held down' while the abortion was carried out. It was a 'nightmare'.[29]

It does not seem to have occurred to Koestler, who preached that the end does not justify the means, least of all where this involved taking human life, and who crusaded against judicial murder, to ask whether there was not something of a contradiction here. As a keen student of the biological sciences he might have considered the possibility that aborting a foetus was the termination of a living organism even if it need not be described emotively as a form of murder. Indeed, in *The Lotus and the Robot* he did inveigh against abortion. He considered the fall in the Japanese birth rate consequent on the permeation of European culture to be one of the worst aspects of the country's break-neck modernisation: 'the result is the slaughter of the unborn with its concomitant ill-effects on women.'[30] His solicitude for the distant women of Japan does not seem to have extended to those females closest to him. His comment on abortion is a grotesque example of hypocrisy. What is unclear is whether it was facilitated by conscious duplicity or self-deception.

Until May, research and writing on the book advanced steadily. But Koestler's life was never peaceful. When he was not buried in work he had to be surrounded by people and commotion. Unlike Cyril Connolly, for example, he was not adept at doing nothing in particular. He regularly worked right up to Christmas and over the New Year holidays. Vacations usually had to be combined with a journalistic assignment to stave off feelings of uselessness and guilt. On Sundays, too, he had to keep busy. Typically, he would meet Henry Green at their favourite pub in the morning. Then he would have a sociable lunch, often a grisly assembly of ex-lovers, followed by a siesta and a frenzied evening. Jefferies noted that after his snooze he would wake up with a 'craving' for company and 'if by chance we were alone, he turned the force of his despair on me'. Koestler had few inner resources. It was as if he had no self on which to fall back when he was alone, or a self that he could face.[31]

His restlessness persisted. In February Wayland Young, the future Lord Kennet and a junior minister in the 1966–70 Labour government, invited him to his Wiltshire country home, the Lacket, near Marlborough. The house was rich with literary associations and drenched in a certain kind of Englishness: Lytton Strachey had written *Eminent Victorians* there. Koestler fell for it and Young agreed to let him use the place for a 'retreat' over the summer. Koestler had been in Montpelier Square for under four years, but he was already searching for a house elsewhere.[32]

At the start of May, Jefferies and Koestler set off on holiday together. The plan was to drive to the Dordogne, then canoe down the river through the country that Koestler had roamed in 1940. As usual, both Koestler and the car were tanked up. He drank champagne at 10 a.m. on the ferry, had a lunch accompanied by wine and brandy in Boulogne, then stopped for coffee and rum in the afternoon. The straight French roads might have been designed to receive him in this condition. The next day began likewise with an 'early morning drink' and further infusions of alcohol to sustain him as he passed through Melun and the areas associated with his residence at Verte Rive with Mamaine. They reached Beaulieu-sur-Dordogne on the third day. Once they set off on the river they followed a more abstemious routine. By day they canoed and picnicked modestly; in the evening they donned casual outfits and sauntered into a local hotel carrying their bags and paddles. On 9 May they celebrated Jefferies's twenty-ninth birthday at an hotel in Souillac, deep in the Périgord region. They drank so much wine and local *digestif* that they meandered out of the dining-room as crazily as the river flowed. But as long as Koestler could work off these excesses in physical exercise he felt anxiety-free and recovered fairly quickly. Although Jefferies spotted grey strands in his hair, he was managing to contain middle-aged spread. Fit and tanned, clad in his sports jacket and flannels from Simpson's or Harrods he cut quite a figure. Jefferies radiated pride to be with him: it was all she wanted out of life.[33]

In the summer, they moved to the Lacket. Attila, Koestler's latest dog and the second of that name, loved the countryside round and about; but Jefferies was brought low with hay fever. Koestler started writing up his research on Kepler, only to find it necessary to add chapters on Copernicus. He became increasingly worried about the dimensions of the book: it got longer and longer. Who was going to read it? Like all his 'retreats', this one was broken up by sociable interludes. Visitors were useful in other ways, too, since they brought supplies of Continental food obtainable only in London, and Koestler was an unhappy man without a regular intake of Polish garlic sausage, smoked cheese and cheesecake. The Lacket, once so 'English', was now home to an eminent and spasmodically gregarious Hungarian.

Frances Partridge, the diarist and veteran of the Bloomsbury set, recalled one of these visitations in her diary. She and her husband Ralph lived in a cottage at Ham Spray, which was nearby, and were invited to dinner along with Pauline and Sylvester Gates – 'a very clever, hard headed man' who combined cultural pursuits with the law and banking. 'The evening became rather uproarious, but I don't think the better of Koestler after it. He is an aggressively male man who likes to have subjugated, pretty women and fawning dogs about him. After dinner he began lecturing us all on relativity in an unconvincing and boring way . . . It was a supremely arrogant performance.' He got on to ESP, about which Ralph Partridge had read widely, but when his guest took a different point of view waved him aside: 'he would brook no disagreement.'[34]

They returned to London in mid–September, but the Lacket had revived Koestler's taste for rural isolation. On a drive through the Kent countryside he saw a property for sale and impulsively bought it. Long Barn was a converted and 'modernised' seventeenth-century farmhouse near Sevenoaks in Kent. The main L-shaped, two-storey building looked gorgeous and was set in beautiful gardens, with a fine lawn tucked into the L. There were also outhouses and service buildings, including chicken houses that were still in use. Montpelier Square was leased for three years and they moved into Long Barn at the end of October. Koestler joked to Margarete Buber–Neumann that he intended 'to live henceforth in the boredom of nature'. However, the attractive exterior concealed a mass of problems: Koestler had learned nothing from his experiences at Island Farm and Ischia. As soon as it got cold they realised that the lack of central heating was a serious deficiency. The place was also too big for just one couple. Koestler thought of dividing it into two self-contained units, and tried to interest Margaret Storm Jameson and Guy Chapman in taking the other half, but they turned down the offer. Before long, he was being plagued by the cold and loneliness.[35]

In October–November 1956 he was briefly drawn back into politics by the turmoil in Hungary. Since Stalin's death the Hungarian Communist leadership had pursued a more liberal line and after Khrushchev denounced Stalin's malign rule the road seemed open to abandoning the Stalinist system altogether. However, the local reformist leadership under Imre Nagy found it had unleashed pent-up feelings of hostility not just against Communism but Russia as well, which had troops stationed in Hungary. Borne along by a tide of liberated public opinion, the government edged towards withdrawal from the Warsaw Pact. This was too much for the Soviet leadership, which ordered its forces to move on Budapest. After days of street fighting in October the Red Army pulled out, pending negotiations. The withdrawal was a feint. The tanks returned and bloodily suppressed the uprising, the reformist leaders were rounded up and shot, while tens of thousands of refugees streamed into Austria.[36]

Koestler was a horrified spectator to these events. Notwithstanding his 1956 oath of abjuration, he indulged in a burst of activism. George Mikes later recalled that early on the morning of 24 October Koestler invited him to join a party of Hungarians who were going to attack the Hungarian legation in London. Mikes told him not to be a fool and proposed organising a protest meeting instead. Koestler was angry that his heroic gesture was treated so rudely, and tossed several bricks through the legation windows in any case. He, Mikes, Zoltán Szabo and Judith Károlyi then worked together to arrange a mass meeting in Denison Hall, Victoria. It was a great success: hundreds attended to hear speeches of varying length and quality from a cast mainly summoned up by Koestler — Henry Green, J. B. Priestley, Sir Jacob Epstein and Hugh Seton-Watson. Green was pathetic and embarrassing. Seton-Watson and Mikes were most pertinent. Koestler ignored adulatory applause and merely said that he was no longer willing to speak on political matters.

Characteristically, he did more effective work in private to help the refugees. He contacted friends in PEN, co-operated with the Sevenoaks Refugee Committee and sent substantial sums to the Hungarian Relief Fund. He also came up with a rather hare-brained scheme to go to Budapest with a group of Western intellectuals to try to mitigate the terror. This was dismissed by Storm Jameson as 'play acting'. She was not to know that Koestler was actually reverting to an idea that had seized him in 1944 when he was trying to save the Hungarian Jews from the Nazis.[37]

At the end of the year, Koestler and Jefferies spent a few days in Cornwall with friends, the St Aubyns, then drove to Cambridge to stay with Celia Goodman and her family. He worked all the way up to New Year's Eve. One of his last journalistic tasks of 1956 was to select his books of the year. He chose *Pincher Martin* by William Golding, the second year in succession that he had picked a Golding novel. Golding was commensurably flattered and they began to correspond occasionally. He was one of the few post-war novelists for whom Koestler had any respect, perhaps because they shared such a bleak perspective on human nature. His tastes were increasingly conservative and he looked on the 'Angry Young Men' writers of the mid- and late 1950s with contempt: 'Among the Angry Young Man–beat generation to go to bed is an act of existential despair; not one of love but of protest. You lug the gin sodden little slag to the bed sitter, do a quick Lucky-Jim, with a grimace in the dark, and look back in anger at the dim performance.'[38]

Conversely, changing tastes affected him. In 1956 the first major book-length study on Koestler appeared, written by John Atkins, a British-born academic who taught in the Sudan. It was badly reviewed, which Koestler took to indicate that he had fallen out of favour. 'I suppose you have to foot the bill for my unpopularity,' he consoled Atkins. Was Koestler being oversensitive? Atkins's book was rather odd. It was shot through with neo-Marxist thinking and was as much about his own thoughts on the crisis of Western civilisation and the need for European unity as it was about Koestler.[39] Yet the mood of the reading public in Britain and the United States was shifting and writers of Koestler's generation were finding it hard to adapt. After the years of struggle against the Nazis and the onset of the Cold War, the appetite for ideologies and novels of ideas waned. Many writers of the Left deserted 'The God That Failed' and thereby lost their muse. 'Mandarin' authors, formed by the public schools and Oxbridge, found society changing as a consequence of the war and the introduction of the welfare state, and were equally disorientated. Many commentators, including Koestler, identified a crisis in fiction writing.[40]

Novelists like Henry Green and Graham Greene responded to the turn from politics by focusing on personal relations and individual dilemmas. Others like Evelyn Waugh, Laurence Durrell and Anthony Powell produced novel series which, like L. P. Hartley's writing, featured ruminations on childhood, schooldays and youth before 1945. Explicitly political writers of the here and now like Koestler were increasingly isolated. Their very fate provoked intro-spection and autobiographical oeuvres.[41] Koestler had anticipated this movement by abandoning the novel and sinking his teeth into autobiography in the early 1950s. But as one who, by his own lights, was identified with the 'Pink Generation', his star was waning.

IV

In 1958 Koestler hit the headlines again, but for a reason he would have preferred to avoid. In January he was arrested in Greenwich, *en route* from Long Barn to London, for reckless driving and driving under the influence of alcohol. Koestler elected to stand trial and pleaded that the incident 'was apparently caused by the combined effects of an acute virus infection, of which I was unaware, and an ambitious young policeman'. Remarkably, in view of his disgraceful record for dangerous driving, he was acquitted after his jury trial in the following June.[42]

For the next few months, however, he behaved in a contrite and sober fashion. He worked steadily on the science book and the American edition of *Reflections on Hanging*, which included the 'Vigil' articles and a new epilogue. His reward came in June when he and Jefferies left for a canoeing holiday on the Loire. They drove to Paris and spent several days there seeing old friends. On 12 June they reached Nevers and unpacked their Canadian kayak. They paddled for six or seven hours each day, but consumed glorious lunches comprising local delicacies. Each evening they dined on the grand scale, consuming a bottle of wine before dinner, two more with the meal, followed by a liqueur with their coffee. At Orleans they took a two-day break and returned to Nevers by train. They picked up the car, drove back to Orleans and started again, continuing for a second week as far as Saumur. They rounded off the trip with a stay in Concarneau in Brittany, where they took the kayak on to the ocean.

Koestler's amusing account of the journey was published in the *Observer* in August. It is interesting for a sidelight it throws on the author's personality. Koestler reiterated his resignation in the face of English culinary obduracy and insularity, and wrote about France, French culture and food with the appearance of an insider. Yet he was, in effect, a tourist. The closer he came to a culture or a country, the more he objectified it and alienated himself from it. His precise and frequently unflattering analysis often had the effect of annoying the 'natives' and giving concrete reality to this estrangement. Koestler could not, or would not, feel at ease anywhere.[43]

Reinvigorated by the trip he resumed his struggle to shape *The Sleepwalkers*, the title he gave to his biography of Kepler, which had now become a study of scientific discovery. But he soon broke off to give a lecture at the Austrian College in Alpbach, at the invitation of its director Dr Fritz Molden. The College was founded in 1946 by Dr Alexander Auer, an anti-Nazi Austrian. Its object was to strengthen the democratic, internationalist elements in Austrian society and to build links with Western Europe. Each year from 1945, Auer and Molden had convened a European Forum of intellectuals in Alpbach, a small ski resort in the Tyrol, which had a number of hotels and guest-houses available for putting up participants during the summer. Molden described their aims as 'the collection of an intellectual and political élite which was to be formed to embrace science, politics and art, in order to create the idea of an "honnête homme" of the 20th century who would be of the widest education and culture and capable of harmonising thought and action. This person was to be the foundation of the intellectual and political unification of Europe.' It was a project that naturally appealed to Koestler. He was impressed by Molden and Auer, and enraptured both by the spirit of the college and its location. The visit began an association with Alpbach that lasted over a decade.[44]

While he was away, Jefferies did her best to cope with Attila the dog, 220 hens, a huge house and no domestic help. The difficulties of maintaining Long Barn now began to oppress Koestler and were compounded by the usual cavalcade of visitors: James Putnam, the Willerts, Moura Budberg, Patrick Gordon Walker, MP, and his wife Audrey, the novelist John Wain, the architect Sir Martyn Beckett and his wife Priscilla, and the Lousadas. After the last of the summer guests had gone he worked like a maniac to revise the first draft of *The Sleepwalkers*. He rose at 8 a.m., had tea and toast, and was at his desk half an hour later. He had a 'snack lunch' at 1 p.m. followed by a siesta or odd jobs until three o'clock, when he would work for another four hours. At about 7.30 p.m. he ended the working day with a very large drink.[45]

Long Barn was freezing that winter and they took refuge in the West Country, seeing various friends. In February, Koestler went to Vienna for a week to deliver a lecture to the European Press Congress. But his chief concern was to complete the book. He was now getting into a typical panic, driving himself and Jefferies even harder. As he was extremely nervous about its potential reception he consulted widely. Through Celia Goodman he made contact with Sir Herbert Butterfield, Master of Peterhouse and author of one of the first histories of science. Butterfield invited Koestler to dine at High Table in Peterhouse, an initiative which Koestler feared his host might have regretted. Such environments put Koestler on the defensive and triggered his inferiority complex. He reacted with a mixture of excitability, aggression and bombast. Afterwards he sent Butterfield a note to thank him, adding: 'I hope my continental intensity didn't wear you down.' The letter betrayed the chip on his shoulder: he relished the experience of dining in Cambridge, although it was 'mingled with the regret of having missed being an undergraduate in England. But Vienna had its points.'[46]

The final draft of *The Sleepwalkers* was completed on 28 February 1958. Koestler then sent portions of the book to friends and colleagues for expert scrutiny. Stuart Hampshire, a reader for Hutchinson, read the entire work and gave it a clean bill of health. To add the last piece of armour plating Koestler asked Butterfield to write an introduction. Butterfield tried to persuade him that the book didn't need one, but consented to 'show alliance in this way, if you wish it'. He finally produced a masterfully ambiguous text, which praised the author while making it clear that he was not in agreement with much of the book's content. Koestler tried to get him to change the wording, but Butterfield politely refused.[47]

The Sleepwalkers was far more than a chapter in the history of science, as Butterfield realised. It was laced with Koestler's own theories about creativity and propagated an essentially political message about the predicament of man. He hoped that the book would blend science and the humanities, identified by C. P. Snow as 'the two cultures', not least because he believed that the rupture was partly responsible for the crisis of mankind. Copernicus, Kepler and Galileo, the major subjects of the study, had wrecked 'the medieval vision of an immutable social order in a walled-in universe together with its fixed hierarchy of moral values, and transformed the European landscape, society, culture, habits and general outlook, as thoroughly as if a new species had arisen on this planet'. By disrupting the account of the universe constructed by the Church fathers they had inadvertently sundered faith from reason and religion from science. Humanity was still reeling from the consequences. Finally, Koestler took these three towering figures of astronomy as case studies in creative thinking. He would also show that scientific progress did not follow a straight line, but moved erratically and often in defiance of all logical thought. Their intellectual odysseys threw light on the working of the mind and might indicate if and how a new 'mutation' of consciousness could occur. [48]

To prove his point about the zig-zag advance of knowledge he began by showing how the Greeks had wrecked the correct heliocentric model of the universe pioneered by the Babylonians and the Egyptians. His villains were Plato and Aristotle, whose ideal universe was geocentric and static. Its mystical and hierarchical nature made it appealing to the Church fathers, most notably Augustine, and for the next two thousand years human intellect was divided between faith and reason. Astronomers wrestled to make the movements of the planets fit the system bequeathed by Aristotle.[49]

The first thinker to challenge the old mental map of the universe was Copernicus, although that was never his intention. Koestler had great fun showing that Copernicus was far from resembling a modern, rational and empirical scientist. Nor was he a martyr to ignorance or religious fanaticism: on the contrary, he was a cleric whose whole career was lived within the confines of the Church. His greatest apprehension was ridicule: he was a coward. However, his half-baked theories did offer fellow thinkers and future generations a notion of the universe as infinite rather than bounded, decentred the earth from planetary motions, and demonstrated that the earth was itself in motion.[50]

Copernicus had little immediate impact. But his work did touch Johannes Kepler, the figure who inspired *The Sleepwalkers* and with whom Koestler identified intensely. Kepler had a poor, miserable childhood. His story was the 'timeless case history of the neurotic child from a problem family . . . How familiar it all is: the bragging, defiant, aggressive pose to hide one's terrible vulnerability; the lack of self-assurance; the dependence on others; the desperate need for approval, leading to an embarrassing mixture of servility and arrogance; the pathetic eagerness for play, for an escape from the loneliness . . . exaggerated standards applied to one's own moral conduct which turns life into a long series of falls into the ninefold inferno of guilt.' Kepler used work as a therapy. He was drawn to working with older men whom he admired and wished to undermine at the same time: he was 'a tortured adolescent, begging to be forgiven by a father whom he hates and loves'. He also had a streak of adventurousness and a penchant for horoscopes: he was a determinist. It was no wonder that Koestler wrote in his diary that 'K=K'.[51]

Like Copernicus, Kepler set out to rescue the medieval world order from the mathematical and empirically observed incoherence to which it was prone: the impetus was irrational and obscurantist. But his use of precise measurement and observation led away from the dogmatic, a priori concepts of the Neoplatonist schoolmen. When the geocentric model did not fit observed reality, he simply scrapped it. Through studying the motion of Mars he stumbled on the principle of gravity.[52]

Kepler was impressed by the discoveries of his contemporary Galileo and wanted to use the telescopes he designed, which had transformed astronomy. However, Galileo snubbed him. Koestler did not like Galileo and the last part of the book is devoted to debunking him. He demonstrated that Galileo, who began his career as a protégé of the Papacy and the Jesuit Order, fell foul of the Holy See only when arrogance and vanity drove him to lampoon the very men who safeguarded his work. Galileo's persecution, dubbed the 'scandal of Christendom', was nothing of the kind; but the myth of the Church suppressing free thought did permanent damage by driving apart the religious spirit and the scientific ethos.[53]

Koestler ended the tome, which ran to over six hundred pages, with a chapter on the implications of his three case studies. He reiterated, in anticipation of Thomas Kuhn and others, that the progress of science and human knowledge in general did not follow a smooth, linear path. It seemed more like 'natural selection', with weird mutations and abrupt leaps of development. He attributed this to a quirk of human evolution which engendered mankind with a capacious brain that it had not yet learned to utilise fully. He then speculated on the patterns of discovery, using the structures presented in *Insight and Outlook*.

In his view all mental leaps followed a pattern of regression prior to an advance. Religion was not intrinsically backward. Yet the popular image developed of the scientist working in opposition to religion: morality and science were deemed to operate in different fields. This perception was heightened by the development of atomic physics and the growing unintelligibility of science. The consequence was political:

> The Philosophy of Nature became ethically neutral, and 'blind' became the favourite adjective for the working of natural law . . . As a result, man's destiny was no longer determined from 'above' by a super-human wisdom and will, but from 'below' by the sub-human agencies of glands, genes, atoms, or waves of probability. This shift of the locus of destiny was decisive. So long as destiny had operated from a level of the hierarchy higher than man's own, it had not only shaped his fate, but also guided his conscience and imbued his world with meaning and value. The new masters of destiny were placed lower in this scale than the being they controlled; they could determine his fate, but could provide him with no moral guidance, no values and meaning.[54]

As if to underline the essentially political drive in this conclusion, Koestler quoted his own words making the same point in *The Yogi and The Commissar*.

The last pages of the book were a tocsin. Man had now acquired the means to destroy the planet. Evolution had granted him a technological capacity far in excess of his spiritual capabilities. 'Thus within the foreseeable future, man will either destroy himself or take off for the stars.' Scientists and non-scientists should heed the message of *The Sleepwalkers* that spirituality and science need not be compartmentalised, before it was too late.[55]

The exertions of the spring and summer had taken their toll of Koestler's health. In mid-May he had to have a hernia operation, which put him out of action for a week. By the beginning of the summer he was exhausted.[56] But at last he could look forward to a long break. On 25 July, he and Jefferies put the car on the 'air ferry' to Le Touquet and set off for Alpbach, where Koestler planned to buy a plot of land and build a summer home.

Alpbach boasted several comfortable Tyrolean guest-houses including the Alpbacherhof and the Böglerhof. The surrounding countryside was ideal for walking. Munich, Innsbruck, Salzburg and northern Italy were all within convenient motoring distance. Koestler could have stayed annually in any one of the hotels, as was the habit of many summer visitors, but he had a compulsion to buy land and property. Every time he did so the experience ended tearfully and Alpbach was no exception. The negotiations for the purchase of land were endless. He quarrelled so violently with the architect he had commissioned that blows were exchanged and he ended up in the local police station.

Even though he hoped to do some writing, he made arrangements to see old friends while he was at the Böglerhof. They included old women friends, some of Berlin vintage, like Eva Schrödinger, and some more recent acquisitions. This was a volatile mixture and, sure enough, after a few days he was enveloped by quarrels which he bizarrely attributed to the 'lesbian' tendencies of his visitors. He contributed to the tempestuous atmosphere by getting drunk almost every night. Inexorably, by mid-August he had descended into a post-book depression. The commencement of building at the end of the month provided a moment of elation, but quickly added new worries as he fretted over every detail. What should have been a peaceful summer became an alpine nightmare. In September they returned to England, but Koestler did not stay for very long.[57]

In December he set off on a three-month tour of India and Japan in pursuit of answers to the questions he had been asking since 1944 and which cropped up again in *The Sleepwalkers*. One leitmotif was the interconnection of science and religion, but Koestler was not just interested in unravelling the nexus in order to clarify the history of science. He was fascinated by the way in which individual thinkers like Pythagoras, Kepler and Copernicus, and their disciples, could entirely reshape human consciousness: 'A study of the evolution of cosmic awareness in the past may help to find out whether a new departure is at least conceivable, and on what lines.' In other words, he was still on the track of the saints–revolutionaries who would provide the new religion or 'cosmic awareness' that would enable mankind to transcend its 'predicament'. He now hoped to find living examples in the East.

V

Koestler flew to Zurich, arriving on Christmas Eve, and stayed for four days to meet his Swiss publishers and check on progress with the house at Alpbach – although it was hard to evaluate since the site was covered with snow and slush. He reached Bombay on 30 December 1958 and plunged into a heavy round of receptions, lectures and research trips. Indian intellectuals greeted him with the same kind of intensity and adulation (or criticism, depending on their political standpoint) that he had met in France in 1946 and in America in 1947. Communism was still a live issue in India. The country was beset by mammoth economic and social problems to which the local Communists offered Marxist solutions. They actually held power in the important state of Kerala. Communist China bordered India to the north and represented a different kind of threat. Indian intellectuals who had avidly devoured Koestler's writings swarmed over him at parties, official functions and public addresses.[58]

He told Jefferies ten days after arrival: 'I am enjoying it madly, and miraculously am not tired. Perhaps it is the excitement, perhaps being on the waggon [sic] helps and gives an additional virtuous boost. Since there is prohibition and you only get, as a foreigner, one bottle (of whisky) per week, which just wets [sic] the appetite, I decided to scrap drink altogether the day after I landed. Very odd how I don't miss it. Must have something to do with the climate (80° to 90° but air conditioning) or with the spicy curries. Whatever it is, it solves a major headache.'[59]

In addition to meetings for research purposes, in the first week in Bombay he spoke at a PEN reception, gave an address for the Congress for Cultural Freedom and a lecture at the university. He was also reacquainted with Ellen Roy, a Berlin-born Jewish woman who was 'still kittenish' and a 'hysteric despite her impressive achievements'. While in Bombay he was oppressed by the overcrowding, the filth and the squalor of the 700,000 street people. The casual acceptance of their plight disgusted him. On 9 January he went by plane to Madras and in the following eight weeks criss-crossed the continent flying in ancient Dakotas, bumping along dirt roads in jeeps and watching the country-side slide by from the windows of antiquated steam trains.

In Madras he visited the university and local temples and inter-viewed the Sankaracharya of Kanchi, leader of one of the 'orthodox' Hindu sects. On 13 January he flew to Trivandrum in the Com-munist-run state of Kerala. Here he had an audience with the swami Krishna Menon Atamanda. But he was unimpressed and having been evicted from his hotel room due to a misunderstanding left after only three days. He returned to Bombay and from there travelled 200 miles north by train and Land-Rover into Rajasthan to seek Acharya Vinoba Bhave, the first of the 'saints'. Vinoba, an early follower of Gandhi, was the founder of the Bhoodan movement which since Indian Independence had persuaded wealthy landowners to give away millions of acres to the landless poor. After less than a week in this poverty-stricken and remote region, he returned to Bombay. In pursuit of yogis and research into yoga, he then went to Lonvala, near Poonah, in the hills south-east of the city. To meet his fourth 'saint', Anandamayee Ma, he travelled first to Benares in the north-east, then to Calcutta, Assam and Bihar between 4 and 18 February. He stayed for several days with the academic Dr Verrier Elwin in Shillong, followed by a visit to the ashram of Jayaprakash (J.P.) Narayan, a former leader of the Indian Socialist Party and a founder of the Indian CCF, near Patna in Bihar. While he was in Calcutta he gave a talk to a symposium on 'Belief and Literature'. Before he left he spent a few glorious days in the foothills of the Himalayas around Darjeeling.[60]

He published his controversial conclusions about India in *The Lotus and the Robot* in 1960. It was largely based on the notes he kept while travelling although, as always with his reportage, the published and private versions diverged when the needs of artistry prevailed over those of veracity. The book was difficult to write because he had made many friends in India, but had harsh things to say about what he saw there. He admired Vinoba's achievement, but saw that his success was fostered by local landowners and the government in order to undermine Communism. His main achievement was to neutralise Communist guerrillas in the region. The other 'saints' left him cold after a short while. Menon preached a system of belief which claimed to lead to the complete collapse of distinctions between the self and the surrounding world. This was symptomatic of the Eastern way of blurring symbol and reality, a world view that had prevailed in the West in pre-Renaissance times. Even if it were

true it could not be translated into Western language, let alone
Western thought. Koestler found the Sankaracharya, the representative of orthodox Hinduism, the most objectionable. His response to
questions was rigid and arrogant, and what he had to say was so at
odds with visible reality as to be useless. The fourth 'saint' was a
woman who ran ashrams all over India. Having squatted at her feet
while she received the devotion of her followers, he retreated in
dismay at what he saw as the degradation, dirt and charlatanry
inherent to her preaching and her followers.[61]

He was no more impressed by his research into yoga. The medical
claims for the practice were untenable. He could find no proof of
supernatural occurrences brought about by meditation, even though
he put his interlocutors at ease by reassuring them that he believed in
telepathy. Whatever he saw could be explained by Western medicine
or psychology. As for the mental state which yoga purported to
induce, he dismissed this as being 'an exercise in death'. In a letter
home he told Jefferies: 'The religious side is disappointing (Hinduism
has degenerated from a philosophy to elementary idolatry and crass
superstition) but the non-orthodox have a special vision and depth
unknown to Europe. It is, alas, I think never exportable.' He thought
he had met a few genuine holy men: they had 'smiles that made me
weep'.[62]

In between, he was engaged in numerous formal events in the
main cities and their universities. Despite forming a close friendship
with J.P. Narayan, he developed a dim view of Indian society and
politics, not unlike the process that occurred during his visit to Israel
in 1948 and for not dissimilar reasons. In his eyes Indian democracy
was a sham, an inappropriate Western system and shibboleth superimposed on a rigid, hierarchical, authoritarian society. The real
influences on the continent were Hinduism and the Hindu family,
which created father-like gods and god-like fathers, reducing all
others to mindless obedience. Hinduism was 'the root of the spiritual
and social crisis, the tragic predicament of India'.[63] In mid-February
when Koestler sat in the Himalayas taking stock, he wrote to
Jefferies: 'I feel that these seven weeks in India were more rewarding
than I expected and will bear fruit in various ways.' The insight was
largely negative: yet again he had been rid of an illusion. A year later
he concluded in *The Lotus and the Robot* that if the West had little to
offer India, then India 'has no spiritual cure to offer for the evils of
Western civilisation'.[64]

Koestler flew to Japan via Hong Kong, where he broke the flight
for two days. In addition to some meetings with local academics and

journalists, he went shopping and had some clothes made. He arrived in Tokyo on 24 February and proceeded to International House, where he stayed most of the time. The visit to Japan was no less frenetic. It included the 'same round of receptions, speeches, parties, and sometimes quite acrimonious struggle to squeeze in an hour of privacy'. For the first few days he stayed put and wrote up some of his thoughts and observations on India. The highlight of this period was a brush with the Japanese PEN, which blew up into a major incident. He was scheduled to address a PEN–CCF meeting in Tokyo which had been arranged long in advance. But he discovered to his fury that the Japanese branch of PEN had recently issued a statement 'condoning the muzzling of Pasternak'. He cancelled his lecture and let his hosts know what he thought of them in an open letter carried on the front page of a national newspaper on 2 March. Mike Josselson was deeply embarrassed by this: 'The SOB has given us a black eye,' he said. But Koestler hoped that it would do some good by alerting the CCF to the influence of pro-Soviet leftists even within its own ranks. He crowed to Jefferies a few days later: 'local controversy ended with complete rout of enemy – now peace and quiet are returning.'[65]

On 8 March he began his touring: to Yokohama, Kyoto, Osaka, Nagasaki and the Unzen Amahusen national park on Kyushu in the south. He spent the last ten days in a retreat on the Miura Peninsula, south of Tokyo, writing an article on India and compiling his observations on Japan. Koestler did not take to the Japanese as he did to certain Indians like Narayan. When Robin Maugham asked if he could suggest some interesting and nice Japanese to meet on a forthcoming trip to Japan, Koestler responded: 'There are no Japs on my list. They are hardly worth talking to – except the bar maidens.' He saw plenty of those. During the days he spent in Tokyo he visited night-clubs almost daily and experimented with a 'Geisha House'. He enjoyed the juvenile 'cockteasers' in geisha attire and not so attired: one of his few pleasures in Japan was naked mixed bathing.[66]

As usual, Koestler stumbled on a congenial drinking partner. The British journalist Quentin Crewe happened to be based in Tokyo and was a stand-by when it came to the bars. Inevitably there was at least one punch-up. Koestler and Crewe were in a Kabuki bar accompanied by Dr Ivan Morris, an American expert on Japanese culture, and his wife Yaki. When the bar owner started flirting with Yaki Morris, Koestler took upon himself the role of Galahad and threw whisky in the man's face. Another time Crewe had to stop Koestler hitting an annoying local journalist. [67]

In writing about Japan, as about India, Koestler displayed an awesome familiarity with local history and culture. To a large extent this was the result of his careful preparation for the trip in the autumn of 1958. There is more than a hint that he had made up his mind before he arrived and interpreted what he saw in the light of his prior reading. This seems most glaring in his analysis of Zen, which relies more on published works than the interviews he conducted with Zen abbots through the mediation of translators he neither trusted nor understood. He treated Zen Buddhism as a vast scam: 'the ultimate evasion'. In extolling the perfection of the act for its own sake (regardless of what it was), its advocates were reduced to spouting 'drivel'. The only role it played was to release Japanese people from oppressive social codes: it offered absolutely no ethical guidance. 'This impartial tolerance towards the killer and the killed; a tolerance devoid of charity, makes me sceptical regarding the contribution which Zen Buddhism has to offer to the moral recovery of Japan — or any other country.'[68]

He argued that the Japanese response to the West was determined by the deep cultural patterns engendered by the hegemony of Buddhism, Confucianism and Shinto. These mental structures were reinforced by the psychological effect of living in an earthquake zone. The Japanese externalised their apprehension of natural disaster by parodying nature in the form of bonsai gardens, deliberately miniaturising and warping nature. They did the same to human nature through education and conditioning, subjecting people to rigid social codes that controlled all conduct. This made life potentially unbearable. It was softened by a habit of ambiguity in language and gesture that enabled an individual to guard against offending another person and humiliating him- or herself. Anything hard and fast was shunned, an attitude of mind sanctioned by the local religions. 'To gain approval and avoid censure is all there is to ethics, because a transcendental system of values does not exist.'[69]

The only redeeming feature of Japan was the very absence of a reconciliation between East and West, of any synthesis between hedonism and stoicism. Koestler argued that the Japanese had never reconciled competition with 'saving face' or individualism with the hierarchical society: they merely set the two systems side by side, negotiating between them using ambiguity. This evidently appealed to a streak in his own character, which found it impossible to reach a compromise between the Spartan life-style and the sybaritic one. It was some kind of answer to the Orwellian reproach, which he never shook off.[70]

Back in England, Jefferies was winding up their tenancy of Long Barn and taking advantage of her free time to see Alan McGlashan, a Jungian analyst who was also a friend of Koestler. The sessions helped her to confront the legacy of her father's suicide, although they were no advertisement for the efficacy of psychoanalysis. She realised how her father's suicide had left a void that she filled by worshipping older men. The corollary of this was that she played up the 'childish and submissive' side of her nature. 'You, of course, know all this,' she wrote childishly and submissively to Koestler. In a similar vein, when he reproached her for not writing for several days, she replied: 'I'll never be so mean again; I hate you to worry. And, also, I hate you to feel guilty; so please don't feel that you must write, because I understand so well.' She took German lessons and cooking lessons while he was away, which were also strikingly submissive gestures. In addition, she did Koestler's accounts and reported on reviews of *The Sleepwalkers* as they appeared during January and February 1959.[71]

To his relief and satisfaction they were broadly positive. Philip Toynbee in the *Observer* counted it the best thing Koestler had written since *Darkness at Noon*, even if it was over-long. *The Times* praised Koestler's ability to make even science dramatic, though sometimes at the price of strict objectivity. *Time* in America considered it an 'animating and dramatic lecture'. Unfortunately, the dyspeptic reviewer for the *New York Times*, Herbert Mitgang, attacked the book for being unoriginal. It was 'lumpy, undigested research' and 'hypnotically somnolent'. This was not the view of the reading public: the book sold well in Britain and the United States, and became a standard work for teachers eager to give their students a readable, absorbing introduction to astrology, astronomy and the history of science.[72]

VI

Koestler arrived back in England in April. He had just enough time to churn out five *Observer* articles on India and Japan before setting off for Alpbach. Once he was installed in the Böglerhof he managed to write up only a small part of the intended book about his trip: instead, the summer was consumed by the building work. He spent hours at the site, discussed the finer points of woodwork with the joiners and disputed endlessly with the builders. Several visitors, including Burnham, whom he had not seen for a while, added to his distractions. Janine Graetz also paid a call. She was angry at the indifference which Koestler displayed towards their child. He could not have been colder: he kept a few pictures of the baby 'in the bottom drawer of his desk' but looked at them as rarely as he spoke of her.[73]

Work on an article about European youth got him temporarily out of the depression that predictably enveloped him. It was not an obvious subject to tackle. Simone de Beauvoir had accused Koestler of having no interest in the young, and until he started giving university seminars in the late 1950s he certainly never spent much time with them – except for girls he wanted to seduce. His analysis for the *Observer* betrayed this lack of direct contact. It was remarkably broad in its scope, but shallow in terms of any experience of youth culture and, ultimately, ambivalent.

He dismissed the hyperbole and moral panic about the 'Teddy Boys' and the 'Peeved [Angry] Young Man'. Despite the self-serving claims of writers such as Colin Wilson (against whom he took a swipe) they were not typical of the mass of youth. Most youngsters were 'earnest, sober, bland'. They were 'uncommitted and non-committal'. The men were focused on professional or technical careers, the women aspired to become 'private secretaries' or mothers. Despite the threat of nuclear war they were 'remarkably un-decadent, unmorbid' and free of the '*mal de siècle*' that infected *his* generation. Nor did they resemble the youth of existentialist Paris: they preferred espresso coffee and careers to alcohol and philosophy. Young people were indifferent to politics and art: they had 'no ideals'. And yet that was an ideal of a kind. In the USA and the USSR they just wanted to get on with life: they were bored with the men and women of the 'Pink Decade'.[74]

He also made a speech at the opening of the annual Alpbach European Forum book exhibition, which gave him a platform for reiterating his ideas about psychological disarmament. Rather presumptuously he criticised the political leadership of Western Europe for neglecting his message and, conversely, the intellectuals for not pressing them hard enough to demand the free exchange of information across the Iron Curtain. Apart from that it was not a particularly productive summer. But when the time came to return to England he had the satisfaction of beholding the finished house – his ashram as he dubbed it while still under the influence of the Indian sub-continent. In a truer indication of his cultural preferences it eventually became known as the *Schreiberhäusl* – the writer's house.[75]

With Long Barn sold they now moved back into 8 Montpelier Square, which was in rather a mess after three years of occupancy by tenants. The resettling process meant that it was a busy autumn, on top of which Koestler gave three lectures at Manchester University. In these he returned to the subject of creativity and began to work again on volume two of *Insight and Outlook*.[76]

He also wrote a curious piece on Vienna for the *Observer*. Koestler recalled the city of his youth and his more recent visits, when he had experienced the 'painful shock' of finding that everyone he knew had either died or departed. This was mainly because his circle had been Jewish. He employed a curious and unflattering metaphor to describe the influence of Jews on Viennese culture: they were 'an iridescent film of oil spread over the surface of a sweet-water pool'. He did not feel, as did many other observers, that the loss of Vienna's Jews had crippled the city. On the contrary, sitting astride the Iron Curtain it had become an 'outpost of Western Christendom' and 'a symbol of Europe's phenomenal powers of regeneration'. The suffering of the war years and the occupation by the Red Army had purged the Viennese of their sins. They had undergone a profound psychological transformation, which enabled them to create a stable politics and a flourishing economy, free of any pining for the Habsburg Empire or Greater Germany.[77] This was a minority view at the time and remains one. Post-war Vienna justifiably acquired the reputation for amnesia, not contrition, and for being one of the dullest cities in Europe.

A visit by J.P. Narayan at Christmas rekindled his interest in India, and gave him the impetus to finish the book he had promised to his publishers. After spending Christmas in Cornwall (where they had a car accident) Koestler and Jefferies hastened back to London for the New Year. For the next four months he hardly set foot outside the house during the day, driving himself on with 'happy pills' (Drinamyl), which he took several times a week. He was so tense he also had to take sleeping pills. On 24 April 1960 the *The Lotus and the Robot* (which until the last moment laboured under the title 'The Fullness and the Void') was completed.[78]

In the midst of this frenzy he made a broadcast for the BBC analysing how humanity had reacted to the dawning of the era of mass destruction. The talk is interesting because it bridges *The Sleepwalkers*, the book on yogis, and anticipated his next major work. The year 1960, he maintained, marked the fifteenth year of an entirely new epoch: pH – post-Hiroshima. Yet the capacity for self-annihilation seemed to have had little effect on the human psyche: to all appearances mankind had hung out a sign inscribed 'Business as Usual'. But Koestler detected the stirrings of change: a new Copernican revolution. Paradoxically, it would come about precisely because mankind was now forced to confront its own mortality. In the Middle Ages humanity had been confident that whatever natural or man-made catastrophe occurred, human civilisation would survive because that was all there was. In the modern era mankind was aware that the Earth was but one planet in a crowded universe in which, possibly, there were other life forms. Mankind could destroy the planet, but the universe would continue serenely. This knowledge, he believed, imparted a humility that might 'rid man of that bio-logical jingoism' which had underpinned his recklessness in the past.[79]

The strain of his schedule told on his relations with Jefferies. He was absorbed in his work, but she had almost no life outside his concerns. When anything involving her went wrong he attributed it to her truculence. Throughout January they squabbled and for a while she retreated to her flat. Koestler was depressed, but did his best to soldier on without her. After a short while he capitulated and they met to discuss how she could 'build up her independence'. There was a brief rapprochement before hostilities resumed and they remained at loggerheads for much of the year, neither able to break permanently with the other.[80]

Once the book on Asia was completed Koestler was liberated to go on his next adventure: a fortnight in Scandinavia. He had a tremendous time. His books had all sold well in the region and he had a number of long-standing academic contacts there, notably Holger Hyden at the University of Gothenburg. His arrival coincided with a tour by Marlene Dietrich and he was tickled to find that he jostled with her on the front pages of the leading Norwegian papers. The object of the tour was to deliver lectures in Oslo and Stockholm, but it soon became an excuse for a binge. He delighted in the Norwegian practice of following each lecture with a *nachspiel*, an informal discussion accompanied by food and drink. Surrounded by adoring Norwegian and Swedish students, he stayed up until 2 or 3 a.m. every other night. 'In Sweden,' he observed with a hint of personal confirmation, 'sex is regarded as an indoor sport, second only in popularity to tennis.' He followed up the visit with two articles for the *Observer* appositely entitled 'Love Affair with Norway'. His depiction of the country was extraordinarily rosy and may be explained as a mirror image of his feelings about England. In Scandinavia he relished the absence of class distinctions and snobbery, the no-frills approach to sex and the role of the state as a patron of the arts.[81]

The proofs of *The Lotus and the Robot* followed hard on his heels when he got back to London. Once they were done he exclaimed: 'Now pressure off for the first time since last autumn.' He caught up with a stack of newspapers and answered five weeks of accumulated mail. At the end of May he and Jefferies left for Austria. The first half of the summer at Alpbach was extremely busy. As well as coping with various guests, he prepared a pioneering analysis of the development of a global culture, which he gave at the 1960 Vienna Festival.

His travels in 1958–60 gave him what was for that time an unusual global perspective on culture as well as politics. The current notion of 'globalisation' as a cultural phenomenon is based on the effect of information technology and mass communication in breaking down spatial and temporal boundaries so that individuals can share instantly in happenings occurring far away. Before technology made it possible to sample diverse cultures while remaining stationary, an individual could achieve the same effect by moving rapidly across political and cultural borders. Koestler thereby stumbled on the concept years before most sociologists, and summarised it, *avant la lettre*, in his Vienna talk.

Koestler constructed a sort of self-regulating Newtonian model for the dynamic of modern cultural transformation. Culture, he argued, was exploding: both the quantity and dissemination of knowledge were expanding exponentially. National frontiers were now porous to external cultural influences, native art forms were declining and uniformity was on the increase. In the process, quantity had altered quality. Thanks to marketing techniques producers were constantly adjusting their output to suit mass tastes. Since their aim was to reduce the risks of selling a new product they relied on 'feedback' to ensure that it was as popular as possible. Consequently, all forms of production were subject to the law of the lowest common denominator. Ironically, the more leisure and spending power that was available to the untutored masses, the more culture was debased. The pious wish of nineteenth-century liberals that education and leisure would result in the refinement of popular tastes was dashed: 'The liquidation of the slum implies a period of cultural slumming.' He maintained that it was pointless to mourn the advent of mass culture: it was a fact that would not go away. However, the situation was not irredeemable. It was constantly being fine-tuned and improved at the margins. 'Lone geniuses' would occasionally burst through banalised popular taste. Mechanical reproduction would enable more high art to reach mass audiences. Finally, the welfare-state sponsorship of the arts would assist the preservation and distribution of more demanding art-forms.[82]

Koestler was thus moderately optimistic, even if his snobbish and conservative assumptions were unmistakable. Theorists like Herbert Marcuse might have developed more sophisticated ideas about the culture of late capitalism, but Koestler had chanced on globalisation and the bilateral role of marketing before many cultural analysts had woken up to these profound changes.

Closeted in the *Schreiberhäusl* after the last guests had left, he finally commenced work on the sequel to *Insight and Outlook*. Late in August, however, Margaret 'Stevie' Stephens called from A. D. Peters to warn him that his mother was seriously ill. After dithering for a day he drove to Munich to catch a flight back to London. He found Adele in a pitiful state, convinced that she had been kidnapped by people who were trying to poison her. She died on 27 August aged ninety-two. Koestler had seen her intermittently, at best, over the previous few years, usually just before and just after a trip abroad. In 1952 a sharp-eyed correspondent for the *Observer* spotted her at a Foreign Press Lunch, giving herself a day out to mark her eighty-first birthday: Koestler was not there. While he was gadding about the world she lived in a boarding-house in Swiss Cottage and spent most of her time playing bridge, reading and telling anyone who would listen that she was the mother of Arthur 'Dundi' Koestler. Now that she was dead her son went through the necessary rituals of filial piety and obtained a liberal rabbi to perform the funeral service at Golders Green Crematorium. Perhaps to his own surprise, he was 'shell-shocked' by Adele's demise and gratefully threw himself into Jefferies's care once he was back at Alpbach.[83]

The latter part of the summer took its usual course. Friends arrived and left every few days, including Wayland Young with his wife, five children and nanny, and the rather more ascetic J.P. Narayan. Additions and repairs were made to the *Schreiberhäusl*. Dr Franz Hammer, an expert on Kepler from the University of Stuttgart, came at Koestler's invitation to share their mutual interest in cosmology. As a break from writing he pottered around the house with his tools doing odd jobs. There were lots of 'huge drinking parties'.[84]

They returned to Montpelier Square at the beginning of October, but in somewhat different circumstances. Koestler was now 'with Cynthia'. From this point, even though Jefferies kept her flat and usually slept there, he accepted that they were a couple. Significantly, from the start of 1961 she began to keep a diary of their life together. To the functions of secretary, cook, housekeeper and mistress she added that of a sardonic Boswell to Koestler's Johnson. Her Pooterish record of the next decade is a splendid counterpoint to Koestler's increasing tendency towards pomposity. It starts with an hilarious account of a trip they made to Shepperton in March 1961 with the intention of locating the riverside house, loaned to Koestler by Walter Layton, where he wrote *Spanish Testament*. He confidently identified the house and other landmarks, until Cynthia timidly made the 'heretic remark' that they were not yet in Shepperton. He fumed, but she was right.[85]

In November he gave an address to the Royal Society of Literature on the occasion of his election to the Fellowship, a gala occasion chaired by Cecil Day Lewis. He aptly chose as his subject the superiority of European culture over the cultures of the Orient, a thin variation on the epilogue to *The Lotus and the Robot*. It gave him the opportunity to display his global scope at its best. European culture, he argued, was superior to Eastern civilisation because it asserted the value of empiricism over transcendence. The split between East and West was not one of materialism versus spiritualism: rather the line of fracture was 'two different approaches to reality – one which relies on intuition, symbolic imagery and essential being – the other, on research, conceptual thinking, logical categories'. Europe managed to blend the two; in India and Japan they were bifurcated. These countries 'lived in a spiritual vacuum'. To the lively approbation of his audience he concluded: 'I went to Asia . . . and came back rather proud of being a European.'[86]

It is notable that in the thumb-nail autobiography he gave in this address Koestler omitted his Jewish roots. European civilisation looked rather less benign from a Jewish point of view and he may quietly have suppressed this aspect of his identity the better to flatter those with whom he wished to integrate himself. The necessity to do so cast some doubt on the notion of Europe as a superior haven typified by 'unity-in-diversity'. In the polytheistic East the Jews had never been persecuted: they had hardly been noticed. In Shanghai the Japanese had even protected a refuge for Jews who had fled the Nazis. Koestler was either unaware of this or chose to omit such discordant but pertinent detail. In any case the absence of an acknowledgement that he was a Jew as well as a European illustrates the extent to which Europe's Christian culture placed limits on diversity. These parameters were sometimes openly accepted; more often they had a tacit presence. Koestler's taciturnity illustrates one response to the constricted diversity of European culture, an intolerance of difference that, as the Jews knew very well, could be lethal.

Chapter 12
The Alpbach Years, 1960–7

During the 1960s Koestler was torn between a taste for respectability and an incapacity to enjoy success or approval. He took risks courting outlandish ideas and even where his arguments were fairly safe he made them out to be dangerously unconventional. He launched an intellectual crusade against Behaviourism, which he rather misleadingly construed as the new orthodoxy explaining all human conduct. Because Behaviourists demeaned consciousness he became even more interested in the brain and its workings. This led him into strange byways, including a flirtation with drugs and an association with Dr Timothy Leary, who was notorious for his advocacy of LSD.

His writing was increasingly monopolised by science. In *The Act of Creation* (1964) he published a revised (though not much improved) version of *Insight and Outlook*. *The Ghost in the Machine* (1967) was ostensibly an assault on Behaviourism in the guise of a book about the workings of the brain and evolution. In fact, both studies dealt with the dilemmas of mankind: what makes humanity tick and why has human society turned out so badly? This was ultimately a political quest: to unravel human nature and show how society could be organised to cope with it or find ways to modify behaviour so as to induce social harmony. From *The Lotus and the Robot* to *The Ghost in the Machine*, in which he recommended giving everyone drugs to eliminate aggression, he traversed all the elements of the counter-culture which flourished in the shadow of the H-Bomb. Koestler moved from Eastern mysticism to the use of chemical compounds to alter consciousness, but years before anyone else.

With his reputation as a science writer buoyed up by *The Sleepwalkers*, Koestler was invited to attend academic seminars and conferences around the world. Notwithstanding his efforts to remain a maverick, honours began to fall on his shoulders. In 1965 he held a prestigious fellowship at the Center for Advanced Studies, Stanford University.

His ambivalence towards domesticity and belonging remained extreme. Koestler and Jefferies migrated annually to rural Austria in a car loaded with books; but their summers were routinely disrupted by waves of fractious visitors: further evidence, if it were needed, that Koestler had a pathological need to wander and to recreate a dysfunctional family around himself wherever he went. He was perversely attracted to people, places and rituals calculated to mark him out as a stranger. Alpbach, for example, lay in the heart of territory closely associated with the Nazis. In 1963 he wrote a belligerent article about the decline of Britain and went on to edit a book of essays, *Suicide of a Nation?*, that could have been pre-meditated to irritate his 'hosts'. It seemed he never let himself feel totally at ease even in England.

He finally married Cynthia Jefferies in January 1965 and lapsed into the habits of middle age, growing increasingly conservative in taste, conduct and politics. It was somehow typical of his slide into carpet-slipperdom that his latest political crusade was devoted to changing the quarantine rules governing the movement of dogs into and out of the British Isles. His single-minded devotion to this quadruped cause almost cost his friendship with David Astor and the *Observer*. As his status (and figure) bulked and his life subsided into the mire of triviality, Koestler's search for the 'tragic plane of existence' became ever more extreme.

I

Dr Timothy Leary, the 'pioneer' of experimentation with 'mind-altering' drugs, had been in correspondence with Koestler since 1959. Leary had been fascinated by Koestler's description of the 'oceanic experience': 'His writings had prepared my life for the "mystic experience" and I wanted to repay him for changing my life.' Koestler, in turn, was drawn to Leary by his drug trials, which seemed to reveal something about the mind and human creativity. The opportunity to meet came when Koestler was invited to a conference on neurology in San Francisco in spring 1960. He intended to break his return journey at Harvard to meet Leary, but before then he paused at the University of Michigan, Ann Arbor, where James (Hans) Meisels, an old comrade from the Ullstein years, was based in the Department of Political Science. At the University, which was also conducting research into drugs, he tried psilocybin (extracted from mushrooms) and had a 'bad trip'. Koestler felt it had tipped him into 'a chemically induced state of insanity' and realised that the same would be true for many other people. Drugs seemed more of a menace than a panacea for a troubled world.[1]

Consequently, when he arrived at Harvard to see Leary he was less than confident about their value. Leary had doubts, too, though not about the drugs. 'I had a few reservations about Arthur as a subject. He was so rational and controlled with little sense of humour. He seemed tormented by an ancient European pessimism.' Koestler's woeful Michigan experience heightened his resistance but the next day he met his bugbear, B. F. Skinner, for lunch and this may have strengthened his resolve. The following evening, after a heavy round of socialising and drinking, Koestler went back to Leary's house and washed down ten 'magic mushroom' pills with a large tumbler of whisky. According to Leary, as they lay back in candle-light listening to Mozart, 'Arthur's face was transfigured. "This is perfection," he murmured. "Everything is so beautiful."' A little later his countenance changed to one of agony, 'his eyes expressing the sorrows of the ages'. Then he said: '"This is wonderful, no doubt . . . But it is fake, ersatz. Instant mysticism. There is no quick and easy path to wisdom. Sweat and toil are the price of knowledge."'[2]

Koestler later recalled that the second experience was not unpleasant, though he remained unimpressed. Listening to music under the influence of drugs was an intense experience, but it was ultimately valueless because he could not recall what seemed special about the music, why he had enjoyed it so much more — or even what piece it was. His subsequent research into writing by authors while they were on drugs confirmed that it did little for creativity. In spite of his penchant for weird ideas, Koestler was too much of a rationalist to be lured by LSD. This incident displayed his horse sense at its best and, though he would have been reluctant to admit it, his commitment to the venerable traditions of European empiricist thought.[3]

During the spring he wrote three major pieces for the *Observer*, which built on his Californian excursion. They heralded several of the themes that he was developing in *Insight and Outlook* volume two and which would preoccupy him for the next decade. In 'Pavlov in Retreat' he claimed that Behaviourism was defunct. Behaviourism was a theory that purported to explain all forms of human activity. It was originated by J. B. Watson, an American zoologist, who claimed that humans acquired behaviour traits in the same way that animals learned to do tricks. Systematic observation would eventually establish all these traits, enable psychologists to predict behaviour and to modify it. By contrast, psychoanalytic theory was undemonstrable and hokum. From the 1920s to the 1950s, Behaviourism dominated American psychological thinking and practice. At its zenith it was advocated by B. F. Skinner, who denigrated any notion of consciousness or the unconscious. Skinner believed that an ideal society could be created merely through appropriate conditioning, without drugs or therapies.[4] But Koestler asserted that from neurologists to philosophers it was becoming apparent that human behaviour could not be explained solely in terms of stimuli and reactions, that the brain and the mind were not the same thing and that man was neither a primitive animal nor a robot.

Behaviourism was Koestler's bugbear, although it is hard to see why. He too was a quasi-determinist who was quite capable of reducing human behaviour to the product of electronic impulses and chemical processes in the body. He used concepts from post-Freudian psychoanalysis, but he never unequivocally endorsed the Freudian notion of the unconscious. If anything, his conflict with the Behaviourists was one of proximity: they were a mite too close to him for his comfort and a little too explicit about their conclusions, which were, in so many respects, the logical extension of his own.

Behaviourism was only one of an interlocking complex of 'doctrines' which, he argued passionately, were 'based on faulty axioms'. These were: 'that biological evolution is the outcome of random mutations preserved by natural selection; that mental evolution is the outcome of random tries preserved by "reinforcements"; and that man is a self-regulating passive automaton, whose actions consist in jerking out adaptive responses to stimuli in the environment.'[5]

He retorted in a number of ways. One tactic was to attack simplistic Darwinism, since he regarded the theory of blind, automatic natural selection as an analogue and foundation of Behaviourism. Using research on flatworms, he demonstrated that species transmitted 'memories' when they bred and that mutations over time were not therefore unconscious or random. Another method was to argue that extra-sensory perception and the paranormal gave evidence of properties of the brain which the theory of stimuli–reaction could not explain.[6] Unfortunately, both lines of attack led into a dense undergrowth of controversy until the original path was completely obscured. An essentially political crusade degenerated into a series of scientific skirmishes around more or less entrenched positions from which no one emerged as a clear winner.[7]

In April *The Lotus and the Robot* appeared, to critical acclaim and commercial success. In buoyant mood, Koestler and Jefferies headed off for Alpbach. *En route* they stayed for three days in Paris and saw

Robert Calmann-Lévy, who was about to publish the book in French, the Winklers, Maxime and Anna. Koestler immediately lapsed into his Parisian mood, staying out late, going to strip clubs, getting drunk every night and arranging meetings with his ex-girl-friends. On one dreadfully hung-over morning he got into a furious row with the concierge at the Calmann-Lévy establishment and smashed the window of his office because he wouldn't allow Jefferies to drive their car into the courtyard. 'A. felt wonderful after that scene,' she recorded sarcastically. They reached Alpbach on 3 May after the usual spate of flat tyres and breakdowns.[8]

Summer in Alpbach was hectic. Michael Polanyi was there when they arrived. He was followed at intervals by Roland Penrose, James Burnham, Melvin Lasky, the conductor Otto Klemperer – whom Koestler had befriended during a recent stay in London – and his wife Lotte, Franz Hammer, Janetta Jackson, her children and her estranged husband Derek, Dr Ivan Morris, Alex Weissberg and Margarete Buber-Neumann, Karl Popper, George Mikes and Holger Hyden. This list, as exhausting as it sounds, is not exhaustive. In between the round of lunches, dinners and drinks, collecting and dropping off, drunken nights and hung-over mornings, Koestler worked on the proofs of his San Francisco paper and the book about creativity. When she was not employed taking dictation, typing, cooking or chauffeuring, Jefferies gardened and sunbathed. Occa-sionally Koestler would ricochet around the house doing odd jobs. There were regular mishaps with the car.

One of the most distinguished visitors was the British-born Cam-bridge professor Paul Dirac, who worked on quantum mechanics. In 1933 he had shared with Professor Erwin Schrödinger the Nobel Prize for working out the mathematical formulation of relativity. Koestler had already made the acquaintance of Schrödinger, a Viennese who taught in Germany until 1933, but he was excited at the prospect of encountering Dirac. His books *What is Life* (1946) and *Science and Man* (1958) had impressed him and he always hoped to garner some secret truth from such geniuses: they might even reveal themselves as his sought-after shaman. But Dirac turned out to be 'extremely narrow, [with] no interests, not even history of science; purely a physicist; teetotaller; non-smoker'. After lunching and dining with him he could make no personal contact and gave up, disgruntled that Dirac was just what he purported to be: a brilliant scientist. The encounter says much more about Koestler's quest for father figures than it does about Dirac's personality.[9]

At the end of June, Koestler and Jefferies motored down to

Bressanone (Brixen) in the Dolomites. On the way their car over-heated and Koestler tried to keep it going by urinating into the radiator, a trick which he had heard saved many a Desert Rat during the war. Not surprisingly, this interesting technique failed to stop the engine boiling up and they turned back. Janetta Jackson arrived for a three-week stay and Koestler fretted about the arrangement she had made to rent the home of one of his neighbours. When the key of the chalet could not be found Koestler dramatically broke in by smashing a window. 'He loved that,' she recalled. Derek Jackson, Janetta's ex-husband, turned up too, and enjoyed talking about physics with him. Frances Partridge, who was accompanying her friend Janetta, recorded a visit by Koestler and 'Angel' (his pet name for Jefferies). They arrived 'swaggering after climbing a mountain, Koestler dressed in beetle-like Austrian uniform – shorts and long socks – yet speaking scornfully in what sounds like a German accent of "krauts"'. He started browbeating Janetta about the landscape, which she claimed not to like, provoking a genteel burst of irritation from Frances Partridge. Once again she observed with exasperation that 'he doesn't listen to other people'.[10]

A few days later Partridge ran into Koestler watching a village procession. She recalled how he stood 'in his best town-suit, head bent, a benign all-embracing, patronising smile on his face, nodding to the grocer or whoever he knew'. When she denigrated the piety of the locals, and their 'stodgy stupidity', he retorted: 'Ah, it fills me with envy.'[11] This vignette shows marvellously well how Koestler liked to blend in, Zelig-like, wherever he was no matter how absurd the effect. And there could be little more incongruous than a short, stout Hungarian Jew trying to be a thigh-slapping Tyrolean peasant when, until quite recently, those very same Tyroleans had been shooting and gassing his ilk wherever they found them. During 1961 Koestler avidly followed the trial of Adolf Eichmann. In Salzburg he scoured the papers for information about the deportation of Hungarian Jews to Auschwitz, which Eichmann had personally organised. Back in Alpbach, he grimaced at the 'ugly krauts' in the Böglerhof as if they alone were to blame for the death of his Aunt Rosa. But Eichmann was an Austrian (he was born in Linz) and so were many of his most zealous lieutenants, a fact which could not have escaped Koestler's attention – consciously, at least.[12]

Jefferies was the patient, infinitely tolerant bystander to these antics. She put up with endless bullying and deprecation, and went in fear of Koestler's wrath, which she could incur for the most trivial of reasons. On 3 August, for example, she recorded a case of his domestic tyranny: 'A. maddened by my forgetting a service utensil; he has become so allergic to my slap-dash table laying. He could not overcome his anger and this spoilt the evening for us.'[13] Neither he nor Jefferies drew the obvious conclusion that Koestler was repeating the patterns of behaviour that prevailed in the Budapest apartments of his childhood, that he was re-enacting the conduct of his mother, the maid and the nannies. The process by which children come to identify with and mimic oppressive parental figures is well known in psychoanalytic writing, particularly among the British post-Freudians such as Winnicott and Bowlby. However, if Koestler was so impervious to his own analysis there is little reason why he should have been susceptible to that of others.

Jefferies was not the sole female object of his violence. Ivan Morris and his Japanese wife Yaki came to stay in August. They went to Vienna together and had dinner at the Sacher, where Koestler got stewed. On the way back to their hotel they were followed by some unruly youths with whom Yaki exchanged words. Koestler took this to be encouraging them and 'gave Yaki a hard slap'. She was so upset by this unprovoked blow that Jefferies had to bundle her into a taxi and take her home. Koestler subsequently reduced the 'Teddy boys' to docility and ended up chatting with them outside the hotel he was staying in. Amazingly, Ivan and Yaki seemed quite reconciled to Koestler the next morning. They spent the next two days viewing places Koestler had frequented in his youth and made a trip to the Hungarian border, where Koestler stared across the fence, choked with emotion. The harmony did not last long. Even Jefferies was terrified by his erratic behaviour. He drank in the bar of the Sacher till the early hours of the morning and only reappeared at their hotel at dawn. She had no idea where he had been.[14]

These trivial events occurred against a tragic backdrop: the construction of the Berlin Wall and an international crisis that seemed to presage a Third World War. Now Koestler could not be restrained from regaling his audiences with comparisons between 1961 and the summer of 1939. Cynthia found his doom-laden pontifications so awful that when he started of an evening she made her excuses and went to bed. He argued so bitterly (and drunkenly) with Alex Weissberg and Fritz Molden, his Austrian publisher, that a sour atmosphere descended over their last days in the *Schreiberhäusl*.[15]

Their departure was delayed by the latest in a succession of automobile mishaps. They eventually set off in a patched-together car and reached Weil-der-Stadt, where Koestler wanted to visit Kepler's house. Then they drove, ate and drank their way through the Black

Forest and into France. Near Nancy they had a 'slight accident'. Jefferies recollected: 'Arthur had to brake suddenly because a car in front braked. We skidded and grazed a tree. I felt quite shaky.' Undeterred, they pressed on towards Paris, quaffing champagne as they went. Once there, they dined and drank with Calmann-Lévy, Aron and the Winklers. Koestler went off to the Monocle, a club favoured by lesbians, about whom he developed something of an obsession. They reached England on 17 September five days after setting off from Austria.[16]

The summer of 1961 at Alpbach was more or less typical of the succeeding dozen summers. Koestler worked and, against the odds, was productive. He invited and welcomed large numbers of guests who stayed in his house or the nearby hotels. His generosity was lavish and his friends returned over and over again. Despite the contretemps and his occasionally boorish conduct, Koestler inspired tremendous affection among his close circle and his more transient visitors. Margarete Buber-Neumann wrote to him after her visit: '*Dein Haus ist wirklich ein Paradies.*' Even Frances Partridge, who was not one of his fans, could see the benign side of his character. One evening he came to the Burglerhof to dine with Derek and Janetta Jackson. As he arrived, she noted 'his face soft like bread soaked in milk'. He argued with Derek Jackson about mathematics, then had a row with Janetta; but no one seemed to get upset. About Janetta, he later told Partridge: 'it was love really.' It is unclear whether the diarist knew about his affair with Janetta Jackson, but the comment and the context are revealing. If Koestler could not let go of ex-wives, mistresses and lovers, they were equally as reluctant to leave him. Perhaps the memory of his charm and benevolence outlasted the scars of bitter quarrels. Or perhaps he attracted a certain kind of masochistic personality for whom he fulfilled a particular need.[17]

There is evidence to suggest the latter. Cyril Connolly reported to Edmund Wilson in 1946 that although Koestler treated Mamaine badly, 'She is madly in love with him and doesn't care how he treats her . . . I am told that Koestler nags and bullies her rather, but she doesn't seem to mind.' To be fair, Connolly added: 'he really is devoted to her.' Jefferies worked out that she was meek and sub-missive towards Koestler, and noted that all his women seemed to share in common the experience of a great hurt that left them vulnerable.[18] Conversely, it may have left them with the compulsion to re-enact that wounding process.

During the autumn, Koestler worked steadily on volume two of

Insight and Outlook, to be called *The Act of Creation*. He was already looking beyond the current book and met Sir Cyril Burt, the then distinguished psychologist, to discuss research into parapsychology. They shared an abundance of interests. Burt, who was a pioneer of industrial, educational and child psychology in Britain, was also a follower of Francis Galton, Karl Pearson and Herbert Spencer. He was a eugenicist and believed in 'breeding'. Another of his mentors was William McDougall, a respected psychologist who had an interest in parapsychology. Burt became active in the Society for Psychical Research in the late 1950s. He was critical of Behaviourism and had ideas about the hierarchical organisation of nature that were close to Koestler's. After Koestler sent him the draft of *Act of Creation* for his comments, Burt provided a glowing Preface. In return, Koestler contributed a chapter to the *Festschrift* in honour of Burt. After his death, however, Burt was enveloped in controversy when it was revealed that he falsified parts of his research into twins and acquired intelligence. There was an element of charlatanry about him and a deep insecurity which may have added to the bond which he and Koestler formed.[19]

Koestler's burgeoning interest in parapsychology and levitation took practical, if rather ludicrous, form. In September he purchased a weighing machine which he intended to use for experiments in levitation by hypnosis. It was delivered to Jefferies's flat, where it sat in her hallway occupying a considerable amount of space. They tried it out in December, but the machine was faulty. It was not a promising start to his psychic research.[20]

The television which Jefferies persuaded him to buy and install did work, however. From this time he became quite an avid TV viewer: *Panorama*, *Play of the Week* and *Z-Cars* were firm favourites. There were many social engagements, too. They saw David Astor, Goronwy Rees and Nicholas Henderson several times. Koestler was introduced to Jacob Bronowski and 'got very excitable and intense' as he was liable to do with academically acclaimed scientists. After a dinner with Otto Klemperer at the Hyde Park Hotel he was so drunk that he fell down the steps into the street, but then insisted on driving home. Jefferies 'felt slightly uneasy' about this. A short while later he had a car accident in Sloane Square, running into the vehicle of an improbably named Mr Croissant. Koestler accepted responsibility and offered to pay for the cost of the damage until he saw the size of the bill. He started quibbling and even claimed, to the consternation of Mr Croissant, that the crash had not been his fault after all. They eventually settled the matter.[21]

In November he developed a passion about the quarantine regulations governing the movement of dogs into and out of the country. These required that dogs (and other pets) brought in from abroad, even animals that were re-entering, had to be held in quarantine for six months. It was an issue he felt keenly since he liked to own a dog, but due to the rules had been forced to leave them scattered all over the world (Attila in Palestine, Sabby in France, Miss Nellie in America) as he shifted from one country and continent to another. He mentioned this to Peregrine Worsthorne over lunch with Melvin Lasky and Constantine Fitzgibbon one day in December. His comments found their way into Worsthorne's column in the *Sunday Telegraph* on Christmas Eve 1960, where they triggered a huge volume of letters from dog-lovers. It was the start of another quixotic episode.[22]

II

Koestler waged his crusade against quarantine with the same rigour as his assault on hanging. He persuaded David Astor to run an article in which he set forth the case for changing the regulations. Astor was less than enthusiastic, not least because Koestler risked debasing his vocabulary and his reputation by applying both to the subject of domestic pets. But Koestler had spent several weeks at the start of the year collecting material. It proved to his satisfaction that the English authorities were gripped by an irrational fear of rabies, as a result of which English-born dogs were forced to endure six months in the canine equivalent of a 'concentration camp' whence they emerged with changed personalities. He urged the government to adopt the practice of certifying dogs vaccinated against rabies before they left the country and giving them a free right of entry when they returned with their owners. This was doubly reasonable, first, since it cohered with the evidence that there was a negligible risk of importing human-life-threatening rabies and, second, because it would actually reduce the chances that infected animals would be smuggled in – which was the real danger.[23]

Despite the 'dotty long-winded doggerers' who quickly monopolised the campaign and threatened to do the same with Koestler's time, he persisted. In conjunction with the Canine Defence League he helped to launch a petition signed by illustrious dog-owners: it was a devastating combination of Münzenberg methods and the English love of animals. Dogs became an 'obsession' which imperilled his long-standing and generally cordial, not to say profitable, relationship with Astor and the *Observer*. Astor admonished that he 'ought to use a bit more British understatement and not get so heated on such a minor subject which would be damaging for future more important issues'. But Koestler could not agree and the two men had to meet several times to stave off a rupture. In the end, Koestler persuaded Astor to run one last article and convinced him that his opposition to the campaign was in some way really about their complex relationship. Following a summit meeting, Astor pleaded with him: 'Don't throw me away. Use your psychological knowledge to see that I have difficulties of my own (not tragic ones, just normal sized ones) which have nothing to do with you, but in which you may have become (unfairly) involved. I have learned much from this episode and I am most grateful for your frankness to me. It will help me to keep things straight . . . I am still your friend and would mind losing the comradely personal relations with you – more than the journalistic side.' As a compromise the final article was accompanied by a pro-reform editorial, but that was the end of the *Observer*'s support. Once again, Koestler was ahead of his times. In June 1997, the British government announced that it would, at last, consider scrapping the six-month quarantine rule and substituting for it certified inoculation against rabies.[24]

In May Koestler went on another lecture tour of Scandinavia, accompanied this time by Jefferies and the writer Joan Henry. He gave one talk at Holger Hyden's research institute in Gothenburg and another at Copenhagen University. It was a merry, drunken spree. Soon after returning, they packed and relocated to Alpbach.[25] Once there it would have been easier for Koestler to concentrate on writing if he had set up a card table and got down to work in Grand Central Station. The traffic through Alpbach included Hyden, Margarete Buber-Neumann, the Hammer family, Paul Dirac, Misi Polanyi, Joan Henry, George Urban, who recorded an interview with him for Radio Free Europe, and an Austrian film crew making a programme about Koestler. Even he was beginning to weary of this cavalcade. He scribbled in his diary after Joan Henry and some others had finally left that he was 'bored' with 'all those hags'. In between these visits and side-trips to Vienna and Venice, he managed to write a considerable amount of the book and joyfully declared the first draft complete three months after arriving. Jefferies observed: 'I have never before seen him work so hard and be so completely physically and mentally exhausted in the evenings.' One night he went to his room at nine o'clock and fell asleep on the bed, book in hand. Sadly, the euphoria wore off when Koestler had to find a way of conjoining volume two with the old volume one. His morale plummeted and he started getting extravagantly drunk.[26]

During this summer Koestler's curious attitude towards Germany revealed itself again when he made a long detour to reach Salzburg from Innsbruck without cutting through Bavaria. On the way back, however, he 'decided not to be squeamish' and not only went via Germany, but visited the ruins of Berchtesgaden – Hitler's alpine retreat. The site left him feeling indefinably disturbed. On 9 October they left Alpbach, travelling home via Switzerland, northern Italy and southern France. They visited Sanary-sur-Mer, where he had paid court to Lion Feuchtwanger in the days of exile, and places which had featured in his wanderings during 1940. In Paris they saw Manès Sperber and Calmann-Lévy, but Koestler went alone to the Monocle to see the lesbians. Jefferies was relieved when he 'came home safe and sound. Paris is too explosive for him.' As soon as he crossed the Channel he began to get melancholy. His unease with England now started to manifest itself in fanatical advocacy of the Common Market and a converse denigration of his country of adoption.[27]

Koestler spent the autumn working on the book, writing a paper for a Nuffield Foundation lunch and moaning about England. He declared to Jefferies: 'if we don't join the Common Market, we should live part of the time near Paris, have three dogs, and only a pied à terre in London.' For her part, she 'saw at last that it would be impossible for him to live here, cut off from Europe'. When Britain's application for membership of the Common Market was rejected at the start of 1963, they 'stayed up late, discussing whether to live in France and like rats desert [the] sinking ship'. Whenever he got into discussion of the issue his temper flared. Once he nearly punched the writer Constantine Fitzgibbon for not being sufficiently pro-European.[28]

His bursts of violence were not confined to politics. Jefferies continued to absorb the worst of them, even though she was pliant in the extreme. Her unquestioning acceptance of his travel plans was one symptom of the subordinate place she occupied in their relationship. Her willingness to forgo children, although it may have coincided with her own desires, was another. In November she became pregnant again and had another abortion, this time in rather more comfortable surroundings. Despite such sacrifices, Koestler would rail against her for the tiniest misdemeanour. On Christmas Day 1962, 'Arthur threw an open bottle of brandy on the floor of the sitting-room because he had to wait for me to let him in with the keys.' She made excuses and allowances for his evil moods, but it was a wearing existence.[29]

The signs of an impending Labour Party victory at the next General Election added impetus to his intention to resettle abroad. Labour's opposition to the Common Market naturally alarmed him, but its policies in general were no longer to his taste. In the 1950s he had continued to meet Labour Party MPs, such as John Strachey and Dick Crossman, but he grew more and more hostile to Crossman who, he believed, was 'blind to moral issues'. As an alternative he tried out other postwar Labour MPs such as Patrick Gordon Walker and Anthony Crosland. There was a mutual interest between Koestler the ex-Communist and these British social democrats. Crosland admired him tremendously: 'Your writings had a crucial influence on me at a critical period. It would be nice if one could repay even 10% of that debt.' Koestler invited Crosland to Long Barn, but his youth and brilliance did not counterbalance Koestler's deepening hostility to the Labour Party.[30]

England had been hospitable to Koestler, but it was not always pleasant to him. He associated with English people who reminded him in a visceral sense that he was an outsider. Henry Green, in particular, represented a vile kind of English xenophobia and Jew-hatred. In May, Koestler recorded an 'Absolutely ghastly evening with Henry – hostile, sneering, pompous, anti-Semitic'. At the end of the year Jefferies noted: 'Dinner at the Yorkes; Henry didn't shave or change, but managed to hold out for the evening . . . made a bloody remark about not having a drop of Jewish blood.'[31] Green was an extreme case, although he was not unique. It is possible to understand why his past brilliance as a novelist and his more recent capacity for consuming alcohol might have attracted Koestler, but there is a suspicion that this friendship had some other function. Like his proclivity for living cheek by jowl with 'ugly krauts' it served to remind Koestler that he was a Jew.

III

Koestler poured his disillusionment with England into an article for the *Observer*. It had been commissioned as one of a series of essays on patriotism, but there was little in his to fit the wider theme. Instead, Koestler dug out his cuttings file labelled 'Suicide of a Nation', a sort of gloomy and negative 'This England' collection, and wrote a scathing piece on the decline of Britain.

He began by recalling his arrival in 1940 and the clash between the keenness of the Continentals in the Pioneer Corps and the institutionalised slothfulness of British tommies on work details. On the basis of this experience he asserted rather spuriously that he 'came to know intimately the lower strata of the working classes'. He learned that they were gripped by class hatred: not a politicised, directed fury, but a sullen resentment against their 'betters'. The dominant element in the British Labour movement comprised the Communist Party, which he claimed was engaged in 'a planned, centralised and extremely well-organised campaign' that succeeded because it drew on this persisting class hostility. The failure of Labour in 1945–51, the poverty of British industrial management and the limitations of British entrepreneurship had resulted in the rising number of strikes and the decline of productivity: Britain was being outstripped by its European rivals and was doomed if change did not come. The patriotic shibboleth for this tirade was his pain at seeing a great country brought low and a few vague panaceas such as 'equal educational opportunities for all' and, of course, membership of the Common Market.

Astor was unhappy with the piece and tried to persuade him to make some changes. Koestler obdurately refused and set off for France, assuming that the article had been spiked. In fact, the proofs and a photographer followed him to the French Riviera. When it appeared it triggered a controversy and, eventually, a book-length sequel.[32]

Koestler thought it would help him finish *The Act of Creation* if he moved to the South of France for a few weeks, so on 25 January he and Jefferies set off for Grassin, near St Tropez. The villa, which they had rented from a friend, turned out to be located in a 'gloomy deserted spot'. It soon snowed heavily, burying the car and trapping them in the freezing house. Both became so miserable that they had to take 'secconol [*sic*] to mute our depressions'. Appropriately enough, Koestler wrote a chapter on 'weeping'. They bumped into Paul Ignotus in St Tropez and Joan Henry came to stay for a week, but nothing lifted their spirits very much. In mid-February they retreated back to London. Koestler then went to a conference on cybernetics in Hamburg, which cheered him up.[33]

In March he completed the first draft of *The Act of Creation* and immediately suggested to Melvin Lasky that *Encounter* run a special issue on the decline of Britain to follow up the interest created by his *Observer* article. Lasky was enthusiastic and quickly arranged a book tie-in. For several weeks Koestler marshalled the contributors, holding almost weekly meetings in his house at 'drinks time'. At first the special issue was going to be humorous; then it turned serious. There were disagreements over the roster of contributors, which eventually divided between professional journalists, experts and Friends of Koestler. The final cast included Henry Fairlie, Malcolm Muggeridge, Goronwy Rees, Michael Shanks, Andrew Shonfield, Austin Albu, MP, Aidan Crawley, John Cole, Hugh Seton-Watson, John Mander, John Grigg, Cyril Connolly, Marcus Cunliffe, Alan McGlashan, Elizabeth Young and John Vaizey. Henry Fairlie, a well-established journalist, caused no end of dissent between Lasky and Koestler because he could hardly see what the problem with England was supposed to be — and said so very persuasively. Koestler contributed an introduction and conclusion, which expanded on the *Observer* article.[34] The revisions of the book were finished in mid-May, the *Encounter* project a few weeks after. Then they were whizzing through Germany, top down, *en route* to Alpbach. Their arrival was marred by evidence of vandalism at the house, but this was soon repaired. Almost immediately, they set off again to tour northern Italy for a week, before settling into the *Schreiberhäusl*. It was very hot. Koestler sweated over the book, rewriting and revising it, while Cynthia gardened. The visitors that summer included Paul Ignotus, Quentin Crewe, the Hydens and the Hammers. But the star turn was provided by the Mayor of Berlin, Willy Brandt, who was holidaying in Alpbach.

Brandt was a social democrat formed in the crucible of the Weimar Republic who had gone into exile in Norway in 1933 and spent the war years with the Norwegian resistance. He returned to Germany in 1945 wearing an Allied uniform and helped rebuild the Social Democratic Party. Brandt admired Koestler's frank autobiographical account of his activities in those troubled times and recalled the part Koestler played in the great demonstration in Berlin in 1950. When Brandt, accompanied by his secretary, walked up the hill from the village to the *Schreiberhäusl* to introduce himself he was paying tribute to a man who had influenced him and touched the life of the city he governed. They got on easily enough and talked about the pre-war years, Berlin and politics. Koestler invited him back for dinner, but the second encounter was more formal and less of a success. Jefferies concluded: 'Willy Brandt obviously not a sociable man.' But Koestler was thrilled that this titan of post-war German politics should choose to make a beeline for his door. He crowed to John Strachey: 'Willy Brandt is here: we get on well.' Brandt enjoyed the meeting enormously and over subsequent years would arrange for Koestler to receive a birthday telegram in his name.[35]

Other reunions had less happy outcomes. He saw Georg Eisler for the first time since the war, had a lot to drink with him, quarrelled and 'fell into a flower bed' on the way back to the house. This was an exceptional incident: for most of August Koestler slaved away. Finally, the typescript was posted to London and they were free to roam once more. They went down into Italy and returned to England via Bavaria, Alsace and Paris (where the brakes gave out again). Koestler immediately got down to a piece on Kepler for the *Encyclopaedia of Philosophy* and moved from that to an article on Galileo for the *Observer* to mark the 400th anniversary of Galileo's birth. The article was a fine distillation of *The Sleepwalkers*, summing up the revolution in knowledge effected by Kepler and Copernicus in a spirited debunking style.[36]

While Koestler was battling to meet his deadline for the *Observer* Jefferies let her flat and moved into the ex–Bachelor Fortress. During the summer they had repeatedly discussed the possibility of living as man and wife; Jefferies finally prevailed. When they threw a big Christmas party she was now more than a part-time hostess. The guests for this end-of-the-year bash included Cyril Connolly, Ernest Gellner, the Viennese-born philosopher, Patrick Gordon Walker, MP and his wife Audrey, the writer Anthony Hobson, the art historian Ernst Gombrich, Goronwy Rees, Andrew Shonfield and the Yorkes.[37]

IV

As Koestler entered his fifty-ninth year he became more and more of a public figure. He had always been well connected, but now many of his youthful acquaintances had achieved eminence and invited him into their illustrious orbit. Through these contacts he ascended the social-intellectual spiral that ran through British society. His friendship with Sir Roland Penrose was a case in point. Penrose was an art collector of genius who had founded the Institute of Contemporary Arts in 1947. They became friendly in the late 1950s while the ICA was still establishing itself. By the 1960s it was part of London's cultural landscape and it was a major event when Koestler was invited to deliver a talk there in February 1964. He worked hard on a presentation of themes from *The Act of Creation*, although in the end he felt it was a waste of time. The hall was packed and hot, and the audience seemed to miss the point.[38]

Another sign of his stature was the series of three broadcasts for the BBC on 'The Act of Creation'. The talks were carved out of the book and were shortly afterwards published in *The Listener*. They transmitted his ideas to a wider audience than ever and helped to boost sales of the book when it appeared the following May. Coincidentally, the page proofs of the book had to be corrected at roughly the same time, subjecting him to enormous strain. For relaxation he and Jefferies embarked on a canal cruise on a boat he had bought at the Boat Show in January. It was a rather cold and damp expedition, but it cleared Koestler's head so that he could get back to the BBC talks.[39]

The Act of Creation came out in May and received generally good reviews. After his experiences with 'volume one' Koestler was hugely relieved. However, the reception of the book was not necessarily a sure sign of its merits. He had sent parts of it to colleagues to guard against obvious errors, but the basic thesis was unchanged from *Insight and Outlook*. Large chunks of it were still almost unreadable and those which could be read easily did not necessarily make any sense. Indeed, when it was republished in the Danube Edition in 1969, Koestler excised the entire second half, which presented his ideas about hierarchy and evolution. But he had acquired a reputation for profound thinking and it took a bold critic to dispute either the general thesis or the details. Many simply summarised the book as best they could and applauded it in general terms. The scientific community was divided. Dr (Sir) Peter Medawar gave it a drubbing from on high. He went for the jugular by pointing out that much of Koestler's technique relied on essentially random analogies between science and art or different branches of science. None of the book's central arguments could be tested in a laboratory: it was all well-informed speculation. Koestler dismissed his authoritative critic as a case of professional jealousy, but a careful reading of other expert reviews showed that they often damned with faint praise or displayed genuine enthusiasm – of the kind Dr Johnson did on seeing a dog walk on its hind legs.[40]

A sure sign of his arrival as a popular writer was a visitation by Melvyn Bragg and a TV film crew from *Writers World*. It took three days to make the programme, but when it was broadcast a new generation of Koestler fans was born.[41] Ironically, few of them would have read *Darkness at Noon* or the autobiographies. To them Arthur Koestler was a benign, middle-aged, Middle European savant whose wisdom was guaranteed by his greying hair and foreign accent.

In fact, he was no less irascible. He lost his temper with Jefferies if she entered his room during his 'quiet reading programme' or put on the 'wrong music', worked himself into a rage over the building work necessitated by her permanent presence in the house and smashed glasses on the floor because there were no friends to see on a Sunday evening.[42] But having fashioned an image of calm sagacity, his mind turned increasingly to protecting his status and his post-humous reputation. One of his cherished projects to this end was a uniform edition of his works. It would enable him to add a preface or epilogue placing each one in its historical context and in the framework of his own development as an author, correct errors, prune ephemera and so establish a time-enduring oeuvre.

In 1958 Koestler had left Collins and signed up with Hutchinson on condition that they agree to fulfil his dream. An accord was reached, despite the scepticism of Bob (Sir Robert) Lusty, who was managing director, with responsibility for Koestler. There were endless knots to untie before the new edition could go ahead, largely due to Koestler's shifting between publishers in the 1940s and 1950s. The publishing rights to his books were held by various houses, notably Cape, and several key titles were still in print. Lusty proposed putting the uniform edition 'in cold storage' until all Koestler's books were out of print, whereupon the rights would revert to him automatically. Koestler exploded when he read this suggestion, since it was crucial to him that the appearance of the first instalments of the series coincide with his sixtieth birthday. Eventually a compromise was patched together by A. D. Peters and Lusty, but at a price. Koestler had to sacrifice his preferred order of republishing and compensate Cape for the loss of royalties if they allowed Hutchinson to reissue *Arrival and Departure*. As a result the 'uniform edition' turned into a dog's breakfast, with novels, autobiographical and non-fiction works appearing in no particular order.[43]

Having smoothed over this crisis, Koestler and Jefferies moved to Alpbach. Then, after a few days to unwind, he travelled on to Japan for a ten-day assignment commissioned by *Life*. He managed to write the piece while also conducting an acerbic correspondence with Hans Eysenck and Peter Medawar in the letter columns of *New Scientist* and *New Statesman* over their reviews of *The Act of Creation*. In mid-July Koestler and Jefferies flew from Munich to Athens, where he took part in a ten-day symposium. It was an imposing congregation of intellectuals from a variety of disciplines, including Buckminster Fuller, Margaret Mead and Barbara Ward. The participants seemed to spend much more time seeing the sights and sunbathing than discussing theories of creativity and art, though. Koestler had great fun, drank a lot of retsina and at one point 'read a poem he composed standing on the main table at dinner'.[44]

That year the visitors to Alpbach included Louis Fischer, Buber-Neumann, the scientist Paul Weiss, Leo Valiani, George Urban, the Hammers and Friedrich von Hayek, who was there to give a lecture at the Austrian College, and a *Newsweek* interviewer writing a profile of Koestler. In the middle of August he was excited to receive an invitation to spend several months in 1965 at the Center for Advanced Studies in the Behavioural Sciences (CAS) at Stanford University. Despite this news his mood went up and down. He nearly got into fights with Germans in the Dolomites and again in Alpbach. Jefferies remarked: 'Arthur feels more than ever [the] closeness of Nazis.' But this could not have been a suitable reason for his altercations with her. One day he got into a temper simply because she had cleared the breakfast table, thereby delaying their morning walk from 8.15 to 8.30 a.m. He was so angered by this that he stormed off alone.[45]

They drove back via Zurich, where they had a long-awaited rendezvous with Abraham Weinshall. It was the occasion for Koestler to tell him honestly why he had not revisited Israel and why he was unlikely ever to do so again. Weinshall had read 'Judah at the Crossroads', but he was shocked by Koestler's bluntness. Koestler may have become more anti-German, but this did not entail being more positive about his Jewishness. He was staking out a peculiar position in no-man's-land.[46]

In November he flew to California for a whirlwind tour of universities, giving lectures and holding seminars. He used the lectures to crusade against Behaviourism and believed that he was inoculating the young against this desiccated doctrine. Another reason for the visit was to locate a house in Palo Alto where he and Jefferies would stay while he was at the CAS. The year ended amid great excitement as they mothballed Montpelier Square and prepared to leave. Koestler was 'once more filled with childish expectations'. As with his journeys to Palestine, the USSR and America in 1950, he began with hopes of discovering some great truth and ended up bitterly disenchanted.[47]

V

Koestler and Jefferies travelled to Palo Alto, via New York and Boulder, Colorado. In New York they were married, in a perfunctory ceremony at the Municipal Building in Manhattan, on 8 January 1965. He was fifty-nine years old; she was just thirty-eight. For Cynthia it was the culmination of a slow, relentless campaign towards a much desired end; for Koestler it was as much a concession to American public morals as a legal recognition of the hardened pattern their relationship had acquired. After a week of seeing friends, celebrating and shopping in New York, Koestler took part in a symposium in Colorado. He gave a televised lecture in San Francisco, visited Ann Arbor again and did not really settle down at Stanford for several weeks.[48]

At his suggestion, the Fellows who were based at the Center for Advanced Studies that year were invited to participate in a seminar series on 'Partly Baked Ideas' or Pbi (a pun on Psi). The seminars started well, in a 'lively' spirit. But after two weeks Koestler began to find them 'claustrophobic'. He particularly objected to the habit that some Fellows had of interrupting speakers and asking them to defend or support a statement they had just made. The number of those attending the Pbi sessions halved and by the end of March Koestler 'felt like cancelling' the series. By mid-May only four faithful chums turned up. He was disappointed, but the reasons for their decline and his disillusion are not hard to find.

At first he was honoured by the invitation and thrilled to be taken seriously by scholars. He told Cynthia: 'The most gratifying thing is, that my various neurological hunches seem to be confirmed.' The San Francisco seminar gave 'time for me to warm up in the discussion, and for the others to realise, gradually – and some reluctantly – that I know, more or less, what I am talking about'. This was flattering, but over a prolonged exposure to the experts Koestler and his ideas tended to wilt: the 'more or less' was a crucial qualifier. He didn't like being challenged to support his hypotheses with empirical detail: it slowed up the flow of his thoughts and, unlike an experimental scientist, he did not feel constrained to substantiate his theories. He tended to dismiss this as 'pedantry' and to accuse his more cautious colleagues of being afraid to dare. Vanity was substituted for rigour as an explanation for their hesitancy, an inverted projection of Koestler's *modus operandi*.

Furthermore, he approached the seminar in a less than collegiate spirit. In May Cynthia learned that he had 'got all he wants out of it'. He used the seminar to confirm his existing hypotheses or to expose untenable positions in order to save his future credibility. If some detail that helped to sustain his grand idea was shown to be wrong, he simply looked for another piece of research to support the architecture. He left with exactly the same basic notions with which he had arrived. These were, in effect, the ideas he had presented in *Insight and Outlook* in 1949. It was typical of his relations with other intellectuals that when he could not win their total concurrence with his point of view he dismissed them. After three months at the CAS he decided that he did not want to return for another stay, which was on offer, because of the 'second rateness of [the] fellows'. According to Cynthia the stay was 'useful to rid Arthur of illusions and looking to scientists'.[49]

The CAS required that the Fellows do some teaching, but if Koestler wasn't much interested in learning he wasn't a very good teacher either. He enjoyed the lively audiences who attended his lectures in Berkeley and San Francisco, but he palled over the long haul. When the postgraduate seminars he gave at Stanford became dull for him he tried to wind them up. He invited the postgraduates to his house for a dinner, but found them 'hard going'. Koestler was a stimulating and entertaining lecturer, and he could inspire students in a seminar situation. But he lacked the patience to listen to *them* and was too arrogant to realise that they might have something to teach him.[50]

Naturally, there was a good deal of heavy socialising while Koestler and Cynthia were in residence. Paul Weiss visited for several days; Eric Erikson, the psychologist, came to give a lecture and stayed for dinner. Koestler met the writers Theodore Draper and Jessica Mitford at a reception for Californian high society and had an uproarious evening with Czeslaw Milosz. He drank heavily and consistently. Cynthia regularly reported that he crawled out of bed late in the mornings with a 'gigantic hangover'. Not all the Fellows approved of his conduct and there was a falling out at the end of term. Koestler wanted to have a *Schlussfest* that would include a skit in the style of his Viennese student days. He obligingly wrote a satire on the CAS and its members called 'Cloudcuckoocamp', but some of his colleagues objected to it. Koestler took umbrage and the concluding feast acquired a more sober hue.[51]

This final spat was consistent with Koestler's behaviour in similar situations: he felt compelled to spoil an experience, to spit in the eye of his hosts and turn himself into an alien. He took a last swing at the CAS when he delivered a paper in Washington the following September. In the course of analysing patterns of creativity he contrasted creative thinking to pedantry, which he characterised as highly specialised thinking and rigid behaviour of the kind found in some animals – such as the koala, a 'charming and pathetic creature'. He commented: 'Some of our departments of higher learning seem expressly designed for breeding koala bears.'[52]

Nevertheless, Koestler accomplished a good deal at Stanford. He started writing his next book, which would emerge as *The Ghost in the Machine*. Initially, he proposed co-writing it with one of the Fellows, the psychologist Karl Pribram, who went so far as to draft a chapter. But Koestler soon realised that he would not be able to work with him and wriggled out of the co-authorship arrangement. Pribram's fault was to demand that Koestler substantiate the generalisations he made in seminars and over the dinner-table. Koestler also wrote a paper for a symposium held at the Brain Research Institute at UCLA in March, a paper for the British Association in Cambridge and the lecture he delivered at the Bicentennial of the Smithsonian Institute in Washington, both in September. The paper he gave at UCLA was superficially about consciousness, but essentially it recapitulated the themes of his last book. It was not all hard grind, though. Koestler and Cynthia took several trips to San Francisco and regional beauty spots, including Monterey, Yosemite National Park and Big Sur.[53]

At the beginning of June they started to pack up and arranged to ship their new car, an Oldsmobile, to England. Cynthia found a tenant for the house, since they were leaving early, and disposed of Tycho, their latest dog. After the graduation ceremony on 12 June, during which Koestler got drunk, they flew to New York. In Manhattan he met his agent, his American publisher and various friends, including Burnham and Ivan Morris. A violent altercation between Koestler and Sally Belfrage, Morris's leftish companion, rather soured the last days. In the course of a conversation in Koestler's hotel room she equated the quality of life in East and West Berlin. Koestler was so enraged by this remark that he 'hit the roof, banged glass on table, threw down Mexican candlestick [and] told her to get out, which she and Ivan did'. A contrite Koestler later wrote to Burnham and the hapless Morris.[54]

They flew back to Paris and stayed in France for several days holidaying and looking for a house. In March Koestler had reviewed Françoise Gilot's memoir of her life with Picasso and he now arranged to meet her. They got on well: Koestler approved of her suggestion that they go to a night-club which boasted a floor show with a naked woman and a bear. To Cynthia's relief this outing had to be postponed. They left Paris on 23 June and began the long drive to Alpbach, stopping off in Switzerland for several fractious days where Koestler had business with his Swiss publishers and translators. For the rest of the summer he worked on the book he had started in California, prepared another volume of essays, *Drinkers of Infinity*, which would appear in 1968, and polished his autumn lectures. Visits by Eva Zeisel and Alex Weissberg disturbed the calm, but these interruptions were briefer than usual. Koestler was preparing for a heavy period of travelling and lecturing.[55]

At the start of September he delivered a paper on evolution to the British Association in Cambridge. Koestler confessed to the traditional annual gathering of scholars and amateur scientific enthusiasts that he was honoured to be invited since he was 'an outsider to the scientific establishment'. He took his presence to be a welcome sign that the 'two cultures' were growing closer. It was certainly a mark of his personal stature. His paper set out the themes of his next book, blending his theories of creativity with concepts of evolution. He suggested that the process of creative thinking was marked by four characteristics: originality, the combination of concepts or actions from different fields, the 'intervention of extra-conscious processes' and the construction of a new thought model, which he called integration. In order to make progress, original thinkers also had to destroy: scientific and artistic revolutions necessarily involved a phase of destruction. This was analogous to the working of evolution by which, he argued, species retreated to a more primitive state before advancing.[56]

A fortnight later he flew to Washington to take part in the Bicentennial of the Smithsonian Institute. The paper he delivered there enlarged on the evolutionary theme. Both creativity and evolution, he maintained, manifested 'a retreat from highly specialised adult forms of bodily structure and behaviour to an earlier, more plastic and less committed stage – followed by a sudden advance in a new direction'. His daring, unified theory of biological and mental processes rested heavily on his notion of hierarchies in nature and relied on argument by analogy rather than any comparative empirical research. The second theme of his presentation was a defence of this method and, as such, it can be read as a response to Medawar's critique of *The Act of Creation*. Koestler wanted to find an explanation for everything. His defence of analogical thinking was: 'It points . . . to a common denominator, a factor of purposiveness, without involving a *deus ex machina*.'[57] This was a classic turn-of-the-century quest of the kind he routinely mocked, which assumed both that the universe had to have a purpose and that it could be found, if it did. His passion for a unified theory also led him into the quagmire of free will and determinism, which he could never resolve satisfactorily. No one, however, could deny the ambition of his enterprise.

Sandwiched between these two important events, Koestler marked his sixtieth birthday. The day itself was 'a sombre *dimanche*', but it was followed by dinner with Bertrand Russell and his wife, whom Koestler unkindly labelled 'half mad', which was rather more fun. The *Sunday Times* marked the occasion with a long interview conducted by Cyril Connolly. Sadly, the printed version lacks the full flavour of the original encounter. The unedited transcript displays Connolly at his most pathetic – envious, indolent and banal – and Koestler at his most bumptious. The transcriber, who was under the impression that Cyril Connolly was a Member of Parliament, had great difficulty because of Koestler's accent and because 'Both speakers frequently interrupt each other making it impossible to hear either.' When Connolly began with an orotund meditation on the effects of ageing, Koestler curtly objected that he made it sound 'as if Johnson were interviewing Boswell'. Connolly promised 'to be as un-Johnsonian as possible', but Koestler didn't understand that he was using an exaggerated interrogative style because the interview would appear verbatim. Koestler thought that the tape would just provide 'raw material' and wanted to 'ramble and waffle'.

At Connolly's invitation, Koestler spent a good deal of time running down England and decrying the 'two cultures' of the middle and working classes. They fell to talking about his time in America, which provoked a daft exchange about national characteristics. Koestler observed that Japanese Americans looked 'American' and echoed one theory that their 'jaw muscles' were affected by enunciating the American accent. Connolly interjected: 'Ah, the jaw muscles. That could be a great many steaks. Chewing proteins.' And so these two sexagenarians rambled on amiably. The conversation flickered to life when Connolly resurrected the critics' question of whether Koestler was a journalist or a writer. He also annoyed him by referring to his recent output as 'popular science'. Koestler insisted sternly that: 'these books are not popular science. They are a reinterpretation.' He chided Connolly, *de haute en bas*, for not being able to grasp this and reiterated that it was necessary to appreciate that he had moved on. 'The seasons of life are so different' he admonished, implying that his interviewer was stuck in one phase – which was not an unfair observation. Connolly, however, showed rather more interest in Koestler's antique furniture and old masters.[58]

During 1966 and 1967 Koestler was preoccupied with *The Ghost in the Machine* and worked single-mindedly on the first draft until early March. To stave off the depression that accompanied the completion of a book he then kept busy supervising the redecoration of Montpelier Square. No new book came to mind. He toyed with another volume of autobiography, but got little further than notes and a thematic outline. In May he and Cynthia, who had been extremely ill with hepatitis earlier in the year, went to Alpbach via France and Germany. In mid-summer Koestler returned to Boulder, Colorado, to give a paper and stayed in the USA for a month.

They were back in London at the start of September when Koestler resumed work revising the book. The first hints of a new direction in his thinking came in two major reviews he wrote of Sir Alister Hardy's Gifford Lectures. Hardy was Professor of Zoology at Oxford, but he had developed an unorthodox view of evolution, which Koestler found fascinating and congenial. Hardy disputed the mainstream Darwinian view that natural selection was a blind, random process. He believed that the evidence of learning across generations suggested the transmission of acquired characteristics, while the rapidly learned patterns of uniform behaviour within species implied a form of telepathy. Hardy suggested that this form of telepathic communication might extend to mankind and might be the medium between humanity and the *anima mundi* or divine being.[59]

On a more mundane level, after years of awful, irresponsible motoring the law finally caught up with Koestler in March 1967. Police stopped his car when it was spotted weaving through Chelsea at five miles an hour in the early hours of the morning as Koestler drove back from a party thrown by Sir Martyn Beckett. When the police asked him to get out of the car he staggered about and was immediately arrested for drunken driving. To make matters worse, he threw a fit when he was taken to Chelsea police station. In his confused and inebriated state, he claimed, he had delusions of falling into the hands of Nazis and flailed wildly. In a subsequent appearance at Marlborough Street Court he admitted to driving under the influence of alcohol, was fined twenty pounds and banned from driving for one year. The newspapers had a field day with the story and he unwisely rose to the bait, firing off letters to *The Times* asserting that he had not been driving dangerously. On the contrary, he had been going at five to ten miles an hour precisely because he knew he was a little intoxicated. Koestler gave the impression of a vain and arrogant man who was always in the right: it was the rest of the world which was wrong. One correspondent to *The Times*, who was evidently familiar with his conduct, added insult to injury by writing: 'Mr Koestler seems to be particularly concerned at the fact that his public image has been adversely affected. He needn't worry. It hasn't.'[60]

In the spring he concentrated on *The Drinkers of Infinity*, his collected essays for 1956–67. In May the couple went to Alpbach and Koestler started the preparations for a symposium that he planned there for the following summer. But the year was dominated by the appearance in August of *The Ghost in the Machine*, causing consternation among many of his closest friends and colleagues.[61]

The Ghost in the Machine had an enormously wide and diverse impact. For example, it supplied the title and some of the material for the 1981 album by the rock group Police. It owed this influence to its essentially political message and the oblique manner in which it addressed the anxieties of the atomic age in the jumpy years after the Berlin Wall and Cuban missile crises. It would be a mistake to see it as a scientific treatise or to ascribe its persuasive power to the scientific argument. Koestler himself described it as dealing with the 'predicament of man' and placed it alongside *The Sleepwalkers* and *The Act of Creation* as the final part of a trilogy: 'the creativity and pathology of the human mind are, after all, two sides of the same model coined in the evolutionary mint.' Mankind was the victim of an evolutionary mistake, 'some built-in error or deficiency that predisposes him towards self-destruction'. To people hungering for an explanation of conflict from the Cold War to the Vietnam War, sweating in their beds at the prospect of all-out nuclear strikes, this book promised an answer. But Koestler warned that it would not be a conventional one. First he had to sweep away the Behaviourist analysis of human conduct and offer 'a new, broader conception of the living organism'. [62]

The book begins with a brilliant and funny attack on 1950s psychology. Behaviourism, which he claimed on rather flimsy evidence dominated academia, was a blight on understanding the crisis of mankind because it banished notions of consciousness and the unconscious: 'It is impossible to arrive at a diagnosis of man's predicament – and by implication at a therapy – by starting from a psychology which denies the existence of mind, and lives on specious analogies drawn from the bar-pressing activities of rats.'[63]

Koestler worked in his own theories to provide an alternative explanation of memory, forgetting, creativity, habitual actions and the problem of consciousness. He argued by analogy with research in various fields, that 'wherever there is life, it must be hierarchically organised'. Open-ended hierarchies were to be found in language, cells and military units. The individual units in these hierarchies were 'holons'; each holon possessed assertive and integrative tendencies and its activity was determined by the assembly of holons on the level above, but freer with respect to those below.[64] To a large extent,

Koestler was just describing existing hypotheses in his own language. He left out anything which didn't fit. Much of what he said repeated his earlier work; his tone was often hectoring and impatient.

In the second part he slated the classic Darwinian account of the ascent of man from a 'blob of slime' by a process of random mutations, the most successful of which survived. In contradistinction he insisted that evolution conformed to purposeful, hierarchical principles: 'there must be unitary laws underlying evolutionary variety, permitting unlimited variations on a limited number of themes'.[65] This was a further sign that Koestler could not abide randomness: for all his denunciation of determinism he wanted life to have a point. The next step in his argument underlined this even more starkly: all evolution was characterised by a pattern of retreat before an advance, *reculer pour mieux sauter*. 'Evolution is a process with a fixed code of rules, but with adaptable strategies. The code is inherent in the conditions of our planet; it restricts progress to a limited number of avenues; while at the same time all living matter strives towards the optimal utilisation of the offered possibilities.'[66]

This is an extraordinary, teleological argument. The notion that a dandelion, for example, 'strives towards the optimal utilisation of the offered possibilities' may possibly be true — but in what sense and could it be proven? Koestler argued by analogy and assertion. Despite his tirades against Behaviourists who argued by analogy from rats to humans, Koestler routinely maintained that what held good for cells and ringworm was equally true for humans.[67]

Having established the 'order' of things, Koestler turned to 'disorder' or the 'predicament of mankind'. The story of humanity illustrated a basic tendency towards destruction and self-destruction. This was not due to a residue of animal aggression, a 'territorial imperative', or a simple response to environmental stimuli. Nor was it a question of a Freudian 'death wish'. Instead, he traced human aggression to an excess of devotion or self-transcendence. Language played a key part in this since it enabled humans, unlike other animals, to differentiate one another, band together and provide reasons for slaughtering other species members. Finally, it was the very awareness of mortality that spurred humans to blood sacrifices. These unique tendencies had biological foundations.[68]

Koestler speculated that 'the delusional streak which runs through our history may be an endemic form of paranoia, built into the wiring circuits of the human brain'. Possibly mankind was a 'biological freak'. Building on the neurological research of Paul McLean he suggested that evolution had superimposed a new rationalising brain on an old emoting brain, but built few connecting mechanisms or hierarchical controls. Hence man was prey to excessive devotion and altruism, an archetypal pattern rooted in species development.[69]

This condition could not persist. Koestler warned that in view of over-population, the knowledge revolution, the capacity for global destruction and the recurrence of armed conflicts it was only a matter of time before humanity wiped itself out. There was no time to wait for man's nature to evolve: it was necessary to intervene directly, using drugs in the same way they had been used to eliminate serious diseases and regulate human reproduction. 'Our present tranquillisers, barbiturates, stimulants, anti-depressants and combinations thereof, are merely a first step towards a more sophisticated range of aids to promote a co-ordinated, harmonious state of mind.'[70]

Koestler even devoted a few pages to how the wonder-drug could be administered and what would happen if some countries adopted it but not others. Yet the treatment of the practical issues was scant, to say the least. Koestler, as ever, was not interested in irritating details. He offered an instant panacea to the world's political problems and many readers fell on his solution like thirsty travellers on a desert oasis. The response to the book is all the more surprising because the first two hundred pages are dense, jargon-ridden, sometimes unintelligible and not really necessary. The crux of the argument was all contained in the third part.

The various strands to the book confused reviewers. The psychologist Anthony Storr, writing in *The Times*, declared it was 'a remarkable book'. But many others couldn't understand why Koestler wanted to explain everything in the universe as well as making some sage observations about human destructiveness. The American historian of medicine Robert Jay Lifton, in the *New York Times Book Review*, saw 'flashes of brilliance in Koestler's ambitious explorations, especially in his general ordering of evolution and in his compelling description of some of the new features of the post-Hiroshima world'. Lifton, who later wrote on Nazi doctors, shared Koestler's interest in the darker side of humanity. 'But,' he continued, 'the book's erratic combination of unfocussed and over-focussed argument eventually renders it tedious.' Leslie Fiedler, in the *New Statesman*, accused Koestler of being out of touch with young people and the new social movements that were going to save the planet. William Sargent, in the *Spectator*, dismissed the book as 'science fiction gone into orbit'.[71]

However, the reading public defied the critics. Koestler's apocalypticism resonated with a genuine fear for the future of mankind, especially among the young. They were also more forgiving towards his penchant for a drug-based salve. But the book has not worn well. With the end of the Cold War the urgency of its message has dissipated and, as a result, the mechanics of the argument look more exposed than ever. *The Ghost in the Machine* represented the bankruptcy of Koestler's political and social thought and the beginning of a move away from empirical realities into mysticism and the occult in the quest for a solution to the 'predicament of mankind'.

VI

Over the previous few years Koestler's interest in the Jews, Zionism and Israel had been muted, but it had not disappeared. In November 1963 he wrote to A. D. Peters: '*Israel.* I would like to go for a few weeks as soon as the page proofs of the new book are finished (presumably February)' and asked him to look out for some assignments that would pay for the journey. He watched Israel's fortunes closely and with concern. In 1964 he responded to Weinshall's prompting by agreeing 'to get together with David Astor and a few other close friends' to see what could be done to present Israel's case.[72]

Several times in 1965 and 1966 he came close to going. He told Weinshall: 'I am pining to see you and Jascha and a very few other old friends and to have a look at the new generation, and so on. But I do not want to get involved in controversies, and that alas seems to be unavoidable.' He said that he 'would go at once if the Hebrew University invited me' and, sure enough, in 1965 he was invited by its president, Eliahu Elath. Koestler asked to defer the visit to early 1966 and a few months later he cancelled the plan. He wrote to Weinshall: 'anybody with a smattering of psychology must suspect that to be prevented for nearly twenty years from re-visiting a country to which one has such close ties can only be explained by some equally strong inner resistance. I do not want to bore you with an attempted analysis of this resistance against stirring up the past; I can only ask for your indulgence for postponing the visit indefinitely.' Even so, when Teddy Kollek, now Mayor of Jerusalem, added his voice Koestler buckled and promised to make his 'long postponed' visit in 1967. It was overtaken by the Six Day War.[73]

The war affected Koestler deeply. He told Tosco Fyvel that 'had Israel been in real danger, he, then in his sixties would have rushed there to fight for her'. When Weinshall wrote plaintively: 'Many friends are asking: where is Koestler? Why is he silent? why does he not raise his voice?' Koestler replied: 'of course you and the country were constantly in my thoughts – we lived by the radio news like millions of others.' But there was no need for him to speak up: public opinion was pro-Israel and he was known to be a fervent Zionist so his words would be discounted. He hoped that Israel's victory would provide the basis for a permanent peace settlement.[74]

Koestler's unwillingness to identify himself as a Jew was paradoxical in many ways. He was perceived as a Jew, certainly by *other* Jews. The leading Anglo-Jewish novelist Louis Golding went so far as to tell him: 'although, dear Koestler, you're not flagrantly Anglo, or luridly Jewish, you're so much the Lord of the Anglo-Jewish scribes'.[75] Some non-Jews also made a point of his Jewishness, such as Evelyn Waugh, who wrote to Nancy Mitford after reading one of Koestler's *Horizon* essays: 'I believe this jew is a chum of S Boots Esq [Cyril Connolly] and all the little bootses.' Koestler was offended by anti-Semitism, yet he continued to associate with Henry Green and didn't hide his Jewishness from him. He signed off one letter to Green 'with rabbinical greetings'. Nor did Koestler conceal his Jewishness from himself. His 1966 notes for a further volume of autobiography make Jewishness a prominent feature. Provisionally dubbed 'A Life Sliced Lengthways' (he had no talent for titles), it would comprise: 'quarrels; crusades; do gooders; alcohol; women I thought I knew; dogs; hangings; author and critics; vanities; honesties; quixotics; guilt; taste; academics; littérateurs; the snob in us; Jews and Hebrews; Houses; Essenes'.[76] Finally, he maintained an ambivalent relationship with Israel and Zionism: never denying his attachment, but not doing much about it, either. If there is a common factor in this it is the negativity of his Jewishness. He would not assert it or stress it. It had no warm or positive connotations to celebrate or nurture. It was a source of discomfort, for example when as a Jew he spent time in Germany and Austria or in Henry Green's company.

Koestler's own experience proved that the solution for the Jewish Question which he mapped out in 'Judah at the Crossroads' was a specious one. He could never assimilate or lose his Jewishness: indeed, the more he attempted to, the more he noted 'Jewish' Jews and was irritated by them. Equally, the harder he tried, the more anti-Semitic slights troubled him. For two decades the Jewish issue was sublimated in the search for an entirely new form of politics and society, in just the same way that for seven years it had been subsumed in the struggle for world revolution. When this solution seemed as distant as ever, Koestler returned to the Jewish Question with a vengeance, making it the subject of his last major authorial endeavour.

Chapter 13
'Reculer pour mieux sauter', 1967–76

In his sixties, with the effects of age and the balm of recognition, Arthur Koestler began to mellow. In 1968 he received the prestigious Sonning Prize from the University of Copenhagen. It was followed by an honorary doctorate from Queen's University, in Kingston, Ontario. In 1972 he became a Commander of the British Empire (CBE) and in 1974 a Companion of the Royal Society of Literature. He was invited to deliver keynote lectures at symposia and conferences around the world and to preside over the cogitations of lofty think-tanks. He was interviewed and profiled on Austrian, German, British and Australian television, and profiled in the international press.

Cynthia wistfully hoped that the CBE would remedy Koestler's itchy feet: 'recognition means strengthening his roots and I hope and pray he won't decide again to leave and live abroad.'[1] She was to be disappointed for a few more years. In 1968 they travelled to Alpbach for the summer, then to Canada, briefly, before making a long trip across the Pacific and through Australasia. This was Koestler's last great geographical adventure, although he continued to oscillate within more limited parameters. He finally tired of Alpbach and sold the *Schreiberhäusl* in 1971, only to exchange it for a villa in the South of France. In the same year he felt the need, too, for a country retreat in England and bought a farmhouse at Denston in Suffolk. During 1972 he made trips to Austria, Iceland, Sweden and Holland, while moving between Montpelier Square and Denston when he was in England. In spring 1973 he yet again retraced his wartime flight through France and, from 1973 to 1976, Koestler and Cynthia spent the winter months at Eze-bord-la-Mer, on the French Riviera.

Public acclaim, like the passing of the years, may have soothed him, but he remained volatile. Cynthia bore the brunt of his obsessions and rages with a stoical humour born out of genuine adoration. His residual intemperance was also evident in his politics: in the 1970s he became a Tory and a keen union basher. At the same time he was generous to needy acquaintances and a thoughtful, amusing companion with a wide circle of impressive friends. Many of these friendships overlapped with his work, which now came to focus on para-science. Koestler gravitated increasingly towards the unconventional and the bizarre, as if he were uncomfortable with his establishment stature and conservative life-style.

In 1968 he organised a heavyweight international symposium in Alpbach, which was intended to bring together the world's leading thinkers to forge an effective challenge to 'reductionism', Behaviourism and other materialistic disciplines that he deemed to be outmoded. The proceedings, which Koestler co-edited, were published under the title *Beyond Reductionism* (1969): it was to be his last dalliance with conventional science. His next book, *The Case of the Midwife Toad* (1971), sought to rehabilitate Paul Kammerer, an outcast from the scholarly community, and provocatively contested neo-Darwinian orthodoxy. It was followed by two studies on parapsychology and the paranormal: *The Roots of Coincidence* (1972) and *The Challenge of Chance* (1973). Koestler also returned to fiction, writing short stories and a novel, *The Call Girls* (1972), although this was in essence a fictionalised version of the Alpbach symposium.

His slowly reviving interest in Israel and Zionism was galvanised by the 1973 Yom Kippur War. Gradually he associated himself with Zionist causes, although he lost none of his ambivalence. In 1973 he published a revised version of 'Judah at the Crossroads', then began his last major original work: *The Thirteenth Tribe* (1976). This controversial study of an obscure aspect of Jewish history arguably provides the key to the final phase of Koestler's life and, by extension, his odyssey through the twentieth century. Koestler believed that a fundamental principle of evolution was *reculer pour mieux sauter*: he could not advance until he had returned to his Jewish roots and resolved their legacy once and for all. But the very fact that he had to go back to his Jewishness was proof that he had not escaped it, and never would, since in so doing he merely drew attention to the anomaly of the Jews and his own anomalous position within that anomaly.

I

On 12 January 1968 Koestler learned that he was to receive the Sonning Prize. It was awarded annually to individuals who the panel of judges at Copenhagen University felt had made an outstanding contribution to European culture. Previous recipients included Albert Schweitzer, Bertrand Russell, Niels Bohr, Karl Barth and Laurence Olivier. In addition to the prestige the prize was worth

140,000 Danish kroner. Koestler was 'deeply moved' by the proffered honour and accepted gracefully. The lavish award ceremony
was held in Copenhagen on 19 April. He spent several weeks
working on his acceptance speech, which took shape as 'The Urge
to Self-Destruction', a reprise of *The Ghost in the Machine*. This
presentation was so much more clearly focused than the book that it
suggests the latter would have been better as an essay.

Contra those who argued that wars were an outcome of a residual
animal aggressiveness, or the 'territorial imperative' to be found
throughout the animal world, he pointed out that most men fight for
a cause: the problem was not aggression 'but an excess of self-transcending devotion'. None of this would happen without language,
which enabled men to express and define differences. In lieu of
abolishing language the only way to curb human destructiveness
would be to re-tool the brain, although in Copenhagen he refrained
from repeating the controversial prescription in *The Ghost in the
Machine* and ended on a speculative note about how advances in
genetic engineering might encourage evolution along its path. The
paper was a perfect summary of politics as science: the relationship
between political thought, the 'pathology of mankind' and the life
sciences to which Koestler had turned after superficially renouncing
political activism.[2]

Apart from some writing and reviewing, he spent the first part of
1968 organising his own symposium on science, due to convene in
Alpbach in the summer. Its aim was to challenge what Koestler saw
as the orthodoxies governing the study of evolution, human
intelligence, cosmology and psychology. Most of those invited were
personal friends, but several, like Jean Piaget, Viktor Frankl and F. A.
von Hayek, were eminent scholars whose attendance was a mark of
the esteem in which Koestler was held by many thinkers. It was
funded by a grant of $1000 from the Ford Foundation and advances
from the three publishers who contracted to bring out the
proceedings: Hutchinson, Macmillan and Fritz Molden Verlag.[3]

The symposium, which took place from 5 to 9 June, involved a
considerable amount of logistical work and endless headaches for
himself and Cynthia. But the tape-recorded discussions show how,
once it was under way, Koestler displayed extraordinary mastery of
not one, but several disciplines and revelled in the learned exchanges.
It might be argued that he was never seriously challenged, since all
those invited were already in broad agreement with the need to
refute Behaviourism and achieve a synthesis of new thinking, but
Koestler and the participants took issue with each other on many

points, big and small, and he gave as good as he got.[4]

Koestler opened the proceedings, which were held in the buildings of the Austrian College, by welcoming his guests and apologising jokingly for being 'a trespasser from the humanist camp'. He explained that he had long felt uneasy about the 'totalitarian claims of the neo-Darwinian orthodoxy' and Behaviourism. But he had discovered in the course of his scholarly travels a wider discontent with 'the insufficient emancipation of the life sciences from the mechanistic concepts of nineteenth-century physics,· and the resulting crudely reductionist philosophy'. No effective riposte would be feasible, however, until scientists had achieved a 'new synthesis'.[5]

The distinguished British zoologist W. H. Thorpe chaired the subsequent papers and discussions while Cynthia operated the tape recorder. Paul Weiss went first. He was followed by Ludwig von Bertalanffy, the pioneer of systems theory; the Swedish neurobiologist Holger Hyden; and Jean Piaget, the renowned child psychologist, with Bärbel Inhelder, a colleague from Geneva University. Blanche Bruner read the paper by Jerome Bruner, a psychoanalyst from Harvard. Koestler delivered a paper summarising his theory of 'holons'. It was praised by Bertalanffy for the 'wealth of ideas'. Weiss said that he was 'in full agreement with practically everything Koestler said'. Viktor Frankl claimed to have said something similar twenty years earlier, but then added that he was not sure it was possible to equate the relations between a cell and an organism with the relations between an individual and society. Weiss appended a gentle criticism of Koestler's use of analogies and was echoed by J. R. Smythies, a psychiatrist from Edinburgh University. Seymour Kety, a Harvard-based psychiatric pharmacologist, was rather more aggressive: 'you made a leap which you did not take time to explain . . . into free will and consciousness, which I do not frankly believe you can fit into your system'.[6]

Smythies next reviewed theories of consciousness, although Koestler thought he treated the matter rather too lightly. Paul MacLean, a neurophysiologist from the National Institute of Mental Health, Bethesda, Maryland, summed up his research into the 'paranoid streak' in man, a theory that had exercised a huge influence over Koestler. David McNeill, professor of psychology at Chicago University, and F. A. von Hayek, whose formal title as Professor of Economics at Freiburg University seriously downplayed his range of learning, gave very dense papers.

Occasionally the debates really came to life. Seymour Kety had a sharp exchange with Koestler, and although it is tempting to see this as Koestler getting his own back for their earlier spat the clash was partly provoked by Kety's misrepresentation of Koestler's ideas.[7] After the British geneticist C. H. Waddington surveyed the history of theories of evolution, Koestler pressed him to admit that neo-Darwinians could not adequately explain the mechanics of evolution and should allow room for Lamarckian principles.[8] Viktor Frankl, the Austrian psychiatrist and concentration camp survivor, ended the symposium with a powerful summation of his view that man was suffering a 'noogenic neurosis' rooted in 'existential frustration'.

At the end of each day the participants retired to the *Weinstuben*, of which Alpbach boasted several, or sat on the terraces of cafés and restaurants conversing animatedly in the late afternoon sun. The symposium spilled over into the streets and inns.

When the guests finally departed Koestler and Cynthia were exhausted. The absence of any ringing conclusion tended to obscure the other aspects of the confabulation and left Koestler deflated. He only began to feel that it had been worthwhile when, during the autumn, he and Smythies came to edit the papers and the transcripts of the discussions. For most readers the published text is almost unintelligible, but the symposium can be experienced vicariously in a more palatable form in *The Call Girls*. The novelised version explicitly voices Koestler's political, almost messianic hopes for the gathering. It also allows him to vent his frustration with some of the participants, several of whom who are caricatured mercilessly. The novel, however, departs significantly from the actual symposium in one respect. No neo-Darwinians or Behaviourists were invited to the Alpbach Symposium, so there was no 'opposition'. In order to add some spice to his fiction, Koestler throws in a couple of hapless Behaviourists. Sadly, this does not do much to help the plot, such as it is.[9]

In addition to the editing work, Koestler and Cynthia prepared for a long journey to Canada and the Pacific region. First they flew to Canada, where Koestler was awarded an Honorary Doctorate in Law by Queen's University, Kingston, Ontario. He also gave a paper to a symposium on 'The University and the Ethics of Change' which took place as part of the celebrations marking the installation of the university's new principal. The symposium was broadcast and later published.[10]

Koestler's paper took up a theme broached to him by Dennis Gabor in the spring. Gabor was a Hungarian-born Jewish physicist who had lived in England since 1934 when he abandoned Germany.

He held a position at Imperial College, London, in the 1950s and was awarded the Nobel prize for physics in 1971 in recognition of his path-breaking work on holography. Gabor and Koestler corresponded and met frequently. Recently, he had remarked to Koestler about the 'terrifying outbreak of irrationality among the students' on American campuses and suggested it as a subject to which he might profitably turn his mind. At first Koestler demurred, remarking that he was a bit long in the tooth to discuss youth. But the student riots in May 1968 in Paris, which he keenly monitored, and their echoes elsewhere, finally convinced him otherwise.

In his address he turned the accepted wisdom upside down, blaming student unrest on the failure of the teaching profession. This was really a device for yet another attack on the alleged 'dominance' of academia by the practitioners of 'reductionism'. In an echo of Viktor Frankl's Alpbach paper he argued that reductionism, Behaviourism, and neo-Darwinism had evacuated meaning from life. Humans were reduced to mere robots; life became the product of a random process of natural selection. The students, he concluded, 'are, simply, hungry for meaning, which their teachers cannot provide'.[11]

From Canada, they embarked on the last of Koestler's great, globe-girdling escapades. It had its origins with an Australian TV company, Crawford Productions, which wanted to make three programmes with Koestler for the HSV–7 TV station in Melbourne. Negotiations on the terms and conditions opened in September 1968. Koestler was offered the cost of the round trip for himself and Cynthia, and a fee of $175 per episode. He also obtained an additional commission from the *Sunday Times*. But the trip turned into a miserable experience. Because they travelled first class, Koestler and Cynthia were efficiently shuttled from one airport lounge to another and one Hilton to another. As a devotee of indigenous arts and culinary traditions, he found this frustrating. The time he spent in Australia was characterised by a series of farcical misunderstanding, which left him angry and embittered.[12]

Koestler accepted the invitation to take part in the *Encounter* television series, a sort of elevated chat show, on condition that the host and programme co-ordinator Barry Jones would 'protect Mr Koestler from other media and from public appearances except as mutually agreed'. Koestler consented to several events for the Congress for Cultural Freedom and the Australian Howard League (since Australia preserved the death penalty), but Jones, who had an interest in the campaign to abolish capital punishment, also tried to get Koestler active in this matter. When he met him and Cynthia at Sydney airport on 21 November, clutching a bunch of orchids, he informed his guest that he had been in discussion with the Australian branch of Amnesty, who wanted to organise a mass meeting in Melbourne to be addressed by Koestler. Somehow Jones had failed to make clear to Koestler that he was booked to give a lecture and Koestler in turn made it clear that he was not happy with the arrangement. Unfortunately, Jones failed to transmit this news to the organisers, with dire consequences. In the meantime, Koestler was whisked from one airport and press conference to another. On the day of his arrival he faced journalists, never a task he relished, in Sydney, Melbourne and at the HSV–7 studios. The programme makers were determined to squeeze as much pre-publicity as possible out of Koestler's fame. But to the ageing and severely jet-lagged savant who had indicated his reluctance to engage in punditry it was deeply irritating. He sank into a foul mood.[13]

The gruelling schedule did nothing to improve things. Koestler made the first recording the very next day and had a filmed rendezvous with students set up two days after that. The third recording session was on 29 November and the last on 3 December. In between he was supposed to give the lecture to Amnesty on 24 November, attend an anti-hanging dinner a few days later, appear at a CCF reception in Sydney on 1 December, then a Howard League dinner. Needless to say, there were additional lunches and dinners with local celebrities. He and Cynthia had only two completely free days. Faced by this marathon it was understandable that he refused to give a formal lecture to Amnesty, for which in any case he had not prepared. Jones frantically improvised an alternative format for the evening, which had already been widely advertised. While over 800 people converged expectantly on the hall of Victoria College of Pharmacy, he called on Sir John Berry, a prominent Melbourne judge, and a handful of academics to man a panel which he himself chaired. Koestler delayed appearing until the last moment and the proceedings started forty-five minutes late. He then refused to make an opening statement and would only answer questions from the floor. Unfortunately the sole roving microphone was ineffectual and half the audience could not hear his answers since the stage mike was not much better. After an hour hundreds of people started to stream out. It was an embarrassing mess, reported in gruesome detail in the local and national newspapers the next morning.[14]

The impression of petulance was confirmed in the minds of Australians when Koestler abruptly cancelled his appearance for the

CCF, claiming that the recordings were taking up all his time. His bad temper showed through in the television encounters with Barry Jones. One reviewer noted that he had no rapport with his interlocutor and seemed to brush off Jones's questions about his youthful adventures in a bid to get on to what interested him, namely science and the human condition. For one programme, filmed at Melbourne University, Koestler was bombarded with questions and declamations from a bizarrely mixed panel of unruly students, politicians and academics. He repeatedly lost patience with the other participants and came across as arrogant and aloof. The press, scenting blood, went for the kill. Profiles of him in the Melbourne and Sydney newspapers were characterised by an undercurrent of ridicule. One concentrated on Cynthia, goading her unwisely into revealing how much she serviced Koestler and exposing him as a pint-sized martinet. It was archly headlined 'Author does not wish to be disturbed'. Another (not the only one) cruelly noted his diminutive stature and middle-aged spread: 'his trousers are worn high over a thick waist, and he is short.' At least this was balanced with a vignette of his generosity, recording how at the airport he patiently signed copies of his books lovingly presented by an elderly displaced European.[15]

Koestler did not recoup his reputation in more intimate encounters. His antipodean fans wanted to discuss his political writings, but he obdurately refused to play ball even with those with whom he had much in common. One member of the televised panel debate was Bob Santamaria, a leading anti-Communist who during the 1940s created a movement to purge the trades unions and the Australian Labour Party. Koestler lunched with him the next day, but Santamaria, a strong Catholic, recalled: 'I wanted to talk about his politics. He wished to talk about my religion.' Although Santamaria was renowned for browbeating people, 'Being the stronger character, he [Koestler] won.' Having wrestled the topic on to his chosen ground, Koestler went on to deride anyone who was a believing Catholic in a way that was bound to offend Santamaria. On the eve of his departure he received a scorching reproof from Rosemary Jones: 'You remarked at a dinner recently that "the trouble with one's enemies is that they have lovable characteristics". Unfortunately, your stay in Melbourne has not been long enough to prove that woolly generalisation true in your case; unless, of course, Mrs Koestler can be classed as a characteristic.'[16]

Mr and Mrs Koestler eventually flew out of Australia on 5 December 1968. But Koestler left a time bomb ticking away behind him. On Christmas Eve the *Melbourne Age* printed a short story he had written on the theme of the crucifixion. It was mildly blasphemous since it speculated on what might have gone through the mind of Jesus as he perished on the cross having intended only to court death so as to jolt an absent, irresponsible deity, his 'father', into saving mankind. God does not make an appearance and Jesus dies in agony, feeling betrayed and knowing that for all his suffering his message would be twisted for evil purposes without restraint from any deity. The story was brazenly at odds with the seasonal mood and triggered dozens of letters to the paper, most of them hostile. It was accused of being a 'corrupt, grossly unintelligent fantasy' and 'anti-Christian'. Although the fiction found some defenders, it left Australians with a sour view of their recently departed guest.[17]

Koestler exacted his revenge on Australia for the inconveniences and indignities he had suffered there by penning a scabrous article for the *Sunday Times* summarising the visit. It was so caustic that it even drew a protest from the Australian High Commissioner in London. Koestler defined the 'Australian character' as 'goodwill devoid of grace, a down-to-earth pragmatism that can be aesthetically offensive, a culture that is deliberately, almost defiantly, suburban'. Unlimited space bred agoraphobia, which in turn promoted conformism: Australians were not only dull, they were all dull in the same way. He detected a looming crisis of identity in Australia: did it want to remain a uniform society that was literally thin on the ground, or did it want to open up to large-scale immigration from Europe and Asia, which would make its society more diverse? This was a stupendous and risky choice to make and brought into play all the psychological factors on which he loved to speculate. In the light of developments in Australia since the 1980s, including the ending of a whites-only immigration policy and the deliberate cultivation of multiculturalism, his observations were actually very prescient. At the time, however, Australians only noted his scathing description of their country and its populace.[18]

The journey back took them to Fiji, Honolulu, Hawaii and the Caribbean. What struck Koestler about the places they visited was not their singularity, but the encroaching sameness. He noted the emerging global culture of airports, hotels, international cuisine and tourist sights. Modern travel and package holidays were destroying the individuality of cultures and societies. This was a perceptive, though not unprecedented, observation. Koestler showed his brilliance as a journalist, however, by burrowing just that bit deeper beneath the patina of a story that had already caught the eye of many travel writers and commentators.

In Fiji he noted the tension between the Polynesians and the Asians who had been brought to the island by the British. He predicted that when the colonial power finally left there would be communal conflict. This *aperçu* led him to a generalisation that was prophetic: 'the world is rapidly moving towards a mass-produced, uniform culture, and yet at the same time both the global confrontations and the venomous local conflicts of religion, language and race are getting not less but more acute.'[19] In one sentence he caught the contradictory and explosive trends within globalisation that were to define the 1990s. But he did it in the 1960s. Sadly, Koestler had such a prejudiced opinion of journalism in general, and his own reportage in particular, that he derived little pleasure or pride from his circumnavigation. By the end of January 1969 his morale was sagging and did not recover until he had delivered the *Sunday Times* articles a few weeks later.

During the spring he thrashed about looking for a subject. For a while he played with the idea of a biography of Mesmer, the eighteenth-century hypnotist, but dropped it. He was in such a brittle mood that he noted telegraphically: 'unable to work unless occupants of the house in harmonious mood. Even the oafish handiman [*sic*] . . .' In February he came up with the idea for a novel about science and scientists, which would eventually mature as *The Call Girls*, although with his unerring ability to invent a bad title his first choice was 'The Parameter of Urgency'. Fiction was recovering its attraction. He was wearied by the need to keep up with scientific literature and longed for the creative freedom which the novel offered. Rather pompously he wrote: 'Time I stopped reading all that psychological stuff. It would add little. Kafka and Dostoievsky [*sic*] did not have to keep up with technical journals.'[20]

In the summer he and Cynthia journeyed by train to Alpbach, where Koestler intended to ease the problems of accommodating his numerous friends and intellectual collaborators by building a guest wing on to the *Schreiberhäusl*. Despite years of knowing Koestler, the village *Bürgermeister* was not co-operative and stood on the planning rules. It was an unhappy contest and engendered the first stages of disillusionment with his Tyrolean retreat. Nevertheless the summer was otherwise fairly peaceful and he wrote a short story that would later appear with *The Call Girls*.[21]

Back in London, Koestler and Cynthia threw a party that was to become an annual event. The guest list included Ivan Morris, the literary agent Pat Kavanagh, the literary editor and translator of

Proust Terence Kilmartin, the novelist Kingsley Amis and the psychiatrist Anthony Storr, a selection that indicated the breadth of Koestler's contacts and the varied fields of his activity. His science writing had brought new friends, some from surprising quarters. Doris Lessing wrote to him in admiration of *The Ghost in the Machine* and *The Act of Creation*: 'You've been digging in the same field as I have.' A new generation of critics, like George Steiner, emerged for whom his current philosophical undertakings were as important as his political background.[22]

Meanwhile, Koestler had to prepare for two major speaking engagements. In November he gave a paper to a symposium on 'Uses and Abuses of Psychiatry' organised by the World Psychiatric Association in London. This was followed by the Cheltenham Lecture, the highlight of the Cheltenham Festival. He took the opportunity of his address to the psychiatric profession to launch another assault on the Behaviourist legacy. It was a bravura performance before such an audience, laying waste to psychiatry by quoting one school against another and showing that a certain type of behaviour would be classed very differently in Britain, America or elsewhere. Psychiatry was in a mess: the fault lay with psychology. His conclusion was, in so many words, psychiatrist heal thyself.

His Cheltenham Lecture was in a more gentle vein. He returned to the problem of creativity and speculated on the phases of literary and cultural development. In order for literature to progress he argued that it was necessary to experiment with, rebel against and reconstruct existing tropes. The range of literary references he deployed was vast: it is extraordinary to juxtapose this cultivated and elegant discourse with the lecture on psychiatry. He may have been wrong in the details and prone to wild generalisation, but it was impossible to gainsay his dizzying erudition.[23]

At the end of the year he was surprised and elated to hear that the House of Lords had finally consented to a bill for the abolition of hanging. He celebrated by getting drunk over dinner. The triumph of the abolitionist cause was a high point in an otherwise rather humdrum period. He tried to work on the novel, but found it hard to settle back into fiction. Instead, he returned to science and pursued a project that had interested him since his student days.

II

Koestler was invited to chair a major symposium on 'Drugs and Drug Addiction' in Zurich in mid-January 1970, so he and Cynthia varied their routine and went to Alpbach in the new year. While he was there he started research on Paul Kammerer, the subject of his next book, intriguingly called *The Case of the Midwife Toad*.[24]

Kammerer was born in Austria in 1880, an only child in a comfortably off family. He was a wunderkind who seemed destined for a career as a musician until he became fascinated by 'the music of the spheres'. At university he studied science and zoology, and in 1903 was taken on as a researcher by a prestigious institute for experimental biology in Vienna. His early work on salamanders was acclaimed, but Kammerer was disturbed by the incoherence in the Darwinian account of evolution and was drawn towards Lamarck's ideas. In a controversial series of experiments he tried to prove the inheritance of acquired characteristics by breeding salamanders, mid-wife toads and sea-squirts under laboratory conditions. This work attracted the hostility of the scientific community, which always viewed him sourly due to his unorthodox background. He added to this opprobrium in 1919 by publishing a book which proposed that coincidences were governed by laws that lay beyond the ken of conventional science. So he already had a reputation as a maverick when, in the 1920s, his pre-war work came under fire from William Bateson, the highly respected English biologist and geneticist.

Bateson pursued him relentlessly, demanding that Kammerer display the laboratory-bred specimens of midwife toad which he claimed were proof that acquired characteristics could be inherited. Bateson implied that the results were falsified. In 1926, *Nature* magazine printed Bateson's claims and the results of tests which appeared to show that Kammerer's specimens had, indeed, been doctored. Shortly afterwards Kammerer was found dead in mysterious circumstances, most likely suicide. Whether this was due to shame or an unhappy love affair was never resolved, although the scientific community assumed the former.[25]

Obviously, as with Kepler, Koestler saw a lot of himself in Kammerer. In January 1970 he wrote to Brian Inglis: 'in England I am in the academic dog-house, but in the USA and on the continent this is not the case.' It was another instance of 'K=K'. Kammerer fascinated him on a number of levels. Kammerer's work fitted with his theories on evolution (set out in *The Ghost in the Machine*) and his distrust of neo-Darwinism. Kammerer was also interested in coincidences and had written a book on the subject, although Koestler wisely decided to treat this subject in a separate volume. The Kammerer story became a vehicle for Koestler to express his contempt for 'the usual hostility of the grey birds in the groves of

Academe against the coloured birds with the too-melodious voice'. In addition it allowed him to indulge in a nostalgic reconstruction of Habsburg Vienna. A further piquant attraction was that the Soviet Union adopted Kammerer as a great scientist, who had been persecuted by wicked capitalists for working along the same lines as the Communist scientist Lysenko; his life was celebrated (and distorted) in an early Soviet film drama which Koestler had seen during his stay in Moscow in the 1930s.[26]

Initially, Koestler planned to write on Kammerer's 'law of seriality' and make it a springboard for an exploration of para-science. But he was diverted by Kammerer's contest with the Darwinians and decided in December 1969 to make that the subject of one book and deal with para-science in another. This would avoid a volume that was too long and pulled in different directions. Koestler pursued his research with customary vigour. He tracked down and corresponded with Kammerer's daughter, as well as dozens of scholars who had witnessed his work. Coincidentally, Holger Hyden and Paul Weiss had both been closely connected with Kammerer. Herta Baresch, a research assistant based at the University of Innsbruck, helped him track down Kammerer's correspondence and other documents, which had never before been used to elucidate the affair. On the basis of his detective work Koestler concluded that the specimens had been tampered with, but that Kammerer was not necessarily to blame for this. And, if he was, the motives might not have been venal. Finally, the case of the midwife toad on its own did not prove or disprove the Lamarckian heresy. The complete body of Kammerer's work remained as a standing challenge to the orthodox followers of Darwin.[27]

The study of Kammerer was eventually completed at the end of 1970, whereupon Koestler returned briefly to the novel. But there were various diversions of a social and an official nature, including an international symposium on 'Functions of Learning', which Koestler chaired. Despite his eminent friends he found it significant that, so far, honour and status had mainly been accorded to him by institutions overseas. His sixty-fifth birthday occasioned a flurry of interviews and celebrations, but in England he still felt an outsider. This was soon to change decisively.[28]

III

For most of spring 1971 he worked up the second book connected with Kammerer, which would emerge as *The Roots of Coincidence*, an examination of para-science and its implications. Koestler knew that he was taking an even greater risk with this one.

He admitted in the opening pages: 'Half my friends accuse me of an excess of scientific pedantry; the other half of unscientific leanings towards preposterous subjects such as extra sensory perception (ESP), which they include in the domain of the supernatural.'[29] For this reason he devoted the opening chapters to explaining why, on the one hand, para-science had changed for the better since the days of charlatans and mediums and, on the other, the certainties of experimental science had evaporated, only to be replaced by theories akin to those once treated as heretical or fantastic. Most recently, research into the brain had apparently uncovered electromagnetic emissions resembling 'brain waves'. 'The rapprochement between the conceptual world of para-psychology and that of modern physics is an important step towards the demolition of the greatest superstition of our age – the materialistic clockwork universe of early nineteenth-century physics.' However, he admitted the unique difficulty of demonstrating the existence of psychokinesis or ESP.[30]

The central chapter expanded on the theories of seriality and synchronicity developed by his hero Kammerer, the psychoanalytical thinker Carl Jung and the physicist Wolfgang Pauli. However, all three thinkers were hampered in Koestler's eyes by attempts to explain coincidences and psychic happenings in terms of the normal patterns of physical causation.[31]

Koestler's solution was to abandon causality as commonly understood: 'coexistent with causality there is an a-causal principle active in the universe, which tends towards unity . . . unlike gravity which acts on all *mass* indiscriminately, this force acts selectively on *form and function* to bring similar configurations together in space and time: it correlates by affinity. By which means this a-causal agency intrudes into the causal order of things – both in dramatic and trivial ways – we cannot tell, since it functions *ex hypothesi*, outside the known laws of physics.' Koestler made clear that his interest in seriality and coincidences derived from his urgent need to prove that there was a unity of all things and that the universe had a purpose. He melded together his previous work on holons, evolution, self-assertive and self-transcendent tendencies to create an apparently seamless theory of parapsychology. ESP was 'the highest manifestation of the integration potential of living matter – which, on the human level, is typically accompanied by a self-transcending type of emotion'. Although, as he confessed, none of this could be proved.[32]

The book ended by returning to the 'oceanic feeling'. Koestler suggested that it occurred, like other psychic events, when the 'filters' installed in the brain that keep out cosmic brain waves were lifted for a moment. The notion of 'filters' was borrowed from Sir Cyril Burt. Koestler's gloss was to maintain that if mankind could learn how to raise and lower them at will, civilisation could be transformed – and saved.[33]

When *The Roots of Coincidence* was completed, Koestler went straight on to *The Call Girls*, but it took another year to finish. In the meantime, his life went through a further upheaval, albeit of a more gentle and beneficent kind than earlier convulsions. In June he sold Alpbach, its attractions having waned to nought. He remarked in his diary: 'Alpbach slowly dying . . . Panorama no longer moves me. For twelve years it did. A landscape can die on one like a love affair'. The advent of tourists, motor bikers, and building developments that encroached on his domain were all nails in the coffin. The house was sold to Fritz Molden, his Austrian publisher. This pleased him, since the thought of having to part with it to a 'Kraut industrialist was unbearable'. As a further compensation Koestler was negotiating to buy a 'cottage' in St Jean-Cap Ferrat on the Côte d'Azur. The purchase ran into complications and over a year passed before he and Cynthia found a villa at Eze, near St Tropez.[34]

Following the sale of the *Schreiberhäusl* they drove through northern Italy to Venice, where Koestler gave a lecture to the Cini Foundation. This is one of the opulent Italian institutions that exist to laud intellectual achievement. The social events surrounding the lecture were lavish and the hosts added to the lustre of the occasion by dubbing their guests 'Sir Arthur and Lady Koestler'. Sir Arthur and Cynthia celebrated his birthday in Milan before driving back through France to Paris and London.[35]

The publication of *The Case of the Midwife Toad* in the autumn was marred by a hitch in the distribution of the *Sunday Times Magazine* which was carrying a feature on the Kammerer story, but this was more than offset by the excellent reviews. George Steiner was respresentative when he called it 'a superb intellectual thriller'. Steiner, like most critics, hedged over whether Kammerer was in the right or not and whether Koestler's plea to exhume Lamarckianism merited action, but he concurred that Koestler had exposed the tyranny of scientific orthodoxy and that more and better-informed debate about evolution was needed. Promotion of the book also benefited from a television tie-in. Benny Green commented on the BBC-made programme: 'Koestler loves and understands the English as only a gifted Hungarian expatriate can, and his programme showed his rare gift for making an abstruse issue like the sex life of the toad a more fascinating whodunit than anything Sherlock Holmes . . . ever got up to.'[36]

Although Koestler had hated television and avoided it during the 1950s, in the 1960s he came to see its potential and discovered that he was actually quite adept at the medium. In June 1971 the BBC series *One Pair of Eyes* broadcast a recorded discussion between Koestler and Anthony Grey, the British journalist who had been imprisoned in China for two years during the Cultural Revolution. After his release Grey had read *Dialogue with Death* and been struck by the similarities between their experiences. He empathised with Koestler's notion of the 'invisible writing' and the two planes of existence, the tragic and the trivial. Through Grey, who was thirty-two, younger people were able to relate to Koestler's Spanish experiences over three decades earlier.[37]

In November Koestler was the subject of an extended interview by Robert Kee. He knew Kee, who had been married to Janetta Jackson, quite well. The interview showed him at his best: relaxed, sagacious and chatty. Koestler aged sixty-five did actually bear a fair resemblance to the Koestler depicted at the age of forty-five in the autobiographical works. Such performances brought him new readers and new fans. One was Russell Hoban, who sent him an adulatory letter that shows how successful Koestler had been in fabricating an identity and projecting it through the new medium. Hoban wrote: 'Never before have I felt so much that a person's way of being was of itself a matter of importance and instruction. Never mind the work, impressive as it is . . . You as a man are the proof of the power and nobility of your thought.' Hoban opined that if he were in a life-or-death situation, he would hope to be in it with a type like Koestler.[38]

Television enabled Koestler to reach a huge audience and cultivate a popular following among a new generation of viewers and readers. It also reinforced his international reputation. During 1971 a German TV company took over his London house for three days to make a programme about him. If anything, his interviews for German and Austrian television had a greater impact, plugging into the first wave of fascination among young Germans for Weimar, the life of the anti-Nazi exiles and the Holocaust. For them, too, Koestler became an iconic figure whose latter-day image bore little relationship to his earlier life.[39]

Nor, in fact, did it have much connection with his life as it was being lived, for he continued to lead a nomadic existence, barely able to settle down and find peace, working in obsessive, frenzied spasms and frequently reducing those around him to misery. While in Australia, Cynthia told a journalist that 'He needs absolute solitude, so I work two floors below. He minds terribly if he is interrupted, so I don't go up to tell him lunch is ready. Instead I buzz him. I stay well out of range.' During the autumn he started hunting for a house outside London, combing the Home Counties and visiting estate agents. He had returned to work on the novella and by November had written the bulk of the first draft, but his productivity owed much to the 'happy pills' which he now consumed regularly. He needed them partly in order to surmount the effect of boozy dinner parties. It was getting harder and harder to cope with late nights: Cynthia often let him sleep till ten o'clock, but he was frequently groggy in the morning and needed a pill to perk him up. He got into an unhealthy cycle of booze, hangovers and drugs.[40]

The greatest tonic was a missive from 10 Downing Street. On 17 November 1971 Sir Robert Armstrong, the Cabinet Secretary, wrote to Koestler informing him that the Prime Minister, Edward Heath, wished to appoint him a Commander of the Order of the British Empire. As a controversial Hungarian-born, ex-Communist, pro-Zionist philanderer, Koestler was perhaps understandably cautious about the exact significance of this offer. He consulted A. D. Peters and Sir Martyn Beckett to make sure that it was, indeed, an honour and not some back-handed compliment that was best avoided. He was reassured and agreed to accept, much to Cynthia's pleasure and relief, since she rather naïvely hoped that such illustrious recognition would deepen his roots in England.[41]

A further sign of his status was another ICA lecture, on 1 December, to a packed house including 'some intense-looking intellectual Jews, Central Europeans, but quite a lot of young and some beardie-wierdoes' [sic]. After the talk Koestler was faced with a persistent questioner who was less than impressed by his *obiter dicta* on 'man's predicament' and undeterred by the speaker's lofty reputation. Was Koestler offering a theory? a scientific analysis? or philosophy? The question penetrated the confusion inherent in Koestler's work. Koestler, who never handled questioners well, lost his temper. He had convinced himself that he was offering humanity a coherent explanation of life and the universe and if it was not understood, well that was humanity's problem. In front of an audience of 300 he curtly asked his interrogator, whom Cynthia loyally deemed to be 'unpleasant and arrogant', if he had listened to the lecture at all. This was hardly an adequate reply, but the question-and-answer session was drawing to a close and he was soon able to escape to dinner with more pliant and agreeable company.[42]

Towards the end of the year the search for a country residence bore fruit. Koestler and Cynthia went to see a farmhouse at Denston, a picturesque Suffolk village. The house was very pretty: clad in pink-painted stucco, oak-beamed, with leaded windows. It was spacious and well-appointed inside, and came equipped with a self-contained guest wing. They fell in love with it and on the spot offered the asking price of £23,000. A few days later he finished the first draft of *The Call Girls*. The CBE, the purchase of the house and the completion of the novel gave cause for much celebration in the new year.[43]

If success and fame had not eradicated his restlessness, nor had they engendered a more settled emotional state. He continued to bully Cynthia and reigned over 8 Montpelier Square like a domestic tyrant. Her diary is filled with instances of his dictatorial behaviour and selfish moods. In late December 1971 she recorded: 'A. very bad tempered this morning. Caught me lying trying to protect myself, because I had forgotten to tell Mrs Martins not to take down the net curtains in his room. I finally had to admit he was right when he accused me of lying.' Some months later he was anxious to hear from the *Sunday Times* about an article he had written. He left a message with Harold Evans, the editor, who failed to call him back. Then, because Cynthia had misread the television schedules, he missed the late night headlines on BBC2. This reduced him to such a state that Cynthia 'thought he was going to kick the set over'.[44] On such occasions one looks in vain for evidence of the 'power and nobility' of Koestler's thought. The fact is it did not translate into reality for those closest to him. He did what he accused Orwell of doing: extending his generosity most easily to acquaintances and 'humanity' at large.

His cruel side was demonstrated by the relentless exclusion of his daughter Christine. She grew up with her mother in glamorous style in Rome and Paris. Janine Graetz sent regular bulletins on her progress and occasional photographs. But Koestler only acknowledged to his oldest and closest friends that he had actually fathered a child. When he did so, he spoke of her with a certain pride. He told von Weisl, for example: 'I have one illegitimate daughter, aged 14 but rather pretty.' Yet he refused to see her. During 1970 Graetz told him that she would be in London for a few days with Christine and asked if he would consent to meet them. She was so eager to get him to agree, and just lay eyes on his offspring, that she even suggested concealing the truth of the relationship. But Koestler would not budge:

'I don't think that a family reunion would be a good idea . . .
Christine might intuitively guess something and one does not know
about what effect this would have. Anyway it would be an
embarrassing situation all round. Don't feel angry or hurt; believe me
this is the best way.'[45]

Two years later Graetz provoked a dénouement by finally
informing Christine who her father was and telling Koestler that now
she knew. Again, she implored him to meet her: 'I believe it is time
that you met Cristina because souffre de ne pas le connaitre [sic].' He
might at least correspond with her. Koestler obliged with a short, off-
putting letter. They were total strangers, he told her; she was
seventeen and he was sixty-seven. Somewhat in contradiction to his
stated belief in the inheritance of characteristics, he said he had never
believed in 'biological bonds' and regarded environment as most
important in shaping a person. If she admired his books, meeting him
would be a disappointment. An encounter would be either a
'Victorian melodrama' or an 'exchange of banalities . . .You might
think that I am a monster – or you might agree with me and heave a
sigh of relief.' And that was that. Graetz's *démarche* irritated Koestler.
Cynthia noted that it was 'a problem for him now to cope with'. He
did not display much concern about Christine's potential problem
concerning her unknown father.[46]

IV

The gulf between the public man of letters and the private figure of
contradictions was masked by the applause which greeted news of
the CBE. Congratulations poured in from far and near, friends old
and new. Among the plaudits he received letters from William
Plomer, who had selected *The Gladiators* for Cape in 1938, and
Douglas Fairbanks, whom he had met briefly in Hollywood during
his IRRC tour in 1948. David Astor shrewdly wrote: 'It gives me
pleasure and I hope it gives you some too.' As if to bear out the
wisdom of Astor's wary acclaim Koestler remarked to Sidney
Bernstein: 'I was more gratified by winning the *Horizon* prize in
1942.' He joked to Jamie Hamilton: 'I was actually expecting to be
made a KE (Knight Errant).'[47]

Success fed Koestler's vanity. When Dennis Gabor was awarded
the Nobel prize Koestler watched him interviewed on television and
unkindly suggested to Cynthia that the honour was making him
pompous. Cynthia noted that 'of course he [Koestler] would like it
[the prize, in order] to have a wider readership'. The desire for a

platform from which to broadcast his philosophy was evident in his plans for a book that would present a definitive summary of his philosophy. This was eventually to be published as *Janus – A Summing Up*, but to begin with it was clumsily titled 'Connect, Always Connect'.[48]

A nervousness about his status in posterity and a concern to explicate his views clearly while he had the chance may not have been unrelated to the appearance of *The Roots of Coincidence* in February 1972. Koestler was aware that by embarking on a crusade for the recognition of parapsychology he was venturing into uncharted and dangerous waters, where many a reputation had sunk without trace. To his relief the reviews were mostly good. A. S. Byatt in *The Times* welcomed it with solid praise. Philip Toynbee, writing for the *Observer*, was more cautious. He objected that despite Koestler's powerful argument and evidence, 'our credulity will only take us so far'. He noted the impossibility of verifying or falsifying most ESP experiments, but nevertheless concluded that Koestler had performed a valuable task in making readers think. Those more familiar with psychology and science were less kind. John Clare gently poked fun at Koestler and Cynthia in an interview in *The Times*. Charles Rycroft, the distinguished psychologist, writing in the *New Statesman*, dismissed Koestler as having nothing new to say and dishonestly making physics seem more paradoxical than it really was in order to make para-science appear more credible.[49]

As part of his continuing research into the paranormal, and to draw attention to the new book, Koestler published a letter in the *Sunday Times* in March 1972 appealing for examples of strange coincidences. The best entries would receive a prize of £100. The contest provoked a cascade of 2000 letters, which the newspaper staff screened. Only the fifty 'best' stories were sent to Koestler, but he soon lost patience with the whole business and told Brian Inglis that he never wanted to read about another coincidence. Cynthia was left to plough through the letters and select the winners.[50]

Work on the first draft of *The Call Girls*, which alternated with the last two science books, was finally completed in spring 1972. It was Koestler's first work of fiction for twenty-two years and, as some critics noted uncharitably, it showed. The prose was rusty, the plotting (what there was) creaked and the characterisation was listless. The novel felt like the product of a worked-out imagination and a weary man. To anyone familiar with *Beyond Reductionism* it was at best a *roman à clef* of personalities and ideas. At worst it was simply repetitious.

The action, if it can be called that, is set in 'Schneedorf', an Alpine resort that is clearly Alpbach. The central figure is a Russian *émigré* physicist called Nikolai Borisovitch Solovief, a bear-sized man with a 'darkly rugged face', 'shaggy head' and Slavic features. He has a self-appointed mission to save humanity and has invited twelve of the world's greatest thinkers, the 'call girls' who travel from conference to conference, to a symposium to hammer out a programme. It takes place against the background of a vague international crisis which threatens to ignite a Third World War.[51]

Solovief has a biography similar to Kammerer, but holds the views of late Koestler. If Rubashov is a reflection of the young Koestler, Koestler as Commissar, Solovief is the expression of Koestler as Yogi. He is how Koestler liked to see himself and how he wanted others to see him: a genial host, a penetrating intellect, a tolerant husband who is sceptical towards monogamy, and an energetic lover. He considers himself, in a distorted echo of Orwell's observation, 'a melancholy hedonist'. In a guilty inversion of Koestler's actual relations with his wives, Solovief's wife has a lover. However, a member of the symposium remarks: 'Without at least two adoring females around he [Solovief] feels depressed.' They comprise his 'harem'.[52]

For six days, resting on the seventh, each savant presents a diagnosis of the crisis and proposes a remedy. The characters are little more than mouthpieces for Koestler's scientific prose: sometimes he quotes himself verbatim. Unlike at Alpbach, he includes a Behaviourist who opens himself up to the ritual attack on 'ratomorphism'. The British are represented by a scientist who resembles Cyril Burt. He is accompanied by a homosexual poet, Sir Evelyn Blood, who may be a caricature of Auden and whose *raison d'être* in the novel is far from clear except to serve as the butt for Koestler's homophobia. There is also a German academic, von Halder, who was a Nazi and articulates the views of Konrad Lorenz on aggression. (Lorenz was a Nazi fellow traveller.) In another departure from the Alpbach model, Koestler includes a woman: a large, sexually omnivorous and ambiguous Kleinian psychoanalyst. She proposes mass administration of a drug against excessive devotion. Koestler's suspicion that only a new religious order will save mankind is embodied by Tony Caspari, a member of the 'Copertinian Order', which seems to be an amalgam of Zen and the Jesuits. The symposium ends inconclusively, although Solovief makes a plea for globally enforced birth control which, for some reason, he thinks will solve the immediate crisis of mankind.[53]

After the manuscript was sent off, with the addition of two short stories which were to flank the novel, Koestler and Cynthia moved into Water Lane Farm House. The transfer involved the usual tribulations which soured his mood and caused numerous quarrels. Cynthia panicked when he announced that the house had 'gone dead on him'. However, he didn't have much time in which to become dissatisfied with his new abode because in early May they took off for Alpbach via Paris and Switzerland. They didn't return to Suffolk for two months. Koestler was then away again, covering the Fischer–Spassky chess match in Reykjavik, contributing to a film with Holger Hyden in Denmark and giving papers at conferences in Amsterdam and Edinburgh.[54]

The expedition to Iceland, on behalf of the *Sunday Times*, was something of a farce because Fischer arrived at the tournament ten days late, by which time Koestler and most of the other journalists had to leave. Nevertheless he produced two substantial articles for the paper. The first, on the history of chess, was based on research and was begun months earlier. The second, which had local colour, compared the contending grand masters and told the story of the opening days. As always, there was a metaphysical and political sub-text. Koestler argued that the ability of players to work out the near-infinite possibilities for moves in a chess game pointed to 'vast untapped faculties of the human mind, potentially many times as powerful as those which we put to use in our everyday routines'.[55] By implication, if mankind learned to tap this unused resource civilisation could be transformed and indeed humanity might ascend to a higher level of existence.

David Pryce-Jones, who had known Koestler for several years and lived nearby, bumped into him *en route* to Iceland where he was also to cover the tournament. In the absence of any games to write about they spent a lot of time with each other. Pryce-Jones later wrote a funny and sensitive account of their Icelandic experience. He recalled that when they first ran into each other Koestler's alertness and hirsute appearance made him think of 'an otter . . . trim, the coat in tip-top condition'. Koestler seemed to know the key members of the tournament organising committee and was full of insider's information, which he shared with a joyful lack of discretion. Journalists and chess experts alike turned to him for an informed view: he was comfortable in all types of company. His only animosity was reserved for the Soviet ambassador and Spassky's entourage. Pryce-Jones also noted that he had a sharp eye for the local women and was not averse to their amorous intentions towards him.[56]

Koestler spent six weeks in Denston writing up the articles and preparing for his coming trips. He and Cynthia flew to Copenhagen, where they were met by Holger Hyden. He took them on his boat to a remote island, and here they featured in a documentary film for Danish TV. Koestler's next stop was in Amsterdam to chair a round-table discussion as part of a conference sponsored by the Para-psychology Foundation. In early September he took the *Flying Scotsman* to Edinburgh for the annual gathering of the Para-psychological Association, where he delivered a keynote lecture. It was later incorporated into *The Challenge of Chance* (1973), which Koestler edited along with Sir Alister Hardy and Robert Harvie, and conveniently summed up his work on the paranormal.

Koestler explained that he understood how, to most people, the claims of para-science seemed outlandish; but then so did the theory of gravity when it was first propounded. The major advances in physics only occurred at the expense of challenging the received wisdom. Nor could conventional science stand on its pride. 'The nineteenth-century clockwork model of the universe is in a sham-bles, and since matter itself has been de-materialised, materialism can no longer claim to be a scientific philosophy.' Modern physics and parapsychology, he asserted, were converging. It was only a question of time before the as yet mysterious substance which enabled thought to be transmitted would be revealed as surely as the existence of the neutrino had been uncovered. New thinking would also help unravel the meaning of coincidences: 'everything in the universe is hanging together, not by mechanical causes but by hidden affinities.' Time would vindicate the belief that everything was connected and nothing was random.[57]

There is a gaping paradox in Koestler's thinking. At the end of his Edinburgh paper he approvingly quoted Spinoza: 'Nature abhors randomness.' Similarly, in a broadcast for the American radio net-work NBC at this time, he concluded that 'both physics and parapsychology point to aspects of reality beyond the reach of con-temporary science – a coded message written in invisible ink between the lines of a banal letter'. So all events had a cause and all life was scripted; it was Koestler's position that para-science would reveal the 'invisible writing', and make sense of the incoherent. Logically, however, once all causes and effects are known, then everything can be predicted and, conversely, all is determined. Koestler *wanted* to live in a clockwork universe, even if the mechanism did not run according to Newtonian principles. What irritated him was the purposelessness of the cosmos and the accidental nature of his survival in it. Access to the other level of reality would give him meaning and a place. Thus the ability to decode the 'invisible writing' was 'exciting and comforting at the same time'.[58]

Between the conferences Koestler and Cynthia went to Morocco for a couple of weeks, staying for most of the time in Marrakesh. On his return he wrote a sprightly travel piece for the *Sunday Times*. It was not terribly complimentary to the Arabs: indeed, he was at pains to show that the Berber inhabitants of the Atlas Mountains were not really Arabs at all. This odd disquisition came about because, while he liked Marrakesh, he disliked Arabs. In her Boswellian role Cynthia recorded that Koestler didn't like Spanish aristocrats because 'they are of Arab descent and therefore not quite human'.[59]

In late September, A. D. Peters celebrated his eightieth birthday at the Savile Club. Koestler was one of those who proposed a toast to this grey eminence of British publishing. When Peters died just a few months later Koestler wrote a fine tribute to him in the *Sunday Times*, revealing much about their enduring relationship. Peters was born in Schleswig-Holstein, where his father was a farmer, but the farm had gone bankrupt when Peters was a boy and he had been placed in the charge of an aunt who sent him abroad, to England, for his education. He had been a journalist before he set up as a literary agent in 1924. With these credentials he could well understand the insecurity and sense of deracination that so often afflicted Koestler. As well as being an acute critic of his work, Peters was a pillar of calm and good sense in the whirling chaos of Koestler's life, a 'father figure' to him, as he was to so many other writers. His death deprived Koestler of an important stabilising influence.[60]

The Call Girls was published in England the next month. It received a mixed reception. David Pryce-Jones called it a 'droll story' in *The Times*, but Gabriel Pearson in the *Guardian* dubbed it a 'disconcertingly bad novel'. The characters were so stiff and their comments so banal that 'this group could not save a novelette let alone a world from disaster'. American reviewers were cutting. Writing in the *New York Times* Anatole Broyard opened: 'Arthur Koestler used to write like a novelist who wanted to be a scientist; now he writes like a scientist who wants to be a novelist.' The prose was 'worse than flat – it is flatness trying to undulate'. The plotting was mechanical and the characters performed like a 'circus of trained bears'. He thought it was 'unfortunate for Mr Koestler that he cannot keep away from the novel'.[61]

Immediately after finishing *The Call Girls* Koestler had commenced work with Sir Alister Hardy and Robert Harvie on a book about coincidences. Initially he wanted to call it 'Smoke Rings', and was again saved from a poor title by his collaborators, who came up with *The Challenge of Chance*. This project, which preoccupied him through the autumn and winter of 1972–3, was a bold effort to give respectability and scientific status to ESP and the paranormal. It was devised jointly by Koestler and Sir Alister Hardy, a distinguished sociologist who had set up and ran the Religious Experience Research Unit at Oxford, with the assistance of Robert Harvie, a psychologist. The first part of the book described and analysed a large-scale experiment in telepathy organised at Caxton Hall in 1967.[62]

Koestler contributed two other parts in which he examined anecdotal as against laboratory evidence for ESP and groped for an explanation of the phenomena. Much of his material came from the correspondence triggered by the appeals for material which he published in the *Sunday Times* in March 1972 and the *New Scientist* in October 1972. On this basis he classified several distinct types of coincidence, such as 'the library angel' which leads by serendipity to the discovery of a needed book. But the real challenge was to explain why coincidences happened and how patterns became discernible. Koestler could not really find an answer: he was much better at sowing doubts about physics with the intention of making it seem as if the line between telepathy and wave particles was so insignificant that their respective study should be treated with equal gravity. He ended with a familiar plea that no progress would be made if research remained trapped by the mechanistic philosophy of science.[63]

As the days closed in he began to pine for the Continent and Cynthia nervously wondered how long he would stay at Water Lane Farm. Fortunately, there were several social occasions to divert his energy. In November the Koestlers threw their annual party, mixing friends and colleagues. This year they invited, among others, Goronwy Rees, Rebecca West, the Becketts, Anthony Storr, Brian Inglis, Kingsley Amis, Robert Kee, Fred Uhlman and Celia Goodman. Storr and Koestler frequently exchanged ideas about psychology and the mind, while Inglis shared Koestler's enthusiasm for the paranormal. Kee had become his portal to the new medium of television; West was an old journalistic comrade-in-arms. Fred Uhlman shared a Central European background and had invited Koestler to write a preface to his autobiographical novella, *Reunion*. Koestler had become friendly with Amis a couple of years earlier, reflecting the transition of two 'Angry Young Men' into sententious middle-aged Conservatives.[64]

V

More and more Koestler's life came to resemble a recapitulation. He obsessively returned to old haunts and well-worn themes. In February 1973, having set to rest his share of *The Challenge of Chance*, he again retraced the route he had taken from Paris to Marseilles in 1940. This time he did more research, speaking to *tabac* owners in the towns through which he had passed to ask what they remembered of the bedraggled soldiers from the routed French armies and the Jewish women from the camp at Gurs. He also went in search of Le Vernet, but could find no trace of it. Some things, however, did not change. In Bergier Koestler got out of the car without looking behind him, causing a motor cyclist to crash into the protruding door. He had to pay the man fifty francs on the spot to calm him down and avoid an incident. When they reached Marseilles they were joined by the Becketts and went house hunting along the coast, but without success. Back in London, he wrote up the piece for the *Daily Telegraph Magazine*, filling in some of the missing details of his escape from France. It also gave him an opportunity to bemoan the change of fortunes between France, which had enjoyed an 'economic miracle', and Britain, whose nationals were looked upon as 'poor relatives' when abroad.[65]

Koestler re-examined his ambiguous relationship with Britain on the occasion of another honour: a lecture to the British Academy in the 'Thank-Offering to Britain' series funded by former Jewish refugees from Nazism. In April, Sir Isaiah Berlin, president of the Academy, wrote to Koestler inviting him to speak. Koestler was initially nervous, but Berlin reassured him: 'Do not dread the Academy: everything you say stirs and stimulates and possesses life-enhancing qualities, as our old friend used to say, far beyond the most distinguished potential members of the audience. You will see this in an instant, as soon as you observe their expectant and somewhat elderly faces.' Berlin went to great lengths to accommodate him, suggesting that they meet in the Athenaeum well before the address so that Koestler could unwind and have a nap in the club's ample armchairs. To Koestler's satisfaction his lecture was a great success.

He opened by announcing that he addressed the Academy as a former refugee and a naturalised Briton. This placed him in a privileged position: at once embedded in British culture, but at the same time able to stand back and view it as a 'continental'. The rest of the lecture was largely a regurgitation of his discussion about the English national character in *Suicide of a Nation?* Class divisions, he repeated, had cost Britain its economic prosperity and international pre-eminence. More in sorrow than in anger he pleaded with his august audience to do something about this canker before it was too late. Dutifully, but not without sincerity, he ended with a paean of praise to Britain and Britishness: 'If, even after thirty years in this country, I still sometimes feel a stranger among its natives, the moment I set foot on the Continent I feel British to the bone.'[66]

An honour of a different kind was an invitation to write the entry on 'Humour and Wit' for the fifteenth edition of the *Encyclopaedia Britannica*. For this he simply extracted the relevant sections from *The Art of Creation*. He also turned out several book reviews for the *New Statesman* and the *Observer*, including one on ESP behind the Iron Curtain and another on a major study of Wittgenstein. He was much more sympathetic to ESP than he was to analytical philosophy, which he accused of 'castrating thought'.[67]

In August Koestler travelled to Geneva for a big international conference on ESP arranged by the Parapsychology Foundation. He had helped to stimulate the conference by suggesting to the head of the Foundation that it arrange a conclave on the relationship of quantum physics to para-science, to show that the gap between conventional science and para-science was narrowing. He made this the subject of his paper. To the reading public he was now becoming identified almost exclusively with this opaque and divisive topic. To give a boost to *The Challenge of Chance*, which appeared in the autumn, he published two large articles on coincidence and chance in the *Sunday Times* in November 1973 and May 1974. They generated a huge mailbag, as did all his journalism and books on the issue. Many people looked upon him as simply a crank who was becoming a victim of his years; yet his work on ESP and coincidence attracted a remarkably wide range of interest and support. It was, for instance, one of the things which bonded his friendship with Kingsley Amis.[68]

Notwithstanding his asseverations of fealty in front of the British Academy he was itching to leave England. During the summer Harold Harris, his editor at Hutchinson, had spent some time in a rented villa on the French Riviera and Koestler asked if he thought it would be suitable for himself and Cynthia. When Harris said he thought it would, Koestler immediately rented it for the winter. He curbed his itchy feet until after the publication of *The Challenge of Chance*, then travelled with Cynthia by train and car to Eze, near St Tropez, and stayed there until the end of January the following year.[69]

VI

They returned to Britain to find it in the grip of an epic miners' strike and a political crisis that would eventually lead to the fall of the Heath government. 'The rats have swum back to sinking ship,' he confided grimly to his diary–notebook. But, as if to prove the country's virtues, its grudging tolerance and decency, Britain continued to heap laurels on Koestler. That month, Lord Butler informed him that he was to be made a Companion of the Royal Society of Literature. Koestler was especially flattered and pleased by this accolade. He thought it evoked the new spirit of Britain's membership of the Common Market that a writer brought up in Austro-German culture could be elected to join the companions of *English* literature. As if to underline the strangeness of the odyssey that had carried him to this pinnacle, at roughly the same time he became a member of the Amicale des Anciens Internés du Camp de Vernet-d'Ariège, the association of ex-inmates of the concentration camp from which he had been released in January 1940. The membership of these two associations in a sense summed up the extraordinary nature of his journey through the latter half of the century.[70]

In the summer, Koestler turned to his last major work, which was to surprise everybody: a study of the origin of the European Jews. He began it at Denston and persevered despite a flood of visitors: 'Happily working on Khazars, in spite of guest-ritis.'[71] If Koestler's work on ESP is not to be marginalised or dismissed, neither is this final monograph, the contents of which will be examined later. It was written at a time of summing up, while he was self-consciously pulling together all the threads of his life and when he felt the tug of posterity on everything he did. It was around then that he and Cynthia started working on a joint autobiography, taking his story on from 1940. He also commenced collaboration with Iain Hamilton on a definitive biography commissioned by Secker and Warburg. Meanwhile, Hutchinson were preparing a *Festschrift* to mark his seventieth birthday, to be edited by Harold Harris. In France the prestigious and influential cultural annual *L'Herne* also planned to devote an issue to Koestler.[72]

Iain Hamilton began work on the biography in autumn 1973. He interviewed Koestler several times and took possession of hundreds of his files, eighty of Mamaine's letters to Celia from the 1940s and 1950s, and her diaries. However, the work took much longer than Hamilton expected. The task was made harder still because a divergence of interests opened up between the biographer and his subject. Koestler was least concerned to document the years before 1955, the period which had attracted Hamilton to the project in the first place. Instead, he gently prodded Hamilton to focus the book on his scientific phase: 'these last twenty years since I stopped writing about politics and turned to natural philosophy, are for me the most important as far as work is concerned.' He told Hamilton that his writing from *The Sleepwalkers* through to *The Roots of Coincidence* formed 'a coherent whole, which asks for a coherent treatment'. This was a problem for Hamilton, who was rather more inspired by Koestler the reformed Communist and Cold Warrior. But Koestler informed him in no uncertain terms: 'what I most resent is being labelled forever as the author of *Darkness at Noon* and other political books at the expense of the second half of my work, which to my mind is the more important.' For a variety of reasons Hamilton could not make much headway with the mass of material and by the start of 1975 it was clear to him and Tom Rosenthal, his editor at Secker and Warburg, that although the birthday publication date was part of the original deal it was unrealistic. This was storing up trouble for the future.[73]

Koestler and Cynthia wintered at L'Horizon Bleu, the villa in Eze. Ensconced within its comfortable precincts he pushed on with his book about the Jews. The second half of 1975 was dominated by the many events surrounding his seventieth birthday. Hutchinson brought out *Astride the Two Cultures*, edited and introduced by Harold Harris, with contributions by Roy Webberley, Mark Graubard, Frank Barron, W. H. Thorpe, John Beloff, Iain Hamilton, Goronwy Rees, John Grigg, Cynthia Koestler, Tosco Fyvel, Kathleen Nott, Renée Haynes and Paul MacLean. The collection reflected Koestler's desired image of himself: it was strong on science and para-science, thin on his novels and pre-1955 writing, and obscurantist concerning his origins. By contrast, the edition of *L'Herne*, edited by Pierre Debray-Ritzen, with contributions by Wolfgang von Weisl, Manès Sperber, Danielle Hunebelle, Alain de Benoist and others, was more balanced and included in-depth appreciations of his Jewish roots and his relationship with Zionism as well as Communism. Even so, it was constrained by a reliance on Koestler's own slippery autobiographical writings and interviews with him. George Steiner wrote an incisive profile for the *Sunday Times*: it was one of the few which drew together, and made some sense of, all the elements in Koestler's life and oeuvre.[74]

In December 1975 Cynthia and Koestler packed up Denston and transferred to Eze. They had to delay their departure while Cynthia had some minor surgery and they had been at L'Horizon Bleu for little more than a month when Koestler became ill. He was diagnosed as needing a major operation on a polyp on his vocal cord. It was his first serious medical set-back and marked the beginning of his physical decline.[75]

VII

Age overtook Koestler suddenly and with a vengeance. In 1969 his hair was still a thick, lustrous dark brown. He wore glasses for reading, but otherwise suffered no physical impediments and was no more ravaged than the average angst-ridden, middle-aged, Central European Jewish intellectual. In 1972 David Pryce-Jones had observed how trim and sleek Koestler appeared; but three years later he was almost entirely grey and his face was scored by deep wrinkles. He moved more slowly and uncertainly, so much so that he wanted to install a lift in the house in Montpelier Square.

Koestler was an unsparing commentator on his own ageing. In 1968 he noted that he still felt very much as he did when he was fifty. But a year later he started to worry that his hair was thinning. Thoughts of decrepitude began to haunt him. In May 1969 he joined the Euthanasia Society, one purpose of which was to facilitate suicide by those who wanted to pre-empt senility or prolonged terminal illness. At the end of 1971 he wrote: 'About a year ago my mind started watching my body – but unable to accept that it is "me".' In dismay he exclaimed: 'My body has become a stranger.' Soon the physical alterations were too great to ignore. 'Last year', he recorded, 'I progressed from upper middle age to lower old age. It was quite a shock.' His seventieth birthday marked a 'brutal transition' and occasioned anguished private reflections. 'Statistically', he mused, 'I am already dead.' He looked in horrified wonder at his reflection: 'the ravaged face in the shaving mirror is not me . . .' In public, however, he maintained a façade of imperturbability. When the novelist Julian Barnes met Koestler in the late 1970s he observed: 'His response to old age [like his attitude to his illnesses] is also scientific and practical.'[76]

His eyes were the first part of his body to show signs of dis-integration. In June 1973 they were troubling him so much that he was driven to see an eye specialist. The following month he went into Moorfields Eye Hospital to have a cataract removed. The operation took place on 17 July and he catalogued his improvement over the next four days from being 'dopey' through 'improving' to 'impatient'. On 24 July he was once more at his desk and 'Back to Full Steam'. This verdict was a little premature. As a consequence of the operation he had to wear special glasses, but they made him dizzy so he went back to wearing his old glasses and covered his bad eye with a patch.[77] In September he was forced to cancel a planned trip to Japan to give the opening address to the eighth Congress of the International Council of Societies of Industrial Design in Kyoto. This was a blow, since he had looked forward to the event. He had told the organisers in the previous March that although he rarely accepted such engagements, in this case 'both the subject and the location are too attractive to refuse'. He worked on his lecture and delayed his final decision until the last minute, when it was clear his eyesight would not permit him to make the journey.[78]

The operation on his throat in 1976 marked a more serious stage in his physical undoing. For two weeks he had what he thought was laryngitis and was prescribed an antibiotic by a French doctor. The symptoms persisted and a second examination revealed a nodule on his right vocal cord. The doctor decreed that it had to be removed at once, although it proved not to be malignant. The possibility of cancer, and the location of the malaise, were doubly terrifying for Koestler. When he was back in England in April he continued to suffer from discomfort in his throat and booked a further round of examinations. To his relief these confirmed that there was no continuing danger, and after a period during which it was hard to talk he recovered enough to give a PEN address in the following August. But it was indicative of his mood as well as his scientific convictions that in 1975 he wrote a chapter on life after death for a book of essays on the subject which he edited with Arnold Toynbee.[79]

Age also took its toll of Koestler's politics: he became crusty and right-wing. He fulminated against the dockers' strike in July 1972: 'England managed to become the only country which established the dictatorship of the proletariat – under a Tory Government.' The miners' strike two years later seemed to confirm his prognosis. Notwithstanding his claim to have achieved knowledge of the working class during his army days, he had no sympathy with their aims and was surprised when close English friends betrayed a stricken conscience on the subject of the pitmen. In March 1977 he joined a break-away union of free-lance journalists that John Grigg helped to found in opposition to the left-wing-dominated NUJ.

By the 1970s the one-time Communist and friend of Nye Bevan, Dick Crossman and Michael Foot had become a Tory voter. In reply to birthday greetings from his MP, Christopher Tugendhat, a pro-

European Conservative, he wrote: 'I hope that there will soon be an opportunity to vote for you again – the sooner the better.' A year later he joined the Conservative Party. His proximity to the Tories was cemented by the leadership of Margaret Thatcher. She was a Cold Warrior to her core and an admirer of Karl Popper and F. A. von Hayek, fellow members of the Central European intellectual migration of the 1930s with whom Koestler enjoyed cordial relations. She counted *Darkness at Noon* as one of the foremost influences on her political career and in 1979, shortly before she took office as Prime Minister, requested that Koestler pay her a visit. According to Celia Goodman, Thatcher ended up going to Montpelier Square, probably because Koestler was too unwell to travel to her. This did not spoil their political tryst, however: 'Arthur rather fell for her: he kept saying "She is very feminine, and she uses it."' He was later invited to one of the first social occasions she initiated after her arrival in 10 Downing Street. Thatcher saw Koestler as a philosophical ally and a potential member of the intellectual circle marshalled by the thinking members of her entourage such as Hugh Thomas. He wrote to Koestler in September 1982 asking if he could persuade him 'to come and have a chat with the PM'. Koestler demurred because of serious ill-health, but he left no doubt where his sympathies lay: 'under different circumstances I would have gladly accepted your invitation.'[80]

According to Julian Barnes, Koestler was aware of the penchant of certain British prime ministers for Central European savants like Thomas Balogh, Peter Bauer and Nicholas Kaldor, but opted not to play a similar role. He was 'flattered by Mrs Thatcher's attention but declined her casting; he told her, "I will not be your Hungarian guru."'[81] This may be what he told Barnes, but his letter to Thomas suggests that he would have seized the opportunity to exert influence at such a level had it come to him when he was younger and in better health. Koestler was no stranger to politics: he had enjoyed long friendships with British politicians and cultivated US government officials, including those he knew were connected with the CIA. It would be inaccurate to cast him as either a naïf or a writer who jealously guarded his autonomy from the dirty stuff of politics. He was never happier than when he felt his words had changed things.

The journey from youthful leftism to right-wing politics was not untypical of Jews of his generation, least of all displaced Central European Jews, but Koestler's ambivalent relationship to Zionism was odd. Jewish intellectuals with a radical background like Norman Podhoretz and Irving Kristol in the United States, Annie Kriegel in

France and Alfred Sherman in Britain usually became fervently pro-Zionist and identified with the Jewish community at the same time as they abandoned their left-wing allegiances. Not so Koestler. In 1976 he astonished those who admired his scientific writings and could recall his earlier commitment to Zionism by publishing a book devoted to showing that the Jews of Europe were not really Jews at all and had no relationship to, let alone any claim on, the Land of Israel.

VIII

To the generations of readers familiar with Koestler's opus since 1955 his interest in Jews and Zionism came as something of a surprise. He had airbrushed the Jewish and Zionist phase of his life out of the potted biographies that accompanied his works. The references to the ancient Israelites or the Holocaust that did occur from time to time in his books, essays and journalism were rarely personal in nature. Yet however much *The Thirteenth Tribe* seemed to come like a bolt from the blue, it had in fact been gestating quietly for many years. Since 1967 Koestler had displayed a more positive interest in Israel and Zionism. This does not mean that he had lost any of his wariness, as indicated by his response to a suggestion from Menachem Begin in 1970 that he write a novel about a hero of the Jewish underground war against the British. 'I have often thought of a sequel to *Thieves in the Night*,' Koestler admitted. 'But it is unlikely that it will materialise. It is very difficult for a writer to go back to a subject a second time without becoming repetitive and a disappointment to the reader.'[82]

When the Zionist Revisionist Organisation (ZRO), Jabotinsky's heirs, asked if Koestler would join their ranks he firmly refused: 'I have never lost my admiration for Vladimir Jabotinsky, with whom I was closely related in the early years of the Movement. But today the situation is quite different and for a number of reasons it is not possible for me to become associated again with the Revisionist Organisation.' Nor would he get involved with the Jabotinsky Institute in Israel, an archive and museum devoted to the eponymous hero, which Jascha Weinshall was helping to build. After a year, however, he relented and allowed his name to be added to the Committee of Friends. In 1980 he became a sponsor of the Jabotinsky Committee in London.[83]

Anti-Israel terrorism in the 1970s and the Yom Kippur War in October 1973 were partly responsible for Koestler's change of heart.

He and Cynthia were 'Terribly shaken . . . with the news of the slaughter of the Israelis' at the Munich Olympics in September 1972. During the Yom Kippur War he was glued to the radio and television news. He told Mala Rossoff, a member of the Weinshall clan: 'we have watched the news from Israel on TV with anxious hearts, as you can imagine.' Cynthia recorded that he 'was unable to start [work] because of obsession and worry over the Israel war'. Months after the fighting had ended he continued to monitor news from the region 'with anguish and bated breath'. He might have turned down an invitation from Rabbi Albert Friedlander to attend the Westminster Synagogue Yom Kippur service in 1973, but he began to lend his name to pro-Zionist fund-raising organisations and the efforts to help Soviet Jews emigrate to Israel.[84]

His comments about the war were not simply polite expressions of concern to old friends in Israel. Nor were his feelings merely visceral or ephemeral. As we have seen, they came at a time when he was tying up the loose ends of his career and shaping his intellectual legacy. This was the context in which, in June 1973, he turned once again to the Jewish Question: it was to remain the focus of his work for the next two years. First, he was invited to contribute an essay to a highbrow coffee-table book on the Jews and the origins of Jewish creativity in the modern world, *Next Year in Jerusalem: Jews in the Twentieth Century*, edited by Douglas Villiers. Instead of turning it down, much as he had rejected requests to contribute to anthologies of Jewish writing in the past, he jumped at the commission.[85]

He produced nothing strikingly new: he simply dusted off 'Judah at the Crossroads', trimmed it a little and added a few barbs aimed at those like Irving Kristol and Isaiah Berlin who had disagreed with him when that essay was first published. But there were two new ingredients. Koestler more explicitly accused modern Jews of practising racialism in the endeavour to preserve their identity and separateness in the Diaspora.[86]

Koestler again quoted Isaiah Berlin, but this time dismissed with greater asperity his argument for tolerating difference and eccentricity. It may have been for this reason that the editor invited a response from Berlin, although in principle all the contributions were intended to be written in ignorance of any of the others. Berlin's reply was correspondingly waspish: 'Arthur Koestler does not do justice to my argument. It is not, to use his words, "that unreason, however irritating or maddening, must be tolerated" or that Jews or anyone else "have the right to be guided by irrational emotion". My thesis was and is that to demand social and ideological homogeneity, to wish to get rid of minorities because they are tiresome or behave "foolishly or inconsistently or vulgarly" (these are indeed my words), is illiberal and coercive and neither rational nor humane.'[87]

Berlin neatly inverted Koestler's argument. Anti-Semitism was not the fault of the Jews, but of those who were unprepared to tolerate them. Whether or not Judaism had any contemporary validity was irrelevant: humans as individuals and in groups had a right to choose how to live, with the caveat that they did not cause harm to others. Berlin went for the jugular: Koestler was thinking like a totalitarian. To rub in the point he ended by complimenting his 'admired friend' and agreeing to differ on his part, although he was less certain that Koestler would follow his example: 'I shall continue to tolerate and, indeed, respect his view, even if he does not consent to tolerate mine.'[88]

While he was working on this 'Jew article', as he termed it, Koestler returned to the idea of a sequel to *Thieves in the Night*. Cynthia noted: 'He wanted to write a novel on Israel, which pinpoints man's dilemma, but he would need to be there for six months.' A few days later he had all but decided to go to Israel for three weeks 'to have a decco with a view to writing his novel'. In the end the novel died, perhaps because he had started to explore modern Israeli fiction and discovered that his role as commentator had been usurped by others in a more advantaged position. Early in 1974 he told Mala Rossoff: 'I have been reading recent Israeli novels – Amos Oz, Yehuda Amichai, and Amos Kollek – and I must say that they are a hopeful counter-argument to your fears of provincialism. We shall see.' He might have added that *his* own prejudiced apprehension that Israel would decline into provinciality had been disproved by the extraordinary fecundity and richness of Israeli literature.[89]

It was against this background that he researched and wrote *The Thirteenth Tribe* between July 1973 and August 1974. The book is ostensibly about the history and legacy of the Khazars, a tribe from the Caucasus that attained considerable regional power in the seventh to ninth centuries and adopted Judaism before going into terminal decline in the eleventh century and fading out of history. The Khazar story had always fascinated Jewish scholars and lay audiences alike, since it appeared to be a tale of success and strength, even if only short-lived, in the mainly lachrymose chronicle of Jewish history. In the twentieth century Jewish and non-Jewish scholars took an interest in the tribe and its conversion, validating some of the historical elements of the story.[90] It was this scholarship, much of it controversial and incomplete, that Koestler plundered for his book. But it would be a mistake to evaluate *The Thirteenth Tribe* purely in academic terms. Koestler's work was not a serious contribution to historical knowledge: it made a selective use of facts for a grossly polemical end.

Its rationale is tucked away in an appendix, a curious practice but one that Koestler had used more then once. Here Koestler repeated his well-established view that since the foundation of Israel Jews in the Diaspora had to make a choice between emigration and assimilation. He hoped to assist those who wished to disappear to overcome their 'tribal loyalty' and pride in their 'race' by showing how, in fact, the majority of Jews in the world stemmed from an obscure Caucasian tribe with no connection to the Biblical patriarchs. If they were descendants of a persecuted people, they had suffered for no good reason and certainly not one worth perpetuating.[91]

The psychological, or propaganda, objective of *The Thirteenth Tribe* was to unhinge the Jews of the Diaspora from Judaism and the Jews of Israel, but Koestler knew that he would not succeed if he attacked entrenched beliefs too overtly. His tried and trusted method was to present his argument with the patina of academic objectivity and authority. So he ransacked the work of several historians to assemble a sketchy history of the Khazars on which to predicate his thesis about the origins of modern Jewry.

His brisk narrative charted the rise, conversion to Judaism, and disintegration of the Khazar kingdom, as a result of which large numbers of Khazars migrated north into southern Russia and north-west into Poland and Lithuania. This much was fairly well sourced, but not his startling assertion that 'the majority of this important part of modern Jewry originated in the migratory waves of Kaber-Khazars'.[92] In reality, Koestler's argument for the Khazar origins of the Jews of East Central Europe rested on little more than a series of analogies. The shtetl resembled Khazar market towns; kaftans were like the coats worn by tribes from the north Caucasian steppes; Uzbeks wore a headgear that was similar to yarmulkas; gefilte fish, a Polish-Jewish culinary favourite, was made of carp, a staple fish in the Caspian region . . . and so forth.[93]

By contrast, there was a crushing weight of archaeological and documentary evidence supporting the standard view that the Jews of East Central Europe had migrated to those lands from the West, voluntarily, or having been driven out of their homes in the Middle Ages. It was equally agreed that these Jewish communities stemmed from the Diaspora of Palestinian Jews. Koestler airily dismissed this vast literature in a few pages, although he had greater difficulty explaining away the origins of Yiddish, the lingua franca of Polish Jewry, a syncretic language of predominantly German character. To accomplish this he attributed Yiddish to a few 'real' Jews from the Alpine countries, Bohemia and eastern Germany who had found their way to Poland and assimilation to the German culture predominant in Polish urban centres. He passed over the fate of the Khazar tongue and the total absence of any Turkic words in the languages and cultural traditions of the Jews who were supposedly descended from them.[94]

The Thirteenth Tribe was slaughtered by knowledgeable reviewers when it appeared in 1976 and not a single Jewish historian has given the slightest credence to Koestler's assertions.[95] Yet however much they may be risible as scholarship, this is not the yardstick by which to judge them. As he showed in *The Case of the Midwife Toad*, Koestler never emancipated himself from a late nineteenth-century conception of race and a neo-Lamarckian belief in the acquisition of characteristics by inheritance. In the final chapter of *The Thirteenth Tribe*, on 'Race and Myth', he fluctuates between a reluctant concurrence with the modern biologists and anthropologists who had demolished the idea of race and the existence of a 'Jewish race' in particular, and an endorsement of those Edwardian researchers who were devoted to the concept. He simply could not accept the contrary scientific evidence: 'intuition tells us that the anthropologists' statistics must be somehow wrong.' His answer was to fall back on a messy, neo-Lamarckian combination of environmental and biological factors.[96]

The key to this was the ghetto. Immured over a period of centuries, Jews had been subjected to inbreeding and 'genetic drift'. Disease and sexual selection in its confines had concentrated the genetic profile of the Jewish population. Finally, persecution and social conditioning, especially child rearing, had inculcated common characteristics that were transmitted down the generations. Notwithstanding his disavowal of race and racism, he concluded: 'there exist certain hereditary traits which characterize a certain type of contemporary Jew.' These characteristics were rooted in the genes.[97]

Once again, aside from the dubious science, the scholarship was wildly adrift. The classic 'ghetto' phase of European Jewish life persisted for three centuries, but it affected only a small proportion of the total Jewish population. The Jews of Britain, France and Holland, for example, stemmed from Spain, where Jews lived in relatively free conditions and never endured ghettoisation. Even the Jewish migrants from Russia and Poland came mainly from villages and small towns in which Jews lived unfettered lives, close to nature. Koestler may have intended to use 'ghetto' as a metonym for endogamy and a close communal life, but he loaded it with so many evolutionary functions that nothing less than the paradigmatic walled enclosure would do. Yet the reality of Jewish life in Europe never conformed to that stereotype.

Not only the history was wrong: more important, the theory was riddled with contradictions. Koestler wanted to have his cake and eat it too: he wished to prove that the Jews were a race, but to disown racialism. He wanted to argue that there was such a thing as an 'authentic' Jewish people, derived from the 'seed of Abraham' with an implicit connection and claim to the Land of Israel. At the same time, he tried to demonstrate that the Jews of North America and Europe were, so to speak, the seed of Khazaria whose genetic descent absolved them of any link with Israel.[98]

There was a deep, personal reason for this bizarre exercise. Koestler was not at pains to demonstrate that he was a true Magyar Hungarian, as Robert Blumstock has suggested.[99] But he was prepared to go to extraordinary lengths to prove that he was not a Jew, or at least a Jew of the 'seed of Abraham'. Koestler could not simply renounce Judaism: he was not a believing Jew and, in any case, saw Jewishness as more than a mere creed – it was a national identity. Indeed, it was even more than that: it was a package of acquired characteristics, a racial type. Given his geneticist convictions the only way in which he could emancipate himself from the 'seed of Abraham' was by tracing his lineage to the loins of the Khazar tribesmen.

The Thirteenth Tribe was exploited by anti-Zionists, who used it as authoritative proof that the Jews had no claim to Israel. Koestler tried to forestall this by maintaining in the controversial appendix that Israel existed on the basis of international law and could not be dismantled except by an act of genocide. By peacefully settling the land and transforming it from a desert into a prosperous country the Jews had earned a right to it that did not rely on Biblical claims. 'Whether the chromosomes of its people contain genes of Khazar or Semitic, Roman or Spanish origin, is irrelevant, and cannot affect Israel's right to exist – nor the moral obligation of any civilised person, Gentile or Jew, to defend that right.' The Khazar 'infusion' was 'irrelevant to modern Israel'. This caveat did nothing to appease the many Jews, including some of Koestler's friends, who saw the damage the book could do. Melvin Lasky, for one, spoke about it with 'utter contempt'.[100]

Looked at with a generous eye, Koestler was trying to help the benighted Jews of the Diaspora to escape the burden of Jewish identity and assimilate, thus ending anti-Semitism. However, it is hard to see how his prescription could have done much good. Whatever Jews thought of themselves, the rest of the world identified them in a certain way and a readjustment of their origins of one thousand years ago was hardly likely to end Judeophobia overnight. Would a pogrom somewhere in the world really be halted if the potential 'Jewish' victims suddenly announced: 'Sorry, case of mistaken identity: we're Khazars, really'? Would a Cohen get into a restricted golf club by telling the secretary that his forebears were really Caucasian? Koestler had given little thought to these matters. It is tempting to see the book as a purely personal act, a part of his tidying up at the end of his life. It was, however, totally counter-productive. It drew attention to his Jewish roots in a way he had avoided for decades. Or perhaps this was what he intended all along: a negative affirmation of his Jewish identity? It is likely that he himself didn't really know what he wanted out of his last proper book. In this he was being wholly consistent with his earlier attitude to being Jewish. Love it or hate it, he couldn't escape it.

Chapter 14
Illness and Exit, 1976–83

Early in 1976 Koestler was diagnosed as having Parkinson's Disease.
From that point the iron laws of age and infirmity governed the rest
of his life. Everything he did was overshadowed by a sense of
mortality. He reserved his energy for publication projects that would
consolidate, codify and perpetuate his political and natural
philosophy: *Janus – A Summing Up* (1978), *Bricks to Babel: Selected
Writings* (1980) and *Kaleidoscope* (1981), a collection of his essays from
1973 to 1980 and as yet unpublished pieces. With posterity in mind
he fretted over Iain Hamilton's still unfinished biography, working
himself into a litigious fury comparable only to his contest against
Sidney Kingsley, a monumental struggle that was also about his
reputation. The summers were spent in the pink-walled confines of
Denston: he did not have enough time or strength for long journeys.
Instead, he exercised mentally by playing Scrabble and chess, and
walked in the gardens that Cynthia tended lovingly.

Death became a practical preoccupation. In a chapter for a book
which he edited with Arnold Toynbee, *Life After Death* (1976), he
speculated on the afterlife. He wrote a pamphlet for the Euthanasia
Society giving its members advice on how to commit suicide. Once
he was sure that his worsening condition left him no other option he
proved to be his own best student. His death by his own hand in
March 1983 came as no surprise to those closest to him, but there was
almost universal consternation that Cynthia, who was only fifty-five
years old and in rude health, took her life with him. Nothing typified
Koestler's life like the manner of his leaving it: the double suicide
triggered a controversy that divided his friends and devotees, and
swirled on for years as protagonists of varying points of view stated
their case and presented new evidence. Their wills proved no less
contentious. Koestler and Cynthia left the better part of a million
pounds to promote research into the paranormal. This was a calculated affront to the scientific establishment and a blow to those who
hoped that his interest in psychical research was ephemeral, leaving

the way clear to consolidate his memory around his more conventional and political writings.

Stephen Vicinczey shrewdly commented that Koestler 'committed suicide twice'. Thanks to his well-publicised interest in ESP and levitation he 'practically made sure no one should suspect this loony Arthur Koestler of having written some of the most lucid and rational books of our time . . .'[1] His reputation took a further battering with the appearance in rapid succession of three books detailing intimate and distressing aspects of his tumultuous personal life. Arthur Koestler receded into a mist of acrimony and misunderstanding.

I

In March 1976 Koestler heard that Leeds University intended to make him an Honorary Doctor of Letters, but when the ceremony took place eighteen months later he was too ill to attend. By autumn 1976 the Parkinson's Disease began to affect him seriously. His concentration span was diminished and he worked under a mantle of anxiety. In early December he noted in his diary: 'shivers pretty bad. Controlled desperation'. A few days later he recorded: 'incredibly hard struggle to control handwriting . . . interferes with thinking. Very exhausting.' He decided to use a typewriter instead, ending a twenty-year-old practice of writing first drafts by hand. It was not a successful experiment and he returned to the pen.[2]

One of his last publishing collaborations was on *Life After Death* with Arnold Toynbee. Various contributors including Crispin Tickell, Renée Haynes and Geoffrey Parrinder covered attitudes towards death and its aftermath, historically and in different cultures. Koestler's chapter, 'Whereof one cannot speak . . .', tried to conceptualise the afterlife in scientific terms. Thanks to quantum physics matter, time and space were now all more or less conjectural; increasingly there were parallels between radiation, wave particles and theories of 'discarnate mental energy' which had been doing the rounds among devotees of parapsychology. Most recently, holograms showed how the entire image of an object could be reconstituted from a particle of it: suppose humans were 'holographic fragments of cosmic consciousness'?[3]

His social life settled down to regular evenings with friends who would come round to play Scrabble and have dinner: Sir Martyn and Lady Priscilla 'Pinkie' Beckett, Mary Benson and George Mikes were his most loyal stand-bys. These logomachic gatherings were often hilarious, since Koestler's undiminished sense of competition reacted with his still eccentric grasp of English to produce screamingly funny neologisms. Harold Harris recalled that during one game against Mikes, Koestler set down VINCE. Mikes naturally challenged him: ' "What's that?" ' Koestler replied 'in his atrocious accent, "You hit me and I vince." '[4]

Once or twice a week, if he felt up to it, he and Cynthia would venture out for a meal at a nearby restaurant alone or with close friends. At the end of the year he began secretly to work on the third volume of his autobiography. To ease the task he dictated to Cynthia, but he found much of the material from the late 1940s hard to bear. Mamaine's letters affected him deeply and his diary notes were 'just awful'. It is significant that the chapters on the break-up of his marriage and Mamaine's death were eventually written by Cynthia. In one fragmentary chapter he confessed that his own illness now made him understand what Mamaine had been through and why he had been so hard to live with: he had been a 'capricious tyrant'. This pathetic insight, so late in the day, of something so elementary was not unlike the revelation he had in the Spanish prison cell when he realised, after talking so freely about liquidating this or that class enemy, what it was like to be a human being on the receiving end of a death sentence. It showed again that despite the patina of self-knowledge, his Spanish experience had not breached the wall of egocentricity that enfolded him.[5]

Janus – A Summing Up also proved to be a 'dreadful struggle' and was not finished until July 1977, forcing Koestler and Cynthia to cancel their hoped-for summer trip to the South of France.[6] Some of the difficulty of the task can be attributed to the dreariness of summarising and condensing texts that he had written and rewritten many times before. Only small parts of *Janus* were fresh: but this was not the point: 'What I hope they show is that they add up to a comprehensive system, which rejects materialism and turns a new light on the human condition.'[7] The organisation and interpretation of the biographical elements in *Janus* exemplified his rewriting of his own life in order to give it a retrospective coherence.

Another reason Koestler decided not to go abroad was his physical condition. His writing was better, but in the second half of the year his walking became unsteady and his doctor started him on the drug L-dopa. Despite invitations from Bob Joyce to stay at his home at Spetsai in Greece, they remained in Denston again during the summer of 1978. Koestler anyway was worried that a barn adjoining his property was up for sale and wanted to ensure against any repetition of the 'Alpbach situation'.[8]

This was not the only cause for anxiety. In the autumn the question of the Hamilton biography boiled over. Hamilton had passed to Koestler the first chunk of the book and he, in turn, had forwarded the manuscript to Celia Goodman, who had vouchsafed to him copies of Mamaine's letters and her diary. Hamilton prized these as a source and pressed them into service. This made Goodman an interested party to the book, but she was not completely happy with what Hamilton had produced. In December 1976 she handed Hamilton a list of corrections and objections, asking that several passages be amended or deleted. Her objections were sometimes highly subjective. For example, she wanted to excise a reference to Adam Watson, a diplomat, because he was 'an old friend of mine and a very nice person'. Nevertheless, Hamilton complied with her requests.[9]

In July 1979 Goodman gave Koestler some more notes. She didn't like the passages about his relations with Simone de Beauvoir and was worried that Mamaine's record of his comments about Sperber and Silone 'might hurt their feelings'. She was especially keen to 'biff' Hamilton's use of de Beauvoir's *The Mandarins*: this would 'lower the tone' of the biography. Several months later she submitted a further string of references, which she wanted eliminated on grounds of 'tone'. These included mention of Dick Wyndham as a former boy-friend of Mamaine; any record of Edmund Wilson's love for her; Mamaine's comments about Peter Russell's claimed adultery; her scathing verdict on a dinner with Sperber and de Beauvoir; and a description of Koestler spending the aftermath of a drunken night 'moaning and gibbering on the bedroom floor'.[10]

Koestler, too, was having misgivings. He did not approve of Hamilton using his Palestine diary as the basis for an account of his 1948 visit to Israel, preferring that Hamilton confine himself to the version printed in *Promise and Fulfilment*. He maintained that the original diary was unsuitable as a source because it was 'jotted down in the emotionally overheated, almost hysterical atmosphere of the Arab−Jewish war'. Without 'critical evaluation' by the biographer it gave a 'one sided and misleading picture of my attitude'. Since a biography is supposed to chronicle its subject's moods, convictions and activity as they occurred, rather than in hindsight, this is a strange reproach. There must be a suspicion that Koestler was looking for a *casus belli*. He told Hamilton that the coverage of 1948 'brought to a head a growing uneasiness' with Hamilton's handling of the project, which had been troubling him for the last five years. His reservations were now accentuated by a fear that he might not survive long enough to screen the final draft. He complained that the book was supposed to have been ready for his seventieth birthday, but it looked more likely to appear posthumously. Finally, he was irked that Hamilton still had a stack of his files and papers. He understood the biographer's problems and realised that he could not hope for the book to be exactly to his taste, but he felt his patience had gone far enough. He had no choice but to put the matter in the hands of Michael Rubinstein, his solicitor.[11]

Hamilton tried to mollify Koestler. He assured him that he had written 225,000 words and hoped to finish the rest of the book in a few weeks. But he insisted on the freedom to quote from various sources, including de Beauvoir, and to determine the ultimate content. Celia Goodman's objections were just her opinion; had not Koestler told him when they started that he wanted the biography to be honest? In a more colloquial vein, according to Rubinstein, Hamilton said that he refused to be a 'hack' and to 'write under your [Koestler's] direction'. Even so, he spent two days with Koestler going over the draft and incorporating many of his suggestions. Cynthia and Koestler were only mildly appeased. In the autumn Rubinstein again pressed Hamilton for the return of Koestler's papers, a definitive deadline and agreement to the final cut. If the book was not completed by May 1979, Koestler would withdraw permission to quote from his papers and writings (thus rendering it unfeasible). Rubinstein reiterated that Koestler was afraid he might die soon and demanded that Hamilton finish the book on time even though this meant writing up the last thirty years of Koestler's career in about six months.[12]

The May 1979 deadline came and went with no sign of the final draft. Hamilton again tried to smooth relations, but Koestler refused to see him even to give a final interview. Relations between biographer and biographee reached their nadir. Hamilton, fed up with being harassed by solicitor's letters, rang Koestler to demand the return of his manuscript. Koestler claimed that he had been aggressive and threatening on the telephone, and ordered Rubinstein to terminate the agreement. A few days later he dissociated himself from the biography. His solicitor wrote to Hamilton revoking permission to quote from his published works and private writings. However, the issue of the permissions was complicated and messy because in the original arrangement for the biography Koestler had agreed that a large amount of his own writing could be included by Hamilton in return for a certain payment. When he revoked his permission he returned the fee, but Tom Rosenthal at Secker and Warburg insisted that Koestler could not act unilaterally in this way. With the book in jeopardy Rosenthal felt compelled to go to lawyers, too, and in August instructed Oswald Hickson and Collier to act in the matter. They summoned the formidable services of Peter Carter-Ruck.[13]

It was a fine legal question and Koestler's solicitors opted to work out a compromise by which Hamilton would soldier on until another deadline. Meanwhile, Koestler seems to have figured out that if he was bound by contract to let Hamilton quote his words, and was therefore powerless to sink the book by withdrawing his permission, Goodman was not. He told her that he would compensate her for any financial losses she might incur if she challenged Hamilton's right to quote from Mamaine's letters and diary. A few months later, during a weekend visit to Denston, Goodman 'hit on the idea of spiking their guns up to a point by editing Mamaine's letters and diaries'.[14]

As always in such legal sagas the means soon took precedence over the ends and the whole thing became mired in technical argument. Neither side had a watertight position. Rosenthal and Carter-Ruck, for example, pointed out that 'time was not of the essence', since Koestler had not objected strenuously when previous deadlines were breached. Moreover, Hamilton had some reasonable excuses for the delay – not the least of which was that since working on the book his Highgate home had been twice burgled and once set on fire. On the other hand, Koestler had good reason to feel wronged. The book was massively overdue. He had agreed to let Hamilton quote about 10,000 of his own words, but so far Hamilton had employed seven times that many. Hamilton used no fewer than 40,000 words from Mamaine's letters and diaries. The book was 320,000 words long and was not yet finished. For all its bulk, Hamilton had spoken to very few of Koestler's friends and hadn't even interviewed Cynthia.[15]

In February 1980 Peter Carter-Ruck went into action on behalf of Secker and Warburg. He demolished Koestler's right to terminate the agreement and refuted the grounds on which he had acted. With legal heavyweights engaged on both sides the stakes and the costs escalated at a terrifying rate. Both sides now sobered up and an interim compromise was reached. In May 1980 the final draft was delivered and a three-month period was agreed for revisions. Carter-Ruck counter-charged that if Koestler refused to co-operate in this arrangement then he was the one causing damage. He dispatched Goodman's right to withhold her permission by showing that when she had allowed Mamaine's papers to be used she had in effect entered a contract. Nor could she claim that 'time was of the essence', since she had continued to accept the arrangement after the 1975 deadline was broken. One year later an 'amicable resolution' was arrived at to resolve all the outstanding issues. None of Cynthia's letters would be quoted without her express permission; up to 20,000 of Koestler's words could be used in the book; other texts from private and published sources would be paraphrased; and Koestler would check the proofs 'on matters of fact'. Celia Goodman made no further interventions.[16]

II

The Hamilton affair consumed a substantial measure of Koestler's diminishing time and energy to little effect. It was a ghostly replay of the Kingsley case, but this time Koestler felt he had more at stake, since he was scared he would die before he could safeguard his legacy. As far as he was concerned time *was* of the essence: in February 1980 he was diagnosed as suffering from chronic lymphatic leukaemia. His doctors did not see any need for immediate treatment and certainly not for chemotherapy, but Koestler had no confidence in his resilience. Even though his mother had suffered from the same illness in her later years and had lived with this slow-moving leukaemia until she was ninety-two, he was oppressed by the imminence of his death.[17]

During 1979–80 he worked on a selection of his writings strung together with commentaries for the benefit of those readers who knew only early or late Koestler. Entitled *Bricks to Babel*, it was another gesture towards posterity. 'I sometimes meet young people', he explained in the Preface, 'who had read in college *The Sleepwalkers* or some other book on natural philosophy written after the "vocational change", and who had no idea that the same author once wrote political novels – and I meet other, more elderly people, who have read a novel called *Darkness at Noon* but never hear of any of the books written in the second period. It makes me feel sometimes as if I had undergone a change of sex. Yet one of the main purposes of this omnibus is to reflect the inseparability of the "two cultures" and the search for a synthesis which would reveal the unitary structures underlying both.'[18]

Koestler again strained to give coherence and purpose to his life and achieved this only with a large measure of hindsight and a good dollop of the paranormal, the 'invisible writing'. Like *Janus*, *Bricks to Babel* included more on the paranormal than Koestler's earlier work and reflected the late flowering of his interest in this arcane department.

This, his latest and last obsession, was reflected in the establishment that year of the KIB Foundation, an acronym for its founders: Koestler, Brian Inglis and Tony Bloomfield, a businessman acquaintance. The purpose of the KIB Foundation (renamed the Koestler Foundation after his death) was to sponsor research 'outside the scientific orthodoxies'. In 1980–1 it lavished £20,000 on the 'Daedalus Project', experiments of uncertain worth intended to prove the existence of levitation. Not content with the railway-station-type weighing machine that he had previously experimented with, Koestler ordered a specially made electronic one that was placed in the basement flat of Montpelier Square. Ruth West, the Foundation's research officer, took up residence with the machine and conducted the 'experiments'. Inglis later explained that Koestler's project 'Daedalus' was 'designed to give people who believe they can levitate the chance to do so on the Foundation's elaborate weighing machine, which measures and records "mood-induced changes in weight", his idea being that it will not be necessary for somebody actually to float, in order to demonstrate objectively the reality of levitation; it will be enough if somebody can "lose" a few ounces that cannot be accounted for by any known form of physical "lift".' The 'experiments' registered one 'success'.[19]

Koestler was 'in purdah' in Denston, working on *Bricks to Babel*, until February 1980. Walking was now quite difficult for him. Sir Martyn Beckett and his wife stopped going on holiday with the Koestlers to the South of France in 1980 because Arthur found it too difficult to walk along the steep roads around their hillside villa in Eze. When Mikes visited Denston that summer he was upset to find Koestler 'shuffling along like a very old man'. The leukaemia had indeed worsened and he had to have blood transfusions and steroid treatment. He abandoned a planned vacation with Holger Hyden in May due to the 'Battle of the Platelets', although later in the year he did manage to deliver a paper to a conference on the life and work of J. B. Rhine organised by the American Institute for Parapsychology.[20]

It was around this time that he wrote a pamphlet on suicide for the Voluntary Euthanasia Society (VES, later EXIT). It was classic Koestler: cool, logical and measured, despite the explosive subject matter. Using the well-tried question and answer method (reminiscent of 'What Do the Friends of Liberty Want?') he began by setting out some reasons for *not* commiting suicide. They are highly pertinent in view of the not too distant fate awaiting himself and, more especially, Cynthia. Those suffering from incurable diseases, he advised, might succeed in finding better pain-killers and care facilities to ease their last months or years. It was also possible that a cure might be found: suicide, as much as 'living in hope', was a risk. Mental illness, depression and loneliness often triggered suicidal impulses, but these could be coped with in a less drastic fashion. 'Suicide is commoner among the unattached, and suicidal thoughts are particularly likely after the death of a spouse. Some people seem better able to cope with the loss of companionship than others, and on common sense grounds it seems likely that those with strong out-side interests are more likely to survive such shocks.' The pamphlet was to carry a list of 'some befriending agencies' to help those rendered bereft of a partner. At this point, Koestler clearly believed that severance from a loved one was not in itself an adequate reason for giving up on life.

He then briefly discussed the history of suicide and the relatively recent prohibition it laboured under. By his lights it seemed a normal, natural and obvious step for someone faced by a debilitating terminal illness, who wanted to pre-empt a lingering death in the course of which he or she was rendered helpless. With admirable clarity and precision he set out a menu of methods for self-killing, taking account of the aesthetic sensibilities of the suicide and his or her family. Hanging, shooting, jumping and drowning were not recommended on these and other practical grounds. Koestler favoured a combination of sedatives and a plastic bag over the head. He went into minute detail to help a suicide get it right: timing was all-important to avoid discomfort on the one hand and discovery on the other. Pills to combat seasickness would help to ensure that the fatal dose of sedatives was not vomited up. It was important to leave an explanatory note. Not surprisingly publication of this section posed legal problems so the pamphlet was specifically intended for circulation only to those who had been members of the Society for at least six months.[21]

The process of literary institutionalisation continued in 1980–1 with the preparation of *Kaleidoscope*, the Danube Edition of his essays, which brought together a selection of his best occasional pieces from 1955 to 1973 and added half a dozen more written up to 1980. He also included five short stories of mixed quality. His Parkinson's Disease was under control thanks to his medication, but the drugs had side effects that often made him 'very tired, depressed and sick'. 'Work', Cynthia told Lacerta Kammerer in May, 'is the best therapy and keeps him going.' He went for monthly blood tests, but as far as the doctors were concerned he was doing well and there was no sign of danger on the horizon. Koestler's attitude of mind seems to have been more problematic. In the spring he wrote to Agnes Knickerbocker to deter her from making a visit to England and spending time with them at Denston. 'This is a difficult letter to write. Cynthia told you some time ago that I have got Parkinson's Disease, something I try to keep strictly secret. It is a condition which at my age progresses slowly, but within this slow deterioration it has its marked ups and downs, depending on one's general state of health. Recently, as a result of a virus infection, I have been feeling very low and still do. After half an hour with visitors, however stimulating, I feel exhausted and talking becomes an effort. Theatre, movies, dinner parties etc, are just not on.'[22]

Due to his medical condition and the treatments Koestler was now afflicted by periodic bouts of exhaustion, muscle weakness, dizziness and back pains. Work was an 'uphill struggle', but he battled on with book reviews, prefaces for new editions of old books, such as *Promise and Fulfilment* which was reissued in 1983, and the fresh volume of autobiography. To make matters worse, Cynthia was temporarily laid up after a bladder operation in the summer.[23]

However, they continued to go out when possible and to entertain, if only for short periods and with intimate friends. Mikes was a stalwart and supplied the connection with *Mitteleuropa* that Koestler so enjoyed and which had become attenuated with the death or indisposition of many of his oldest friends from the years of emigration and exile. In 1982 Mikes had the idea of buying a pig, having it slaughtered, prepared in the Hungarian manner and served as a special Christmas treat. Since one pig went a long way he recruited Emeric Pressburger, the eminent film-maker, and his friend Julian Schoepflin to join this enterprise. Koestler became an enthusiastic supporter of the scheme and initiated the 'Anglo–Hungarian Pig Committee' to arrange *faux* meetings and the ultimate banquet. Sadly, his ill-health precluded participation in the feast.[24]

Julian Barnes, who spent a week at Denston in the summer of 1982 while he was writing *Flaubert's Parrot*, provides a fine portrait of Koestler in his last year. Barnes had got to know him a few years earlier: his partner Pat Kavanagh had taken the place of A. D. Peters as Koestler's literary agent. Barnes admired Koestler hugely, and the two struck up a warm friendship based on shared cosmopolitan tastes and a passion for chess. When he saw Koestler in Suffolk he was struck by how old and frail he looked. Koestler lamented that the Parkinson's Disease 'knocks me sideways'. His right hand shook, his eyesight was poor, he became dizzy if he sat for too long, but could only take exercise if he walked with a stick. He went to bed at quarter past nine in the evening. Yet his mind was as sharp as ever and he won three out of five chess games against Barnes, who was less than half his age, in perfect health and no mean player.[25]

There is no reason to doubt the accuracy of Barnes's account of Koestler's condition, but around this time there is a discrepancy between Koestler's medical records, the opinion of his doctors and his general demeanour. In January 1982 his doctor described 'mild Parkinsonian features'. After an examination a specialist told his regular doctor that 'I do not think anything very serious has been happening here . . . I have reassured him that I am convinced that he will recover.' When Koestler complained of feeling exhausted after 9 p.m. each day his doctor asked what he ate and drank in the evening. When he heard Koestler's typical intake of food and drink at dinner time he pointed out that after two double whiskies and several glasses of wine most fit people would feel a little drowsy. On top of that, the consumption of 'happy pills', namely Dexedrine, reacted negatively with the alcohol. He advised Koestler to accept that depression was 'a basic state with him' and learn to handle it without medication. His Parkinsonism was 'well controlled'.[26]

The likely explanation for these discrepancies is that both chronic conditions fluctuated, aggravated by any minor ailment affecting Koestler and by his state of mind. Each set-back seems to have left him less psychologically resilient. He was repeatedly unable to work, and when that happened he descended into a pit of despair. For a while in November Cynthia had to engage a day nurse to provide blanket baths because he could not get out of bed or walk to the bathroom. Early in the new year of 1983, an examination revealed a swelling in the groin, which suggested that the cancer was accelerating. His doctor advised that he go into hospital for further tests without delay. This was the last straw for Koestler. His physical and mental resources were close to exhaustion. If he wanted to act according to the advice for the terminally ill he had given in his EXIT pamphlet, he had to act now.[27]

III

The appointments diary Cynthia kept for 1983 is full for the whole of January and February. Almost every day they saw people either at Montpelier Square or out: Mary Benson, John Grigg, the Becketts, the Rumbolds, Harold Harris, George Mikes and others. At the end of January the *Observer* published a piece by Koestler to mark the fiftieth anniversary of Hitler's assumption of power. In the course of preparing the article Koestler was as conscientious and assiduous in the craft of journalism as he ever had been. Not content to rely on his own memories or reading, he consulted Tony Rumbold, the son of Sir Horace Rumbold, who had been British ambassador in Berlin in 1933, to see what he could recall of his father's response to Germany's political earthquake. He and Cynthia scrupulously replied to the latest fan mail, dispatching dozens of letters over those eight weeks.[28]

But some visitors to Montpelier Square in late February left with a feeling of uneasiness. Harold Harris recalled: 'He was unable to stand, his speech was disjointed, and he clearly found it difficult to concentrate on what was being said to him.' Harris, who knew of Koestler's determination to die at home, in his own time and in circumstances of his own choosing, worried that 'he may have left it too late'. The next day he spoke to Cynthia, who reported that Koestler was feeling better, but she later cancelled their weekend appointments. Mikes was supposed to go round for dinner and Scrabble on 27 February, but Cynthia deterred him. When Mikes put down the telephone he had the feeling that something was not quite right about her tone. She also told Julian Barnes that they would not be able to go to the Gay Hussar on the twenty-eighth. But there was nothing unusual about this, since they had often been forced to cancel engagements over the previous few years.[29]

On the morning of Tuesday, 1 March, Amelia Marino, the Spanish home help whom they had shared with the Becketts for several years, arrived at 8 Montpelier Square. She didn't see Koestler or his dog, David. Cynthia told her that she had given the dog to friends because she could not cope with it at the same time as nursing Koestler. In fact, that morning she had taken the animal to be put down by a vet. Marino returned to Montpelier Square on Thursday, 3 March. She found a note on entering. It said: 'Please do not go upstairs. Ring the police and tell them to come to the house.' Instead, she called the Becketts, who in turn summoned the police. Inspector David Thomas and a colleague quickly arrived and proceeded up to the living-room on the first floor. They found Koestler sitting upright in his armchair, with a whisky glass in his hand. He was dead. Cynthia was reclining on the sofa at right angles to the chair, facing him. She too was dead. Two wine glasses with a residue of powder in them and a jar of honey, to sweeten the contents, stood on the coffee table parallel to the sofa. The powder was Tuinal, a powerful barbiturate. They had been dead for about thirty-six hours, which suggested that they had jointly killed themselves on the evening of 1 March. It was a textbook suicide: neat, flawlessly timed and tranquil. George Mikes rightly commented: 'Koestler organised his death to perfection'.[30]

Few of Koestler's closest confidants were surprised by the news. Brian Inglis, for example, told Norman Lebrecht that Koestler 'was falling apart'. As a vice-president of EXIT, whose views on euthanasia were well known, it would have been hard to expect otherwise. But most were stunned to hear that Cynthia was also dead. Harris, who was called upon to identify the bodies, remembered: 'I do not think it had occurred to a single one of us that she intended to take her life at the same time as Arthur.'

However, even before their joint suicide notes were made public a line crystallised among Koestler's staunchest friends. Celia Goodman summed it up just two days after the news broke: 'I would not have expected it of Cynthia. On the other hand, she couldn't have lived without him.' The same occurred to Mikes: 'everyone who knew them well can see the logic, almost the inevitability of her decision.' But if it was so obvious, why had Koestler taken no steps to end his life alone and in such a way that Cynthia might be rescued and comforted by friends in the aftermath of his demise? He had noted in his pamphlet on suicide that bereavement and loneliness could tip a person into suicide, but that grief and loneliness did not have to be the triggers for taking one's life. If he was prepared to supply strangers with a list of 'befriending agencies', why had he not arranged for his wife to be befriended? These were questions which would erupt once the formalities of interment and commemoration were over.[31]

The funeral was held on a cold, wet day at Mortlake Crematorium in South London on 11 March. Only thirty people attended, including two officers of EXIT who read from Koestler's pamphlet on suicide and fielded enquiries from the clamorous media. His death was his last act of propaganda. Melvin Lasky recalled that the bodies were held in 'two plain coffins with handwritten labels . . . No religion, no prayers, no Bible, no music, no farewell'. But there was one moment of black comedy when the conveyor got stuck and the passage of the coffins juddered to a halt. The inquest was held some two weeks later at Westminster Coroner's Court and recorded a verdict of suicide. It heard about Koestler's worsening condition and his determination not to suffer a slow, painful and undignified death. Thanks to the helpful notes left by him and Cynthia it all made perfectly good sense. Or did it?[32]

The suicide notes have been referred to frequently, but never in their entirety. Koestler left a handwritten note post-dated June 1982. Cynthia, as revealed at the inquest, had added a typewritten postscript of her own. What has been largely ignored by subsequent commentators is that sandwiched between the two was a crucial sentence typed by Cynthia and initialled by Koestler. It completely alters the meaning of her subsequent words. Koestler wrote:

To whom it may concern.

The purpose of this note is to make it unmistakably clear that I intend to commit suicide by taking an overdose of drugs without the knowledge or aid of any other person. The drugs have been legally obtained and hoarded over a considerable period.

Trying to commit suicide is a gamble the outcome of which will be known to the gambler only if the attempt fails, but not if it succeeds. Should this attempt fail and I survive it in a physically or mentally impaired state, in which I can no longer control what is done to me, or communicate my wishes, I hereby request that I be allowed to die in my own home and not be resuscitated or kept alive by artificial means. I further request that my wife, or physician, or any other friend present should invoke *habeas corpus* against any attempt to remove me forcibly from my home to hospital.

My reasons for deciding to put an end to my life are simple and compelling: Parkinson's Disease and the slow-killing variety of leukaemia (C.C.L.). I kept the latter a secret even from intimate friends to save them distress. After a more or less steady physical decline over the last years, the process has now reached an acute state with added complications which make it advisable to seek self-deliverance now, before I become technically incapable of making the necessary arrangements.

I wish my friends to know that I am leaving their company in a peaceful frame of mind, with some timid hopes for a de-personalised after-life beyond the confines of space, time, and matter, and beyond the limits of our comprehension. This 'oceanic feeling' has often sustained me at difficult moments, and does so now, while I am writing this.

What makes it nevertheless hard to take this final step is the reflection of the pain it is bound to inflict on my few surviving friends, and above all my wife Cynthia. It is to her that I owe the relative peace and happiness that I enjoyed in the last period of my life – and never before.[33]

Cynthia had typed at the bottom of the page her own parting statement:

> I fear both death and the act of dying that lies ahead of us. I should have liked to finish my account of working for Arthur – a story which began when our paths happened to cross in 1949. However, I cannot live without Arthur, despite certain inner resources.
>
> Double suicide has never appealed to me; but now Arthur's incurable diseases have reached a stage where there is nothing else to do.[34]

This codicil is well known and has fed speculation about Cynthia's immediate state of mind, her personality as a whole and the nature of her relationship with Koestler. It is worth dwelling upon.

The first point to note is the plethora of ambivalence. The opening phrase is an echo, perhaps a parody, of the preface which Koestler wrote for the Voluntary Euthanasia Society publication. In this he opined that: 'When people talk of "the fear of death", they often fail to distinguish between two types of fear which may be combined in experience but are separate in origin. One is the fear of the *state* of death (or non-existence); the other the fear of the *process* of dying.' Death, he nonchalantly asserted, should hold no terrors because it was no different from the pre-natal state. If the process of dying was the only alarming aspect, then a few careful preparations could ensure a serene, tidy and foolproof farewell.[35] Koestler's Olympian prose evidently offered no comfort to his wife. Perhaps she saw that his argument against the terror of being dead was nonsensical since a baby, newborn or foetal, has nothing to miss and no imagination with which to fear 'non-existence'. Hers was the voice of a frightened person. She also clearly felt that she had much to live for: she wanted to finish the book she was writing. Although she said that she could not endure without him, she acknowledged that she was not completely helpless: she had 'certain inner resources'. On top of all this havering, she mocked the notion of 'double suicide'. She at least shared with Koestler an unsentimental view of such things as 'death pacts' between star-crossed lovers. But she was resigned to her fate because in the light of his terminal illness 'there was nothing else to do'.

Yet surely Koestler would have had something to say about that. After all, in the suicide pamphlet he cautioned that the death of a loved one need not be the trigger for self-destruction. 'Some people seem better able to cope with the loss of companionship than others, and on common sense grounds it seems likely that those with strong outside interests are more likely to survive such shocks.' *Only* those who were elderly and with no interests in life might be expected to give up the ghost: his advice on suicide techniques was addressed to them.[36]

Cynthia was young and fit. She had 'strong outside interests'. It is significant that in March 1979 when Goodman visited Denston she 'mentioned to Cynthia that should Arthur happen to die before her I would be glad to have her live with me if she would consider it. (I'd told K. this already, and he said the evening before he'd spoken to her about it.) She said she would love to.'[37] If she had indicated to him that she wanted to die, too, he could have given her the advice he offered to others and reminded her of the unfinished memoir as well as Goodman's offer to befriend her. Instead he dictated the following:

> Since the above was written in June, 1982, my wife decided that after thirty-four years of working together she could not face life after my death.[38]

There is no indication of an attempt to dissuade her. Either he disagreed with her decision, but accepted it with uncharacteristic meekness, or else he did not contest it. Koestler was ill-famed as a bully; everyone who knew of his relations with Cynthia agreed that he dominated her. The inevitable conclusion is that he consented to her decision to end her life in concert with his suicide. His appended sentence implicitly abrogating any effort to cajole her into living on, to follow the advice he prescribed for strangers, was Cynthia's death-warrant.

IV

The suddenness of Koestler's death meant that memorial events were hastily improvised several weeks after the funeral. The first was held at the Royal Academy of Arts. It was chaired by Sir Hugh Casson, president of the Academy and ex-chairman of the Koestler Award Trust. A galaxy of Koestler's intimate allies and collaborators recalled him and Cynthia: David Astor, Mary Benson, Maurice Cranston, Holger Hyden, Brian Inglis and George Mikes. A service was held at St Nicholas's Anglican Church in Denston and a requiem mass was pronounced at the Roman Catholic church in Alpbach. The *Jewish Chronicle* carried a lengthy obituary, but ironically there was no Jewish religious or secular ceremony to mark his passing. Of his close friends in Israel, all but Kollek were now dead.[39]

In June his will was proved, to widespread consternation and merriment. He left £319,105 net, of which £7000 was devoted to personal bequests. The cash beneficiaries included Mary Benson and the aged, infirm Paul Ignotus. He left *objets d'art* to Holger Hyden, Daphne (Hardy) Henrion and Christine, the sole acknowledgement of his illegitimate daughter. The London Library inherited his books. The Trustees who were to administer the residue of his estate were charged with founding a Chair in Parapsychology at a university in Britain. Conjoined with the residue of his estate for this purpose was £100,000 bequeathed by Cynthia out of the £111,300 net which she left. This was not all that was expected to accrue for use towards the study of parapsychology: there was also the sale of property, assets abroad and royalties. The house in Montpelier Square was valued at £250,000 and Denston at £80,000. To this was added the sum accruing from the disposal of overseas investments and the continuous earnings of royalties from his publications. The total fell not far short of one million pounds.[40]

However, the Universities of Oxford and Cambridge, King's College, London, and University College, London, which were approached to set up such a chair, did not display much enthusiasm for this potentially magnificent gift. The subject matter to which it was to be devoted was regarded as ridiculous and the bequest was treated as a likely source of derision as much as enrichment. In the end, Edinburgh University reached an agreement with the Trustees to set up a chair on the lines required. This consummation was greatly assisted by the presence there of Dr John Beloff, a well-respected psychologist with a special interest in the paranormal who had come to know Koestler well over the previous decade.[41]

But the controversy over the legacy was as nothing compared with the acrimony over Cynthia's death, which flared up repeatedly over the next five years. The attempts to explain her suicide called into question her character and Koestler's, and the nature of the tie that bound them together. Koestler, the champion against totalitarianism and the opponent of capital punishment, was on trial for tyranny and murder.

Harold Harris agonised over her end. 'Why had this intelligent, healthy woman of fifty-five ended her life? Why had she written "I cannot live without Arthur."' He found the answer, he believed, in the unfinished draft of the joint autobiography, which they were writing before their twin deaths. He discovered it on Koestler's desk and subsequently edited and published the manuscript as *Stranger on the Square* (1984). It showed how 'his life became hers, that she *lived* his life. And when the time came for him to leave it, her life too was at an end.' It was an elegant resolution of the conundrum, but it cast Cynthia in a dim light: love is one thing, but love to the point of self-negation is altogether different. And what of the man who accepted such pathological devotion? Harris was aware of the problem. Looking back over her life as a self-effacing amanuensis to the Great Man, he acknowledged: 'of course there is an element of sadness in all this [the aborted pregnancies, her lack of any life of her own], just as there is in the way that she surrendered her life to his on an all-inclusive scale.' However, in view of the fact that suicide ran in her family and that she had contemplated it in the past, her final choice 'seems logical and almost inevitable'. He speculated that Koestler 'might indeed have felt some remorse or even guilt because of Cynthia's decision, but that was an emotion with which he had been familiar all his life'.[42]

In a similar vein, George Mikes concluded in *Arthur Koestler: The Story of a Friendship* (1983): 'everyone who knew them can see the logic, almost the inevitability of her decision.' Cynthia had consciously dedicated her life to the service of a man she considered a genius, whom she worshipped: 'She was Arthur's appendix and – according to her – that was her role in life.' Koestler dominated her. He was overbearing, dictatorial, intolerant, insulting and patronising: 'Arthur treated Cynthia abominably.' This pattern was most acute early in their relationship, but his irritability towards her and her unquestioning subservience towards him continued even after their marriage. Cynthia strained to serve him and would not even allow a major operation in 1979 to stop her taking his dictation. Mikes noticed that as Koestler aged and became ill, Cynthia gained in confidence, and he went so far as to claim that 'Arthur became Cynthia's prisoner'.[43] If so, it was a comfortable incarceration and in the end the jailer opted to join the convict on the gibbet, a strange way for a jailer to behave.

Mikes saw a tragic paradox in the alleged slackening of Koestler's hold over Cythia: as he mellowed their mutual love deepened and so her eventual choice to die with him became even more explicable. 'Cynthia had no life of her own: she lived through Arthur.' He did not 'take her with him' when he killed himself, 'she went of her own free will'.[44] Given Koestler's notion of free will, that last phrase may be read in two very different ways. Those who knew of his strength of will and crushing personality, compared with Cynthia's frail, almost transparent persona, derided the notion that she had any choice in the matter.

The Hungarian-born *émigré* novelist Stephen Vicinczey, in a review of Mikes's book, unambiguously pronounced 'Koestler's moral responsibility for his wife's premature death'. He berated Harris's interpretation as 'a prime example of both male chauvinism and the *Herrenvolk* mentality of the intellectual classes'. For Vicinczey their mutual love and Cynthia's consecration of her life to Koestler offered no justification for her end: he could have ensured that she was able to live beyond his death, but chose not to do so. 'He may have had the right to end his own life, but it was his duty to protect Cynthia's by every means, to give her the chance to survive the first shock of his death and perhaps to find out that it was possible to live without him after all.'[45]

With the appearance of more memoirs detailing Koestler's life and, for the first time, explicitly documenting his moods, his vicious temper and his unhappy affairs with women, his relationship with Cynthia seemed to darken and her fate appeared to take on a different hue. Harris's roseate picture of the enthralled lovers passing away together in their nest paled. Edward Pearce, writing in 1985 about *Living with Koestler*, connected Koestler's frequently violent and abusive treatment of his second wife with the death of his third. He read Mamaine's letters and diary, edited by Celia Goodman, as a chronicle of ill-treatment by a selfish, boorish, pseudo-intellectual of the worst order. Koestler was 'a man who at the end was to sacrifice his feebly devoted last wife on his own dogmatic deathbed – a case of suttee among the thinking folk'.[46]

In 1986 Mikes muddied the waters by revealing that Vicinczey had told him years earlier that a doctor informed him that Cynthia was also suffering from cancer. If this was true, 'Instead of being seen as his victim she can be seen to have chosen to share the dignity of his end.' This revision, occasioned by the reprinting, but in amended form, of Vicinczey's review, triggered a bombardment of criticism from Harris and others. Harris insisted that there was no evidence that Cynthia had cancer and, indeed, her medical records confirm that to be true. In the course of his counterblast Harris repeated the version of the fatally entwined lovers.[47] But this line was wearing thin. Even sympathetic witnesses like Julian Barnes would not deny that Cynthia's relationship with Koestler was an unequal one and that such an imbalance had to affect an evaluation of her death. 'That she lived entirely for him nobody doubted; that he could be tyrannical was equally clear. Did he really bully her into killing herself? This was the unmentionable, half-spoken question that their friends came up against.' Barnes had pondered her suicide message carefully and saw

that she had no predilection for a 'suicide pact'. So why didn't
Koestler exert his forceful personality to encourage her to plod on?
Barnes shied away from an unequivocal answer: at such a juncture
'speculation becomes impertinent'. Yet his vignette of Cynthia in
1982 revealed very clearly how much of a cipher she was, running to
and fro at Koestler's behest, hardly giving the impression that she had
any needs and wants of her own.[48]

While the men slugged it out in male fashion, perhaps the sagest
and most sensitive analysis came from Anita Brookner in a review of
Stranger on the Square. She noted how Cynthia had not written a joint
autobiography: she practically vanished from sight in its pages. Even
the most wrenching personal episodes, such as her failed marriage
and the abortions, were skimmed in order to concentrate on
Koestler. Nothing mattered that was not about him. She might have
loved him, but 'that great love contained a pathological element'.
Simone de Beauvoir had also dedicated her life to a great man and a
great mind, and her 'autobiography' was likewise really his story. But
in the end she surmounted the death of Sartre. She had a life – it was
one of the things which endeared her to Sartre and which bound
them so tightly. They were two independent people united by shared
interests, passions and mutual respect. The contrast to the ligatures
binding Cynthia and Arthur Koestler could not be more painful.[49]

Ultimately, it is an indictment of Koestler that he lived with a
woman who was a vacuum. Celia Goodman used the German term
kontaktlos to describe her: she had no friends of her own or contact
with other people outside Koestler's circle. Goodman regarded her
as almost childlike and totally dependent on Koestler. It is worth
recalling the excoriating observation on Koestler by another woman
observer, Frances Partridge: 'He is an aggressively male man who
likes to have subjugated, pretty women and fawning dogs about
him.'[50] It was Koestler's will that he should be accompanied through
life by these selfless handmaidens. The more they abrogated independence of mind, of course, the more he despised and ill-treated
them. But he could not tolerate dissent or defiance. In order to
achieve 'perfection' in his cooking and his domestic environment, to
avoid being queried in the full flight of his obsessions and manias, he
had to have someone who was masochistically devoted to him.
Cynthia served that role for over thirty years.

The true and enormous tragedy is that she was a woman of intelligence and humour, who saw through Koestler and knew exactly
what she was doing with her own life. In her diary – kept, to be fair
to Koestler, with his encouragement – she constantly jabbed at the

bubbles of his pomposity, recorded in gruesome thoroughness escapades that deserved to miscarry, and unsparingly detailed conduct that merited reproach. The true indication of how heavily Koestler's domestic tyranny pressed on her is that he knew of her vivacity and brightness, and that it had to be suppressed for their relations to persist; and that Cynthia knew this, too, and connived in an act of self-abnegation that was finally to be her downfall. If she could not live without Koestler, if this was how she wanted it, he did not object. It is this negation of another human being that casts a pall over the life, work and reputation of Arthur Koestler.[51]

While the meaning of their deaths will always remain elusive, whichever way the event is viewed it can be seen as a logical out-come of Koestler's flawed personality, lack of identity and homelessness. A person with a sense of self-worth, who loved himself and others to a reasonable and normal degree, who knew who he was and whence he came, would be at ease with other personalities or on his own. Koestler's sense of self was so fragile that unless he could see himself in another he was in almost physical agony. This was a man who could not bear to be alone unless he was completely absorbed in work. Ironically, in view of their respective destinies, unlike Cynthia, he had few 'inner resources'. Yet the time he spent with equally forceful people only reminded him of his interior uncertainty. In public he appeared confident, opinionated, literally full of himself. Once alone he deflated. As his diaries show, he became a maundering, confused sixteen-year-old not sure who he was or what he was supposed to be doing, projecting this adolescent angst on to the meaning of life and the universe in general. Cynthia was a reassuring reflection of his being, and their suicide notes can be read mirror-wise. Her life was the counterpart, the guarantee, the validation of his own. He could not bear to live without her. Perhaps he could not bear to die without her.

Conclusion

The Homeless Mind

Arthur Koestler died just a year before the accession to power of Mikhail Gorbachev and the consequent fulfilment of all his hopes and predictions about Communism and the Soviet Union. But in the celebrations that followed the humbling of Soviet power his name was barely mentioned, and he was virtually always omitted from the pantheon of those who had helped to undermine Communism.[1] This neglect is astonishing in view of Koestler's participation in the Cold War, a commitment of energy and intellect that only a few surviving contemporaries seemed able to appreciate. Raymond Aron, for example, recalled his front-line role in the 'war of ideologies and intellectuals' as 'one of the last and greatest of those *intellectuels engagés*'. Sidney Hook counted him 'an exemplary European "freedom-fighter", loyal, courageous, conscientious, self-sacrificing'.[2]

Koestler was a paradoxical casualty of the West's victory in the Cold War. His early works lost their relevance; without a shared awareness of the urgency that drove *Darkness at Noon* its vitality paled. However, as he reiterated with increasing irritability from middle age onwards, anti-Communism represented only a fraction of his life's work.

Yet he was his own worst enemy when it came to ensuring his legacy in other respects. He reinvented himself as a man of science in the 1950s, but then threw himself into para-scientific studies. Rationality was a key to his stature as a science writer; his perceived irrationality jeopardised that. The more he summed up his *Weltanschauung*, the more he tried to unify his life and work, centred on his belief in the paranormal, the more he defeated his bid for intellectual longevity. Christopher Booker, reviewing *Janus – A Summing Up* in the *Spectator*, dismissed it as a 'chaotic jigsaw'. Koestler was revealed as 'talking pure gibberish'. Alex Comfort called it a 'self-indulgent muddle'.[3]

Finally, the circumstances of his death and the inquests into his relationship with Cynthia, subsequently extrapolated to embrace all his personal relations, guaranteed that Koestler's troubled personality would overshadow his entire life and opus. He went from being a bold outsider to a maverick and ended as an embarrassment.

Now that the dust from the collapse of the Berlin Wall has settled and fifteen years have passed since his death the time has come for a reassessment of his life, his personality and his accomplishments. In the light of his private papers it is clear that previous commentators and biographers have missed perhaps the most fundamental element of his story: that Koestler was a Jew. Far from being a particularistic observation that leads nowhere, his Jewishness makes him supremely representative of our age. To continue to neglect it is to distort his life and to undervalue his importance.

I

Koestler's achievements were not limited to anti-Communism. He wrote five major novels, one of which instantly became a classic; two marvellous autobiographical volumes that charted the first half of the century and spoke to millions of people; two brilliant works of reportage which stand among the best ever written by a journalist; a powerful contribution to the history of science which still has the capacity to electrify readers; several volumes of essays and a considerable body of writing on subjects as varied as psychology, neurology, evolution and genetics. The scope of his interests, catholicity of tastes and polymathic skills is in itself remarkable.

On the eve of the Second World War he was recognised as one of the world's leading foreign correspondents, a reputation that was consolidated by his wartime writing. André Gide recorded in his diaries in the 1960s that 'Koestler is a supreme journalist, and I like him best when he is simply recording facts, as in *Spanish Testament* and *Scum of the Earth*'. For Sidney Hook 'he was one of the foremost political journalists of our time, who had been to hell and back and knew the face of the enemy in all his totalitarian guises'.[4] Sadly, Koestler looked down on his journalism and aspired to greatness first as a writer of fiction, then as a master of scientific fact.

Whatever the long-term value of his novels, there is little doubt that he was one of the greatest writers ever to adopt English as a second or third language. Michael Foot placed him on a par with Joseph Conrad (an author with whom Koestler has a lot in common, not least a distrust of utopias and political violence). Equally distinctive was his attempt to bridge the 'two cultures' of science and the humanities. Here, too, he mastered different grammars and vocabularies and translated from one into another. The political philosopher Maurice Cranston marvelled at the way Koestler 'collected knowledge over a wide range'. George Steiner, one of the few of his intellectual peers with a similar breadth of interest, recognised how 'Koestler sought to give to the interactions between the humanities and the exact sciences a logic, a recognition of reciprocities, which the mechanistic conventions of classic physics and biology had eroded'. Honoured several times for his contribution to the humanities, Koestler was also nominated three times for the Nobel prize. He craved recognition as a scientific innovator, a second Darwin. Of course, Darwin gave birth to a social and political outlook and Koestler aspired to do no less.[5]

If Koestler had little success in this respect it was because he was a synthesiser of ideas and not a researcher or an original thinker. The distinguished American scientist Frank McConnell, reviewing *Janus*, observed that he was 'always a wonderful assimilator and less than satisfactory originator'. John Maynard Smith, a leading zoologist and expert on evolution, commenting on *The Act of Creation* fourteen years earlier, noted that 'at no point does Koestler attempt to formulate a scientific theory of originality'. In 1964 Peter Medawar, the Nobel prize-winning zoologist and long-standing adversary of Koestler, complained that he had 'no real grasp of how scientists go about their work'. He accused him of amateurishness: above all, he failed to subject his own theories to rigorous self-criticism or objective experimentation. Koestler wanted recognition as a scientific thinker, but ignored basic rules of scientific procedure.[6]

There is anyway a question mark over the originality of his major scientific-political ideas from the 1940s. Literary critics and scientists contested the finer points of Koestler's oeuvre, but few noted the inspiration he derived from less well-known figures. Olaf Stapledon and Michael Polanyi, in particular, were crucial to his intellectual development in the years 1940 to 1950. Both were quite modest men and seemed to have been content to subsist out of the limelight. But others resented the way that Koestler appropriated their ideas. After the death of Polanyi his widow, Magda, wrote bitterly to Koestler reproaching him for exploiting what had seemed an innocent and productive relationship with her husband. 'You should hear what people say about you – don't you care about that? "He is known for stealing other people's ideas" said to me a famous and important literary personality a couple of years ago. It would be time to repair your reputation, instead of PERSEVERING TO LIVE ON OTHER PEOPLE'S – mainly Michael's – ideas.'[7]

Whatever their accuracy, validity or exact provenance, his

scientific writings were hugely influential. *The Sleepwalkers* became a standard work on Copernicus, Galileo and Kepler, and conceptually anticipated Thomas Kuhn's work on the structure of scientific revolutions. *The Ghost in the Machine* educated a generation growing up in the 1960s about debates around evolution, genetics and neurology, relating them to the arms race and the fear of nuclear war. Its effect may be gauged by the fact that Sting (Gordon Sumner), lead singer and song-writer of the 1980s super-group Police, used the title of the book and its ideas for his group's 1981 album *Ghost in the Machine*. Two years later he drew on Koestler again for the album *Synchronicity*. It is impossible to read Martin Amis on nuclear war without detecting echoes of Koestler's declamations on the sources of human self-destructiveness.[8]

In *Insight and Outlook* (also *The Act of Creation*) and *The Ghost in the Machine* Koestler attempted to refound politics on biological foundations. His struggle to reconcile ethics with biology and devise moral systems that accorded with human nature anticipated the work of E. O. Wilson, Richard Dawkins, Peter Singer and Steven Pinker. They have achieved greater recognition because their writing is grounded in profound knowledge of their subjects and garnished with academic respectability. But Koestler's autodidactic gropings deserve greater acknowledgement. He caused controversy by advocating the use of drugs to alter behaviour patterns, but today it is acceptable discourse to speak about a 'gene for crime' that, if isolated, could be eliminated. Koestler may yet have the last laugh on the 'grey birds' of academe.

II

Koestler's volcanic personality casts such a shadow over his life that it is hard to reach a balanced assessment of the kind of man he was. Opinions of him were sharply polarised: even his friends equivocated about his character. Arthur Schlesinger Jr grasped Koestler's kaleidoscopic make-up in an essay on his autobiographical writing, dating from 1970: 'For all his occasional posturing, self-dramatisation, conceit, and cheapness of metaphor and argument, here is the testament of a brave, bright, prickly, reckless, impatient, witty, hostile man.'

Mary Benson, who was close to Koestler in the second half of his life, wrote of him: 'Along with his brilliance, his humanity and his ironic sense of humour, there was the demonic side to his nature – the pendulum swing into despair, the drinking and the violent tempers.' Sidney Hook, who respected him tremendously, was nevertheless repelled by his selfishness, brutality and sexism: 'Koestler was too indulgent of his own emotional quirks and had been spoiled by those who are always making allowances for his *Geniemoral*, especially women.'[9]

Long before he felt free to act as he chose by dispensation of his genius he displayed a behaviour pattern that was liable to get out of control. As well as being unusually sedulous, Langston Hughes remembered him in 1932 as restless, miserable, obsessive and fussy. His enthusiasm for ideas easily turned into arrogance, his zeal into boorishness. Koestler's insistence that he be treated as a philosopher maddened A. J. Ayer, whose opinion on such matters was not to be taken lightly. 'There have been times when we have been good friends, but longer periods of estrangement in which, on my side, at least, our intellectual differences have been emotionally tinged. This extends to my judgement of him as a writer. I think highly of his autobiographical books and continue greatly to admire the psychological and political insight of *Darkness at Noon*. At the same time, I cannot help wishing that he would leave philosophy alone.'[10]

Once he was famous, wealthy and independent Koestler became overbearing and dogmatic. Ayer's comments may be held to reflect more badly on their author than their target, but they differ little from those of Frances Partridge, a gentle soul with no vested interest in the matter. She complained with uncharacteristic asperity that 'There's no means of discussing ideas with Koestler, as Ralph [Partridge – her husband] long ago found out. You can either listen to him haranguing or not. He won't listen to you. I don't think the better of him for that, clever though he undoubtedly is.'[11] The journalist and anti-hanging campaigner C. H. Rolph recalled that 'there were no grey figures in Arthur's world: they were black, or white or invisible'. His quarrels were legendary and he rarely forgave a disputant. Rolph was more than once a witness to the 'bitterness and spite . . . the deftness with which he reduced reputations to tatters'. George Mikes, a loyal friend, admitted: 'He was quarrelsome, he could be rude, he was obstinate and occasionally obsessive . . . his rudeness could be stupendous.'[12]

Established in a domestic setting in which he was the supreme authority, Koestler became tyrannical. In an unfinished chapter of the uncompleted third volume of memoirs, he acknowledged this himself: Mamaine decided to leave him because of 'the urge to lead her own life – painting, playing the piano, cultivating her own friends (most of whom I disapproved of, as they disapproved of me) – all of which, she felt, was impossible in a household ruled by a capricious tyrant. I saw her point only too clearly.'[13]

Even when there was room for a piano to be located far away from Koestler's sensitive ears, Mamaine was usually so busy servicing his needs that she never had a chance to practise on it: Koestler was *very* demanding. Cynthia recalled an incident that showed how the fussiness which amused Langston Hughes could, in changed conditions, turn into persecution. One day on Island Farm he noticed that weeds had attacked the herbaceous border. 'Arthur was furious when he saw the devastation . . . How could Mamaine allow such a thing to happen? . . . He brooded about it and there was no way of placating him. His mood was spoilt and, once spoilt, could not be changed.'[14]

At the time of this floral tiff Mamaine was recovering from a severe illness, which was not assisted by the insalubrious conditions on the island. But Koestler refused to accept that his insistence on living in damp, humid locations aggravated her condition.

Koestler was a bully. On the eve of Cynthia's departure for America in 1950, he took her and Mamaine to dinner at the Ivy. 'He looked at Mamaine and urged her to eat more. He did his best to tempt her with her favourite food . . . But she had been through this determined cajoling too many times in the past and was sick of it . . . As he was getting nowhere he turned to me. I could not eat another thing, but I was bullied into have [sic] a mousse *au chocolat* and plied with wine. He offered me half of his dessert and then plonked nearly all of it on my plate with a dollop of crème Chantilly. My protests were ignored.'[15]

Genius, certified by his success, conferred an ugly imperiousness on Koestler. Woodrow Wyatt commented that 'like many men of towering talent he could not flourish unless the entourage subordinated themselves to his godlike whims'. Julian Barnes perceived the same dynamic at work at Denston, even though Koestler was old and ill: 'Domestically, he is a frail dictator.'[16]

The kind of women with whom Koestler enjoyed sustained relationships are a barometer of his egomania. According to one of her oldest friends Dorothea Ascher, Koestler's first wife, was 'an intellectual person, a serious person' who was independent-minded and 'not someone who would submit to his being'.[17] Daphne Hardy was highly cultured, artistically gifted and strong-willed. Mamaine was clever and talented, but lacked self-confidence. Cynthia was a mere cypher. Dorothea, Daphne and Mamaine more or less left Koestler once they found him impossible to live with any longer. Cynthia was too weak to take that step. Their respective fates, like the wives of Henry VIII, have some bearing on the dynamic between them and him: survived, survived, died, suicide.

Koestler's sexual affairs were capable of generating heat years after his death. In 1984 Woodrow Wyatt angrily recalled that Koestler swiped one of his girlfriends during the war. This was a symptom of his insatiable appetite for women: 'A steady supply of them was as necessary to him as alcohol which he also consumed in large quantities.' Even Mary Benson, a firm ally, deprecated his 'pathological promiscuity'. His defenders, chiefly George Mikes, regarded the 'charge of "womanising" [as] downright ridiculous'. Koestler simply practised the mores of his birthplace: 'In Central Europe every woman was regarded as fair game. She could always say "no" and — after several renewed attempts to persuade her to change her mind — her *no* would be taken for an answer, even if grudgingly.' A woman might have seen things differently and, in any case, Koestler does not seem to have taken 'no' for an answer. Simone de Beauvoir, having been pestered by him, found it easier to say 'yes'. Jill Craigie not only said 'no', she struggled without a scintilla of ambiguity to repel his unwanted attention. There is evidence that as well as his consistent violence against women Koestler was a serial rapist.[18]

Despite his appalling treatment of many (but not all) women, he remained on good terms with several ex-lovers, most former wives and a number of past mistresses: they liked him and valued his company despite his faults. The fact that he was the author of textbooks on sexual practice and interpersonal relations that were progressive for their time, and are enlightened even by today's standards, is just another indication of the massive contradictions in his personality.

What is beyond doubt, though, is his failure to allow the good to mitigate the bad. Mamaine did not excuse her husband's licentiousness by reference to the cultural mores of Hungarian males; she preferred to blame Ma. She wrote to Cynthia: 'One thing K agreed about was that he couldn't live with any women, however perfect, and he agreed with my analysis of his attitude as being a hostility to women derived from his hatred of his mother.'[19] If they could agree on this diagnosis, rightly or wrongly, why couldn't Koestler do anything about it? The inference must be that he was either not in control of himself for much of the time or wilfully suspended his self-knowledge and the insight he had gained from the study of psychology.

Indeed, although Koestler was celebrated for his candid auto-biographical writings, to many critics he could seem oddly blind to his own character. 'Many years ago', Ayer recounted in 1982,

'Koestler told me that he aspired to become "the Darwin of the twentieth century". I did not laugh at him then and I do not now. Nevertheless I think he showed a lack of self-knowledge. He has proved himself to be a man of exceptional gifts, but his mind has displayed a religious rather than a scientific bent.' In fact, Koestler did toy with religion. At a dinner with Nicholas and Mary Henderson in 1963, he asserted to Frances Partridge: 'There is no longer a basis for rejecting religion.' He once rang up Janetta (Jackson) Parladé and astonished her by saying in all seriousness that he was going to become a Catholic. Parladé suspected that this fad was due to a liaison with a certain woman; it certainly led to nothing.[20]

For all his ultra-rationalism Koestler was driven to look for a supernatural meaning in life: unlike the existentialists, he was unable to live in a universe devoid of transcendent purpose. Having turned his back on Judaism, rejected conventional religion *tout court* and spurned dialectical materialism, he turned to spiritualism and mysticism. He eventually concocted a pseudo-rationalistic version of the supernatural and the immortality of the soul, exemplified by his suicide note. Life after death was transmogrified into the merging of individual consciousness back into a 'psychic universe'.

If he was intemperate, obsessive, egomaniacal, bullying, petty, selfish, arrogant, lecherous, duplicitous and self-deluding, there was another side to him. Koestler was lauded for his warmth, kindness and generosity. He could be immensely charming, funny and interesting.

In her memoirs, Storm Jameson recounted 'An incident [which] taught me about Arthur Koestler that neither his formidable intelligence nor his black temper nor his natural charm lie as near his bones as his kindness'. When Orwell was staying at Bwlch Ocyn his son, Richard, woke up early one morning and started to cry: 'to keep him quiet, so that Orwell could sleep on, Arthur sat beside the cot for an hour and amused him silently by pulling faces.' His charitable nature was perhaps more easily extended to those who were least proximate to him. In 1956 an old lady, who was Attila Jozsef's last lover, wrote to him from Haifa to say that she had suffered an accident and sought his help. He could have dismissed this request out of hand since he had never met the woman, but instead he wrote to Abraham Weinshall asking him to divert some of his Israeli royalties to her. When he got a new television, he didn't just throw out the old one: he contacted a girls' borstal in Aylesbury and offered it for the amusement of the inmates.[21]

Melvin Lasky recalled that 'He had enormous loyalties to old friends. . . .He was very warm: you always wanted to have Arthur as an uncle because he would always be reliable with warmth unless he had a "prickly Tuesday" day and then for no good reason you were on the out.' Raymond Aron put on record Koestler's loyalty to his former comrades. He might no longer agree with them, but he rarely turned down a plea for assistance from a fellow inmate of Le Vernet or the exile circle in Paris.[22]

Koestler was constantly providing financial support to relatives, friends and old comrades. He set up funds, mainly from his own pocket, to help refugee intellectuals and reward talented prisoners. Sometimes these aims blurred and got him into trouble. In 1951 the Fund for Intellectual Freedom made a 200,000-franc loan to Manès Sperber to help him buy a flat. Sperber was the largest individual recipient of funding in the financial year 1951–2; it was partly this kind of assistance that worried men like Budd Schulberg and undermined their confidence in Koestler's management of the FFIF. Less problematically, he asked A. D. Peters to buy the rights to a volume of poems by Ivan Blatny, an East European refugee writer, even though he knew they would never find a publisher. He knew Blatny needed money, but didn't want him to suffer the indignity of being offered charity.[23]

Koestler's hospitality in London, Alpbach or Denston was renowned. He always had a supply of fine wine on hand and prided himself on offering haute cuisine. (Although Cynthia had to do the cooking: Koestler ordained that she take a cookery course in order to supply dishes of a sufficiently high standard.)[24] He was enchanting company when relaxing on holiday in the South of France with the Becketts or taking them out on his boat *Socrates* on the Thames. While he 'would pick an argument at the drop of a hat' and often ended up drunk after dinner, his boorishness has to be balanced against his abundant charm.[25]

Celia Goodman, Mamaine's twin, remains a stout advocate of Koestler's many virtues. The man she knew was 'incredibly generous' as well as 'tremendously brave, both physically and morally . . . He was such fun to be with, he had such a good sense of humour, he was so affectionate and nice, such a terribly nice person. Always interesting, always full of new ideas. Chat away about anything: he was frightfully easy to talk to. The thing about Arthur was that he made life fun, that's to say, if he was in a good mood: he always liked having fun.'[26]

When he was on form Koestler was tremendously good fun to be with. Maurice Cranston revelled in 'his charm and his restlessness, and sometimes absurd enthusiasm'. David Astor, who fell for him from the moment they met in Cyril Connolly's house, regarded him as 'one of the most lively writers I've ever known'. For all his reservations about his at times 'appalling' conduct 'I loved Arthur both because I admired him and also because he was a little boy – there was something boyish and winning about him which made him irresistible to me. I would forgive him any bad behaviour in the way you do forgive a child bad behaviour. I think he had a wonderful heart and there was so much of the spirit and the lovable about him.' Even though Janetta (Jackson) Parladé found him ultimately too demanding, she stressed that 'he was fascinating really. I loved his company . . . he was very glorious to be with, a very original and very exciting person to have to talk to.'[27]

III

The picture of Koestler that emerges from his own published and unpublished writing, the letters and diaries of other people who knew him, memoirs and oral history, is of a sharply conflicted personality. He was keen to trace his flaws to his upbringing, yet the picture he paints of his childhood and youth does not entirely support this. The times through which he lived may share some of the responsibility. C. H. Rolph observed that 'at the centre of his unchangeably distorted nature was a hatred of authority, a distrust of the officials who represented it, and a certainty that authorities hated him'. This may be explained as much by the wars and revolutions that shattered his family life and domestic security, as the more usual explanations that point a finger at tyrannical nannies and governesses.[28]

The chaotic events he witnessed, no less than the erratic emotional currents in his home life, may also account for his ultra-rationality, which was both a strength and a weakness of his character. As Hook noted, many people found him exasperating in argument because of his relentless, sometimes absurd logic and his inability to compromise on principles. After lunching with Koestler in February 1946 Malcolm Muggeridge confided to his diary that he 'Found him interesting and piquant, picking up things so quickly – English slang even; so perceptive – too perceptive perhaps; all antennae and no head'. Timothy Leary realised that Koestler would never understand drug-induced mysticism or 'altered states of consciousness' because he remained locked into a positivist, nineteenth-century scientific mentality.[29]

His unbending attitude was related to his apocalypticism. Again, this can only be understood against the background of European history and the modern Jewish experience. Having survived one revolution, two world wars and experienced two anti-Semitic totalitarian systems at uncomfortable propinquity (of which one was responsible for the murder of half his family, the other of half his friends), Koestler the Jew might well have felt nervous about the prospects for political stability and his own safety. This had an immediate effect on his thinking and his life-style. In a typical letter from the late 1940s, he wrote to Michael Polanyi: 'time is running short and I feel a categorical imperative to concentrate ruthlessly on my work, which is my *raison d'être* on this earth. If I succeed I shall wait with a clean conscience for the devil to take us all.' According to Guy de Rothschild, Koestler had a nightmare in which he was 'Koestler the prophet: knowing the truth, but unable to convince others, whether it was alerting the world to the massacre of the Jews or unmasking the Soviet regime'. When Barbara Skelton, then Cyril Connolly's wife, read *Arrow in the Blue* in 1953, she noted: 'He hears his voice as a warning to the world.'[30]

Convinced that civilisation would end imminently unless drastic action was taken to turn away the barbarians at the gate, he had no time for the niceties of intellectual debate. He was impatient with the minutiae of political manifestos, social programmes or laboratory experiments. He formulated broad principles and stuck by them rigidly (some to a greater or lesser degree). From these he was able to deduce answers to any and every social or political question; they could even be applied to literary or artistic criticism. This gave his system of thought a patina of unity and immense persuasive power; but it often fell apart at the level of detail. By that time, however, he had usually moved on to a new cause, a new book, a new enthusiasm, a new home.

War, revolution, exile were responsible for more than his urgency. Koestler knew only too well the plight of the displaced persons, the refugees and the stateless: the condition of homelessness was at the root of much of his anxiety and led to many absurdities. On holiday with Koestler in Cornwall in the new year 1954, Janetta Jackson was puzzled to find Koestler taking cold baths in the morning. She discovered he did this because he believed it was the way Englishmen were brought up in public schools and he wanted to be like them, to belong. All his moving was, paradoxically, driven by the desire for a home. Paul Willert claimed that the incident in Hammersmith when Koestler got into an altercation with a policeman occurred not only because he was tight, but due to the policeman's assumption that Koestler was a foreigner. He so wanted to be accepted as English that he lost his temper and lashed out. David Astor thought that the cottage in Suffolk and the dogs were all symbolic of his efforts to Anglicise. [31]

But the more Koestler tried to fit in, be it in Britain, America, France or Austria, the more he was conscious of his exteriority. Contrary to the view of even his closest companions, a specific Jewish sensibility was never far beneath the surface. At the end of January 1955 he noted ruefully in his diary that BOAC (the forerunner of British Airways) had been obliged to order American-made planes. Britain was 'generally losing ground . . . As a Jew and therefore more British than the Britons, it breaks my heart.' To those who were never deceived by his charades and for whom he remained a deracinated Central European Jew, his attempts to assimilate seemed distinctly ridiculous. Julian Barnes, for instance, was puzzled that Koestler contributed to the fund to restore Denston's Anglo-Saxon parish church. When Koestler told him 'It is expected', Barnes wondered at his insouciance, 'as if I should not be surprised at an agnostic Hungarian Jew taking up his squirearchical English responsibilities'.[32]

If Koestler deliberately blurred his ethnicity in the 1950s, from the 1960s it became increasingly difficult to discuss Jewish matters with him at all. When Sperber was composing an essay on '*Mein Judensein*', he told Lasky not to let Koestler know the subject since it would annoy him. Koestler briskly dismissed Hyam Maccoby, who broached *The Thirteenth Tribe* when they met at a party, and many of Koestler's intimate friends cannot recall his Jewish origins ever coming up in conversation. And yet Jewishness was always there, expressed through anxieties and neurotic behaviour patterns: the classic symptoms of displacement and repression. George Steiner commented shrewdly that 'Koestler was one of the great Central European Jews in a time which saw the annihilation of the breed. Almost from boyhood, he was a survivor, with a survivor's resilience and scars.'[33]

One of the factors which may be cited as mitigating judgement on his conduct was his Jewish heritage, although he virtually barred that from consideration of his life history. His Jewishness, like that of other survivors of Central European Jewry, connoted self-abasement, deracination, exclusion and trauma: it did much to explain, if not to condone, eccentric and even extreme behaviour.

IV

Koestler's obfuscation of his Jewish past and his Jewish identity deceived many commentators. Of the early critics who paid him attention only Joseph Nedava, a follower of Jabotinsky who had encountered Koestler in Palestine in the 1940s, placed Koestler's Jewish roots in the foreground.[34] John Atkins, whose critical study appeared in 1956, treated Koestler reverentially as a great European author and eschewed any mention of his Zionist activism. A major study of Spanish Civil War literature in 1967 referred to him as being of 'Austrian-Hungarian extraction'.[35]

In 1968 Jenni Calder published a monograph comparing Koestler and Orwell. She accepted Koestler's description of himself as a representative figure, but noted that his writing was most alive when he dealt with Jewish issues. She explained this partly by the fact that he was 'an exile from the faith that had sustained his ancestors'. This exile, combined with his emigration and renunciation of Communism, deepened his isolation and affected his use of language.[36]

The first substantial examination of Koestler that appeared in the wake of *The Thirteenth Tribe* was by Sidney Pearson, a political scientist interested in what happened to politics after the 'death of God'. Pearson slotted *The Thirteenth Tribe* into this framework: if, as Koestler averred, the Jewish God was deceased then there was no point in Jews remaining Jewish. Far from seeing Koestler as a Jewish writer or even an author concerned with Jewish questions, Pearson reconstructed him as a quasi-Christian thinker.[37]

Between Koestler's seventieth birthday and his death in 1983, several collections of essays and a large-scale biography appeared. Koestler's publisher Harold Harris edited a book of essays in 1975, not one of which discussed Koestler as a Jew, even though the Jews were the subject of his next book. Only one contributor, Iain Hamilton, mentioned Koestler's Jewish background. Hamilton was then at work on his biography of Koestler. The final version was riddled with errors and lacunae, and bore the marks of surgical attention by Koestler, Cynthia and Celia Goodman. Hamilton was spoonfed by Koestler and brusquely replicated his subject's own version of his origins. It seems from documents in the Koestler archive which Hamilton saw, and from the transcripts of interviews which Hamilton conducted with Koestler, that important insights into his Jewishness were omitted or played down.[38]

A useful collation of critical articles spanning Koestler's writing career edited by Murray A. Sperber in 1977 contained several key pieces about Koestler and Palestine, but otherwise reproduced the barrenness of commentary on Koestler the Jew.[39] It was not until 1983, after Koestler's death, that the first essay appeared which discussed him solely in a Jewish context. This path-breaking study by Hyam Maccoby set out to explain why Koestler had launched the vicious assault on Jewish loyalties in *The Thirteenth Tribe*. He concluded that Koestler was abysmally ignorant of Judaism and had such a dim view of the religion and its bearers that he desperately wanted to be shot of both. 'The ironic thing is that Arthur Koestler was a Jew to his finger-tips, not only in physical appearance, but in his whole habit of thought. The search for truth, the concern for justice, the this-worldly messianism . . . all put him in the great tradition of Enlightenment Jews from Solomon Maimon, Heine to Freud.'[40]

On the tenth anniversary of Koestler's death Krisztina Koenen published an insightful biographical article in the *Frankfurter Allgemeine Zeitung*. She noted that Koestler never explored his Jewish roots or his relations to Judaism with the same intensity that he analysed his entry into and exit from other movements or ideological 'homes'. Koenen attributed his attraction to Utopian and universalist movements as a flight from Jewishness in search of a new community. He was horrified by the Jews he saw around him and wanted to 'solve' the Jewish problem in his own way. Zionism, Communism and assimilation were the three chief options. He settled in England because he believed it was the country least likely to force him to recall the self-perceived stigma of his origins. In this he was mistaken.[41]

Today it is possible to view Koestler as a Jew as much as an Hungarian or European figure. Koestler was the classic homeless mind: the *émigré* in search of roots, the secular sceptic yearning for a faith and a Messiah. He was the embodiment of 'extraterritoriality', that condition identified by George Steiner as the loam of twentieth-century creativity. Celebrating Koestler's seventieth birthday, Steiner observed that the honours bestowed on him in Britain 'hardly disguise the characteristic figure of the perpetual outsider, of the wanderer who brings scandal and provocation in his battered valise, of the unhoused questioner who has voluntarily engaged the savagery of the times'.[42]

What Steiner wrote about Vladimir Nabokov applied equally to Koestler: 'A great writer driven from language to language by social upheaval and war is an appropriate symbol for the age of the refugee. No exile is more radical, no feat of adaptation and new life more demanding. It seems proper that those who create art in a civilization of quasi-barbarism which has made so many homeless, which has torn up tongues and peoples by the root, should themselves be poets unhoused and wanderers across language.' The progenitors of modernism, with its fragmented and sceptical sensibility, its play on language and interest in the fluidity of identities, shared with Koestler 'the characteristically alert and tentative gait of one who walks along frontiers'.[43]

One may go further and suggest that the condition personified by Koestler is that of the post-modern, too. Homi Bhabha observes that 'It is the trope of our times to locate the question of culture in the realm of the *beyond*. . . . Our existence today is marked by a tenebrous sense of survival, living on the borderlines of the "present", for which there seems to be no proper name other than the current and controversial shiftiness of the prefix "post": *postmodernism, post-colonialism, postfeminism* . . .' In this in-between situation all borders are collapsed or porous. Formerly hard, resisting categories are dissolving; culture is global, multi-ethnic, fluid and constantly metamorphosing. Population upheavals have provided the social bases and impulsion for this cultural moment. 'For the demography of the new internationalism is the history of postcolonial migration, the narratives of cultural and political diaspora, the major social displacements of peasant and aboriginal communities, the poetics of exile, the grim prose of political and economic refugees. It is in this sense that the boundary becomes the place from which *something begins* . . .'[44]

The Jews were among the colonised of Europe's great domestic empires. Koestler grew up in Austria-Hungary and saw the empire dissolve. Estranged from his ancestral faith and a community bonded by religion, he threw himself into the emancipatory national movement of the Jews that subsequently mounted one of the first successful modern anti-colonial struggles. Koestler later embarked on a Messianic project to dissolve all religious and ethnic tensions by creating a fraternity based on Marxist universalism. In the process he was condemned to the life of a wanderer. Finally, for the sake of psychic survival he had to invent a new identity and new roots for himself. But he did so in highly specific historical conditions: the Cold War.[45]

Koestler's relationship with his Jewishness is fundamental to understanding the man and his work and, by extension, the conditions of post-modernity or what Stuart Hall has called 'cultures of hybridity'. However, even the protagonists of the post-modern who recognise that exile and migration are central to the contemporary imagination miss a vital part of this experience which helps to explain the conduct of their culture heroes. The cult of the exile, the *émigré*, the migrant, the transient, the rootless tends to overlook just how awful it was to be deracinated: how demoralising, debilitating, corrosive, embittering, wasteful and soul-destroying.[46]

Koestler's homelessness, beginning with his estrangement from Jewish tradition, may explain his confused personal morality as much as the legendary virility of the Hungarian male. His fleeting relationships and rushed couplings may have been groping for temporary security in the flesh, a product as much of circumstances as individual psychology. They were conducted between men and women on the move, whose future was uncertain. The men were pitiful Casanovas whose infidelity reflected the impermanence of their existence. Koestler may or may not have been constitutionally able to contract a stable, long-term relationship, but one can be certain that between 1919 and 1949 he was rarely in one place long enough to find out. War, migration, exile were not of his making; he and his relationships were victims of a frenetic world and an apocalyptic sensibility.

Unlikely as it may seem, Koestler's apocalypticism is not so far removed from today's *Zeitgeist*. The mentality that came from exile and dispersion prefigured globalisation: Koestler personified a condition that is now too familiar. Globalisation has turned us into nomads without our having to leave our living-rooms. The electronic media bring us information almost instantly from every corner of the world; we are constantly crossing borders and cultures even as we remain stationary. But this sharpens the question: who are we and where do we belong? As our cities become more multi-cultural, multi-ethnic and cosmopolitan the notion of home becomes more fluid. If home connotes a certain kind of sovereignty we are all more or less displaced, our cities and countries locked into transnational associations and economic networks over which we have no control.

With the end of the grand narratives of progress, socialism and liberalism, we are not sure what we believe in, or even if there is anything to believe in at all. But the longing for faith is undiminished: the truth, it is said, is out there. Koestler's conviction that there was another plane of existence, one which made sense of the diurnal round, prefigures the current passion for conspiracy theories coupled to the paranormal. His notion of the 'language of destiny' that spoke through coincidence, for example, echoes the belief that signs and signals are coming to us from other realms be they via *ET* or *The X-Files*.

Nor is the world so much safer than it was in Koestler's lifetime, despite the partial demobilisation of nuclear stockpiles. The threat of atomic apocalypse has been replaced by the fear of environmental catastrophe, global warming, unstoppable human-engineered viruses and rampaging mutant genes. Koestler's analysis of the human predicament is still relevant: the quest to understand human destructiveness, rooted in human nature, continues.

If Koestler's life and work resonate with contemporary experience and bear on current debates surrounding human nature, evolution, genetics and ethics, their relevance cannot be detached from his ethnic-religious roots. Because intellectual homelessness, physical exile and vulnerability sharpened his sensibility and drove him to try to understand the world his Jewishness is a key to understanding the man as well as his times.

Koestler was uncomfortable being a Jew. This was a social more than a psychological condition and derives from the context in which the Jews were placed by European society in the modern era. As Paul Mendes-Flohr has observed: 'Self-hatred is a product of assimilation. Locked for a length of time in a house of distorting mirrors and bereft of an alternative perception of oneself one would perforce accept the phantasmagoric images refracted by the mirrors as true.' But Mendes Flohr cautions that 'To identify the crazed victim of this house of mirrors with its proprietor only magnifies the distortion . . . Rather we should speak of ambivalence towards oneself and community. This complex emotion has undoubtedly affected the Jew as he was torn from his primordial community in the accelerated process of assimilation that has characterised his entrance into modernity.'[47] So Koestler's notorious ambivalence may be related to the troubled encounter between a minority ethnic-faith group and modernity, a far from isolated happening in this century.

Koestler was divided between being an Hungarian and a Jew. His Jewish side was denigrated: it was even life-threatening. In flight from this unappealing and perilous Jewishness he sought other homes. Complete renunciation of Jewish identity would have been cowardly, so he adopted Jewish nationalism, which offered an attractive, secular variant of Jewishness as well as claiming to solve the Jewish Question by rooting the Jews in their own land. When he realised it would be a long, hard job to make this happen, and that he would have to accept no more than a bit-part, while in the process shedding his hard-won European culture, he balked. Since finding a home among other Jews in a particularistic sense seemed impossible, he sought to dissolve Jewishness completely by entering a confraternity based on universal values: socialism and inter-nationalism. Ironically, although the Communist Party decried ethnicity, it was heavily populated by Jews and from the late 1920s was perceived by them as a shield against anti-Semitism.

However, the Communist project was visibly at odds with reality. Because Koestler was attracted to it for instrumental reasons, when he saw it was not working and was actually lethal to all concerned, he backed away. After he left the Party he drifted into Zionism again, although with even greater unease than before. His extreme ambivalence about Jews, Judaism and Jewishness ultimately frustrated the possibility that he would settle in Israel in 1948. From then on he lived as a wanderer, in a permanent state of self-denial. His lack of self-worth, his habitual duplicity and his homelessness, which made him behave so terribly towards others, are thus rooted in his origins and his inability to resolve his identity.

In Koestler's 'theory of everything' set out in *Insight and Outlook* and interminably repeated, all life forms are organised hierarchically and exist relative to each other in a tense state of equilibrium between self-assertion and self-transcendence. In contrast to Konrad Lorenz, Robert Ardrey, Freud and the post-Freudians, who traced the origins of war to human aggression, Koestler blamed the urge to transcend the self, to join a cause and to belong. In other words, he stigmatised the longing for home. Yet he clearly felt this urge himself: why else was he constantly acquiring causes, houses, properties and ménages? His entire scientific and social thought seems a radical act of self-denial. Perhaps it was too painful to contemplate home. After all home represented the secure bourgeois domesticity swept away by the Great War; home was a country that rejected him and connived in the slaughter of his family; home was a community united by history, tradition, creed and culture that he despised.

So Koestler condemned himself to homelessness. All that remained were the ideas he dragged about with him like Job, a favourite biblical figure, from place to place. Home finally was mind; home was homelessness; Koestler was the homeless mind.

Works by Arthur Koestler

Koestler's books have been published in many different editions. The Danube Edition was an attempt at standardisation but it is incomplete and Koestler sometimes amended the original version of the texts that did appear under this imprint. I have used the first edition of his books, where possible, or the most available edition. For exhaustive details of Koestler's writing, interviews, lectures and broadcasts, as well as reviews, critical commentaries and works about Koestler, see Reed Merrill and Thomas Frazier, *Arthur Koestler. An International Bibliography* (Ann Arbor, MI, 1979) and Frank Day, *Arthur Koestler: A Guide to Research* (New York, 1987).

Koestler's major publications are listed below chronologically. Where a different edition was the one consulted the date of publication is given in square brackets (the place of publication is always London) along with an abbreviation if it is cited frequently.

Von Weissen Nächten und Roten Tagen (Kharkov, 1933) [VWNRT]
Encyclopaedia of Sexual Knowledge, with others, (London, 1935)
L'Espagne ensanglantée (Paris, 1937)
Spanish Testament (London, 1937) [ST]
'A Sentimental Journey Through Palestine', in Wilfred Hindle (ed.) *Foreign Correspondent* (London, 1939), pp.51–79 [SJ]
The Gladiators, trans. Edith Simon (London, 1939) [1949; TG]
The Practice of Sex, with others, (London, 1940)
Darkness at Noon, trans. Daphne Hardy (London, 1940) [1947; DAN]
Scum of the Earth (London, 1941) [1955; STE]
Dialogue with Death (London, 1942) [DWD]
Arrival and Departure (London, 1943) [1966; AAD]
The Yogi and The Commissar (London, 1945) [YAC]
Twilight Bar (London, 1945)
Thieves in the Night (London, 1946) [TIN]
Insight and Outlook (New York, 1949) [IO]
The God That Failed: Six Studies in Communism, with others, ed. Richard Crossman (London, 1950) [TGF]
Promise and Fulfilment. Palestine 1917–1949 (London, 1949) [PAF]
The Age of Longing (London, 1951) [AOL]
Arrow in the Blue (London, 1952) [1969; AIB]
The Invisible Writing (London, 1954) [IW]
The Trail of the Dinosaur and Other Essays (London, 1955) [TOD]
Reflections on Hanging (London, 1956) [1970; ROH]

The Sleepwalkers: A History of Man's Changing Vision of the Universe (London, 1959) [SW]

The Lotus and the Robot (London, 1960) [LAR]

Suicide of a Nation (London, 1963)

The Act of Creation (London, 1964) [AOC]

'Motivation: A Biased Review', in Charlotte Banks and P. L. Broadhurst (eds), *Stephanos: Studies in Psychology Presented to Cyril Burt* (London, 1965), pp.39–53

The Ghost in the Machine (London, 1967) [GIM]

Drinkers of Infinity: Essays 1955-1967 (London, 1968) [DOI]

Beyond Reductionism: The Alpbach Symposium. New Perspectives in the Life Sciences, ed. with R. J. Smythies (London, 1969) [BR]

The Case of the Midwife Toad (London, 1971) [CMT]

The Roots of Coincidence (London, 1972) [ROC]

The Call Girls: A Tragicomedy with a Prologue and Epilogue (London, 1972) [CG]

The Challenge of Chance: A Mass Experiment in Telepathy and Its Unexpected Outcome, with Sir Alister Hardy and Robert Harvie (London, 1973) [COC]

The Heel of Achilles: Essays 1968-1973 (London, 1974) [HOA]

'The Vital Choice', in Douglas Villiers (ed.), *Next Year in Jerusalem* (London, 1976), pp.98–106

The Thirteenth Tribe: The Khazar Empire and Its Heritage (London, 1976) [TT]

Life After Death, ed. with Arnold Toynbee (London, 1976)

Janus: A Summing Up (London, 1978)

Bricks to Babel (London, 1980)

Kaleidoscope: Essays from 'Drinkers of Infinity', and 'The Heel of Achilles' and later pieces and stories (London, 1981)

Stranger on the Square, with Cynthia Koestler, ed. Harold Harris (London, 1984) [SOS]

Notes and Sources

Unless otherwise indicated in the notes all unpublished material is held by the Koestler Archive, Edinburgh University Library. Files are numbered from MS2301 to MS2461. See *The Koestler Archive in Edinburgh University Library: A Checklist* (Edinburgh University Library, Edinburgh). Other archives:

CCHDC   Centre for the Conservation of Historical Documentary Collections, Moscow

EWC   Edmund Wilson Correspondence, Beinecke Rare Book and Manuscript Library, Yale University Library

PRO   Public Record Office, Kew, London

If not stated otherwise interviews were conducted by the author.

David Astor, London, 8 June 1995
Sir Martyn and Lady Priscilla Beckett, London, 27 May 1998
Marion Bieber, London, 1 June 1998
Jill Craigie, London, 1 August 1998
Anita von Etzdorf, London, 1 June 1998
Michael Foot, London, 1 August 1998
Celia Goodman, Cambridge, 7 April 1998
Daphne (Hardy) Henrion, Cambridge, 8 June 1998
Elizabeth Jane Howard, telephone, 4 August 1998
Jan Karski, London, 30 March 1995
Melvin Lasky, Berlin, 13 March 1994
Janetta (Jackson) Parladé, London, 29 May 1998
Hon. Miriam Rothschild, Ashton Wold, 4 April 1998
Lord Weidenfeld, London, 2 April 1998
Paul Willert, London, 28 August 1994

Abbreviations of frequently cited works:

BCM   de Beauvoir, Simone, *Beloved Chicago Man: Letters to Nelson Algren 1947–64*, comp. and with a preface by Sylvie Le Bon de Beauvoir (London, 1998)

L'Herne   Debray-Ritzen, Pierre (ed.), *L'Herne*, Cahiers No.27, *Arthur Koestler* (Paris, 1975)

LWK   Goodman, Celia (ed.), *Living with Koestler: Mamaine Koestler's Letters 1945–51* (London, 1985)

ATC   Harris, Harold (ed.), *Astride The Two Cultures: Arthur Koestler at 70* (London, 1975)

In general throughout the notes the authors and recipients of letters are referred to by their surname. However, to avoid confusion due to name changes in correspondence with Arthur Koestler Dorothea Ascher (later Koestler, aka 'Nicole') is referred to as Dorothea; Daphne Hardy (later Henrion) as Daphne; Mamaine Paget (later Koestler) as Mamaine; Celia Paget (later Kirwan, later Goodman) as Celia; Cynthia Jeffries (later Koestler) as Cynthia; Janetta Jackson (later Parladé) as Janetta; and Janine Graetz as Janine.

INTRODUCTION

1   See Tony Judt, *Past Imperfect. French Intellectuals, 1944–1956* (Berkeley, 1992); David Caute, *Communism and the French Intellectuals* (London, 1964) and *The Fellow Travellers: A Postscript to the Enlightenment* (New York, 1973).

2   See, for example, Steven Pinker, *How The Mind Works* (London, 1998); Steven Rose, *Lifelines: Biology, Freedom, Determinism* (London, 1998); Peter Singer, 'Evolutionary Workers Party', *Times Higher Educational Supplement* [*THES*], 15 May 1998 and his *The Expanding Circle: Ethics and Sociobiology* (Oxford, 1981). On para-science and the paranormal, see Richard Wiseman, 'Investigating the paranormal', lecture to the Royal Society, 7 May 1998, published in amended form as 'Money for Old Rope', *THES*, 8 May 1998 and Catherine Bennett, 'Would You Believe It?', *Guardian*, Sec. 2, 14 June 1996. For a report on the work of the Koestler Institute, see Robert Matthews, 'The Truth about ESP', *Sunday Telegraph*, 30 March 1989 and John Davies, 'Psycho bubble', *THES*, 14 November 1997.

3   On postmodernism, see David Lyon, *Postmodernity* (Buckingham, 1994); Steven Connor, *Postmodernist Culture* (Oxford, 1989); cf. Keith Tester, *The life and times of post-modernity* (London, 1993). On the role of Jews as cultural avatars see especially Zygmunt Bauman, *Intimations of Postmodernity* (London, 1992), pp.226–7.

4   George Steiner, 'Extraterritorial' (1969), in his *Extra-Territorial: Papers on Literature and the Language Revolution* (London, 1972), pp.3–11; Ian Chambers, *migrancy culture identity* (London, 1994); Homi K. Bhabha, 'The postcolonial and the postmodern: the question of agency', in his *the location of culture* (London, 1994), pp. 171–97.

5   John Atkins, *Arthur Koestler* (London, 1956); Jenni Calder, *Chronicles of Conscience: A study of George Orwell and Arthur Koestler* (London, 1968); Wolfe Mays, *Koestler* (Guildford, 1973); Sidney Pearson, *Arthur Koestler* (Boston, 1978); Iain Hamilton, *Koestler* (London, 1982); Mark Levene, *Arthur Koestler* (New York, 1984).

6   There are honourable exceptions to the de-Judaisation of Koestler: Emanuel Litvinoff, 'Europe's Cassandra', *Jewish Observer and Middle East Review*, 14 September 1956; Lothar Kahn, 'Arthur Koestler: Dejudaized Zionism', in his *Mirrors of the Jewish Mind* (New York, 1968), pp.146–59; Hyam Maccoby, 'Jew', *Encounter*, September-October 1983, pp.50–3; John Milfull, '"Die Wonnen der Gewöhnlichkeit": Arthur Koestler and Zionism', *Jahrbuch des Instituts für Deutsche Geschichte*, Vol. 14 (Tel Aviv, 1985), pp.359–70; Krisztina Koenen, 'Arthur Koestler', *Frankfurter Allgemeine Zeitung*, magazine, 26 November 1993; Louis Gordon, 'Koestler revisited', *Midstream*, February-March 1994, pp.13–15.

CHAPTER 1: 'A GOOD JEWISH CHILD', 1905–22

1   On autobiography see Laura Marcus, *Auto/Biographical Discourses: Theory, Criticism, Practice* (Manchester, 1994).

2   In *Arrow in the Blue* [AIB] Koestler changed this to 3.30 p.m. to produce a coincidence between the hour of his birth and the signing of a diplomatic treaty. His birth certificate is in MS2302/3.

3   For personal documents, see MS2302/3. Such was the nature of Central European patronymics and the handwriting of the time that his mother's family name is variously rendered Zeiteles, Feitels, Teitels or even Jeiteles. The French secret service opted for Zeiteles, the FBI for Feitels.

4   AIB, pp.33, 34–5; *The Invisible Writing* [IW], p.376.

5   AIB, pp.23–5. Heiman (Henrik) Koestler's birth certificate, MS2302/3. Due to migration and translation, the family name was spelled variously until the 1920s. Raphael Patai, *The Jews of Hungary: History, Culture, Psychology* (Detroit, 1996), p.296.

6   AIB, pp.25–9.

7   Ibid., p.44; 'Micromemoirs', *Encounter*, September-October 1983, p.57, John Lukacs, *Budapest*

1900 (London, 1988), pp.60–1.

8   AIB, pp.42–4, 55.

9   'Micromemoirs', p.57.

10   AIB, pp.45–6; unpublished autobiographical fragment, MS2342/1.

11   AIB, pp.43–4.

12   Ibid., p.47

13   Ibid.

14   Ibid., pp.46, 49–50.

15   Ibid., p.35; *Janus: A Summing Up*, p.92.

16   AIB, pp.57–9.

17   Ibid., pp.58, 74–7.

18   See Laura Marcus, *Auto/Biographical Discourses*.

19   AIB, pp.15–22.

20   Ibid., pp.20, 22.

21   *The Fall of Dr Icarus: A play in 3 acts*, MS2325/4.

22   Adele to Arthur Koestler, 19 March 1950 and reply on 21 February 1950, MS2302/1.

23   Mamaine's diary, 2 December 1949. Celia Goodman (ed.), *Living with Koestler: Mamaine Koestler's Letters 1945–51* (London, 1985) [LWK], p.118.

24   Poem dated June 1919; Arthur to Adele Koestler, 25 June 1919, MS2302/3.

25   Arthur to Adele Koestler, 30 July 1918 and 25 June 1921, MS2302/3.

26   Ibid. and Arthur to Adele Koestler, (25) June 1919, MS2302/3.

27   IW, pp.217–18, where Willy and Ferenc appear camouflaged as Theodore and Freddie. In August 1945 a former playmate wrote to him recalling their days together in Szív út. elementary school and the games they played together on Erzsébet Térez: Arthur Kallos to Koestler, 15 August 1945, MS2373/4.

28   J. A. C. Brown, *Freud and the Post-Freudians* (London, 1961), pp.38–41. Manès Sperber who was Koestler's closest friend in the 1950s was a student of Adler and did much to popularise Adlerian psychology. Sperber even 'analysed' Koestler. This may have added to the self-ascription of an Adlerian personality type in his autobiography.

29   AIB, p.134. Between 1871 and 1910, 175,000 Jews immigrated to Budapest from the north-east. Some had already migrated once from further east and acculturated during their sojourn in the Austro-Hungarian portion of Galicia, but not all shed the old ways. Despite the rapid Magyarisation of the new arrivals, in 1910, twenty-five per cent of Hungarian Jews gave Yiddish or another language as their mother-tongue. Patai, *The Jews of Hungary*, p.431.

30   William O. McCagg Jr, *Jewish Nobles and Geniuses in Modern Hungary* (New York, 1972), p.30; Lukacs, *Budapest 1900*, pp.95–6, 183–7.

31   Lakacs, *Budapest 1900*, pp.36, 44–6; Robert Blumstock, 'Going Home: Arthur Koestler's Thirteenth Tribe', *Jewish Social Studies*, 48:2 (1986), pp.98–9.

32   Lewis Herman to Koestler, 10 December 1943, MS2372/3.

33   Transcript of interview between Arthur Koestler and Iain Hamilton, 14 March 1974, MS2436/5, pp.1–2.

34   AIB, pp.23–4. In the interview with Iain Hamilton in 1974, Koestler denied that his grandfather kept a kosher kitchen.

35   AIB, pp.134–5. See Sander L. Gilman, *Jewish Self-Hatred: Anti-Semitism and the Hidden Language of the Jews* (Baltimore, 1986), pp.332–6. Steven Aschheim, *Brothers and Strangers: The East European Jew in German and German Jewish Consciousness, 1800–1923* (Madison, WI, 1986).

36   Koestler to Rabbi Kokotek, 3 September 1960, MS2383/4. He arranged for the proceeds resulting from the sale of her effects to go via the rabbi to an Israeli charity. Koestler to Rabbi Kokotek, 12 September 1960, MS2303/2.

37   Mary Gluck, *Georg Lukács and his Generation 1900–1918* (Cambridge, MA, 1985), pp.45–6.

38   Marsha Rozenblit, *The Jews of Vienna: Assimilation and Identity 1867–1914* (Albany, 1983); Patai, *The Jews of Hungary*, pp.435–41.

39   AIB, p.119.

40   Lukacs, *Budapest 1900*, pp.188–94; Patai, *The Jews of Hungary*, pp.347–57, 447–57.

41   Lewis Herman to Koestler, 10 December 1943, MS2732/3.

42   Unpublished autobiographical fragment, MS2342/1.

43   AIB, p.67.

44   Ibid., p.78.

45   Ibid., p.29.

46   Ibid., pp.29–31.

47   Tibor Hajdu and Zsuzsa Nagy, 'Revolution, Counterrevolution, Consolidation', in Peter Sugar,
     Peter Hanak, Tibor Frank (eds), *A History of Hungary* (London, 1990), pp.295–318.
48   Lukacs, *Budapest 1900*, pp.185–96; cf. AIB, p.83.
49   AIB, pp.79–91.
50   Ibid., pp.86–7.
51   Ibid., p.91; Patai, *The Jews of Hungary*, pp.461–76; Hajdu and Nagy, 'Revolution,
     Counterrevolution, Consolidation', pp.295–318.
52   AIB, pp.50–2.
53   Ibid., pp.52–3, 61–3.
54   Ibid.
55   Ibid., pp.93–6, 98.
56   Arthur Koestler to Adele Koestler, 26 May and 8 June 1921, MS2302/3. Somehow, Koestler
     also crossed paths with the Rabbi of Baden and his family. The son of Rabbi Reich later
     chanced on him in Palestine in what proved an auspicious meeting: AIB, p.191.
57   Arthur Koestler to Adele Koestler, 8 June 1921, MS2302/3.
58   Arthur Koestler to Adele Koestler, 22 August 1921, MS2302/3.
59   Arthur Koestler to Adele Koestler, 25 June 1921, MS2302/3.
60   AIB, p.77.
61   Ibid, p.91; Hajdu and Nagy, 'Revolution, Counterrevolution, Consolidation', pp.295–318;
     Gluck, *Georg Lukács and his Generation*, pp.194–212; Lukacs, *Budapest 1900*, pp.209–13.
62   Arthur Koestler to his parents, nd 1922, MS2302/3.
63   Koestler to his parents, 1 and 4 July 1921, MS2302/3. A few weeks later Koestler travelled to
     Vienna to see a performance by Alexander Moissi, the well-known German-Jewish actor. On
     Kafka's reactions to the Yiddish theatre, see *The Diaries of Franz Kafka 1910–1923*, ed. Max Brod
     (London, 1972), pp.64–70.
64   Arthur Koestler to Adele Koestler, 26 May 1921, MS2302/3.

CHAPTER 2: ZIONISM AND PALESTINE, 1922–9

1   AIB, p.127.
2   Gilman, *Jewish Self-Hatred*, pp.112, 180.
3   AIB, pp.112, 118.
4   John Haag, 'Blood on the Ringstrasse: Vienna's Students 1918–33', *Wiener Library Bulletin*,
     39/40 (1976), pp. 29–34; Harriet Pass Freidenreich, *Jewish Politics in Vienna 1918–1938*
     (Bloomington, IN, 1995) pp.183–4.
5   Haag, 'Blood on the Ringstrasse', p.32.
6   AIB, pp.107–21; Marsha Rozenblit, 'The Assertion of Identity: Jewish Students and Nationalism
     at the University of Vienna before the First World War', *Leo Baeck Institute Year Book*, 27 (1982),
     pp.171–83.
7   AIB, p.118. George Weidenfeld, *Remembering My Good Friends. An Autobiography* (London,
     1995), p.58.
8   Wolfgang von Weisl on Koestler, in Joseph Nedava, *Arthur Koestler: A Study* (London, 1948),
     p.18; theatre programme, MS2302/3.
9   AIB, p.145.
10   Ibid., pp.148–51.
11   Ibid., pp.140–6; Lucy Adler-Wiener to Koestler, 15 January 1945, MS2373/3. Joseph
     Schechtman, *Fighter and Prophet: The Vladimir Jabotinsky Story. The Last Years* (London, 1961),
     pp.34–5.
12   Arthur Koestler interview with Iain Hamilton, 14 March 1974, p.1, MS2436/5.
13   AIB, p.109; Helmut Gruber, 'Red Vienna and the "Jewish Question"', *Leo Baeck Institute Year
     Book*, 38 (1993), pp.105–6 and fn. 22.
14   AIB, pp.112, 118–19.
15   Rozenblit, 'The Assertion of Identity', p.182; Patai, *The Jews of Hungary*, chap.36.
16   Walter Laqueur, *A History of Zionism* (New York, 1976), pp.339–53.
17   Laqueur, *History of Zionism*, pp.456–68.
18   Gideon Shimoni, *The Zionist Ideology* (Hanover, NH, 1995), pp.236–49, 252–6.
19   Entry on Wolfgang von Weisl in Geoffrey Wigoder (ed.), *Encyclopaedia of Zionism and Israel*
     (London, 1994).
20   AIB, pp.142–3.

21 See Laqueur, *History of Zionism*, pp.339–46; Schechtman, *Fighter and Prophet*.
22 Chaim Weizmann, *Trial and Error* (London, 1949), p.63.
23 Oskar Rabbinowitz to Koestler, 21 June 1955, MS2380/1.
24 AIB, pp.72, 140.
25 Ibid., pp.123–4.
26 Ibid.
27 Ibid., pp.140–6; Arthur to Henrik Koestler, nd probably 1925, MS2302/3.
28 AIB, pp.128–33.
29 Ibid., pp.153–8.
30 Ibid., pp.156–60.
31 Schechtman, *Fighter and Prophet*, pp.40–2.
32 See Amos Elon, *The Israelis: Founders and Sons* (London, 1971).
33 AIB, pp.161–2.
34 Entry on Abraham Weinshall in Wigoder (ed.), *Encyclopaedia of Zionism and Israel*.
35 Entry on Heftzi-Bah in Wigoder (ed.), *Encyclopaedia of Zionism and Israel*.
36 Laqueur, *History of Zionism*, pp.308–14, 320–5.
37 Ibid.
38 AIB, p.168. Nedava, *Arthur Koestler*, p.20.
39 For this and other references to his experiences, see AIB, pp.170–1.
40 Cf. 'A Sentimental Journey Through Palestine' [SJ], in Wilfred Hindle (ed.), *Foreign Correspondent* (London, 1939), p.52, to *Thieves in the Night* [TIN], p.257.
41 TIN, pp.54–5.
42 Laqueur, *History of Zionism*, pp.314–16.
43 AIB, pp.176–86.
44 Ibid., pp.188–92.
45 Ibid., pp.195–201.
46 Entry on Avigdor Hameiri in Glenda Abramson (ed.), *Blackwell Companion to Jewish Culture* (Oxford, 1989).
47 AIB, pp.199–203. Nedava, *Arthur Koestler*, p.20.
48 AIB, pp.204–5.
49 Ibid., pp.206–8.
50 Ibid., pp.208–9; Schechtman, *Fighter and Prophet*, pp.79–80.
51 Hermann Ullstein, *The Rise and Fall of the House of Ullstein* (London, 1939).
52 AIB, pp.216–19.
53 Ibid., pp.224–32.
54 Louis Gordon, 'Arthur Koestler and His Ties to Zionism and Jabotinsky', *Studies in Zionism*, 12:2 (1991), pp.153–4; Gordon, 'Koestler revisited', pp.13–15; Nedava, *Arthur Koestler*, p.21.
55 AIB, pp.242–3; Schechtman, *Fighter and Prophet*, pp.94–7.
56 Nedava, *Arthur Koestler*, pp.18–21.
57 AIB, pp.244–5; Adolph Gourevitch, 'Jabotinsky and the Hebrew Language', in Schechtman, *Fighter and Prophet*, pp.597–9.
58 AIB, pp.233, 237–8, 244.
59 Ibid., p.244; Nedava, *Arthur Koestler*, pp.18–21.
60 SJ, pp.51–3, 56, 64–6.
61 Koestler to Mamaine, 30 January 1945 and 16 February 1945, MS2303/2.
62 Ullstein, *The Rise and Fall of the House of Ullstein*, p.148. Ullstein mistakenly attributes the wounding to the 1921 riots, when von Weisl was not an Ullstein reporter.

CHAPTER 3: TOWARDS THE 'NEW PROMISED LAND', 1929–33

1 See Robert Wistrich, *Revolutionary Jews from Marx to Trotsky* (London, 1976); Zvi Gitelman, *A Century of Ambivalence: Jews in Russia and the Soviet Union, 1881 to the Present* (New York, 1988).
2 AIB, p.247.
3 *Stranger on the Square* [SOS], pp.22–3.
4 AIB, pp.245–6.
5 Alfred Kantorowicz, *Deutsches Tagebuch*, Vol.1 (Berlin, 1980), p.22.
6 On the Paris bureau, see AIB, pp.249, 251–5, 272–3.
7 Ullstein, *The Rise and Fall of the House of Ullstein*, pp.177–8.
8 AIB, p.277.

9   Ibid., pp.248–50, 250–1, 255–6, 278–9.
10 Ibid., pp. 257–64; Lisa Luria Klebanow to Koestler, 10 February 1978, MS2391/2. Amazingly, she survived in the USSR and returned to Israel via the USA in the 1970s.
11 AIB, pp.261–70.
12 Ibid., p.282.
13 Hans Mommsen, *The Rise and Fall of Weimar Democracy* (Chapel Hill, 1996).
14 Ullstein, *The Rise and Fall of the House of Ullstein*, pp.177–8.
15 AIB, pp.288–90.
16 IW, p.21; *The God That Failed: Six Studies in Communism*, ed. Richard Crossman (London, 1950) [TGF], p.41; AIB, p.284; Manès Sperber, 'Koestler il y a vingt ans', in Pierre Debray-Ritzen (ed.), *L'Herne*, Cahiers No.27, *Arthur Koestler* (Paris, 1975, hereafter *L'Herne*), p.9 (first published in *Arts*, 12 June 1953).
17 AIB, pp.341–3, 346–8 and see his article, 'The World as Grenade', *Vossische Zeitung*, 17 March 1931.
18 IW, p.215. By a coincidence that escaped Koestler's eye for bizarre juxtapositions, Willi Münzenberg, the Communist propaganda boss who would later play a major role in Koestler's life, rented office space from Hirschfeld.
19 His regular columns in *Vossische Zeitung* were 'Wo hält die Forschung' and 'Tagebuch der Forschung', see *Vossische Zeitung*, 19 April 1931; AIB, p.351–5.
20 *Vossische Zeitung*, 23, 24, 26, 27, 28 splash, 29 and 30 July, front page. The various Ullstein papers carried successive bulletins in their morning and evening editions.
21 AIB, pp.383–406. The fullest account is in his 'lost' book published in Russia in 1934, *Von Weissen Nächten und Roten Tagen*, pp.7–72.
22 AIB, p.407.
23 Manès Sperber, *Until My Eyes Are Closed With Shards*, trans. Harry Zohn (New York, 1994), p.47; AIB, pp.283–5.
24 AIB, pp.286–8.
25 Ibid., pp.288–91.
26 Ibid., pp.301–6.
27 TGF, pp.29–30; AIB, p.306; IW, pp.26, 233; Simone de Beauvoir, *Force of Circumstance*, trans. Richard Howard (London, 1965), p.108.
28 AIB, pp.296, 350; SOS, p.50.
29 AIB, p.319.
30 TGF, pp.25–33.
31 AIB, pp.322–3.
32 Ibid., p.392.
33 Ibid., pp.407–9.
34 In this sense, his description of his 'conversion' corresponds to the process described by William James in the *The Varieties of Religious Experience* [1902] (London, 1985), chapters 9–10.
35 AIB, pp.410–12.
36 Ibid., pp.411–12.
37 Ibid., pp.297, 324.
38 Ibid., pp.409–10.
39 Ibid., pp.392–3.
40 Ibid., pp.376–7; Gordon, 'Arthur Koestler and His Ties to Zionism and Jabotinsky', p.154.
41 Alexander Weissberg, *Conspiracy of Silence*, trans. Edward Fitzgerald (London, 1952), pp.207–8.
42 Sperber, *Until My Eyes*, p.48.
43 Ibid., p.44–5. Otto Bihaly was probably Otto Biha, former editor of *Die Linkskurve*, an intelligent if hard-line Marxist literary journal published in Berlin by Hungarian (mostly Jewish) exiles from 1929 to 1933: Lee Congdon, *Exile and Social Thought: Hungarian Intellectuals in Germany and Austria, 1919–1933* (Princeton, NJ, 1991), pp.86, 88.
44 IW, pp.15–17; TGF, p.35.
45 IW, p.17; TGF, pp.42–6.
46 Kantorowicz, *Deutsches Tagebuch*, Vol.1, p.26.
47 IW, pp.37–8; Ullstein, *The Rise and Fall of the House of Ullstein*, pp.15–16.
48 TGF, pp.46–50; IW, pp.19–20.
49 TGF, pp.44, 48–9; IW, p.19.
50 IW, p.19.
51 Kantorowicz, *Deutsches Tagebuch*, Vol.1, pp.31–2.
52 Gustav Regler, *The Owl of Minerva: The autobiography of Gustav Regler*, trans. Norman Denny

(London, 1959), pp.143–6.

53　TGF, pp.50–2; IW, pp.22–4, 38, 44. Kantorowicz, *Deutsches Tagebuch*, Vol.1, mocked Koestler's claims to have been involved in self-defence operations in the Red Block.

54　TGF, pp.63–4; IW, pp.25–6.

55　IW, p.33.

56　Ibid., p.44. The story, 'Wie ein Mangobaumwunder', was credited to Koestler and Andor Németh, MS2336/3. In his memoirs Koestler recalled writing a crime novel with Németh, but in Hungary in 1933. However, the address given on the title page is Bonner-Strasse which was the location of the Red Block where he had lived in 1932.

57　Cf. his comment about Becher many years later in a letter to an editor at Simon and Schuster, 'I hope he will break his neck some day, but I don't want to be the cause of it': Koestler to Schwed, 23 May 1951, MS2377/1.

58　TGF, pp.64–5; IW, pp.43–6.

59　TGF, pp.64–7; IW, pp.49, 54, 61. Weissberg, *Conspiracy of Silence*, pp.208–9.

60　TGF, pp.64–7; IW, pp.61–3.

61　Weissberg, *Conspiracy of Silence*, p.210.

62　TGF, p.67; IW, p.64.

63　Caute, *The Fellow Travellers*, chap.2.

64　Pierre Debray-Ritzen, 'Un croisé sans croix: Deuxième partie: Communisme (1930–1950)', in *L'Herne*, pp.154–8; Koestler interview with Debray-Ritzen, *L'Herne*, p.142.

65　AIB, p.388; IW, pp.152–3.

66　IW, pp.66–9. On the famine, see Robert Conquest, *The Harvest of Sorrow* (London, 1988). *Von Weissen Nächten und Roten Tagen* [VWNRT], pp.78–82.

67　Langston Hughes, *I Wonder as I Wander* (New York, 1956), pp.112–13. See also, Arnold Rampersad, *The Life of Langston Hughes*, Vol.1, *I Too, Sing America* (New York, 1986), pp.242–62 and Faith Berry, *Langston Hughes: Before and Beyond Harlem* (New York, 1983), pp.173–9. Koestler wrongly identified the artist as Sophie Tucker, an interesting slip since she was famous for her Yiddish jazz songs such as 'My Yiddishe Momma'.

68　Hughes, *I Wonder as I Wander*, pp.113–14; cf. IW, pp.111–12.

69　Ibid., pp.114–15.

70　IW, pp.116–20; Hughes, *I Wonder as I Wander*, pp.116–17.

71　Hughes, *I Wonder as I Wander*, pp.118–20.

72　Ibid., pp.126–31.

73　Ibid., pp.137–8. Cynthia Koestler recounts the episode and quotes Hughes in *Stranger on the Square*, but she colludes in the effacement of Koestler's Jewish identity and comments rather oddly that the incident showed 'Arthur's rather unnerving way of pouncing on seemingly ordinary, decent sentiments and exposing their hypocrisy', pp.163–4.

74　IW, pp.111, 129, 136–9.

75　Hughes, *I Wonder as I Wander*, pp.142–3; IW, pp.79–81, 90–107, 111–12, 142–8; Weissberg, *Conspiracy of Silence*, p.210.

76　IW, pp.149–51; Debray-Ritzen, 'Un croisé sans croix', p.157; Weissberg, *Conspiracy of Silence*, p.210.

77　VWNRT, pp.7–17, 27–8, 35–6, 72.

78　Ibid., pp.75–82.

79　Ibid., pp.82–8, 89–101.

80　Ibid., pp.112–14.

81　Ibid., pp.119–27, 130–41, 143–58, 170–81.

82　TGF, pp.68–9; IW, pp.79–81, 134–5.

83　IW, pp.71–4, 84–6, 90–107.

84　Ibid., pp.90–107.

85　Ibid., pp.45–6, 107, 120.

86　TGF, pp.68–9; IW, pp.150–2.

87　Weissberg, *Conspiracy of Silence*, pp.210–11.

88　IW, pp.152–3; Weissberg, *Conspiracy of Silence*, p.211.

89　IW, pp.155–9.

90　Ibid., pp.158–9; The play was called *Twilight Bar* in its subsequent English version [TB], p.6.

91　IW, pp.153–4; Weissberg, *Conspiracy of Silence*, pp.211–12.

92　Weissberg, *Conspiracy of Silence*, pp.210–11.

93　IW, pp.163–5.

94　Ibid., p.165–6.

95 Ibid., pp.168–73, 185–7.
96 Ibid., pp.175–81.

CHAPTER 4: RETREAT FROM COMMUNISM, 1933–8

1   Sperber, *Until My Eyes*, pp.48–9.
2   IW, p.193.
3   See the excellent textual analysis in Murray A. Sperber, 'Looking Back on Koestler's Spanish War', in Murray A. Sperber (ed.), *Arthur Koestler: A Collection of Critical Essays* (Englewood Cliffs, NJ, 1977), pp.109–21.
4   IW, p.189.
5   Sperber, *Until My Eyes*, pp.48–9.
6   IW, p.247.
7   Sperber, *Until My Eyes*, pp.69–70.
8   IW, p.174.
9   Ibid., pp.249–51.
10 Jorgen Schleimann, 'The Life and Work of Willi Münzenberg', *Survey*, 55 (April 1965), pp.64–91; Helmut Gruber, 'Willi Münzenberg's German Communist Empire 1921–1933', *Journal of Modern History*, 38:3 (1966), pp.278–97; Babette Gross, *Willi Münzenberg: Eine Politische Biographie* (Stuttgart, 1967) (English translation by Marion Jackson, Michigan, 1974); *Willi Münzenberg. 1889–1940: Un Homme Contre*, Colloque International, Organisé par Bibliothèque Méjunes L'Institute de L'Image (Marseilles, 1993).
11 Sperber, *Until My Eyes*, p.90.
12 Regler, *The Owl of Minerva*, p.163.
13 Ibid., p.163. On the Reichstag fire and trial, see Christopher Andrew and Harold James, 'Willi Münzenberg, the Reichstag Fire and the Conversion of Innocents', in D. A. Charters and M. A. Tugwell (eds), *Deception Operations: Studies in the East-West Context* (London, 1990), pp.25–52.
14 Regler, *The Owl of Minerva*, p.163.
15 IW, p.205; Arthur Koestler foreword to Gross, *Willi Münzenberg*, pp.8–9.
16 See Andrew and James, 'Willi Münzenberg'.
17 IW, pp.194, 198.
18 Ibid., p.193.
19 Ibid., pp.211–12.
20 AIB, p.93; Regler, *The Owl of Minerva*, p.173.
21 IW, pp.211–12.
22 Regler, *The Owl of Minerva*, p.173.
23 See manuscript dated April 1934, MS2336/2.
24 For example, *Encyclopaedia of Sexual Knowledge*, pp.38–46, 83–4, 153–5, 168.
25 IW, pp.213–23. An English version was published in 1935 as *Encyclopaedia of Sexual Knowledge* by Drs A. Costler, A. Willy and others under the general editorship of Norman Haire Ch.M, MB. Haire pointed out that some of its recommendations were in his opinion unwise and in the case of anal intercourse in England, at least, illegal. For the German manuscript see MS2324/4.
26 IW, pp.224–5; Gross, *Willi Münzenberg*, p.255.
27 IW, pp.224–30.
28 'Die Erlebnisse des Genossen Piepvogel und seiner Freunde in der Emigration', pp.7, 9–11, 21, 26–7, 59–61, 221–3, MS2325/1.
29 IW, pp.225–30, 231–6; Alfred Kantorowicz, *Politik und Literatur im Exil* (Hamburg, 1978), pp.147–94.
30 IW, p.234.
31 Ibid., pp.234–6.
32 Ibid., pp.242–9.
33 Ibid., pp.255–6.
34 Sperber, *Until My Eyes*, pp.49, 55.
35 IW, p.256. Sperber, *Until My Eyes*, p.56.
36 See letters between Koestler and Malraux, MS2345/1.
37 IW, pp.244, 246–7, 262; tribute to Ascher by Gerhard Schoenberner, 11 May 1992, MS at Wiener Library, and interview with Marion Bieber, 1 June 1998.
38 IW, pp.262–6. The story was not wholly original: Flaubert had treated it in *Salammbô*.

39   IW, pp.269–73.
40   Regler, *The Owl of Minerva*, p.221.
41   *Das Neue Tagebuch*, No.2 (1935), pp.40–1; Sperber, *Until My Eyes*, p.61.
42   IW, pp.264–5; Debray-Ritzen, 'Un croisé sans croix', pp.166–7.
43   IW, pp.276–9.
44   Julius Hay, *Born 1900*, trans. and abridged J. A. Underwood (London, 1974), p.145. See also Congdon, *Exile and Social Thought*, pp.92–6.
45   IW, pp.279–80.
46   Hay, *Born 1900*, p.146.
47   IW, p.282; Hay, *Born 1900*, p.146.
48   IW, pp.213–14; Paul Ignotus, *Political Prisoner: A Personal Account* (New York, 1964), p.45.
49   IW, pp.286–300.
50   Ibid., p.283.
51   Koestler dubs him Alex Rado. Koestler's epitaph on Rado in *The Invisible Writing* was premature. He reached the Eastern bloc after the war and lived into old age in Hungary, making maps. Sandor Rado, *Code-name Dora* (London, 1977); Ruth Werner, *Sonya's Report*, trans. Renate Simpson (London, 1991), pp.214–17.
52   IW, pp.301–4.
53   Ibid., pp.283, 313–14.
54   Gross, *Willi Münzenberg*, pp.288–9; IW, pp.313–17.
55   *Spanish Testament* [ST], pp.17–28; VWNRT, p.3.
56   ST, pp.32–4.
57   Ibid., pp.17–40; IW, pp.318–23.
58   Andrew Graham Yoll, *Arthur Koestler: Del Infinito al Cero* (Madrid, 1978), pp.21–6, 34–40.
59   K. W. Watkins, *Britain Divided: The Effect of the Spanish Civil War on British Political Opinion* (London, 1963).
60   IW, pp.323–4; John Costello, *Mask of Treachery* (London, 1988), pp.169, 295–8. According to Oleg Tsarev and John Costello, Donald Maclean, the 'second man', warned Moscow as early as March 1937 that Münzenberg's circle had been penetrated by a British agent. See John Costello and Oleg Tsarev, *Deadly Illusions* (London, 1993), pp.203–4.
61   Ibid., pp.328–32.
62   Ibid., pp.333–5.
63   Regler, *The Owl of Minerva*, p.172.
64   Gross, *Willi Münzenberg*, pp.298–302.
65   IW, pp.333–5; Simone de Beauvoir, *Letters to Sartre*, trans. and ed. Quintin Hoare (London, 1991), p.131. Sartre appreciated it no less. See de Beauvoir to Sartre, 2 December 1939, *Letters to Sartre*, p.192.
66   IW, pp.226–7.
67   Stanley Weintraub, *The Last Great Cause: The Intellectuals and the Spanish Civil War* (London, 1968), pp.66–7; Frederick Benson, *Writers in Arms, The Literary Impact of the Spanish Civil War* (London, 1968), *passim*.
68   IW, pp.325–8.
69   ST, pp.178–93.
70   Ibid., pp.193–201.
71   Sir Peter Chalmers-Mitchell, *My Fill of Days* (London, 1938), pp.257–8.
72   Luis Bolin, *Spain: The Vital Years* (London, 1967), pp.241–2.
73   Chalmers-Mitchell, *My Fill of Days*, p.404.
74   For Koestler's account, see ST pp.222–31 and IW, pp.338–44.
75   IW, pp.338–40. In Chalmers-Mitchell's account of the fall of Malaga, Koestler spent the whole day in his company. There is no mention of his attempt to leave with Colonel Alberto or his return. See Sir Peter Chalmers-Mitchell, *My House in Malaga* (London, 1937), pp.260–8.
76   Chalmers-Mitchell, *My House in Malaga*, pp.262–7, 273.
77   Ibid., pp.113–20, 132–9, 193–203.
78   Ibid., pp.269–79.
79   Bolin, *Spain: The Vital Years*, pp.242–53.
80   Chalmers-Mitchell, *My House in Malaga*, pp.261–2, 278.
81   Ibid., pp.280–91.
82   Hugh Thomas, *The Spanish Civil War* (London, 1977), pp.572–6; cf. Raymond Carr, *The Spanish Tragedy* (London, 1976), pp.161–2.

83 This information and all subsequent details come from the previously unseen 'Report on proceedings of HMS *Basilisk* at Malaga on 9–11 February 1937', FO371/21285, Public Record Office, Kew [PRO].

84 FO minutes regarding Parliamentary Question by R. Sorenson MP, FO371/21302, PRO.

85 ST, pp.283–8.

86 Ibid., pp.288–91, 295–7.

87 Ibid., pp.305, 308, 315–19, 327, 336–9.

88 IW, pp.360–1; ST, pp.376–8.

89 Kantorowicz, *Deutsches Tagebuch*, Vol.1, p.59; Sperber, *Until My Eyes*, pp.108–9.

90 IW, pp.365–6; Koestler Collection, Centre for the Conservation of Historical Documentary Collections, Moscow [CCHDC], 619/1/1–11.

91 Sheila Grant Duff, 'A Very Brief Visit', in Philip Toynbee (ed.), *The Distant Drum: Reflections on the Spanish Civil War* (London, 1976), pp.76–86. See also Dorothea Koestler to Duff, 26 April 1937 and reply, CCHDC, 619/1/2.

92 Variously titled 'Bericht über den Stand der Aktion für Arthur Koestler' or 'Bericht aus London' (Situation report), 1 March 1937 to 13 May 1937, CCHDC, 619/1/8.

93 Situation reports dated 1, 8–21 and 22–8 March 1937, 7–20 April 1937, 29 March-7 April 1937, CCHDC, 619/1/8.

94 Situation reports, 22–8 March 1937 and 13 May 1937, CCHDC, 619/1/8. For individual letters see CCHDC, 619/1/2. On Churchill, see also Martin Gilbert to Koestler, 18 January 1982, MS2393/2.

95 Situation reports, 24 April 1937, CCHDC, 619/1/8; ST, p.381. Most of the Foreign Office documents relating to the episode have been destroyed, but the record of correspondence and files it generated has survived. See *Foreign Office Index to General Correspondence*, 1937, vol. E-L, PRO.

96 Sperber, *Until My Eyes*, pp.108–9; Harold Nicolson, *Diary and Letters 1930–1939*, ed. Nigel Nicolson (London, 1966), p.298.

97 Dorothea Koestler to Arthur Koestler, 9 March, 15 April and 3 May 1937, CCHDC, 619/1/1; Dorothea Koestler to M. Coullbas, 4 May 1937, CCHDC, 619/1/2.

98 Marcel Junod, *Warrior Without Weapons*, trans. Edward Fitzgerald (London, 1951), pp.124–5.

99 TGF, p.76; Koestler mistakenly attributes the phrase to Goethe. Arthur Koestler to Henrik Koestler and reply, 15 May 1937, CCHDC, 619/1/2.

100 IW, pp.367–8; *News Chronicle*, 22 May 1937, front page. See Yoll, *Arthur Koestler*, p.119 for a sarcastic gloss.

101 Tangy Lean, *News Chronicle*, to Koestler, 25 May 1937, CCHDC, 619/1/1; Victor Gollancz to Koestler, 27 May 1937, CCHDC, 619/1/1.

102 These included letters to Rudolph Olden of PEN, Professor Vámbéry, Sylvia Pankhurst, the Press Association, Vyvyan Adams MP, Harold Nicolson MP, Henry Wickham Steed and the Newspaper Proprietors Association, CCHDC, 619/1/1. IW, p.368.

103 See Murray Sperber, 'Looking Back on Koestler's Spanish Civil War', pp.109–21.

104 Ibid., pp.109–13. The first pages of *L'Espagne ensanglantée* anyway begin with Koestler's departure from Southampton and are quite personal: see *L'Espagne ensanglantée*, pp.9–12.

105 ST, pp.41–60.

106 Ibid., pp.84, 177.

107 Ibid., p.11.

108 Murray Sperber, 'Looking Back on Koestler's Spanish Civil War', p.116.

109 ST, pp.240, 265.

110 *Dialogue with Death* [DWD], pp.195–6; ST, pp.375–6.

111 TGF, pp.75–6.

112 André Malraux, *Antimemoirs*, trans. Terence Kilmartin (London, 1968), p.423.

113 Sperber, *Until My Eyes*, pp.108–9, 134.

114 Ibid., p.134.

115 IW, pp.348–9.

116 Ibid., pp.359–60.

117 Ibid., pp.350–2.

118 Ibid., pp.352–3.

119 Ibid., pp.353–4.

120 Ibid., p.370.

121 See Pierre Debray-Ritzen, 'Un croisé sans croix', p.170.

122 IW, p.358.

123 Ibid., pp.366–7. See *Manchester Guardian*, 26 June 1937. Hilda Spiel recalled meeting him at the flat of Paul Frischauer, a Viennese writer then living in London, with a number of other *émigrés* and exiles, *Frankfurter Allgemeine Zeitung*, 5 March 1983.
124 IW, pp.370–4, 375–6.
125 Ibid., pp.376–81; SJ, pp.51–2.
126 IW, pp.378–9.
127 Ibid., p.379.
128 SJ, pp.51–79.

CHAPTER 5: WAR, 1938–42

1 Ruth Dudley Edwards, *Victor Gollancz: A Biography* (London, 1987), pp.269–70.
2 IW, pp.382–4. Albrecht Betz, 'La Problemtatique du renégat: Münzenberg, Sperber et Koestler à la fin des années trente', in *Willi Münzenberg. 1889–1940: Un Homme Contre*, Colloque International, Organisé par Bibliothèque Méjunes, L'Institut de L'Image (Marseilles, 1993), pp.135–43.
3 IW, pp.385–7; Weissberg, *Conspiracy of Silence*, pp.x–xi; Alfred Kantorowicz, *Exil in Frankreich* (Bremen, 1971), pp.17, 167.
4 IW, pp.386–9.
5 See Michael Scammell, 'Arthur Koestler Resigns', *New Republic*, 4 May 1998, pp.27–33. Scammell made the find and the translation is his.
6 Ibid. IW, pp.388–90.
7 TGF, pp.71–3; Gross, *Willi Münzenberg*, pp.299–309, 311–13; Harald Wessel, *Münzenbergs Ende* (Berlin, 1991), pp.136–42, 143–50; R. N. Carew Hunt, 'Willi Münzenberg', in David Footman (ed.), *International Communism*, St Antony's Papers, No. 9 (London, 1960), pp.72–87.
8 IW, pp.365, 386, 406.
9 IW, p.393. Münzenberg contracted to publish the German version, but the printing was overtaken by the war.
10 TG, pp.156, 169, 333–53.
11 IW, p.411. Weissberg, *Conspiracy of Silence*, pp.71–2.
12 Kantorowicz, *Deutsche Tagebuch*, Vol.1, pp.59, 340; Ludwig Marcuse, *Mein Zwanzigstes Jahrhundert* (Munich, 1960), p.244.
13 IW, p.393. See also publication proposal, probably for Jonathan Cape, MS2308/2.
14 Sperber, *Until My Eyes*, p.134.
15 Ibid., p.138.
16 Gross, *Willi Münzenberg*, pp.323–4, 325–8; Wessel, *Münzenbergs Ende*, pp.200–17.
17 Marcuse, *Mein Zwanzigstes Jahrhundert*, p.234.
18 IW, pp.406–8; Sperber, *Until My Eyes*, p.138.
19 Interview with Paul Willert, 28 August 1994. See also Stephen Koch, *Double Lives: Stalin, Willi Münzenberg and the Seduction of the Intellectuals* (London, 1995), pp.82, 93, 308–9; Sam Tanenhaus, *Whittaker Chambers: A Biography* (New York, 1997), pp.134–5, 137, 147–8, 149.
20 IW, pp.214, 222, 401; Sperber, *Until My Eyes*, p.134.
21 Drs A. Willy, A. Costler, R. Fisher and others, *The Practice of Sex* (London, 1940), Introduction and pp.48–9, 111–12.
22 Ibid., pp.86–91, 103–7, 438, 451–4.
23 Koestler to Heinz Grueber, 29 November 1971, MS2387/2; Sperber, *Until My Eyes*, pp.151–2.
24 IW, p.413.
25 SOS, p.24; *Scum of the Earth* [STE], p.58. Interview with Daphne (Hardy) Henrion, 8 June 1998.
26 STE, pp.1, 6–10, 16–18.
27 Ibid., pp.20–1, 24–32.
28 Ibid., pp.32–3.
29 Ibid., pp.35–40.
30 The following account of Koestler's internment is based on STE, unless otherwise indicated.
31 STE, pp.97; Regler, *Owl of Minerva*, pp.333–4, 352–3.
32 Regler, *Owl of Minerva*, pp.336–7.
33 STE, pp.105–6; IW, p.416; Regler, *Owl of Minerva*, p.350.
34 STE, pp.107, 111–19.
35 Ibid., pp.99–102; Regler, *Owl of Minerva*, p.350.
36 Interview with Daphne (Hardy) Henrion, 8 June 1998. Daphne to Cape, 10 October 1939;

Daphne to Atholl, 14 October 1939; Atholl to Daphne, 21 October 1939 and 5 January 1940, CCHDC, 619/1/3.

37   Dorothea Koestler to Eden, 31 October 1939; Dorothea Koestler to Vansittart, 1 November 1939, CCHDC, 619/1/3.

38   STE, pp.141–5; IW, p.142; Mowrer cable to Nicolson, nd, probably November 1939; Malraux guarantee, 27 November 1939; Paulhan to Daphne, 12 December 1939; Rupert Hart-Davis to Daphne, 10, 22, 23, 25 November 1939, CCHDC, 619/1/3. Curtis Cate, *André Malraux: A Biography* (London, 1995), p.274.

39   Interview with Paul Willert, 28 August 1994. Regler also benefited from the intercession of the French politician Georges Mandel, Ernest Hemingway, whom he had known well in Spain, Eleanor Roosevelt and Martha Gelhorn. Regler, *Owl of Minerva*, pp.340, 349, 352–3.

40   STE, pp.146–8. Regler, *Owl of Minerva*, pp.342–3.

41   Le Troquer to Daphne, 28 November 1939 and Ministère des affaires étrangères to Le Troquer, 30 November 1939, CCHDC, 619/1/3.

42   STE, pp.158–62; Cate, *André Malraux*, p.274.

43   STE, pp.162–7, 172.

44   Ibid., p.167. Daphne Hardy gave the novel its famous English title when she was handling it for Cape and Koestler was *incommunicado* in France. Interview with Daphne (Hardy) Henrion, 8 June 1998.

45   STE, pp.171–4; Sperber, *Until My Eyes*, p.161.

46   Koestler to Gisele Freund, 5 October 1955, MS2380/3; STE, pp.175–9 and preface to Danube Edition (London, 1968), pp.8–9; IW, p.420.

47   STE, pp.179–88. A few of the papers of 'Private Albert Dubert' survive in MS2308/2. His demobilisation documents record 16 June 1940 as his date of enlistment in Limoges.

48   See diary 1939–40, MS2304. The following narrative is based on the memoir of the fall of France in *Scum of the Earth* and the unpublished version of the diary. Where the text of the diary coincides more or less with the version published in *Scum of the Earth* the page references to the published version are given. Koestler wrote a third version for a *Daily Telegraph* magazine article, 17 August 1973, reprinted as 'A Sentimental Pilgrimage', in *Kaleidoscope* (London, 1981), pp.285–305. Several details differ in this narrative. Daphne disappears from it completely.

49   For the following paragraphs see diary and STE, pp.193–261.

50   Sperber, *Until My Eyes*, p.183; Kantorowicz, *Exil in Frankreich*, p.187.

51   STE, p.278; IW, pp.420–1; 'A Sentimental Pilgrimage', p.303; Martin Domke to Koestler, 12 October 1941, MS2371/2. For minor inconsistencies in the two accounts of this meeting, see Ingrid and Konrad Scheurmann (eds), *For Walter Benjamin*, trans. Timothy Nevill (Bonn, 1993), pp.275–6.

52   Varian Fry, *Surrender on Demand* (New York, 1945), pp.76–9, 105–13. Koestler's name and that of his wife appear on a list of 'clients' prepared by Fry around 1941; information from Dr Elizabeth Berman, Guest Curator, 'Assignment: Rescue' exhibition at United States Holocaust Memorial Museum June 1994–January 1995. In 1967, Koestler was considered for writing a preface to a book celebrating Fry's wartime work, Document 10, Varian Fry Papers, ed. Karen J. Greenberg, *Archives of the Holocaust*, Vol.5, *Columbia University Library* (New York, 1990), p.129.

53   Richard Newman to Daphne Hardy, 9 December 1940, MS2371/1; reference to Lt Hopkins, 8 September 1940 and for the voyage, see 3–6 September 1940, diary 1939–40, MS2304. Koestler to Miss Fitzgerald, 26 June 1942, MS2372/1, refers to a Jack Pollock. Ian McCallum to Koestler, 29 October 1946, MS2374/4.

54   E. E. Bullen to Koestler, 12 September 1978; Koestler to Bullen, 30 September 1978, MS2391/2. According to Norman Bentwich, Etzdorf deserted from the German army in 1938 or 1939 and was interned in France when war broke out. Norman Bentwich, *I Understand the Risks* (London, 1950), p.102. Interview with Anita von Etzdorf, 1 June 1998.

55   Proposed Sending of British ex-soldiers to Martinique from Casablanca, 12 October 1940, FO371/24303, PRO. Communications between the acting consul in Casablanca listed Koestler among sixteen British personnel. Strangely, the FO correspondence places them in Casablanca in October 1940, a month *after* Koestler's diary. Koestler was described as a 'naturalized British subject' with Palestinian nationality dating back to March 1928.

56   Preface to the Danube Edition, STE (London, 1968), p.11; unpublished memoir by Rudiger von Etzdorf, courtesy of Anita von Etzdorf.

57   See diary 1939–40, MS2304; IW, p.407; Wessel, *Münzenbergs Ende*.

58   Ellen Hill to Koestler, 31 August 1941, MS2371/1. See also Ellen Hill to Daphne Hardy, 27

February 1941, MS2371/1.

59   IW, p.421; Koestler to D. R. Darling, 8 September 1973, MS2388/3.

60   *News Chronicle* to Koestler, 2 October 1940, MS2308/2; 15 October 1940, diary 1939–40, MS2304.

61   *News Chronicle* to Koestler, 21 October and 1 November 1940; Kesler to Koestler, 22 October 1940, MS2308/2; 22 and 29 October 1940, diary 1939–40, MS2304; Daphne to Koestler, 6, 24 and 31 October 1940, MS2308/2 and undated telegram from Daphne to Koestler, MS2301/3.

62   Leonard Mins to Koestler, 28 October 1940. Early in December 1940 the Committee recommended that Koestler's visa application receive 'expeditious consideration'. Harry Donaldson to Koestler, 13 December 1940, MS2414/1.

63   Koestler to British Passport Control Officer, Lisbon, 21 September 1940, MS2414/1. The dating is probably an error.

64   Koestler to Sir Henry King, November 1940, MS2414/1. See also Sir Henry King to Koestler, 11 March 1953 and Koestler to King, 24 March and 8 April 1953, MS2332/5.

65   IW, pp.421–2. Koestler to Aliens Department, Home Office, 29 December 1940, MS2372/1. He claimed that the governor of Pentonville said that his belongings had been sent to MI5: Koestler to Aliens Department, Special Branch, 29 December 1940, MS2372/1; Koestler to Bristol Police, 23 December 1940, MS2372/1. Koestler insisted it was a KLM plane, but other documents refer to a BOAC airliner.

66   See letter, author unknown, to Under Secretary of State, Home Office, 3 December 1940, MS2308/2. Letter to Major Sinclair, 9 December 1940, MS308/2. According to Tom Bower, Koestler did do work briefly for MI5; see Tom Bower, *The Perfect English Spy: Sir Dick White and the Secret War 1935–50* (London, 1995), pp.46–7.

67   Laski to Koestler, 21 December 1940, MS2371/1.

68   Wickham Steed to Koestler, 25 December 1940 and Strachey to Koestler, 23 January 1941, MS2371/1; Koestler to Kingsley Martin, 2 April 1941, MS2414/1.

69   For a useful guide to the various critical studies, see Frank Day, *Arthur Koestler: A Guide to Research* (New York, 1987).

70   IW, p.394. Schneour Zalman Rubashov (1889–1974), who became Salman Shazar in Israel, was born in White Russia and emigrated to Palestine in 1924. He was a leading figure in the Palestinian labour movement and an editor of *Davar*, its main daily paper, until he became its chief editor from 1944 to 1949. He was Minister of Education in two Labour cabinets and twice served as President of Israel from 1963 to 1973.

71   Pearson, *Arthur Koestler*, pp.56, 66–7.

72   *Darkness at Noon* [DAN], pp.210–11.

73   See Jonathan Frankel, *Prophecy and Politics: Socialism, Nationalism and the Russian Jews 1862–1917* (Cambridge, 1981); Robert Wistrich, *Revolutionary Jews from Marx to Trotsky* and *Socialism and the Jews* (Oxford, 1982); Gitelman, *A Century of Ambivalence*; W. D. Rubinstein, *The Left, the Right and the Jews* (London, 1982).

74   Sperber, *Until My Eyes*, pp.157–9.

75   IW, pp.394–401.

76   Sperber, *Until My Eyes*, p.158. Sperber, unlike Koestler, goes on to acknowledge that they had been wrong about the 'confession theory'.

77   Stephen F. Cohen, *Bukharin and the Bolshevik Revolution: A Political Biography, 1888–1938* (New York, 1975), pp.372–80.

78   DAN, pp.18, 40, 65.

79   Ibid., pp.81–4, 90.

80   Ibid., pp.124–8, 186–90.

81   Ibid., pp.206–7.

82   Michael Foot, *Loyalists and Loners* (London, 1986), p.217.

83   Koestler to Gollancz, 23 December 1940; Gollancz to Koestler, 26 December 1940, MS2371/1; Koestler to Gollancz, 7 January 1941, MS2372/1.

84   Iain Hamilton interview with Arthur Koestler, 5 March 1974, p.10, MS2436/5; SOS, p.25; Daphne to Koestler, 31 May 1941, MS2301/3.

85   Documents pertaining to Koestler's alien status and application to join the British army are in MS2308/2. On 22 December 1940 the foreign editor of the *News Chronicle* wrote to the officer in charge of the No. 3 Recruiting Centre for Aliens confirming that Koestler had acted as a reporter for the paper and reiterating his anti-Fascist credentials, MS2414/1. Although, even now, Koestler hedged his bets. Early in December 1940 the Exiled Writers Committee in New York had recommended that Koestler's visa application receive 'expeditious consideration'. On

4 January 1941 he wrote to them to explain that since he had reached Britain he had no *immediate* need of the fare money or entry visa to the USA. 'I have no desire to leave this country as long as I am allowed to be at liberty and to do my share. But I am a Hungarian subject and Hungary, as part of the Axis, might reenter [*sic*] the war at any moment. This might mean internment again . . . So it would be a great reassurance if I could know that the way to the USA was open to me, should such an emergency arise': Koestler to Miss Sherman, secretary, Exiled Writers Committee, 4 January 1941, MS2414/1.

86   Lilian Herbert (of Cape) to Koestler, 31 January 1941 and Jonathan Cape to Koestler, 14 February 1941, MS2342/3; Army Recruitment Office to Cape, 12 February 1941, MS2371/1; Iain Hamilton interview with Arthur Koestler, 5 March 1974, p.10, MS2436/3.

87   Nicolson to Koestler, 27 January 1941, MS2371/1; see also 'A Sentimental Pilgrimage' in *Kaleidoscope*, p.300; interview with Miriam Rothschild, 4 April 1998.

88   Koestler to Jonathan Cape, 19 and 26 February 1941, MS2372/1; Gollancz to Koestler, 7 March 1941, MS2371/1; Koestler to Gollancz, 28 March 1941; Koestler to Nicolson, 1 April 1941, MS2372/1; Nicolson to Koestler, 7 April 1941; Gollancz to Koestler, 2 April 1941; Gollancz to Koestler, 5 May 1941, MS2371/1.

89   STE, pp.16–17, 42–50, 244–5.

90   STE, pp.66–7, 78–83, 89–91, 119–22.

91   Koestler to Gollancz, 26 February and 2 April 1941, MS2372/1; Trevor/Phyllis Blewitt to Koestler, 29 March 1941, 6 May 1941, 28 May 1941, 31 July 1941, MS2371/1.

92   Koestler to Jonathan Cape, 26 February 1941; Koestler to Gollancz, 28 March 1941, MS2371/1.

93   Haffner to Koestler, 3 March 1941; Neumann to Koestler, 19 March 1941, MS2371/1; Koestler to Laski, 12 February 1941, MS2372/1; 8–9 March 1941, diary 1941, MS2304.

94   Warburg to Koestler, 7 and 20 January 1941, MS2371/1; 4, 5 and 17 February 1941, MS2371/1; Fyvel to Koestler, 13 and 27 February 1941, MS2371/1; Koestler to Fyvel, 15 February and 18 April 1941, MS2372/1; 11 February 1941, diary 1941, MS2304.

95   Attestation and enlistment forms, 15 April 1941, MS2308/2; Koestler to Fyvel, 18 April 1941, MS2372/1.

96   Koestler to Daphne, 10 May 1941, MS2301/3; Daphne to Koestler, 21 April 1941, MS2301/3.

97   Koestler to Willert, 1 July 1941, MS2372/1; Strachey to Koestler, 11 July 1941, MS2371/1; Koestler to Neumann, 13 August 1941, MS2372/1.

98   Hugh Thomas, *John Strachey* (London, 1973), pp.209–10; John Strachey, *The Strangled Cry* (London, 1962), pp.11–12.

99   'The Lion and the Ostrich', Lecture to the British Academy 'Thank-Offering to Britain Fund', 27 June 1973, reprinted in *Kaleidoscope*, pp.275–7.

100 Koestler to Sheila, 26 August 1941; Koestler to Willert, 4 September 1941, MS2372/1.

101 Koestler to Willert, 4 September 1941, MS2372/1; Capt. S. B. Denison, Education Corps to Koestler, 6 November 1941, MS2371/2.

102 Koestler to Dobrée, 30 September 1941, MS2414/1; Koestler to Chapman, 28 October 1941, MS2372/1; diary-notebook [DN], 28 October 1941, MS2305.

103 Jameson to Koestler, 18 and 26 August 1941, MS2371/1; Jameson to Koestler, 15 September 1941, MS2372/1; see also diary 1941, MS2304; Iain Hamilton interview with Arthur Koestler, 5 March 1974, pp.14, 19, MS2436/5.

104 Iain Hamilton interview, pp.19–20.

105 Ibid., pp.18–24; Strachey to Koestler, 1 April 1942, MS2371/3; Koestler to Strachey, 9 April 1942, MS2372/1; Rothschild to Koestler 19 April and 27 April 1942; Koestler to Rothschild, 28 April 1942, MS2372/1; DN, 8 April 1942, MS2305; 30 June and 30 July 1942, diary 1942, MS2304; Foot, *Loyalists and Loners*, pp.215–20; Guy de Rothschild, *The Whims of Fortune* (London, 1985) p.137; A. J. Ayer, *Part of My Life* (London, 1977), pp.244–5. Interview with Miriam Rothschild, 4 April 1998.

106 Interview with David Astor, 8 June 1995.

107 Report on injury, 20 September 1941, Oakley Camp Farm, MS2307/1; DN, 29 September 1941, 29 September 1941 to 22 May 1943, MS2305; DN, 8, 17, 19 October 1941, MS2305.

108 Daphne to Koestler, 21 April, 6 May 1941; Koestler to Daphne, 10 May 1941; Daphne to Koestler, 28 May, 4 June 1941, MS2301/3.

109 Daphne to Koestler, 8, 10, 27 June 1941, MS2372/1; Koestler to Willert, 4 September and to Connolly, 19 September 1941, MS2372/1.

110 Koestler to Willert, 2 October and to Helen Lidiski, 17 October 1941, MS2372/1; Strauss to Koestler, 8 October 1941, MS2371/2.

111 Diary, 10 August 1941, MS2304; Koestler to Gollancz, 2 and 4 August 1941; Koestler to

Neumann, 13 August 1941; Koestler to Cape, 4 September 1941, MS2372/1; diary, 11 and 13 September 1941, MS2304; Connolly to Koestler, 16 September 1941, MS2371/2; Koestler to Forster, 26 September, 1 and 17 October 1941, MS2372/1; diary, 2/3 November 1941, MS2304.

112   Christopher Salmon, BBC, to Koestler, 16 October and 19 November 1941, MS2372/1; Trevor Blewitt, BBC, to Koestler, 13 January 1942, MS2371/3. For 'Europe in Revolt', see MS2363/2. Iain Hamilton interview with Arthur Koestler, 5 March 1974, p.14, MS2436/5.

113   Koestler to Trevor/Phyllis Blewitt, 2 May 1941; Koestler to Cape, 3 May and 30 July 1941, MS2372/1; Gollancz to Cape, 5 May and 11 June 1941, MS2371/1. For praise of the book, see Storm Jameson to Koestler, 8 July 1941, MS2371/1. Robert Hewison, *Under Siege. Literary Life in London 1939–45* (London, 1988), pp.42–4.

114   Strauss to Koestler, 8 October 1941, MS2373/2; Strauss to Koestler, 16 December 1941, MS2371/2; Strauss to Koestler, 20 January and 18 May 1942, MS2371/3; Laski to Koestler, 22 September and 1 October 1941, MS2371/2; Koestler to Laski, 28 September 1941, MS2372/1.

115   See MS2371/2. Weiczen to Koestler, 24 December 1941, MS2371/2.

116   DN, 7 November 1941, MS2305. Michael Sheldon, *Friends of Promise: Cyril Connolly and the World of Horizon* (London, 1990), p.71.

117   'Scheme for the rescue of Alien Refugees in Unoccupied France and French North Africa' encl. with Koestler to Paul Strage, Secretary of the Friend's Service Council, nd, probably September 1941, MS2413/2. See also Eleanor Rathbone to Koestler, 28 September 1941 and 14 October 1941, MS2371/2.

118   Koestler to Laski, 28 September 1941, MS2372/1; Astor to Koestler, 1 October 1941, MS2413/2; Edith Pye, International Committee for War Refugees in Great Britain, to Koestler, 20 October 1941, MS2371/2; Koestler to Rathbone, 9 November 1941; Koestler to Astor, 9 November 1941, MS2413/2; DN, 7 November 1941, MS2305.

119   Koestler to Astor, 23 November 1941, MS2732/1; Einstein to Koestler, 28 November 1941, suggesting a meeting between them; Astor to Koestler, 25 November 1941; Rathbone to Koestler, 12 December 1941; Rathbone to Koestler, 18 December 1941, MS2371/2; Koestler to Rathbone, 7 January 1942, MS2372/1; Rathbone to Koestler, 24 January 1942, MS2371/3; interview with David Astor, 8 June 1995.

120   Koestler to CO, 24 and 25 November 1941; Koestler to Connolly, 26 November 1941; Koestler to Calder-Marshall, 26 November 1941, MS2372/1. Sheldon, *Friends of Promise*, pp.83–4.

121   Calder-Marshall to Koestler, 7, 22, 28 November and 1 December 1941, MS2371/2; Koestler to Calder-Marshall, 26 November 1941 and to George Campbell, MOI Films Div., 26 November 1941, MS2372/1.

122   Koestler to Károlyi, Koestler to Neumann, 6 December; Koestler to Sir Herbert Read, 23 December; Koestler to Carus Wilson, 25 December 1941, MS2372/1; Daphne to Koestler, 4 and 20 December 1941, MS2301/3; Notes for discharge, MS2307/1.

123   Kingsley Martin to Koestler, 2 December 1941, Arthur Calder-Marshall to Koestler, 5 December 1941; Astor to Koestler, 10 December 1941; Strauss to Koestler, 23 December 1941, MS2371/2.

124   Calder-Marshall to Koestler, 5, 12 and 18 December 1941; Paul Willert to Koestler, 16 December 1941, MS2371/2.

125   Koestler to Daphne, 27 December 1941, MS2301/3.

126   Calder-Marshall to Koestler, 29 December 1941, MS2371/2; Crossman to Koestler, 1 January 1942; Calder-Marshall to Koestler, 6 January 1942, MS2371/3; Koestler to Phyllis Bottome, 13 February 1942, MS2372/1; Army Discharge Notice, 10 March 1942, MS2308/2.

CHAPTER 6: HOLOCAUST, 1942–4

1   Hewison, *Under Siege*, ch.4.

2   Ibid.; Bernard Bergonzi, *Wartime and Aftermath: English Literature and its Background 1939–1960* (Oxford, 1993).

3   See transcript of Cyril Connolly interview with Arthur Koestler for the *Sunday Times*, 5 September 1965, pp.18–19, MS2304/1; Iain Hamilton interview with Arthur Koestler, 5 March 1974, p.20, MS2436/5; Clive Fisher, *Cyril Connolly: A Nostalgic Life* (London, 1995), pp.205, 214–15. See also Jeremy Lewis, *Cyril Connolly: A Life* (London, 1997), pp.364–5.

4   DN, 18 January 1942, 27 March 1942, MS2305; Koestler to Strachey, 9 April 1942, MS2372/1.

5   DN, 3 June 1944, MS2305; Quennell to Koestler, nd, 1944, MS2373/2. See Peter Quennell,

The Wanton Chase: An Autobiography from 1939 (London, 1980), p.21.

6   Fisher, *Cyril Connolly*, p.223. See also Connolly to Wilson, 19 March 1945, cited in Lewis, *Cyril Connolly*, p.364.

7   David Astor, 'Crusader', *Encounter*, July-August 1983, p.32; Rothschild, *The Whims of Fortune*, p.137.

8   Interview with Arthur Koestler, Imperial War Museum [IWM], Department of Sound Records, 005393/03, reels 1–2; draft of 'Regiment With No Traditions', MS2340/2.

9   Draft proposal for 'Those Who Escaped', MS2340/2.

10 Script of *Lift Your Head Comrade*, MS2340/2; see Tony Kushner, *The Holocaust and the Liberal Imagination* (Oxford, 1994); Ian McLaine, *The Ministry of Morale: Home Front Morale and the Ministry of Information in World War II* (London, 1979).

11 *Lift Your Head Comrade*. There is a rare copy of the film in the IWM Film Archive.

12 Draft letter to Miriam or Victor Rothschild, May 1942, MS2372/1.

13 Bentwich, *I Understand the Risks*, pp.56–7; interview with Koestler, IWM, Department of Sound Records, 005393/03, reel 2.

14 *News Chronicle*, 12 December 1945; *Reynolds News*, 13 December 1942; *Spectator*, 18 December 1942.

15 'Protective Custody', MS2340/3.

16 *The Black Gallery*, No.5. 'Julius Streicher', broadcast on BBC Home Service, 11 June 1942; No.7, 'Heydrich', broadcast on BBC Home Service, 25 June 1942. Tapes are held in the BBC Sound Archive, London. See also draft outlines, MS2340/3.

17 Script for 'Europe in Revolt', MS2402/5. See also correspondence with the BBC in MS2363/2.

18 DN, 8, 19, 23 April and 6 October 1942, MS2305; Koestler to Lehmann, 1 May 1942, MS2371/3; Koestler to Strauss, 2 July 1942, MS2372/1. It was republished in *The Yogi and the Commissar* [YAC], pp.9–20.

19 Reprinted in YAC, pp.9–20.

20 Ibid., p.10.

21 'Scum of the Earth 1942' and 'Revolt in the prison camp', *Evening Standard*, 3, 4 June 1942; 'The Idle Thoughts of Sidney Sound (Your Neighbour on the Underground)', *Evening Standard*, 10, 17, 25 July 1942; Koestler to Foot, 10 June and 8 July 1942, MS2372/1; Foot to Koestler, 11 June 1942, MS2371/3. See also MS2393/5. Interview with Michael Foot, 1 August 1998.

22 Reprinted in YAC, pp.43–4. See Richard Cockett, *David Astor and the Observer* (London, 1991).

23 Reprinted in YAC, pp.100–5; notes, MS2414/1.

24 See diary 1942, MS2304; Rothschild, *The Whims of Fortune*, p.139; Ayer, *Part of My Life*, pp.244–5.

25 Anthony Howard, *Crossman: The Pursuit of Power* (London, 1990), pp.32–4, 51; Mervyn Jones, *Michael Foot* (London, 1994), pp.47, 60–4. Interview with Michael Foot, 1 August 1998.

26 Iain Hamilton interview with Arthur Koestler, 5 March 1974, pp.12–13, 16, MS2346/3; DN 27 March 1942, MS2305; Polanyi – 17 April 1942, Gordon Walker – 24 June and 29 August 1942, Crossman – 1 July and 27 November 1942, Laski – 6 August and 9 October 1942, diary 1942, MS2304.

27 See Edward J. Doherty, 'Michael Polanyi: Physician to the Modern Mind', unpublished paper, 1994; Lee Congdon, *Exile and Social Thought*, pp.10, 23.

28 Daphne to Koestler, 7 August, 7, 11, 14 December 1942, MS2301/3.

29 Treatment advice, 28 August 1942; Plesch to Koestler, nd; Pathological Report on request of Dr Plesch, nd, 1942, MS2307/1; Koestler to Weiczen/Valiani, 14 September 1942, MS2372/1; Koestler to 'Misi' (Michael Stricker), 25 September 1942, MS2344/7.

30 Ould to Koestler, 21 November 1942, MS2371/4; Valiani to Koestler, 15 April 1942, MS2371/3; Valiani to Koestler, 1 August 1942, MS2371/4; Koestler to Erika Mann, 14 September 1942; Koestler to Valiani, 14 September 1942, MS2372/1.

31 Elizabeth Ascher to Koestler, 2 October 1940, MS2308/1; Koestler to Lucas, prob. December 1940; Unitarian Service Committee to Koestler, 14 January 1941, MS2371/1.

32 Neumann to Ould, 24 January 1941; Koestler to Elizabeth Ascher, 9 February 1941, MS2371/1; Bedrich Heine, Unitarian Service Committee, Lisbon, to Koestler, 20 April 1941, MS2301/1; Koestler to Elizabeth Ascher, 28 April 1941, MS2372/1; Elizabeth Ascher to Koestler, 30 April 1941, MS2301/1; Koestler to Heine, 2 July 1941, MS2372/1.

33 Koestler to Jim Putnam, 27 September 1941; Elizabeth Ascher to Koestler, 17 November 1941; Koestler to Mr Nievergelt, Bank Manager, 29 December 1941, MS2372/1; Elizabeth Ascher to Koestler, 25 January and 23 March 1942; Emily Hughes, Friends Service Committee, to

Koestler, 4 March 1942, MS2371/3.

34 Koestler to Elizabeth Ascher, 25 August 1944; Koestler to 'Nicole' (Dorothea), 21 November 1944, MS2372/4.

35 *Daily Herald*, 30 June 1942; *News Chronicle*, 2 September 1942. See press cuttings kept by Koestler in MS2414/1. Flyer advertising meeting, MS2371/4.

36 Interview with Jan Karski, 30 March 1995; Iain Hamilton interview with Arthur Koestler, 5 March 1974, p.18, MS2436/5. On Karski and his mission, see David Engel, *In the Shadow of the Holocaust: the Polish government-in-exile and the Jews 1939–42* (Chapel Hill, 1987) and E. Thomas Wood and Stanislaw M. Jankowski, *Karski: How One Man Tried to Stop the Holocaust* (New York, 1994).

37 Koestler to Newsome, 28 June 1943; Koestler to Karski, 12 October 1943, MS2372/4. See also Martin Gilbert to Koestler, 29 February 1980 and reply, 15 May 1980, MS2393/1.

38 The artist Feliks Topolski invited him to his studio in May 1943 to meet two 'interesting Poles from over there': Topolski to Koestler, 17 May 1943, MS2372/2; appointments diary, 1943, MS2304; Rathbone to Koestler, 11 August 1943. MS2372/2.

39 Rathbone to Koestler, 11 August 1943; Ould to Koestler, 10 August 1943; Bracey to Koestler, 17 June and 3 August 1943, MS2372/2; 'Suggested Plan for providing asylum for Jewish refugees from Nazi Occupied Territory', 4 June (1943), MS2413/2.

40 For a recent account of Hillary's life and death, see Sebastian Faulks, *The Fatal Englishman* (London, 1997).

41 Richard Hillary, *The Last Enemy* (London, 1942, republished 1997). The fiancée of a dead pilot, who was Hillary's closest friend, plays a role in the book similar to that of Maria Kloepfer in Koestler's memoirs, positing a supernatural explanation of events against the narrator's ultra-rationalistic one.

42 Hillary Trust papers, MS2339/4; Lovat Dickson, *Richard Hillary* (London, 1950), pp.vii-viii, 155–6 and pp.183 and 191 for examples of Koestler's influence on Hillary.

43 Koestler's essay was reprinted as 'In Memory of Richard Hillary' in YAC, pp.46–56.

44 Ibid., pp.66–7.

45 Ibid., pp.63, 67; DN, 6 April 1944, MS2305.

46 Koestler to Michael Hillary, 9 January 1943; Koestler to unknown, 7 July 1943, MS2372/4. In a touching gesture he sent flowers to the family on Richard's birthday in April 1943: Michael Hillary to Koestler, 20 April 1943, MS2372/1.

47 Iain Hamilton interview with Arthur Koestler, 5 March 1974, pp.15, 17, MS2436/5.

48 Reprinted in YAC, pp.21–7; Lewis, *Cyril Connolly*, pp.376–8.

49 Reprinted in YAC, pp.106–12. Compare with C. S. Lewis, 'It is the logic of our times / No subject for immortal verse / That we who live by honest dreams / Defend the bad against the worst.'

50 Koestler to Willert, 16 March 1943, MS2372/4; Blit to Koestler, 31 May 1943, MS2372/2; Blit to Koestler, 24 September 1943, MS2372/2; Blit to Koestler, 6 October 1943, MS2372/3.

51 Blit to Koestler, 28 October 1943; Bottome to Koestler, nd, probably late October 1943, MS2372/3; Lewis, *Cyril Connolly*, p.365.

52 Koestler to Connolly, 22 November 1943, MS2372/4; *Horizon*, December 1943; Peter Watson to Koestler, nd, probably November 1943, MS2372/3; Sheldon, *Friends of Promise*, pp.83–4.

53 Koestler to Connolly, 14 February 1944, MS2372/4; Reprinted in YAC, pp.94–9.

54 *Arrival and Departure* [AAD], postscript to Danube Edition, pp.190–2.

55 Ibid., pp.20–2, 69–70, 74–5, 92–6.

56 Ibid., pp.35, 77–87, 107–8. See Pearson, *Arthur Koestler*, pp.83–4, 149–50.

57 AAD, pp.136–50, 141–2, 144–5.

58 Ibid., pp.158–62, 176–7.

59 Ibid., pp.176, 187–9.

60 George Orwell, *The Collected Essays, Journalism and Letters*, Vol.3, *As I Please, 1943–1945*, ed. Sonia Orwell and Ian Angus (London, 1970), pp.278–82.

61 SOS, p.128. Koestler made the point more explicitly in his obituary for Orwell.

62 Jameson to Koestler, 27 November 1943; Rotha to Koestler, 28 December 1943; Willert to Koestler, 1 December 1943 and correspondence to *New York Times*, MS2372/3; *Times Literary Supplement*, 18 November 1943; *Evening Standard*, 26 November 1943; *New York Times Book Review*, 28 November 1943; *New Yorker*, November 1943.

63 Unfinished sequel to AAD, hereafter AAD II, pp.11, 22, MS2317/2.

64 Ibid., pp.45–52.

65 Notes, MS2317/2.

66 YAC, pp.80–1, 84.
67 Leslie Fielder, *Olaf Stapledon: A Man Divided* (New York, 1983); Robert Crossley, *Olaf Stapledon* (Liverpool, 1994).
68 Olaf Stapledon, *Saints and Revolutionaries* (London, 1939), pp.18–21.
69 DN, notes during 1943, MS2305.
70 Stapledon to Koestler, 7 and 30 April, 20 March, 20 May, 28 May, 23 June, 27 July, 24, 26 and 29 November 1943; Postgate to Koestler, 27 May 1943, MS2372/2; Koestler to Postgate, 2 November 1943 and 5 January 1944, MS2372/4; memorandum on discussion between Koestler, Postgate and Stapledon on the current crisis, October 1943, MS2414/2. See also Koestler to Jameson, 4 February 1944, MS2372/4; Stapledon to Koestler, 7 July 1944, MS2373/2; Ould to Koestler, 16 October 1944, MS2373/2; Crossley, *Olaf Stapledon*, pp.307–8.
71 Koestler to Mr Cooper, 1 June 1944, MS2372/4; 24, 29 June 1944, DN, MS2305; Koestler to Dewar, 11 June 1944, MS2372/4; Dewar to Koestler, 13 June, 10, 16 July 1944, MS2372/2.
72 DN, 19 April, 20 May 1943, MS2305. For names and dates of encounters see diary 1943, MS2304.
73 Strachey to Koestler, 2 January 1943; Jameson to Koestler, 20 May 1943; Connolly to Koestler, 11 May 1943, MS2372/2.
74 Hewison, *Under Siege*, p.96; DN, 29 February 1944, MS2305.
75 See DN 1944, MS2305.
76 AAD, pp.55 and 39, 69, 116, 164–5.
77 As an example of the 'split mind' or the persistence of an illusion he included 'the psycho-analyst who gets married': YAC, p.121.
78 AAD, p.55.
79 Annette to Koestler, nd and 9 June 1942, MS2371/3.
80 Marie to Koestler, nd late 1942, MS2371/4.
81 Koestler lunched or dined with Rothschild on 18 and 31 January, 2 February, 19 May, 26 June, 11 September, diary 1943, MS2304. Miriam Rothschild to Koestler, 23 November 1942, 6 February, 24 March, 7 June, 14 October 1943, MS2372/2; interview with Miriam Rothschild, 4 April 1998.
82 Invitation, 25 January 1944, MS2372/1; DN, 10 March 1944, MS2305; Father d'Arcy to Koestler, 21 February 1944, MS2373/1; Koestler to d'Arcy, 23 February 1944, MS2372/4; on Berlin, DN, 29 April 1944, MS2305; interview with Miriam Rothschild, 4 April 1998 and information generously provided by Berlin's biographer Michael Ignatieff.
83 Plesch, 2, 10, 18 March 1944; row with Peters, 10 March 1944; drunken evening with Beaverbrook, DN, 17 March 1944, MS2305. See also Koestler to Beaverbrook, nd; to Astor, 6 April 1944; to Lovat Dickson, 17 April 1944, MS2372/4; Crossman, Rumbold and Hemingway evenings, DN, 24, 25, 31 May 1944, MS2305.
84 DN, 28 February, 6, 7, 10, 14 March, 14, 29 April 1944, MS2305.
85 Koestler to Dobrée, 15 January 1944; Koestler to Lamda, 14 February 1944; Koestler to Ould, 23 March 1944 and Koestler to Connolly, 31 March 1944, MS2372/4; Ould to Koestler, 23 June 1944, MS2373/2; Koestler to Ould, 24 June and 24 August 1944, MS2372/4; Arthur Koestler interview with Iain Hamilton, 5 March 1974, p.18, MS2346/3.
86 Koestler to Oxford Club, 14 February 1944, MS2373/1; details of army lectures in MS2372/4 and DN, 7 March, 10 June 1944, MS2305; Koestler to Dr Jacobs, 31 May 1944, MS2372/4; correspondence with Jewish Committee for Relief Abroad, 6 February, 14 March 1944, MS2362/3.
87 Koestler to Ellen Wilkinson, 28 February 1944, MS2372/4; DN, 28 February, 9, 10 March, 29 April, 26 May and 2 June 1944, MS2305; H. A. Finch to Koestler, 22 March 1944, MS2372/1.
88 DN, 10, 11, 23, 26 March, 6, 29 April, 1944, MS2305; Bottome to Koestler, 30 March and 11 April 1944, MS2373/1.
89 Alison Wood to Koestler, 11 April 1944, MS2373/1; T. T. Scott, UNRRA, to Koestler, 12 May 1944, MS2372/2; DN, 29 April, 8, 28 May, 3, 6, 29 June 1944, MS2305.
90 DN, 10, 22 March and 8 May, 17–18, 24, 25, 28 June, 1, 10 July 1944, MS2305; Connolly to Koestler, nd, MS2373/2. 'I wish I knew what exactly happened after we left Korda . . . I am very fond of you Mary; cross my heart'; note to Mary Dunn, nd, MS2372/4.
91 DN, 28 March, 7, 29 April, 8 May, 29 June 1944, MS2305; Rothschild to Koestler, 9 April 1944, MS2373/1; Koestler to Gollancz, 17 May 1944, MS2372/4.
92 DN, 26 June 1944, MS2305; correspondence between Koestler, Connolly, Jonathan Cape and Bluth re. Kavan, MS2412/2; DN, 21 July 1944, MS2305.
93 Miriam Rothschild to Weizmann, 24 March 1943, MS2372/1; Guy de Rothschild to Koestler,

24 June 1943, MS2372/2.

94 Diary, 3 January 1943, MS2304; Koestler to Bentwich, 8 January 1943; Bentwich to Eric Mills, Palestine Administration, nd, MS2372/2.

95 Meetings with Weizmann, Sieff, Shertok, see diary 1944, MS2304; Anglo-Palestine Committee minutes, 21 February, 6, 15, 30 March, 6 April 1944, MS2403/1; DN, 29 February, 9, 19 March 1944, MS2305; Koestler to Pakenham, 15 March and to Martin, 15 March 1944, MS2372/4; interview with David Astor, 8 June 1995.

96 DN, 19 March, 29 April 1944, MS2305; John Hampden to Lovat Dickson, 28 April 1944, MS2402/4; Polanyi to Koestler, 6 and 8 January 1944, MS2344/7.

97 DN, 22 March 1944, MS2305.

98 Stricker to Koestler, 17 August 1942, MS2371/4; Koestler to Adele, 25 September 1942, MS2302/1. Bergman, Jewish Agency for Palestine (JAP) to Koestler, 3 April 1944 and Koestler to Aldor, 31 July 1944, MS2414/2. DN, 26 June 1944, MS2305. Brockway to Koestler, 1 July 1944 and Laski to Koestler, 13 July 1944; Francis Aldor to Koestler, 7 July 1944, MS2373/2. Rather curiously, Koestler was maintaining an elaborate pretence via Stricker to convince his mother that he was safe in the USA and not in Britain, Koestler to 'Misi' (Michael Stricker), 25 September 1942 and 29 March 1944, MS2344/7.

99 Agenda for meeting 8 May 1944, MS2402/4; Sieff to Koestler (circular), 22 June 1944, MS2402/4. DN, 8 and 25 May, 10 and 21 June 1944, MS2305. Notes of conversation, Shertok-Brand, 11 June 1944, Aleppo, MS2403/1. See Bernard Wasserstein, *Britain and the Jews of Europe 1939–1945* (Oxford, 1979), pp.168–9, 249–70.

100 DN, 8 July 1944, MS2305; Koestler to Shertok, 19 July 1944, MS2372/4; Yehuda Bauer, *Jews for Sale? Nazi-Jewish Negotiations, 1933–1945* (New Haven, 1994), pp.145–95; David S. Wyman, *The Abandonment of the Jews: America and the Holocaust, 1941–1945* (New York, 1984), pp.235–54, 288–307.

101 DN, 11 July 1944, MS2305; 'The case for bombing the Extermination camps in Upper Silesia by the American Air Force', 11 July, 1944, MS2403/1. Doris May to Koestler, 13 July 1944, MS2402/4. See David Cesarani (ed.), *Genocide and Rescue. The Holocaust in Hungary 1944* (Oxford, 1997).

102 DN, 8, 10 July 1944, MS2305; Koestler to Aldor, 11 July 1944, MS2372/4.

103 DN, 12, 13 July 1944, MS2305.

104 DN, 13, 15, 17 July 1944, MS2305; Foot to Koestler, 11 July 1944, MS2402/4.

105 DN, 21, 22 July, 25 August 1944, MS2305.

106 DN, 21 July 1944, MS2305.

107 LWK, pp.7–19.

108 SOS, pp.33–4; Mamaine to Koestler, 15, 21 February 1944, MS2303/2; DN, 9 March, 25 May, 3 and 7 June 1944, MS2305.

109 Mamaine to Koestler, 8 June and July 1944, MS2303/2; DN, 15, 25, 28 June 1944, MS2305.

110 DN, 9, 10 July 1944, MS2305; Mamaine to Koestler, nd 1944, MS2303/2.

111 DN, 11, 12, 13, 15 July 1944, MS2305.

112 DN, 21, 22, 25 July and 25 August 1944, MS2305; Mamaine to Koestler, 27 July and undated notes July–August 1944, MS2303/2.

113 DN, 10, 22, 25, 27 July, 6 August 1944, MS2305.

114 Koestler to José, 11 August 1944, MS2372/4; DN, 15 August 1944, MS2305. José or Josephine was an ex-girlfriend. In July she offered to take him in: 'If you don't know where to go for rest or a weekend, come with a lady if you like. If without, I promise not to expect you to seduce me', Josephine to Koestler, 24 July 1944, MS2373/2.

115 YAC, pp.121–35.

116 Ibid., pp.136–200.

117 Ibid., pp.201–26.

118 Ibid., pp.227–9.

119 Ibid., pp.229–34.

120 Ibid., pp.234–41.

121 Ibid., pp.248–54.

122 Ibid., pp.254–6.

123 Ibid., p.256.

124 DN, 1 July 1944, MS2305; Koestler to Brunius, 10 September 1944, MS2372/4.

125 Koestler to Phyllis Bottome and to Milo Sperber (brother of Manès Sperber), 6 December 1944, MS2372/4; Koestler to Elizabeth Ascher, 25 August and to 'Nicole' (Dorothea), 21 November 1944; Koestler to Dorothea, 12 November 1944, MS2372/4; Guy de Rothschild to Koestler, 18

December 1945, MS2301/1; Paul Willert also helped: in 1944 he was air attaché at the British embassy in Paris, Ayer, *Part of My Life*, p.282.
126 Koestler to Mr Tyerman, 17 November, to Lovat Dickson, 20 December to Mr Lutheran, nd, to Wylie, 20 December 1944, MS2372/4; Mamaine to Koestler, 31 December 1944, MS2303/2.

CHAPTER 7: PALESTINE, FRANCE AND SCIENCE, 1945-7

1 IW, pp.380–1.
2 Rothschild, *The Whims of Fortune*, p.138; Michael Polanyi to Koestler, 6 and 8 January 1944, MS2344/7.
3 Mamaine to Koestler, 30 January 1945, MS2303/2.
4 Nicholas Bethell, *The Palestine Triangle* (London 1979), pp.153–93, 191–2; SOS, pp.36–9.
5 Iain Hamilton interview with Koestler, 14 March 1974, pp. 6–7, 9, MS2436/5. For the travel arrangements, see MS2414/2 and the record of the trip in Koestler's 1945 diary, MS2304.
6 1945 diary, MS2304; Arnold Zweig to Koestler, 16 July 1945, MS2373/3. Zweig gave Koestler a manuscript of a story, 'Napoleon of Jaffa', which he hoped to see published in England. Brod invited Koestler to give a lecture and to see the Habimah Theatre with which he was involved; see letters 19 January 1945, 26 June 1945, 8 July 1945, MS2373/3.
7 Ernst Eppler to Koestler, 11 January 1945, MS2373/3 and reply, 17 January 1945, MS2374/1; Koestler to Mamaine, 30 January 1945, MS2303/2. For correspondence and meetings over this period, see MS2373/3 and 1945 diary. Sieff to Koestler, 28 November 1945, enclosing a copy of the Haggadah which had been read at the seder 'when you were with me', MS2373/4. Rothschild, *The Whims of Fortune*, p.260.
8 Koestler to Yona Yani, 9 July 1945, MS2374/1.
9 Menachem Begin, *The Revolt*, trans. Samuel Katz (London, 1951), pp.308–10; SOS, pp.36–9.
10 Koestler to Mamaine, 30 January 1945 and 16 February 1945, MS2303/2.
11 Koestler to Daphre, 11 February 1945, MS2301/3 and Koestler to Mamaine, 30 January 1945, MS2303/2. Judith Weinshall could not understand how he could say he was 'homesick' for England and asked plaintively what Palestine lacked: Judith Weinshall to Koestler, 4 October 1945, MS2373/4.
12 Koestler to Mamaine, 15 April 1945, MS2303/2; Koestler to Daphne, 3 May 1945, MS2301/1; Koestler to Rubinstein, 14 April 1945, MS2309/1.
13 Koestler to Jim Wylie, 15 April 1945, MS2309/1; Koestler to Mamaine, 10 June 1945, MS2303/2.
14 Mamaine to Koestler, 8 and 19 January, 12, 15 and 29 March, 10 April 1945, MS2303/2. On the leasing of Bwlch Ocyn, see letters to Harold Rubenstein, MS2374/1.
15 Koestler to Mamaine, 16 February and 15 April 1945, MS2303/2; Mamaine to Koestler, 10 April 1945; Koestler to Mamaine, 15 April 1945, MS2303/2.
16 Koestler to Mamaine, 10 June 1945, MS2303/2. 'I often wish I had not done away with the prospective junior – I am sure I shall never have the courage to start anything again. I could have lived peacefully in some back street and contented myself with the thought that the offspring is bound to be a genius.' Rather pathetically, at this time she was working as a writer of children's stories: Anny Rothwell to Koestler, 7 January 1948, MS2375/2. (She had married the journalist Bruce Rothwell.)
17 See correspondence in MS2373/3 and Anny to Koestler, 27 November 1945, MS2373/4; Anny to Koestler, 5 May 1946, MS2374/3.
18 Mamaine to Koestler, 15 June 1945, MS2303/2; Edmund Wilson, *The Forties: From Notebooks and Diaries of the Period*, ed. Leon Edel (New York, 1983), p.148 and Wilson to Mamaine, 28 April 1945, Edmund Wilson, *Letters on Literature and Politics 1912–1972*, ed. Elena Wilson (London, 1977), pp.147–8. See also letters in May–June 1945, Wilson, *Letters*, pp.418–21; Jeffrey Myers, *Edmund Wilson: A Biography* (New York, 1995), pp.279–82.
19 Wilson, *The Forties*, pp.107, 111–12; Wilson, *Letters*, pp.427, 430, 454, 485–6; Mamaine to Wilson, 26 July 1945, Edmund Wilson Correspondence, Beinecke Rare Book and Manuscript Library, Yale University (hereafter EWC). For his exquisite portrait of Mamaine, see Edmund Wilson, *Europe Without Baedeker* (London, 1947), p.212.
20 Mamaine to Koestler, 15 and 23 June, 5 and 13 July 1945, MS2303/2.
21 Koestler to Daphne, 1 February 1945, MS2301/3; Koestler to Mamaine, 15 April 1945, MS2303/2.

22   Air Ministry Travel Warrant, 27 July 1945, MS2373/3; 1945 diary, MS2304; *The Times*, 26 and 28 September 1945; Koestler to Kollek, 25 March 1946, MS2374/1. Koestler to Dick Wyndham, 29 August 1946, MS2374/1 and Iain Hamilton interview with Arthur Koestler, 14 March 1974, pp.8–9, MS2436/5.

23   R. Zaslani to Koestler, 2 October 1945, MS2373/4. Koestler was furious when Dick Wyndham disclosed his identity as the author of the article.

24   LWK, p.21; Mamaine to Edmund Wilson, 7 September 1945, EWC.

25   Koestler to Harold Rubinstein, 14 April 1945, MS2309/1; Neumann to Koestler, 26 December 1945, MS2309/1; Koestler to Wylie, 13 October 1945, MS2309/1; Mamaine to Celia, 6 November 1945, LWK, p.23.

26   Mamaine to Celia, 6 November 1945, LWK, p.23; Koestler to Tom Hopkinson, 15 September 1945; Koestler to Korda, November 1945, MS2374/1.

27   Koestler to Orwell, 18 October 1945, MS2374/1; Bethell, *The Palestine Triangle*, pp.202–10.

28   Gollancz to Koestler, 1 October 1945; Koestler to Gollancz, 2 October 1945, MS2345/1.

29   Koestler to H. Lubinski, New Zionist Organisation, 3 October 1945; Koestler to Rossoff, 24 November 1945 and to Guy de Rothschild, 9 December 1945, MS2374/1.

30   *Thieves in the Night* [TIN], pp.74–6.

31   See Gilman, *Jewish Self-Hatred*, pp.332–3; cf. Eliezer Schweid, 'The Rejection of the Diaspora in Zionist Thought: Two Approaches', *Studies in Zionism*, 5:1 (1984), pp.43–70.

32   TIN, pp.9, 16–17, 90.

33   Ibid., pp.55, 71.

34   Ibid., p.150.

35   Ibid., p.275.

36   Ibid., p.175.

37   Ibid., pp.100, 150; Iain Hamilton interview with Arthur Koestler, 14 March 1974, p.13, MS2436/5.

38   Goldman to Koestler, 16 and 21 October 1945, MS2373/4; Koestler to Goldman, 20 and 30 October 1945, MS2374/1. At the same time, Koestler was disengaging from Hungarian expatriate affairs. In December 1945 he resigned from the Hungarian PEN Club in London and declined election to the Hungarian-Jewish Kadimah Society: Koestler to Koermedi, 9 December 1945, and to B. Szego, 17 April 1946, MS2374/1.

39   TIN, pp.10, 12, 37, 57.

40   Ibid., pp.181, 187, 267–9.

41   Ibid., pp.293–6, 297–8.

42   Cf. DAN, p.206.

43   Mamaine to Celia, 4 January 1946, LWK, pp.24–5; Koestler to Mamaine, 26 February 1946, MS2303/2; Koestler to Linden [Jo Linton], 23 March 1946, MS2374/1; Mamaine to Wilson, 9 December 1954, EWC.

44   Mamaine to Celia, 6 November 1945, LWK, pp.23–4; Daphne to Koestler, 9 October 1945, MS2301/3; Lys to Koestler, 12 November 1945, MS2373/4.

45   Hopkinson to Koestler, 3 November 1945, MS2373/4; Koestler to Hopkinson, 9 November 1945, MS2374/1. Dr John Lewis and Reginald Bishop, *The Philosophy of Betrayal: An Analysis of the Anti-Soviet Propaganda of Arthur Koestler and Others* (London, 1945); Harold Rubinstein to Koestler, 22 October 1945, MS2373/4.

46   King-Hall was trying to aid the anti-Soviet underground in Eastern Europe, many of whom were former Nazi collaborators being manipulated by the British and American secret services. Koestler declined to get involved too deeply, but he did suggest promoting anti-Soviet propaganda from a left-wing point of view and identified some anti-Soviet *émigrés* who might help. Storrs to Koestler, March 1946, MS2374/2; Koestler to Storrs, 17 March 1946, MS2374/1; E. Dangerfield to Koestler, 10 May 1946, MS2374/1; Koestler to Orwell, 12 April 1946, MS2345/2; King-Hall to Koestler, 9 April 1946, MS2374/3; Koestler to King-Hall, 12 April 1946, MS2374/1.

47   Mamaine to Koestler, 10 May 1945, MS2345/2; Liddell Hart to Koestler, 14 May 1945, MS2373/3; Guy de Rothschild to Arthur Koestler, 30 May 1945, MS2373/3; Koestler to Rothschild, 3 July 1945, MS2374/1.

48   Orwell to Koestler, 17 October 1945, MS2345/2; Koestler to Orwell, 18 October 1945, MS2374/1.

49   Iain Hamilton interview with Arthur Koestler, 5 March 1974, pp.23–4, MS2346/5; Koestler to David Walton, 6 July 1977, MS2391/1. In this letter, Koestler maintains that Orwell was tainted by anti-Semitism: 'One can of course be anti-Zionist without being anti-Jewish, but the

emotional bias was unmistakenly present.'

50   Koestler to Tom Hopkinson, 8 December 1945, MS2374/1; Bernard Crick, *George Orwell: A Life* (London, 1980), pp.483–4; Michael Sheldon, *Orwell: The Authorised Biography* (London, 1991), p.442. Cf. the recollection by Storm Jameson who claimed that Koestler got up early one morning and entertained Richard Orwell by silently making faces at him so that his father could sleep for another hour: *Autobiography of Storm Jameson: Journey from the North*, Vol.2 (London, 1984), p.131.

51   Orwell to Koestler, 2 January 1946, MS2345/2; Crick, *George Orwell*, pp.497–8, refers to a different version of the manifesto.

52   Reprinted in *The Trail of the Dinosaur* [TOD], pp.17–24.

53   SOS, p.41; Orwell to Koestler, 2 January 1946, MS2345/2; Ayer, *Part of My Life*, p.307; Mamaine to Wilson, 27 January 1944, EWC.

54   Koestler to Orwell, 9 January 1946, MS2345/3; Mamaine's diary, 10 January 1946, LWK, pp.25–6.

55   Crawshay-Williams to Koestler, 21 January 1946; Orwell to Koestler, 11 and 27 February 1946, MS2345/2; Polanyi to Koestler, 19 February 1946, MS2344/7; Koestler to Mamaine, 5 February 1946, MS2302/2.

56   Koestler to Phillips, 14 March 1946, MS2345/2; Koestler to Sperber, 14 March 1946, MS2374/2; Koestler to Orwell, 19 March 1946, MS2345/2.

57   Orwell to Koestler, 10 March 1946; Slater to Koestler, MS2345/2; Koestler to Celia, 21 March 1946, MS2301/2; Koestler to Orwell, 23 March 1946; Koestler to Sperber, 22 March 1946, MS2345/2.

58   SOS, p.41; Koestler to Orwell, 23 March 1946; Orwell to Koestler, 31 March 1946; Koestler to Storm Jameson, 23 April 1946, MS2345/2; Koestler to Russell, 16 April 1946, MS2374/1; Storm Jameson to Koestler, 27 April 1946, MS2374/3; Mamaine's diary, 14 April 1946, LWK, p.29.

59   Mamaine to Celia, 23 April 1946, LWK, pp.30–1; Koestler to Russell, 26 April 1946 and Russell to Koestler, 3 May 1946, MS2345/2.

60   Koestler to Russell, 6 May 1946, MS2345/2.

61   SOS, pp.42–3; Russell to Koestler, 13 and 16 May 1946, MS2345/2.

62   Koestler to Orwell, 12 June 1946, MS2374/1; Koestler to Sperber, 17 April 1946 and 2 August 1946, MS2374/1; Edwards, *Victor Gollancz*, pp.564–5.

63   Mamaine to Koestler, 4 August 1946, LWK, p.33.

64   Mamaine to Koestler, 9 October 1950, MS2303/2; Koestler to Mamaine, 14 October 1950. Koestler told this to George Mikes in 1956: George Mikes, *Arthur Koestler: The Story of a Friendship* (London, 1983), p.19.

65   Mamaine to Celia, 6 November 1945, LWK, pp.23–4; Mamaine to Wilson, 7 September, 24 November and 9 December 1945, EWC; Wilson to Mamaine, 11 September 1945, cited in Myers, *Edmund Wilson*, p.283.

66   Daphne to Koestler, 30 October 1945, MS2301/3.

67   Daphne to Koestler, 12 December 1945, MS2301/3.

68   Mamaine to Celia, 11 January 1946, LWK, pp.25–6.

69   Mamaine to Koestler, 25 January, 4, 7, 13, 24 February 1946, MS2303/2 and note by Celia Goodman, LWK, p.26; Mamaine to Wilson, 17 February 1946, EWC.

70   Koestler to Mamaine, 5 and 12 February 1946, MS2302/2.

71   *Listener*, 21 March 1946, reprinted in Rupert Crawshay-Williams, *The Challenge of Our Time* (London, 1948), pp.11–12, 15–19 and TOD, pp.11–16; Koestler to Mamaine, 26 February 1946, MS2303/2.

72   Crawshay-Williams, *The Challenge of Our Time*, p.73; Mamaine to Celia, 18 March 1946, LWK, p.28.

73   Mamaine to Celia, 17, 30 April, 12 June 1946, LWK, pp.29–30, 31, 32. In one day she had to deal with thirty letters: Mamaine to Wilson, 10 April 1946, EWC.

74   Bergman, JAP, to Koestler, 3 April 1944 and Koestler to Aldor, 31 July 1944, MS2414/2; Koestler to Aldor, 9 October 1944, MS2372/4; Francis (Ferenc) Aldor to Koestler, 23 October 1944, MS2373/2. Irene Aldor in Switzerland sent him information in July and August 1944 about his mother's presumed whereabouts: telegrams 10 July and 18 August 1944, MS2363/4.

75   Adele to Irene Aldor, 15 April 1945, MS2302/1; Koestler to Daphne 3 May 1945, MS2301/3, Irene Aldor to Koestler, 22 April 1945, MS2373/3.

76   K. B. Cohen to Koestler, 29 October 1945, MS2373/4; Koestler to Adele, 5 September 1945, MS2302/1; Adele to Koestler, 31 January 1946, MS2302/1; Koestler to P. C. F. Dalton, FO

Consular Department, nd, 1945, MS2302/2.

77 Koestler to Irene Aldor, 5 September and 11 December 1945, MS2301/3; Koestler to Foreign Office, 5 September 1945, MS2374/1; Koestler to American Joint Distribution Committee, London, 12 November 1945, MS2302/2; Dalton to Koestler, 19 November 1945, MS2302/2. See correspondence between Koestler and FO in MS2302/2.

78 Paul Ignotus, *Political Prisoner* (London, 1964), p.46.

79 See correspondence in MS2302/1 and MS2302/2.

80 Koestler to Nicole, 15 May and 24 December 1945; Koestler to Willert and Rothschild, 9 April 1946, MS2374/1; Nicole to Koestler, 13 September 1945, MS2373/4 and 26 January 1946, MS2374/1; Nicole to Koestler, 2 April 1946, MS2374/3; Koestler to Elizabeth Ascher, 5 April 1946, MS2374/1.

81 Eva Tay to Koestler, 20 October 1945, MS2373/4; Koestler to Tay, 24 November 1945, MS2374/1; Valiani to Koestler, 8 January 1946, MS2374/2; Valiani to Koestler, 29 April 1946, MS2374/3; Valiani to Koestler, 4 November 1946, MS2374/4.

82 Koestler to Weissberg, 4 May, 11 June, 8 September, 23 September and 6 November 1946, MS2374/1; Weissberg to Koestler, 8 May, 15 June, 1 July 1946, MS2374/3.

83 Orwell to Koestler, 5 and 22 March, 13 April 1946; Koestler to Orwell, [March?] 1946, MS2345/2.

84 Mamaine to Celia, 18, 24 March 1946, LWK, p.28; Mamaine's diary, 6, 8 April 1946, LWK, p.29; Koestler to Anny, 10 May 1946, MS2374/2.

85 Koestler to Will Morris (Red Flag Fellowship), 8 May 1946, MS2374/1; Koestler to Bertrand Russell, 13 May 1946, MS2374/1; Mamaine to Koestler, 27 May 1946, MS2303/3; Koestler to Connolly, 8 June 1946, MS2374/1; Connolly to Koestler, 14 June 1946, MS2374/3. Koestler to Sperber, 17 June 1946, MS2374/1.

86 Bethell, *The Palestine Triangle.*

87 Howard, *Crossman*, pp. 112–19, 125–6.

88 Ibid., pp.125–6; Jones, *Michael Foot*, pp.145–7. Interview with Michael Foot, 1 August 1998.

89 Koestler to Crossman, 12 June 1946, MS2374/1.

90 Crossman to Koestler, 19 June 1946, MS2375/3; Koestler to Crossman, 2 and 22 July 1946, MS2374/1; Howard, *Crossman*, p.125; Jones, *Michael Foot*, p.146.

91 Crossman to Koestler, 19 June 1946, MS2375/3; Koestler to Kollek, 29 June 1946 and Koestler to Kollek, 23 September 1946, MS2374/1; Crossman to Koestler, 25 July 1946, MS2374/3.

92 Mamaine to Celia, 4 and 10 August 1946, LWK, pp.34–5; Kollek to Koestler, 23 August 1946, MS2374/3; Crossman to Koestler, 25 August 1946, MS2374/3.

93 Connolly to Koestler, 6 August 1946, MS2374/4; Koestler to Connolly, 9 August 1946, MS2374/1.

94 Crossman to Koestler, 25 August 1964, MS2374/3; Kollek to Koestler, 6 September 1946, MS2374/1.

95 Guy de Rothschild to Koestler, 13 September 1946; Randolph Churchill to Koestler, 26 September 1946; Mills to Koestler, 27 September 1946; Samuel to Koestler, 2 October 1946; Storm Jameson to Koestler, 19 October 1946, MS2374/4; Montague to Koestler, 18 October 1946, MS2376/2.

96 Daphne to Koestler, 4 January 1947, MS2301/3.

97 Koestler to Daphne, 27 January 1947, MS2301/3.

98 IW, p.381; Tuvia Arzi to Koestler, 4 November 1946; Kollek to Koestler, 24 September 1946, MS2374/4; Koestler to Yonah, 23 December 1946, MS2374/1; MS2374/4.

99 Crossman to Koestler, 3 September 1946, MS2374/4; Koestler to Kollek, 3 September 1946, MS2374/1; Mamaine's diary, 26 September 1946, LWK, p.39.

100 Mamaine to Celia, 10 August 1946, LWK, pp.34–5; Koestler to Mamaine, 31 July 1946, MS2374/1; Mamaine to Celia, 4 August 1946, LWK, pp.33–4; Koestler to Insurance Company, 18 August 1946, MS2414/3.

101 Koestler to Strauss, 7 August 1946, MS2374/1; Strauss to Koestler, 22 August 1946, MS2374/4; Koestler to Foot, 23 August 1946, MS2374/1; Koestler to Gates, 29 August 1946, MS2374/1; Koestler to Under Secretary of State, Foreign Office, 5 September 1946, MS2414/4. Nye's response came too late: 14 September 1946, MS2374/1.

102 SOS, pp.65–6; Koestler to Gollancz, 28 June 1946, MS2374/1; Gollancz to Koestler, 1 July 1946, MS2374/3; Koestler to Rubinstein, 23 August 1946, MS2374/1; Koestler to Malraux, 30 April 1946, MS2374/1.

103 Mamaine to Celia, 30 April 1946, LWK, p.31. For the background see Antony Beevor and Artemis Cooper, *Paris After the Liberation 1944–1949* (London, 1995), chs 19–21. Postscript to the

Danube Edition of DAN, pp.272–3. See also Guy de Rothschild to Koestler, 19 July 1946 and Sperber to Koestler, 12 June 1946, MS2374/3; Mamaine to Celia, 16 August 1946, LWK, p.35.

104 Mamaine to Celia, 22 September 1946, LWK, p.38; 1–2 October 1946, Paris diary, MS2304/4.

105 Unless otherwise stated, the details of the visit are based on Koestler's 1946 Paris diary, MS2306/4.

106 SOS, pp.65, 73; Koestler to Mamaine, 9 October 1946, MS2302/4. This phrase was cut out of the published version of the letter in SOS, p.66.

107 Manès Sperber, *Until My Eyes*, pp.231–2, 234–49.

108 Mamaine to Celia, 23 October 1946, LWK, p.41; Koestler to Mamaine, nd, prob. 9 October 1946, MS2303/2; Paris diary, MS2306/4.

109 IW, pp.414–17.

110 Koestler to Mamaine, 9 October 1946, MS2302/2.

111 Cate, *André Malraux*, pp.352–8. Paul Willert also knew Malraux: Ayer, *Part of My Life*, p.282.

112 Mamaine to Celia, 26 October 1946, LWK, pp.41–2.

113 Herbert Lottman, *Albert Camus: A Biography* (London, 1997) and Olivier Todd, *Camus: A Life* (London, 1997); cf., Patrick McCarthy, *Camus* (London, 1982), p.217.

114 SOS, p.67, Koestler to George Berkely, 14 June 1973, MS2391/4; Jean Cau, *Croquis de Mémoire* (Paris, 1985), p.133.

115 SOS, pp.67–9.

116 Koestler to Mamaine, 14 October 1946, MS2303/2; Mamaine's diary, 17 October 1946, LWK, p.39.

117 See Paris diary, MS2306/4.

118 Ronald Hayman, *Writing Against: A Biography of Sartre* (London, 1986), p.237; Lottman, *Albert Camus*, pp.426–7; Todd, *Albert Camus*, pp.231–2.

119 Mamaine to Celia, 1 November 1946, LWK, pp.43–4; Simone de Beauvoir to Nelson Algren, 28 September 1947, Simone de Beauvoir, *Beloved Chicago Man: Letters to Nelson Algren, 1947–64* (London, 1998) [BCM], pp.70–3. Simone de Beauvoir, *Force of Circumstance*, trans. Richard Howard (London, 1965; first published in France in 1963), p.140.

120 de Beauvoir, *Force of Circumstance*, pp.140–1.

121 SOS, p.72.

122 Mamaine to Celia, 23 October 1946, LWK, p.40; de Beauvoir, *Force of Circumstance*, pp.18, 68–9, 89.

123 de Beauvoir to Algren, 30 October 1947, BCM, pp.73–5; de Beauvoir, *Force of Circumstance*, pp.108–9.

124 Deirdre Bair, *Simone de Beauvoir: A Biography* (London, 1990), p.316; de Beauvoir to Algren, 28 September 1947, BCM, pp.70–3.

125 Paris diary, MS2306/4; Mamaine to Celia, 23 October 1946, LWK, p.40.

126 Simone de Beauvoir, *Adieux: A Farewell to Sartre*, trans. Patrick O'Brien (London, 1984), p.270; Simone de Beauvoir, *The Mandarins*, trans. Leonard Friedman (London, 1994; first published in France in 1954), pp.29, 43–4. She told Nelson Algren: 'I put a lot of things into it . . . some of Koestler, Camus, Sartre and myself.': de Beauvoir to Algren, 13 October 1952, BCM, p.481.

127 de Beauvoir, *The Mandarins*, pp.45–6, 48.

128 de Beauvoir, *The Mandarins*, pp.50–1, 89–93.

129 Ibid., pp.95–7.

130 Ibid., pp.98–9.

131 Ibid., pp.28, 43, 137–42.

132 Paris diary, MS2306/4. Todd, *Albert Camus*, pp.233–4. The French edition gives sources: *Albert Camus: Une Vie* (Paris, 1996), pp.424–5 and n.30–6, p.803. Celia Goodman did not give the author access to Mamaine's letters and diaries for this crucial period, but confirmed the details orally, interview, 7 April 1998.

133 Koestler to Mamaine, 10 October and 11 November 1946, MS2303/2; 6, 7, 8 November 1946, diary 1946, MS2304.

134 Orwell to Koestler, 5 and 22 March 1946, MS2345/2; Orwell to Rahv, 4 February 1948, quoted by Crick, *George Orwell*, p.537.

135 Reprinted in TOD, pp.25–35.

136 Koestler to Mamaine, 11 November 1946, MS2303/2; 26 November 1946, diary 1946, MS2304; Sperber to Koestler, 2 December 1946, MS2374/4; Crossman to Koestler, 4 December 1946, MS2374/4; Koestler to Sperber, 5 December 1946, MS2374/1; Kollek to Koestler, 22 December 1944, MS2374/4.

137 Sperber to Koestler, 25 February 1947, MS2375/1; Koestler to Sperber, 7 March 1947,

MS2376/1; Mamaine to Celia, 31 May 1947, LWK, pp.53–4.

138 Mamaine to Celia, 19 February and 18 March 1947, LWK, pp.47–9; Koestler to Sperber, 7 March 1946, MS2376/1. Also Hilda Stricker to Koestler, 14 and 28 April and 25 June 1947, MS2375/1. She sent ham, eggs, salami.

139 Mamaine to Celia, early February 1947, LWK, pp.45–6.

140 Ibid., and 24 March 1947, LWK, pp.45–6. 49–50.

141 Mamaine to Celia, 18 and 24 March 1947, LWK, pp.28–50.

142 Mamaine to Wilson, 19 June 1947, EWC; 2–15 May 1947, diary 1947, MS2304.

143 Mamaine to Celia, 22 May 1947, LWK, p.50.

144 Reprinted in TOD, pp.35–6.

145 26 May 1947, diary, MS2304; Mamaine to Celia, 26 May 1947, LWK, p.51. The version of this letter printed by Iain Hamilton, *Koestler*, p.124, differs significantly from the one that appears in LWK, the collection of correspondence edited by Celia Goodman. Goodman omitted the sentence 'I always have . . .' Mamaine to Celia, 27 May 1947, LWK, pp.51–2.

146 Mamaine to Celia, 27 May 1947, LWK, p.51–2.

147 Mamaine to Celia, 16 June 1947, LWK, p.56; Camus to Koestler, 13 August 1947, MS2345/1; Koestler to Voigt, 12 August 1947, MS2376/1. See also Koestler to Mme Labin, 6 January 1947, MS2376/1; Eliot to Koestler, 7 February 1947, MS2345/1; Norris Chipman to Koestler, 31 March 1947, MS2375/1.

148 Mamaine to Celia, 31 May and 3 June 1947 and Mamaine to Celia, (?) February 1947, LWK, pp.46, 54–5; Kollek to Koestler, 2 May 1947, MS2375/1; Dr S. Bernstein, Zionist Organisation of America to Koestler, 16 June 1947, MS2376/2; Koestler to Crossman, 14 July 1947, MS2375/1.

149 *New Statesman*, 16 August 1947; Koestler to Gollancz, 28 August 1947, MS2375/1; Koestler to Martin, 1 September 1947, MS2402/4. For letters, see MS2376/2. Mamaine told Wilson they did not think anyone would publish it: Mamaine to Wilson, 8 August 1947.

150 Koestler to Voigt, 12 August 1947; Koestler to Elizabeth (?), 8 September 1947, MS2376/1; Elizabeth (?) to Koestler, 12 September 1947, MS2375.

151 IW, pp.380–1.

152 Mamaine to Celia, 10 September 1947, LWK, pp.57–8, 23–8 September 1947, diary 1947, MS2304.

153 Beevor and Cooper, *Paris*, pp.331–45, 346–54, 359–61, 361–78.

154 Mamaine's diary, 1 October 1947, LWK, pp.58–9.

155 Paris diary, MS2306/4; Mamaine's diary, 8 October 1947, LWK, pp.59–60. Koestler was responsible for setting up meetings between Malraux and Camus and Norris Chipman of the embassy: Koestler to Chipman, 19 October 1947, MS2376/1 and Chipman to Koestler, MS2375/1; de Beauvoir to Algren, 9 October 1947, BCM, pp.78–80.

156 Sartre to Koestler, nd, 1947, MS2345/2: reprinted SOS, pp.69–70.

157 Mamaine's diary, 9 and 10 October 1947, LWK, pp.60–1; Mamaine to Wilson, 1 November 1947, EWC.

158 de Beauvoir to Algren, 3, 9, 10 and 14 October 1947, BCM, pp.73–5, 78–82.

159 Mamaine to Celia, 4 November 1947, LWK, pp.62–3. Simone de Beauvoir seems to confuse this with two articles on the incipient Cold War which appeared in *Carrefour*: de Beauvoir, *Force of Circumstance*, p.141.

160 See MS2341/2; *L'Herne*, pp.240–7.

161 Mamaine to Celia, 4 November 1947, LWK, p.62.

162 *Insight and Outlook* [IO], p.vii.

163 Ibid., pp.3–35.

164 Ibid., pp.36–70.

165 Ibid., pp.113–29, 130–49.

166 Ibid., pp.158, 163–4, 166–7.

167 Ibid., pp.177–8.

168 Ibid., p.189.

169 Ibid., pp.198–9.

170 Ibid., pp.190–4.

171 Ibid., pp.239–370, 371–80.

172 Ibid., p.xi.

173 Mamaine to Celia, 11 and 24 November 1947, LWK, pp.63–4, 66–7.

174 Mamaine to Celia, 18 and 25 November 1947, LWK, pp.64–5, 68–9.

175 Mamaine to Celia, 11 November and 2 December 1947, LWK, pp.64, 69.

176   Mamaine to Celia, 19 December 1947, LWK, pp.70–1.
177   Mamaine to Celia, 18 and 24 November, 12 December 1947, LWK, pp.65, 67, 70–1; Adele Koestler to Koestler, 21 December 1947, MS2302/1.

CHAPTER 8: FRANCE, AMERICA AND ISRAEL, 1947–9

1   SOS, p.47.
2   France 1948 diary, 1–8 January 1948, MS2304; Beevor and Cooper, *Paris*, pp.361–73.
3   France 1948 diary, 8–29 January 1948, MS2304; Mamaine's diary, 7 January 1948, LWK, p.72.
4   Mamaine's diary, 9, 13 and 15 January 1948, LWK, pp.72–3. Cate, *André Malraux*, pp.366–8.
5   de Beauvoir, *Force of Circumstance*, p.140; see also de Beauvoir to Algren, 13 January 1948, BCM, pp.144–7.
6   Mamaine's diary, 22 January 1948, LWK, pp.73–4; de Beauvoir, *Force of Circumstance*, p.140; de Beauvoir to Algren, 20 January 1948, BCM, pp.149–51.
7   See in an amended form, 'Land of Bread and Wine', TOD, pp.40–3; Koestler to Winkler, 11 February 1948, MS2376/1; Koestler to Crossman, 13 February 1948, MS2375/2.
8   Mamaine's holiday diary, MS2306/4; Mamaine to Celia, 3, 10, 19 February 1948, LWK, pp.74–8.
9   SOS, p.46.
10   Mamaine to Celia, 29 February 1948, LWK, p.79; Koestler's diary of the trip, MS2306/4.
11   *Le Rassemblement*, 28 February 1948, cited in Cate, *André Malraux*, pp.366–8.
12   France 1948 diary, 27, 28, 29 February and 1 March 1948, MS2304/6.
13   de Beauvoir to Algren, 28 February 1948, BCM, pp.178–81.
14   de Beauvoir, *Force of Circumstance*, pp.139–40.
15   1948 diary, MS2304; holiday diary, 3–9 March 1948, MS2306/4; Koestler to Mamaine, 6 March 1948, MS2303/2.
16   Orwell to Koestler, 16 March 1946, MS2345/2; Henson to Koestler, 20 June 1946, MS2374/3; Koestler to Crossman, 13 February 1948, MS2375/2; holiday diary, 29 February 1948, MS2306/4; France 1948 diary, 10, 11, 12 March 1948, MS2306/4; press release, MS2413/4.
17   FBI file, MS2308/2.
18   France 1948 diary, 11–15 February 1948, MS2306/4.
19   Unless otherwise stated, this account is based on his 1948 US diary, MS2306/4.
20   A version of this speech was printed in TOD, pp.47–52. Contemporary press reports give a verbatim account.
21   For this account of the trip, see 1948 US diary, MS2306/4.
22   Koestler to Mamaine, 1 April 1948, MS2303/2; *New Yorker*, 3 April 1948.
23   *New Yorker*, and *P.M.*, 3 April 1948; *Chicago Tribune*, 4 April 1948, MS2413/4.
24   1948 US diary, MS2306/4; cable, MS2413/3.
25   Koestler to Mamaine, nd, MS2413/4.
26   Koestler to Eri Jabotinsky, nd, MS2413/3.
27   Mamaine to Koestler, 1, 12 and 26 March, 6, 12 and 16 April 1948, MS2303/2.
28   1948 US diary, 12–14 May 1948, MS2304; Mamaine to Celia, 15 May 1948, LWK, pp.82–3.
29   1948 US diary, MS2306/4.
30   Koestler to Kollek, 19 October 1947, MS2376/1; Koestler to Fyvel, 26 December 1947, MS2375/1; Kollek to Koestler, 31 December 1947, MS2375/1; France 1948 diary, 24 February 1948, MS2306/4.
31   LWK, pp.83–4. According to Celia Goodman, Mamaine also encouraged Koestler to go to Israel: interview, 7 April 1998.
32   SOS, p.47.
33   1948 US diary, MS2306/4; Koestler to Wylie, 30 May 1948, MS2376/1; Koestler to Dunn, 30 May 1948, MS2376/1.
34   Palestine diary (hereafter PD), 1 June 1948, MS2306/3; Koestler to Ben-Gurion, 21 September 1948, MS2376/1.
35   See MS2331/2 for the deletions.
36   PD, 4–6 June 1948.
37   Ibid., 6–8 June 1948.
38   Ibid., 9, 11, and 12 June 1948.
39   Ibid., 8 and 11 June 1948.
40   Ibid., 16, 21, 24, 27–8 June 1948.

41   Ibid., 13–17 June 1948.
42   Ibid., 19 June 1948.
43   Ibid., 26–8 June 1948. See also Mamaine to Celia, 26 June 1948, LWK, pp.85–6.
44   PD, 4–5 July 1948.
45   Ibid., 27–30 June 1948. On 1 July he wrote: 'Fascinated by the striking conformity to the pattern of the development of this embrionic [*sic*] totalitarianism.' He saw Begin often: PD, 3, 4 July 1948.
46   PD, 26–8 June 1948. See also Mamaine to Celia, 26 June 1948 and 2 July 1948, LWK, pp.85–6, 88–9.
47   PD, 5 and 23 July 1948; Mamaine to Celia, 7 July 1948, LWK, p.90. He soon got into a 'feud' with the people in the flat below: 18 July 1948. See correspondence, MS2413/2.
48   PD, 11 and 15 July 1948.
49   Ibid., 15 July 1948, 4 August 1948.
50   Mamaine to Celia, 21 July 1948; PD, 18, 30 July 1948.
51   PD, 14 August 1948. The allusion to the Latin proverb is suggestive. In full it is *Post coitum omne animal triste*. The implication is that his affair with Zionism and Palestine had an erotic or sexual quality.
52   PD, 25 July 1948. Kollek was no less browned off with Israel than Koestler and in 1948 hoped to spend at least a year studying at Harvard. He was cajoled into returning by Ben-Gurion. See Teddy Kollek with Amos Kollek, *For Jerusalem: a life* (London, 1979), p.104. Tellingly, he makes no mention of his row with Koestler. See Crossman to Koestler, 2 September 1948, MS2375/2. Such was Koestler's mood about England that he heartily approved a proposal by Menachem Begin that Israel should intern British citizens in Israel as a reprisal for the detention of 1200 Jews in Cyprus. PD, 21 September 1948.
53   Mamaine to Celia, 10 September 1948, LWK, p.92.
54   PD, 13 and 24 September 1948. He met Shertok the next day. He, too, launched a fusillade of complaints against *Thieves in the Night* and hoped that Koestler's next book would show Israel in a favourable light.
55   PD, 14, 17, 18 September 1948.
56   Ibid., 28 September and 3 October 1948; Mamaine to Celia, 21 September 1948, LWK, p.93.
57   PD, 21, 22, 23 September 1948; Mamaine to Celia, 21 September 1948, LWK, p.93.
58   PD, 1, 2, 3, 4, 8 and 10 October 1948. Shabtai Teveth, *Moshe Dayan* (London, 1974), p.172.
59   SOS, pp.48–9; Crossman to Mamaine, 3 November 1946, MS2375/2; Koestler to Crossman, 6 November 1948, MS2376/1. It is notable that his certificate of naturalisation gave his nationality as 'Palestinian' rather than Hungarian: naturalisation certificate, MS2308/2.
60   PD, 25 August 1948; Koestler to Abraham Weinshall, 25 December 1948, MS2376/1; Mamaine to Celia, 25 November and 6 December 1948, LWK, pp.96, 98.
61   Mamaine to Celia, 14 November 1948 and 26 January 1949, LWK, pp.94–5, 99; SOS, p.49.
62   1949 diary excerpt, MS2306/1.
63   *Promise and Fulfilment* [PAF], p.ix.
64   Ibid., pp.11–34.
65   Ibid., pp.46–93.
66   Ibid., pp.133–84.
67   Ibid., pp.232, 252–4.
68   Ibid., pp.289–302, 306–9. See Gideon Shimoni, *The Zionist Ideology* (Hanover, NH, 1995), pp.231–2.
69   PAF, pp.311–15, 324–31.
70   Ibid., pp.319–23.
71   Ibid., p.331.
72   Ibid., pp.332–4.
73   Ibid., pp.334–5.

CHAPTER 9: COLD WARRIOR, 1949–52

1   TGF, p.7; SOS, p.50.
2   1949 diary excerpts, 7–12 February 1949, MS2306/1.
3   *Time*, 14 February 1949. Hermes Agenda planning diary [HA], 13–26 February 1949, MS2304 and MS2306/1; Koestler to Mamaine, 16 February 1949, MS2302/2 and Mamaine to Koestler, 20 February 1949, MS2303/2.

4   de Beauvoir to Algren, 19 February 1949, BCM, pp.268–9.
5   de Beauvoir, *Force of Circumstance*, p.141. This version is close to that which Spender recorded Koestler telling him: Stephen Spender, *The Thirties and After* (London, 1978), 14 April 1950, p.170.
6   1949 diary excerpts, 26 February 1949, MS2306/1; Mamaine to Celia, 26 February and 2 March 1949, LWK, pp.99–100, 101–2; Koestler to Malraux, 12 March 1949, MS2376/3.
7   See SOS, pp.57–8; Mamaine to Celia, 26 February and 2 March 1949, LWK, p.100; 1949 diary excerpts, 27, 28–9 February 1949, MS2304.
8   Mamaine to Celia, 7, 11 and 21 March 1949, LWK, pp.103–4, 105, 106–7.
9   Mamaine to Celia, 7, 11, and 21 March 1949, LWK, pp.103–4, 105, 106–7; diary, 12 March 1949, MS2306/1.
10 Mamaine to Celia, 18 and 21 March, 9 and 12 May, 1949, LWK, pp.106, 106–7, 108, 108–9; Koestler to A. D. Peters, 26 May 1949, MS2351/4.
11 Mamaine to Koestler, 3 June 1949, MS2303/3; diary, 3–4 March 1949, MS2306/1; Koestler to Putnam, 16 April 1949; Koestler to Jascha Weinshall, 26 October 1949, MS2376/3. See proofs, MS2331/3.
12 Cynthia to Koestler, 27 May 1949, MS2303/1; diary, 20, 27 May, 1, 17, 26 June 1949, MS2304; Koestler to Mamaine, 7 June 1949, MS2303/3.
13 SOS, pp.53–7.
14 Ibid., p.65.
15 Koestler to Mamaine, 7 and 12 June 1949, MS2303/3; Koestler to 'Stevie', 4 June 1949, MS2351/4.
16 Mamaine to Wilson, 14 June 1949, EWC.
17 Mamaine to Koestler, 1, 3, 4, 10, 12 June 1949, MS2303/3. These letters were omitted from the volume published by Celia Goodman.
18 Mamaine to Koestler, 14, 21 June, 5, 10, 11, 13, 14, 17, 22, 24 July, 4 August 1949, MS2303/3; Koestler to Mamaine, nd, July 1949, MS2303/3; Dr F. Croxon-Deller to Koestler, 10 August 1949, MS2375/4.
19 See 1949 diary, MS2304; DN, 12 and 21 July 1949, MS2305; Koestler to Mamaine, July 1949, MS2303/3; Crossman to Koestler, 20 July 1949, MS2375/2; Jill Craigie to Koestler, 2 August 1949, MS2375/4.
20 Mamaine to Celia, 13 September 1949, LWK, p.112.
21 Mamaine to Celia, 13 August and 13 September 1949, LWK, pp.110, 112–13.
22 Mamaine to Celia, 22 September, 29 October 1949; and diary, 30 October 1949, LWK, pp.113–14, 117, 118; Mamaine to Koestler, 14 October 1949, MS2303/3.
23 Mamaine to Koestler, 12 and 15 November 1949 and Koestler to Mamaine, nd, November 1949, MS2303/3. Barley Alison and Willert overlapped at the Paris embassy. Barley was 'a small, dark intelligent, vivacious girl' who had served in SOE, Ayer, *Part of My Life*, pp.271, 282.
24 Mamaine to Koestler, 15 November 1949, MS2303/3; Mamaine to Celia, 20 October and 10 December 1949; diary, 29 November and 16 December 1949, LWK, pp.115–17, 118, 119–20; Koestler to Weissberg, 15 December 1949, MS2376/3.
25 SOS, p.80.
26 Mamaine to Celia, 28 December 1949, LWK, pp.120–2.
27 Mamaine's diary, 29 December 1949 and 1 March 1950, LWK, pp.120–3, 122–3; Koestler to Mamaine, 7, 10 and 14 January, 13 February 1950, MS2303/3; DN, 26 January 1950, MS2305; Mamaine to Koestler, 16 February 1950, MS2303/3.
28 Koestler to Crossman, 11 February 1948, MS2376/1; Jamie Hamilton to Koestler, 16 April 1948, MS2413/3; Crossman to Koestler, 2 September 1948, MS2375/2.
29 TGF, pp.26, 29.
30 Ibid., pp.29–30, 30–1.
31 Ibid., pp.32, 43.
32 Ibid., pp.46, 52.
33 Ibid., p.7.
34 Ibid., p.199.
35 Frankel, *Prophecy and Politics*; Wistrich, *Revolutionary Jews*.
36 Crossman to Koestler, 17 June 1949, MS2351/4.
37 Muggeridge to Koestler, 14 January 1950, MS2376/3; Schöpflin to Koestler, 20 April 1950, MS2376/4; Wesker to Koestler, 21 August 1952, MS2378/2.
38 *Spectator*, 1 July 1949; *Observer*, 19 June 1949; *New Statesman*, 30 July 1949; *Jewish Chronicle*, 17 June 1949.

39 Mamaine to Koestler, 13 and 14 June 1949, MS2303/3; A. D. Peters to Koestler, 11 July 1949, MS2351/5; Koestler to Strauss, nd, February 1950, MS2376/3; Strauss to Koestler, 16 February 1950, MS2376/4.

40 A. D. Peters to Koestler, 9 August 1949, MS2351/5; Mamaine to Koestler, 11 October 1949, MS2303/3 and 20 October 1949, LWK, p.116; Koestler to Adele Koestler, 26 October 1949, MS2302/1; A. D. Peters Jr to Koestler, 28 September 1949.

41 Koestler to A. D. Peters, 11 August and 2 November 1949 and to James Putnam, 22 August 1949, MS2351/5; A. D. Peters to Koestler, 4, 16 and 30 November 1949, MS2351/5; Koestler to Peters, 10 November and 5 December 1949, MS2351/5. See also DN, 25–9 May 1950, MS2305.

42 Koestler to Mamaine, 17 and 21 February 1950, MS2303/3; Koestler to Paul Winkler, 25 March 1950, MS2376/3; Mamaine to Celia, 18 April 1950, LWK, p.136.

43 *New York Times Magazine*, 19 February 1950, reprinted in extended form in TOD; Mamaine to Celia, 14 March 1950, LWK, pp.129–30. Koestler to 'Stevie', 12 May 1950, MS2376/3. See Tanenhaus, *Whittaker Chambers*.

44 Koestler to Orwell, 26 August and 24 September 1949, MS2376/3; Koestler to Mamaine, January 1950, MS2303/3; *Observer*, 29 January 1950 (repr. TOD, pp.102–4); Sonia Orwell to Koestler, nd, 1950, MS2376/5.

45 Joel Carmichael to Koestler, 6 May 1950, MS2376/4; Paul Graetz to Koestler, 1 and 9 December 1949, MS2375/4; Koestler to Graetz, 8 December 1949, MS2376/3; Paul Graetz to Koestler, 13 and 28 March 1950, MS2376/4; Mamaine to Celia, 2 and 10 April 1950, LWK, pp. 131, 133.

46 Mamaine's diary, 2 January to 28 February, 1 March, 27 May 1950, LWK, pp.124–7, 127–8, 138–9; Mamaine to Koestler, 1 February 1950; Koestler to Mamaine, 21 January, 2 February 1950, MS2303/3; Mamaine's diary, 15 March 1950, LWK, p.130; Mamaine to Celia, 7 and 28 March and 2 April 1950, LWK, pp.128–9, 130–2.

47 Koestler to Maître Blumel, 29 October 1947, MS2376/1; Koestler to Mamaine, nd, July 1949 and Mamaine to Koestler, 2 July 1949 and 13 February 1950, MS2303/3; Mamaine to Celia, 13 August and 20 October 1949, 2 April 1950, LWK, pp.110, 116; Koestler to 'Stevie', 31 August 1949, MS2351/5; Mamaine's diary, 15 December 1949, LWK, p.120.

48 HA, 15 April 1950, MS2304; Mamaine to Celia, 18 April 1950, LWK, pp.134–5; SOS, pp.85–6. In his biography of Koestler Iain Hamilton gets the date of the marriage wrong.

49 DN, 11, 17 and 30 April 1950, MS2305.

50 DN, 28, 29 April, 6–7 May 1950, MS2305; Daphne to Koestler, 21 June 1950, MS2301/3; Koestler to Camus, 11 May 1950, MS2376/3.

51 DN, 7 May 1950, MS2305.

52 Mamaine to Celia, 1 June 1950, LWK, p.139; HA, 4 May-26 June 1950, MS2304.

53 See Koestler's introduction to Weissberg, *Conspiracy of Silence*.

54 Weissberg to Koestler, 19 May 1948, MS2375/1; Weissberg to Koestler, 24 January and 10 May 1949, MS2375/3; Koestler to Weissberg, 21 June 1949, MS2376/3; Weissberg to Koestler, 3 September 1950, MS2376/5; Koestler to Hamilton, 23 May 1951, MS2377/2; Koestler to Weissberg, 16 June 1951; Mamaine to Celia, 28 September 1949, LWK, pp.114–15.

55 Koestler to Eliot, 7 March 1949; Koestler to Malraux and to Burnham, 12 March 1949, MS2376/3; Eliot to Koestler, 15 February and 14 March 1949, MS2345/1.

56 July 1949, *Le Figaro littéraire* (repr. TOD, pp.60–5). Thorez was the leader of the French CP.

57 Koestler to Norris Chipman, 12 December 1949, MS2376/3; Foreign Office to Koestler, 17 March 1950 and Comm. F. B. Watt to Koestler, 30 February 1950, MS2376/4.

58 Peter Coleman, *The Liberal Conspiracy: The Congress for Cultural Freedom and the Struggle for the Mind of Post-War Europe* (London, 1989), pp.3–8.

59 Ibid., pp.15–16.

60 Ibid., pp.16–21.

61 Ibid., pp.4, 160–2.

62 Lasky to Koestler, 20 July 1949, MS2375/3; Ruth Fischer to Koestler, 4 October 1949, MS2375/4; Koestler to Lasky, 3, 14 and 22 March 1950, MS2395/3.

63 Mamaine's diary, 4 May 1950, pp.136–7; DN, 30 May, 19 and 21 June 1950, MS2305; Koestler to Burnham, 3 June 1950, MS2395/3; Lasky to Koestler, 12 June 1950, MS2395; SOS, pp.93–4.

64 The account of the Congress is taken from Mamaine's diary, 23 June to 2 July 1950, LWK, pp.140–8 and Koestler's Berlin diary, MS2306/4.

65 Koestler to Lasky, 3 March 1950, MS2395/3.

66 See Silone's contribution to TGF, pp.83–119; Coleman, *The Liberal Conspiracy*, pp.22–5.

67   Koestler's Berlin diary, MS2306/4; Ayer, *Part of My Life*, pp.244–5, 306–7.
68   Sidney Hook, *Out of Step: An Unquiet Life in the Twentieth Century* (New York, 1987), p.443.
69   For text, see TOD, pp.183–5.
70   Hook, *Out of Step*, pp.436–7; A. J. Ayer, *More of My Life* (London, 1988), pp.63–4.
71   Mamaine's diary, 26 June 1950, LWK, pp.142–3.
72   Text in TOD, pp.186–95.
73   Mamaine's diary, 28 June 1950, LWK, p.144; Hook, *Out of Step*, pp.437–8.
74   Ayer, *More of My Life*, pp.63–4; Hook, *Out of Step*, pp.440–1, 444.
75   For text, see TOD, pp.179–82. Clause 13 was inserted by Ayer and Trevor-Roper. A third
     sentence in clause 5 of the original Koestler–Sperber draft was deleted at their insistence. It read:
     'Totalitarian ideologies which deny intellectual freedom have no right of citizenship in the
     republic of the spirit.' The English delegation took this to be a declaration of intolerance and a
     back-door route to suppression and censorship, a view which won some support partly due to
     problems of translation, although it would clearly have been incompatible with the spirit and
     substance of the manifesto as a whole to suggest that advocates of totalitarian ideologies should
     lose their citizenship.
76   Koestler's Berlin diary, MS2306/4.
77   Mamaine's diary, 30 June 1950, LWK, p.146 and Koestler's Berlin diary, MS2306/4.
78   Text of interview, 24 June 1950, MS2395/5.
79   Iain Hamilton interview with Arthur Koestler, 19 February 1974, pp. 3–7, MS2436/5; SOS,
     p.96; Koestler to Mr Eldridge, 5 July 1950, MS2395/3.
80   *Guardian*, 28 June and 10 July 1950; *New Statesman*, 15 July 1950: see MS2396/3 for further press
     reports.
81   Mamaine's diary, 1–2 July 1950, LWK, pp.147–8 and Koestler's Berlin diary, MS2306/4.
82   Coleman, *The Liberal Conspiracy*, pp.33–5.
83   Koestler to Burnham, 2 July 1950; Koestler to Lasky, 4 July 1950, MS2395/3; Mamaine's diary,
     26 July 1950, WK, p.149; Koestler to *New York Herald Tribune*, 27 July 1950, MS2395/3.
84   For the abridged text, see TOD, pp.196–203. For the many drafts and the final pamphlet, see
     MS2395/4. Koestler to Lasky, 25 July 1950, MS2395/3.
85   Mamaine's diary, 27 July, 2, 10, 14 and 16 August 1950, LWK, pp.149, 150–1, 152, 153, 154;
     papers for CCF executive meeting, Paris, 5 August 1950, MS2395/5; Koestler to Brown, 7
     August 1950, MS2395/3.
86   Koestler to Bondy and to Sperber, 18 August 1950, MS2395/3; Mamaine's diary, 17 August
     1950, LWK, pp.153–4.
87   Koestler to Burnham and Brown, 3 and 18 August 1950; Burnham to Koestler, 2 September
     1950; Koestler to Bondy, 9, 13, 16 September 1950, MS2395/3; DN, 7 October 1950, MS2305;
     Koestler to Sperber, 21 September 1950, MS2395/3.
88   SOS, p.97; Iain Hamilton interview with Arthur Koestler, 19 February 1974, pp. 3–7,
     MS2406/5; Spender, *The Thirties and After*, pp.161–3; Nicholas Nabokov, *Bagazh: Memoirs of a
     Russian Cosmopolitan* (London, 1975), pp.240–6; Coleman, *The Liberal Conspiracy*, pp. 219–34.
89   Bob Joyce CV, MS2394/1; 16 April 1951, USA diary 1951, MS2306/4. See also a reference to
     similar information vouchsafed by Norris Chipman, DN, 29 February 1954, MS2305. See
     Coleman, *The Liberal Conspiracy*, pp.220–1. On the wider role of Wisner, Thayer and Bohlen,
     see Trevor Barnes, 'The Secret Cold War: The CIA and American Foreign Policy in Europe',
     Pts 1 and 2, *Historical Journal*, 24:2 (1981), pp.399–415 and 25:3 (1982), pp.649–70 and
     Christopher Simpson, *Blowback: America's Recruitment of Nazis and Its Effects on the Cold War*
     (London, 1988).
90   Koestler to Father John Dittberner, 27 September 1972, MS2395/3; Iain Hamilton interview
     with Arthur Koestler, 19 February 1974, pp.3–7, MS2436/5; Koestler to Jay Lovestone, 29
     January 1951, MS2395/3.
91   Mamaine to Celia, 21 July 1950, LWK, pp.148–9; HA, July–August 1950, MS2304; Mamaine's
     diary, 27 and 30 July, 7 and 14 August 1950, LWK, pp.149–50, 151, 152–3; DN, 19[?] August
     1950, MS2305.
92   Mamaine's diary, 7, 8, 10 and 18 August 1950, LWK, pp.151–2, 154.
93   Mamaine's diary, 25 August to 3 October 1950, LWK, pp.155–8.
94   Ibid., 20 September 1950, LWK, p.161; Koestler to Mamaine, 9 September 1950, MS2303/3,
     telling her that he 'went back on the waggon [*sic*] the moment you left'.
95   Mamaine's diary, 18 September 1950, LWK, pp.159–60 and 16 April 1950, p.132.
96   Mamaine's diary, 18 September 1950, LWK, pp.159–60; DN, 7 October 1950, MS2305; Zita
     Crossman to Koestler, 20 September 1950; Dick Crossman to Koestler, nd, prob. 22 September

1950, MS2395/3; Strachey to Koestler, 28 October 1950, MS2377/3; Mamaine to Koestler, 8 December 1950, MS2303/3. See also, Howard, *Crossman*, pp.151–2.

97 See correspondence between Sidney Hook and Crossman, and between Hook and Koestler about the article, March–April 1951; Koestler to Hook, 5 April 1951, MS2377/2; Zita Crossman to Koestler, nd, 1952; Crossman to Koestler, 24 July 1952, MS2378/2.

98 DN, 11 April, 7 October 1950, MS2305; Koestler to Mamaine, 9 September 1950, MS2303/3; SOS, p.98.

99 HA, October 1950, MS2304; DN, 7 October 1950, MS2305; Koestler to Mamaine, 24 September, 1 and 4 October 1950, MS2303/3.

100 *New York Times*, 8 October 1950 (repr. TOD, pp.204–14).

101 DN, 7 October, 10–20 October 1950, MS2305; Koestler to Mamaine, 10 and 14 October 1950, MS2303/3.

102 Koestler to Greene, 21 September 1950, MS2395/3; Koestler to Mamaine, 10 and 14 October 1950, MS2303/3; DN, 7 October 1950, MS2305; on CCF party, see MS2395/3.

103 DN, 28 October 1950, MS2305; Koestler to Mamaine, 30 October 1950, MS2303/3.

104 SOS, p.98.

105 Mamaine to Koestler, 8 November 1950, MS2303/3.

106 Mamaine's diary, 6 February 1951, LWK, p.163. Mamaine to Koestler, 5 and 21 October, 8, 9, 15 November, 8 December 1950, MS2303/3.

107 DN, 1–11 November 1950, MS2305; Koestler to Mamaine, 5 December 1950, MS2303/3.

108 Koestler to Mamaine, 17 November and 6 December 1950, MS2303/3; Mamaine to Celia, 27 and 28 December 1950, LWK, pp.163–4.

109 Mamaine to Celia, 27 and 28 December 1950, 4 January 1951, LWK, pp.163–4.

110 Mamaine to Celia, 18 January 1951, LWK, p.169; DN, 8 January 1951, MS2305.

111 Mamaine to Celia, 30 January 1951, LWK, p.171.

112 Mamaine's diary, 6, 14 February 1951, LWK, p.172; Mamaine to Celia, 4, 18 January and 12 February 1951, LWK, pp.167, 172.

113 SOS, pp.102–3.

114 DN, 31 January 1951, MS2305; Mamaine's diary, 4 February 1951, LWK, p.174.

115 Koestler to Cynthia, 9 February 1951; Cynthia to Koestler, 13 February 1951; MS2303/1; SOS, pp.103, 108–11.

116 SOS, pp.111–12.

117 DN, 23 March 1951, MS2305; Mamaine's diary, 1 March 1951, LWK, p.174.

118 See Preface to the Danube Edition and SOS, pp.75–6.

119 *The Age of Longing* [AOL], pp.46, 158–9.

120 Ibid., pp.33–4, 97–8, 168–9.

121 Ibid., pp.174–6, 436–7.

122 Ibid., pp.171–4.

123 Ibid., pp.100–16 and *passim*.

124 SOS, p.76.

125 Mamaine to Koestler, 9 October 1950; Koestler to Mamaine, 14 October 1950, MS2303/3; Koestler to Malraux, 31 August 1951, MS2378/1.

126 *New Statesman*, 28 April 1951; *Jewish Chronicle*, 4 May 1951; *Tatler*, 18 April 1951; Collins to Koestler, 24 April 1951, MS2377/1.

127 Koestler to Mary Astor, 26 March 1951, MS2377/1; Koestler to Rougemont, to Jay Lovestone and to Bob Joyce, 29 January 1950; Koestler to Rougemont, 1 February 1951; Koestler to Nabokov, 30 July 1951, MS2395/3; Koestler to Burnham, 8 February 1951, MS2377/1; Koestler to Sperber, 25 April 1951, MS2377/3; Mamaine's diary, 14 February 1951, LWK, p.184. For the Waldorf meeting see MS2395/3; for Freedom House, see MS2396/2; for Humphrey see Kruger to Koestler, 5 June 1951, MS2395/3. There was no love lost between Koestler and Nabokov, see Nabokov, *Bagazh*, p.240.

128 SOS, pp.103–6.

129 Koestler to Mamaine, 12 November 1950, MS2303/3; Koestler to Einstein (about Milosz), 26 February 1951, MS2377/1 and Storm Jameson to Koestler, 16 March 1951, MS2377/3; Storm Jameson, *Autobiography*, pp.263–4.

130 Mamaine to Celia, nd, March 1951, LWK, pp.175–6; Koestler to Schulberg, 13 March 1951, MS2332/5; Koestler to Hook, 19 April 1951, MS2395/3.

131 Schulberg to Koestler, 8 November 1951, MS2377/1.

132 Bob Joyce CV, MS2394/1; Scout Master to Koestler, 29 March 1949, MS2375/3; DN, 3 November 1950, MS2305; Bertram Wolfe to Koestler, 19 January, February and 8 March 1951,

MS2377/1; 17 April 1951, Diary Notes 1951, MS2306/4. See Coleman, *The Liberal Conspiracy*, pp.220–1. On the wider role of Wisner, Thayer and Bohlen see Barnes, 'The Secret Cold War' and Simpson, *Blowback*.

133 See correspondence January 1951 to August 1951, with Bob Morris and Martin Richard (lawyers), Senator Lodge and Senator Brewster, MS2309/5. Mamaine to Celia, 4, 18 January and 25 March 1951, LWK, pp.166, 168, 177; Koestler to Brewster, 3 April 1951, MS2377/1; Koestler to Mamaine, 19 July 1951, MS2303/4.

134 DN, 16 and 17 April, 1951, MS2306/4.

135 SOS, pp.106–7, 115, 129–30.

136 Koestler to Mamaine, 4 October 1950, MS2303/3; DN, 31 January 1951, MS2305; Mamaine to Celia, 30 January 1951, LWK, p.168; Koestler to Mamaine, 30 and 31 July 1951, MS2303/4. See *New York Times*, 9 August 1951 and *Jewish Chronicle*, 31 August 1951. See Sidney Kingsley, *Darkness at Noon: A Play in Three Acts*, based on the novel by Arthur Koestler (New York, 1950). Claude Raines starred as Rubashov.

137 Mamaine to Celia, nd, March, 5 April 1951, LWK, pp.175–6, 179–80; Mamaine's diary, 25 March 1951, p.179; SOS, p.118.

138 Mamaine's diary, 11–16, April 1951, pp.182–4; Mamaine to Celia, 25 April 1951, LWK, p.185; Koestler to Dr Grant, 25 April 1951, MS2377/2.

139 Mamaine to Celia, 25 March, 5 April 1951, LWK, pp.178, 179–80; Mamaine's diary, 8 April 1951, p.181; 9 April 1951, Diary Notes 1951, MS2305/6.

140 SOS, pp.101–2. DN, 7 and 20 October, 9, 12 and 30 November 1950,

141 DN, 24 December 1950, 8 January, 26 February 1951, MS2305; SOS, p.100; Mamaine's diary,·2 and 8 April 1951, pp.179, 181.

142 Mamaine to Celia, 24 May 1951, LWK, p.188; notes, 7 April 1951, MS2308/4; Mamaine's diary, 29 April and 27 June 1951, pp.185–6; SOS, pp.112, 191–2, 117.

143 Mamaine's diary, 8, 14 July 1951, LWK, p.192; HA, 27 June–14 August 1951, MS2304; Koestler to Mamaine, 16 and 30 July 1951, MS2303/4; Koestler to Al Hart and to Budd Schulberg, 13 July 1951, MS2309/5; DN, 22 and 30 July 1951, MS2304.

144 Mamaine to Koestler, 18, 22 and 25 July 1951, MS2303/4.

145 Cynthia's account in SOS, pp.138–9; HA, 15–17 August 1951, MS2304; DN, 19 August 1951, MS2305.

146 DN, 19 August and 25 September 1951, MS2305.

147 Koestler to Mamaine, 20, 22 and 25 August 1951, MS2303/4; Koestler to Peters, 22 August 1951, MS2351/5.

148 Koestler to Peters, 29 August 1951; Koestler to Mamaine, 31 August 1951, MS2303/4; MS2303/4; HA, 18 August–14 September 1951, MS2304.

149 DN, 26 September 1951, MS2305.

150 Koestler to Bonsal, 5 September 1951 and Bonsal to Koestler, 13 September 1951, MS2309/5; Koestler to Mamaine, 7 September 1951, MS2303/4. See also correspondence in MS2344/5.

151 DN, 26 September, 11 October 1951, MS2305; HA, 22 September–23 November 1951, MS2304; Koestler to Mamaine, 5 and 14 October, 1, 7 and 21 November 1951, MS2303/4; Koestler to Cynthia, 10 December 1951, MS2303/1.

152 DN, 20, 21 October 1951, MS2305.

153 DN, 5, 11 November 1951, MS2305.

154 Paul Graetz to Koestler, 15 April 1951, MS2377/2; Koestler to Janine, 25 April 1951, MS2377/2; Janine to Koestler, 17 September and 3 November 1951, MS2377/4; Koestler to Jack Newsom, 8 September 1951, MS2344/6; HA, 1–2, 8–9, 14–15, 20–2 December 1951, MS2304; Koestler to Mamaine, 21 December 1951, MS2303/4.

155 Koestler to Mamaine, 10 and 21 December 1951, 27 January 1952; Mamaine to Koestler, 23 and 31 December 1951, 5 January 1952, MS2303/4.

156 HA, 1 December 1951–31 January 1952, MS2304; DN, 31 December 1951, 24 January 1952, MS2305; Koestler to Mamaine, 31 December 1951, MS2303/4.

157 Koestler to Mamaine, 27 January 1952, 24 February 1952, 8 March 1952, MS2303/4.

158 HA, 1 March–15 April 1952, MS2304; DN, 26 February 1952, MS2305; Koestler to Mamaine, 8 March 1952, MS2303/4.

159 DN, 17 March 1952, MS2305.

160 Charles Sawyer to Koestler, 2 October 1952, MS2377/1; Yale diary 1952, MS2306/4.

161 HA, 17 March–15 April 1952, MS2304; Koestler to Peters, 4 April 1952, MS2351/4.

CHAPTER 10: 'MY HAREM IS BEGINNING TO WEAR ME OUT', 1952–5

1   Koestler to Mamaine, 4 April 1952, MS2303/4; SOS, pp.149–50. Cynthia was living in a rented room in a house in Hans Place.
2   DN, 22 April, 6 May 1952, MS2305.
3   HA, 16 April–29 May 1952, MS2304; DN, 6 May 1952, MS2305.
4   In Koestler's Hermes Agenda on 4 May 1952 there is a scribbled, almost illegible entry: 'House hunting, Gill', MS2305. In his diary–notebook in the entry for 6 May 1952 there is a reference to seeing 'Gill' and Foot, MS2305.
5   Interview with Michael Foot and Jill Craigie, 1 August 1998. Due to attitudes towards women at the time, Craigie told no one, not even her husband, about the rape. She merely said that she had been in a terrible fight with Koestler. She waited nearly fifty years to tell the truth.
6   HA, 7–29 May 1952, MS2304; DN, 28 May, 6 June 1952, MS2305.
7   HA, 30 May–5 August 1952, MS2304; DN, 15, 21 June, 2 and 10 August 1952, MS2305.
8   DN, 21 June, 10 August 1952, MS2305; Koestler to Mamaine, 20 July 1952, MS2303/4.
9   HA, 8 August–19 October 1952, MS2304; DN, 21 September, 19 October 1952, MS2305; Christine to Koestler, 1 July 1952, Priscilla to Koestler, 12 July 1952; Connolly to Koestler, 11 September 1952, MS2378/2.
10 DN, 22 July 1954, MS2305, cited SOS, pp.192, 222.
11 See note 7 and DN, 16 September and 16 October 1952, MS2305.
12 HA, 20 October–1 November 1952, MS2304; DN, 19, 20 October 1952, MS2305.
13 Koestler to Rubinstein, 30 October and Rubinstein to Koestler, 3 November 1952, MS2332/5; Stephen Spender, 'Koestler's Story of his Fervent Quest for Utopia', *New York Times Book Review*, 21 September 1952 (repr. Murray Sperber (ed.), *Arthur Koestler*, pp.100–5; *New York Times*, 22 September 1952.
14 AIB, pp.15–22, 37–41.
15 Ibid., pp.29–30.
16 Ibid., pp.42–63.
17 Ibid., pp.65–73.
18 Ibid., pp.93–94.
19 Ibid., pp.107–46, 165–204.
20 Ibid., pp.248–56, 271–83, 286–91.
21 Ibid., pp.257–70.
22 Ibid., pp.295–340.
23 *The Fall of Dr Icarus: A play in 3 Acts*, MS2325/4; DN, 25 November–15 December 1952, 1–4 January, 16 March 1953, MS2305.
24 HA, 22–31 December 1952, MS2305; DN, 1, 4 January 1953, MS2305.
25 Koestler to Gould, 6 March 1953 and Gould to Koestler, 17 March and 1 April 1953, MS2332/5; Koestler to Eric Strauss, 8 March 1953, MS2379/1; DN, 16, 22 March 1953, MS2305.
26 Eugene Loebel (ed.), *Sentenced and Tried: The Stalinist Purges in Czechoslovakia* (London, 1969), esp. pp.151–8, and Karel Kaplan, *Report on the Murder of the General-Secretary*, trans. Karel Kovanda (Columbus, OH, 1990); DN, 26 November 1952, MS2305.
27 HA, 4–15 January 1953, MS2305; DN, 16, 22 March 1953, MS2305.
28 HA, 26 March–9 May 1953, MS2305; Koestler to Gross, to Franz Borkenau, 8 April 1953; Koestler to Gross, 17 April 1953, MS2379/1. See also 1953 correspondence with Sperber, Jupp Füllenbach and Babette Gross in MS2342/3.
29 DN, 25 April, 9 May 1953, MS2305.
30 DN, 1 January, 22 March, 30 April, 7 May and 18 October 1953, MS2305.
31 HA, 1 May–30 August 1953, MS2305; DN, 30 May, 14, 25, 27 June, 11 July, 25 August 1953, MS2305; Koestler to Margarete Buber-Neumann, 18 May and 1 July; to Babette Gross, 27 July; to Harold Nicolson and Lord Farringdon, 30 June; to Willy Forrest, 1 July 1953, MS2379/1; Mikes to Koestler, 27 July 1953, MS2378/3.
32 HA, 27, 28, 29 July 1953, MS2304; DN, 25 August 1953, MS2305; Cynthia to Koestler, 19 August 1953, MS2303/1; SOS, pp.150, 153, 159–60, 165, 170–1.
33 DN, 20 August 1953, MS2305.
34 DN, 18 September 1953, MS2305; Koestler to Jack Newsom, 18 October 1953, MS2344/6.
35 DN, 29 November, 19 December 1953, 3 January 1954, MS2305.
36 HA, 2 December 1953–1 January 1954, MS2305; DN, 29 November, 19, 25 and 16 December 1953, MS2305; Barbara Skelton, *Tears Before Bedtime and Weep No More* (London, 1993), p.75.

37   HA, 1–4 January 1953, MS2305; DN, 19 October, 26 December 1952, 5 February 1954,
     MS2305; Ayer, *More of My Life*, p.64; interview with Janetta Parladé, 29 April 1998.
38   Koestler to Henderson, 18 January 1954, MS2379/1; Henderson to Koestler, 29 January 1954,
     MS2379/2; Janetta to Koestler, 22 and 23 February 1954, MS2379/2; HA, 27 February 1954,
     MS2304; DN, 18 February, 18, 20, 21 March 1954, MS2305. Koestler to Henderson, 18 January
     1954, MS2379/1; interview with Janetta Parladé, 29 April 1998.
39   DN, 19 January 1954, MS2305.
40   HA, 14 March 1954, MS2304; DN, 6, 15, 27 March, 6 April 1954, MS2305; Koestler to Janetta,
     nd, March 1954, MS2379/1.
41   HA, 7–15 April, MS2304.
42   HA, 16–25 April, MS2304; DN, 27 April 1954, MS2305.
43   HA, 26 April–18 May 1954, MS2304.
44   Mamaine to Koestler, 27 September, 10 October, 14 November 1951, 17 January, 12 February,
     7 April, 29 September 1952, MS2303/4. Koestler to Mamaine, 14 October 1951, MS2303/4;
     DN, 21 May 1952, MS2305
45   HA, 2–7 June 1954, MS2304; Mamaine to Koestler, 27 and 30 April, 15 and 19 May 1954;
     Koestler to Mamaine, 14 October 1951, 30 April 1954, MS2303/4; DN, 1 and 6 April, 19 May
     1954, MS2305.
46   Celia's statement to Iain Hamilton, May 1974, MS2303/4 and LWK, p. 193. Dr Csato to
     Koestler, 22 February 1955, MS2380/1; interview with Janetta Parladé, 29 April 1998. He knew
     this and noted in his Hermes agenda, 3 September 1954: 'Entirely wrong impression at funeral.'
47   HA, 8 June–20 July 1954, MS2304; DN, 15 June, 20 and 22 July 1954, MS2305. Ischia
     novel–fragment, MS2342/5.
48   HA, 21–26 July 1954, MS2304; DN, 24 July 1954, MS2305.
49   HA, 17 July–17 August 1954, MS2304; DN, 24 and 29 July 1954, MS2305.
50   DN, 27 July, 4, 5, 7, 9, 11, 12 August 1954, MS2305.
51   HA, 12–31 August 1954, MS2304.
52   Koestler to Orwell, 24 September 1949, MS2376/3; DN, 14 May 1953, MS2305; Koestler to
     Mamaine, 19 May 1954, MS2304.
53   *New York Times Book Review*, 10 October 1954; *New Statesman*, 3 July 1954; *Sunday Times*, 2
     July 1954.
54   IW, pp.189–91, 428.
55   Ibid., pp.186–96.
56   Ibid., pp.348–58.
57   Ibid., p.19.
58   Ibid., pp.50–148, 198–212.
59   Ibid., p.33.
60   Ibid., p.235.
61   Ibid., p.251.
62   Ibid., pp.425–30.
63   Ibid., p.430.
64   HA, 1 September–5 October 1954, MS2304; DN, 6 and 21 September, 5 October, 7
     November 1954, MS2305. SOS, pp.194–5.
65   HA, 6–28 October 1954, MS2304; DN, 6/5, 22 and 29 October 1954, MS2305. The final, final
     rupture with Janetta came in late October because she had forgotten to keep an evening free for
     when he returned from a weekend out of town and 'who wants to come back from the country
     on a Sunday evening and be left alone?' So he made alternative arrangements and 'kicked her
     out'.
66   Senika Taskiranel to Koestler, 9 July 1954, nd, October and 13 October 1954; DN, 16 October
     1954, MS2305.
67   HA, 1 November–31 December 1954, MS2304; DN, 14, 28 November and 5 and 19
     December 1954, MS2305.
68   HA, 6–10 May, 30 August, 25 September–28 October 1954, 5 February, 30 July 1955, MS2304.
     DN, 2 August 1955, MS2305; June Pryce-Jones to Koestler, October 1954, MS2379/4 and to
     Koestler nd, 1954–5, MS2380/2; Janine to Koestler, 11 February 1955, MS2308/1; Janine to
     Koestler, 8 December 1954, MS2379/4. SOS, pp.194–5.
69   HA, 1 January–27 February 1955, MS2304; SOS, pp.155–6, 158, 189.
70   Interview with Elizabeth Jane Howard, 4 August 1998 and undated correspondence between
     Howard and Koestler concerning the abortion, MS2380/2.
71   Elizabeth Jane Howard, *After Julius* (London, 1994), pp.232–3.

72 HA, 1 November–31 December 1954, MS2304; DN, 5 and 24 October, 14 and 28 November, 19 December 1954, MS2305.
73 TOD, pp.vii–viii.
74 Ibid., pp.95–101.
75 Ibid., pp.142–7.
76 Ibid., pp.69–94.
77 Ibid., pp.106–41.
78 Koestler to Berlin, 16 and 25 November 1954, MS2379/1; Berlin to Koestler, 18 and 30 November 1954, MS2379/4.
79 TOD, pp.215–31.
80 Ibid., pp.232–53.
81 HA, 1 November–31 December 1954, MS2304; DN, 5 and 24 October, 14 and 28 November, 19 December 1954, MS2305.
82 Cynthia to Koestler, 1 September, 18 October 1955, 12 November 1953, 18 June 1954; Koestler to Cynthia, 2 and 18 January 1954, MS2303/1; SOS, pp.172–7.
83 Cynthia to Koestler, 30 November 1954, 5 January 1955; Koestler to Cynthia, 4 September, 20 October 1954 and 10 and 29 January and 11 February 1955, MS2303/1; SOS, p.193.

CHAPTER 11: HANGING AND SCIENCE, 1955–60

1   Preface to Danube Edition, of *Trail of the Dinosaur/Reflections on Hanging*, p.viii.
2   *Reflections on Hanging* [ROH], p.169; Koestler to President Eisenhower, 16 June 1953, MS2379/1; DN, 27 June 1953 and 14 July 1955, MS2305. See John Grigg, 'The Do-Gooder from Seville Gaol', in Harold Harris (ed.), *Astride The Two Cultures: Arthur Koestler at 70* (London, 1975) [hereafter ATC], pp.123–6, for the background.
3   Koestler to Cynthia, 14 July 1955, MS2303/1; SOS, p.193.
4   HA, 17 July 1955, MS2304; Koestler to Gollancz, 18 July 1955, MS2400/1; SOS, p.193. Edwards, *Victor Gollancz*, p.637.
5   C. H. Rolph, *Further Particulars* (London, 1987), pp.112–13; Edwards, *Victor Gollancz*, p.640.
6   Koestler to Gollancz, 13 August 1955, MS2400/1. For documents and minutes relating to Koestler's role in the NCACP, see MS2400/1. See also, Edwards, *Victor Gollancz*, p.368.
7   Edwards, *Victor Gollancz*, pp.368–9.
8   Koestler to Gardiner, nd, 1956; Edwards, *Victor Gollancz*, pp.369–70.
9   ROH, pp.175–206.
10 Ibid., pp.235–44.
11 Ibid., pp.245–51, 257–72.
12 Ibid., pp.284–5.
13 Ibid., pp.170, 287.
14 David Astor to Koestler, 11 November 1955, MS2400/1; SOS, p.210; Edwards, *Gollancz*, p.340.
15 Astor to Koestler, 28 October 1955; Priestley to Astor, 18 November 1955; Koestler to Gollancz and to Woodrow Wyatt, 27 November 1955; Koestler to Priestley, 3 December 1955; Priestley to Koestler, 5 December 1955; Koestler to Astor, 5 December 1955, MS2400/1.
16 Koestler to Astor, 31 December 1955; Koestler to Ken Oban, *Observer*, 8 January 1956; Koestler to Astor, 25 January 1956; and general correspondence, MS2400/1; SOS, pp.214–15, 217–20; ROH, p.274.
17 Astor to Koestler, 17 February and 10 March 1956, MS2400/1.
18 Koestler to Astor, 30 January; and to Gollancz, 24 February 1956; Minutes of NCACP executive meeting, 21 February 1956, MS2400/1; Edwards, *Victor Gollancz*, p.643.
19 Koestler to Gollancz, 14 March and Gollancz to Koestler, 16 March 1956, MS2400/1; Grigg, 'The Do-Gooder from Seville Gaol', in ATC, pp.128–9; Edwards, *Victor Gollancz*, p.644.
20 Koestler to Duff, 7 April 1956; Koestler to Astor, 9 April 1956; Duff to Koestler, 18 April 1956; Koestler to Astor, 9 July 1956; Koestler to Gardiner, 27 July 1956; minutes of NCACP executive meeting, 1956, 1958, MS2400/1.
21 Rolph, *Further Particulars*, pp.149–53; Grigg, 'The Do-Gooder from Seville Gaol', in ATC, p.130. For correspondence and papers connected with the Koestler Award, see MS2409 and 2410.
22 Jascha Weinshall to Koestler, 24 May 1960, MS283/4; Cynthia's diary [CD], 28 May 1961, MS2305; Koestler to Prof. Sommerlet, 20 April 1961, MS2384/1.
23 Koestler to Gollancz, 12 April and 28 December 1961 and 5 January 1962, and to Gardiner, 27

December 1961; Gardiner to Koestler, 20 April 1961, MS2384/2; Gollancz to Koestler, 4 January 1962, MS2402/1; CD, 2 January 1962, MS2305; Edwards, *Victor Gollancz*, pp.690–1.

24   Cynthia to Koestler, 2 September 1955, MS2303/1; SOS, pp.196–200, 201–2.

25   Koestler to Mikes, 6 September 1955, MS2380/3; DN, 20 October 1955, MS2305; SOS, pp.202, 205–10.

26   Koestler to Cynthia, 3 October and 10 November 1955, and to Al Hart, 10 November 1955; Cynthia to Koestler, 5, 14 and 24 October, 7 November 1955, MS2303/1; HA, 12–20 November 1955, MS2304; SOS, pp.211–12.

27   DN, January 1956, MS2305. He was found not guilty of a drink-driving offence on 18 January 1956. SOS, pp.212–15.

28   Reprinted in *Drinkers of Infinity: Essays 1955–1967* [DOI], pp.49–52, 53–57.

29   Anthony Lousada to Koestler, 28 March 1956, MS2381/1; Koestler to Janine, 2 June 1956, MS2380/3; Koestler to Eva (Zeisel), 18 October 1975, MS2390/1; HA, 16 and 29 March 1956, MS2304; SOS, p.219.

30   *The Lotus and the Robot* [LAR], p.168.

31   SOS, pp.221–2.

32   Young to Koestler, 10 January 1956, MS2380/3; SOS, pp.223.

33   SOS, pp.223–9.

34   HA, 4 July 1955, MS2304; Koestler to Moura Budberg, 7 August 1956, MS2380/3; Cynthia Koestler, 'Twenty-five Writing Years', in ATC, pp.138–40; Frances Partridge, *Everything to Lose: Diaries 1945–1960* (London, 1985), 13 August 1956, pp.256–7.

35   HA, 29 October 1956, MS2304; Koestler to Buber-Neumann, 20 November 1956 and to Storm Jameson, 6 December 1956; Cynthia to Lorna St Aubyn, 30 November 1956, MS2380/3.

36   Peter Sugar, Peter Hannak and Tibor Frank (eds), *A History of Hungary* (London, 1990).

37   Koestler to Harold Nicolson, 15 November 1956, MS2380/2; Koestler to Sevenoaks Refugee Committee, 24 November 1956, MS2381/1; Koestler to Storm Jameson, 1 December 1956, MS2380/3; Mikes to Koestler, 1 January 1958, MS2382/3; Mikes, *Arthur Koestler*, pp.17–20.

38   HA, 23–31 December 1956, MS2304; Golding to Koestler, 14 October 1956, MS2381/3 and 24 February 1957, MS2381/2. See DN, 4 November 1958, MS2306.

39   Atkins, *Arthur Koestler*; Koestler to Atkins, 11 September 1956, MS2380/3. In America the book was attacked in the left-wing press for 'whitewashing' Koestler's involvement with the State Department. See Atkins to Koestler 28 May 1957, MS2381/3.

40   See for example his paper 'Artist on a Tightrope' delivered in Calcutta, February 1959, repr. DOI, pp.32–8.

41   Bergonzi, *Wartime and Aftermath*, pp.81–101, 111–33; Robert Hewison, *In Anger: Culture in the Cold War 1945–60* (London, 1981), pp.24–36, 85–98.

42   Koestler to Mr James, 6 February 1957, MS2382/1 and messages of congratulations, MS2381/3.

43   *Observer*, 11 August 1957, repr. DOI, pp.125–34; SOS, p.228.

44   Correspondence, MS2382/1; Dr Alexander Auer CV and speech by Fritz Molden at Europe House, London, 30 March 1960, MS2383/4.

45   See HA, 1957, MS2304. Cynthia to Lorna St Aubyn, 25 August and 12 December 1957, MS2382/1.

46   Koestler to Lorna St Aubyn, 3 February 1958 and Cynthia to St Aubyn, 28 February 1958, MS2383/1; Herbert Butterfield to Koestler, 2 February 1958 and Koestler to Butterfield 28 February 1958, MS2382/3; correspondence and arrangements for Vienna lecture, 23 February–1 March 1958, MS2382/4.

47   Koestler to Butterfield, 16 June 1958, MS2383/1; Butterfield to Koestler, 8 August and 14 October 1958, MS2382/4; Koestler to Peters, 19 August 1948, MS2352/2.

48   *The Sleepwalkers* [SW], pp.9–12.

49   Ibid., pp.26–105.

50   Ibid., pp. 125–56, 194–222.

51   Ibid., pp.229–47, DH, 2 March 1955, MS2305.

52   SW, pp.257–67, 289–339.

53   Ibid., pp.431–503.

54   Ibid., p.550.

55   Ibid., pp.523–53.

56   Correspondence, May 1958, MS2383/1.

57   HA, 24 June to 18 September 1958, MS2304; Koestler to Joshi, 6 September 1958, MS2383/1; Koestler to Bronowski, 25 September 1958, MS2382/4.

58   See notes on trip to India and Japan, 30 December 1958–28 March 1959, MS2306/2.

59 Koestler to Cynthia, 11 January 1959, MS2303/1.
60 Notes on trip to India and Japan, 30 December 1958–28 March 1959, MS2306/2.
61 LAR, pp.15–80.
62 Ibid., pp.101–30; Koestler to Cynthia, 11 January 1959, MS2303/1.
63 Ibid., pp.145–50, 155–62.
64 Koestler to Cynthia, 17 February 1959, MS2303/1; LAR, p.162.
65 Koestler to Cynthia, 3 March 1959, MS2303/1. Coleman, *The Liberal Conspiracy*, p.187.
66 Notes on trip to India and Japan, 30 December 1958–28 March 1959, MS2306/2; Koestler to
   Maugham, 18 November 1960, MS2383/5.
67 Quentin Crewe, *Well, I forget the rest* (London, 1991), pp.143–5.
68 LAR, pp.227–75.
69 Ibid., pp.174–225.
70 Ibid., pp.205–12, 274.
71 Cynthia to Koestler, 30 December 1957, 12 and 25 January, 2 and 8 February, 1 and 7 March
   1959, MS2303/1.
72 *Observer*, 25 January 1959; *The Times*, 29 January 1959; *Time*, May 1959; *New York Times*, 19
   May 1959.
73 See *Observer*, 26 April, 3, 10, 24 and 31 May 1959. Koestler to Maugham, 18 November 1960,
   MS2383/5; Koestler to Frau Lena, 8 May 1959, MS2382/2; HA, 2 July–22 September 1959,
   MS2304; Janine to Koestler, 12 and 13 June 1959, MS2383/3; 1959, MS2383/2. On the
   building of the house, see MS2309/1. SOS, p.195.
74 *Observer*, 16 August 1959, repr. DOI, pp.69–101.
75 See DOI, pp.112–14. Koestler to Elwin Verrier, 14 October 1959 and to Roger St Aubyn, 23
   September, MS2382/2.
76 Zdanek Kopal to Koestler, 29 October 1959, MS2383/2.
77 *Observer*, 18 October 1959, repr. TOD, pp.135–40.
78 HA, 24–30 December 1959, MS2304; Cynthia Koestler, 'Twenty-five Writing Years', in ATC,
   pp.140–1.
79 Broadcast 25 February 1960, repr. DOI, pp.39–45.
80 HA, 1–31 January 1960, MS2304. See also New Year reflections, 4 January 1961, DN MS2305.
   Koestler and Cynthia took short breaks in Cornwall in April and May: HA, 16–18 April, 5–9
   May 1960, MS2304.
81 HA, 11–24 May 1960, MS2304; Koestler to Cynthia, 14 May 1960, MS2303/1; 'Love Affair
   with Norway', *Observer*, 26 June and 3 July 1960, repr. DOI, pp.115–24.
82 'Culture in Explosion', International Symposium on Art in Modern Society, Vienna Festival,
   repr. DOI, pp.103–11.
83 HA, 30 June–3 October 1960, MS2304; *Observer*, diary, 1952.
84 Koestler to Joan Henry, 6 August 1960, MS2383/4.
85 HA, 3–7 October 1960, MS2304; CD, 16 March 1961, MS2305.
86 Repr. DOI, pp.87–95.

CHAPTER 12: THE ALPBACH YEARS, 1960–7

1 Leary to Koestler, 27 November and 4 December 1959; Koestler to Leary, 2 December 1960,
   MS2383/2; Leary to Koestler, 8 March 1960, MS2383/4. Timothy Leary, *Flashbacks: An
   Autobiography* (London, 1983), pp.56–7.
2 Ibid., pp.59–60.
3 'Mystical Hallucinations . . .', *Sunday Telegraph*, 12 March 1961, repr. DOI, pp.201–12.
4 For useful summaries, see Richard L. Gregory, *The Oxford Companion to the Mind* (Oxford,
   1987).
5 See Kathleen Nott, 'The Trojan Horse: Koestler and the Behaviourists', in ATC, pp.162–74.
6 *Observer*, 23, 30 April and 7 May 1961; repr. DOI, pp.213–34.
7 Prof. John Cohen to Koestler, 21 April 1961, MS2384/2.
8 DN, 4 January 1961, MS2305; CD, 24 April–3 May 1961, MS2305.
9 CD, 24 June 1961, MS2305.
10 Ibid., 28 June–15 July 1961, MS2305; Koestler to Janetta, 8 June 1961, MS2383/5; Janetta to
   Koestler, 11 June 1961, MS2384/2; CD, 16–26 July 1961, MS2305. Frances Partridge, *Hanging
   On: Diaries 1960–1963* (London, 1990), 28 July 1961, p.63; interview with Janetta Parladé, 29
   April 1998.

11   Partridge, *Hanging On*, 6 August 1961, pp.65–6. The village priest was a regular visitor to the
     Schreiberhäusl and actually blessed it shortly after construction was completed.

12   CD, 28 May, 3 June 1961, MS2305. Janetta Parladé recalled that 'He used to run the Germans
     down' saying 'they can't do without their sausage.'

13   CD, 16 March, 3 August 1961, MS2305.

14   Ibid., 12–22 August 1961, MS2305.

15   Ibid., 22 August–12 September 1961, MS2305.

16   Ibid., 12–17 September 1961, MS2305.

17   Buber-Neumann to Koestler, 12 September 1961, MS2384/2; Partridge, *Hanging On*, 7 August
     1961, p.66.

18   Myers, *Edmund Wilson*, p.284; SOS, p.222.

19   Arthur Koestler, 'Motivation: A Biased Review', in C. Banks and P. L. Broadhurst (eds),
     Stephanos (London, 1965), pp.39–54; L. S. Hearnshaw, *Cyril Burt: Psychologist* (London, 1979),
     pp.203–4, 221–6.

20   CD, 28 September, 18 November and 1 December 1961, MS2305.

21   CD, 13 October–19 December 1961, MS2305; Klemperer had been a guest at Montpelier
     Square the previous April, an evening which turned out to be euphoric, squalid and chaotic,
     CD, 5 April 1961, MS2305. See Peter Heyworth, *Otto Klemperer, his life and times*, Vol.2,
     1933–73 (London, 1996), p.281. Interestingly, Klemperer suggested that Koestler write a libretto
     for an opera based on the life of Anne Frank. Peter Croissant to Koestler, 10 and 22 January
     1962, MS2384/3; Koestler to Mr Croissant, 19 January 1962, MS2384/4.

22   See *Sunday Telegraph*, 24 December 1961.

23   *Observer*, 1 and 22 April 1962, repr. DOI, pp.58–73.

24   CD, 9–17, April 1962, MS2305; Astor to Koestler, 18 April 1962, MS2384/3. See
     correspondence and material in MS2404/2–3 and MS2405/4; *Independent*, 7 June 1997.

25   CD, 13–20 May 1962, MS2305.

26   Ibid., 21 May–12 September 1962, MS2305; HA, 6 August 1962, MS2304.

27   CD, 12 September–20 October 1962, MS2305.

28   Ibid., 25 October and 4–6 September 1962, and 30 January 1963, MS2305.

29   Ibid., 22–29 November and 25 December 1962, MS2305.

30   DN, 15 December 1952, MS2305; Crosland to Koestler, nd (prob. November) 1958,
     MS2382/4.

31   HA, 10 May 1962, MS2304; CD, 25 December 1962, MS2305.

32   *Observer*, 10 February 1963, repr. DOI, pp.74–83; CD, 19–23, 27 January 1963, MS2305.

33   CD, 24 January–26 February 1963, MS2305.

34   Ibid., 10 March, 13–18 May, 4 June 1963, MS2305.

35   Ibid., 14–18 June 1963, MS2305; Koestler to Strachey, 24 July and Brandt to Koestler, 19
     August 1963, MS2384/5.

36   *Observer*, 2 February 1964, repr. DOI, pp.18–31; CD, 18 August–18 December 1963, MS2305.

37   CD, 4 and 22 March 1963, MS2305; Christmas party list, 1963, MS2384/5. He had first met
     Gellner in March and was discomfited to find that one so wise was so young. Soon after, he
     effected a reconciliation with Ayer, another philosopher.

38   CD, 19 February 1964, MS2305.

39   *The Listener*, 14, 21, 28 May 1964; CD, 24 February–10 March, 16 March–1 April 1964,
     MS2305. He named the boat *Socrates*.

40   See positive reviews by Cyril Connolly, *Sunday Times*, 31 May 1964; Brian Inglis, *Guardian*, 29
     May 1964; Kathleen Nott, *Observer*, 24 May 1964; and negative ones by John Maynard Smith,
     Listener, 28 May 1964; Peter Medawar, *New Statesman*, 19 June 1964.

41   CD, 26–28 May 1964, MS2305.

42   Ibid., 22 January, 24, 25 May 1964, MS2305.

43   Koestler to Peters, 27 January, Lusty to Peters, 27 April, Peters to Lusty, 21 May, Lusty to
     Peters, 22 May, Koestler to Lusty, 22 May 1964; Peters to Lusty, 22 May, Peters to Lusty, 26
     May 1964, MS2354.

44   CD, 2 June–23 July 1964, MS2305.

45   Ibid., 23 July–30 August 1964, MS2305.

46   Ibid., 2 September 1964, MS2305.

47   Ibid., 21 November 1964, MS2305; Koestler to Burnham, 25 November 1964, MS2385/1; DN,
     19 December 1964, MS2305.

48   Marriage Certificate, MS2308/2.

49   Koestler to Cynthia, 31 January 1965 and nd (January 1965), MS2303/1; CD, 4 and 11 March, 9

April, 4, 14 and 18 May 1965, MS2305.
50   CD, 29 March, 27 April 1965, MS2305.
51   Ibid., 14 and 24 May, 12 June 1965, MS2305.
52   'Biological and Mental Evolution: an Exercise in Analogy', repr. DOI, pp.261–74.
53   CD, 6 April and 24 May 1965; 4 and 6 May and 11 June 1965; 13 March, 20–22 March, 2–3 June 1965, MS2305; 'The Daemon of Socrates', repr. DOI, pp.235–47.
54   Burnham to Koestler, 23 July 1965 and Morris to Koestler, 27 June 1965, MS2385/2. CD, 20 May–18 June 1965, MS2305.
55   CD, 20 June–20 July 1965, MS2305.
56   'Evolution and Revolution', repr. DOI, pp.248–60.
57   'Biological and Mental Evolution: An Exercise on Analogy', in *Knowledge Among Men: Eleven Essays on Science, Culture and Society* (New York, 1966), repr. DOI, pp.261–74.
58   HA, 5 and 7 September 1965, MS2304. For the unedited version, see MS2440/1.
59   DN, 8 March 1966, MS2305; Koestler to Louis Fischer, 18 June 1966, MS2385/3; *Sunday Times*, 14 November 1965; *New Scientist*, 29 December 1966, repr. DOI, pp.166–77.
60   DN, 6 April 1967, MS2305; *Daily Mail, Evening News*, 18 March 1967; *The Times*, 22, 25, 28, 31 March 1967.
61   Alan McGlashan to Koestler, 30 August 1967, MS2385/5.
62   *The Ghost in the Machine* [GIM], pp.xi–xiv.
63   Ibid., pp.3–18, 19–41.
64   Ibid., pp.45–51.
65   Ibid., pp.115–26, 129–48, 152–3.
66   Ibid., pp.166–70.
67   Ibid., pp.177–90.
68   Ibid., pp.299–312.
69   Ibid., pp.225–92.
70   Ibid., pp.313–36.
71   *The Times*, 15 October 1967; *New York Times Book Review*, 7 April 1968; *Spectator*, 27 October 1967; *New Statesman*, 27 October 1967.
72   Koestler to Peters, 12 November 1963, MS2352/4; Koestler to Weinshall, 9 September 1964, MS2385/1.
73   Koestler to Abraham Weinshall, 24 September 1963, MS2384/5; to Mala Rossoff, 6 November 1963 and to Eliahu Elath, 17 July 1965; Koestler to Weinshall, 21 January 1966; Koestler to Weinshall, 12 September 1964, MS2402/4; Kollek to Koestler, 7 April and Koestler to Kollek, 22 April 1966, MS2402/4.
74   *Jewish Chronicle*, 11 March 1983; Weinshall to Koestler, 27 June 1967; Koestler to Weinshall, 8 August 1967, MS2402/4.
75   Louis Golding to Koestler, 12 March 1956, MS2381/1.
76   Waugh to Mitford, 28 January 1946, *Letters of Evelyn Waugh*, ed. Mark Amory (London, 1980), p.220; Koestler to Green, 9 February 1960, MS2383/5; DN, March 1966, MS2305.

CHAPTER 13: *'RECULER POUR MIEUX SAUTER'*, 1967–76

1   CD, 19 November, MS2305.
2   Prof. Fog to Koestler, 12 January and Koestler to Fog, 18 January 1968, MS2308/2. For 'The Urge to Self-Destruction' see *The Heel of Achilles* [HOA], pp.11–25.
3   For the planning, see MS2395/2. The results were published in a volume edited by Koestler and R. J. Smythies, *Beyond Reductionism: New Perspectives on the Life Sciences* (London, 1969) [BR]. The participants were: Professor Ludwig von Bertalanffy (SUNY), Professor Jerome Bruner (Director, Center for Cognitive Studies, Harvard University), Professor Viktor Frankl (psychiatry, University of Vienna), Professor F. A. von Hayek (economist, Freiburg University), Professor Holger Hyden (neurobiologist, Gothenburg University), Professor Bärbel Inhelder (developmental psychologist, Geneva University), Professor Seymour Kety (psychiatry, Harvard), Paul D. MacLean (Head of Laboratory of Brain Evolution and Behavior, NIMH, Bethesda, Maryland), Professor David McNeill (psychology, Chicago University), Professor Jean Piaget (psychology, Geneva University), Professor J. R. Smythies (psychiatry, Edinburgh University), Dr W. H. Thorpe (zoologist, Cambridge University), Professor C. H. Waddington (genetics, Edinburgh University), Professor Paul Weiss (Rockefeller University, New York).
4   See BR and correspondence in MS2395/2.

5   BR, pp. 1–2. See this volume for all the papers and discussions.

6   Ibid., pp.192–224.

7   Ibid., pp.346–53, 355.

8   Ibid., pp.382–8.

9   Unfortunately Cynthia's diary does not cover this period, but see the comments, 30 December 1971, MS2305, and *The Call Girls* [CG].

10 *The Ethics of Change: A Symposium* (CBC, 1969). The other participants were René Dubois, Martin Myerson and Northrop Frye.

11 Dennis Gabor to Koestler, 5 June and Koestler to Gabor, 17 June 1968, MS2386/1; HA, 24 May and 30 June 1968, MS2304. The paper was printed in *The Political Quarterly*, October–December 1969 and repr. HOA, pp.26–37.

12 Crawford Productions to Koestler, 8 October 1968, MS2411/1. For details of the trip, see MS2411/1.

13 *Sydney Sun*, 21 November 1968; undated memo from Barry Jones to Koestler, November 1968; press release, Victorian Section of Amnesty International, nd; Barry Jones, *On Arthur Koestler, Amnesty International and Communications Failure*, 26 November 1968, MS2411/1.

14 See itineraries, MS2411/1; *Melbourne Age* and *The Australian*, front page, 25 November 1968.

15 *Sydney Morning Herald*, 26 November 1968; *Australian*, 27 November 1968; *Melbourne Age*, 23 November and 4 December 1968; *The Australian*, 14 December 1968.

16 B. A. Santamaria, *Australia at the Crossroads* (Melbourne, 1987), pp.236–7; Rosemary Jones to Koestler, 3 December 1968, MS2411/1. I am grateful to Professor Louis Waller for bringing the Santamaria reference to my attention.

17 The story also appeared in *Encounter*, 31 (December 1968). *Melbourne Age*, 24, 26, 27 December 1968 and 3 January 1969.

18 See 'The Faceless Continent', *Sunday Times*, 25 May 1969, repr. HOA, pp.163–72.

19 'Farewell to Gauguin', *Sunday Times*, 13 April 1969, repr. HOA, pp.163–72. For angry correspondence, see MS2386/4.

20 DN, 26 February and 2 May 1969, MS2305; Cynthia Koestler, 'Twenty-Five Writing Years', ATC, pp.144–5.

21 DN, 1–25 July 1971, MS2305 and MS2386/3. They no longer drove to Alpbach. Instead, his Oldsmobile was garaged in Austria and they travelled there by train: Koestler to Julius Hay, 6 February 1971, MS2387.

22 Lessing to Koestler, 14 March and Steiner to Koestler, 24 August 1969; note of guests, 30 October 1969, MS2386/3.

23 See HOA, pp.28–44, 117–32.

24 DN, 19 December 1969, MS2305; Cynthia Koestler, 'Twenty-Five Writing Years', ATC, p.145.

25 *The Case of the Midwife Toad* [CMT], pp.14–27, 49–121.

26 Koestler to Inglis, 22 January 1970, MS2386/5. See CMT, pp.18–26.

27 CMT, pp.128–32; Cynthia Koestler, 'Twenty-Five Writing Years', ATC, pp.145–6.

28 See MS2386/5; interview in *L'Express*, 30 August 1970.

29 *The Roots of Coincidence* [ROC], p.11.

30 Ibid., pp.53–81.

31 Ibid., pp.85–101.

32 Ibid., pp.86, 108–14.

33 Ibid., pp.127–33.

34 DN, August 1971, MS2305; Koestler to von Weisl, 25 July 1973, MS2388/3; Koestler to Bob Joyce, 21 June 1971, MS2387/2; CD, 30 and 31 August 1971, MS2305. They had holidayed in Switzerland earlier in the year rather than in Austria.

35 CD, 2–3, 4, 5–8 September 1971, MS2305.

36 *Sunday Times Magazine*, 20 September 1971; *Sunday Times*, 3 October 1971; *Jewish Chronicle*, 8 October 1971.

37 CD, 19 September–1 October 1971, MS2305. For transcript, see *The Listener*, 1 July 1971, repr. HOA, pp.151–9.

38 Hoban to Koestler, 14 November 1971, MS2387/3.

39 CD, 6–9, 10–30 October, 30 October–2 November 1971, MS2305.

40 *Sydney Morning Herald*, 27 November 1968; CD, 5, 9–12 November 1971, MS2305.

41 CD, 18–25 November, 1 December 1971, MS2305.

42 Ibid., 1 December 1971, MS2305.

43 Ibid., 28, 30 December 1971 and 1 January 1972, MS2305.

44 Ibid., 30 December 1971; 29–31 September 1972, MS2305.
45 Janine to Koestler, nd, 1970 and Koestler to Janine, nd, 1970, MS2386/5.
46 Janine to Christine, 1 October 1972 and Koestler to Janine, with enclosure to Christine, 2 October 1972, MS2387/4; CD, 7–9 September, 1 October 1972, MS2387/4.
47 Letters from Plomer, Hamilton, Fairbanks, Bernstein, 7 January 1972 and correspondence in MS2387/4. He also received a letter of congratulations from Mark Carlisle, MP, the Minister of State at the Home Office responsible for prisons, 18 January 1972, MS2387/4.
48 CD, 12 January–25 April 1972, MS2305.
49 *The Times*, 7 and 10 February 1972; *Observer*, 6 February 1972; *New Statesman*, 11 February 1972.
50 Brian Inglis, *The Unknown Guest: The Mystery of Intuition* (London, 1987), pp.9–10.
51 CG, pp.25–9, 42–5.
52 Ibid., pp.30, 40–1, 46–54.
53 Ibid., pp.84–158, 161–81.
54 CD, 27 April, 5 May–20 July 1972, MS2305.
55 See MS2411/2 and *Sunday Times*, 2 July, 3 September 1972, repr. HOA, pp.195–217.
56 David Pryce-Jones, 'Chess Man', *Encounter*, July–August 1983, pp. 25–8.
57 CD, 6 July–11 August, 14–19 August, 22–8 August, 2–6 September 1972, MS2305; 'Science and Parascience', printed in HOA, pp.133–47.
58 'Science and Reality', printed in HOA, pp.148–50.
59 'Marrakesh', *Sunday Times*, 8 September 1972, repr. HOA, pp.183–94; CD, 3 November 1971, MS2305.
60 For tribute, see *Sunday Times*, 4 February 1973, repr. HOA, pp.111–14.
61 *The Times*, 16 October 1972; *Guardian*, 19 October 1972; *New York Times*, 3 April 1973.
62 *The Challenge of Chance* [COC], pp.24–118.
63 Ibid., pp.227–75.
64 CD, 10–12 September, 2 November 1972, MS2387/4; Cynthia Koestler, 'Twenty-Five Writing Years', ATC, pp.144–8; CD, 1972.
65 CD, 15–24 March 1973, MS2305; *Sunday Times*, 17 August 1973, repr. as 'A Sentimental Pilgrimage' in *Kaleidoscope*, pp.285–305. For associated correspondence, see MS2388/3.
66 Berlin to Koestler, 18 April 1973, MS2388/3; HA, 13, 27 and 28 June 1973, MS2304. The address was published as *The Lion and the Ostrich* (London, 1973) and reprinted as 'Going Native' in *Kaleidoscope*, pp.273–84.
67 The text can also be found in *Bricks to Babel* (London, 1980), pp.326–42. *New Statesman*, 4 May 1973; *Observer*, 3 June 1973; repr. HOA, pp.102–10.
68 *Sunday Times*, 25 November 1973 ('Beyond our Understanding') and 5 May 1974 ('The Mysterious Power of Chance'); Amis to Koestler, 5 May 1974, MS2389/1; DN, 25 August 1974, MS2305; John Beloff, *Parapsychology: A Concise History* (London, 1993), pp.219–20.
69 CD, 1–17 November 1973, MS2305.
70 DN, 5 February 1974, MS2305; Lord Butler to Koestler, 15 February and Koestler to Butler, 26 February 1974, MS2389/1; Amicale des anciens internes du camp de Vernet-d'Ariège to Koestler, 20 March 1973, MS2389/1.
71 DN, 24 August 1974, MS2305.
72 CD, 31 October 1973, MS2305; von Weisl to Koestler, 22 July 1973, MS2388/3; John Grigg to Cynthia, 16 September 1974, MS2389/1.
73 Hamilton to Koestler, 21 September 1973, 23 January and 15 February, 4 May, 11 October 1974; Koestler to Hamilton, 24 October 1974, MS2370/2; Rosenthal to Hamilton, 27 January 1975, MS2370/2.
74 See ATC, *L'Herne*; George Steiner, 'Koestler's Quest', *Sunday Times*, 31 August 1975.
75 For operation on 30 January 1976, see medical records, MS2390/2.
76 HA, 21 May 1968, MS2305; DN, 13 February 1969, 16 December 1971, 29 July 1972, 15 June and 17 September 1975, MS2305; Secretary of the Euthanasia Society to Koestler, 1 May 1969, MS2409/1; Julian Barnes, 'Playing Chess with Arthur Koestler', *Observer Review*, 3 July 1988.
77 Correspondence with Eye Hospital, 11 July 1973, MS2388/3 and HA, 16–25 July 1973, MS2304; Koestler to Rebecca West, 17 August 1975. MS2390/1.
78 International Council of Societies of Industrial Design to Koestler, 16 March 1973; Sir Paul Reilly to Koestler, 3 September 1973, MS2412/4.
79 Cynthia to Eva Zeisel, 30 January 1976, MS2390/2; Koestler to Dr Freedman, 28 April 1976, MS2390/2; medical correspondence, 15 April and 19 May 1976, MS2307/1; 'Life After Death', in Arnold Toynbee and Arthur Koestler (eds), *Life After Death* (London, 1976), repr. *Kaleidoscope*, pp.313–38.

80 DN, July 1972, MS2305; HA, 1 February 1974, MS2304; Grigg to Koestler, 17 March 1977, MS2390/5; Koestler to Tugendhat, 9 September 1975, MS2390/1; Conservative Party membership correspondence, 1976, MS2390/2; Celia Goodman to Peg Hessen, 4 March 1979, in possession of Celia Goodman; Prime Minister to Koestler, 12 May 1980; Thomas to Koestler, 17 September 1982; Koestler to Thomas, 20 September 1982, MS2392/4; Margaret Thatcher, *The Path to Power* (London, 1995), pp.57–8.

81 Barnes, 'Playing Chess with Arthur Koestler'.

82 Menachem Begin to Koestler, 2 July 1970 and Koestler to Begin, 22 July 1970, MS2386/5. In the early 1950s Koestler had toyed with a sequel to *Thieves in the Night*. Provisionally entitled 'Seen in Daylight', the draft outline covered Israel's struggle for independence, with the focus on Begin and the Irgun. See MS2343/4.

83 ZRO to Koestler, 19 October 1970, MS2386/5; Weinshall to Koestler and reply, 10 December 1970, MS2386/5; I. Benari to Koestler, 15 February and reply 27 March 1971, MS2387/2; Weinshall to Koestler and reply, 29 May and 12 June 1973, MS2388/3; Koestler to Benari, 24 March 1973, CZA, A330/409; Jabotinsky Committee to Koestler and reply, 13 August and 19 August 1980, MS2392/4.

84 CD, 6 September 1972 and 31 October 1973; Koestler to Kollek, 9 October and to Mala Rossoff, 18 October 1973, MS2388/3; Koestler to Mala Rossoff, 16 February 1974, MS2389/1; Koestler to Mizrachi Women's Organisation, 27 November 1973, MS2388/3; signature to petition on behalf of Soviet Jews, *The Times*, 25 November 1974, MS2390/1; Koestler to Women's Campaign for Soviet Jewry, 11 September 1976 and 6 April 1977, MS2390/2; Friedlander to Koestler, 1 October 1973 and reply, MS2388/5.

85 HA, 13, 12 and 12 June 1973, MS2304.

86 'The Vital Choice', in Douglas Villiers (ed.), *Next Year in Jerusalem: Jews in the Twentieth Century* (London, 1976), pp.98–106.

87 Berlin to Villiers, 11 July 1973, ibid., p.106.

88 Ibid.

89 CD, 4 and 18 November 1973, MS2305; Koestler to Rossoff, 16 February 1974, MS2389/1.

90 On the enduring fascination of the Khazars and Koestler's unfortunate influence on serious scholarship about the subject, see *Jerusalem Report*, 7 September 1995.

91 *The Thirteenth Tribe* [TT], p.226.

92 Ibid., pp.141–4.

93 Ibid., pp.152–6.

94 Ibid., pp.159–69, 172–7.

95 Leon Wieseltier, 'You Don't Have to be Khazarian . . . .', *New York Review of Books*, 28 October 1976; Edward Grossman, 'Koestler's Jewish Problem', *Commentary*, December 1976; Chimen Abramsky, 'The Khazar Myth', *Jewish Chronicle*, 9 April 1976.

96 TT, pp.181–95.

97 Ibid., pp.196–200.

98 Ibid., pp.15–16.

99 Robert Blumstock, 'Going Home: Arthur Koestler's Thirteenth Tribe', *Jewish Social Studies*, 48:2 (1986), pp.93–104.

100 TT, p.233. For Lasky's reaction, see Josselson to Koestler, 31 August 1975, MS2390/2.

CHAPTER 14: ILLNESS AND EXIT, 1976–83

1 Stephen Vicinczey, review of Mikes, *Arthur Koestler, Sunday Telegraph*, 9 October 1986.

2 Correspondence with Leeds University about D.Litt. (Hon.), conferred *in absentia*, 17 November 1977, MS2308/2; Iain Hamilton to Koestler, 18 March 1976, MS2390/2; HA, 26, 27 November and 4, 6, 7, 8 and 21 December 1976, MS2304.

3 Arthur Koestler, 'Whereof one cannot speak . . .', in Toynbee and Koestler (eds), *Life After Death*, pp.238–9, repr. *Kaleidoscope*, pp.313–38.

4 BBC1, *Everyman*, 19 February 1984.

5 Koestler to Pinkie Beckett, 9 September 1976, MS2390/2; HA, 18 December 1976, MS2304; SOS, pp.233–4.

6 Cynthia to Marcia Wilson, 6 July 1977, MS2390s.

7 *Janus: A Summing Up* (London, 1978), Preface, p.vii.

8 Medical correspondence, 24 August and 5 December 1977, MS2307/1; Koestler to Joyce, 14 June 1978, MS2391/2.

9 Celia to Koestler, 6 December and 21 December 1976, MS2301/2.

10 Celia to Koestler, 3 July, 15 October, 3, 12 and 17 December 1978, MS2301/2.

11 Koestler to Hamilton, 12 October 1978, MS2370/2.

12 Hamilton to Rubinstein and to Koestler, Rubinstein to Koestler, 16 October 1978; Cynthia to Hamilton, 20 October; Koestler to Hamilton, 27 November 1978; Rubinstein to Hamilton, 23 October and 8 and 12 December 1978 and 25 January 1979, MS2370/2.

13 Koestler to Hamilton, 7 May, to Rubinstein, 3 June 1979 and Rubinstein to Hamilton, 6 June 1979; Rubinstein to Tom Rosenthal, 25 June 1979, Rosenthal to Rubinstein, 28 June and 20 August 1979, MS2370/2. See contract, 2 March 1974, Hutchinson archive, Random House, London.

14 Koestler to Celia, 14 March 1979, MS2370/2; Celia to Koestler, 4 June 1979, MS2301/2. Celia Goodman's diary, 30 July 1979, in possession of Celia Goodman.

15 Koestler to Rubinstein, 3 June 1979, MS2370/2. For Hamilton's own remarkably even-handed account of the affair, see Iain Hamilton, 'Biographee', *Encounter*, August–September 1983, pp.18–22.

16 Carter-Ruck to Rosenthal, 6 February, 21 May, 9 June, 10 October 1980, 5 February, 15 May 1981, MS2370/2.

17 Medical notes, 20 February 1980, MS2307/1. See note of his anxiety, Celia Goodman's diary, 30 July 1979.

18 *Bricks to Babel*, pp.9–10.

19 On the Koestler Foundation and Operation Daedalus see MS2146/1–2 and MS2306/2. Brian Inglis, 'Parapsychology', *Encounter*, September–October 1983, pp.55–6; Inglis, *The Unknown Guest*, p.161.

20 Koestler to Hyden, 23 May, to Fitzgibbon, 28 May 1980, to Lacerta Kammerer, 13 August MS2392/4; Mikes, *Arthur Koestler*, pp.72–3; interview with Sir Martyn and Priscilla Beckett, 27 May 1998; 'Rhine's impact on philosophy', 28 November 1980, repr. *Kaleidoscope*, pp.309–12.

21 'Draft for Suicide Pamphlet', MS2409/3. See BTB, p.580.

22 Cynthia to Lacerta Kammerer, 6 May 1981; Koestler to Knickerbocker, nd, 1981; Dr John Shanks to Koestler, 7 and 16 May 1981, MS2393/2; medical correspondence, 23 March, 1 July, 30 November 1981, MS2307/1.

23 Medical notes, 31 October 1982, MS2307/1; Cynthia to Knickerbocker, 29 March 1982, MS2394/1.

24 'Minutes', Anglo-Hungarian Pig Committee, 29 August 1982, MS2394/1; Mikes, *Arthur Koestler*, pp.30–3; Kevin Macdonald, *Emeric Pressburger* (London, 1994), pp.409–10; medical notes, 31 October 1982, MS2307/1.

25 Julian Barnes, 'Playing Chess with Arthur Koestler'; Barnes to Cynthia, 13 June 1980, MS2392/4 and to Koestler, nd (June) 1982, MS2394/1.

26 Medical correspondence, 9 and 15 January, 22 February 1982, MS2307/1.

27 Cynthia note, 26 May 1982; arrangements for day nurse, 24–7 November and 25 December 1982 onwards, MS2307/1. Testimony by Dr Ian West and Dr John Creightmore at the inquest for Arthur and Cynthia Koestler, Westminster Coroner's Court, 30 March 1983, *The Times*, 31 March 1983.

28 Appointments diary, 1983, MS2304; *Observer*, 30 January 1983; Koestler to Rumbold, 12 January 1983; correspondence in MS2394/1.

29 Harris, introduction, SOS, p.10; Mikes, *Arthur Koestler*, p.3; interview with Sir Martyn and Priscilla Beckett, 27 May 1998; Barnes, 'Playing Chess with Arthur Koestler'.

30 Evidence from the inquest for Arthur and Cynthia Koestler, Westminster Coroner's Court, 30 March 1983, *The Times*, 31 March 1983; Harris, Introduction, SOS, pp.10–11; Mikes, *Arthur Koestler*, pp.76–8. 'Pinkie' Beckett, too, noted strange hints in her conversations with Cynthia such as 'if you ring in a few days you may not get me': interview, 27 May 1998.

31 *Sunday Times*, 6 March 1983; Harris, Introduction, SOS, p.11; Mikes, *Arthur Koestler*, p.78. For VES/EXIT membership, see MS2390/2 and MS23409/1.

32 *Guardian*, 12 March 1983; *The Times*, 31 March 1983; Lasky in *Encounter*, September–October 1983, p.64. Among others the mourners included Celia and Arianne Goodman, the Becketts, Harold Harris and Lasky.

33 Suicide notes, MS2308/1.

34 Ibid.

35 'Draft Preface to VES booklet', MS2409/1.

36 'Draft for Suicide Pamphlet', MS2409/3, pp.2–3.

37 Celia Goodman's diary, 19 March 1979, in the possession of Celia Goodman.

38 Suicide notes, MS2308/1.
39 *The Times*, 7 April 1983, 9 April 1983.
40 For the wills, see MS2432/1. Koestler's wills reflect his changing relationships and interests. In 1941 the chief beneficiaries were Dorothea, Sperber and Weiczen/Valiani. In 1954, the bulk of his estate was to go to charity with small amounts to ex-wives and lovers. In 1973 it was amended so that forty per cent of the estate would go to the Koestler Award, an equal amount to the VES and twenty per cent to the Society for Psychical Research for 'non-statistical' investigative projects. In July 1976, he set in motion the mechanisms which would lead to the academic endowment.
41 *Sunday Telegraph*, 13 March 1983; *The Times*, 21 June 1983.
42 Harris, Introduction, SOS, p.14, and Epilogue, p.232.
43 Mikes, *Arthur Koestler*, pp.42–7.
44 Ibid., pp.77–8.
45 Stephen Vicinczey, *Sunday Telegraph*, 9 October 1983; and letters, *Observer*, 17 August 1986.
46 *Sunday Telegraph*, 19 February 1986.
47 George Mikes, 'Who Killed Cynthia Koestler?', *Observer*, 3 August 1986; Harold Harris, 'For the love of Arthur', *Observer*, 10 August 1986; Mikes, letters, *Observer*, 31 August 1986; and Vicinczey, *Observer*, 17 August 1986.
48 Barnes, 'Playing Chess with Arthur Koestler'.
49 *Sunday Times*, 19 February 1984.
50 Interview with Celia Goodman, 7 April 1998; Partridge, *Everything to Lose*, 13 August 1956, p.256.
51 For a similar argument see Bernard Avishai, 'The Dangers of Devotion', *New Yorker*, 6 January 1997.

CONCLUSION: THE HOMELESS MIND

1   For example, he is not mentioned in Bernard-Henri Lévy, *Adventures on the Freedom Road* (London, 1995).
2   Raymond Aron, 'A Writer's Greatness', *Encounter*, July–August 1983, pp.9–12; Sidney Hook, 'Cold Warrior', ibid., pp.12–16; John Wain, 'From Diagnosis to Nightmare', *Encounter*, September–October 1983, pp.45–50.
3   Christopher Booker, *Spectator*, 4 March 1978; Alex Comfort, *Guardian*, 23 February 1978; George Steiner, *Sunday Times*, 19 February 1978.
4   Hook, *Out of Step*, p.443. His reportage has been disgracefully overlooked in recent anthologies.
5   Maurice Cranston, 'In the Tradition of Daniel Defoe', *Encounter*, July–August 1983, pp.16–18; George Steiner, *Sunday Times*, 8 March 1983; obituary, *The Times*, 4 March 1983.
6   Frank McConnell, '*Janus*', *New Republic*, 13 May 1978; P. B. Medawar, 'Koestler's theory of the creative act', *New Statesman*, 19 June 1964; John Maynard Smith, 'Theories and Connections', *The Listener*, 28 May 1964. Compare this with the sympathetic essays by Frank Barron, W. H. Thorpe and John Beloff in ATC.
7   Magda Polanyi to Koestler, 25 August 1980, MS2344/7.
8   For an evaluation of his impact see Mark Graubard, '*The Sleepwalkers*: Its Contribution and Impact', in ATC, pp.20–49 and Alain de Benoiste, 'Koestler et la pensée contemporaine', in *L'Herne*, pp.454–63.
9   Arthur Schlesinger, 'Cassandra Revisited', *Vogue*, 156 (1970); Mary Benson, *Guardian*, 23 February 1984; Hook, *Out of Step*, p.443.
10 Ayer, *Part of My Life*, p.245.
11 Partridge, *Hanging On*, 6 March 1963, pp.150–1.
12 Rolph, *Further Particulars*, p.154; Hook, *Out of Step*, p.438; Mikes, *Arthur Koestler*, pp.25–6.
13 SOS, pp.233–4. Enjoying a chance to practise while Koestler was in America, Mamaine complained to Edmund Wilson: 'Of course, when I am with Koestler I never get a chance anyway, because he is always working and the piano is just underneath his room', Mamaine to Wilson, 20 October 1950, EWC.
14 SOS, p.118.
15 Ibid., pp.61, 170.
16 Woodrow Wyatt, *The Times*, 23 February 1984; *Observer*, 3 July 1988.
17 Interview with Marion Bieber, 1 June 1998.
18 *The Times*, 23 February 1984; Mikes, *Arthur Koestler*, pp.25–8.

19 Mamaine to Celia, nd, March 1951, LWK, p.176.
20 A. J. Ayer, 'Koestlerkampf', *London Review of Books*, 20 May–2 June 1982; Partridge, *Hanging On*, 7 March 1963, pp.150–5; interview with Janetta Parladé, 29 April 1998.
21 Koestler to Weinshall, 5 March 1956; Koestler to Klari Lorant, 14 April 1956, MS2380/3; Joan Martyn to Koestler, 16 April 1956, MS2381/1.
22 Interview with Melvin Lasky, 14 March 1994; Aron, 'A Writer's Greatness', p.9.
23 FFIF Annual Report, 15 March 1952, MS2397/3; Koestler to Peters, 16 July 1951, MS2379/4.
24 CD, September–October 1961, MS2305.
25 Harold Harris, 'Author', *Encounter*, July–August 1983, pp.23–5; interview with Sir Martyn and Priscilla Beckett, 27 April 1998.
26 Interview with Celia Goodman, 7 April 1998.
27 Cranston, 'In the Tradition of Daniel Defoe', pp.16–18; interview with David Astor, 8 June 1995; interview with Janetta Parladé, 29 April 1998.
28 Rolph, *Further Particulars*, p.53; Malcolm Muggeridge, *Like it was: The Diaries of Malcolm Muggeridge*, ed. John Bright-Holmes (London, 1981), 1 February 1946, p.208.
29 Hook, 'Cold Warrior', pp.13–15; Leary, *Flashbacks*, p.56.
30 Koestler to Polanyi, 24 September 1949, MS2344/7; Rothschild, *The Whims of Fortune*, p.138; Skelton, *Tears Before Bedtime*, p.159.
31 Interview with Janetta Parladé, 29 April 1998; interview with Paul Willert, 28 August 1994; interview with David Astor, 8 June 1995.
32 DN, 31 January 1955, MS2305; Barnes, 'Playing Chess with Arthur Koestler'.
33 Interview with Melvin Lasky, 14 March 1994; Hyam Maccoby, 'Jew', *Encounter*, September–October 1983, pp.50–3; Steiner, *Sunday Times*, 8, March 1983.
34 Nedava, *Arthur Koestler*.
35 Atkins, *Arthur Koestler*; F. R. Benson, *Writers in Arms* (New York, 1968), p.73. In Weintraub, *The Last Great Cause*, p.120, he is identified as 'a Hungarian émigré Communist'.
36 Calder, *Chronicles of Conscience*, pp.276–8; cf. Raymond Mortimer, 'The Art of Arthur Koestler', *Cornhill*, 146 (Winter 1946), pp.213–22; V. S. Pritchett, 'Absolutitis', *New Statesman*, 18 August, 1956.
37 Pearson, *Arthur Koestler*.
38 Iain Hamilton, 'Wonderfully Living; Koestler the Novelist', in ATC, pp.97–8; Iain Hamilton, *Koestler* (London, 1982).
39 Murray A. Sperber (ed.), *Arthur Koestler*. See also *L'Herne*.
40 Hyam Maccoby, 'Jew', *Encounter*, pp.50–3. See also Maccoby's review of *The Thirteenth Tribe*, *The Listener*, 8 April 1976: 'this book represents one more stage in his struggle to exorcise his own Jewishness.'
41 Koenen, '*Arthur Koestler*', pp.63–70. I would like to thank Walter Laqueur for bringing this article to my attention.
42 George Steiner, 'Koestler's Quest'.
43 Steiner, *Extra-Territorial*, p.11 and his tribute to Koestler, *Sunday Times*, 8 March 1983.
44 Bhabha, *the location of culture*, pp.1, 5.
45 Koestler is also a salutary reminder that dislocation, minority status and exposure to the catastrophes of the twentieth century does not *necessarily* result in a progressive literary politics. There is a book to be written about right-wing and culturally conservative exiles (Henry Kissinger, Peter Bauer, Nikolaus Pevsner etc.).
46 Robin Cohen, *Global Diasporas* (London, 1997), p.133; Stuart Hall, 'New Ethnicities', in J. Donald and A. Rattansi. *'Race' Culture and Difference* (London, 1992), pp.252–60.
47 Paul Mendes-Flohr, 'The Throes of Assimilation: Self-Hatred and the Jewish Revolutionary' in his *Divided Passions: Jewish Intellectuals and the Experience of Modernity* (Detroit, 1991), pp.67–8.

Select Bibliography

(Place and date of publication refer to the edition consulted).

Andrew, Christopher and James, Harold, 'Willi Münzenberg, the Reichstag Fire and the Conversion of Innocents', in D. A. Charters and M. A. Tugwell (eds), *Deception Operations: Studies in the East-West Context* (London, 1990), pp.25–52.

Appleyard, Bryan, *Understanding the Present* (London, 1992).

Aron, Raymond, 'A Writer's Greatness', *Encounter*, July–August 1983, pp.9–12.

Aschheim, Steven, *Brothers and Strangers: The East European Jew in German and German Jewish Consciousness, 1800–1923* (Madison, WI, 1986).

Astor, David, 'Crusader', *Encounter*, July–August 1983, pp.31–3.

Atkins, John, *Arthur Koestler* (London, 1956).

Avineri, Shlomo, *The Making of Modern Zionism* (London, 1981).

Avishai, Bernard, 'The Dangers of Devotion', *New Yorker*, 6 January 1997, pp.32–9.

Ayer, A. J., 'Koestlerkampf', *London Review of Books*, 20 May–2 June 1982.

Ayer, A. J., *More of My Life* (London, 1988).

Ayer, A. J., *Part of My Life* (London, 1977).

Bair, Deirdre, *Simone de Beauvoir: A Biography* (London, 1990).

Banks, Charlotte and Broadhurst, P. L., *Stephanos: Studies in Psychology Presented to Cyril Burt* (London, 1965).

Julian Barnes, 'Playing Chess with Arthur Koestler', *Observer Review*, 3 July 1988.

Barnes, Trevor, 'The Secret Cold War: The CIA and American Foreign Policy in Europe', Pts 1 and 2, *Historical Journal*, 24:2 (1981), pp.399–415 and 25:3 (1982), pp.649–70.

Barron, Frank, 'Bisociates: Artist and Scientist in *The Act of Creation*', in Harold Harris (ed.), *Astride The Two Cultures: Arthur Koestler at 70* (London, 1975), pp.37–49.

Bauer, Yehuda, *Jews for Sale?: Nazi-Jewish Negotiations, 1933–1945* (New Haven, 1994).

Bauman, Zygmunt, *Intimations of Postmodernity* (London, 1992).

Beevor, Antony and Cooper, Artemis, *Paris After the Liberation: 1944–1949* (London, 1995).

Begin, Menachem, *The Revolt*, trans. Samuel Katz (London, 1951).

Beloff, John, 'Koestler's Philosophy of Mind', in Harold Harris (ed.), *Astride The Two Cultures: Arthur Koestler at 70* (London, 1975), pp.69–83.

Beloff, John, *Parapsychology: A Concise History* (London, 1993).

Beloff, John, 'Psychologist', *Encounter*, July–August 1983, pp.28–31.

Bennett, Catherine, 'Would You Believe It?', *Guardian*, Sec. 2, 14 June 1996.

Benoist, Alain de, 'Koestler et la pensée contemporaine', in Pierre Debray-Ritzen (ed.), *L'Herne*, Cahiers No.27, *Arthur Koestler* (Paris, 1975), pp.453–63.

Benson, Frederick, *Writers in Arms: The Literary Impact of the Spanish Civil War* (London, 1968).

Benson, Mary, 'Angel', *Encounter*, July–August 1983, pp.33–6.

Bentwich, Norman, *I Understand the Risks* (London, 1950).

Bergonzi, Bernard, *Wartime and Aftermath: English Literature and its Background 1939–1960* (Oxford, 1993).

Berry, Faith, *Langston Hughes: Before and Beyond Harlem* (New York, 1983).

Bethell, Nicholas, *The Palestine Triangle* (London, 1979).

Betz, Albrecht, 'La Problématique du renégat: Münzenberg, Sperber et Koestler à la fin des années trente', in *Willi Münzenberg. 1889–1940: Un Homme Contre*, Colloque International, Organisé par Bibliothèque Méjunes L'Institute de L'Image (Marseilles, 1993), pp.135–43.

Bhabha, Homi K., 'The postcolonial and the postmodern: the question of agency', in Homi K. Bhabha, *the location of culture* (London, 1994), pp.171–97.

Bhabha, Homi K., *the location of culture* (London, 1994).

Blumstock, Robert, 'Going Home: Arthur Koestler's Thirteenth Tribe', *Jewish Social Studies*, 48:2 (1986), pp.93–104.

Bolin, Luis, *Spain: The Vital Years* (London, 1967).

Bower, Tom, *The Perfect English Spy: Sir Dick White and the Secret War 1935–50* (London, 1995).

Brown, J. A. C., *Freud and the Post-Freudians* (London, 1961).

Bukowsky, Vladimir, 'Introduction' to Arthur Koestler, *Darkness at Noon* (London [Folio Society Edition], 1980), pp.7–15.

Burnham, James, *The Managerial Revolution* (London, 1942).

Calder, Jenni, *Chronicles of Conscience: A study of George Orwell and Arthur Koestler* (London, 1968).

Carew Hunt, R. N., 'Willi Münzenberg', in David Footman (ed.), *International Communism*, St Antony's Papers, No.9 (London, 1960), pp.72–87.

Carr, Raymond, *The Spanish Tragedy* (London, 1976).

Cate, Curtis, *André Malraux: A Biography* (London, 1995).

Cau, Jean, *Croquis de Mémoire* (Paris, 1985).

Caute, David, *Communism and the French Intellectuals* (London, 1964).

Caute, David, *The Fellow Travellers: A Postscript to the Enlightenment* (New York, 1973).

Cesarani, David (ed.), *Genocide and Rescue: The Holocaust in Hungary, 1944* (Oxford, 1997).

Chalmers-Mitchell, Sir Peter, *My House in Malaga* (London, 1937).

Chalmers-Mitchell, Sir Peter, *My Fill of Days* (London, 1938).

Chambers, Ian *migrancy culture identity* (London, 1994).

Charters, D. A. and Tugwell, M. A. (eds), *Deception Operations: Studies in the East–West Context* (London, 1990).

Cockett, Richard, *David Astor and the Observer* (London, 1991).

Cohen, Robin, *Global Diasporas* (London, 1997).

Cohen, Stephen F., *Bukharin and the Bolshevik Revolution: A Political Biography, 1888–1938* (New York, 1975).

Cohen-Solal, Annie, *Sartre: A Life* (London, 1991).

Coleman, Peter, *The Liberal Conspiracy: The Congress for Cultural Freedom and the Struggle for the Mind of Post-War Europe* (London, 1989).

Congdon, Lee, *Exile and Social Thought: Hungarian Intellectuals in Germany and Austria, 1919–1933* (Princeton, NJ, 1991).

Connor, Steven, *Postmodernist Culture* (Oxford, 1989).

Conquest, Robert, *The Great Terror* (London, 1968).

Conquest, Robert, *The Harvest of Sorrow* (London, 1988).

Costello, John and Tsarev, Oleg, *Deadly Illusions* (London, 1993).

Costello, John, *Mask of Treachery* (London, 1988).

Cranston, Maurice, 'In the Tradition of Daniel Defoe', *Encounter*, July–August 1983, pp.16–18.

Crawshay-Williams, Rupert, *The Challenge of Our Time* (London, 1948).

Crewe, Quentin, *Well, I forget the rest* (London, 1991).

Crick, Bernard, *George Orwell: A Life* (London, 1980).

Crossley, Robert, *Olaf Stapledon* (Liverpool, 1994).

Davies, John, 'Psycho bubble', *Times Higher Education Supplement*, 14 November 1997.

Dawkins, Richard, *The Blind Watchmaker* (London, 1991).

de Beauvoir, Simone, *Adieux: A Farewell to Sartre*, trans. Patrick O'Brien (London, 1984).

de Beauvoir, Simone, *Beloved Chicago Man: Letters to Nelson Algren 1947–64*, comp. and with a preface by Sylvie Le Bon de Beauvoir (London, 1998).

de Beauvoir, Simone, *Force of Circumstance*, trans. Richard Howard (London, 1965).

de Beauvoir, Simone, *Letters to Sartre*, trans. and ed. Quintin Hoare (London, 1991).

de Beauvoir, Simone, *The Mandarins*, trans. Leonard Friedman (London, 1994).

Debray-Ritzen, Pierre, 'Un croisé sans croix: Deuxième partie: Communisme (1930–1950)', in Pierre Debray-Ritzen (ed.), *L'Herne*, Cahiers No.27, *Arthur Koestler* (Paris, 1975), pp.139–208.

Debray-Ritzen, Pierre (ed.), *L'Herne*, Cahiers No.27, *Arthur Koestler* (Paris, 1975).

Dickson, Lovat, *Richard Hillary* (London, 1950).

Donald. J. and Rattansi, A. *'Race' Culture and Difference* (London, 1992).

Edwards, Ruth Dudley, *Victor Gollancz: A Biography* (London, 1987).

Elon, Amos, *The Israelis: Founders and Sons* (London, 1971).

Engel, David, *In the Shadow of Auschwitz: the Polish government-in-exile and the Jews 1939–42* (Chapel Hill, 1987).

Faulks, Sebastian, *The Fatal Englishman* (London, 1997).

Faure, Jean-Louis and Pachet, Pierre, *Bêtise de l'intelligence* (Paris, 1995).

Fiedler, Leslie, *Olaf Stapledon: A Man Divided* (New York, 1983).

Fisher, Clive, *Cyril Connolly: A Nostalgic Life* (London, 1995).

Foot, Michael, *Loyalists and Loners* (London, 1986).

Footman, David (ed.), *International Communism*, St Antony's Papers, No.9 (London, 1960).

Frankel, Jonathan, *Prophecy and Politics: Socialism, Nationalism and the Russian Jews 1862–1917* (Cambridge, 1981).

Friedenreich, Harriet Pass, *Jewish Politics in Vienna 1918–1938* (Bloomington, IN, 1995).

Friedenreich, Harriet, *The Jews of Vienna during the First Republic* (Bloomington, IN, 1990).

Fry, Varian, *Surrender on Demand* (New York, 1945).

Fyvel, T. R., *George Orwell: A Personal Memoir* (London, 1982) .

Fyvel, T. R., 'Arthur Koestler and George Orwell', in Harold Harris (ed.), *Astride The Two Cultures: Arthur Koestler at 70* (London, 1975), pp.149–61.

Gilman, Sander L., *Jewish Self-Hatred: Anti-Semitism and the Hidden Language of the Jews* (Baltimore, 1986).

Gitelman, Zvi, *A Century of Ambivalence: The Jews in Russia and the Soviet Union, 1881 to the Present* (New York, 1988).

Gluck, Mary, *Georg Lukács and his Generation 1900–1918* (Cambridge, MA, 1985).

Goodman, Celia (ed.), *Living with Koestler: Mamaine Koestler's Letters 1945–51* (London, 1985).

Gordon, Louis, 'Arthur Koestler and His Ties to Zionism and Jabotinsky', *Studies in Zionism*, 12:2 (1991), pp.149–68.

Gordon, Louis, 'Koestler revisited', *Midstream*, February–March 1994, pp.13–15.

Gould, Stephen Jay, *Ever Since Darwin* (London, 1991).

Gourevitch, Adolph, 'Jabotinsky and the Hebrew Language', in Joseph Schechtman, *Fighter and Prophet: The Vladimir Jabotinsky Story. The Last Years* (London, 1961), pp.597–9.

Grant Duff, Sheila, 'A Very Brief Visit', in Philip Toynbee (ed.), *The Distant Drum: Reflections on the Spanish Civil War* (London, 1976).

Graubard, Mark, 'The Sleepwalkers: Its Contribution and Impact', in Harold Harris, (ed.), *Astride The Two Cultures: Arthur Koestler at 70* (London, 1975), pp.20–36.

Greenberg, Karen J. (ed.), Varian Fry Papers, in *Archives of the Holocaust*, Vol. 5, *Columbia University Library* (New York, 1990) .

Gregory, Richard L., *The Oxford Companion to the Mind* (Oxford, 1987).

Grigg, John, 'The Do-Gooder from Seville Gaol', in Harold Harris (ed.), *Astride The Two Cultures: Arthur Koestler at 70* (London, 1975).

Gross, Babette, *Willi Münzenberg: Eine Politische Biographie* (Stuttgart, 1967) [English translation by Marion Jackson, Michigan, 1974].

Gruber, Helmut, 'Red Vienna and the "Jewish Question"', *Leo Baeck Institute Year Book*, 38 (1993), pp.99–118.

Gruber, Helmut, 'Willi Münzenberg's German Communist Empire 1921–1933', *Journal of Modern History* 38:3 (1966), pp.278–97.

Haag, John, 'Blood on the Ringstrasse: Vienna's Students 1918–33', *Wiener Library Bulletin*, 39/40 (1976), pp.29–34. .

Hajdu, Tibor and Nagy, Zsuzsa, 'Revolution, Counterrevolution, Consolidation', in Peter Sugar, Peter Hanak, Tibor Frank (eds), *A History of Hungary* (London, 1990), pp.295–318.

Hall, Stuart, 'New Ethnicities', in J. Donald and A. Rattansi, *'Race' Culture and Difference* (London, 1992), pp.252–60.

Hamilton, Iain, *Koestler: A Biography* (London, 1982) .

Hamilton, Iain, 'Wonderfully Living; Koestler the Novelist', in Harold Harris (ed.), *Astride The Two Cultures: Arthur Koestler at 70* (London, 1975), pp.84–101.

Harris, Harold (ed.), *Astride The Two Cultures: Arthur Koestler at 70* (London, 1975) .

Harris, Harold, 'Author', *Encounter*, July–August 1983, pp.23–5.

Hay, Julius, *Born 1900*, trans. and abridged J. A. Underwood (London, 1974).

Hayman, Ronald, *Writing Against: A Biography of Sartre* (London, 1986).

Hearnshaw, L. S., *Cyril Burt: Psychologist* (London, 1979).

Hewison, Robert, *In Anger: Culture in the Cold War 1945–60* (London, 1981).

Hewison, Robert, *Under Siege. Literary Life in London 1939–45* (London, 1988).

Heyworth, Peter, *Otto Klemperer, his life and times*, Vol. 2, *1933–73* (London, 1996).

Hidegkúti, Béla, *Koestler Emlékkönyv* (Melbourne, 1992).

Hillary, Richard, *The Last Enemy* (London, 1942; republished 1997).

Hook, Sidney, 'Cold Warrior', *Encounter*, July–August 1983, pp.12–16.

Hook, Sidney, *Out of Step: An Unquiet Life in the Twentieth Century* (New York, 1987).

Howard, Anthony, *Crossman: The Pursuit of Power* (London, 1990).

Howard, Elizabeth Jane, *After Julius* (London, 1994).

Howe, Irving, 'Malraux, Silone, Koestler: The Twentieth Century', in Irving Howe, *Politics and the Novel* (New York, 1992).

Hughes, Langston, *I Wonder as I Wander* (New York, 1956).

Ignotus, Paul, *Political Prisoner: A Personal Account* (New York, 1964).

Inglis, Brian, *Coincidence: A Matter of Chance – or Synchronicity?* (London, 1990).

Inglis, Brian, 'Parapsychology', *Encounter*, September–October 1983, pp.50–3.

Inglis, Brian, *The Unknown Guest: The Mystery of Intuition* (London, 1987).

James, William, *The Varieties of Religious Experience* [1902] (London, 1985).

Jones, Mervyn, *Michael Foot* (London, 1994).

Judt, Tony, *Past Imperfect. French Intellectuals, 1944–1956* (Berkeley, 1992).

Junod, Marcel, *Warrior Without Weapons*, trans. Edward Fitzgerald (London, 1951).

Kafka, Franz, *The Diaries of Franz Kafka 1910–1923*, ed. Max Brod (London, 1972).

Kahn, Lothar, 'Arthur Koestler: Dejudaized Zionism', in Lothar Kahn, *Mirrors of the Jewish Mind* (New York, 1968), pp.146–59.

Kantorowicz, Alfred, *Deutsches Tagebuch*, Vols 1 and 2 (Berlin, 1980).

Kantorowicz, Alfred, *Exil in Frankreich* (Bremen, 1971).

Kantorowicz, Alfred, *Politik und Literatur im Exil* (Hamburg, 1978).

Kaplan, Karel, *Report on the Murder of the General-Secretary*, trans. Karel Kovanda (Columbus, OH, 1990).

Kingsley, Sidney, *Darkness at Noon: A Play in Three Acts*, based on the novel by Arthur Koestler (New York, 1950).

Koch, Stephen, *Double Lives: Stalin, Willi Münzenberg and the seduction of the Intellectuals* (London, 1995).

Koenen, Krisztina, 'Arthur Koestler', *Frankfurter Allgemeine Zeitung*, magazine, 26 November 1993.

Koestler, Cynthia, 'Twenty-five Writing Years', in Harold Harris, (ed.), *Astride The Two Cultures: Arthur Koestler at 70* (London, 1975), pp.136–48.

Kollek, Teddy with Kollek, Amos, *For Jerusalem: a life* (London, 1979).

Kramnick, Isaac and Sheerman, Barry, *Harold Laski: A Life on the Left* (London, 1993).

Kushner, Tony, *The Holocaust and the Liberal Imagination* (Oxford, 1994).

Laqueur, Walter, *History of Zionism* (New York, 1976).

Lasky, Melvin, 'Remembering', *Encounter*, September–October 1983, pp.59–64.

Leary, Timothy, *Flashbacks: An Autobiography* (London, 1983).

Levene, Mark, *Arthur Koestler* (New York, 1984).

Lévy, Bernard-Henri, *Adventures on the Freedom Road* (London, 1995).

Lewis, Jeremy, *Cyril Connolly: A Life* (London, 1997).

Lewis, Dr John and Bishop, Reginald, *The Philosophy of Betrayal: An Analysis of the Anti-Soviet Propaganda of Arthur Koestler and Others* (London, 1945).

Litvinoff, Emanuel, 'Europe's Cassandra', *Jewish Observer and Middle East Review*, 14 September 1956.

Loebel, Eugene (ed.), *Sentenced and Tried: The Stalinist Purges in Czechoslovakia* (London, 1969).

Lottman, Herbert, *Albert Camus: A Biography* (London, 1997).

Lottman, Herbert, *The Left Bank: Writers in Paris From the Popular Front to Cold War* (London, 1982).

Lukacs, John, *Budapest 1900* (London, 1988).

Lyon, David, *Postmodernity* (Buckingham, 1994).

Maccoby, Hyam, 'Jew', *Encounter*, September–October 1983, pp.50–3.

Macdonald, Kevin, *Emeric Pressburger* (London, 1994).

Madsen, Axel, *Malraux: A Biography* (London, 1977).

Malraux, André, *Antimemoirs*, trans. Terence Kilmartin (London, 1968).

Marcus, Laura, *Auto/Biographical discourses: Theory, criticism, practice* (Manchester, 1994).

Marcuse, Ludwig, *Mein Zwanzigstes Jahrhundert* (Munich, 1960).

Matthews, Robert, 'The Truth about ESP', *Sunday Telegraph*, 30 March 1989.

Mays, Wolfe, *Koestler* (Guildford, 1973).

McCagg Jr, William O., *Jewish Nobles and Geniuses in Modern Hungary* (New York, 1972).

McCarthy, Patrick, *Camus* (London, 1982).

McLaine, Ian, *The Ministry of Morale: Home Front Morale and the Ministry of Information in World War II* (London, 1979).

Mendes-Flohr, Paul, 'The Throes of Assimilation: Self-Hatred and the Jewish Revolutionary', in Paul Mendes-Flohr, *Divided Passions: Jewish intellectuals and the experience of modernity* (Detroit, 1991), pp.67–76.

Merleau-Ponty, Maurice, 'Koestler's Dilemmas', in Murray A. Sperber (ed.), *Arthur Koestler: A Collection of Critical Essays* (New Jersey, 1977), pp.89–85.

Mikes, George, *Arthur Koestler: The Story of a Friendship* (London, 1983).

Milfull, John, '"Die Wonnen der Gewöhnlichkeit": Arthur Koestler and Zionism', *Jahrbuch des Instituts für Deutsche Geschichte*, vol. 14 (Tel Aviv, 1985), pp.359–70.

Milosz, Czeslaw, *The Captive Mind* (London, 1985).

Mommsen, Hans, *The Rise and Fall of Weimar Democracy* (Chapel Hill, 1996).

Mortimer, Raymond, 'The Art of Arthur Koestler', *Cornhill*, 146 (Winter 1946), pp.213–22.

Muggeridge, Malcolm, *Like it was: The Diaries of Malcolm Muggeridge*, ed. John Bright-Holmes (London, 1981).

Myers, Jeffrey, *Edmund Wilson: A Biography* (New York, 1995).

Nabokov, Nicholas, *Bagazh: Memoirs of a Russian Cosmopolitan* (London, 1975).

Nedava, Joseph, *Arthur Koestler: A Study* (London, 1948).

Nicolson, Harold, *Diaries and Letters 1930–1939*, ed. Nigel Nicolson (London, 1966).

Nott, Kathleen, 'Trojan Horses: Koestler and the Behaviourists', in Harold Harris (ed.), *Astride The Two Cultures: Arthur Koestler at 70* (London, 1975), pp.162–74.

Orwell, George, *The Collected Essays, Journalism and Letters*, Vol. 1, *An Age Like This 1920–40*, ed. Sonia Orwell and Ian Angus (London, 1970).

Orwell, George, *The Collected Essays, Journalism and Letters*, Vol. 2, *My Country Right or Left, 1940–43*, ed. Sonia Orwell and Ian Angus (London, 1970).

Orwell, George, *The Collected Essays, Journalism and Letters*, Vol. 3, *As I Please, 1943–45*, ed. Sonia Orwell and Ian Angus (London, 1970).

Orwell, George, *The Collected Essays, Journalism and Letters*, Vol. 4, *In Front of Your Nose 1945–50*, ed. Sonia Orwell and Ian Angus (London, 1970).

Partridge, Frances, *Everything to Lose: Diaries 1945–1960* (London, 1985).

Partridge, Frances, *Hanging On: Diaries 1960–1963* (London, 1990).

Patai, Raphael, *The Jews of Hungary: History, Culture, Psychology* (Detroit, 1996).

Pearson, Sidney, *Arthur Koestler* (Boston, 1978).

Pinker, Steven, *How The Mind Works* (London, 1998).

Preston, Paul, *The Spanish Civil War* (London, 1986).

Pritchett, V. S., 'Absolutitis', *New Statesman*, 18 August 1956.

Pryce-Jones, David, 'Chess Man', *Encounter*, July–August 1983, pp.25–8.

Quennell, Peter, *The Wanton Chase: An Autobiography from 1939* (London, 1980).

Rado, Sandor, *Code-name Dora* (London, 1977).

Rahv, Philip, 'Koestler and Homeless Radicalism', in Philip Rahv, *Image and Idea* (New York, 1949).

Rampersad, Arnold, *The Life of Langston Hughes*, Vol. 1, *I, Too Sing America* (New York, 1986).

Regler, Gustav, *The Owl of Minerva: The autobiography of Gustav Regler*, trans. Norman Denny (London, 1959).

Roazen, Paul, *Freud and His Followers* (London, 1979).

Rolph, C. H., *Further Particulars* (London, 1987).

Rose, Steven, *Lifelines: Biology, Freedom, Determinism* (London, 1998).

Rothschild, Guy de, *The Whims of Fortune* (London, 1985).

Rozenblit, Marsha, 'The Assertion of Identity: Jewish Students and Nationalism at the University of Vienna before the First World War', *Leo Baeck Institute Year Book*, 27 (1982), pp.171–83.

Rozenblit, Marsha, *The Jews of Vienna: Assimilation and Identity 1867–1914*.

Rubinstein, W. D., *The Left, the Right and the Jews* (London, 1982).

Santamaria, B. A., *Australia at the Crossroads* (Melbourne, 1987).

Schechtman, Joseph, *Fighter and Prophet: The Vladimir Jabotinsky Story. The Last Years* (London, 1961).

Scheurmann, Ingrid and Konrad (eds), *For Walter Benjamin*, trans. Timothy Nevill (Bonn, 1993).

Schleimann, Jorgen, 'The Life and Work of Willi Münzenberg', *Survey*, 55 (April 1965), pp.64–91.

Schlesinger, Arthur, 'Cassandra Revisited', *Vogue*, 156 (1970).

Schweid, Eliezer, 'The Rejection of the Diaspora in Zionist Thought: Two Approaches', *Studies in Zionism*, 5:1 (1984), pp.43–70.

Sheldon, Michael, *Friends of Promise: Cyril Connolly and the World of Horizon* (London, 1990).

Sheldon, Michael, *Orwell: The Authorised Biography* (London, 1991).

Shimoni, Gideon, *The Zionist Ideology* (Hanover, NH, 1995).

Silone, Ignazio, *Emergency Exit* (London, 1969).

Simpson, Christopher, *Blowback: America's Recruitment of Nazis and Its Effects on the Cold War* (London, 1988).

Singer, Peter, 'Evolutionary Workers Party', *Times Higher Education Supplement*, 15 May 1998.

Singer, Peter, *The Expanding Circle: Ethics and Sociobiology* (Oxford, 1981).

Skelton, Barbara, *Tears Before Bedtime and Weep No More* (London, 1993).

Spender, Stephen, 'Koestler's Story of his Fervent Quest for Utopia', *New York Times Book Review*, 21 September 1952.

Spender, Stephen, *The Thirties and After* (London, 1978).

Sperber, Manès, 'Koestler il y a vingt ans', in Pierre Debray-Ritzen (ed.), *L'Herne*, Cahiers No. 27, *Arthur Koestler* (Paris, 1975), pp.9–11.

Sperber, Manès, *Until My Eyes Are Closed With Shards*, trans. Harry Zohn (New York, 1994).

Sperber, Murray A. (ed.), *Arthur Koestler: A Collection of Critical Essays* (New Jersey, 1977).

Sperber, Murray A., 'Looking Back on Koestler's Spanish War', in Murray A. Sperber (ed.), *Arthur Koestler: A Collection of Critical Essays* (Englewood Cliffs, NJ, 1977), pp.109–21.

Stapledon, Olaf, *Saints and Revolutionaries* (London, 1939).

Steiner, George, 'Extraterritorial' (1969), in George Steiner, *Extra-Territorial: Papers on Literature and the Language Revolution* (London, 1972), pp.3–11.

Steiner, George, *Extra-Territorial: Papers on Literature and the Language Revolution* (London 1972).

Steiner, George, 'Koestler's Quest', *Sunday Times*, 31 August 1975.

Storm Jameson, Margaret, *Autobiography of Storm Jameson: Journey from the North*, Vol. 2 (London, 1984).

Storr, Anthony, *The Dynamics of Creation* (London, 1986).

Strachey, John, *The Strangled Cry* (London, 1962) .

Sugar, Peter, Hanak, Peter and Frank, Tibor (eds), *A History of Hungary* (London, 1990).

Tanenhaus, Sam, *Whittaker Chambers: A Biography* (New York, 1997).

Tester, Keith, *The life and times of post-modernity* (London, 1993).

Teveth, Shabtai, *Moshe Dayan* (London, 1974).

Thomas, Hugh, *John Strachey* (London, 1973).

Thomas, Hugh, *The Spanish Civil War* (London, 1977).

Thorpe, W. H., 'Arthur Koestler and Biological Thought', in Harold Harris (ed.), *Astride The Two Cultures: Arthur Koestler at 70* (London, 1975), pp.50–68.

Todd, Olivier, *Albert Camus: A Life* (London, 1997).

Toynbee, Arnold and Koestler, Arthur (eds), *Life After Death* (London, 1976).

Ullstein, Hermann, *The Rise and Fall of the House of Ullstein* (London, 1939).

Urban, George (ed.), *Scaling the Wall: Talking to Eastern Europe. The Best of Radio Free Europe* (Detroit, 1964).

Villiers, Douglas (ed.), *Next Year In Jerusalem: Jews in the Twentieth Century* (London, 1976).

Wain, John, 'From Diagnosis to Nightmare', *Encounter*, September–October 1983, pp.45–50.

Wasserstein, Bernard, *Britain and the Jews of Europe 1939–1945* (Oxford, 1979).

Watkins, K. W., *Britain Divided: The Effect of the Spanish Civil War on British Political Opinion* (London, 1963).

Waugh, Evelyn, *Letters of Evelyn Waugh*, ed. Mark Amory (London, 1980).

Weber, Eugene, *The Hollow Years: France in the 1930s* (London, 1995).

Weidenfeld, George, *Remembering My Good Friends: An Autobiography* (London, 1995).

Weintraub, Stanley, *The Last Great Cause: The Intellectuals and the Spanish Civil War* (London, 1968).

Weissberg, Alexander, *Conspiracy of Silence*, trans. Edward Fitzgerald (London, 1952) .

Weizmann, Chaim, *Trial and Error* (London, 1949).

Werner, Ruth, *Sonya's Report*, trans. Renate Simpson (London, 1991).

Wessel, Harald, *Münzenbergs Ende* (Berlin, 1991).

Willi Münzenberg, 1889–1940: Un Homme Contre, Colloque International, Organisé par Biblioteque Méjunes L'Institute de L'Image (Marseilles, 1993).

Wilson, Edmund, *The Forties: From Notebooks and Diaries of the Period*, ed. Leon Edel (New York, 1983).

Wilson, Edmund, *Letters on Literature and Politics 1912–1972*, ed. Elena Wilson (London, 1977).

Wilson, Edmund, *Europe Without Baedeker* (London, 1977).

Wiseman, Richard, 'Money for Old Rope', *Times Higher Education Supplement*, 8 May 1998.

Wistrich, Robert, *Revolutionary Jews from Marx to Trotsky* (London, 1976).

Wistrich, Robert, *Socialism and the Jews* (Oxford, 1982).

Wolpert, Lewis, *The Unnatural Nature of Science* (London, 1992).

Wood, E. Thomas and Jankowski, Stanislaw M., *Karski: How One Man Tried to Stop the Holocaust* (New York, 1994).

Wyman, David S., *The Abandonment of the Jews: America and the Jews 1941–1945* (New York, 1984).

Yooll, Andrew Graham-, *Arthur Koestler: Del Infinito al Cero* (Madrid, 1978).

Index